MW00762900

Cisco Press

Staying Connected to Networkers

We want to hear from **you**! Help Cisco Press **stay connected** to the issues and challenges you face on a daily basis by registering your book and filling out our brief survey.

Complete and mail this form, or better yet, jump to **www.ciscopress.com** and do it online. Each complete entry will be eligible for our monthly drawing to **win a FREE book** from the Cisco Press Library.

Thank you for choosing Cisco Press to help you work the network.

Name _____

Address _____

City _____ State/Province _____

Country _____ Zip/Post code _____

E-mail address _____

May we contact you via e-mail for product updates and customer benefits?
❑ Yes   ❑ No

Where did you buy this product?

❑ Bookstore	❑ Computer store	❑ Electronics store
❑ Online retailer	❑ Office supply store	❑ Discount store
❑ Mail order	❑ Class/Seminar	

❑ Other _____

When did you buy this product? _____ Month _____ Year

What price did you pay for this product?
❑ Full retail price   ❑ Discounted price   ❑ Gift

How did you learn about this product?

❑ Friend	❑ Store personnel	❑ In-store ad
❑ Catalog	❑ Postcard in the mail	❑ Saw it on the shelf
❑ Magazine ad	❑ Article or review	❑ Used other products
❑ School	❑ Professional Organization	

❑ Other _____

What will this product be used for?
❑ Business use   ❑ Personal use   ❑ School/Education

❑ Other _____

How many years have you been employed in a computer-related industry?
❑ 2 years or less   ❑ 3-5 years   ❑ 5+ years

www.ciscopress.com

Cisco Systems
Cisco Press

www.ciscopress.com

Which best describes your job function?
- ❐ Corporate Management
- ❐ Network Design
- ❐ Marketing/Sales
- ❐ Professor/Teacher
- ❐ Systems Engineering
- ❐ Network Support
- ❐ Consultant
- ❐ IS Management
- ❐ Webmaster
- ❐ Student

- ❐ Other _____

What is your formal education background?
- ❐ High school
- ❐ College degree
- ❐ Vocational/Technical degree
- ❐ Masters degree
- ❐ Some college
- ❐ Professional or Doctoral degree

Have you purchased a Cisco Press product before?
- ❐ Yes
- ❐ No

On what topics would you like to see more coverage?

_____

_____

Do you have any additional comments or suggestions?

_____

_____

Cisco Internetwork Design (1-57870-171-6)

Cisco Press
201 West 103rd Street
Indianapolis, IN 46290
www.ciscopress.com

Place
Stamp
Here

Cisco Press
Customer Registration
P.O. Box 189014
Battle Creek, MI 49018-9947

Cisco Internetwork Design

Matthew H. Birkner, CCIE # 3719, Editor

CISCO SYSTEMS

CISCO PRESS

Cisco Press
201 West 103rd Street
Indianapolis, IN 46290 USA

Cisco Internetwork Design

Matthew H. Birkner, Editor

Copyright © 2000 Cisco Systems, Inc.

Cisco Press logo is a trademark of Cisco Systems, Inc.

Published by:
Cisco Press
201 West 103rd Street
Indianapolis, IN 46290 USA

Printed in the United States of America 1 2 3 4 5 6 7 8 9 0

Library of Congress Cataloging-in-Publication Number: 99-61719

ISBN: 1-57870-171-6

Warning and Disclaimer

This book is designed to provide information about designing Cisco networks. Every effort has been made to make this book as complete and as accurate as possible, but no warranty or fitness is implied.

The information is provided on an "as is" basis. The author, Cisco Press, and Cisco Systems, Inc., shall have neither liability nor responsibility to any person or entity with respect to any loss or damages arising from the information contained in this book or from the use of the discs or programs that may accompany it.

The opinions expressed in this book belong to the author and are not necessarily those of Cisco Systems, Inc.

Trademark Acknowledgments

All terms mentioned in this book that are known to be trademarks or service marks have been appropriately capitalized. Cisco Press or Cisco Systems, Inc. cannot attest to the accuracy of this information. Use of a term in this book should not be regarded as affecting the validity of any trademark or service mark.

Feedback Information

At Cisco Press, our goal is to create in-depth technical books of the highest quality and value. Each book is crafted with care and precision, undergoing rigorous development that involves the unique expertise of members from the professional technical community.

Readers' feedback is a natural continuation of this process. If you have any comments regarding how we could improve the quality of this book, or otherwise alter it to better suit your needs, you can contact us through e-mail at ciscopress@mcp.com. Please make sure to include the book title and ISBN in your message.

We greatly appreciate your assistance.

Publisher	John Wait
Executive Editor	John Kane
Cisco Systems Program Manager	Jim LeValley
Managing Editor	Patrick Kanouse
Acquisitions Editor	Brett Bartow
Development Editor	Christopher Cleveland
Project Editor	Jennifer Nuckles
Copy Editor	Keith Cline
Technical Editor(s)	John Cavanaugh, Scott Morris, Tom Thomas
Team Coordinator	Amy Lewis
Book Designer	Gina Rexrode
Cover Designer	Louisa Klucznik
Compositor	Gina Rexrode
Indexer	Tim Wright
Proofreader	Sheri Replin

CISCO SYSTEMS

CISCO PRESS

Corporate Headquarters
Cisco Systems, Inc.
170 West Tasman Drive
San Jose, CA 95134-1706
USA
http://www.cisco.com
Tel: 408 526-4000
   800 553-NETS (6387)
Fax: 408 526-4100

European Headquarters
Cisco Systems Europe s.a.r.l.
Parc Evolic, Batiment L1/L2
16 Avenue du Quebec
Villebon, BP 706
91961 Courtaboeuf Cedex
France
http://www-europe.cisco.com
Tel: 33 1 69 18 61 00
Fax: 33 1 69 28 83 26

Americas Headquarters
Cisco Systems, Inc.
170 West Tasman Drive
San Jose, CA 95134-1706
USA
http://www.cisco.com
Tel: 408 526-7660
Fax: 408 527-0883

Asia Headquarters
Nihon Cisco Systems K.K.
Fuji Building, 9th Floor
3-2-3 Marunouchi
Chiyoda-ku, Tokyo 100
Japan
http://www.cisco.com
Tel: 81 3 5219 6250
Fax: 81 3 5219 6001

Cisco Systems has more than 200 offices in the following countries. Addresses, phone numbers, and fax numbers are listed on the Cisco Connection Online Web site at http://www.cisco.com/offices.

Argentina • Australia • Austria • Belgium • Brazil • Canada • Chile • China • Colombia • Costa Rica • Croatia • Czech Republic • Denmark • Dubai, UAE Finland • France • Germany • Greece • Hong Kong • Hungary • India • Indonesia • Ireland • Israel • Italy • Japan • Korea • Luxembourg • Malaysia Mexico • The Netherlands • New Zealand • Norway • Peru • Philippines • Poland • Portugal • Puerto Rico • Romania • Russia • Saudi Arabia • Singapore Slovakia • Slovenia • South Africa • Spain • Sweden • Switzerland • Taiwan • Thailand • Turkey • Ukraine • United Kingdom • United States • Venezuela

About the Editor

Matthew H. Birkner, CCIE #3719, is a Network Consulting Engineer and works for Cisco Systems in the NSA (Network Supported Accounts) Program. Currently, he works a network consulting engineer, supporting and designing enterprise networks. He has been a network design engineer, network operations center engineer, and technical support specialist. Matt holds a B.S. degree from Tufts University, where he majored in electrical engineering. Additionally, he is a Cisco Certified Internetwork Expert (CCIE), Cisco Certified Design Professional (CCDP), Certified Netware Engineer (CNE), and a Bay Networks Certified Specialist (BNCS). In his spare time, Matt enjoys golfing and fishing.

About the Technical Reviewers

John Cavanaugh, CCIE #1066, is a Senior Consulting Engineer in Cisco's NSA organization. John is involved with network design and review for many of Cisco's largest customers. His position requires in depth knowledge of routing protocols and staying abreast of emerging technologies. John also works with the university community and was a member of the team that designed and built the Internet2 Abilene network. Prior to joining Cisco in 1993, John worked as an engineer for Boeing Computer Services in Seattle. He worked on a variety of networking assignments.

Scott Morris, CCIE #4713, is the Information Services Manager for Tele-Tech Company, Inc., where he is responsible for telecommunications services and computer and security systems for the entire company. His current position requires Scott to be involved with LAN, WAN, and remote networking design, configuration, implementation, configuration, and maintenance. Previous to joining Tele-Tech, Scott ran his own consulting and systems integration company, for which he provided network analysis and design services covering all OSI layers, as well as Cisco network configuration, packet-level analysis, and diagnostic work.

Thomas M. Thomas II is President and CEO of NetCerts, a virtual community for Networkers who desire to learn and practice their networking skills. NetCerts empowers its members so that they can obtain their Cisco Certifications by offering technical questions and networking labs relating directly to certification. NetCerts provides Internet portal services and a variety of other resources for every visitor as well. Previously, Tom has been a Course Designer in Cisco Systems' Worldwide Training Division and a Senior Network Engineer and Group Leader of the Advanced Systems Solutions Engineering Team for MCI's Managed Network Services. He has extensive experience in network support and design consulting. He is a member of the OSPF Working Group and author of the Cisco Press publication *OSPF Network Design Solutions*.

Dedications

I dedicate this book to my wife, Tiffany, and my son, Matthew, Jr., for all their patience, love, and encouragement while I wrote this book. If not for your unending support and encouragement during the many late nights that I spent writing, I'm certain that this book would not be in print today.

I can only dream that I can be as supportive to you as you've both been to me.

Forever Yours,

Matt

Acknowledgments

Numerous individuals have helped make this book a reality. First, I want to thank my Mom and Dad for buying me my first computer system back in 1981. While I did not realize it at that time, I now can clearly see that was the beginning of my thirst for technology. Dad, our many visits to MIT for the Inventor's Society meetings have always kept the spirit of innovation burning inside of me. Through both of your encouragement, I eventually chose to get my electrical engineering degree and continue that pre-established passion for technology.

I want to thank Rob Roy, an old friend of mine, who, many years ago, told me that if I wanted to get into networking as a career, I needed to just GO FOR IT and not look back. Rob, thanks for those words of wisdom, as they have stuck with me for all these years; today, I now encourage others with those same words.

I want to thank Helen Work for all your encouragement to pursue certifications and information technology many years back. I always felt thankful to get insight from you after you spent all those years at GTE.

Thanks, Walt and Barb Ross, for your never ending support, prayer, and encouragement (not to mention the infinite number of hours babysitting your grandson, Matthew Jr., so that I could get this book finally completed.)

I would like to thank John Kane, Brett Bartow, Amy Lewis, and especially Chris Cleveland from Cisco Press for all your hard work that you put into this project. Chris, if it was not for your constant dedication to perfection, I can say that this project would have failed. You are a great editor to work with, for which I am extremely grateful to you. Brett, I have worked with you before on other projects, and, as always, this project has been a pleasure. Your professionalism (and occasional nagging) helped keep me focused on completing this book.

Tom Thomas, Scott Morris, and John Cavanaugh, thank you all for your tremendous efforts as technical reviewers. While sometimes I wish I could strangle you, your comments were always top notch. Tom, my good friend, thanks for your candid comments, especially on the OSPF Chapter ;-). Scott, you always shot from the hip and your comments were dead-on in technical accuracy. And John, you have been a mentor to me since I started at Cisco. You are truly the best in the business—a very rare breed—"A technical guy who is smoother than a sales guy" and am really happy that you helped review this book.

Most of all, I want to thank The Lord Jesus Christ for granting me the ability and strength to write this book and balance time with my family, home, and work.

I wish you, the reader, best of luck in your pursuit of Cisco certification or career enhancement in the area of network design.

Feel free to e-mail me any comments and Second Edition suggestions!

—Matt Birkner (mbirkner@cisco.com)

CCIE #3719
CCDP
CNE
BNCS
BSEE

Contents at a Glance

Table of Contents

Figure Icons Used in This Book

Throughout this book, you will see the following icons used for networking devices:

Router

Bridge

Workgroup Switch

ATM Switch

Multilayer Switch

DSU/CSU

Communication Server

PIX Firewall

Gateway

Throughout this book, you will see the following icons used for peripherals and other devices:

PC

Workstation

Macintosh

Terminal

Printer

File Server

IBM Mainframe

Front End Processor

Cluster Controller

Host

Throughout this book, you will see the following icons used for networks:

Line: Ethernet

Token Ring

FDDI

Line: Serial

Line: Switched Serial

Network Cloud

Introduction

Internetworks are growing at a fast pace, supporting more protocols and users, and becoming more complex. The proper design of these networks is therefore becoming more crucial to the optimal operation and management of the network. Cisco Systems, as the premier designer and provider of internetworking devices, is committed to supporting network designers, implementers, and administrators in the use of its products.

The content, objectives, and organization of this book are based on the current *Cisco Internetwork Design (CID)* instructor-led course. This book provides a reference and reinforcement of ideas in this course, as students prepare for their Cisco Certified Design Professional (CCDP) exam and Cisco Certified Internetworking Expert (CCIE) exam.

This book provides the reader with a framework and process to follow when designing internetworks, to ensure that all essential issues necessary to design an optimal network are considered. The process includes steps for defining what the network requirements are, the decisions that need to be made in the design process, and how to document and test the design.

Case studies are used to provide you with an opportunity to evaluate your understanding of, and to practice applying, the concepts presented. The chapters in the book also contain *Design Rules*, *Tips*, and *Notes* to emphasize critical details, and other supplementary information to provide useful background and reference information.

Who Should Read This Book

Cisco Internetwork Design can be used as a general reference for the design of internetworks, as well as a specific reference for designing with Cisco devices. People reading this book are typically internetwork designers and systems engineers who have experience implementing networks and are currently involved in designing architectures for complex, multiprotocol internetworks. If you are planning to take a Cisco certification exam, particularly the CCDP or the CCIE lab exam, this book provides you with in-depth study material.

Before reading this book, it is assumed that you have working knowledge of internetworking and Cisco products. You should have both theoretical and hands-on experience with multiprotocol internetworks. You should also have an understanding of typical routing algorithms, including distance vector, link-state, split horizon, and the concept of convergence. A detailed understanding of the IP protocol, including addressing, subnetting, and routing protocols such as RIP, IGRP, and OSPF is also needed. You should be able to recognize routing and bridging issues in the AppleTalk, IPX, and NetBIOS environments. You should have a knowledge of WAN protocols including Frame Relay, ISDN and X.25, and an understanding of typical bridging algorithms, including source-route bridging, transparent bridging, and the Spanning-Tree Algorithm. You should have a working knowledge of protocol behavior, such as broadcasting, multicasting, keepalives, flow control, resource discovery, connectionless versus connection-oriented services, connection establishment, and media access methods.

If you lack experience with internetworking technologies and Cisco products, it is recommended that you review Cisco's interactive, self-paced *Internetworking Multimedia CD-ROM*, or read the *Internetworking Technologies Handbook* (Cisco Press), before starting this course.

Objectives for This Book

Upon completion of the readings and exercises this book, you will be able to design a network that meets a customer's requirements for performance, security, capacity, and scalability, and assemble Cisco devices into an end-to-end networking solution. The case studies used at the end of the book allow you to test your knowledge at each step in the design process.

After you finish this book, you might choose to become certified by completing the CCDP exam through your local Sylvan Testing Center. The CCDP Sylvan-administered examination will verify that you have met the objectives of this book.

Parts of the Book

This book is organized in eight parts, as described in the following sections.

Part I: Introduction to Internetwork Design

Chapter 1, "Internetwork Design Overview," provides a review of key internetworking technology information. Chapter 1 also includes excerpts from Cisco's interactive, self-paced *Internetworking Multimedia CD-ROM*, and the *Internetworking Technologies Handbook* (Cisco Press). The objectives for this chapter are as follows:

- List internetwork design goals
- Identify key requirements of internetwork design
- Describe a methodology for internetwork design

Chapter 2, "Hierarchical Internetwork Design," provides a framework that you can use to easily analyze customer network problems and create Cisco scalable solutions. The objectives for this chapter are as follows:

- Describe the benefits of using a hierarchical design model
- Identify the three tiers that make up the hierarchical model
- Describe the functions typically performed at each tier
- Describe variations on the three-tier hierarchy using only one or two tiers of the model

Part II: Campus LAN Design

Chapter 3, "Campus LAN Overview," defines the design, technical, and business considerations that you must wrestle with before jumping in and deploying a campus LAN design. The objectives for this chapter are as follows:

- Identify the technical considerations in campus LAN design
- Identify the business considerations in campus LAN design
- Describe the evolutionary approach to campus LAN design

Chapter 4, "Campus LAN Technology," focuses on the LAN technologies most commonly used in campus LANs, including the various flavors of Ethernet, Token Ring, FDDI, and ATM. This chapter also discusses the concepts of bridging, switching, routing, and VLANs. The objectives for this chapter are as follows:

- Summarize the technology options available for campus LAN design
- Describe the operation of Ethernet, Token Ring, Fiber Distributed Data Interface (FDDI), and Asynchronous Transfer Mode (ATM) as technologies supporting the network design model
- Compare bridging/switching and routing as interconnection and segmentation techniques
- Discuss the deployment of VLANs and LANE

Chapter 5, "Campus LAN Design Models," discusses cabling topologies typically used in campus LANs. In addition, you learn about what the best backbone design is for your campus LAN as well as how to properly deploy VLANs. Finally, the chapter wraps up with coverage of how to migrate to ATM in the campus LAN. The objectives for this chapter are as follows:

- Describe cabling topologies used in campus LAN designs
- Describe and implement distributed backbone designs in campus LANs

- Describe and implement collapsed backbone designs in campus LANs
- Describe deployment of VLANs and LANE in campus LANs
- Determine where to use switches, where to use bridges, and where to use routers in segmenting campus LANs

Part III: TCP/IP Network Design

Chapter 6, "TCP/IP Design Overview," delves into IP addressing and all the trappings that come with it. In addition, this chapter focuses on routing protocols and considerations as well as the security considerations that you need to consider with a TCP/IP network. The objectives for this chapter are as follows:

- Describe aspects of design relating to TCP/IP networks
- Understand limitations inherent in IP addressing
- Distinguish private from public network addressing
- Describe the purpose of IP subnetting
- Describe the function of Internet routing protocols
- Describe the security requirements in a TCP/IP network

Chapter 7, "TCP/IP Addressing Design," focuses on the various addressing choices you have when designing a TCP/IP network and how to manage your IP addressing option. This chapter also covers multicast addressing considerations and TCP/IP security. The objectives for this chapter are as follows:

- Choose an appropriate IP addressing scheme based on business and technical requirements
- Identify IP addressing problems and describe strategies for resolving them
- Describe different address management tools and techniques, including DNS and DHCP
- Understand the mechanics of multicast addressing
- Describe methods for implementing TCP/IP security features

Chapter 8, "Routing Protocol Design," describes basic routing concepts and the different types of routing protocols (those directly affecting host routing, interior routing protocols, and exterior routing protocols). This chapter also explains aggregation, convergence, and route redistribution. The objectives for this chapter are as follows:

- Business and technical requirements for routing protocol design
- Routing concepts
- Routing protocol categorization
- Route summarization (aggregation)
- Routing convergence
- Route redistribution

Chapter 9, "OSPF Design," focuses on IGP, link-state protocol, OSPF, and those topics associated with OSPF, including: the mechanics of how the protocol works, summarization, OSPF areas, OSPF backbone design, and the scalability of OSPF networks. The objectives for this chapter are as follows:

- Describe how to use modular design and summarization features to design scalable Open Shortest Path First (OSPF) internetworks

- Describe how to allocate IP addresses in contiguous blocks so that OSPF summarization can be used

Chapter 10, "IGRP/EIGRP Design," explains the mechanics, routing characteristics, and convergence of EIGRP and its predecessor, IGRP. The objectives for this chapter are as follows:

- Determine IGRP convergence time for various internetwork configurations
- Describe how to use IGRP for path determination in IP internetworks
- Describe how to use EIGRP for path determination in internetworks that support IP, IPX, and AppleTalk

Part IV: Desktop Protocol Design

Chapter 11, "Desktop Design Overview," focuses on the fundamentals of desktop protocols, including: IPX, AppleTalk, and Microsoft Windows. Specifically, the chapter covers the client/server models and broadcast technology as they apply to these three common desktop protocols. The objectives for this chapter are as follows:

- Explain the requirements of the client/server model as implemented by different desktop protocols
- Explain how clients send out broadcasts to locate servers for Novell IPX, AppleTalk, and Microsoft Windows networks
- Describe the elements involved in desktop protocol design

Chapter 12, "IPX Design," discusses the protocols, encapsulations, routing specifics, and configuration considerations indigenous to IPX networks. This chapter also tackles RIP and SAP issues that you might encounter in an IPX network. The objectives for this chapter are as follows:

- Examine a client's requirements and construct an appropriate IPX design solution
- Choose the appropriate routing protocol for an IPX internetwork
- Describe how to design scalable and manageable IPX internetworks by controlling RIP and SAP traffic

Chapter 13, "AppleTalk Design," focuses on the business and technical requirements for an AppleTalk network, as well as the protocol, routing, and administrative choice issues that come with planning an AppleTalk network design. In addition, this chapter discusses the network and zone information filtering options available to AppleTalk. Tunneling AppleTalk in IP-only networks is also covered. The objectives for this chapter are as follows:

- Examine a sample client's requirements and construct an appropriate AppleTalk design solution
- Determine which addressing and naming conventions are used to build manageable and scalable AppleTalk internetworks
- Describe how to use Cisco IOS software features to design scalable AppleTalk internetworks

Chapter 14, "Windows Networking Design" focuses on general Windows Networking concepts, specifically, the mechanics, components, and transport protocols associated with NetBIOS. The chapter also tackles the multifaceted topic of name resolution and concludes with several Windows Networking design examples. The objectives for this chapter are as follows:

- Identify the design requirements of deploying Windows-based internetworks
- Describe the network architecture used by Microsoft clients and servers
- Describe the operation of the NetBIOS and NetBEUI protocol stacks
- Identify the operational impact that NetBIOS and NetBEUI have on network design
- Describe design practices that allow efficient deployment of NetBIOS and NetBEUI

Part V: WAN Design

Chapter 15, "WAN Design Overview," discusses basic WAN design issues as well as how to optimize core WAN availability and performance. This chapter also covers WAN backbone routing protocol choices. The objectives for this chapter are as follows:

- List common concerns that customers have about WAN designs
- Examine sample customer statements and distinguish issues that affect the choice of WAN designs
- Describe how to design core WAN connectivity to maximize availability and optimize utilization of resources

Chapter 16, "Design Using Dedicated Lines," provides an invaluable overview of leased lines, including the required components/connections and general line usage guidelines. This chapter also covers the serial line encapsulations deployed with dedicated lines as well as the ideal WAN architecture design for use with dedicated lines. The objectives for this chapter are as follows:

- Identify the components required for leased line connections
- Compare different leased line topology methods
- Describe different encapsulation methods and the benefits of each

Chapter 17, "Frame Relay Design," provides a general overview of Frame Relay networks, including coverage of the advantages, access devices, services, and switching operations associated with Frame Relay. In addition, this chapter covers router interaction, NBMA, and subinterfaces in Frame Relay networks. The chapter concludes with the various Frame Relay topology options. The objectives for this chapter are as follows:

- Understand Frame Relay terminology
- Describe the components and terminology used in Frame Relay networks
- Compare different topology options available in Frame Relay designs, recognizing the costs and the benefits of each

Chapter 18, "X.25 Design" focuses on using X.25 switching to provide X.25 services over an integrated IP backbone, using static routing and static SAPs over reliable X.25 WAN circuits, using the hierarchical design to scale an X.25 NBMA WAN, and using point-to-point subinterface configuration for robust routing over an X.25 WAN core. The objectives for this chapter are as follows:

- Design scalable internetwork WANs with NBMA X.25
- Design a scalable, robust internetwork WAN with X.25 subinterface configurations
- Describe how to use X.25 switching to provide X.25 service over an integrated IP backbone

Chapter 19, "Remote Access Design," covers using dial-up remote access through analog and ISDN, the different types of remote access methods, the equipment at both the central and remote site needed to deploy remote access. In addition, this chapter provides an in-depth look at the various protocols required to deploy remote access and the security and Internet considerations you need to make before deploying remote access. The objectives for this chapter are as follows:

- Identify the major business and technology issues that relate to remote access
- Describe the two dialup connection methods and the benefits of each
- Identify three methods to connect remote users
- Select equipment to be deployed at the remote user site
- Select equipment to be deployed at the central site
- Describe security and Internet design options

Chapter 20, "ATM Internetwork Design," covers ATM concepts, routing, and implementation in LANs and WANs. The chapter also covers SMDS concepts and implementation issues. The objectives for this chapter are as follows:

- Describe issues related to using cell-based services for WAN connections
- Describe how to implement router- and ATM-based designs for ATM WAN connectivity
- Describe how to deploy SMDS technology in a WAN design

Part VI: SNA Design

Chapter 21, "SNA Design Overview," in addition to providing a comprehensive overview of SNA, focuses on the hardware, software, link, and gateway components of an SNA network. This chapter also covers complex SNA internetworking concepts such as SDLC tunneling, remote source-route bridging (RSRB), data-link switching (DLSw), and the Cisco Channel Interface Processor (CIP). The chapter concludes with a detailed look at topology considerations for SNA internetworks. The objectives for this chapter are as follows:

- Identify the components that make up the SNA environment and the function of each
- Compare different methods of doing SNA internetworking and list the benefits of each
- Describe different topologies used in SNA designs

Part VII: CID Course Summary and Case Studies

Chapter 22, "Internetworking Design Summary," wraps up the main chapters of the coursebook with a reflection on internetwork design goals, steps for designing internetworks, and the tools needed to determine that your internetwork design works. The objectives for this chapter are as follows:

- Summarize the major concepts covered in the rest of the book
- Recall the steps for internetwork design
- Describe methods for monitoring your internetwork design
- Return to your environment with fresh ideas and plans for internetwork designs

Chapter 23, "Case Studies," provides the framework for six different network scenarios. Each case study specifies the current network setup as well as the criteria needed for a new network design. Your task is to apply the knowledge you've gained from the book to design new networks for each case study.

Part VIII: Appendixes

Appendix A, "Answers to Chapter Review Questions," repeats the questions found at the end of each chapter and provides the correct answers.

Appendix B, "Solutions to Case Studies," provides viable solutions to the case study problems found in Chapter 23. Although there are probably several solutions for these case studies, the solutions provided in this appendix are a litmus test to ensure that your design solutions are on the right track.

Appendix C, "Design and Implementation Guide: Frame Relay," is a document previously available to internal Cisco employees only. This design and implementation guide was originally posted internally at Cisco in 1996 by Adrien Fournier. It has been updated and included as a valuable supplement to this coursebook.

Appendix D, "Design and Implementation Guide: Designing Networks with Windows Networking," is another document previously available to internal Cisco employees only. This design and implementation guide was originally posted internally at Cisco in 1996 by Rohan Mahy. It has been updated and included as a valuable supplement to this coursebook.

Appendix E, "Design and Implementation Guide: OSPF," is a popular resource written by Bassam Halabi, which you can also find at http://www.cisco.com/warp/public/104/1.html. This design guide has been updated and included as a valuable supplement to this coursebook.

Foreword

In April 1998, Cisco Systems, Inc., announced a new professional development initiative called the *Cisco Career Certifications*. These certifications address the growing worldwide demand for more qualified and better trained computer networking experts. Building upon our highly successful Cisco Certified Internetwork Expert (CCIE) program—the industry's most respected networking certification vehicle—Cisco Career Certifications enable you to be certified at various technical proficiency levels.

Cisco Internetwork Design presents, in book format, all the topics covered in the challenging, instructor-led certification preparation course of the same name. The Cisco Internetwork Design (CID) exam is one of four required to become a Cisco Certified Design Professional (CCDP). Whether you are studying to become CCDP certified, or if you just need a better understanding of the framework and processes that ensure optimal network design, you will benefit from the insights this book offers.

Cisco Systems, Inc., and Cisco Press present this material in text-based format to provide another learning vehicle for our customers and the broader user community in general. Although a publication cannot replace the instructor-led environment, we must acknowledge that not everyone responds in the same way to the same delivery mechanism. It is our intent that presenting this material through a Cisco Press publication will enhance the transfer of knowledge to our audience of networking professionals.

This is the sixth book in a series of course supplements planned for Cisco Press, following *Introduction to Cisco Router Configuration, Advanced Cisco Router Configuration, Building Cisco Remote Access Networks, Cisco Internetwork Troubleshooting,* and *Designing Cisco Networks*. Cisco will present existing and future courses through these Coursebooks to help achieve Cisco Worldwide Training's principal objectives: to educate Cisco's community of networking professionals and to enable that community to build and maintain reliable, scalable networks. The Cisco Career Certifications and classes that define these certifications are directed at meeting these objectives through a disciplined approach to progressive certification. The books Cisco Systems, Inc., creates in partnership with Cisco Press will meet the same standards for content quality demanded of our courses and certifications. It is our intent that you will find this and subsequent Cisco Press certification and training publications of value as you build your networking knowledge base.

Thomas M. Kelly
Director, Worldwide Training
Cisco Systems, Inc.
September 1999

Introduction to Internetwork Design

Nothing in this world can take the place of persistence. Talent will not; nothing is more common than unsuccessful people with talent. Genius will not; unrewarded genius is almost a proverb. Education will not; the world is full of educated derelicts. Persistence and determination alone are omnipotent. The slogan "Press On" has solved and always will solve the problems of the human race.

—Calvin Coolidge

Upon completion of this chapter, you will be able to do the following:

- List internetwork design goals
- Identify key requirements of internetwork design
- Describe a methodology for internetwork design

CHAPTER 1

Internetwork Design Overview

If you have ever been tasked with a network design project, whether large or small, undoubtedly you have had to make several difficult design decisions. You may have even found several "right answers" to the problem, but then needed to select the best "right answer." What, then, is the best "right answer?" It depends on how well you and your team know your customer and their requirements. The truth is, you can approach a network design in several ways. However, most network designs (the successful ones, at least) follow some fundamental guidelines.

This chapter focuses on the goals of internetwork design, including the technical and business trade-offs you must understand prior to making design choices. Sometimes, you and your team may be diverted from the topic into business issues that may not necessarily be technically oriented. As a network designer, you must remember to keep the team focused and gather the relevant information to make the design meet the customer's goals. This chapter provides you with an internetwork design methodology road map for use when approaching an internetwork design to keep your project on track.

Internetwork Design Goals

An internetwork can be generally defined as two or more local-area networks (LANs) interconnected by one or more Layer 3 devices (ordinarily routers). An internetwork may be contained within a single building, or may span the globe. Although there are specific differences between LANs and wide-area networks (WANs), in general terminology (and in this book) the word *network* refers to either type.

The first step in designing an internetwork is to establish and document the goals of the design. These goals will be particular to each organization or situation. Certain requirements tend to always show up in any good network design, however. They are as follows:

- Functionality
- Scalability
- Adaptability
- Manageability
- Cost effectiveness

Functionality

First and foremost, you cannot design a network without first fully knowing what you are trying to accomplish. Gathering all the requirements is often a very difficult task, but when the network is deployed, it must work as designed. There is absolutely no room for negotiation here. The network must enable users to meet their individual job requirements in such a way that the overall business requirements of the organization are met. The network must provide end-to-end application availability at some specified level of service (defined by management as the optimal compromise between functionality and cost). An MCI executive once told me that, before you embark on a new challenge, you must know the answer to the question, "How do you measure your success?" I urge you to ask yourself this same question of your network design on a regular basis, because it leads to an overall understanding of the tasks you are trying to achieve and keeps you focused on success.

Scalability

The network must be able to grow as the organization grows, and as more of the organization is included in the network. The initial design must be scalable across several orders of magnitude of network growth.

Take company XYZ, for example. They have been acquiring new companies at a rate of three to five per year. As a measure of your success, the network infrastructure must scale in a modular fashion so that new acquisitions "snap in" to their existing infrastructure. If scalability is not present in company XYZ's network, the network absorption of this new company will undoubtedly fail or will become a management nightmare. I have seen many networks in the past which, due to poor planning for scalability, had become a jumbled "spaghetti net." It is vital, therefore, to ensure that a design will scale in the future, even if large-scale expansion is not necessarily required today.

Adaptability

The network should be designed with an eye toward future technologies and should not include any design elements that would limit adoption of new technologies as they become available. There may be trade-offs between this and cost effectiveness throughout a network design/implementation. For example, Voice over IP (VoIP) and multicast are new technologies rapidly being adopted in many internetworks. Network designs should certainly be able to support these technologies without requiring a "forklift upgrade." This is done by provisioning hardware and software that has future-proofed options for expansion and upgradability.

Manageability

The network should be designed to facilitate proactive network monitoring and management, to ensure ongoing stability of operation and availability of resources (see the sidebar later in this chapter, "Total Cost of Ownership"). You should consider a network management strategy as carefully as you consider the network design. What this means is that the network must work as designed, but it also must be *supportable*. If a highly complex design is delivered to the network-management team, it may require an excessive amount of your time and support to work with network-operations personnel. The key is to remember that another organization or individual may support the network you designed. Your reputation as a designer is on the line and, as the adage says, "Perception is reality."

Cost Effectiveness

The benefits of the network to the organization, however quantified, must equal or outweigh the costs. The cost of implementing the network design must be within agreed-upon budgetary constraints. For example, a design requirement may implicitly exceed the financial commitment of the customer. If that is the case, you must identify this and find an alternative solution, if one exists. If an alternative does not exist, this must be communicated back to the customer with his options so that he can make an informed decision.

Key Design Issues and Requirements

The cost trade-offs involved in internetwork design can be viewed in two ways:

- The costs could be categorized according to the technology, whether it be WAN or LAN design.
- The costs could be divided between one-time, fixed costs, and costs that recur on a regular (often monthly) basis.

In the WAN environment, the fixed costs typically are for equipment purchases, such as modems, channel service unit/data service units (CSU/DSUs), and router interfaces, as well as for any circuit-provisioning costs and network-management tools and platforms such as NetView and HP OpenView. The recurring costs are the monthly circuit fees from the service provider. Additionally, recurring costs are those for support and maintenance of the WAN, including any network management center personnel.

In the LAN environment, the fixed costs again include equipment purchases—such as routers, switches, and hubs—and the purchase and installation costs of the physical cabling for the network. The recurring costs are the salaries of administration staff who attend to daily network operations. Day-to-day operational tasks include user moves, adds, and changes related to end stations, along with the growth, maintenance, and troubleshooting of the network infrastructure.

The real cost of ownership of a network is most often overlooked in the preliminary phases of network design. Typically, recurring costs such as cost of circuits and staff tend to predominate in LAN and WAN environments. When weighing trade-offs between cost and benefit, you should first consider changes that offer the potential for reducing recurring costs. As previously stated, however, neglecting the real cost of ownership is a trap that many network designers fall into.

Total Cost of Ownership

According to a survey conducted by The Gartner Group (described further at www.cisco.com/warp/public/779/smbiz/solutions/t1.shtml), the miscalculation of labor costs involved in setting up and managing WANs has left many organizations underestimating network Total Cost of Ownership (TCO) by half. The study suggests labor accounts for a whopping 43% of some networks' TCO, with the rest of the money covering such items as training, end-user downtime, disaster prevention, and information recovery.

Design Methodology

The flowchart in Figure 1-1 outlines a simple methodology that you can use in your network design. Notice that the first three steps to be completed are one-time and sequential. The initial steps of designing the network topology and of devising addressing and naming conventions should be completed early, and should not require major revision later. These foundational steps are very important for the next steps to successfully occur. The next three steps are a recurring loop that never goes back beyond the fourth step. Keeping router Internetworking Operating System (IOS) code current through online bug searches and tools available on Cisco Connection Online (CCO), www.cisco.com, should be viewed as an ongoing task. Much like code maintenance, capacity planning and maintenance should also be an area of ongoing attention.

Figure 1-1   *Design Methodology*

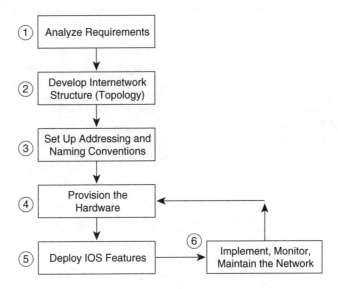

Step 1: Analyze Requirements

Step 1 in the design methodology is to analyze the requirements of the network and its users. Network user needs constantly change, both in response to changing business conditions and in response to changes in technology itself. As more voice and video-based network applications (for example, Cisco IP/TV) become available, for example, the pressure to increase network bandwidth intensifies. Needs analysis includes not only the business case (cost/benefit analysis) for adopting such bandwidth-hungry applications, but also a detailed analysis of the procedures and costs required to upgrade the network to provide the needed bandwidth. Similar examples might include extending the corporate network to include regional and international offices, or integrating a telephone system into what was previously a data-only network.

Step 2: Develop the Internetwork Structure

Step 2 in the design methodology is to develop the overall network topology using a three-tiered hierarchical model. In this model, the network is divided into core, distribution, and access tiers. These tiers describe a set of discrete functions performed at each tier, as well as a network topology typically associated with each tier. Each tier within the topology has its own function. By keeping the tiers separate, the hierarchical design method produces a highly flexible and scalable network. Figure 1-2 shows an internetwork structure that follows the hierarchical model of network design.

Figure 1-2 *Develop the Internetwork Structure*

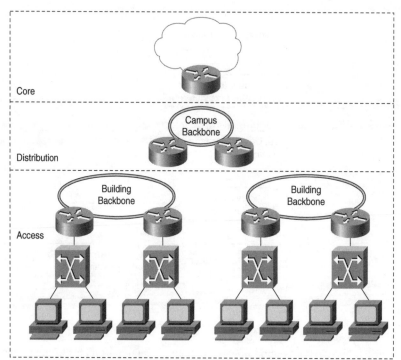

In the hierarchical model, the core tier primarily provides the wide-area links between geographically remote sites, tying a number of campus networks together in a corporate or enterprise WAN. Hosts are rarely in the core tier; core services are typically leased from a telecom service provider (for example, T1/T3, Frame Relay, SMDS, and ATM). In fact, placing hosts in the core is not generally recommended.

NOTE
The use of the word *tier* here is unrelated to the seven-layer OSI reference model. The three-tiered model describes a network design methodology, not a protocol stack. It is worth noting, however, that a boundary between topological tiers is usually created with an OSI reference model Layer 3 device (for example, a router).

The distribution tier generally refers to the distribution of network services to multiple LANs within a campus network environment. This tier is where the campus backbone network is found and is typically based on FDDI, Fast or Gigabit Ethernet, or sometimes campus ATM. In Figure 1-2, the distribution tier is implemented as a FDDI ring. This tier is often where network policy is implemented as well (that is, security, access lists, and so on). In many corporate networks, for example, you'll find that the distribution tier is commonly where company-wide servers (such as e-mail, Internet proxy, firewalls, demilitarized zones [DMZs], and so on) are placed.

The access tier is usually a LAN or a group of LANs, typically Ethernet or Token Ring, that provides users with first-line access to network services. The access tier is where almost all hosts are attached to the network, including servers of all kinds as well as user workstations.

Step 3: Set Up Addressing and Naming Conventions

Step 3 in the design methodology is to develop the overall addressing scheme by assigning blocks of addresses to portions of the network, thus simplifying address administration and producing a more scalable internetwork. In the TCP/IP example in Figure 1-3, IP address 10.0.0.0 with 16 bits of subnetting is used throughout the organization. This campus has been allocated a contiguous block of 254 of these addresses. The address is then further allocated, with each building receiving approximately 16 contiguous subnets.

Figure 1-3 *Set Up Addressing and Naming Conventions*

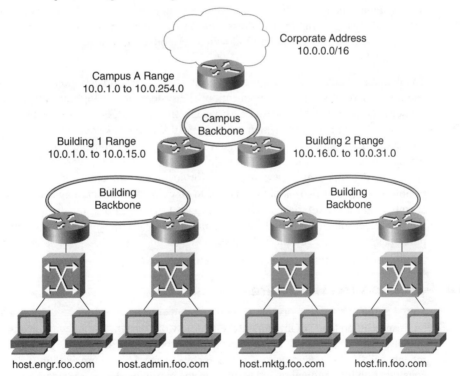

If the routing protocols used in the internetwork support variable-length subnet masking (VLSM), you can deploy a true hierarchical addressing scheme. In a generic TCP/IP example, an 8-bit subnet mask can be in use at the core tier, a 16-bit mask can be in use at the distribution tier, and a 24-bit mask can be applied to the access tier. Careful allocation of addresses in a hierarchical design can result in efficient summarization of routes in the routing tables.

Consider 10.0.0.0 as a sample network number that you are assigned. Your network will consist of 50 regions. An example of an 8-bit subnet mask will be chosen at the core for summarization. The subnet and subnet mask at the core location would be 10.0.0.0 255.0.0.0. The result is that all the specific route entries at the access and distribution tiers will not be seen to the outside world. After you do this, the core basically says to any external network, "If your IP packet destination is '10.anything,' come to me." At the distribution tier, a 16-bit mask is used to identify each region without allowing all the specific routes at the access layer to be propagated to other distribution layer routers. A typical subnet and mask combination at the distribution tier would be 10.1.0.0 255.255.0.0.

After you do this, the distribution tier router basically says to any external network, "If your IP packet destination is '10.1.anything,' come to me." Finally, the access tier uses a 24-bit mask. A typical subnet and mask combination at the access tier would be 10.1.1.0 255.255.255.0. As you migrate down the hierarchical model, your subnet masks become more granular (more specific), and, as you move back to the top, the masks become less specific. By using hierarchical addressing to fit your hierarchical model, the result is *scalability* and *stability*. Networks following this model can scale to thousands of nodes and be extremely stable.

The naming scheme is also designed in a systematic way, with common prefixes used for naming components within an organization. The systematic naming convention also makes the network more scalable and easier to manage. In Figure 1-3, each site has a named prefix that identifies the domain to which it belongs. All admin hosts contain admin.foo.com in their name, for example. Generally, onto this name you will prepend a name such as tiffany.admin.foo.com for a specific user's workstation (Tiffany's workstation) within the hostadmin domain. This proves invaluable for documentation and subsequent troubleshooting and also should be applied to other areas where naming is important, such as router names and interface descriptions. In the future, as more sites are added, you have room to select some unused addresses within a preallocated range. Also, the names become predictable and organized for optimal support.

Step 4: Provision the Hardware

Step 4 in the methodology is to use vendor documentation to select the LAN and WAN hardware components, to implement the internetwork design. LAN devices include router models, switch models, cabling systems, and backbone connections. WAN devices include modems, CSU/DSUs, and remote access servers. The selection process typically includes consideration of the function and features of the particular devices, including their expandability and management capabilities. The initial cost of the equipment is always part of the decision process.

An example of a hierarchical hardware design uses a Cisco 7200 class router at the core tier, a Cisco 3600 class router at the distribution tier, and a Cisco 2600 class router at the access tier. An excellent tool available on CCO can assist you in router product selection. You can find this tool at www.cisco.com/public/reseller_mktplace/select.html. Note also that the IOS version may be impacted by the type of hardware selected; certain hardware features require specific levels of software. An example would be the new NPE-300 CPU for the 7200 platform. This CPU requires a minimum IOS of 12.0 to operate and may impact (in a positive or negative way) your ultimate hardware decision.

Step 5: Deploy Cisco IOS Software Features

Step 5 in the methodology is to deploy Cisco IOS features as appropriate. Many of these features, such as access lists, proxy features, traffic shaping, queuing, QoS, and compression, are available to support bandwidth management. Other features provide support for security, general network management, tariff management, and bandwidth management.

Initial deployment of Cisco IOS features is directly related to the applications in use on host machines. Consideration for protocol types is critical. You might consider asking yourself some of the following questions:

- Are the protocols routable, like IP and IPX?
- Are the protocols nonroutable, like NetBIOS and SNA, DEC MOP (Maintenance Operation Protocol) or LAT (local-area transport) traffic?

Such planning will ensure that NetBIOS doesn't get added as an afterthought—for example, when users of Windows machines accept the defaults. Also, you need to understand which mechanisms are in place to do remote management and router discovery. If so, where are the network-management systems (NMSs) located, and how often will they poll the network?

Additional deployment of features is based on the three-tier hierarchical model. The access tier interconnect devices often employ static definitions, proxy services, and first-cut filtering. The distribution tier typically uses features providing compression, congestion control, and security. Finally, the core tier generally focuses on QoS (Quality of Service) features (for example, WRED—Weighted Random Early Detection). For more information on WRED, check out www.cisco.com/univercd/cc/td/doc/product/software/ios111/cc111/wred.htm.

Step 6: Implement, Monitor, and Manage the Network

The last step in the methodology is to deploy the network. If possible, model and test the new design in a lab environment prior to full deployment. A very good way to do this is to use a modeling tool called Netsys. Netsys enables you to see the network impact of proposed configuration changes before they are made. A good general-reference Web page for Netsys can be found at www.cisco.com/warp/public/458/54.html. Later on, during actual deployment, you should use a phased approach to reduce the impact on the user communities. Perform operational data gathering continuously so that planning for higher-bandwidth applications can occur proactively. A number of SNMP and RMON tools that allow for proactive network management are available today. Deploy new hardware and Cisco IOS software features as required to support new applications. Remember to have solid test and contingency plans before you implement any new design!

Summary

A successful network design requires persistence. As a designer, you are responsible for making your network design a success. This chapter covered a number of issues that you should consider when approaching any internetwork design and outlined an internetwork design methodology to keep you focused on providing a fully functional network design solution. The better you understand your design goals and requirements, the more successful your design will be.

Chapter Review Questions

1   List and describe five goals of a sound network design.

2   What is the key trade-off that must be made in most network designs?

3   Describe the steps that need to take place in a good network design methodology.

4   At which tier of the hierarchical model is QoS usually deployed?

5   Why is scalability so important in good network design?

6   Why is adaptability so important in good network design?

7   At which tier of the hierarchical model are firewalls most often deployed?

More than 200 years ago, the Industrial Revolution changed the fortunes of people, companies, and countries. Similarly, the Internet Revolution of today is driving change and economic growth. Our industry is rapidly maturing with the convergence of data, voice, and video over a single network. As a New World economy begins to evolve, the Internet is being used as a tool to communicate, shop, educate, conduct business, and more.

—John Chambers, President and CEO, Cisco Systems

Upon completion of this chapter, you will be able to do the following:

- Describe the benefits of using a hierarchical design model
- Identify the three tiers that make up the hierarchical model
- Describe the functions typically performed at each tier
- Describe variations on the three-tier hierarchy using only one or two tiers of the model

CHAPTER 2

Hierarchical Design

There really is no "one size fits all" when it comes to network design. All the contributing technologies are complex and changing rapidly, so design tools are often too simplistic or out of date. The interaction of so many complex protocols will produce unique (and often negative) results for every network. Bandwidth-hungry applications are already driving many corporate network architectures to their knees, without even considering a multitude of intranet and Internet applications such as Voice over IP (VoIP), for example. Some engineers are in a position to design a new network infrastructure from the ground up; others need to meld the new technologies into an existing infrastructure. I think it is certainly clear that the Internet Revolution will impact many areas of business and our lives. As Internet services become more and more prevalent, however, Internet-based products and applications will also drive how networks are designed. As a designer, are you ready for this revolution?

This chapter describes the hierarchical model for structuring an internetwork. Although precise models are scarce, the models that do exist are vital for analyzing large, complex internetworks. As stated in Chapter 1, "Internetwork Design Overview," general rules make the complex job of internetwork design easier than it might otherwise be. These rules provide a foundation from which you can build a network to your customers' requirements.

NOTE   The use of the word *tier* in this book was chosen to avoid confusion with the seven-layer OSI reference model. In the three-tier model, we describe a network design methodology, not a protocol stack. It is also worth noting, however, that a boundary between topological layers is usually created by an OSI reference model Layer 3 device (that is, a router) or by other devices that separate broadcast domains.

Components of the Three-Tier Hierarchical Model

The three-tier model consists of core, distribution, and access tiers, with each having specific functions in a hierarchical network design. Figure 2-1 shows the three tiers of the hierarchical network design model and how they all relate to the large internetwork.

Figure 2-1 *Three-Tier Model Components*

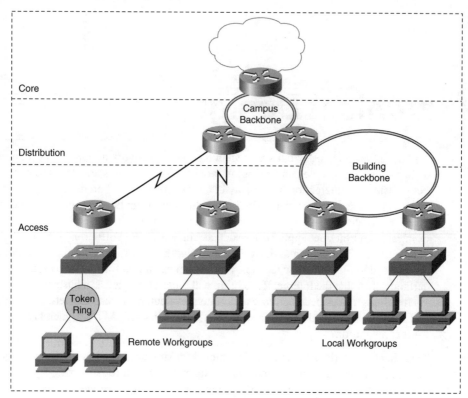

The sections that follow describe the characteristics of each tier. The section titled "Functions of Each Tier" discusses how each tier of the model has its own function that is independent in purpose from the other tiers in the hierarchical model.

Core Tier

The core tier provides optimal wide-area transport between geographically remote sites, tying a number of campus networks together in a corporate or enterprise WAN. Core links are usually point to point, and there are rarely any hosts in the core tier. Core services (for example, T1/E1, T3/E3, OC-12, Frame Relay, ATM, SMDS, and so on) are typically leased from a telecom service provider. The core tier design mission should be to focus on redundancy and reliability. You should examine each component of the core and analyze the tradeoffs between cost and reliability, while bearing in mind the cost of downtime.

NOTE   Many companies measure the real cost of any outage in dollars because of revenue lost. With the advent of the Internet electronic commerce (E-Commerce), many companies are doing millions of dollars of business online each day. The cost of a catastrophic outage could be immense, not including the immeasurable consequences resulting from customer dissatisfaction and bad press. (Making the headlines of the *USA Today* with *<Insert Your Company's Name Here>'s Network Suffers Extended Outage* is *not* a way to get a promotion.)

Spending extra money for redundancy is much like buying car insurance. Most of the time, redundancy is not necessary. Like car insurance, the level of risk you decide to incur will vary from network to network (and even tier to tier within the hierarchy), but it should be an item of considerable forethought and analysis.

Distribution Tier

The distribution tier connects multiple networks within a campus network environment. This tier is where the campus backbone network is found, typically based on FDDI, Fast Ethernet, Gigabit Ethernet, or ATM. This tier is often where network policy is implemented as well (for example, security with IOS firewall feature set, access lists, Network Address Translation, network naming and numbering conventions, and encryption). Network evolution is occurring at a very rapid pace, and as newer and faster technologies evolve, the ones they displace move downward in the hierarchical model. In the not-too-distant future, it will not surprise me to see Gigabit Ethernet at the access tier and Terrabit Ethernet at the distribution or core tiers.

Access Tier

The access tier is usually a LAN or a group of LANs, typically Ethernet or Token Ring, that provides users with local access to network services. The access tier is where almost all hosts are attached to the network, including servers of all kinds and user workstations.

Functions of Each Tier

Each tier of the model has its own function that is independent in purpose from the other tiers in the hierarchical model. However, each tier must be designed to be fully compatible and complementary to the other tiers in the structure.

Core Tier Functions

Simply put, the core tier's primary function is to provide optimal transport between remote sites. The core tier is, therefore, usually implemented as a high-speed WAN, normally ATM, T1/T3, or Frame Relay. Figure 2-2 depicts a common core network that connects multiple geographic networks. An example of a common core router interfaces is High-Speed Serial Interface (HSSI), with speeds reaching more than 50Mbps.

Figure 2-2   *Core Tier Topology*

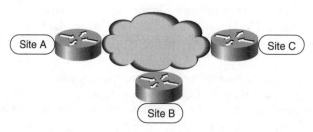

The wide-area character of the link may indicate the need for redundant paths, so that the network can withstand individual circuit outages and continue to function. Load sharing and rapid convergence of routing protocols are generally considered important core design features. Because of provider tariffs, efficient use of bandwidth in the core is nearly always a concern. Efficiencies can be achieved through the use of Cisco IOS software features that reduce bandwidth consumption or prioritize traffic. If a router sends 2000 routes and updates to its neighbors every 90 seconds, there is a certain amount of update overhead that the circuits must carry all the time. If these routes are summarized (you can think of summarization as "network shorthand") into a list of 500 routes, however, your circuit would realize a 75% savings of bandwidth in update traffic.

Some features commonly found in core network designs are Cisco Express Forwarding (CEF), Weighted Random Early Detection (WRED), and route aggregation via Border Gateway Protocol (BGP). As good network design practice, do not put end stations (such as servers) in the core. This allows the core to act strictly as a transit path for traffic between workgroups in different buildings, or from workgroups to campus-wide servers.

DESIGN RULE   Design the core for optimized transport.

Distribution Tier Functions

The distribution tier includes the campus backbone with all its connecting routers. Because network policy is typically implemented at this level, we can say that the distribution tier provides policy-based connectivity. *Policy* in this sense includes the following items:

- Network naming and numbering conventions
- Network security for access to services

- Network security for traffic patterns through definition of path metrics
- Restriction of network advertisements by routing protocols, including route summarization

Typically, distribution tier devices serve a region by acting as a concentration point for many of its access tier sites. Figure 2-3 shows a typical distribution tier layout.

Figure 2-3   *Distribution Tier Topology*

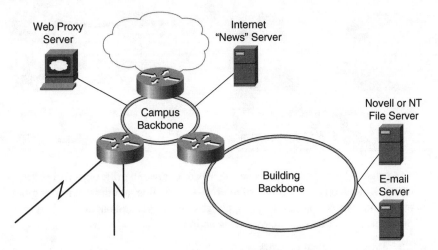

As stated later in the chapter, a big benefit of the hierarchical model (in particular at the distribution tier) is fast problem isolation due to network modularity. A well-designed distribution tier device insulates the rest of the enterprise network from events (link flapping and so forth) that may be occurring within its region.

DESIGN RULE   Implement policy at the distribution layer.

Access Tier Functions

The access tier connects users into LANs, and LANs into campus backbones. This approach enables designers to distribute services across the CPUs of devices operating at this tier. LANs can consist of several different topologies, including Ethernet, Token Ring, and FDDI. Figure 2-4 shows a typical access tier setup. Note that to achieve access tier–to–access tier connectivity, you need to define a connection to the distribution tier (in Figure 2-4, the campus backbone).

Figure 2-4 *Access Tier Topology*

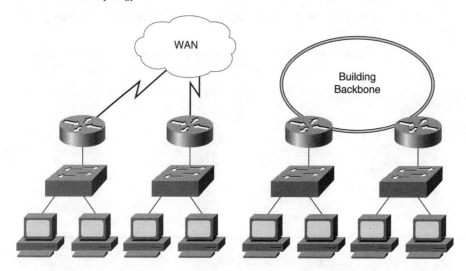

The principal function of the access tier is to connect workgroups (users grouped on the network based on a community of interest—marketing, administration, engineering, and so on) to the distribution tier and, if applicable, its associated backbone. In turn, this function of the access tier carries the following actions:

- Provides logical network segmentation
- Isolates broadcast traffic based on the workgroup or LAN
- Distributes services among multiple CPUs

Traditionally, network segmentation at the access tier is based on organizational boundaries (marketing, administration, and so on). Remote (dialup) users are also often connected at the access tier, and they are generally connected as a separate broadcast domain for performance and easy problem isolation. If a bandwidth utilization problem occurs on the local network, for example, the remote access users are not necessarily impacted because they are in a separate broadcast domain. Furthermore, this isolation is especially important when a problem impacts the remote access users only and an outage window is required to correct it. In this model, only a single group is impacted by the downtime, as opposed to the entire organization.

DESIGN RULE   Move user servers and services down to the access layer.

Benefits of a Hierarchical Design Model

Network designs generally tend to follow one of two general design strategies: mesh or hierarchical. In a mesh structure, the net topology is flat and non-hierarchical; all routers perform essentially the same functions, and there is usually no clear definition of where specific functions are performed, nor is there generally a notion of tiers. Expansion of the network tends to proceed in a haphazard, arbitrary manner, with little or no attention to impact on the network as a whole entity. In a hierarchical structure, the network is organized in tiers that each have one or more specific functions. Characteristics/benefits of a hierarchical model include the following:

- Scalability
- Ease of implementation
- Ease of troubleshooting
- Predictability
- Protocol support
- Manageability

The sections that follow elaborate on these six characteristics/benefits of a hierarchical model.

Scalability

Networks that follow the hierarchical model can grow much larger without sacrificing control or manageability because functionality is localized and potential problems can be recognized more easily. A simple example of a large-scale, scalable, hierarchical network design is that of the Public Switched Telephone Network (PSTN). Of course, the PSTN has had its fair share of growing pains over the years, but additional area codes have been added, successfully scaling this design that has been in service for more than half a century. Regardless of what you think about the PSTN, if your network could scale as well as the PSTN has scaled for the past 50 years, you would be doing quite well.

DESIGN RULE Build hierarchical networks for maximum scalability.

Ease of Implementation

A hierarchical design assigns clear functionality to each tier, thereby making network implementation easier. When deploying a large hierarchical network, for example, a phased approach is generally most effective due to the cost of resources. In brand-new networks, for example, the design team generally begins network deployment at the core, followed by distribution tier routers at concentration locations. These steps are generally followed by the addition of access routers at remote locations, which attach to the distribution routers. A key benefit to this approach is that it allows for efficient allocation of engineering resources during each phase of network deployment.

Ease of Troubleshooting

Because the functions of the individual tiers are well defined, the isolation of problems in the network is less complicated. Temporary segmentation of the network to reduce the scope of a problem is also easily accomplished without requiring a full-scale enterprise outage. This is known as a "divide-and-conquer" approach for troubleshooting. Additionally, areas of troubleshooting responsibility can easily be defined and service levels can be written for each level within the hierarchy. If a problem is isolated to a remote access router, for example, the core network engineers would not necessarily need to be involved in troubleshooting such a problem.

Predictability

The behavior of a network using hierarchical tiers is much more predictable and ultimately makes capacity planning for growth considerably easier. For example, hierarchical design facilitates modeling of network performance for analytical purposes. What that really means is that in a true, hierarchical design, each tier can be analyzed and monitored independently or in conjunction with the other tiers. This is especially important for capacity planning. "How much load is seen at the distribution tier?" or "How much load is seen at the core tier under a given high-traffic condition?" are common questions that a hierarchical design helps answer. Because you can focus on a given tier, you can quickly and easily get your hands around any issue that occurs at any tier. Engineering planning tools such as Netsys are invaluable in helping plan network growth and are well suited for networks with clearly defined boundaries.

Suppose, for example, that you plan to increase network capacity by adding in a parallel circuit between two existing routers. To confirm that load balancing will occur properly before the change occurs, you can load the proposed router configuration files into Netsys and simulate traffic flow between routers. That way, prior to the hot-cut, you have "known" working configurations, ultimately leading to a smoother project implementation.

Protocol Support

The mixing of current and future applications and protocols will be much easier on networks that follow the principles of hierarchical design because the underlying infrastructure is already logically organized. Suppose, for example, that your client acquires another company. Because of the modular nature of a hierarchical network, your client should be able to integrate the new company's network at a predefined connection point and address space range. In multicast network designs, a hierarchical network model bodes well, because the group members are usually located at the access tier, and the multicast content servers are generally located at the distribution tier. Also, as you deploy Internet class applications, new protocols will more easily integrate into your framework.

Manageability

The direct result of following a hierarchical design in the manner described is greater manageability of the network. When it comes time to implement network management instrumentation, for example, your deployment strategy will likely follow the same hierarchy of the network. Many probe deployments involve placing the probes at core and distribution tier router circuits. This same type of model applies often to the network-management system (NMS) model. The NMS "mid-level managers" are often placed at several distribution tier locations and fed back to a centralized location. Therefore, a good hierarchical network design yields hidden benefits for network-management strategies. The network-management staff will thank you for letting them take back control of the network (instead of it being the other way around).

Variations on the Three-Tier Model

A three-tier model can usually meet the needs of most enterprise networks. However, not all environments require a full three-tier hierarchy—a one- or two-tier design may be adequate. Even in these cases, however, a hierarchical structure should be maintained to allow these one- or two-tier hierarchical networks to expand to three tiers as the need arises.

This section identifies three variations of the three-tier model. As a network designer, you should select the model that works best within your environment, because each variation has its own pros and cons.

One-Tier Design—Distributed

Not all networks require a three-tier hierarchy. In fact, a single-tier design will suffice in many smaller networks. Figure 2-5 shows remote networks connecting to a pseudo-core that connects directly to each remote site.

Figure 2-5   *Distributed Design*

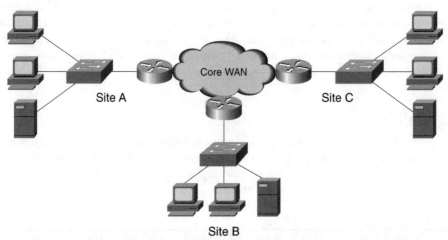

You will typically see this setup when there is an any-to-any connectivity requirement, without the immediate or long-term need for a high level of scalability. An example of a network that may utilize this design would be a small sales organization that does not have a centralized server location. Every night, each salesperson must FTP each other's documents and synchronize personal digital assistant (PDA) data so that all data is updated at the end of each day. The network in Figure 2-5 has a very minimal number of router hops between end devices, which adds to faster overall response time between peers and simplicity in architecture. The beauty of this model is that it is simple and cost effective, but still offers the capability for expansion to support a future core insertion, if the need arises. (Most of all, it gets the job done!)

A key design decision is the placement of corporate servers. They may be distributed across multiple LANs, for example, or concentrated in a central "server farm" location. Figure 2-5 depicts a distributed server design whose major benefits are survivability and lower bandwidth requirements between sites. The downside of this design, however, is the loss of centralized management control because responsibilities such as server backups and network documentation are delegated to the access site. Additionally, higher management cost might result because of the duplicated management functions and personnel skill sets at each site. You could argue that standardization of equipment and best practices tend to get lost or abandoned in this model because there is a lack of centralized control.

One-Tier Design—Hub and Spoke

A hub-and-spoke design is typically deployed in cases where servers are located in central farms. This design has the advantage of increased management control because the servers are centralized; simultaneously, however, there may be concerns regarding single points of failure and bandwidth aggregation. In this design, the server farm network itself makes use of a higher-bandwidth LAN technology (for example, FDDI, Fast Ethernet, Gigabit Ethernet). This design approach, shown in Figure 2-6, enjoys simplicity of structure, but at the same time, it "future-proofs" the network for an upgrade to a higher level of hierarchy if customer requirements change. Future-proofing your network with upgradable and expandable technologies is an essential ingredient to long-term network scalability.

Figure 2-6   *Hub-and-Spoke Design—One Tier*

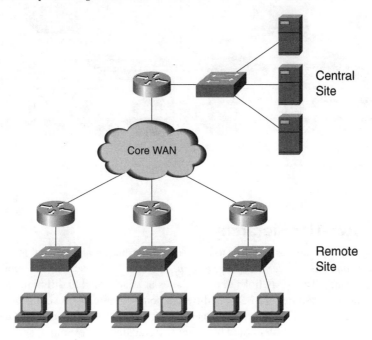

Two-Tier Design

In a two-tier design, a campus backbone interconnects separate buildings. Inside the building, you can implement a single logical network or bridge multiple logical networks. As you will see in Chapter 4, "Campus LAN Technology," you can also use a technology called virtual LANs (VLANs) to create separate logical networks without requiring additional routers. Functionally, VLANs are nothing more than broadcast domains, as previously discussed. Instead of requiring a separate hub for each broadcast domain, however, VLANs can be defined per port within one device. VLANs are very efficient, because they eliminate the need to purchase a new hub for every segment in your network. Figure 2-7 shows a typical two-tier design model.

Figure 2-7 *Two-Tier Design*

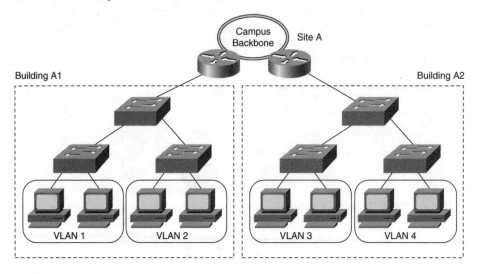

Redundant Two-Tier Hierarchy

Figure 2-8 illustrates one way to use the two-tier hierarchical model in a method called the *redundant two-tier hierarchy design*. The core LAN backbone is duplicated for total redundancy. The WAN links to remote sites are duplicated to different core routers. A number of failures can occur at different points without losing connectivity. Redundancy at each tier of the model maximizes network uptime and survivability. One of the WAN links to an access router could be a Frame Relay link, for example, and the other could be dial-backup or ISDN.

Figure 2-8 *Redundant Two-Tier Hierarchy Design*

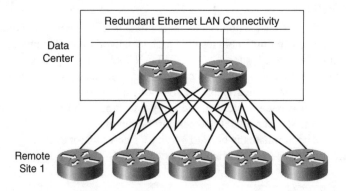

This configuration provides cost-effective redundancy because LAN media is inexpensive relative to WAN media. In other situations where ISDN may be unavailable, the remote site often chooses to back up the Frame Relay link with another Frame Relay circuit with Zero Kilobytes Committed Information Rate (0 K CIR).

Hierarchical Design Guidelines

The use of a hierarchical model facilitates a design rollout where similar topologies are replicated at many sites and a modular architecture facilitates gradual migration to technologies. Guidelines for effective use of the hierarchical design model are as follows:

- **Choose a hierarchical model that best fits your requirements**—This boundary serves as an isolation point for broadcasts as well as a focal point for network control functions, such as access control lists.

- **Do not always completely mesh all tiers of the network**—Meshing would occur if access tier routers were directly connected, or if distribution routers at different sites were directly connected (not through backbones). Core connectivity, however, will generally be meshed for circuit redundancy and network convergence speed.

- **Do not place end stations on backbones**—A backbone without end stations improves the reliability of the backbone, facilitates traffic management, and makes planning for increased bandwidth easier. Placement of stations on the network backbone can also lead to longer convergence and potential route-redistribution problems.

- **Workgroup LANs should be "well behaved" by keeping as much as 80% of their traffic local to the workgroup**—Proper workgroup behavior is accomplished by positioning the server on the workgroup LAN. The so-called 80/20 rule for LANs with servers should still apply here.

- **Use specific features at the appropriate hierarchical level**—The hierarchical design model vastly facilitates deployment of Cisco IOS software features, but you need to choose the features carefully, based on the need that you are trying to address.

Summary

Hierarchical models for internetwork design help you design, implement, and manage scalable internetworks by using a tiered approach. This model is very powerful because the concepts can be applied to virtually any internetwork, from small to large.

A hierarchical network design consists of the core tier, distribution tier, and access tier. Each tier represents functionality that needs to exist in a network. In some cases, a particular tier can be omitted altogether; for optimal network performance, however, you should always maintain some form of hierarchy.

As technology heads into the 21st century, network requirements will undoubtedly continue to grow. By using sound hierarchical design practices, you will be able to scale the network as needs change and most importantly, maintain control of the network (instead of it controlling you).

Chapter Review Questions

1 What three components comprise the hierarchical model?

2 What is the primary function of the core tier in a hierarchical network design?

3 Describe the functions performed at the distribution tier of a hierarchical network design.

4 Describe the elements that comprise the access tier of a hierarchical network design.

5 Identify six benefits of using a hierarchical design model.

6 List some common variations on the three-tier hierarchy using only one or two tiers of the model.

7 What are the general hierarchical design guidelines?

8 What are some IOS features commonly found in the core tier design?

Campus LAN Design

When change is inevitable, you must recognize it, embrace it, and find ways to make it work for you.

—Bill Gates, Chairman and CEO of Microsoft Corporation

Upon completion of this chapter, you will be able to do the following:

- Identify the technical considerations in campus LAN design
- Identify the business considerations in campus LAN design
- Describe the evolutionary approach to campus LAN design

CHAPTER 3

Campus LAN Overview

The first step in any campus network design is to identify the technical and business considerations that surround the project. Traditional bridges, switches, and routers are still commonplace in many designs, but newer switches such as the Cisco 8500 series and the Cisco 4000 and Cisco 6000 series are becoming more prevalent in campus designs models. As demonstrated in Chapter 2, "Hierarchical Design," networks are continually evolving to meet new customer needs. As this chapter demonstrates, however, regardless of the current trends, many similar types of issues need to be considered for any campus design to be successful. The best solution always boils down to this question: What problem am I trying to solve? As a network design engineer, you should challenge yourself to answer that question for each issue you face. Before making any kind of technical analysis, you must be able to determine the characteristics of the issue you are tasked with solving. The conclusions you can draw from these questions will be very helpful to ensuring your design's success.

Campus LAN Design Considerations

When designing a campus LAN, you must take into account several common technical considerations, which are generally defined by the following areas:

- Client end-station issues
- Server end-station issues
- Network infrastructure issues
- Cable design choices
- Network management issues
- Business issues

Before we proceed with these issues, however, a brief overview of a campus LAN topology is in order. Figure 3-1 shows a typical campus LAN topology.

Figure 3-1 *Typical Campus LAN Topology*

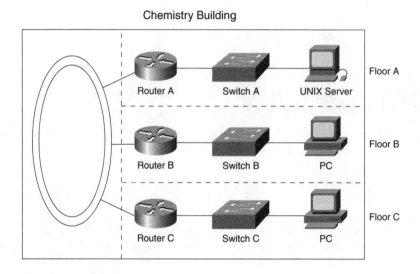

In this example, we have a university Chemistry building with three floors. Each floor has end-user devices (PCs and UNIX machines) attached to a designated floor switch. A floor router in turn is connected to both the floor switch and the campus FDDI backbone segment, which provides floor-to-floor and floor-to-other building connectivity. A typical packet is sourced from a user on the third floor (we'll call it Subnet C) in the Chemistry building and is destined for a UNIX database server on the first floor (we'll call it Subnet A) in the Chemistry building. First, the user's PC on the third floor creates a packet with a destination IP address on Subnet A of the UNIX machine. When the packet arrives in the third floor switch (that is, Switch C), because Switch C does not have a local MAC address entry for the UNIX device, the packet is switched out the port to Router C. After Router C receives the packet, it examines the destination IP address of the UNIX machine, and quickly realizes that, because the UNIX machine is on a different subnet than it is (that is, Subnet A), it follows the best router path to get the packet to Subnet A. In this case, Router C sends the packet to Router A, and then Router A sends it through Switch A, which has a MAC address and port mapping for the UNIX host. The packet then arrives at the UNIX machine.

The discussion now turns to each of the design issues that need to be dealt with as you design a campus LAN topology.

Client End-Station Issues

Client end-station issues can be both hardware- and software-relevant. Some of the main client end-station issues include the following:

- Application support, specifically:
  - Bandwidth demand
  - Quality of Service (QoS)
- Platform upgrades
- Network interface cards (NICs)

End-station issues include hardware and software issues. Software issues regarding the operating system (OS) include the network transport mechanism used, and how much this mechanism relies on broadcasts in its operation.

Examples of OS choices include whether to deploy Windows 98, Windows NT, Macintosh, or OS/2. Of course, today the majority of the market is PC-based, but there are still many organizations (in particular, publishing companies) that have large deployments of Macintosh end-station systems. Chapter 13, "AppleTalk Design," discusses AppleTalk design in further detail, including some OS upgrades that may be necessary for optimal Macintosh network resource utilization. After you decide on the type of end station, the use of broadcasts by the client for device discovery and normal operation also comes into play, especially if there is some wide-area network (WAN) connectivity in between end systems. Windows 98 and NT both have several options for their client transport and, as you will see in Chapter 14, "Windows Networking Design," can have serious network impact that must be understood. As a design engineer, you need to know how to find solutions for these software issues as well as how to effectively communicate what impact they may have on the network design.

End-station application issues include anticipating current and future bandwidth demands that the application will present, as well as any requirements for QoS guarantees. QoS is a set of capabilities that enable you to create differentiated services for network traffic, thereby providing better service for selected network traffic. With QoS, for example, you can increase bandwidth for critical traffic, limit bandwidth for noncritical traffic, and provide consistent network response, among other things. This enables you to use expensive network connections more efficiently and to establish service-level agreements (SLAs) with customers of the network.

To implement QoS, you define QoS properties and policies on device interfaces. The policies can differentiate traffic based on its source, destination, or type. For example, you can recognize traffic based on the network host, port, protocol, or even IP precedence and TOS values in the packets. Real-time voice and video applications increase the importance of QoS because of their dedicated bandwidth requirements.

End-station hardware issues include plans for upgrades to more powerful platforms, which can place more demand on the network infrastructure. If 100 client machines are slated to upgrade to Fast Ethernet NICs, and your router has only a 10 MB NIC currently installed, for example, you will need to design your campus infrastructure to support these requirements. Otherwise, the switches or routers in your campus design will definitely be a performance bottleneck.

Of course, hardware problems can really be a factor anywhere in your network, and they often can be the most difficult problems to find. Diagnostic tools, such as probes, LAN meters, and network sniffers, are invaluable for readily identifying hardware problems. A typical LAN-based meter is made by Fluke and is shown in Figure 3-2. You can also visit Fluke's Web site at www.fluke.com. Netscout Systems, a leading manufacturer of LAN and WAN probes, has a Web site at www.netscout.com, and Network Associates has a Web site for their sniffer products at www.nai.com.

Figure 3-2   *Fluke's LANMeter®—One of Many Diagnostic Tools That Can Identify Network Hardware Problems. Reproduced with Permission of the Fluke Corporation.*

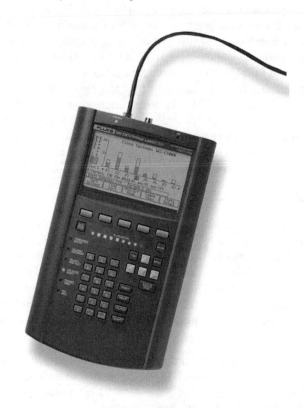

Server End-Station Issues

Server end-station issues and decisions are similar to those required by clients and include the following:

- Application support, specifically:
  - — Bandwidth demand
  - — NICs
- Software issues
- Broadcast issues
- Server placement
- QoS

End-station bandwidth requirements for servers are higher due to the centralized location and the servicing of multiple, concurrent user requests. The need for dedicated bandwidth via a switch port and access via a high-performance backbone—such as Fast Ethernet, Gigabit Ethernet, Fast EtherChannel (FEC), or Gigabit EtherChannel (GEC)—is reinforced by the requirements of many high-power applications. The bottom line is that if a file server is slated to have multiple NICs installed for more connections or FEC support, you will need to design your campus infrastructure to support these requirements.

Server-related software issues regarding the network operating system (NOS) include to what degree a server relies on broadcasts in its operation. A Novell NetWare server, for example, will broadcast service advertisements (SAPs) every 60 seconds by default. This behavior is important to recognize, because SAPs can quickly deplete available bandwidth. It is not uncommon to observe large Novell SAP tables consuming 20–30% of a low-speed serial link. Chapter 12, "IPX Design," covers this and other key issues surrounding IPX network design.

Like client issues, server-oriented application issues include anticipating current and future bandwidth demands that the application will present, and any requirements for server QoS guarantees. This is especially true of the Cisco IP/TV application server, because its content (video streams) may require a level of QoS. You can find more information on IP/TV at www.cisco.com/univercd/cc/td/doc/pcat/171.htm.

Server placement is a critical consideration because of the differing needs of the protocol suites and applications being supported. Servers are required to be continuously accessible, and avoidance of circuit outages such as WAN links and whether to provide a single- or dual-homed connection should be part of the design strategy. Simply put, a single connection always guarantees a single point of failure, whereas a dual connection provides a redundant path. In practice, this decision of whether to run single or dual-homed connections boils down to risk versus availability. After all, a network is only as strong as its weakest link. Therefore, you must consider and determine how much redundancy (that is, availability) you can afford to have. Sometimes, managers like to phrase the question in slightly different terms: How much redundancy can you afford *not* to have? The answer is often driven by business rather than technical reasoning.

Network Infrastructure Issues

Network infrastructure issues include the following considerations:

- Whether to deploy a distributed or collapsed backbone
- The bandwidth requirements of the backbone, along with the technology type that will be deployed
- The costs and benefits of deploying bridging, switching, or routing

The sections that follow discuss the details of each of these issues.

Distributed Versus Collapsed Backbone Deployment

Whether distributed or collapsed, each type of backbone has its benefits and drawbacks. It is important to first define what we mean when we say distributed and collapsed backbones and how they differ for a building that contains 10 floors.

A distributed backbone would define each floor's router in a building directly connected to the centralized backbone, essentially attaching each floor's backbone router across a building or campus. This configuration, where each device is serially attached to one another, lends itself well for maximum fault tolerance when deployed as a FDDI ring. Distributed backbones require extra input and output ports for each component of the distributed backbone. These extra ports can have an adverse impact on cost, especially with some of the newer technologies such as Gigabit Ethernet. You may find that some devices need to have forklift upgrades to support the core technology being distributed. The tradeoff is that faults can generally be quickly corrected by the process of isolation, and can also generally be classified as a backbone problem or a localized segment problem much more quickly than if you are dealing with a collapsed backbone.

On the other hand, a collapsed backbone has a single concentration point where all user traffic flows from each floor. All floor-to-floor connectivity would need to pass through the backbone component (usually a Catalyst 5500 switch and high-end router such as a Cisco 7513) before being sent to the destination floor. A collapsed backbone makes problem isolation relatively simple, but actually finding a problem's root cause can sometimes be difficult or may require network-wide downtime because any troubleshooting changes can potentially impact other segments attached to the same device. Furthermore, in a collapsed backbone, you can make changes relatively easily because all users are directly attached to the central concentration point. This can have an adverse affect on cost, however, because more cabling is required to support this topology.

You can use a variety of techniques to introduce a redundant, cost-effective, and reliable LAN backbone. A robust, hierarchical FDDI backbone includes dual-attached concentrators and dual-homed routers. Concentrators are just hubs that are generally designed with the capability to collapse a large number of user traffic in one fault-tolerant box. Typically, the concentrators are located together, possibly in the same rack. Locating the concentrators together gives the advantage of a collapsed backbone but is superior to the type of collapsed backbone that relies on just one router or one concentrator, because there is no single point of failure.

Also, without redundancy (as with this design choice), the oft-dreaded "single point of failure" problem exists.

Backbone Bandwidth Requirements

Backbone bandwidth requirements generally include the terms *high speed* and *reliable* somewhere in the specification. To achieve this level of service, technologies and architectures that allow for redundancy are critical. For example, dual-ATM paths for backup are commonly deployed in backbones. In the event that one path fails, the other path can switch and carry all the load. Often, it is helpful to first decide what your bandwidth requirements are, and then to create a matrix that classifies the available technologies. Your selections then should be narrowed down to a select few.

Bridging, Switching, and Routing Deployment: Cost and Benefits

The adage "Route where you can; bridge where you have to" is still valid today. Routing is still more expensive in most situations than switching, but it enables you to logically separate your network into broadcast domains. There is no doubt that switching is also very useful, especially in the workgroup. Layer 3 decisions cannot be made by a Layer 2 switch, however, unless you introduce multilayer switching (MLS) technology. With MLS, you can combine routing and switching in a single box, essentially providing you with the best of both worlds. In MLS, a special cache maintains flow information for all active flows. Instead of requiring the route processor for every packet in a flow, subsequent packets are switched, yielding much faster throughput than if each packet were individually routed. You can find more information on MLS at www.cisco.com/univercd/cc/td/doc/product/lan/cat5000/rel_4_1/netflow/index.htm.

Cable Design Choices

The physical cable is one of the most important issues to consider when designing a network. You may ask why cabling is so important. Studies have shown that more than 50% of all network disruptions are related to cabling. Design issues include the type of cabling to be used (typically copper or fiber) and the overall structure of the cable plant. In addition to distance limitations, carefully evaluate the strengths and weaknesses of various wiring topologies. Be certain, especially when looking at Gigabit Ethernet, that your cable infrastructure meets or exceeds specifications.

Table 3-1, from www.gigabit-ethernet.org/technology/overview/compsum.html, provides an overview of the distance limitations and wiring configurations of several different cabling options for Ethernet.

Table 3-1   *Ethernet Cabling Technology Options*

	Copper-Based Cabling		Fiber-Optic Cabling	
	Coaxial (10Base2)	Twisted-Pair (10BaseT)	Single-Mode Fiber	Multimode Fiber
Distance Limitations	300 m	100 m	< 25 km	< 2 km
Strengths	Inexpensive	Ubiquitous, and its cabling requires less skill to install.	Has a much higher capacity and allows greater distances than multimode fiber.	Typically used in applications such as campus LANs, extending their network diameters up to 2 km.
Weaknesses	Prone to bad connections. Also, you need repeaters if the cable length exceeds 185 meters.	Slightly more expensive than 10Base2 cable.	Expensive to implement and may require attenuators.	Limited only to distances < 2 km, susceptible to modal noise and unpredictable bandwidth performance.
Physical Wiring Configuration	Bus	Star		

One of the strengths of 10Base2, known as Cheapernet, is that it is inexpensive. It is prone to bad connections, however, and you need repeaters if the cable length exceeds 185 meters. A key strength of 10BaseT cable is that it is ubiquitous and its cabling requires less skill to install; however, 10BaseT is limited to only 100 meters per cable. In the world of optics, multimode fiber is typically used in applications such as LANs, at distances less than 2 km, whereas single-mode fiber is generally used in telco networks that require long-distance (5–25 km) connectivity and cable TV access.

NOTE   To ensure that your cabling is within specifications, it should be TIA/EIA 568-compliant. This standard, although published in the early 1990s, is still a work in progress. This specification covers cabling, connectors, and patch panels. A very good reference for these specifications is located at www.eia.org and www.tiaonline.org.

Network Management Issues

Network management issues include the following:

- Network management platform
- Network management tools
- End-user administration and preparation for network growth

Your options for a network management system (NMS) include centralized or distributed network management, and where to deploy tools based on the Simple Network Management Protocol (SNMP) and Remote Monitoring (RMON). For small- to medium-size networks (100–500 nodes), centralized management often makes sense. Here, SNMP and RMON data are polled from remote devices through Management Information Bases (MIBs) for analysis at a central location. This model implies that there will be much network bandwidth consumed by polling; for networks of this size, however, the cost of purchasing and managing distributed servers is not always cost-effective.

For larger-size networks (500+ nodes), distributed management is often a requirement. In the distributed NMS model, the majority of RMON and SNMP management traffic is kept regionalized, where it is analyzed by the local RMON or SNMP manager. Only exceptions and post-analysis data are sent to a centralized NMS server. This model greatly saves on bandwidth costs, because you no longer need to poll the entire network from a centralized location. Of course, the downside is the cost of the additional poller servers (generally UNIX boxes) and the cost to administer multiple systems.

As a design engineer, you should consider general issues of user end-station administration. An example of administration could include a strategy for modifying the physical configuration of the network (moves, adds, and changes) as users move to different locations and your network grows. Network growth will most likely include a deployment of virtual LAN (VLAN) technology as well. VLAN technology is widely deployed in many customer networks. As discussed in Chapter 2, VLANs are the functional equivalent of broadcast domains, but instead of requiring a separate hub-per-broadcast domain, VLANs can be defined per port within a single switch.

Business Issues

Business issues include budgetary considerations such as the cost of equipment and software purchases, the cost of maintenance, and the cost and benefits of preserving your investment in existing network components. As mentioned in Chapter 1, "Internetwork Design Overview," the Total Cost of Ownership (TCO) centers around recurring costs, such as salaries and training for administrators, monthly tariffs on WAN circuits, and other operating charges. Typically, you will confront other issues, such as adhering to corporate and industry standards and developing guidelines for adoption of emerging technologies. Meeting the current network requirements and planning for growth are also critical business issues.

Designing Campus LANs for New Applications and Technologies

As shown in Figure 3-3, traditional LAN designs will undoubtedly need to be modified as new applications put more demands on current implementations.

Figure 3-3   *Campus LAN Design Evolution: New Network Applications*

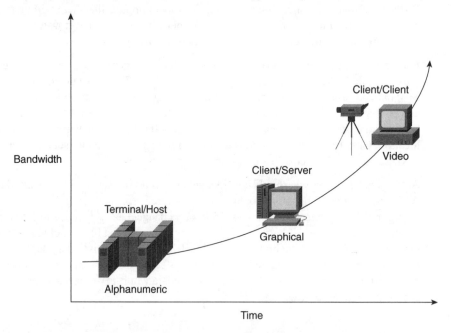

During the past 20 years, bandwidth requirements have increased from simple terminal/ host communications to client/server graphics and are increasing steadily to serve video-based client/server applications. Bandwidth is proving itself to be the "mother of all applications." Multicast traffic—for example, carrying a video broadcast—can conceivably consume nearly all your available bandwidth, if not properly managed. QoS protocols such as Resource Reservation Protocol (RSVP) may be required to guarantee critical applications the bandwidth they require. In addition to new applications, other changes affecting networks include the increase in CPU power at workstations and servers, organizational restructuring, and the internationalization of companies. Without proper bandwidth planning today, your network's growth options will be short-lived tomorrow.

Campus LAN design professionals ask "What now?" Should you use hubs, LAN switches, bridges, routers, Gigabit switches, ATM switches, or all of the above? Where should you use the different devices, and to what extent? The answer comes back to this simple question: What problem are you trying to solve? As the adage says, "You should always compare apples to apples." The same holds true for network design choices. Some network hardware decisions are just overkill for a particular requirement. For example, deployment of Catalyst 6000 Gigabit Ethernet switches at a three-user office that connects via 56 kbps to the parent company may be unnecessary.

The sections that follow discuss how to tackle the issue of designing a campus LAN for evolving and new technology based on the following procedures: how to determine the problem at hand, how to categorize the problem, and how to solve the problem based on how it is categorized.

Determining the Network Problem

Simply stated, the decision to use an internetworking device depends on which problems you are trying to solve for your client.

Media contention refers to excessive collisions on Ethernet or long waits for the token in Token Ring or FDDI caused by too many devices, all with a high offered load for the network segment. The number of broadcasts becomes excessive when there are too many client packets looking for services, too many server packets announcing services, too many routing table updates, too many bridge protocol data units (BPDUs), or too many other broadcasts dependent on the protocols. Some protocols were designed for small workgroups and do not scale well in large campus LANs. Examples of these protocols include AppleTalk and NetBIOS.

Network layer addressing issues include running out of IP addresses, the requirement to use variable-length subnet masks, the need for physically discontiguous subnets, and other issues dependent on the protocols.

An issue facing many internetwork designers is the lack of trained personnel to configure and manage new devices, because specialized switches may require advanced configuration knowledge and retraining costs. A related issue is the need to simplify moves, adds, and changes as corporate structures change.

The need to transport new payloads includes the need to offer voice and video network services. These services will most likely require much more bandwidth than is available on the network or backbone.

An underlying issue that always affects design is the need to provide cost-effective solutions. The importance of saving money varies from company to company. Some companies will offer you a blank check for a network project; others will waffle for weeks on whether they should upgrade DRAM on a router from 16 MB to 32 MB. Do not get caught up in politics. Be a diplomat. Most of all, your responsibility is to make sure the design works and is an overall success.

Categorizing and Proposing Solutions for Network Problems

As shown in Figure 3-4, network problems and potential solutions can be categorized into one of three areas:

- **Media**—The network load is too high, causing congestion. If your problems involve media contention, use LAN switching. Examples of Cisco LAN switches include the 5500 and 2900 series switches. Switch selection will depend on a number of factors, including number of ports required, scalability, and cost effectiveness of the proposed solution.

- **Protocols**—Some protocols do not scale well, which causes a different type of congestion. For example, some protocols send an excessive number of broadcasts. This is the case with NetBIOS and IPX. If your problems are protocol-related, you can find a solution by dividing a network into separate segments using one or more routers. Typical routers include the Cisco 2600, 3600, 7200, and 7500 series routers. Like switch selection, router selection will depend on a number of factors, including traffic loads required, features required, scalability, and cost effectiveness of the proposed solution.

- **Transport**—Voice and video need much more bandwidth than traditional applications. Often, the backbone capacity cannot handle the new transport requirements. Voice and video also require support for low latency and predictable latency. Voice and video require isochronous services, where the amount of time required to access the network is always the same, unlike Ethernet and Token Ring networks, where latency depends on traffic and number of stations. If you need to transport payloads that require high bandwidth and predictable low latency, use ATM switching or consider Gigabit Ethernet. Examples of these switches include the Catalyst 8500, 5500, and LightStream models—again, selection depends on the characteristics of your data (constant stream requirements), speed (packets-per-second switching requirements), and feature (that is, QoS) requirements.

Figure 3-4   *Categorizing Network Problems*

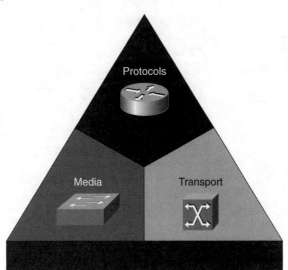

Media Problems: Use Switches to Reduce LAN Congestion

Microsegmentation means using bridges and switches to boost performance for a workgroup or a backbone. Typically, boosting performance in this manner involves Ethernet or Token Ring switching, generally using the Cisco Catalyst products such as the Catalyst 5000 switching system, Catalyst 1900/2820/2900 Ethernet switches, or Catalyst 3900 Token Ring switch. Switches can be used with regular hubs to provide the appropriate level of performance for different power users and servers. Figure 3-5 shows a typical microsegmentation using switches.

In this Figure 3-5, availability is tailored to the special needs of the attached devices. The servers are connected with dedicated switch ports, for example, because they will generally have a large bandwidth requirement. The end stations, on the other hand, share a hub. The hub is cascaded from the local switches, providing what is known as *segment switching*.

Figure 3-5 *Microsegmentation Using Switches*

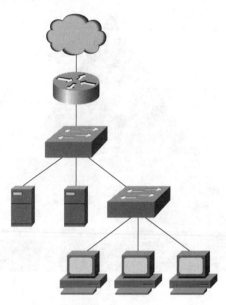

DESIGN RULE Use switches to solve media contention problems.

More Media Problems: Broadcast Radiation

As stated earlier in the chapter, hubs, switches, and bridges forward broadcasts and multicasts. Desktop protocols, such as AppleTalk, NetBIOS, IPX, and IP, require broadcasts or multicasts for resource discovery and advertisement.

Broadcast radiation refers to the way that broadcasts and multicasts radiate from the source to all connected LANs in a flat network, causing all hosts on the LAN to do extra processing.

Consequently, in a flat-switched network, there is an upper limit to its size before broadcast radiation overwhelms the CPUs of the hosts. Table 3-2 lists these limits based on protocol.

Table 3-2 *Scalability Constraints for Flat (Switched/Bridged) Networks*

Protocol	Maximum Number of Workstations
IP	500
IPX	300

Table 3-2   *Scalability Constraints for Flat (Switched/Bridged) Networks (Continued)*

AppleTalk	200
NetBIOS	200
Mixed	200

The numbers in Table 3-1 are provided as a guide. Actual station limits depend on factors such as broadcast/multicast load, IP addressing constraints, inter-VLAN routing requirements, management and fault-isolation constraints, and traffic-flow characteristics. These numbers apply to the number of stations in a LAN or VLAN. When connecting LANs or VLANs via one or more routers, it is important to understand the characteristics of the network traffic. It is also important to understand the performance of the router(s) you plan to use in the network design.

Campus LANs are easiest to design when the traffic obeys the 80/20 rule, which states that 80% of traffic is local to a LAN or VLAN and only 20% of the traffic goes to a different LAN or VLAN. This is the case when users primarily access departmental servers and the LANs or VLANs are subdivided by department. With the emergence of server farms and corporate Web servers, however, the 80/20 rule does not always apply. In these cases, it is important to provision bandwidth and routers carefully so as to avoid congestion and poor performance.

DESIGN RULE   Broadcast radiation affects CPU usage on all hosts on a flat network.

Protocol Problems: Broadcasts

Stated simply, protocol problems are caused by protocols that do not scale well. For example, some protocols, like NetBIOS, send many broadcasts. The number of broadcasts becomes excessive when there are too many clients looking for services, too many servers announcing services, or just too many BPDU frames coming from bridges and switches.

The majority of protocol problems occur when customers attempt to deploy protocols that were designed for small workgroups that do not scale with the enterprise business model.

Protocol problems are solved with routers. Routers terminate the broadcast domain and allow for a logical network-numbering model to be used for optimum network bandwidth efficiency and scalability.

Transport Problems: Quality of Service

The need to transport large payloads includes the need to offer multicast video over the network. These services may require much more bandwidth than is available on a customer's network or backbone. Multicast video will need more bandwidth than standard data. Multicast video may also require support for low and predictable latency. Therefore, QoS is often a requirement for this type of application. QoS is supported in many different aspects in Cisco IOS. WRED, WFQ, and traffic shaping are all QoS mechanisms that are part of Cisco IOS. You can find out more about these technologies at www.cisco.com/univercd/cc/td/doc/cisintwk/ito_doc/qos.htm.

Now that you have an understanding of some typical types of problems and their solutions, the remaining sections in the chapter discuss some good rules of thumb for designing scalable networks.

Design Rule 1: Use Routers for Scalable Internetworks

In the past, flat, bridge-based networks were commonplace. Because of broadcast issues inherent with bridge technology, however, routers became popular in enterprise networks. Defined simply, routers are devices designed to forward packets based on logical network numbers. They adapt best into a hierarchical network-numbering scheme. Routing technology filters data-link broadcasts and multicasts. By adding router ports with additional subnet or network addresses, the internetwork can be segmented as required.

Routers also convert cleanly between media. Media conversion is simple because routers discard and regenerate the data-link encapsulation each time a packet is switched.

Network protocol addressing and routing provide built-in scaling. Cisco IOS software provides hundreds of value-added features that make it easier to scale internetworks. Some of these features include the following:

- Hierarchical addressing
- Communication between dissimilar LANs
- Fast convergence
- Policy routing
- QoS routing
- Security
- Broadcast filtering
- Redundancy and load balancing
- Traffic-flow management
- Multimedia group membership

When deciding whether to use routers or switches, remember to ask, "What problem am I trying to solve?" If your problems are protocol-related rather than media-contention–oriented, routers are appropriate. Routers solve problems with excessive broadcasts, protocols that do not scale well, security issues, and network layer addressing issues such as discontiguous subnets. However, routers are more expensive and harder to configure than switches.

Design Rule 2: Use Routers to Impose Logical Structure

As shown in Figure 3-6, routers permit greater scalability because they serve as firewalls for broadcasts. In addition, routers permit greater scalability because Layer 3 addresses have structure. In this figure, the router forwards traffic to separate subnets of the main network number. Here, network 131.108.1.0, 131.108.2.0, and 131.108.3.0 are all segments that the router separates. The end result is a logical structure that is easy to troubleshoot and scale as demand warrants.

Figure 3-6   *Routers Impose Logical Structure*

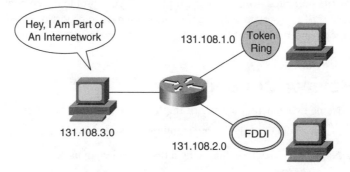

With bridges and switches, all unknown addresses must be flooded out every port.

With routers, hosts using protocols with network layer addressing can solve the problem of finding other hosts without flooding. If the destination address is local, the sending host can encapsulate the packet in a data-link header and send a unicast frame directly to that station. The router does not see the frame and, of course, does not need to flood the frame. The sending host might have to use the Address Resolution Protocol (ARP), causing a broadcast; the broadcast is just a local broadcast, however, and is not forwarded by the router.

If the destination is not local, the sending station transmits the packet to the router. The router sends the frame to the destination or to the next hop, but does not need to flood the packet as a bridge or switch might need to do.

A Token Ring bridged or switched environment usually uses source-route explorer frames to find stations, but does not scale well. A Token Ring–routed environment serves as a firewall for broadcasts and scales to a larger size than a network with only bridges and switches.

Given the routing functionality mentioned, it is clear that large, scalable LANs need to incorporate some routers. Design considerations and constraints for building campus networks are discussed in the next two chapters.

Summary

The first step in any campus network design is to identify the technical and business considerations that surround the project. Traditional bridges, switches, and routers are still commonplace in many designs, but newer "Layer 3 switches" such as the Cisco 8500 series and the 6000 series are becoming prevalent in campus design models.

When trying to find the best solution to a given requirement, remember to ask, "What problem am I trying to solve?" If your problems are protocol-related rather than media-contention–oriented, routers are appropriate. If your problems are contention-oriented, switches are appropriate. Finally, if your problem is transport-oriented, use ATM or some other high-speed transport that delivers low latency and predictable data delivery.

Chapter Review Questions

1 Name two general methods of implementing campus backbones.

2 Name a benefit of deploying a collapsed campus backbone.

3 Name a drawback of deploying a distributed campus backbone.

4 What is an end-user issue as you design a campus LAN topology?

5 What is a server issue as you design a campus LAN topology?

6 What are the general design recommendations for implementation of cabling in campus network designs?

7 Compare bridging/switching and routing as interconnect methods.

8 What is a typical media problem, and how can it be corrected?

9 What is a typical protocol problem, and how can it be corrected?

10 What is a typical transport issue, and how can it be corrected?

Ethernet works in practice, but not in theory.

—Dr. Robert Metcalfe, a co-inventor of Ethernet and founder of 3Com, in reference to the probabilistic rather than deterministic model of Ethernet

Upon completion of this chapter, you will be able to do the following:

- Summarize the technology options available for campus LAN design

- Describe the operation of Ethernet, Token Ring, Fiber Distributed Data Interface (FDDI), and Asynchronous Transfer Mode (ATM) as technologies supporting the network design model

- Compare bridging/switching and routing as interconnection and segmentation techniques

- Discuss the deployment of VLANs and LANE

CHAPTER 4

Campus LAN Technology

Undoubtedly, you have already faced or will be faced with network designs that work with Ethernet, Token Ring, FDDI, and ATM as technologies supporting the network design requirements. This chapter addresses each of these technologies from a design perspective, in addition to comparing bridging and routing as interconnection and segmentation techniques. Finally, we will look at the deployment of virtual LANs (VLANs) and LAN Emulation (LANE) and see how each fits into a campus network design.

LAN Technology Options

In today's networks, the most common LAN network technologies that you will work with are as follows:

- **Ethernet**—The most widely deployed LAN technology because of its operational simplicity and low cost. Traditional Ethernet runs at 10 Mbps. However, Fast Ethernet (100 Mbps) and Gigabit Ethernet (1000 Mbps) are next-generation technologies that are supplanting the installed base of traditional 10-Mb Ethernet.

- **Token Ring**—Originally developed by IBM, this LAN technology passes tokens over a ring topology running at 4 or 16 Mbps. Token Ring has lost favor in many new installations but is still present in legacy environments, especially those with AS/400 or mainframe connectivity.

- **FDDI**—Offers a well-known, stable technology operating at 100 Mbps with inherent redundancy. This technology generally runs over fiber, but it can also be deployed over copper. FDDI is still deployed in many networks, although Gigabit Ethernet is beginning to make its move over new FDDI installations.

- **ATM**—A hardware and software architecture that switches small, fixed-length units of data called *cells*. ATM is a multiplexing and switching technology designed for both flexibility and performance. ATM can run at speeds as low as T1 (1.544 Mbps) up through OC-48 (2.4 Gbps) in some of the newer implementations. ATM has a large installed base and is usually on the shortlist of technology options for networks that have bandwidth service-level requirements.

The sections that follow provide greater coverage of each of these LAN technology options.

Ethernet

Ethernet is the most widely deployed LAN technology, and its use continues to grow because of its simplicity and low cost. Ethernet's main disadvantage is that it is probabilistic based on CSMA/CD (Carrier Sense Multiple Access/Collision Detection), which is a bus arbitration scheme with the side effect of rapid degradation of available bandwidth in heavy traffic conditions. A bus arbitration scheme just defines the mechanism by which a station wants to transmit data across the wire (the bus). However, this limitation can be overcome through the use of Ethernet switching. CSMA/CD is also associated with the creation of a collision domain, a concept unique to the Ethernet environment.

Ethernet Technology—Operation

Ethernet remains a logical bus topology, even though the physical configuration since the advent of 10BaseT describes not a bus but a physical star. In older 10Base2 and 10Base5 networks, the configuration was a physical bus/logical bus. In a logical bus/physical bus network, every packet travels the length of the bus and is seen by every device attached to the bus. Unfortunately, the biggest problem in physical bus/logical bus environments was that of improper segment termination. If, for example, a 75-ohm terminator was not applied to the end of a 10Base2 segment, an "open circuit" would exist, and no connectivity could occur. In a logical bus/physical star, the "bus" is the backplane of the hub. As shown in Figure 4-1, the hub represents a single collision and broadcast domain. Bridging and switching can segment the network into multiple collision domains, but even a switched Ethernet remains a single broadcast domain.

Figure 4-1 *Broadcast/Collision Domains in an Ethernet Network*

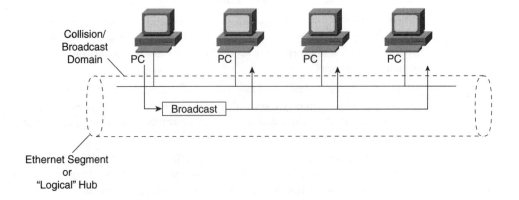

The use of collision detection to control media access constitutes the major disadvantage of Ethernet. As traffic increases on the shared media, the rate of collisions will also increase. Collisions therefore decrease the amount of usable bandwidth, because the data that collided needs to be retransmitted when the Ethernet is available for transmission again. Figure 4-2 shows how a collision typically occurs on Ethernet.

Figure 4-2   *Typical Ethernet Collision*

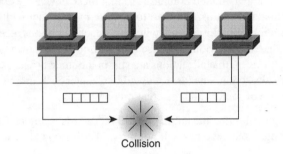

Although collisions are normal events in Ethernet, an excessive number of collisions will further (sometimes dramatically) reduce available bandwidth. In reality, the actual available bandwidth of Ethernet due to collisions is reduced to a fraction (about 35 to 40%) of the theoretical 10 Mbps. This reduction in bandwidth can be remedied by segmenting the network using bridges, switches, or routers (as discussed in the following section).

With the advent of more-powerful end stations and more-demanding applications, it is now necessary to dedicate bandwidth to smaller groups of users and even to individual users. Figure 4-3 gives some rough bandwidth estimates that indicate when you should consider changing the topology or the transmission medium to accommodate user demands. Ethernet switching technology provides a relatively simple solution to the LAN bandwidth problem.

Figure 4-3   *Increased Demand for Bandwidth*

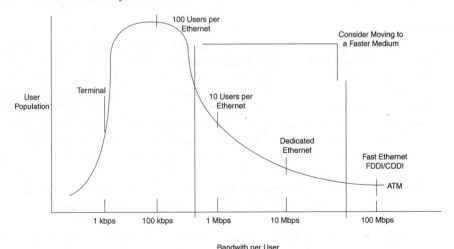

Ethernet Technology—Segmentation

Segmentation is the process of splitting a single collision domain into two or more collision domains. Layer 2 bridging and switching are both used to segment the logical bus topology and create separate collision domains. Adding these devices results in the creation of multiple collision domains, and therefore, more overall bandwidth is made available to individual stations. For the case of switching, attached stations receive dedicated bandwidth rather than shared bandwidth, because each station is in its own collision domain. Remember, however, that all stations are still in the same broadcast domain. The method to break up broadcast domains (as discussed in Chapter 3, "Campus LAN Overview") is through the use of routers and the creation of VLANs.

Notice in Figure 4-4 that the entire bus still represents a single broadcast domain, because although bridges and switches will not forward collisions, they will forward broadcast packets.

Figure 4-4   *Segmented Ethernet Network*

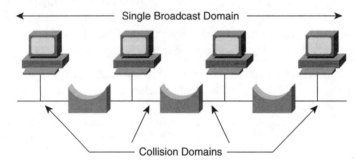

Ethernet Switching

Ethernet switches are devices that microsegment a collision domain. An excellent feature of a switch is that the switch can maintain the same physical positioning and rack space as the supplanted shared hub. In other words, conversion from hub to switch technology for a given hub generally doesn't require any major cabling changes (outside of the expected moving of workstation cables from the hub ports to the respective switch ports). Therefore, conversion from hub to switch technology for a given hub is usually done in a short period of time. The end result of microsegmentation with switches is that it eliminates the impact of packet collisions. End users generally notice a positive impact after a switch has been installed, so a measurable difference can be seen. An Ethernet switch dedicates full bandwidth (10, 100, or 1000 Mbps) to each of its ports; the switch backplane, meanwhile, has bandwidth at least equal to the aggregate bandwidth of all its ports. This is called a *non-blocking switch*. Some switches are designed to accommodate a single machine per port; others assume a switch port will be assigned to an entire segment of the LAN. This technique is generally referred to as *segment switching*. Figure 4-5 shows how an Ethernet switch microsegments a collision domain.

Figure 4-5   *Switched Ethernet Network*

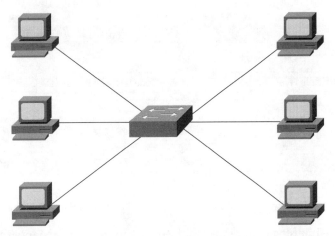

Ethernet switches employ one of two kinds of switching methods: cut-through or store-and-forward.

As shown in part A of Figure 4-6, in *cut-through switching*, the frame is forwarded as soon as the first 48 bits (that is, the destination address, or DA) are read, which means that no packet integrity or cyclic redundancy check (CRC) functions are performed. Furthermore, a cut-through switch forwards frames at the fastest possible rate but may proliferate errors (and retransmissions) throughout the network by its failure to perform error checking.

In store-and-forward switching, as shown in part B of Figure 4-6, the entire frame is copied into a buffer, where frame checks are performed before the frame is forwarded to its destination. Although the raw frame-forwarding rate is lower with this type of switch, actual data throughput will generally be higher due to the greater capability to trap error packets.

Figure 4-6   *Switching Methods*

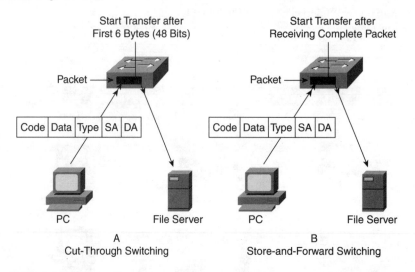

Table 4-1 illustrates the primary differences between store-and-forward and cut-through switching.

Table 4-1   *Ethernet Switching Method Comparison*

Cut-Through Switching	Store-and-Forward Switching
Forwards after receiving first 64 bytes	Stores entire frame in buffer, checks for frame integrity, and then forwards frame
No CRC performed on frame	CRC performed on frame
High speed	Medium speed
Low latency (15 to 60 microseconds)	Medium latency (80 to 100 microseconds), but depends on the type of packet transferred

Fast Ethernet

Fast Ethernet is Ethernet that has been upgraded to 100 Mbps. Fast Ethernet uses the standard Ethernet broadcast-oriented logical bus topology that we see in 10BaseT, along with the familiar CSMA/CD method for Media Access Control (MAC). However, Fast Ethernet has smaller allowable repeater counts and a smaller network diameter. There are two classes of repeaters in Fast Ethernet, and, as a network designer, you must understand the capabilities and limitations of each. Class I repeaters are electrical-signal repeaters that generally have a latency of .70 microseconds or less, whereas Class II repeaters have a forwarding latency of .47 microseconds or less. Therefore, Class II repeaters are generally preferred because their propagation delay times are 35% shorter than Class I repeaters.

For copper-based and fiber-based Fast Ethernet, if you use a Class I repeater, only one repeater hop is allowed; if you use a Class II repeater, two repeater hops are permitted. The allowable cable distances of fiber are greater than that of copper. For example, copper segments cannot exceed 100 meters in length, whereas fiber segments cannot exceed 412 meters for half duplex and 2000 meters for full duplex.

The Fast Ethernet standard is actually three different standards: two based on copper-pair wire (100BaseTX, 100BaseT4) and one on fiber (100BaseFX). There is no Fast Ethernet version for copper coaxial cable.

Gigabit Ethernet

The Gigabit Ethernet standard (802.3z), approved in 1998, is becoming increasingly popular in many networks. Gigabit Ethernet runs at 1000 Mbps and is based on familiar CSMA/CD technology. Gigabit uses a signal-encoding scheme called 8B/10B, which was originally part of the ANSI Fibre Channel Technology. The Fibre Channel Technology was essentially attached to the existing Fast Ethernet MAC layer, clocked at 10 times Fast Ethernet, and voilà—Gigabit Ethernet. This description is oversimplified, of course, but it gives you an understanding of this technology. Additionally, as you may imagine, similar to Fast EtherChannel (FEC), Gigabit EtherChannel (GEC) is also becoming popular. Gigabit EtherChannel enables you to bundle up to eight single 1 Gbps links, forming one aggregate link speed equal to 8 Gbps. Even if you decide not to deploy Gigabit Ethernet yet, you should consider running fiber to all locations where Gigabit Ethernet might be deployed in the future.

NOTE   An excellent resource for Gigabit Ethernet is the Gigabit Ethernet Alliance Web site at www.gigabit-ethernet.org, which contains interoperability test results and excellent technical white papers.

Token Ring

Token Ring networks run at 4 or 16 Mbps. A collision-avoidance scheme, token passing, is used for access control on the shared media. This method results in higher utilization of the available bandwidth (typically more than 90%) compared to Ethernet. Congestion in Token Ring networks usually occurs at the points at which multiple rings converge on a backbone ring. The bridge device (as shown in Figure 4-7) traditionally had been a simple PS/2 computer containing two Token Ring network interface cards (NICs). Today, in many networks, the same functionality is built into the IOS of a Cisco router and yields much better throughput than a PC-based bridge. Note that because MAC is accomplished by collision avoidance rather than collision detection, the concept of a collision domain does not apply. Token Ring networks speak instead of bandwidth domains. Figure 4-7 shows an example of a Token Ring topology.

Figure 4-7 *Typical Token Ring Network Topology*

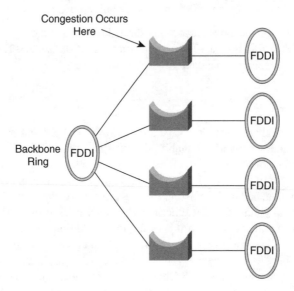

Token Ring Switching

Token Ring switches can relieve the backbone-access bottleneck by employing cut-through backbone switching. As shown in Figure 4-8, the switch reduces the bottleneck by providing connectivity for traffic between the individual Token Rings; by handling inter-ring traffic, the switch reduces the volume of traffic reaching the backbone ring.

Like Ethernet, Token Ring switches can also be configured to provide dedicated bandwidth per port. Figure 4-8 depicts the typical placement of a switch in a Token Ring network. The Catalyst 3900 and 5500 with the Token Ring line card are examples of Token Ring switches commonly deployed in many networks.

Figure 4-8   *Token Ring Switching*

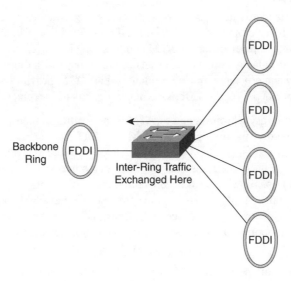

FDDI

FDDI offers a 100-Mbps token-passing, dual-ring LAN using fiber-optic cable. FDDI is frequently used as high-speed backbone technology because of its support for high bandwidth and greater distances than copper. Further, FDDI uses a dual-ring architecture (one ring is called the primary, and the other ring is called a secondary), with traffic on each ring flowing in opposite directions (called counter-rotating). During normal operation, the primary ring is used for data transmission, and the secondary ring remains idle. The dual rings provide rock-solid reliability and robustness.

This technology generally runs over fiber, but it can also be deployed over copper and is known as Copper Distributed Data Interface (CDDI). Most high-end LAN switches offer FDDI interfaces and support translational, transparent, and source-route bridging over the FDDI link. Today, however, FDDI is at a crossroads and is slowly losing favor for most new installations. FDDI is considered a legacy transport technology and is slowly being replaced by ATM and Gigabit Ethernet. A good Web site for FDDI is at www.cisco.com/warp/customer/90/index.shtml.

ATM Technology

ATM is a standards-based network architecture that switches small, fixed-length units of data in 53-byte components or *cells*. In addition, ATM is a switching technology designed for flexibility and performance. ATM combines the benefits of circuit switching (guaranteed capacity and constant transmission delay) with those of packet switching (flexibility and efficiency for intermittent traffic). ATM provides scalable bandwidth from a few megabits per second (Mbps) to many gigabits per second (Gbps).

Because of its asynchronous nature, ATM is more efficient than synchronous technologies, such as time-division multiplexing (TDM). With TDM, each user is assigned to a time slot, and no other station can send in that time slot. If a station has a lot of data to send, it can send only when its time slot comes up, even if all other time slots are empty. If a station has nothing to transmit when its time slot comes up, however, the time slot is sent empty and is wasted. Because ATM is asynchronous, time slots are available on demand with information identifying the source of the transmission contained in the header of each ATM cell. ATM supports Quality of Service (QoS) options for flexibility and high-bandwidth options (up to Gbps) for performance. ATM networks are connection-oriented.

ATM offers both permanent virtual circuits (PVCs), as when an engineer sets up static connections, and switched virtual circuits (SVCs), which are automatically set up and torn down as communicating end nodes require.

ATM supports environments in which applications with different performance requirements are executed on the same computer, multiplexer, router, switch, and network. The flexibility of ATM means that voice, video, data, and future payloads can be transported.

ATM has worldwide support. The ATM Forum (www.atmforum.com), an industry forum made up of many companies including Cisco Systems, works with other standards bodies to determine ATM specifications. This Web site is a very good resource for updated and emerging ATM standard information. Another good site for ATM resources, including links to the ATM Forum, ITU, and an excellent paper from Cisco called "Designing ATM Internetworks," is at www.netcerts.com/netres.asp.

ATM Internetworking

There are a few design rules to follow when designing ATM-based networks:

- Use a full-mesh virtual circuit (VC) configuration between routers. Each router can transmit directly to every other router over ATM.

- Use of a full mesh is almost always a requirement, because a full-mesh topology avoids an extra router hop that introduces latency because of repeated segmentation and reassembly (SAR).

- The interface between the router and the switch is defined by the User-Network Interface (UNI) specification. This is the case on most routers and switches today, but some older boxes out there may still require your attention.

Figure 4-9 illustrates internetworking within an ATM network, applying the preceding design rules.

Figure 4-9   *ATM Internetworking*

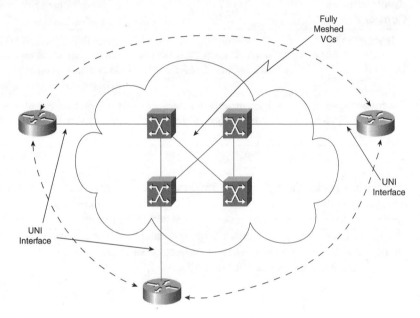

LAN Interconnection Methods

Table 4-2 shows the two logical interconnection methods that exist for network designs: bridging (also known as "slow switching") and routing. Each method has its strengths and weaknesses, and deployment should occur only after careful consideration of design objectives.

Table 4-2   *Comparison of LAN Interconnection Methods*

	Bridging/Switching	Routing
OSI Model Orientation	Layer 2	Layer 3
Addressing Scheme	MAC	Logical Network Numbering
Broadcast-Handling Method	Flooding	Blocking

continues

Table 4-2 *Comparison of LAN Interconnection Methods (Continued)*

	Bridging/Switching	Routing
Loop-Prevention Method	Spanning Tree	Routing protocols can't help prevent loops. Only careful configuration and close attention to design detail can.
Administrative Control	MAC layer	Network/Upper layer
Advantages	Simple configuration, ease of implementation, low latency (with switch deployment)	Scalability, logical address space that can be assigned to organizational units within a company, simple to troubleshoot
Disadvantages	Lack of scalability, flat address space, difficult to troubleshoot	Configuration complexity, higher latency with lower throughput

NOTE   Latency of a packet through a Cisco 7500 router is generally measured in microseconds, depending on the switching mechanism configured on the router interfaces. Very often, customers are concerned about packet latency within the router or switch device. When the true router latency figures are understood, customers are less concerned about "device latency" and focus more on other areas of latency, such as Frame Relay services from the service provider, usually measured in milliseconds.

Bridging/Switching Operation

The primary function of bridges and switches is to filter or forward frames. As shown in Figure 4-10, LAN switches and bridges work by examining frames "seen" on the network and building a table that pairs the source hardware address of the frame with the bridge/switch port on which it was seen. Thus the bridge/switch "knows" which devices are physically attached to each of its own ports. Now the switch can selectively filter (that is, discard) frames when forwarding is not required (as when both source and destination address are attached to the same port) or forward frames as required (as when source and destination addresses are on different ports). By keeping local traffic local, bridges and switches can dramatically cut traffic on individual segments and improve overall network performance.

Figure 4-10 *Transparent Bridge Functionality*

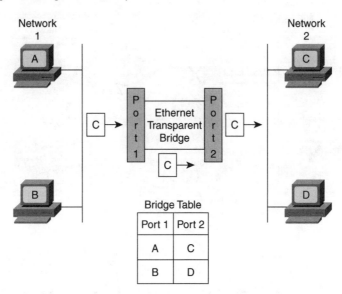

In Figure 4-10, the bridge learns the addresses of Stations A and B on Network 1, as well as the addresses of Stations C and D on Network 2. The bridge stores this learned information (MAC addresses) in a table with the port number that it learned each address on. When the bridge receives a packet, it forwards or drops packets based on the destination address comparison to the address table. The bridge will automatically drop packets that are determined to belong to the same LAN.

Note that Ethernet collision packets are always filtered, but broadcast packets are always forwarded, or "flooded," out all ports.

Routing Operation

Like bridges and switches, routers use tables of addresses to forward packets to their proper destination; however, the similarity stops there. Where bridges and switches track Layer 2 (hardware) addresses, routers maintain tables of Layer 3 (logical) addresses; router configuration is therefore protocol-specific. Unlike switches, routers use specialized protocols to share information about routes and destinations among each other. With routers, broadcast packets are typically not forwarded (unless specific "helper addresses" have been configured for that purpose in the router). Routers are highly configurable, and packet forwarding occurs in a very controlled manner. Figure 4-11 illustrates a typical routing operation.

Figure 4-11 *Routing Operation*

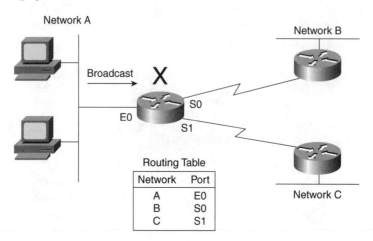

Considerations for Scaling a Switched Network

In a single flat network, as stated in Chapter 3, a good rule of thumb is to avoid having more than 500 IP-based workstations or 300 IPX stations due to broadcast radiation and performance degradation.

The scalability of a switched network depends on a number of factors, the most important being the protocols in use. Among others, AppleTalk and NetBIOS networks are susceptible to problems, especially as they approach up to 200 workstations per segment. AppleTalk has many multicast operations, the most common one being the Chooser, which is used to find services. When a Chooser user clicks on a zone and service, numerous multicasts are sent until the Chooser is closed. The exact behavior of the Chooser depends on the Macintosh system version. Fortunately, Version 7.x and higher backs off on the number of multicasts sent when the Chooser is left open, but there remains multicast overhead, even in the newer MacOS system updates.

NetBIOS stations send broadcasts to verify their own names and to find other named stations. These broadcasts are sent using the source-route bridging option *Single Route Broadcast/All Routes Broadcast Return*. All Routes Broadcast Return means that the response takes all possible paths, hence affecting all rings and switches in the LAN. NetBIOS uses broadcasts, not multicasts, meaning all stations process NetBIOS name frames.

Novell IPX networks can be larger, perhaps as large as 500 stations. IP networks can often be as large as 1000 stations, as long as the stations are well-behaved. Turn off the remote WHO (RWHO) daemon and make the ROUTE daemon silent on UNIX stations. The

RWHO UNIX utility produces a list of users who are logged in for all machines on the local network. If no report has been received from a machine for 5 minutes, RWHO assumes the machine is down, and doesn't report users last known to be logged in to that machine. (ROUTED should listen to, but not send, RIP frames. This is usually configured with the **routed -q** option.)

Finally, you should consider whether the NIC and driver support accepting selected multicasts. Most NICs today do support it, but you'll need to implement driver software to use this feature if it is a requirement.

VLANs

The deployment of LANs is traditionally tied to locality: All the end stations attached to a LAN must be in close physical proximity, and the LAN itself cannot extend beyond strictly defined cable-length limitations. This deployment can become problematic in an organization with a highly mobile workforce. When accessing e-mail at a remote office, the mobile user could inadvertently connect to an unauthorized LAN segment. Virtual LANs (VLANs) offer a solution by allowing users in any location to participate in any LAN. The assignment of VLAN membership is done in the switch and can be based on physical port association, MAC address, network address, or other packet characteristics. A key characteristic of VLANs is that every VLAN represents a separate broadcast domain. Furthermore, for VLAN-to-VLAN connectivity, a router is required. (This point is often forgotten or overlooked!)

In Figure 4-12, physical port association is used to implement VLAN assignment. Ports P0, P1, and P4 have been assigned to VLAN 1. VLAN 2 has ports P2, P3, and P5. Communication between VLAN 1 and VLAN 2 can occur only through the router.

Figure 4-12 *VLAN Operation*

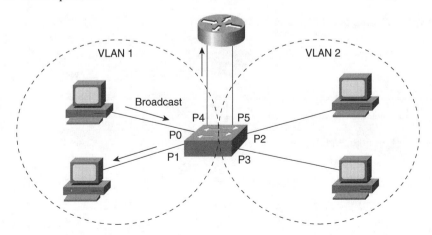

When more than one switch is connected together (a technique called *trunking*), VLAN information often needs to be passed between switches. With trunking enabled, every switch knows about every VLAN in the network and can be configured to add its own ports to an existing VLAN. Two Ethernet trunking options are available on Cisco products; the choices of which to use are discussed in the next section.

Ethernet Trunking Considerations in VLANs

When multiple workgroups are connected by a single switch, the port-association method works well. A problem arises, however, when those workgroups must communicate across switches. The VLAN membership information must be conveyed to the switch receiving the frame by a VLAN identifier field carried in the MAC frame.

In the past, Cisco switches used only a proprietary method called Inter-Switch Link (ISL) (see Figure 4-13). The ISL field is similar to 802.10; it consists of a 30-byte field that contains a 2-byte VLAN ID. There is no support for trunk lines based on 10BaseT, because adequate bandwidth is not available to handle VLAN operation.

In practice, this meant that VLAN deployment was proprietary. Second, the VLAN ID addition to the header can result in a "giant" frame, which Ethernet interprets as an error. This anomaly is also handled in a vendor-specific way, implemented in vendors' proprietary hardware drivers. The biggest problem, however, with large installed VLAN implementations is that you were locked in to a single vendor VLAN solution, due to lack of compatibility between switch vendors. For example, a Cisco switch running ISL could not talk to a 3Com or Cabletron switch running its own proprietary VLAN protocol. Today, thankfully, more and more vendors, including Cisco, are implementing the 802.1Q standard. ISL is a superset of 802.1Q functionality. The bottom line is that if you require multivendor VLAN interoperability, you should look to implement 802.1Q in your network.

Figure 4-13 *Fast Ethernet Trunk Lines*

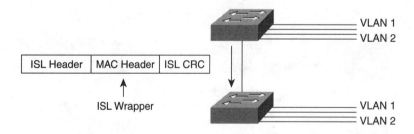

FDDI Trunking Considerations in VLANs

Cisco switches implement the 802.10 Secure Bridging field on FDDI links. This is a 16-byte field added between the MAC header and the LLC header. This field contains a 4-byte VLAN ID.

The IEEE 802.10 specification addresses "Secure Transport for Ethernet." A portion of that specification was implemented for use with VLANs because a true VLAN specification was not yet adopted. As already stated, 802.1Q has since been adopted. Fortunately, Cisco switches support frame formats from both specifications, which makes designing and migrating from existing networks easier.

ATM LANE

LANE emulates a LAN over ATM. LANE creates a single "logical wire" out of multiple physical wires, and similarly creates a single logical broadcast domain. Cisco 7000 series and 4000 series routers with an ATM Interface Processor (AIP) or the newer PA-A3 (VIP ATM port adapter) module provide a gateway function when LANE is configured. LANE allows existing LAN end stations to transparently interface an ATM cell relay network with Cisco workgroup switches.

LANs can use connectionless service; however, ATM is always a connection-oriented service. Figure 4-14 shows a typical LANE configuration with several components identified.

Figure 4-14 *LANE Components in an ELAN*

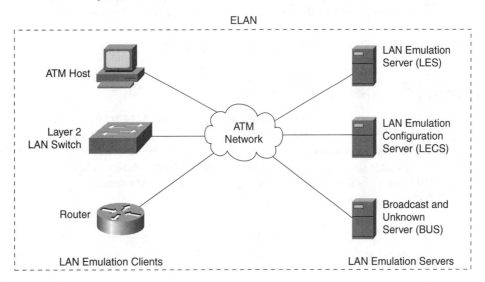

LANE defines the operation of a single emulated LAN (in a similar style to a VLAN), also known as an ELAN. An ELAN emulates either an Ethernet or a Token Ring LAN and consists of a LAN Emulation Client (LEC), a LAN Emulation Server (LES), a Broadcast and Unknown Server (BUS), and a LAN Emulation Configuration Server (LECS). The LEC is a software client that resides in an end station (such as a workstation, LAN switch, or router). The LEC performs data forwarding and receiving, address resolution, and other control functions for a single endpoint in a single ELAN. A LES provides a central control point for LECs to forward registration and control information; the BUS is a multicast entity, used to flood unknown DA traffic and to forward multicast and broadcast traffic to clients within a particular ELAN. Finally, the LECS maintains a database of LECs and the ELANs to which they belong. It accepts queries from LECs and responds with the appropriate ELAN identifier. LANE in and of itself is a complex topic. For more information on LANE, consult www.cisco.com/univercd/cc/td/doc/product/atm/c8540/q_config/lane.htm.

LAN Emulation uses point-to-multipoint connections to service the connectionless broadcast service required by LAN protocols. Under LANE, users can run their existing LAN-based protocols and applications across ATM links without modification.

When using ATM switching, no change in LAN functionality is apparent to existing higher-layer protocols and applications.

LAN Emulation for IP, IPX, and AppleTalk Phase 1 and 2 are supported in Cisco IOS Release 11.0 and later releases.

Finally, today many network designs that traditionally had LANE deployed are moving toward Multiprotocol Over ATM (MPOA). MPOA is a relatively new IOS feature, supported in Cisco IOS Release 11.3(4) WA4(6) and later. For your reference, more information on MPOA can be found at www.cisco.com/univercd/cc/td/doc/product/software/ios120/12cgcr/switch_c/xcprt7/xcmpc.htm.

Summary

It is no revelation that Ethernet, Token Ring, FDDI, and ATM are the building blocks from which many networks are built today. Before you approach a network design, it is extremely important that you fully understand the underlying fundamentals of each of these technologies. In addition to exploring these topics from a design perspective, this chapter also listed several Web resources for you to bookmark and maintain in your technical archives.

Also, this chapter compared bridging and routing as interconnection and segmentation techniques. We also examined VLANs and LANE. We certainly will continue to see more VLANs in our designs; most likely, several will use the recently ratified 802.1Q standard.

Chapter Review Questions

1 Describe the operation of Token Ring.

2 What is a cut-through switch?

3 What is a store-and-forward switch?

4 What is a key characteristic of a VLAN?

5 What is an ELAN?

6 Why is the 802.1Q standard important?

7 What are some ATM design guidelines?

8 What is a major topological difference between 10Base2 and 10BaseT?

I see designs by technologists who fall in love with specific technologies and cause problems because of overemphasizing them. I like candy, but candy for breakfast, lunch, and dinner can become unappealing, not to mention unhealthy. Networks are the synthesis of both Layer 2 and Layer 3 technologies, and the best designs are a balance of these technologies.

—Bill Kelly, Chief Network Architect, Cisco Systems

Upon completion of this chapter, you will be able to do the following:

- Describe cabling topologies used in campus LAN designs
- Describe and implement distributed backbone designs in campus LANs
- Describe and implement collapsed backbone designs in campus LANs
- Describe deployment of VLANs and LANE in campus LANs
- Determine where to use switches, where to use bridges, and where to use routers in segmenting campus LANs

CHAPTER 5

Campus LAN Design Models

Campus LANs have their own set of design ground rules, which, when understood and implemented, can produce positive results. However, I have seen many network designers ignore key areas of campus LAN design, such as cabling topologies, or perhaps unknowingly let VLAN management get out of control. The result is always the same—unplanned outages and unnecessary network downtime. The techniques presented in Chapters 1–5 are the network design building blocks and the litmus test for any network designer, regardless of the protocols, topologies, or devices used. The fundamentals discussed in these chapters are paramount to network success, yet oddly, these are the very areas that are most frequently skipped.

Sample Building Layout

Figure 5-1 shows a typical building layout that is referenced throughout the rest of the chapter.

This sample building layout assumes that user end stations (clients) must access servers and other end stations. The servers may be identified as those that are local to a workgroup or a floor, and those that are used more widely (building, campus, or enterprise-wide). End-station connections will be required for the workgroup, which, as shown in Figure 5-1, is isolated to a floor. A wiring closet is available on each floor to connect the client workstations and floor (local) servers. The riser goes between floors and provides a cable path to interconnect workgroups located throughout the building. The basement houses a data center, where the most heavily used servers are located, along with cable connections to other buildings and sites as required.

Figure 5-1   *Sample Building Layout*

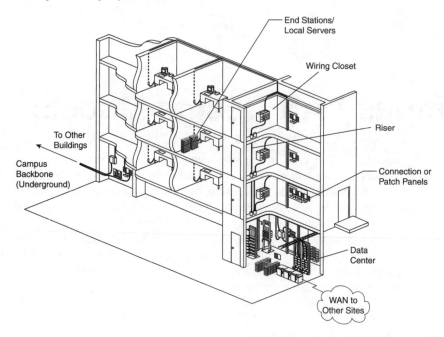

Cabling Issues

Cabling recommendations in general call for multimode fiber in the risers between floors and in the tunnels that typically connect buildings in a campus environment. Fiber allows the bandwidth to be scaled up as far as necessary (FDDI, 100BaseFX, fiber-based ATM, Gigabit Ethernet) while providing reliable links that are resistant to sources of electromagnetic interference (EMI). As shown in Figure 5-2, network interconnection devices (hubs, bridges, switches, routers) are typically located in the network closet on each floor, and in the data center in the basement. Category 5 unshielded twisted-pair (UTP) in most cases should be used to link desktop clients and local servers to the active components in the network closets. A Category 5 UTP segment is generally considered to be usable at speeds up to 100 Mbps, over a maximum distance of 100 meters.

Figure 5-2   *Building Cabling Schematic*

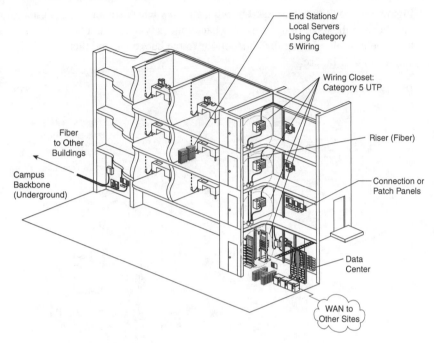

End Stations/
Local Servers
Using Category
5 Wiring

Wiring Closet:
Category 5 UTP

Riser (Fiber)

Fiber
to Other
Buildings

Connection or
Patch Panels

Campus
Backbone
(Underground)

Data
Center

WAN to
Other Sites

Distributed Backbones

Distributed backbones are a somewhat less-flexible approach to wiring a building, but they also spread your risk of a problem over several devices or topologies. Therefore, distributed backbones generally do not contain a single point of failure. Just like any other design approach, however, if not selected and designed carefully, there can be several points of failure. (This situation is often corrected by deploying a second router running Hot Standby Router Protocol [HSRP] at each backbone location because HRSP automatically detects a network or router failure and subsequently switches to the alternate router without the end-user systems noticing that a problem has ever occurred.)

DESIGN RULE   Use HSRP to eliminate a single point of failure at the router.

Distributed Backbones in Buildings

Figure 5-3 shows the distributed backbone model where routers on each floor connect to a backbone in the riser. In this case, the backbone is typically an FDDI ring. This design has the benefit of distributing the connections to the backbone and thereby eliminating any single point of failure.

Figure 5-3   *Distributed Backbone in a Building*

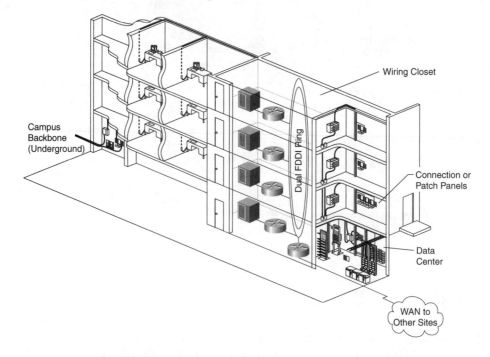

This design also has drawbacks. Multiple IP network numbers within a building reduce the ease with which user adds, moves, and changes can be made. Furthermore, this design tends to be more expensive and does not always migrate easily to switching.

Note that in this design, no end stations are attached to the backbone. This is an important design guideline that we should continue to follow. The backbone should be used only as a transit path between local networks, and not as a host-based network itself. This guideline keeps the backbone more stable, facilitates traffic management and capacity planning, and enhances overall scalability for future redesign. Possible exceptions include heavily utilized servers (such as servers providing Domain Name System [DNS] or Simple Mail Transfer Protocol [SMTP]); however, these servers need to be closely monitored. If you have a bad server NIC on the backbone, for example, it could potentially cause a network outage, with far-reaching impact. This is because many servers, unlike routers and switches, do not have advanced system utilities to quickly correct and isolate network problems. Therefore, servers on the backbone are not generally recommended.

NOTE   Note that we already discussed this principle in Chapter 2, "Hierarchical Design," when we stressed that distribution layer services should be kept separate from the access layer.

Distributed Backbones on the Campus

The distributed backbone on the campus is a more resource-efficient solution than in a building. As depicted in Figure 5-4, this solution involves a single router per building, typically located in the basement, with a combination of hubs and switches providing user access throughout the building. Using fewer logical networks per building increases the ease of user adds, moves, and changes. The only drawback is the lack of flexibility in connecting to other buildings on the campus. Switching could easily be deployed in the building, but not across the campus.

Figure 5-4   *Distributed Backbone on the Campus*

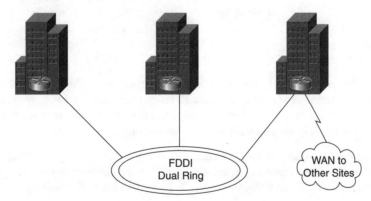

Collapsed Backbones

Collapsed backbones generally represent a much more flexible and cost-effective approach to wiring a building. For example, Figure 5-5 shows the traditional ring or bus backbone collapsed inside a single switch or router (Figure 5-5 shows a router), making the device backplane act as the backbone network. Hubs on each floor connect to the end stations in the workgroup, and each hub attaches to a separate LAN interface on the router.

Figure 5-5 *Collapsed Backbone—Router/Hub Design*

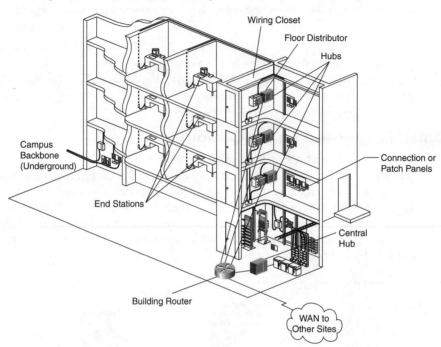

This design would make moving users a little easier than in the distributed backbone model, but the solution is not yet ideal. Also, the router represents a single point of failure. This situation could be corrected by deploying a second router that attaches to the hub and uses the HSRP and redundant hubs running Multigroup HSRP (MHSRP).

In another option, as shown in Figure 5-6, the hub in the preceding design could easily be replaced with an Ethernet switch to provide more bandwidth to the workgroup. However, the use of a single router represents a bottleneck in the traffic flow and a single point of failure.

Figure 5-6   *Collapsed Backbone—Router/Switch Design*

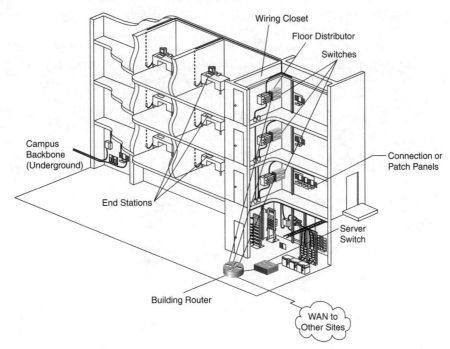

The collapsed backbone design can easily be extended to accommodate VLANs, just by adding another Ethernet switch in the data center. Figure 5-7 shows the backplane of the switch now becoming the collapsed backbone for the building. In this case, the router has a separate Ethernet port for each VLAN, and communication between VLANs can occur only through the router. The router also provides the edge connection point to access other building networks, as before. Again, it is recommended to use multiple hubs and multiple routers for best redundancy.

Figure 5-7   *Collapsed Backbone—Building VLAN*

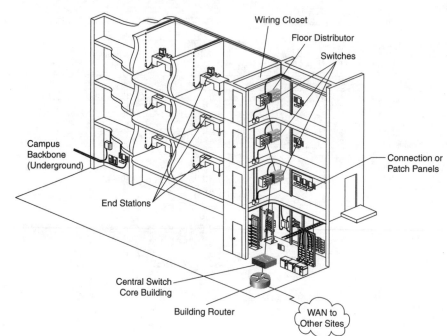

Deploying VLANs Within a Building

The use of VLANs provides more flexibility in the physical positioning of end stations and servers. User workstations can be physically placed anywhere in the building and still remain in the same LAN. In addition, a user workstation can remain in its current physical location and still move to a new logical LAN (VLAN) assignment. All the servers in the building can be placed in one physical location (server farm) but still remain logically in separate LANs. Figure 5-8 shows a typical collapsed backbone VLAN.

Figure 5-8   *Collapsed Backbone—VLAN*

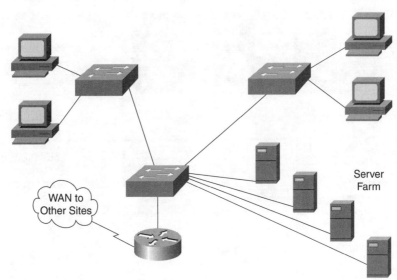

The trunk links between the floors should then be FDDI or Fast Ethernet, and all frames would carry the VLAN ID. The router connection to the backbone switch could also be FDDI or Fast Ethernet and would then receive the VLAN ID. Separate subinterfaces could then be set up for each VLAN, and the router would route between them accordingly.

Deploying VLANs Across a Campus

The collapsed backbone concept could be taken further to include the entire campus. As Figure 5-9 shows, one switch would act as the backbone for the entire campus, which would allow maximum flexibility in moving users around the campus, either physically or logically. All servers on the campus could then be placed in one location for ease of administration.

Figure 5-9 *Collapsed Backbone—Campus VLAN*

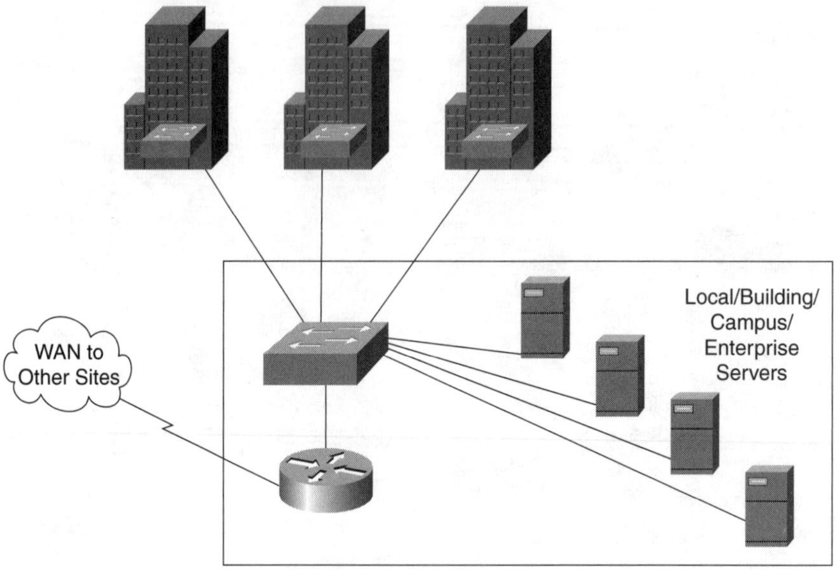

The potential for growth should always be considered an important variable in any network design, so you should choose your VLAN assignments carefully and follow a naming convention that is easy to troubleshoot, as discussed in Chapter 1, "Internetwork Design Overview." Also, note that the potential for wide-scale problems increases if you do not manage your VLAN implementation carefully. I have recently seen cases where VLAN trunking problems have caused a ripple effect of network instability across an entire VLAN domain, which could be a global enterprise network. This type of problem can be avoided, however, with proper planning, regular design reviews, and effective change-management processes and procedures.

DESIGN RULE   Choose your VLAN assignments carefully. Whenever possible, assign stations to VLANs such that only 20 percent of their traffic is destined to other VLANs.

Migrating to ATM in the Campus LAN

Migration to ATM would be needed when routinely transferring large amounts of data, and will typically follow one of two strategies:

- Using a distributed campus backbone
- Using the LANE model

As Figure 5-10 shows, in the case where a distributed campus backbone is used, the ATM switch (or switches) replaces the FDDI ring. In this case, the ATM network generally is fully meshed and represents one logical subnet, just as the FDDI ring did in Figure 5-4.

Figure 5-10 *Migrating to ATM—Distributed Campus Backbone Model*

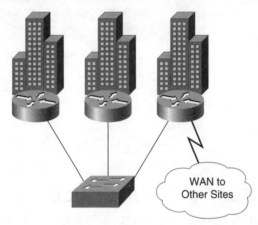

The second strategy is to use a LANE model. You can achieve increased flexibility by going to the LANE model. In essence, LANE describes an architecture of VLANs deployed in ATM environments. The router still would act as the interconnection point for traffic traveling between VLANs. Figure 5-11 illustrates a typical LANE network diagram.

NOTE   You can find more detailed information about ATM LANE at www.atmforum.com.

Figure 5-11 *Migrating to ATM with the LANE Model*

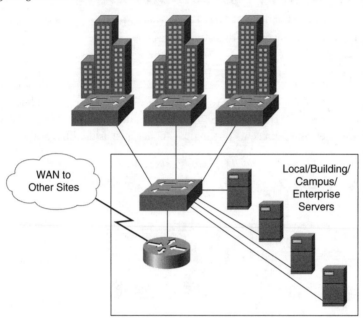

Dynamic Host Configuration Protocol

Dynamic Host Configuration Protocol (DHCP) is a reliable method for automatically assigning IP addresses to hosts on your network. Rather than assigning static IP addresses to hosts, they are dynamically configured by a DHCP Server. The DHCP Server provides a master listing of IP addresses and host information for all registered hosts. DHCP is discussed further in Chapter 7, "TCP/IP Addressing Design," but it is important to note that subsequent to DHCP, the impact of simplifying the add/move/change process with the benefits of small broadcast domains could be had. DHCP completely conceals the complexity of the addressing structure.

In a nutshell, as shown in Chapter 7, DHCP permits the ease of configuration of a Layer 2 network with the protections and performance of a Layer 3 design.

DESIGN RULE If possible, implement DHCP in your network today.

Summary

Much like the other design techniques discussed in previous chapters, campus LANs have their own set of guidelines, which, when properly followed, increase the likelihood of long-term network stability. You will face issues such as cabling topologies and whether to use distributed or collapsed backbone design strategies. You will also need to consider the deployment of VLANs and LANE in campus LANs. In many cases, you'll find that your final design uses a balance of Layer 2 and Layer 3 technologies. Without such a balance, your network could get a major "stomachache" from overloading on one particular technology or approach for something other than technical reasons.

Chapter Review Questions

1 An organization requires a network that will permit any user within a building to be in any logical workgroup. It also requires that all servers in the building be centrally located. What design would you recommend to meet these needs?

2 How would you extend the design in Question 1 so that a user could be located anywhere within a campus?

3 What is DHCP?

4 Why do cabling recommendations in general call for multimode fiber in the risers between floors and in the tunnels that typically connect buildings in a campus environment?

5 What is LANE?

6 What is Hot Standby Router Protocol (HSRP), and how can it be used in a VLAN design?

7 What is a widely deployed high-speed upgrade path for existing legacy FDDI distributed backbones?

TCP/IP Network Design

My great-great-grandchildren may well read this screen by the illuminating rays of an Internet light bulb and smile at their great-great-grandfather's limited vision and striking timidity.

—Vint Cerf, Father of the Internet, on the inability to predict the future of this ever-changing technology. April, 1996

Upon completion of this chapter, you will be able to do the following:

- Describe aspects of design relating to TCP/IP networks
- Understand limitations inherent in IP addressing
- Distinguish private from public network addressing
- Describe the purpose of IP subnetting
- Describe the function of Internet routing protocols
- Describe the security requirements in a TCP/IP network

CHAPTER 6

TCP/IP Design Overview

TCP/IP. You use it every day when you connect to the Internet through a Web browser. One of the most important decisions to be faced in a TCP/IP network design is how to handle IP addressing. It still amazes me how well IP has scaled over the past few decades. As a designer, knowing and understanding IP's benefits and limitations will play a tremendous role in your network's design. Before we get into routing protocols, there are a few more building blocks upon which we will build. This chapter addresses these IP design issues, with an eye toward network scalability. Effective IP addressing strategies today will allow your network to scale as more devices such as IP telephones are added to your network.

Physical Versus Logical Networks

A physical network is defined with reference to Layer 2 concepts, sometimes as a single collision or bandwidth domain, but more often as a single broadcast domain.

To allow hosts on other networks to locate and identify this network, every physical network also requires at least one logical network number. Logical network numbering is, therefore, protocol-specific. In other words, the number of protocols you add to a given segment is proportional to the number of logical network numbers required.

In general, one or more logical net numbers can be assigned to a physical network. Routing information between networks (that is, internetworking) relies on both networks and nodes being properly configured with intelligible Layer 3 addresses. Figure 6-1 shows a typical network design depicting both physical and logical networking components. For TCP/IP-based networks, a fundamental part of the logical network design is the IP addressing and subnetting scheme. Although often overlooked, this component is an absolute essential building block of the IP network. If you do not choose an IP strategy carefully, it may later need to be reengineered, which is a very painful (and embarrassing) process. In short, the important message behind an IP addressing scheme can be likened to a home construction project—you can't easily rebuild the foundation with the house already in place.

Figure 6-1   *Network Design: Physical and Logical Components*

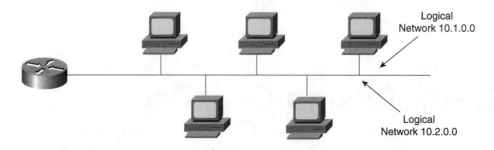

IP Addressing and Subnetting

IP addresses can be defined by the following characteristics:

- IP addresses are 4-byte logical representations written in dotted-decimal format.

- Each IP address contains a network/host pair. Some of the 4 bytes represent the logical network number; the rest represent the individual host. Taken together, the IP address identifies a unique host located on a uniquely identified logical IP network.

- Public IP addresses are licensed, and private IP address ranges are universally available.

Figure 6-1 shows some typical IP addresses with their corresponding network/host pair. These are the default network/host numberings for each type (called a class) of IP address. As discussed later, we can modify the network/host pair information by using subnet masks.

Table 6-1   *IP Addresses Broken Down by Network/Host Pair*

IP Address	Network Portion	Host Portion
10.16.127.104	10.	16.127.104
131.16.82.97	131.16.	82.97
195.31.72.123	195.31.72.	123

In the simplest (and default) cases, the network portion of the address consists of the first byte, the first two bytes, or the first three bytes of the IP address. These cases correspond to Class A, B, and C network addresses, respectively. Class A networks allocate the first byte of the address for network identification and the last three bytes for host identification. Therefore, there are very few Class A networks, but each can have a very large number of hosts. Conversely, there are many Class C networks, but each one can have only a limited number of hosts. Chapter 7, "TCP/IP Addressing Design," describes classful IP addressing in more detail.

The public, global Internet is based on the principle that every network number (and every host number) is unique. Without address uniqueness on the Internet, there would be no way to reliably route packets to a given destination. A situation of a duplicate IP address would be analogous to having two mailing addresses. To which would the Post Office deliver your mail? It is evident that method would not work very well. The Internet Assigned Numbers Authority (IANA) is the central authority that assigns "legal" IP addresses to networks that want to be part of the global Internet. The following is from the IANA home page (www.iana.org):

The new independent IANA organization will have responsibilities in three interrelated areas: Internet Protocol addresses, domain names, and protocol parameters. This will include the root server system and the work carried out currently by the existing IANA. The new IANA's goal is to 'preserve the central coordinating functions of the global Internet for the public good.'

However, not all networks need or want to participate in the global Internet—these networks can use nonunique or private IP addresses without any problem. Firewalls and other proxy devices have been developed to translate private IP address into public IP addresses. PIX firewalls, for example, support Network Address Translation, known simply as NAT. Note that IOS Releases 11.2 and higher also support NAT.

As shown in Table 6-2, networks can be further divided into subnets by borrowing bits from the host portion of the address to further describe the location of the network. In the simple case, an entire byte can be allocated for subnetwork identification. (For example, the second octet can provide multiple subnets in a Class A network environment, or the third octet in a Class B environment.)

Table 6-2   *IP Addresses Divided into Subnets*

IP Address	Network Portion	Mask	Host Portion
10.16.127.104	10.16.0.0	255.255.0.0	127.104
131.16.82.97	131.16.82.0	255.255.255.0	97

You may ask, "Why is subnetting important?" Simply stated, subnetting enables you to make the most efficient use of your granted IP address space. Suppose, for example, that you are given an Internet-registered Class C network, such as 198.100.2.0. The cost alone of this IP address block may be a financial drain on your budget, so you need to understand how to make the most efficient use of it. This technique is called subnetting and is arguably one of the most powerful (and often misunderstood) features of the IP protocol. To further expand address space efficiency, many corporations locally administer subnet policies at the access tier location, because the requirements at each remote location may vary. It is not uncommon for a remote site to be granted a block of addresses to subnet as they see appropriate. Chapter 7 describes subnetting in detail.

In the more complex case, subnets are designated by borrowing bits from within a single byte of the host portion of the address. For example, the first two-and-a-half bytes might be used to identify the network portion of the IP address. Chapter 7 describes the use of variable-length subnet masks (VLSM) in more detail. An understanding of VLSM and subnetting is valuable as you carefully consider how to make the most efficient use of a newly assigned or existing IP address space. We'll now take a look at the considerations that you need to take into account as you map out your IP address scheme with these tools.

DESIGN RULE   Spend the time to master VLSM.

Addressing Considerations

One of the first decisions to be faced in a TCP/IP network design is how to handle IP addressing. Generally, you have two options for address selection:

- You can use addresses issued by the IANA.

- You can use private addresses as specified in RFC 1918 and the earlier specification, RFC 1597.

If you elect to use private addresses and plan to have Internet access, you must have some method of doing address translation as part of the design. The address method choice may be further complicated by the presence of a preexisting addressing scheme and the need to support automatic address assignment.

Many networks still statically assign IP addresses to end systems, for example. If your new network design requires the network to be completely renumbered, or if the subnet mask needs to be changed slightly for most efficient use of address space, all end devices will require this change applied to them. This technique is very time-consuming and prone to human configuration error. Believe it or not, in the not-too-distant past, I saw the "fear" of static readdressing deter many otherwise solid network changes from ever occurring. Fortunately, DHCP provides the capability to dynamically assign end-station IP addresses on-the-fly. Therefore, a large benefit of DHCP is that it allows complete network addressing changes to occur, transparent to the end users. On Friday your IP address could be 10.1.10.55, for example, and when you arrive back to work on Monday, your address could be 192.1.1.12—and your e-mail still works as well (or hopefully better, provided the other changes made some positive improvements) as ever! In general, address organization must support very large-scale networks to ensure growth of the network.

DESIGN RULE   Use addresses from the private network address space for hosts that do not need access to other enterprises or directly to the Internet.

NOTE   An excellent Web source for RFCs is located at www.cisco.com/public/rfc/RFC/. Another good site for RFCs is at www.freesoft.org/CIE/index.htm. Also, a great Cisco design guide for IP address space subnetting (good for CCIE lab study) can be found at www.cisco.com/univercd/cc/td/doc/cisintwk/idg4/nd20a.htm.

Routing Protocols

Routers are the devices responsible for transmitting information from one local network to another. You can also think of a router as a packet switch that forwards traffic based on Layer 3 logical addresses. A router generally has two or more interfaces corresponding to two or more networks, and the router's job is to forward packets from one network to another. In the simplest case, a router's function is basically to accept a packet in one interface and to route it out another.

To perform this function, routers maintain tables of network addresses. In some cases, depending on the protocol, routers maintain topology databases of the network structure. They have the capability to determine the paths a packet must follow to reach those destinations. Routers on the same internetwork constantly update each other about the location and condition of all the possible links to all the internetwork's member networks.

Example 6-1 shows a typical routing table of a router called Thunder.

Example 6-1 *Sample Routing Table*

```
Thunder>show ip route
Codes: C - connected, S - static, I - IGRP, R - RIP, M - mobile, B - BGP
       D - EIGRP, EX - EIGRP external, O - OSPF, IA - OSPF inter area
       N1 - OSPF NSSA external type 1, N2 - OSPF NSSA external type 2
       E1 - OSPF external type 1, E2 - OSPF external type 2, E - EGP
       i - IS-IS, L1 - IS-IS level-1, L2 - IS-IS level-2, * - candidate default
       U - per-user static route, o - ODR
       T - traffic engineered route

Gateway of last resort is not set

     130.127.0.0/24 is subnetted, 7 subnets
C       130.127.128.0 is directly connected, Ethernet4/0
```

continues

Example 6-1   *Sample Routing Table (Continued)*

```
D        130.127.101.0 [90/409600] via 130.127.128.3, 2d11h, Ethernet4/0
C        130.127.100.0 is directly connected, Loopback0
D        130.127.40.0 [90/283648] via 130.127.128.3, 2d11h, Ethernet4/0
C        130.127.30.0 is directly connected, ATM3/0.1
D        130.127.20.0 [90/283648] via 130.127.128.3, 2d11h, Ethernet4/0
C        130.127.10.0 is directly connected, ATM1/0.1
```

The far-left column of this display shows two kinds of routes in the routing table—**D** routes and **C** routes. The **C** (connected) routes are automatically defined for all attached interfaces. In this example, there are two connected ATM interfaces, one connected loopback interface, and one connected Ethernet interface. Additionally, the **D** (EIGRP) routes are those that are learned via EIGRP. Chapter 11, "Desktop Design Overview," explores EIGRP in detail, but this example serves as a good reference as a typical routing table.

Routing protocols are the language by which routers exchange this routing information. Like network protocols (IP, IPX, and so on), a number of routing protocols exist, each with various strengths and weaknesses.

Examples include Open Shortest Path First (OSPF), Interior Gateway Routing Protocol (IGRP), Routing Information Protocol (RIP), and Enhanced IGRP (EIGRP). Internetwork designers must choose from among them in designing a functioning internetwork. The remaining chapters in Part III, "TCP/IP Network Design," discuss the routing protocols in detail.

Routing protocols can be broadly grouped into Interior Gateway Protocols (IGPs) versus Exterior Gateway Protocols (EGPs). IGPs are responsible for locating networks within an area of management control—for example, inside a company. A group of routers under a common administration are said to be part of the same autonomous system (AS). IGPs are discussed in detail in Chapter 9, "OSPF Design," and Chapter 10, "IGRP/EIGRP Design." EGPs are used when connecting autonomous systems, as is the case with the Internet.

Most internetworks are designed with multiple possible paths between a given source and a given destination. One job of routing protocols is to determine which is the best path to follow for a given transmission. Different protocols use different methods and different metrics for determining the best path, which is a source of some complexity in internetwork design. Route redistribution, the translation of path metrics between different routing protocols, is discussed in Chapter 8, "Routing Protocol Design."

Routing protocols can be broadly categorized into two groups:

- **Link-state protocols**—Routers advertise to the internetwork only those networks physically attached to it.

- **Distance vector protocols**—Routers advertise remote networks learned about through other routers' advertisements, sometimes also referred to as "routing by rumor."

Table 6-3 lists the IP-based routing protocols and whether they are considered IGPs or EGPs and whether they are link-state or distance vector protocols.

Table 6-3   *IP-Based Routing Protocol Characteristics*

	Interior Gateway Protocols	Exterior Gateway Protocols
Link-state protocols	OSPF	None
	IS-IS	
Distance vector protocols	RIP	BGP
	RIP v2	EGP
	IGRP	
	EIGRP[1]	

1. EIGRP is actually a hybrid protocol because it has properties of both link-state and distance vector. For the sake of this table, however, it is classified as a distance vector.

Routers can be configured statically; that is, a network manager can manually enter paths to other networks into a routing table, which is then not updated by any process other than further manual input. Configuring routers statically works in some small internetworks and for some special purposes but, in general, it does not scale well to internetworks of even moderate size and complexity. Of course, the alternative to static routing is dynamic routing. The routing protocols discussed in the next few chapters are all dynamic routing protocols.

Routing Considerations

In addition to selecting a scalable IP addressing scheme, selecting the most appropriate routing protocol is another major consideration for you when designing a TCP/IP network. The protocol must support fast convergence in response to topology changes while consuming as few network resources as possible. The protocol should also support flexibility in addressing, including support for VLSM and prefix-based summarization. You can use several protocols to do interior and exterior routing. Each offers benefits and caveats that must be well understood.

A classic example of mixing interior and exterior protocols is that of a single OSPF-based AS that has a requirement to connect to another OSPF AS (IGP-to-IGP). The connectivity between the two ASs will often use BGP, which is by far the most common EGP deployed today. Additionally, connectivity to the Internet from each region is achieved through BGP touchpoints to each regional Internet service provider (ISP).

Security Considerations

The key to implementing IP security is the establishment of a corporate policy. After the policy is clearly defined, you can accomplish the tasks of implementation. Firewall systems and access lists that handle many or all of the necessary functions to implement the established policy are available.

Firewall systems and other products perform the following functions:

- Network address translation
- Applications proxy
- Packet filtering
- Audit trails
- Login protection

The most challenging part of security can sometimes be that of security policy identification and agreement. Often, the groups that manage the security aspects of the network differ from those designing the network. You may find that it truly takes a collaborative (and sometimes diplomatic) effort to engage all security groups and implement it in your design. You need to be aware that as much as network designs are technical, they also often revolve around corporate politics.

Summary

By far, one of the most important decisions you will face in a TCP/IP network design is how to efficiently handle IP addressing. This chapter discussed fundamental IP design issues of addressing and high-level routing protocol selection that every network designer needs to understand. More and more, IP-based security will become an issue as sites are exponentially being connected to the Internet. Because IP hosts will undoubtedly increase, the need to design your network with a highly scalable IP addressing strategy is of utmost importance.

Chapter Review Questions

1 What are some major issues in strategic design of TCP/IP networks?

2 Name two general choices for selection of IP addresses.

3 Name three considerations for routing protocols.

4 What is subnetting?

5 What is a routing protocol?

6 Name a commonly deployed Exterior Gateway Protocol.

7 What is the key to implementing IP security?

8 What is the difference between a distance vector and a link-state routing protocol?

9 Why is IP address uniqueness important?

Q: Is the IP number shortage real?

A: Yes, but not as severe as we once thought. We have instituted a more efficient use of Internet numbering and project that the current numbering space will last until something like 2008. This is the so-called IPv4 classless interdomain numbering plan (CIDR). In addition, we are in the process of approving a new numbering plan, IPv6 which allows 128-bit addresses (IPv4 allowed 32-bit numbers). This increases the maximum address space from 4 billion sites to more sites than there are electrons in the universe. We don't think we will run out of these.

—Vint Cerf, inventor of TCP/IP, 1997

Upon completion of this chapter, you will be able to do the following:

- Choose an appropriate IP addressing scheme based on business and technical requirements
- Identify IP addressing problems and describe strategies for resolving them
- Describe different address-management tools and techniques, including DNS and DHCP
- Understand the mechanics of multicast addressing
- Describe methods for implementing TCP/IP security features

CHAPTER 7

TCP/IP Addressing Design

Choosing an appropriate IP addressing scheme based on business and technical requirements is probably the most important aspect of network design. Identification of current IP addressing problems and describing strategies for resolving them are all key areas that you will need to address during this critical phase of network design. Also, security features such as access lists and inclusion of firewall technologies are vital toward making your network secure. This chapter covers addressing decisions you will need to make, including variable-length subnet masks (VLSMs), multicast technology, and security techniques that make your design fit your requirements.

Addressing Decisions

You will have to make several IP addressing decisions as you design your IP addressing scheme. Certainly, every design will differ, but the following addressing tools are invaluable resources:

- Hierarchical addressing
- Prefix routing
- VLSM
- Secondary addressing

Whether you deploy hierarchical addressing in your network will determine how scalable your network ultimately can and will be. Furthermore, if, for example, you have a very limited amount of address space to work with, and have many workstations and interfaces that require IP addresses, a technique called *classless routing*, combined with variable-length subnet masks might make sense. Finally, if you are in the process of transitioning an existing network number to a new network numbering scheme, you may decide to use a technique called *secondary addressing*. The following sections describe each of these techniques.

Hierarchical Addressing

Hierarchical addressing really is not a new concept; for example, the telephone system has handled hierarchical routing for many years. A telephone switch in California does not need to know how to reach a specific line in Virginia. As shown in Figure 7-1, it just needs to recognize that the call is not adjacent.

Figure 7-1   *Hierarchical Addressing*

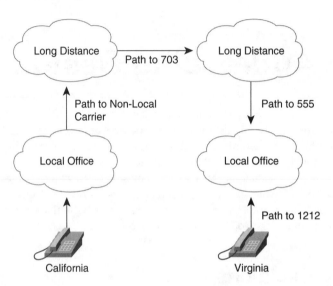

As illustrated in Figure 7-1, the local office in California recognizes the 703 prefix as a prefix that is not local, so it forwards the call to its local long distance carrier in California. The California long-distance carrier recognizes that 703 is the area code for Virginia, but does not need to know the details of how to reach the specific local line in Virginia. When the Virginia-based long-distance carrier, also called a Point of Presence (POP), forwards the call to the Virginia local office (555), the call is in turn sent to the end user's telephone (1212) in Virginia. The telephone circuit is then established for the call.

Prefix Routing

Like hierarchical addressing, a technique called *prefix routing* is not new in the IP environment. However, it is an extremely important concept to master as you lay out your addressing plan. The most important thing to remember is that a router needs to know only how to reach the next hop. It does not need to know all the details (router hops) of how to reach an end node that is not local. *Prefix routing* is really a generic term for how a router forwards packets. Prefix routing consists of two methods: classful prefix routing and classless prefix routing. The kind of prefix routing that you will deploy depends on the routing protocol you have running and your addressing scheme. Classless prefix routing, as you will see, provides much more addressing flexibility; classful prefix routing, on the other hand, has many limitations. Before prefix routing can be further discussed, a deeper understanding of subnetting and classful versus classless routing is in order.

Subnetting

Traditional IP hosts knew about only three prefix lengths: 8, 16, and 24 bits. When subnetworks were introduced, a host (or router) could be configured to understand that the local prefix length was extended by the use of a subnet mask. In Figure 7-2, for instance, 172.16.0.0, a Class B network (which normally uses 16 bits to designate the network number) has extended its subnet mask an additional 7 bits. This extension allows the Class B network to be divided into 126 (this is calculated by $2^7 - 2$ or $128 - 2 = 126$) separate subnets. The hidden cost of this extension is that the maximum number of nodes on each subnetwork is limited to 510 (derived by $2^9 - 2$ or $512 - 2 = 510$). In most designs, however, this is a more than adequate number of hosts per subnet.

Figure 7-2   *Subnetting Extends Prefixes*

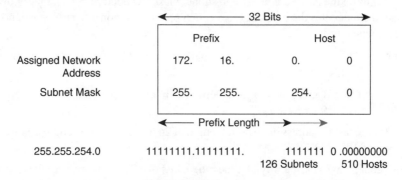

Hosts have a limited capability to understand prefix lengths. They know the length for local configurations, but not for remote configurations. As stated earlier, the key to remember about classful routing is that the router does not transmit any information about the prefix length (that is, the subnet mask is not transmitted in routing updates).

Classful Versus Classless Routing

The original IP specification, RFC 760, did not use any classes. The network number was defined as the first octet. The first octet was a prefix. Classful addressing was introduced when more than 254 networks threatened to collapse the Internet. Classful addressing is specified in RFC 791, which is usually considered the standard IP specification.

As shown in Figure 7-3, the three customary IP address classes each define a prefix (which denotes the network that a host is on) of a certain length are called Class A, Class B, Class C, and Class D IP addresses.

Figure 7-3   *Prefix Length Determined from Context*

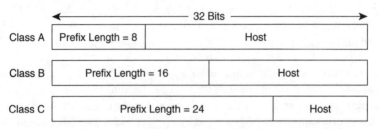

All IP addresses have two components: network and host. The length of each component depends on the class of address and subnet mask. As documented in the following bulleted list, the *n* denotes the network (also called prefix) component, and the *h* denotes the host component of the IP address.

- A Class A address has a prefix length of 8 bits. All Class A addresses are in the format of 0–127.*h.h.h*

- A Class B address has a prefix length of 16 bits. All Class B addresses are in the format of 128–191.*n.h.h*

- A Class C address has a prefix length of 24 bits. All Class C addresses are in the format of 192–223.*n.n.h*

A subnet mask is just a way of allocating *n* bits of a 32-bit address as identifying a network number and (32-*n*) bits as identifying a device or host number. The prefix length varied even before subnet masks were introduced. The prefix length used to be determined by the first few bits in an address, which identify the class of address. As shown in Figure 7-3, the prefix length is determined from the context of the address. For each class of address, the binary bit patterns of the first few bits are an easy way to determine the class of IP address being used. For example,

- A Class A address always starts with a bit pattern of 0.

- A Class B address always starts with a bit pattern of 10.

- A Class C address always starts with a bit pattern of 110.

NOTE   A very good Web site for assistance in subnet calculation is at www.ccci.com/tools/subcalc/
index.html. This can come in handy while you are designing your network (or if someone
asks you a question on the spot!).

A prefix is an IP address and an indication of the leftmost contiguous significant bits
within the address. The indication of the leftmost contiguous part, or the prefix, was
conventionally done with a subnet mask. More recently, a length indication has followed a
network number and slash, for example, 192.10.168.0/21. This type of routing is classless,
which means that the mask is not necessarily the default length. Instead of writing 10.0.0.0
255.0.0.0, for example, a "network shorthand" way of writing the same network is 10.0.0.0/
8. The "slash 8" means that there are 8 bits applied as the prefix mask. This makes sense,
because 11111111 (8 binary bits) is the same as 255 (decimal).

As discussed earlier, each class of addresses has different prefixes. When a router sees a
packet with a destination of 150.100.1.2 255.255.0.0, for example, it always knows to
forward this packet to the 150.100.0.0 network. This is classful routing because the subnet
mask follows the standard 255.255.0.0 format. Standard distance-vector routing protocols,
such as RIP-1 and IGRP, do not advertise subnet masks in the routing-protocol updates.
These classful routing protocols always perform route summarization at major network
class boundaries. If major subnets in a network become separated by another network, the
automatic summarization feature causes the major subnets to become discontiguous. As
shown in Figure 7-4, devices in the core network 192.168.1.0 separating the discontiguous
major subnets 131.108.0.0 will become confused because conflicting advertisements about
the same destination network are received on different interfaces—that is, the routing tables
on the 192.168.1.0 show that network 131.108.0.0 was learned on two different interfaces.
This causes ambiguous routing, which is not a good thing! Therefore, if you need to support
discontiguous subnets, you need to use a protocol that supports it such as OSPF or EIGRP.
Subnets must be contiguous when using classful routing protocols.

Figure 7-4   *Classful Routing Protocols*

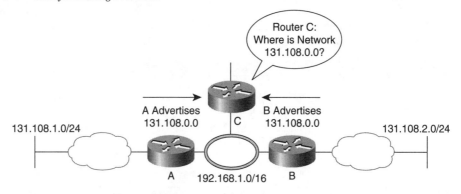

On the other hand, *classless routing* is a technique where the routers examine both the destination IP address and the subnet mask before making a routing decision. OSPF, EIGRP, IS-IS, and RIP-2 are examples of classless routing protocols.

Rule: The Router Always Looks for the Longest Match

If more than one entry in the routing table matches a particular destination, the longest prefix match in the routing table is used. Several routes might match one destination, but the longest matching prefix is always used. The route that has the longest match is often called the most specific route. Regardless of whether the route is classful or classless, routers will always prefer the more specific route to a given destination over a less specific route to that same destination.

VLSM

Link-state and hybrid routing protocols advertise subnet masks when their processes exchange routing table information. Advanced protocols can interpret the differences in subnet masks; this concept is known as variable-length subnet masks (VLSMs).

VLSM relies on providing prefix-length information explicitly with each use of an address. The length of the prefix is evaluated independently at each place it is used. This method is really no different from traditional routing, where a subnet mask within a network is hidden from the outside internetworks.

As shown in Figure 7-5, the capability to have a different prefix length at different points supports more efficient use of the IP address space and reduces routing traffic. The capability to use different subnet masks at different locations in the network enables the designer to tailor the addressing allocation to the host density required for each subnet. Enhanced IGRP (EIGRP), ISO's IS-IS, OSPF, and RIP-2 support VLSM design, which in the end, enables you to have a very flexible addressing design.

Figure 7-5   *Classless Routing Protocols*

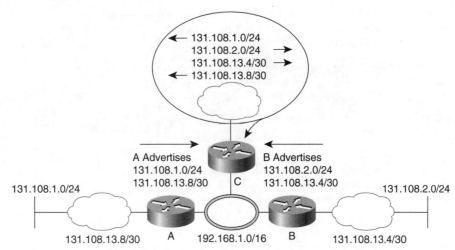

Link-state and hybrid routing protocols handle discontiguous subnets much more easily than classful routing protocols. EIGRP requires a small amount of additional configuration to support discontiguous subnets. EIGRP's default is to summarize at major network boundaries, but this "auto summary" feature can be disabled to allow manual summarization on arbitrary boundaries. The capability to manually summarize on arbitrary boundaries is a characteristic of many classless routing protocols.

VLSM Uses Address Space Efficiently

In addition to many other places throughout your network, VLSM is often used to number serial lines. Serial lines each need a distinct subnet number, even though each serial line has only two host addresses. This requirement wastes subnet numbers that are very scarce under traditional classful IP subnetting. Therefore, VLSM makes the most efficient use of your address space.

In Figure 7-6, VLSM is used to number all the serial links in the core. Regular subnet 131.108.13.0 is further subnetted with six additional bits. The six additional subnet bits make 62 additional subnets available, each capable of supporting up to two hosts. For example, 131.108.13.4 is a valid subnet with two valid host addresses. The aggregate route for all the subnets in the core is 131.108.13.0. In traditional classful networks, you would normally have had to waste a whole Class B network address or whatever was the largest mask you were using. Quite simply, use VLSM whenever possible because it saves address space, especially on serial links.

Figure 7-6   *VLSM Uses Address Space Efficiently*

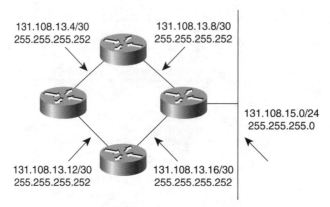

Classless Routing Using CIDR

RIP and IGRP always summarize routing information by major network numbers. Again, they are called classful routing protocols because they always consider the IP network class. As already discussed, this is not always the most efficient and flexible way to aggregate routing information.

As shown in Figure 7-7, the Boston Router is running BGP4 (RFC 1771) and uses a technique called classless interdomain routing (CIDR) to aggregate blocks of Class C networks (192.108.168.0 through 192.108.175.0) as a single route (192.108.168.0/21) and sends them to the Peabody Router. CIDR reduces the number of routes advertised throughout the Internet.

Figure 7-7   *Classless Routing*

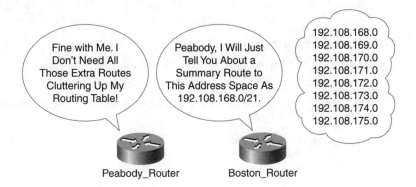

NOTE   CIDR is considered the "lifeline" of the Internet. Without it, the Internet routing table would have grown beyond the memory capabilities of most routers. Even CIDR'ized, the Internet routing table is about 67,000 entries in size. If you want to see what the Internet routing table is really like, you can Telnet to route-server.cerf.net and enter any Cisco **show** command (like **show ip bgp**). Be prepared to press the Spacebar often!

Similar to BGP, EIGRP and OSPF can support classless prefix routing. If correctly configured, contiguous blocks of subnets can be consolidated as a single route. This characteristic also allows for specific host routes. I like to think about CIDR as network addressing "shorthand."

To summarize, the following are general characteristics of classless and prefix routing:

- One routing entry might match a block of host, subnet, or network addresses.
- Routing tables can be much shorter.
- Switching performance can be faster.
- Routing protocol traffic is reduced.

Rule: Use Route Summarization (Aggregation) When Possible

Route summarization, also called aggregation or supernetting, is the key to scaling routed internetwork designs. Whenever possible, use route summarization at key concentration points in your hierarchy, usually at the core and distribution layers. Route aggregation refers to allocating multiple IP addresses in a way that allows aggregation of multiple networks into a smaller number of routing table entries. Summarization reduces memory usage on routers and routing protocol network traffic. Summarization is described in RFC 1518. Classless interdomain routing (CIDR) is one application of route summarization. For summarization to work correctly, the following requirements must be met:

- Multiple IP addresses must share the same high-order bits.

- Routing tables and protocols must base their routing decisions on a 32-bit IP address with a prefix length that can be up to the entire 32-bit length of the field.

- Routing protocols must carry the prefix length, or subnet mask, in a separate field along with the 32-bit IP address.

The bottom line is, really regardless of size, it is good practice to use summarization whenever possible to scale your network.

Secondary Addressing

Cisco routers support a secondary addressing feature. This feature allows multiple IP subnets to exist on the same router port. Secondary addressing is most frequently required in a "flat" network design where multiple switches interconnect end stations, or during network migrations from one addressing scheme to a new one. This allows multiple logical networks to exist on the same physical media. The router in Figure 7-8 uses secondary addresses. Hosts on the 172.16.1.0 and the 172.16.2.0 networks can both communicate with each other by either setting up the router as their default gateway, or the hosts may communicate directly, using ARP for learning. The Cisco IOS Ethernet interface configuration of this router is as follows:

```
!
interface e1
ip address 172.16.1.1 255.255.255.0
ip address 172.16.2.1 255.255.255.0 secondary
!
```

Figure 7-8   *Secondary Addressing*

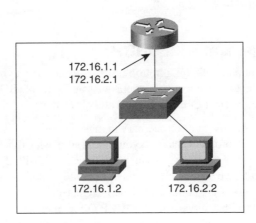

172.16.1.1
172.16.2.1

172.16.1.2   172.16.2.2

NOTE   In general, secondary addressing is considered bad nonoptimal design practice. Many legacy networks still use this technique today, however, because of user density per segment or if they are doing an IP address migration and need to temporarily allocate some new IP addresses.

Rule: Only Use Secondary Addressing When Absolutely Necessary

Secondary addressing can effectively connect discontiguous subnets, but this design approach is inefficient and can negatively impact router performance. Secondary addressing should generally only be used as a temporary solution. These solutions will increase network overhead, degrade throughput, and consume greater memory and CPU resources of the router. Only use these approaches as a last resort to doing it the right way. Quite often
(and unfortunately), the removal of the "temporary" secondary addresses is forgotten. Secondary addressing can be your friend, but the key is to remember to remove the secondary addresses if they are not in use.

Address Management

Proper IP address management is a key facet in a network of any size. In the past, "Old World" networks would use static assignment of IP addresses. Today, through the use of DHCP, this process can be automated. With this automation, there becomes less administrative overhead, and less room for error. Furthermore, these tools, such as

DNS/DHCP Manager and Network Registrar, when implemented properly, can save a corporation much time and money.

IP Address Management with DHCP

To reduce the number of configuration tasks, you can use a dynamic host address-assignment protocol—for example, the Bootstrap Protocol (BOOTP) or the much more common Dynamic Host Configuration Protocol (DHCP).

Renumbering IP hosts may be necessary to make better use of CIDR. To prepare for CIDR and other future IP protocol changes, you should start using dynamic IP address assignment in your network designs today. As shown in Figure 7-9, with dynamic host assignment, a client does not have a statically assigned IP address. Rather, when it boots up, it dynamically requests an address from the DHCP server. Basically, the client's "DHCP Request" is met with a server-based "DHCP Offer" message, which the client uses after it goes through steps to ensure that the IP address is unique. When your network is running DHCP, you can change addresses very easily, if necessary. Most importantly, these changes are transparent to the end user.

Figure 7-9   *IP Address Assignment with DHCP*

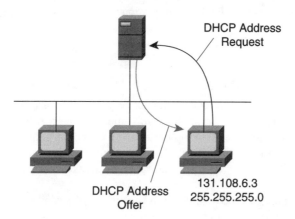

IP Address Management with the DNS/DHCP Manager and Network Registrar

When managing IP addresses in a dynamic environment, it may be necessary to update the domain name server after an IP address is assigned. The Cisco DNS/DHCP Manager (CDDM) has traditionally been a software tool that can be deployed on several platforms including Sun Solaris, HP-UX, IBM-AIX, Windows NT, and OpenVMS. The DNS/DHCP Manager's capabilities include management of domain names and synchronization of IP addresses. Multiple logical subnets (secondary addressing) are supported on the same router interface, which makes DNS/DHCP Manager suitable to the types of environments that often need DHCP most.

A relatively new Cisco product, called Cisco Network Registrar (acquired in 1998 from American Internet Corporation), is a scalable DNS and DHCP system for very large IP networks, including large enterprises, cable Internet service providers, and Internet service providers. CDDM will be replaced by Cisco Network Registrar (CNR). CNR supports Solaris and Windows NT, and support for HP-UX and IBM AIX on PowerPC platforms is coming. Among other things, Network Registrar enables you to

- Stabilize the IP infrastructure
- Automate network services
- Prepare for policy networking

CNR is currently deployed in many large organizations and cable companies.

You can learn more about Network Registrar at www.cisco.com/univercd/cc/td/doc/product/rtrmgmt/ciscoasu/nr/index.htm.

Multicast Issues

The rising need for multicast communication presents an interesting challenge for protocol designers. Emerging multimedia applications such as IP/TV, collaborative computing, and desktop conferencing depend on the capability to communicate from one to many or from many to many hosts. Routing protocols have traditionally been designed to provide the optimal route from one network to another. Multicast routing requires routers to efficiently locate the route to many networks simultaneously. Class D addressing is the first step toward solving the problem of accessing multiple networks simultaneously. Figure 7-10 shows a typical multicast topology setup.

Figure 7-10 *Multicast Addressing*

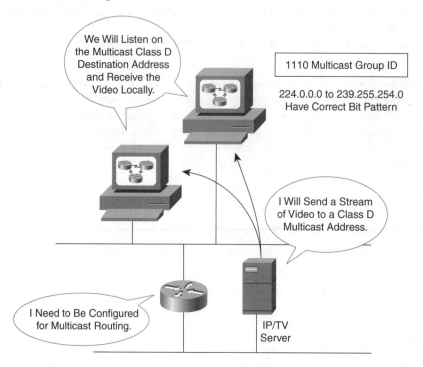

The server sends out multicast data to the address range of the Class D address. Here, a Class D multicast group address is identified by those starting with the bit pattern 1110. This corresponds to the IP address range 224.0.0.0 through 239.255.255.255. The router needs to be configured to forward multicast traffic, generally using a protocol called PIM. PIM is discussed in more detail later in this chapter.

When a station needs to send a frame to an IP group identified by a Class D address, the station takes the low-order 23 bits of the Class D address and inserts them into the MAC layer destination address. As shown in Figure 7-11, the top 9 bits of the Class D address are not used, including the 1110 that identifies an address as being in the D class. The MAC prefix of a multicast address can be easily identified in a Sniffer trace by the IANA-assigned 01:00:5e:XX:XX:XX pattern. The XX's are the low-order 23 bits from the Class D IP address. For example, a common IP address used for multicast is one packet that OSPF uses for Hello packets: 224.0.0.5, which translates to 01:00:5e:00:00:05 as the multicast MAC address. IP multicasting uses the MAC address range 01:00:5e:00:00:00 through 01:00:5e:7f:ff:ff.

Figure 7-11 *Class D Address Maps to a MAC Address*

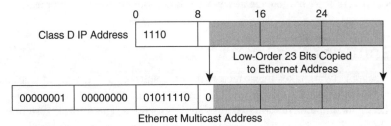

Joining a Multicast Group

When multicasting in an internetwork, routers need to know whether they should forward a frame with a Class D destination address. Multicast switches often use the Internet Group Management Protocol (IGMP) to learn whether any hosts on a given segment belong to a given multicast group. Note that if IGMP is not configured on the switch, the switch will always flood all multicast packets out all ports, which is not a good thing for users who are not running multicast!

Another protocol, the Cisco Group Management Protocol (CGMP), is worth mentioning here as well. CGMP works with the Internet Group Management Protocol (IGMP) and requires a connection to a router running CGMP and IGMP. When the router receives an IGMP request (leave or join) from a client, it forwards this information to the switch in a CGMP packet. The switch uses this information to alter its forwarding behavior. You can learn more about CGMP at www.cisco.com/warp/public/cc/cisco/mkt/gen/tech/cgmp_wp.htm.

Determining the Best Path for IP Multicasts

Cisco implemented Protocol-Independent Multicast (PIM) in Cisco IOS Release 10.2 as a pivotal routing component of its IP multicast support.

PIM provides a scalable, multi-enterprise solution for multicast capability that enables networks running any unicast routing protocol to support IP multicast. PIM can be integrated into existing networks running IGRP, EIGRP, IS-IS, OSPF, or RIP routing protocols.

Cisco routers running PIM can interoperate with routers using DVMRP. Other multicast routing protocols are available, including core-based trees (CBT) and Multicast OSPF (MOSPF), however, even John Moy, the inventor of OSPF, acknowledges that MOSPF has some major scaling problems that need to be worked out.

Some other excellent links to multicast and PIM information can be found at the Networkers 1999 home page at www.cisco.com/networkers/nw99_pres/.

TCP/IP Security

A secure network takes many factors into account, but at the heart of a good design is a security policy that is simple and efficient. After the policy addresses "who, when, and where," the implementation becomes straightforward. The firewall system in the diagram in Figure 7-12 is being used as a generic item rather than as a single solution. A security implementation can include firewall products (both hardware and software), bastion hosts, demilitarized zones (DMZ's, isolation LANs, access lists in routers, and so on). Note that an in-depth technical discussion of firewalls is beyond the scope of this book. You can, however, find valuable information at Cisco's Web site, as well as in *Designing Network Security* by Merike Kaeo, published by Cisco Press.

Business and Technical Requirements

The engineer responsible for designing, specifying, implementing, and overseeing the installation of a security system should follow a few basic design steps.

The first and most important design step is to determine the security goals and policy of your company or organization. What are the objectives for the security system? Is a firewall being put in place to explicitly deny all services except those critical to the corporate mission, or is the firewall just to audit network access? Or is it a combination of both? There are degrees of risks between these positions. The final stance of your firewall may be a business decision rather than an engineering decision.

The second question is what level of monitoring, redundancy, and control do you want? Having established the acceptable risk level by resolving the first issue, you can form a checklist of what should be monitored, permitted, and denied.

The third issue is financial. It is important to try to quantify any proposed solution in terms of how much it will cost to buy and to implement. A complete firewall product may cost between $100,000 at the high end and next to nothing (other than staff time and the cost of the router) at the low end. The systems-management overhead is also a consideration. It is important to build a system that does not require constant updating and has room for growth and expansion.

NOTE	Note that Cisco IOS has a special version called the Firewall Feature set that is available. More information is available at www.cisco.com/warp/public/cc/cisco/mkt/security/iosfw/index.shtml.

Firewalls, Access Management, and Host Security

Firewalls usually refer to setting up access control lists on routers. Firewalls also refer to topologies that lessen the risk of unwanted access, such as the three-part firewall system that we will discuss.

Firewalls are just one part of designing secure networks. *Access management* refers to controlling asynchronous mobile users, branch offices, and telecommuters by requiring authorization and authentication. It also refers to authenticating routes received from access routers and other routers.

Host security refers to physical security of hosts, user accounts, data software, access rights on data, and following policy with regard to sharing host data. Encryption can include packet encryption or data encryption, depending on whether the risk involves hackers doing protocol damage or hackers changing confidential data.

Firewall System

As shown in Figure 7-12, two isolation LANs provide a buffer between the corporate internetwork and the outside world. A hacker on the outside has direct access only to the DMZ and the public servers on it. For security purposes, the DMZ has a unique network number that differs from the corporate network number. Only the DMZ network is visible to the outside world.

Figure 7-12 *Firewall System with Isolated LANs*

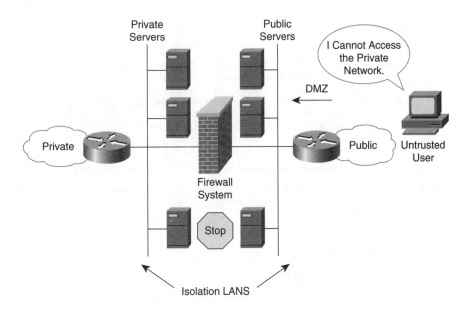

Some services available to the outside world are located on the DMZ, for example:

- Anonymous FTP server
- World Wide Web (WWW) server
- Domain Name Service (DNS)
- Telnet server

Firewall systems vary in their capabilities. You should educate yourself as to the many available security options prior to deployment. You can find information on security and related security standards at the following Web sites:

> www.rsa.com/standards/
> www.checkpoint.com/

You should also look for some additional functionality in a firewall product, including the following:

- **Network address translation**—Substitutes public addresses for private addresses.
- **Application proxy**—Provides centralized source for application access.
- **Packet filtering**—Examines packets to verify security fields.
- **Audit trails**—Keeps accounting statistics for usage (very useful in the event of an attack).
- **Login protection**—Provides addition security with an extra layer of passwords.

Protocol Filtering in the Firewall

As a general rule, the outside filter router should be as simple as possible. Do not allow connections to it and do not enable any unnecessary services. Doing this keeps the policy simple and also helps with firewall packet-forwarding performance.

Although not all-inclusive, a list of suggestions for the outside filter router follows:

- Turn off Telnet access (no virtual terminals defined).
- Use static routing only.
- Do not make it a TFTP server.
- Use password encryption.
- Turn off proxy ARP service.
- Turn off finger service.
- Turn off IP redirects.
- Turn off IP route caching.
- Do not make it a MOP server (used rarely anymore).

- Do not make it a MacIP server (rarely used anymore).

As depicted in Figure 7-13, you should allow outside connections only to specific services on specific servers on the DMZ. Also, you should be very specific about the services you do allow. In this example, if you do not require remote VTY's, TFTP, or finger access, make certain to disable these features on the router.

Figure 7-13 *Only Permit Necessary Services*

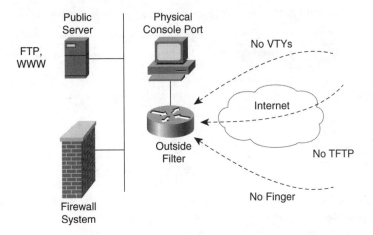

There is an old story that is a favorite of mine about the "Fishnet" versus the "Iron Wall" of firewall management. Put bluntly, the Fishnet approach is a bad one. In this approach, you are constantly denying services against new applications (that is, SATAN scans) and are vulnerable to new attacks all the time. It is a reactive, losing battle, as well as an administrative nightmare.

In the Iron Wall approach, you start off denying all services, while permitting just those you define. Although cumbersome, this is a very good security method. The Iron Wall approach always requires a good reason to "drill" (that is, configure) a hole in the wall. Figure 7-14 shows the Iron Wall approach to security. Here, FTP, HTTP, and DNS are allowed only to certain specific hosts, making this a very secure configuration.

Figure 7-14 *The Iron Wall Approach to Firewall Management*

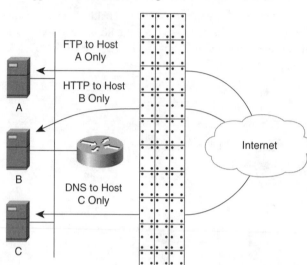

Table 7-1 lists some well-known ports that you may need to block or permit at your firewall.

Table 7-1   *Ports to Block/Permit at Your Firewall*

Application	Protocol	Transport	Port Number
E-mail	SMTP	TCP	25
Domain Name System	DNS	UDP or TCP	53
Terminal access	Telnet	TCP	23
File transfer	FTP	TCP	20, 21
File transfer	TFTP	UDP	69
Web browser	HTTP	TCP	80

You can also find an excellent list of well-known UDP/TCP ports at www.netanalysis.org/docs/portnumbers.txt.

Firewall routers and hosts should not be automatically trusted by any other system. The firewall routers and hosts themselves are likely to be a jumping-off point for unauthorized users. This means that you need to make sure that the firewall router is extremely secure, because it likely will be the first target of outside attack or interrogation.

The essence of this defense is that any packets coming from the outside that claim to be from your network are dropped, thereby preventing the style of attack known as *IP spoofing*. As shown in Figure 7-15, when using IP source-address spoofing, an attacker illegitimately uses a trusted machine's IP address in conjunction with a mechanism that does address-based authentication. For example, an attacker could use remote UNIX protocols such as rsh and rlogin to spoof a trusted host. These protocols allow an administrator to establish a list of trusted remote hosts whose users do not need to supply a password.

If filtering is not set up correctly on the border router, the outside host can combine the IP spoofing with other hacking methods and compromise internal hosts. The bottom line is to deny packets from outside your network that claim to have a source address inside your network.

Figure 7-15 *Avoid IP Spoofing*

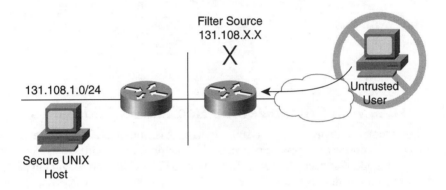

NAT and Cisco Private Internet Exchange

Network Address Translation (NAT) allows hosts on networks using a private addressing scheme to connect to and through the Internet without renumbering using a registered, public address space. Ordinarily, all hosts connected to the Internet require globally unique, registered IP addresses. NAT devices (such as Cisco's Private Internet Exchange (PIX) firewall, shown in Figure 7-16, a security gateway offering NAT capability) can substitute a registered public address for an unregistered private one in the source-address field of an outbound IP packet; they do the same for the destination-address field of an inbound IP packet. A single registered address can therefore serve as an "alias" for multiple sessions between multiple hosts on either side of the NAT device. The alias feature allows networks using a private address space access to the Internet, and it enhances network security at the same time.

Figure 7-16 *Cisco PIX*

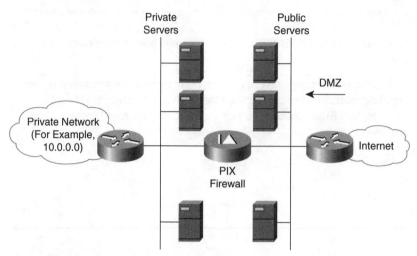

Security Issues with Private Versus Registered Addresses

The Internet Assigned Numbers Authority (IANA) of the InterNIC has reserved three blocks of addresses for private networks. An enterprise that decides to use IP addresses from this address space, defined in RFC 1918/RFC 1597, can do so without any coordination with IANA or an Internet registry. Thus, the address space can be used by many enterprises. Three address blocks are reserved for private networks: 10.0.0.0 through 10.255.255.255; 172.16.0.0 through 172.31.255.255; and 192.168.0.0 through 192.168.255.0. Addresses within this private address space are only unique within an enterprise. Enterprises using the reserved-addressing approach must encapsulate, translate, or proxy their private addresses into registered, unique addresses before accessing the public Internet.

The obvious advantage of using private address space is that the globally unique address space is then conserved for the rest of the Internet.

Enterprises themselves also enjoy many benefits from their use of private address space. They gain flexibility in network design by having more address space at their disposal than they could obtain from the globally unique pool, which makes addressing more convenient and enables smoother growth paths. In fact, probably the most popular private address space usage is the 10.0.0.0 network. It is no wonder, because using a Class A does not inhibit growth!

Summary

IP addressing is probably the most important aspect of network design. No matter how fast your hardware, proper summarization techniques to reduce the number of routes advertised can make or break your network. VLSM makes more efficient use of subnet addressing space, and secondary subnets can be used if not enough host addresses are on a particular subnet. As IP-based multicasting becomes more popular, consider using IGMP and PIM to implement IP multicasting. Security is a key element of any good network design. Access lists, NAT, and PIX firewalls are all good proactive methods to ensure that your network is not only well designed, but also very safe. Remember that IP addressing takes time. If planned well, many future headaches can be avoided.

Chapter Review Questions

1 What is meant by classful routing?

2 Give examples of classless routing protocols.

3 What is Network Registrar?

4 What is the first and most important design step to determine the security policy of your company or organization?

5 What is IGMP and what is its importance?

6 What is meant by route summarization?

7 What are two key benefits of route summarization?

8 What routing protocol is commonly used in implementing IP-based multicasting?

9 Describe general functionality requirements that are important to look for in a firewall system.

10 What are some commonly blocked ports on a firewall?

We can't solve problems by using the same kind of thinking we used when we created them.

—Albert Einstein

Upon completion of this chapter, you will be able to understand the following:

- Business and technical requirements for routing protocol design
- Routing concepts
- Routing protocol categorization
- Route summarization (aggregation)
- Routing convergence
- Route redistribution

CHAPTER 8

Routing Protocol Design

Choosing the right IP routing protocol based on your network requirements can be a very difficult task. Selection should be based on convergence time requirements, protocol overhead, and topology requirements. This chapter covers the business and technical requirements you will face as you define your routing design. Route summarization and route redistribution are building blocks you will use when scaling your network. As Voice over IP (VoIP, pronounced v-oyp) networks become a more realistic standard in today's and tomorrow's networks, these issues will become even more critical. In light of these new requirements, the message is clear: Get your networks ready for prime time now.

Routing Concepts

A router has two separate tasks: relaying or switching packets, and path determination. It is important to understand these terms and how they differ. The following sections discuss these differences.

Switching

The steps for switching (or relaying) packets through a router are as follows:

Step 1 A packet or frame comes into an internetwork device.

Step 2 The address or virtual circuit number in the header is examined.

Step 3 A table lookup operation determines where the packet or frame should be sent.

Step 4 Header information may (in the case of unicasts) or may not (in the case of broadcasts) be changed.

Step 5 The packet or frame is transmitted out an interface.

Figure 8-1 shows where each of the procedures documented in the preceding list occur in the router.

Figure 8-1   *Switching Steps in a Router*

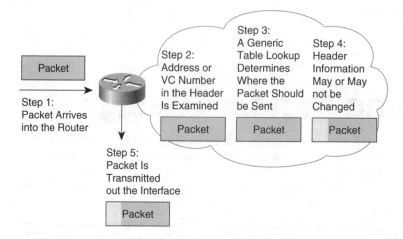

Switching Paths Overview

Cisco routers can switch packets through IOS devices in several different ways. The general
concept of switching uses what is called IOS switching paths. To best understand how
switching works, it helps to first understand basic router architecture and where various
processes occur in the router. Before delving into the various available switching paths,
however, an overview of basic router architecture and processes is needed.

Overview of Basic Router Platform Architecture and Processes

Fast switching is enabled by default on all interfaces that support fast switching. If you have
a situation where you need to disable fast switching and fall back to the process-switching
path, understanding how various processes affect the router and where they occur will help
you determine your alternatives. This understanding is especially helpful when you are
troubleshooting traffic problems or need to process packets that require special handling.
Some diagnostic or control resources are not compatible with fast switching or come at the
expense of processing and switching efficiency. Understanding the effects of those
resources can help you minimize their effect on network performance.

Figure 8-2 illustrates a possible internal configuration of a Cisco 7500 series router. In this
configuration, the Cisco 7500 series router has an integrated Route Switch Processor (RSP)
and uses route caching to forward packets. The Cisco 7500 series router also uses Versatile
Interface Processors (VIPs), RISC-based interface processors that receive and cache
routing information from the RSP. The VIP card uses the route cache to make switching
decisions locally, which relieves the RSP of involvement and speeds overall throughput.

This type of switching is called *distributed switching*. Multiple VIP cards can be installed in one router.

Figure 8-2   *Basic Router Architecture*

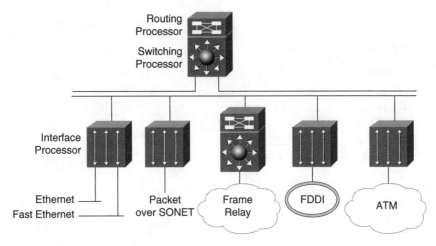

Cisco Routing and Switching Processes

The routing, or forwarding, function comprises two interrelated processes to move information in the network:

- Making a routing decision by routing
- Moving packets to the next-hop destination by switching

Cisco IOS platforms perform both routing and switching, and there are several types of each.

Routing

The routing process assesses the source and destination of traffic based on knowledge of network conditions. Routing functions identify the best path to use for moving the traffic to the destination out one or more of the router interfaces. The routing decision is based on a variation of criteria, such as link speed, topological distance, and protocol. Each separate protocol maintains its own routing information.

Routing is more processing intensive and has higher latency than switching as it determines path and next-hop considerations. The first packet routed requires a lookup in the routing table to determine the route. The route cache is populated after the first packet is routed by the route-table lookup. Subsequent traffic for the same destination is switched using the routing information stored in the route cache. Figure 8-3 illustrates the basic routing process.

Figure 8-3   *The Routing Process*

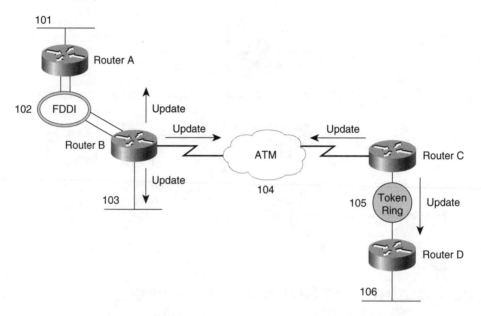

A router sends routing updates out each of its interfaces that are configured for a particular protocol. It also receives routing updates from other attached routers. From these received updates and its knowledge of attached networks, it builds a map of the network topology.

Switching

Through the switching process, the router determines the next hop toward the destination address. Switching moves traffic from an input interface to one or more output interfaces. Switching is optimized and has lower latency than routing because it can move packets, frames, or cells from buffer to buffer with simpler determination of the source and destination of the traffic. It saves resources because it does not involve extra lookups. Figure 8-4 illustrates the basic switching process.

Figure 8-4   *The Switching Process*

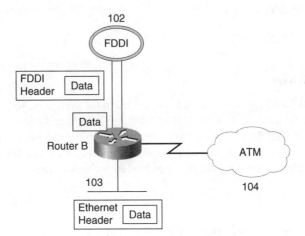

In Figure 8-4, packets are received on the Fast Ethernet interface and destined for the FDDI interface. Based on information in the packet header and destination information stored in the routing table, the router determines the destination interface. It looks in the protocol's routing table to discover the destination interface that services the destination address of the packet.

The destination address is stored in tables, such as ARP tables for IP and AARP tables for AppleTalk. If there is no entry for the destination, the router will either drop the packet (and inform the user if the protocol provides that feature), or it must discover the destination address by some other address-resolution process, such as through the ARP protocol. Layer 3 IP addressing information is mapped to the Layer 2 MAC address for the next hop. Figure 8-5 illustrates the mapping that occurs to determine the next hop.

Figure 8-5   *Layer 3–to–Layer 2 Mapping*

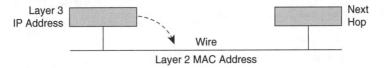

Basic Switching Paths

On a Cisco router, the following switching paths are available:

- Process switching
- Fast switching

- Distributed switching
- NetFlow switching
- Process switching

Process Switching

In process switching, the first packet is copied to the system buffer. The router looks up the Layer 3 network address in the routing table and initializes the fast-switch cache. The frame is rewritten with the destination address and sent to the exit interface that services that destination. The same switching path sends subsequent packets for that destination. The route processor computes the cyclic redundancy check (CRC).

Fast Switching

When packets are fast switched, the first packet is copied to packet memory and the destination network or host is found in the fast-switching cache. The frame is rewritten and sent to the exit interface that services the destination. Subsequent packets for the same destination use the same switching path. The interface processor computes the CRC.

Distributed Switching

Switching becomes more efficient the closer to the interface the function occurs. In distributed switching, the switching process occurs on VIP and other interface cards that support switching. For model numbers and hardware compatibility information, refer to the Cisco Product Catalog. Figure 8-6 illustrates the distributed switching process on the Cisco 7500 series.

The VIP card installed in this router maintains a copy of the routing cache information needed to forward packets. Because the VIP card has the routing information it needs, it performs the switching locally, making the packet forwarding much faster. Router throughput is increased linearly based on the number of VIP cards installed in the router.

Figure 8-6   *Distributed Switching on Cisco 7500 Series Routers*

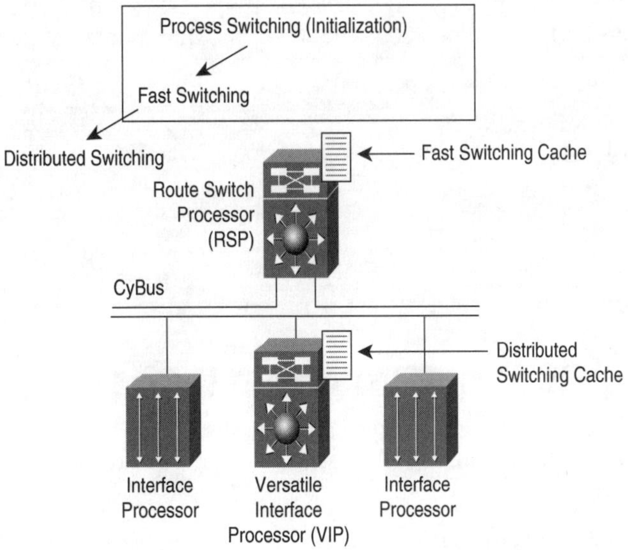

NetFlow Switching

NetFlow switching enables you to collect the data required for flexible and detailed accounting, billing, and charge-back for network and application resource utilization. Accounting data can be collected for both dedicated line and dial-access accounting. NetFlow switching over a foundation of VLAN technologies provides the benefits of switching and routing on the same platforms. NetFlow switching is supported over switched LAN or ATM backbones, allowing scalable inter-VLAN forwarding. NetFlow switching can be deployed at any location in the network as an extension to existing routing infrastructures.

Platform and Switching Path Correlation

Depending on the routing platform you are using, availability and default implementations of switching paths varies. Table 8-1 shows the correlation between Cisco IOS switching paths and routing platforms.

Table 8-1   *Switching Paths on RSP-Based Routers*

Switching Path	Cisco 7200	Cisco 7500	Comments	Configuration Command
Process switching	Yes	Yes	Initializes switching caches	**no protocol route-cache**

continues

Table 8-1 *Switching Paths on RSP-Based Routers (Continued)*

Switching Path	Cisco 7200	Cisco 7500	Comments	Configuration Command
Fast switching	Yes	Yes	Default (except for IP)	*protocol* **route-cache**
Distributed switching	No	Yes	Using second-generation VIP line cards	*protocol* **route-cache distributed**
NetFlow switching	Yes	Yes	Configurable per interface	*protocol* **route-cache flow**

Categorizing Routing Protocols by Usage

You can characterize the many specialized routing-related protocols for IP according to where they are used. With this criteria, the three principal categories of IP routing protocols are as follows:

- Host routing protocols
- Interior Gateway Protocols (IGPs)
- Exterior Gateway Protocols (EGPs)

Figure 8-7 illustrates these three different types of routing protocols and where they are normally found.

Figure 8-7 *Different Classes of IP Routing Protocols*

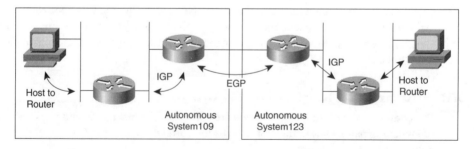

Host-to-router protocols are found on the LAN, for example, and IGPs are found within an autonomous system (AS). EGPs, on the other hand, connect ASs together. A very common example of an EGP is the Border Gateway Protocol (BGP), with the most common implementation being BGP v4.

Host Routing Protocols

Hosts can be configured in a number of ways to participate in a routed internetwork environment. Hosts are often configured with a default gateway. This is a static configuration that fails if the gateway fails. Cisco's Hot Standby Router Protocol (HSRP [RFC 2281]) can be implemented in this case to provide redundancy. With HSRP, two or more routers communicate to provide a single gateway address that is always available as long as one router is up. A standby gateway router becomes active within seconds after the first gateway fails. This convergence timer is configurable with the **standby timers** command. (Actually, with newer IOS code versions, you can tweak this timer to milliseconds, if that level of failover is required.)

Alternatively, hosts can run Gateway Discovery Protocol (GDP) or ICMP Router Discovery Protocol (IRDP) to dynamically determine a gateway router. This technique is not often used. Figure 8-8 shows a router running GDP or IRDP as one possibility and another running HSRP (more popular.)

Figure 8-8   *Host Routing Options*

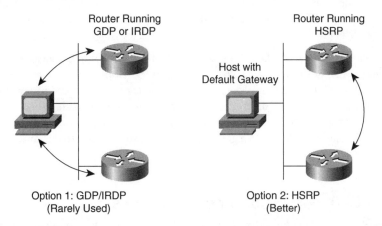

Another alternative is to configure hosts with no default gateway so that the host always sends an Address Resolution Protocol (ARP) request for every destination. The condition where the host always sends an ARP is found in some older versions of vendor TCP/IP stacks. In this case, the router is configured to respond to any ARP if it has a route in its routing table, which is called proxy ARP. Proxy ARP is not recommended because the router is effectively spoofing when it responds on behalf of hosts that may or may not be present and reachable. Proxy ARP is on by default on a Cisco router.

Although still an option, having the hosts listen to RIP is not a preferred solution either, because routers must generate RIP broadcasts. If a routing protocol other than RIP is used, route redistribution to RIP is required. Route redistribution is discussed later in this chapter. Also, among other things (some mentioned in the following note), because RIP is classful, subnet mask information is not carried in its update packets.

NOTE   RFC 1923, "RIP1: Applicability Statement for Historic Status," was published in 1996. It declares RIP Version 1 a historic document and essentially restates that RIPV1 is an "Old World" protocol with no support of classless updates. This is an important document to show to prospective customers who insist on staying with RIPV1 in their networks. It is well worth your time to give this brief RFC a read.

IGPs Used Within an Autonomous System

IGPs are, as their name implies, used within an AS. Examples of IGPs include RIP, IGRP, OSPF, and IS-IS. Each type of IGP has its own inner workings, but each can be classified into either the category of distance vector or link state.

RIP and IGRP are both distance vector protocols (also known to "old-timers" as Bellman-Ford protocols), so they receive their routing table information from their adjacent neighbors. After the update is received from the neighbor, the cost or metric to reach that neighbor is just added to the received metric and the best route (cheapest cost) is placed in the routing table. The metric used in RIP is hop count; whereas the metrics used for IGRP include bandwidth, delay, MTU size, reliability, and load.

OSPF and IS-IS are link-state protocols, which means that in broadcast environments such as LANs, they receive link-state packet information from a router that functions as the designated router (DR). The received link states are then stored in a database local to the router. Each link-state router then calculates its own routing table to each destination in the network based on the link-state costs. The mathematical algorithm used to calculate a routing table is known as Dijkstra's algorithm, which is also often referred to as just the shortest past first (SPF) algorithm.

EGPs Used Between Autonomous Systems

EGPs are used to connect ASs together. A common example of an EGP is BGP. BGP performs interdomain routing in TCP/IP networks. BGP is an EGP, which means that it performs routing among multiple autonomous systems or domains and exchanges routing and reachability information with other BGP systems.

BGP was developed to replace its predecessor, the now obsolete EGP, as the standard exterior gateway routing protocol used in the global Internet. BGP solves serious problems with EGP and scales to Internet growth more efficiently.

As with any routing protocol, BGP maintains routing tables, transmits routing updates, and bases routing decisions on routing metrics. The primary function of a BGP system is to exchange network reachability information, including information about the list of AS paths, with other BGP systems. This information can be used to construct a graph of AS connectivity from which routing loops can be pruned and with which AS-level policy decisions can be enforced.

Each BGP router maintains a routing table that lists all feasible paths to a particular network. The router does not refresh the routing table, however. Instead, routing information received from peer routers is retained until an incremental update is received.

BGP devices exchange routing information upon initial data exchange and after incremental updates. When a router first connects to the network, BGP routers exchange their entire BGP routing tables. Similarly, when the routing table changes, routers send the portion of their routing table that has changed. BGP routers do not send regularly scheduled routing updates, and BGP routing updates advertise only the optimal path to a network. BGP uses a single routing metric to determine the best path to a given network. This metric consists of an arbitrary unit number that specifies the degree of preference of a particular link. The network administrator typically assigns the BGP metric to each link. The value assigned to a link can be based on any number of criteria, including the number of autonomous systems through which the path passes, stability, speed, delay, or cost.

Routing Overhead

Routing is an overhead activity for a router or any device functioning as a router. It consumes network, CPU, and memory resources. In addition, routers consume bandwidth, the amount of which can be estimated by answering the following questions:

- How often are routing updates transmitted?
  - Updates are transmitted as a function of the update timer.
  - Updates might be triggered by events.
- How much data is transmitted?
  - Data might include the whole routing table.
  - Data might include only changes to the routing table.
- Where are routing updates distributed?
  - To neighbors
  - To a bounded area
  - To all routers in the AS
- How and where are static and default routes used?

The Routing Table

Cisco routers build the IP routing table based on several factors, including the following:

- Static routing entries
- Local interface configuration
- Local interface status, including the following:
    - Status of the Carrier Detect (CD) lead
    - Keepalive counters and timers
- Dynamic routing protocols and routing metrics
- Redistribution between routing protocols
- Policy decisions implemented with access lists

Each of these mentioned items affects how the routing tables are built. When a change occurs within a network, such as link failure or port shutdown, for example, that network path becomes invalidated. In RIP networks, for example, after a holddown time is reached (180 seconds after the problem occurs), the next update advertises the network with a distance of 16, signifying that the network is unreachable.

In OSPF, for the same type of problem, a link-state change is first detected by the attached router. Next, it floods this update to its DR. The DR then tells all routers it knows about its metric information, from which they promptly recalculate their routing tables. If access lists are deployed with a feature known as "distribute lists," certain networks are blocked from being advertised. The result is that the recipient of the update does not populate its routing table with the route because it was never received.

How Routers Make Routing Decisions

Figure 8-9 shows a router that continually polls several types of inputs to help it make a routing decision. Because these inputs are dynamic, the routing decisions can change depending on the current state of the network inputs.

Figure 8-9 *A Routing Process Has Many Inputs*

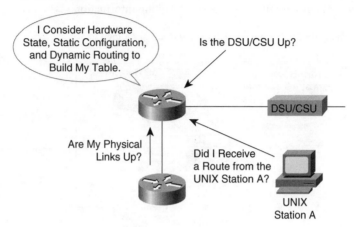

A part of the internetwork that can only be reached by one path is called a *stub*. Manually configured static routes are often used to connect to a stub. An example of a stub is an AS that connects to the Internet. For example, the ISP could use static routing to direct traffic to the stub. Static routes provide a high degree of control over data flow in the internetwork. However, the tradeoff with only one way in and out is that redundancy is severely limited because you have a single point of failure.

Also, because static routes have a manually configured routing entry, they must be carefully administered. A default route is one example of a static route. Static routes are preferred to dynamically determined routes because of what is known as their lower administrative distance. The administrative distance is a measure of the "trustworthiness" of a routing information source and can be altered by using the **distance** command (but this is not recommended). Example 8-1 demonstrates how to set the value of OSPF routing updates to 200. This may be useful during a RIP-to-OSPF migration.

Example 8-1 *Setting the OSPF Administrative Distance*

```
!
router ospf 90
network 150.100.1.0 0.0.0.255 area 0
distance 200
!
```

NOTE   With Bay (Nortel) routers, this is not true. Static routes assume lowest administrative priority by default. This is an important design issue to remember in mixed-vendor environments.

As shown in Figure 8-10, Cisco uses an integer called *administrative distance* (*AD* or *distance*) to differentiate sources of IP routing information.

Figure 8-10 *Use Administrative Distance to Implement Routing Policy*

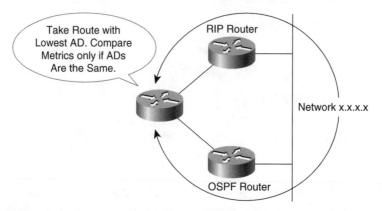

Several routing protocols can provide routing information for a particular network, even while using incompatible metrics. Path determination to a network always uses the source of information with the lowest AD. AD is like a measure of confidence in the protocol that sourced the route information. AD has an integer value up to 255. If an RIP route and a IGRP route exist to the same destination, for example, the IGRP takes precedence because its AD is 100, but RIPs AD is 120.

DESIGN RULE The route derived from the protocol with the lowest AD is always used. In the case where the ADs are equal, the route with the best metric is used.

Table 8-2 provides examples of standard or default AD integer values.

Table 8-2 *Default/Standard Administrative Distances by Route Type*

Route Type	Standard/Default Administrative Distance
Directly connected interface	0
Static route	1
EIGRP summary route	5
External BGP	20
Internal EIGRP	90
IGRP	100

Table 8-2   *Default/Standard Administrative Distances by Route Type (Continued)*

Route Type	Standard/Default Administrative Distance
OSPF	110
IS-IS	115
RIP	120
EGP	140
External EIGRP	170
Internal BGP	200
Unknown	255

Routing Metrics and Administrative Distance

Routing protocols determine the best path to a destination network by exchanging routing metrics. Examples of routing metrics are bandwidth and delay (EIGRP and IGRP), hop count (RIP), and cost (OSPF). Figure 8-11 shows the criteria that each routing protocol uses to make its "best" forwarding decisions. As you deploy different types of routing protocols in the same network, you need to have a good understanding of how these decisions are made.

Figure 8-11 *Different Protocols May Use Different Metrics*

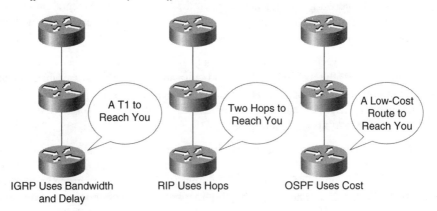

IGRP Uses Bandwidth and Delay   RIP Uses Hops   OSPF Uses Cost

Routing Protocol Scalability and Convergence

Routing protocols can be characterized according to whether classful or classless routing is supported. Routing protocols can also be characterized by what information is exchanged between routing peers. Some protocols send periodic updates and some have separate "hello" or keepalive mechanisms. On the other hand, some protocols exchange information about routes and some exchange information about link states.

Link-state routing protocols are also known as "routing by propaganda." By this, we mean that routers broadcast routing information about directly connected links only. On the other hand, distance vector routing protocols are also known as "routing by rumors," meaning that routers pass routing information gathered from neighbors.

RIP uses hops as a routing metric. Although the hop count is a 32-bit value, meaning that RIP in theory could support 2^{32} as the largest metric, in reality, the greatest metric is 16, which is considered to be infinity or unreachable. Figure 8-12 shows RIP's scalability.

Figure 8-12 *RIP Scalability Limited by Diameter*

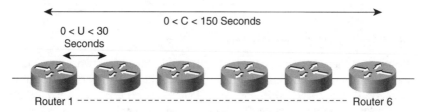

Figure 8-12 demonstrates that no RIP-based internetwork can have a diameter greater than 15 hops. (Diameter is just a term that refers to the maximum number of router hops that a network can have.) In this figure, U is the update interval of RIP (30 seconds by default). C refers to the network convergence time required for Router 6 to receive an update that was sourced by Router 1. In this case, it would take five update times (150 seconds) for an update sourced on Router 1 to reach Router 6.

Other distance vector protocols have more sophisticated metrics. For example, IGRP uses a compound 24-bit metric based on bandwidth and delay. EIGRP uses the same metric, but is multiplied by a factor of 256 ($2^8 = 256$) for finer granularity. To accommodate this extra granularity of 8 bits, the metric field in the EIGRP packet was increased from 24 bits to 32 bits (24 bits + 8 bits = 32) long.

When a topology change occurs, the time it takes for all routers to agree on network reachability is known as *convergence*. Convergence time is a function of diameter and complexity. Routing information must propagate from one edge of the internetwork to the other. Convergence time in a 15-hop internetwork can be quite long. The diameter of the internetwork should be kept consistent and small. The section, "Routing Convergence," describes the concept of convergence in greater detail.

Scalability with link-state internetworks is a complex problem and is affected by the following factors:

- The number of routing nodes in an area
- The number of networks in an area

- The number of areas
- How the address space is mapped
- Whether effective use of route aggregation exists
- The overall stability of links

Route Summarization (Aggregation)

Route summarization is important to all routing protocols. To scale an internetwork, routing information must be summarized. IP internetworks should be hierarchical; without summarization, there is a flat address space with a specific route for every host being transmitted, which means large routing tables and large router updates. Routers summarize at several levels. Figure 8-13 metaphorically illustrates the steps for route summarization as the street, address, city, and state of a given router.

Figure 8-13 *Route Summarization Determines Scalability*

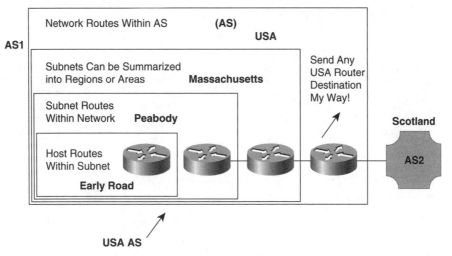

In the case of Figure 8-13, the router is located at Early Road, Peabody, Massachusetts. The local router announces to its upstream router (city router) that it is located on Early Road. To do this, the local router announces via a summary address that it contains all the Early Road host addresses. Again, instead of telling the specifics of every street that it knows about, the "Peabody Router" then summarizes to the Massachusetts Router that it knows how to get to all the Peabody addresses. This summarization continues to the AS boundary, where the USA router tells other countries (other ASs) that it can reach any USA-based host. Although very simplified, this is the very same concept that IP address summarization uses. An example using real IP addresses is presented later in this section. But, to summarize (no pun intended):

Step 1 Hosts are grouped into subnetworks.

Step 2 Subnetworks are grouped into major networks.

Step 3 Subnets and networks can be collected in areas or regions.

Step 4 With prefix routing, networks can be grouped into ASs.

This hierarchical structure allows networks to be scaled. As a general rule of thumb, always think in terms of hierarchy for maximum scalability of your design.

Figure 8-14 depicts an example where all subnets are visible to all routers within a major network. There is no summarization. As more major network numbers are added, more consolidation can take place. Each router tracks 254 local subnets. Other Class B networks appear as a single entry in the routing table. True impact of summarization is seen more and more as major network numbers are added. What this really means is that, as subnets are added to remote networks, no new routes are added because they are already covered in the existing summary range.

Figure 8-14 *Summarization Reduces Size of Routing Table*

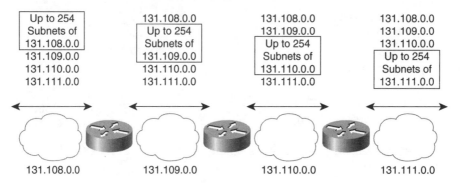

DESIGN RULE Always plan for scalability. Scalability doesn't just happen. To achieve scalability, you need to plan summarization.

Routing Convergence

As mentioned earlier, convergence is the time it takes when a route currently in the forwarding table is invalidated until an alternate is installed. During the interim, packets will be discarded or may loop.

Convergence is a critical design constraint for many applications. This constraint is especially true if time-sensitive protocols, such as Systems Network Architecture (SNA), are being transported. TCP and some desktop protocols are more tolerant of long or unpredictable convergence. Details surrounding convergence with dynamic routing protocols, such as OSPF, IGRP, and EIGRP, are covered in later chapters.

Convergence is not an issue if the internetwork never experiences a failure. In that case, static routing could be used. However, cases where internetworks never fail are nonexistent. Let me repeat: No network today truly has 100% uptime.

Convergence has two components:

- The time it takes to detect the link failure
- The time it takes to determine a new route

Fault detection depends on the data link and topology. For serial lines, fault detection is immediate if the CD lead drops. Otherwise, two to three keepalive times (20–30 seconds) will trigger a fault condition.

For Token Ring and FDDI, the time to detect a problem is almost immediate due to beacon protocol. A Token Ring algorithm called *beaconing* detects and tries to repair certain network faults. Whenever a station detects a serious problem with the network (such as a cable break), it sends a beacon frame, which defines a failure domain. This domain includes the station reporting the failure, its nearest active upstream neighbor (NAUN), and everything in between. Beaconing initiates a process called *auto-reconfiguration*, where nodes within the failure domain automatically perform diagnostics in an attempt to reconfigure the network around the failed areas. Physically, the multistation access unit (MSAU) can accomplish this through electrical reconfiguration.

With Ethernet, fault detection is generally about two to three keepalive times (20–30 seconds) or immediate if caused by local or transceiver failure.

If the routing protocol uses hellos, hellos will supersede keepalives if the hello timer is shorter than the keepalive timer.

Distance Vector Routing Convergence

As shown in Figure 8-15, the routing table propagates step by step with distance vector routing. Convergence is a function of how frequently the routing table is advertised, and across how many hops new information must propagate.

Figure 8-15 *Distance Vector Convergence*

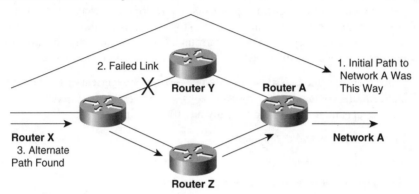

The fastest convergence takes place with load balancing. If the routing table has multiple paths to a destination, all traffic will be immediately routed over the remaining paths. In this example, Router X has a primary path to get to Network A via Router Y. When the link between Router X and Router Y fails, however, the next best path to Network A is through Router Z.

DESIGN RULE   For a fault-tolerant design, always design with backup paths whenever possible. Furthermore, routing over multiple, equal-cost paths is optimal for best fault tolerance.

Link-State Routing Convergence

Link-state protocols were designed to converge quickly. For example, OSPF was designed to converge faster than RIP. When a link changes state (as shown in Figure 8-16), a link-state advertisement (LSA) is transmitted and propagates to all routers throughout the area. As the LSA propagates, it must be acknowledged. The acknowledgement of LSAs ensures that the link-state database is synchronized on all routers within the area. When a router receives an LSA, it calculates a routing table independently via the SPF algorithm (that is, each router derives its own routing table).

Figure 8-16 *Link-State Convergence*

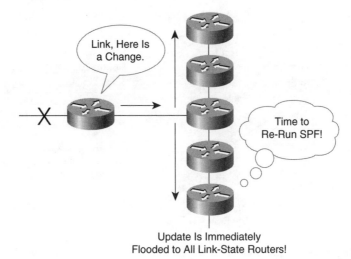

Link, Here Is a Change.

Time to Re-Run SPF!

Update Is Immediately
Flooded to All Link-State Routers!

The entire process takes only a few seconds. Note that like distance vector protocols, link-state protocols also converge faster if there is load balancing over multiple paths. It takes several update periods for new routes to propagate with classical distance vector protocols. Therefore, although much more CPU intensive, OSPF and other link-state protocols will always converge much faster than a distance vector protocol like IGRP or RIP.

Preventing Routing Loops During Convergence

A routing loop occurs when routers disagree about the best path to a given destination. In Figure 8-17, for example, routers disagree if their routing tables are inconsistent. The protocol's routing algorithm will take a certain amount of time to converge after a change in internetwork topology. During convergence, routing tables are inconsistent and routed data can be lost. Routing loops can almost be thought of as the traditional, "I've got it! No, you've got it!" that occurs when amateur (and sometimes professional) baseball infielders react when an infield pop fly is hit. The result is that the ball is dropped, resulting in an error.

Figure 8-17 *Routing Loop: A Routing Disagreement*

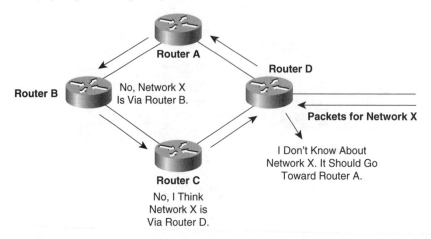

Routing loops do not often cause the internetwork to completely fail. Usually, there is a temporary traffic surge until the loop is resolved. IP datagrams can traverse a maximum of 255 routing nodes, as dictated by the Time To Live (TTL) field in the IP header.

NOTE   TTL is an end-system responsibility and is usually set to 32. Packets, such as TTY session packets, that originate from the router have the TTL set to 32 by default.

Distance vector protocols use several methods to prevent routing loops. These mechanisms include the following:

- Holddown timers
- Split horizon
- Poison reverse

Link-state protocols attempt to minimize the number of routing loops by using reliable updates and converging quickly.

In Figure 8-18, a holddown timer is used to prevent general routing loops. When the route to Network B fails, Router X puts the effected route into holddown. While the route to Network B is in holddown, Router X ignores all advertised routes to Network B, which allows time for the changed information about Network B to propagate to all the routers in the AS. After the changed information has reached every router, false routes are no longer advertised. After the holddown timer expires, Router X will accept routes to Network B.

Figure 8-18 *Holddown Prevents Routing Loops*

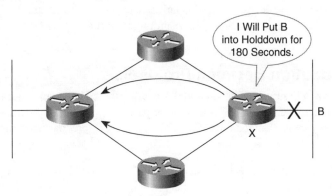

Split horizon prevents the short routing loop because routers do not advertise a route back to the original source. Put simply, split horizon enforces the rule that a router should never re-advertise a route out the same interface it learned it on.

The holddown timer is set long enough for routing information to propagate all the way across the internetwork, and convergence takes at least as long as the holddown timer value. The lessening of the holddown timer can speed convergence time, but this lessening makes the internetwork susceptible to temporary routing loops.

While routes to a network are in holddown, packets to that destination are thrown away.

You can adjust the RIP update timer using the **timers basic** command, the syntax for which is as follows:

```
timers basic update time invalid timer holdown timer flush timer [sleeptime]
```

For example, the default settings for RIP are **timers basic** *30 180 180 24*. This means that RIP uses 30-second updates, marks a route invalid at 180 seconds, and sets holddown, finally flushing the route at 240 seconds. If a few routers are set to provide fast convergence (**timers basic** *5 15 15 30*), the results are catastrophic. Routers in the border between the two different timers will be flushing routes and re-adding them continually. This is not the desired result.

DESIGN RULE   Do not modify timer settings unless you have a good reason to do so. If you do change them, make sure to change the settings throughout the AS.

Route Redistribution

Route redistribution is a Cisco IOS software feature. Redistribution is the exchange of routing information between two different routing processes (that is, two different routing protocols). It is useful if you have separate routing domains within your AS and you need to exchange routes between them. The engineering department might be running RIP, for example, and the accounting department might be running IGRP.

Route Redistribution Between Protocols

As shown in Figure 8-19, when routes are redistributed between major networks, no subnet information is required. The router participates in two routing processes (RIP and OSPF) and routes are exchanged internally. The router, therefore, has a routing table that contains RIP and OSPF routes.

Figure 8-19   *Route Redistribution Between Protocols*

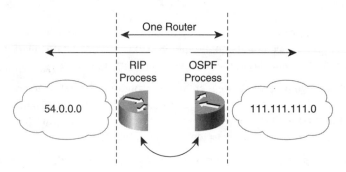

Example 8-2 shows a router with both types of routes.

Example 8-2   *Router Participating in Two Routing Processes (RIP and OSPF)*

```
MICKEY#show ip route
Codes: C - connected, S - static, I - IGRP, R - RIP, M - mobile, B - BGP
       D - EIGRP, EX - EIGRP external, O - OSPF, IA - OSPF inter area
       N1 - OSPF NSSA external type 1, N2 - OSPF NSSA external type 2
       E1 - OSPF external type 1, E2 - OSPF external type 2, E - EGP
       i - IS-IS, L1 - IS-IS level-1, L2 - IS-IS level-2, * - candidate default
       U - per-user static route, o - ODR

Gateway of last resort is 172.16.65.1 to network 0.0.0.0

C    10.0.0.0/8 is directly connected, Ethernet1
C    15.0.0.0/8 is directly connected, Serial0
C    20.0.0.0/8 is directly connected, TokenRing0
     54.0.0.0/8 is variably subnetted, 2 subnets, 2 masks
R       54.0.0.0/8 [120/5] via 20.1.1.2, 00:00:16, TokenRing0
R       54.0.0.0/16 [120/5] via 20.1.1.2, 00:00:16, TokenRing0
     111.0.0.0/24 is subnetted, 1 subnets
O       111.111.111.0 [110/12] via 20.1.1.2, 00:01:13, TokenRing0
C    192.68.15.0/24 is directly connected, Loopback6
     172.16.0.0/27 is subnetted, 1 subnets
```

Example 8-2   *Router Participating in Two Routing Processes (RIP and OSPF) (Continued)*

```
C       172.16.65.0 is directly connected, Ethernet0
S*   0.0.0.0/0 [1/0] via 172.16.65.1
MICKEY#
```

Route Redistribution Within the Same Network

Routes can also be redistributed within the same major network number, as illustrated in Figure 8-20.

Figure 8-20   *Route Redistribution in the Same Network*

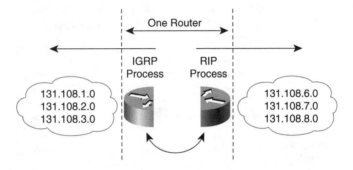

In this case, block the IGRP advertisements into the RIP cloud with the **passive-interface** command. Likewise, you can block the RIP advertisements into the IGRP cloud with the **passive-interface** command, as illustrated in Example 8-3.

Example 8-3   *Blocking RIP Advertisements with **passive-interface***

```
router igrp 1

    network 131.108.0.0

    passive-interface serial 1.1

    passive-interface serial 1.2

    passive-interface serial 1.3
```

Subnets are automatically redistributed between RIP and IGRP within the same major network. In other cases (for example, RIP-to-OSPF), subnet information might need to be forced with the **subnets** keyword, as demonstrated in Example 8-4.

Example 8-4   *Forcing Redistribution of Subnets with the **subnets** Keyword*

```
!
router ospf 90
```

continues

Example 8-4 *Forcing Redistribution of Subnets with the **subnets** Keyword (Continued)*

```
network 150.100.1.2 0.0.0.0 area 0
redistribute rip subnets metric 3
!
```

Route Redistribution to RIP for Hosts

As shown in Figure 8-21, UNIX-based workstations might need to hear RIP routing updates to populate their local routing table.

Figure 8-21 *Redistribute to RIP for Hosts*

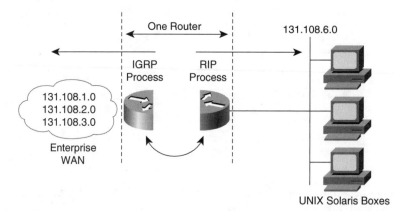

These workstations can run the routed daemon in passive mode to listen to routing updates without advertising them into the RIP process. (You can configure passive mode by using the **-q** option). On a Sun Solaris 2.5 box, for example, you would type in the following:

```
/usr/sbin/in.routed -q
```

WARNING You should take extreme care to prevent host-generated RIP advertisements from being redistributed into the protocol, such as IGRP in this example. A misconfigured workstation whose updates are redistributed into the router's protocol can subvert routes for the entire network by continuously changing default route information. Controlling host-generated routing information is a growing problem that you can manage by filtering for devices from which updates will be accepted, or you can manage by protocol authentication methods, and so on.

Accommodating Routing Protocol Inconsistencies During Route Redistribution

Different routing protocols have many inconsistencies, such as how each handles the default route, as well as each routing protocol having differing metric values. When redistributing, it is important to accommodate these differences.

For example, RIP and IGRP handle default routes differently. RIP uses network 0.0.0.0 as the universal default route. IGRP advertises and selects from several candidate default networks. The 0.0.0.0 route must be filtered when redistributing from RIP to IGRP. In Figure 8-22, if IGRP has a candidate default network (that is, 131.108.7.0) in the routing table, it will be translated to a 0.0.0.0 route when redistributing to RIP. Otherwise, you can configure a 0.0.0.0 route statically.

Figure 8-22 *Configure Default Routes: RIP to IGRP*

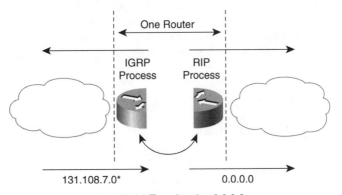

The appropriate use of default routes is a very important design consideration, and not something arbitrarily applied to solve a problem. A preferable strategy is to have defaults originate at selected exit points of the network. Originate a 0.0.0.0 route at Internet links, for example, originate a network-level summary route at the core WAN router, and so on.

Different routing protocols use different metrics. Translation of the RIP metric to the IGRP metric is a problem because all redistributed routes are assigned the same metric due to the format of the **default-metric** command. For example, all IGRP-derived routes might be assigned a hop count of 1. This metric mismatch could be a bad thing because IGRP calculates its metric from a series of steps (default IGRP metric = BW + delay) and the metrics are usually much larger than those of RIP (max metric is 15). A route may get inadvertently used if you are not careful with the metric values.

The metric substitution is a problem if you allow routes to redistribute back across the boundary because the original IGRP metric was lost. To prevent metric substitution, impose split horizon with route filters or a technique known as route maps. Otherwise, a problematic, iterative routing failure called *route feedback* occurs.

NOTE   A route map is an advanced feature to redistribute routes or to subject packets to policy routing. For more information on route maps, check out www.cisco.com/univercd/cc/td/doc/product/software/ios112/112cg_cr/5rbook/5riprout.htm#xtocid12003185.

IP access lists are normally used to filter routes when redistributing. As noted previously, route maps are a powerful route-filtering feature that can also be used when redistributing. Redistribution filters are crucial in keeping your network from looping, as illustrated by Figure 8-23. In this example, the IGRP process allows in only what it does not send to RIP. The RIP process allows in only what it did not send to IGRP. Other protocol-specific options include OSPF tags and manual configuration of split horizon.

Figure 8-23   *Filter to Avoid Redistribution Feedback*

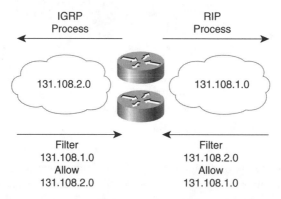

Table 8-3 summarizes the characteristics of the most common IP routing protocols. Each routing protocol has advantages that make it useful in an integrated network design.

Table 8-3   *IP Routing Protocol Characteristics*

Protocol	Type	Proprietary	Function	Updates	Metric	VLSM	Summarization
RIP	Distance vector	No	Interior	30 seconds	Hops	No	Automatic
RIPV2	Distance vector	No	Interior	30 seconds	Hops	Yes	Automatic

Table 8-3   *IP Routing Protocol Characteristics (Continued)*

Protocol	Type	Proprietary	Function	Updates	Metric	VLSM	Summarization
IGRP	Distance vector	Yes	Interior	90 seconds	Composite based on: bandwidth, delay, MTU, reliability, load	No	Automatic
EIGRP	Advanced distance vector	Yes	Interior	Triggered	Composite based on: bandwidth, delay, MTU, reliability, load	Yes	Manual or automatic
OSPF	Link-state	No	Interior	Triggered	Cost	Yes	Manual
IS-IS	Link-state	No	Interior/ Exterior	Triggered	Cost	Yes	Manual
BGP	Distance vector	No	Exterior	Triggered	Cost	Yes	Manual

Summary

Routing protocols can be characterized by where they are used, what resources they need, what metrics they use, and what information the routers exchange. Routing protocols determine the best path based on a metric or a combination of metrics. Summarization of routing information allows routing protocols to scale. When doing route redistribution, block routes from redistributing back to the source. This type of precaution is well worth it, even if it saves your network just one outage in the future.

Chapter Review Questions

1 What are the tasks that a router must accomplish?

2 What is the difference between process switching and fast switching?

3 What does the term "routing by rumors" mean and what is an example of a protocol that uses this mechanism?

4 What is meant by administrative distance?

5 Describe the operation and purpose of the split horizon mechanism.

6 What is meant by convergence time?

7 What is an EGP and give an examplex of a common EGP?

8 What is the significance of RFC 1923?

The development of OSPF began in 1987 as a replacement for the Internet's Routing Information Protocol (RIP), which was showing signs of wear in many networks. Since that time, OSPF has been refined and extended to support additional features, such as multicast routing and efficient operation over dialup links.

—John Moy, creator of OSPF

Upon completion of this chapter, you will be able to perform the following:

- Describe how to use modular design and summarization features to design scalable Open Shortest Path First (OSPF) internetworks

- Describe how to allocate IP addresses in contiguous blocks so that OSPF summarization can be used

CHAPTER 9

OSPF Design

Building scalable OSPF internetworks is a challenge that you will eventually have to face, if you haven't already. This chapter presents how to use modular design and summarization features to design scalable Open Shortest Path First (OSPF) internetworks. Essential areas of OSPF network design include how and when and where to use OSPF summarization. Other key factors in scaling OSPF include where and how many routers to place in an area. This chapter addresses these and other issues. You will also find several key design links for your further OSPF enlightenment.

OSPF Protocol

OSPF version 1 (and its replacement, version 2), is a standard, nonproprietary, routing protocol for IP. Unless otherwise specified in this book, OSPF refers to OSPF version 2. As a replacement for Routing Information Protocol (RIP), OSPF was designed to overcome the limitations of RIP, which, as seen in Chapter 8, "Routing Protocol Design," included limited scalability, slow convergence, and susceptibility to routing loops. Furthermore, OSPF is a link-state routing protocol, whereas RIP is a distance vector protocol. In review, link-state protocols receive link-state packet information and store it in a database local to the router. Each link-state router then calculates its own routing table to each destination in the network, based on the link-state costs. The mathematical algorithm used to calculate the routing table is known as *Dijkstra's algorithm*, which is also often referred to as just the *shortest path first (SPF) algorithm*.

OSPF is classified as an Interior Gateway Protocol (IGP), which means that it distributes routing information between routers that belong to a single autonomous system (AS).

OSPF version 2 is described by RFC 2328. OSPF is an evolving protocol, with new enhancements being added as needed. Note that although new features are added in newer RFCs, downward compatibility is always preserved.

NOTE   You can find RFCs and some very useful OSPF information at www.freesoft.org/CIE/ index.htm. In addition, a "living reference" tied to the OSPF IETF committee and that lists the current RFCs can be found at www.ietf.org/html.charters/ospf-charter.html.

OSPF Network Types

As shown in Figure 9-1, three types of network connection types are defined for the OSPF routing protocol:

- Point-to-point—Describes network types where neighbor relationships are formed only with the other router on the point-to-point link. Both routers can independently communicate with all other OSPF routers. An example of a point-to-point network is an ISDN or T1 connection.

- Broadcast multiaccess—Describes network types where a so-called designated router (or DR) communicates with all other OSPF routers regarding the LAN network. That router shares learned information with other local routers. Neighbor relationships are formed based on a dynamic learning process using multicast Hello packets. An example of a broadcast multiaccess network is Ethernet.

- Nonbroadcast multiaccess—Describes network types where all routers might not communicate with other OSPF routers. Because multicasts are not available in a nonbroadcast environment (for example, Switched Multimegabit Data Service (SMDS) environment), neighbor relationships are typically formed by a manual configuration process or some other configuration. Another example of a nonbroadcast multiaccess network is Frame Relay.

Figure 9-1   *OSPF Network Types*

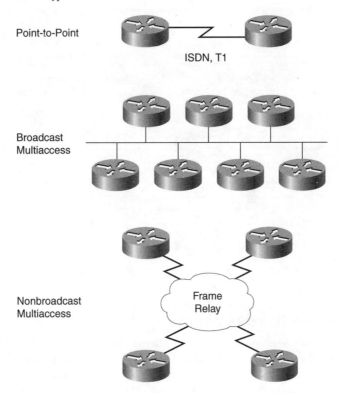

Point-to-Point

ISDN, T1

Broadcast
Multiaccess

Nonbroadcast
Multiaccess

Frame
Relay

OSPF Router Types

Just as different network types are used in OSPF, Figure 9-2 shows that there are also four classes of OSPF router types, as follows:

- Internal OSPF Router—Router with all directly connected networks belonging to the same area. (Also includes routers with only backbone interfaces.)

- Area Border Router (ABR)—Router that attaches to multiple areas, including area 0. ABRs also can perform summarization from its attached area(s) into the backbone area 0.

- Backbone Router (BBR)—Router that has an interface to the backbone. Includes ABRs and routers with all interfaces connected to the backbone (which are also considered internal routers).

- Autonomous System Boundary Router (ASBR)—Router that exchanges routing information with routers belonging to other autonomous systems. ASBRs can also be configured to perform summarization of its external links into area 0.

Figure 9-2   *Classification of OSPF Routers*

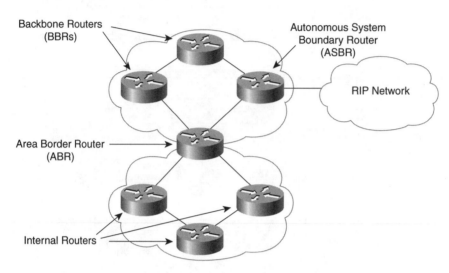

OSPF Link-State Advertisements

OSPF routers communicate link status changes with link-state advertisements (LSAs). LSAs are always acknowledged and tagged with a sequence number. Sequencing is the critical piece that OSPF uses to converge reliably; it also guarantees the integrity of the OSPF link-state database. If an LSA is not acknowledged in a set time (default timer is 5 seconds), for example, the source router will retransmit the LSA. This value for retransmission can be set on a "per-interface" basis. Example 9-1 sets the retransmit interval value to 7 seconds:

Example 9-1   *Setting the OSPF Router Retransmit Interval*

```
!
interface ethernet 1/1
 ip ospf retransmit-interval 7
!
```

Figure 9-3 depicts the different types of LSAs, which are described as follows:

- Router links advertisement—Contains information about the sending router's links to neighbor routers. Router links are also known as Type 1 LSAs.

- Network links advertisement—Contains list of routers connected to a network segment. Sent by the designated router on behalf of all routers on a multiaccess network, such as Ethernet. Network links are also known as Type 2 LSAs.

- Summary link advertisement—Describes networks reachable from outside the area. Routes to these networks are injected into an area by an ABR. In Figure 9-4, you can see the summary LSA getting generated from the ABR that connects to both area 0 and area 1. Summary links are also known as Type 3 (sourced by ABR) and Type 4 (source by ASBRs) LSAs.

- External link advertisement—Describes a route to a destination in another AS or separate routing process. Note in Figure 9-4 that the external routes are injected here into area 0 from an ASBR. External links are also known as Type 5 LSAs.

NOTE   RFC 2370 introduces a newer LSA type that is called the opaque LSA. This LSA type (LSA Type 8) is for the future use of OSPF to support other application-specific information. As a design engineer, it is important to understand that OSPF, although a standard, is not standing idle. It is ever-changing and improving. You will also later see that not-so-stubby-areas use Type 7 LSAs.

Figure 9-3   *Types of Link-State Advertisements*

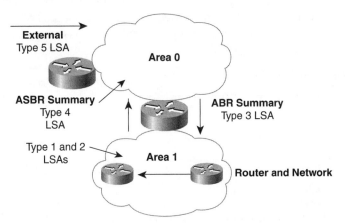

As shown in Figure 9-4, all OSPF routers in an area have an identical link-state database that consists of all the LSAs heard within that particular area. The type of link-state information depends on the source of the LSA. The benefit of having all routers with an identical database is that any change will be propagated to all OSPF routers sharing a broadcast domain.

Figure 9-4   *All Routers in the Same Area Have Identical Link-State Databases*

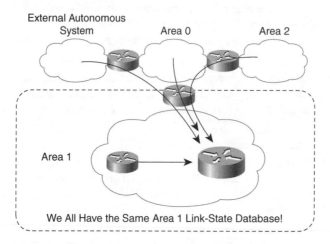

When a link changes state, directly connected routers generate an LSA. The LSA is sent to neighbor routers. The designated router, if present, forwards the LSA to other routers in the area to which it is adjacent. The term *adjacent* means an OSPF router with which another OSPF router has formed a neighbor relationship and exchanged link-state databases. OSPF routers go through several stages prior to establishing an adjacency, as shown in the following list.

Step 1   Initialization

Step 2   Establish two-way communication

Step 3   Exstart state

Step 4   Exchange state

Step 5   Loading state

Step 6   Full state

When 2 OSPF routers are in "full state," it means that they have successfully established an adjacency.

When a router gets an LSA, it updates its link-state database. It then uses the SPF algorithm with the new database to generate a new routing table. After the router finishes recalculating, it generates a new routing table and the router switches over to the new routing table.

NOTE   The SPF algorithm is also called the Dijkstra algorithm, named after the computer scientist who invented it.

As shown in Figure 9-5, sometimes a link, such as a serial line, will go up and down rapidly. This condition, known as link flapping, can generate a series of LSAs, which would cause routers to repeatedly recompute a new routing table. This repeated recalculation condition could be so serious that the routers would never converge.

Figure 9-5   *When a Link Changes State*

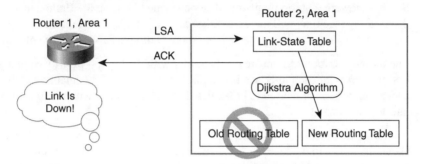

Each SPF calculation uses resources from the CPU to process, based on the new LSA information. The **timers spf** *spf-delay spf-holdtime* command was added to prevent routers from computing a second routing table any more frequently than every 10 seconds. This value for *spf-holdtime* can be configured to values between 0 and 65,535. The value of *spf-delay* defines the delay time, in seconds, between when OSPF receives a topology change and when it starts a SPF calculation. It can be an integer from 0 to 65,535. The default time is 5 seconds. A value of 0 means that there is no delay—that is, the SPF calculation is started immediately.

NOTE   In Figure 9-5, there is an LSA ACK (acknowledgement) after the LSA was sent. As mentioned earlier in the chapter, this is key to the reliability of OSPF.

Designated and Backup Designated Routers

A broadcast LAN is designated as an OSPF multiaccess network. A multiaccess network has a designated router (DR) and a backup designated router (BDR). You may ask, "What, then, is a DR and BDR?"

The DR represents the multiaccess network in the sense that it sends LSAs on behalf of all the routers on the network. The designated router is a consolidation point for LSAs for a given broadcast network (that is, it gets an LSA via a multiaccess network then forwards it out).

The *backup designated router (BDR)* will automatically become the DR in the event that the DR fails or becomes unreachable.

Each area router forms an adjacency to both the DR and the BDR. Adjacent routers regularly exchange Hello messages to verify reachability. This frequency is determined by the Hello interval, which defaults to 10 seconds. The Hello interval can be modified by using the command **ip ospf hello interval** *interval*, where the *interval* is in seconds. The default setting is 10 seconds. Increasing this interval is sometimes necessary over heavily congested links. If there is much congestion on a given link, you may miss Hello messages because they are sent too frequently. The downside to setting the Hello interval too high is that convergence time will increase. Likewise, the smaller the Hello interval, the faster topological changes will be detected, but more Hello traffic will fill up your links.

The designated router for an area is the router with the highest priority (router ID). The OSPF priority for each interface is a numeric value, set to 1 by default; and the highest IP address on the router is used to break ties. Priority can be set with the **ip ospf priority** interface command.

As shown in Figure 9-6, you want to selectively choose which router will become the DR. Generally, this will be the most powerful (memory, CPU, and so forth) router on the broadcast network. You can, therefore, set other routers that you want not to be the DR to have an OSPF priority set to 0 on each interface where the router will not participate as DR/BDR. Every router on the multiaccess segment is adjacent to the designated router.

Figure 9-6 *Designated Router on a Multiaccess Link*

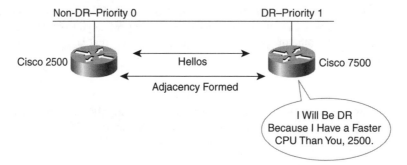

The Hierarchical Nature of OSPF

OSPF is typical of link-state routing protocol in that participating networks must be hierarchically arranged. The backbone area is designated area 0 (or 0.0.0.0). All other areas attach to the backbone by one or more ABRs. All interarea traffic must go across the backbone. As shown in Figure 9-7, OSPF areas must follow a strict hierarchy. If the areas are not set up hierarchically, the network will have discontiguous areas, which will cause inconsistent routing or most likely result in the complete failure of any interarea routing.

Figure 9-7 *All ABRs Must Be Connected to the Backbone Area*

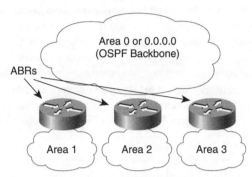

Interarea routing occurs when a packet is destined to a device in a different area from which it belongs. Interarea routing travels from the local area, through area 0, and finally to the destination area. Intra-area routing, on the other hand, occurs when a packet is destined to a device within the same area. The packet does not travel through area 0 for intra-area routing and is considered as an optimal routing scenario.

ABR-s attach the backbone (area 0) to other areas. Further, note that all routers within an area share the same link-state database.

Virtual Links in OSPF Networks

As depicted in Figure 9-8, special connections called *virtual links* pass through a non-0 area (in this case, area 1, known as the transit area) to provide connectivity to the nearest ABR for area 2. Virtual links act like tunnels, which maintain connectivity to the backbone when failures occur.

Figure 9-8 *Virtual Links in an OSPF Network*

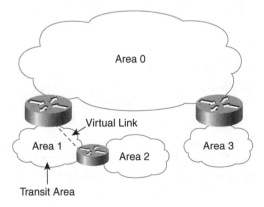

The performance of virtual links is slower than that of normal links. Virtual links also add complexity to network design and configuration. Also, some older versions of IOS code (pre-11.2 code) had problems with virtual links and required the routers to be rebooted to make virtual links work properly. The general suggestion, therefore, is to avoid using virtual links unless absolutely necessary. One example may be in the case of a disaster recovery. If your ABR link is down, you may have no choice but to create a virtual link through a different transit area. This should only be a temporary solution to keep the network up. If your design requires virtual links, you may want to reexamine whether OSPF is the most appropriate protocol to be using in your network.

DESIGN RULE   OSPF designs should avoid using virtual links.

OSPF Summarization

For optimal OSPF network performance, IP address ranges should be grouped by area. After you have grouped IP address ranges by area, OSPF summarization is flexible and can be configured. Summarization for OSPF is a manual process. There is no concept of "automatic summarization," as is seen in some protocols, such as RIP v2 or EIGRP. "Legal" OSPF area configurations could have any of following characteristics:

- Single major network number
- Single fixed-mask subnet
- Several major networks
- Several fixed-mask subnets
- Combination of major networks and subnets of different major networks
- Random assortment of networks, fixed and variable subnets, and specific host addresses

Address Space Allocation

It is important that hosts, subnets, and networks be allocated to areas in a controlled way. Optimally, all the addresses in an area should be contiguous so that summary LSAs can represent the entire address space as efficiently as possible.

Allocate blocks of addresses in powers of two so that a block can be represented by a single summary link advertisement. Use the **area** *area id* **range** *address mask* command on ABRs to summarize contiguous blocks of subnets with one summary link advertisement. To minimize the number of summary blocks, make each block as large as possible. Summary

LSAs that represent an entire area's address space, for example, will be injected into the backbone area 0, as shown in Figure 9-9.

Figure 9-9   *Injecting Summary LSAs into Area 0*

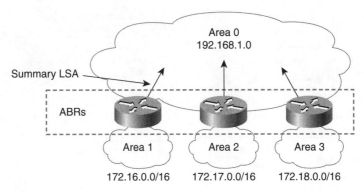

Example 9-2 shows the router configuration to summarize contiguous blocks of subnets with one summary link advertisement on an ABR.

Example 9-2   *Summarizing Subnets with One Summary Link Advertisement on an ABR*

```
!
router ospf 90
network 192.168.1.0 0.0.0.255 area 0
network 172.16.0.0 0.0.255.255 area 1
area 1 range 172.16.0.0 255.255.0.0
!
```

In Figure 9-9, Class B address ranges are summarized at each ABR. Therefore, specific IP address information of each area never traverses the backbone. Only a summary address is sent across the backbone for each area. This methodology of summarization is highly recommended for OSPF to scale in large internetwork designs, especially international OSPF networks, which often have fault-prone WAN links (that is, links that are prone to errors).

Bit Splitting

To divide a major network number across more than one area, you should use a technique known as *bit splitting*.

Bit splitting borrows some subnet bits to designate areas. Bit splitting is best achieved when subnets are grouped in contiguous blocks. To differentiate two areas, split 1 bit. To differentiate 16 areas, split 4 bits. The example in Figure 9-10 uses 4 bits for the area and uses 32-bit numbers to represent 4 of the 16 possible areas. The area numbers appear in dotted-decimal notation and look like subnet numbers. In fact, the 32-bit area number corresponds to the summary advertisement that represents the area. It is equally valid to just call the areas 1, 2, 3, and 4.

Figure 9-10 *Bit Splitting the Address Space*

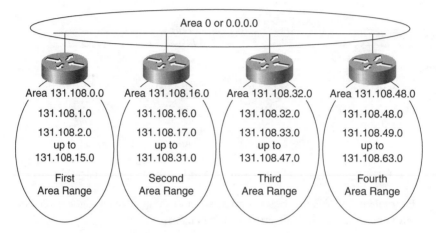

As shown in Figure 9-10, if you divide a Class B network into 16 areas with 16 subnets in each, you get the following:

- Range mask 255.255.240.0
    - Area bits: 4
- Subnet mask 255.255.255.0
    - Total subnet bits: 8
    - Leftover subnet bits: 4
    - Subnets per area: 16
- Address bits advertised to the backbone: 11111111.11111111.11110000.00000000
- Address bits hidden within the area: 00000000.00000000.00001111.11111111

IP Address Mapping for VLSMs

Mapping the IP address space for variable-length subnet masks (VLSMs) is similar to the preceding bit splitting example. In Figure 9-11, notice which part of the address space is advertised and which is hidden within the area:

- Advertised: 11111111.11111111.11110000.00000000
- Hidden: 00000000.00000000.00001111.11111111

The hidden address space bits can be used for VLSM. For maximum summarization benefit, it is important to keep the VLSM subnets together in contiguous blocks. One of the key benefits of VLSM is that is enables you to increase the number of subnets that you have to assign for serial links. The bottom line is that VLSM makes the most efficient use of your address space and should be used in your OSPF network.

Figure 9-11 *Map OSPF Address Space for VLSMs*

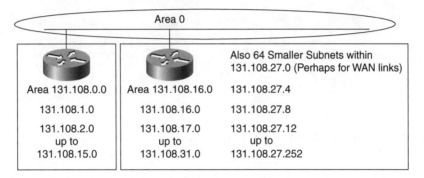

Discontiguous Subnets

Subnets become discontiguous when they are separated by one or more segments represented by a different major network number. Discontiguous subnets are supported by OSPF because subnet masks are part of the link-state database (LSDB). The backbone area 0 could be a Class C address, and all the other areas (all subnets of the same network) could be address blocks from a Class B major network.

One nice benefit of OSPF is that discontiguous subnets are supported whether or not summarization is configured. As shown in Figure 9-12, the network 131.108.0.0 is discontiguous because it has components (as Class C's) within area 3 and within area 2. Again, OSPF can take care of this problem because the LSDB carries mask information. RIP or IGRP, for example, can not support discontiguous subnets.

Figure 9-12 *OSPF Supports Discontiguous Subnets*

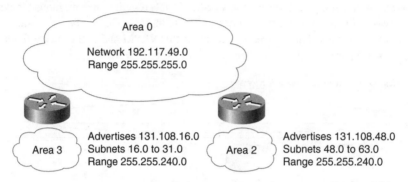

Configuring Summarization on ABRs

The ABR between the backbone and another area consolidates routing information between areas. This means that specific routes within a summarized range are not injected into the backbone of the network. Note, too, that an area can have one or more ABRs (good design practice and often done for redundancy). The consolidation is configured manually with the previously discussed **area** *area id* **range** *address mask* command under the **router ospf** section of the router configuration. Figure 9-13 shows a network where area 1 and area 2 ABRs can summarize their area network ranges into area 0, thereby consolidating updates into the backbone.

Figure 9-13 *ABR Consolidates Updates to and from Area 0*

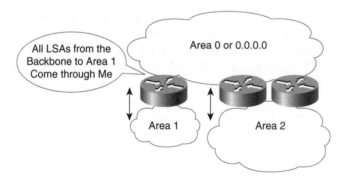

If summarization is not configured on ABRs, all specific link information propagates out to the backbone. If a link is flapping, a stream of LSAs is generated out to the backbone and throughout the autonomous system, which can cause serious traffic and router CPU overhead. Figure 9-14 shows that all specific LSAs from areas 1, 2, and 3 are injected "non-summarized" into the backbone. Every router must compute the CPU-intensive SPF algorithm to build a new routing table every time a link state changes anywhere in the OSPF AS.

Figure 9-14 *No Summarization: Specific-Link LSA*

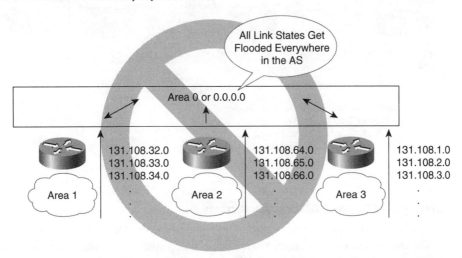

The **spf holdtime** command limits how often the SPF algorithm is computed. By default, the SPF hold time is 10 seconds. LSAs are collected for a period of 10 seconds before a new routing table is calculated. Today, many networks still do not employ route summarization. When link flaps occur, designs are a network disaster waiting to happen. Simply put, OSPF networks not deploying summarization are poorly designed.

DESIGN RULE   Summarize your OSPF network for maximum stability and scalability.

With properly configured summarization, only summary-link LSAs propagate into the backbone, which is important for scaling because specific link-state changes do not propagate to the backbone and cause every router to compute the SPF algorithm. More summarization means more stability. Summarization is the key to scaling any large internetwork with OSPF. As shown in Figure 9-15, summarization hides link flaps within a given area. Note that all intra-area OSPF routers still see the link state, but other interarea OSPF routers will not.

Figure 9-15 *Summarization Hides Link Changes*

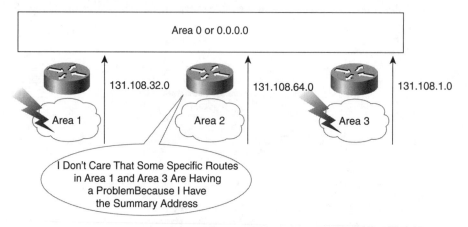

Configuring Summarization on ASBRs

Just as the ABR can summarize internal OSPF networks, the ASBR can inject specific external links or summary external links into the AS. The decision to inject this route is determined by whether the **default-information originate** command is configured on the ASBR. As a general rule, summarize external links with **default-information originate** if there is only one ASBR.

Example 9-3 specifies a metric of 50 for the default route redistributed into the OSPF routing domain.

Example 9-3 *Specifying a Metric for the Default Route Redistributed into the OSPF Routing Domain*

```
!
router ospf 90
 redistribute igrp 90 metric 50 subnets
 default-information originate metric 50
!
```

If more than one ASBR exists, you must make a tradeoff. Use the **default-information originate** command to minimize the external routing information injected into the AS. Each router in the AS uses the closest ASBR as an external gateway because it does not have complete information on specific external links.

In Figure 9-16, an ASBR is receiving BGP routes from an ISP and then summarizing these externally learned routes with a default route into the local OSPF domain. Allowing all Internet routes into your network is not recommended as it could easily overwhelm your routers with excessive routing tables. If you have multiple ASBRs all injecting defaults, the tradeoff is that you could encounter non-optimal routing because you will not have "specific" routes. This tradeoff is not really a "bad thing," but just an item to remember when doing route summarization.

Figure 9-16 *ASBRs Consolidate External Routes*

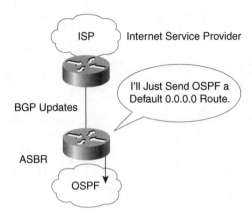

NOTE   External OSPF routes are transmitted one packet at a time. This makes flooding of these LSAs extremely bandwidth intensive. Because of this, it is recommended to do default route injection or configure OSPF stub areas, as discussed later in this chapter.

OSPF Areas

As shown in Figure 9-17, the ABR of a regular (non-summarized) OSPF area is promiscuous, which means that the ABR processes all LSAs from the backbone and its locally attached areas. No default LSA is injected. The LSAs from the backbone could be any combination of the following, depending on how summarization is configured on other ABRs:

- Specific-link LSAs from other areas
- Specific-link LSAs representing links within the backbone area
- Specific external LSAs from an ASBR
- Summary-link LSAs from other areas
- Summary-link LSAs representing links within the backbone area
- Summary external-link LSAs from an ASBR

Figure 9-17 *The Non-Summarized Area Is Promiscuous*

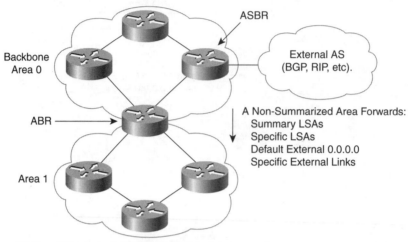

There are different types of OSPF areas and each has a special purpose. Each type of area is discussed in the following sections.

Stubby Areas

Figure 9-18 depicts what is known as a *stub area*. A stub area summarizes all external LSAs as a default LSA. This advertisement applies only to external links (these are called OSPF Type 5 LSAs) from outside the AS. A stub area sees all the specific-link and summary-link LSAs advertised within the AS. The stub ABR is therefore an LSA Type 5 filter for all areas below it in a hierarchy. The net result of all external LSAs is a simple default route (0.0.0.0) that is propagated to all routers in the stub area. A stub area can generate any of the following:

- Specific-link LSAs from other areas
- Specific-link LSAs representing links within the backbone area
- Summary-link LSAs from other areas
- Summary-link LSAs representing links within the backbone area
- Default LSA represents all external links (0.0.0.0)

Figure 9-18 *Stub Areas Consolidate External Links*

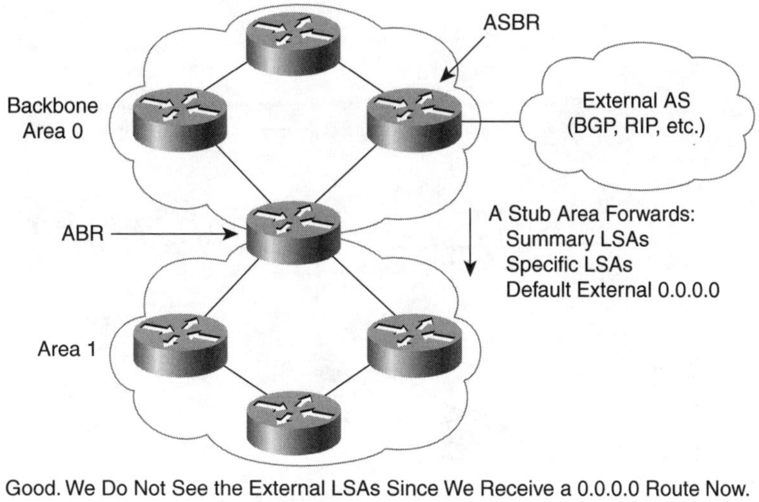

Good. We Do Not See the External LSAs Since We Receive a 0.0.0.0 Route Now.

Totally Stubby Areas

If an area is configured as *totally stubby*, only the default summary link 0.0.0.0 is injected into the area by ABRs. Each router picks the closest ABR as a gateway to everything outside the area. The **area** *area-id* **stub** [**no-summary**] command is available in Cisco IOS Release 9.1. and later.

The totally stubby area (TSA), shown in Figure 9-19, is a Cisco-specific feature. Therefore, totally stubby areas are not part of the RFC standard. Be careful if you are mixing vendors across the same OSPF domain. An AS gateway router cannot be configured in a totally stubby area because external routing information is not supported. Similarly, redistribution from other routing protocols cannot take place on any router in a TSA. TSAs are recommended for building highly scalable Cisco-based OSPF designs.

DESIGN RULE   Whenever possible, use TSAs in your design.

Figure 9-19 *Totally Stubby Area Injects Default Only*

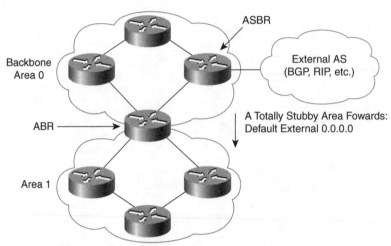

Even Better. We Do Not See the External or Summary LSAs
Since We Receive a 0.0.0.0 Route Now.

Not-So-Stubby Areas

An area configured as a Not-So-Stubby-Area (NSSA) summarizes or filters a limited
number of external routes (known as Type 5 LSAs). The number of routes is limited to those
required to provide connectivity between backbone areas. When you define an NSSA, you
can import specific external routes as Type 7 LSAs into the NSSA. In addition, when
translating Type 7 LSAs to be imported into nonstub areas, you can summarize or filter the
LSAs before importing them as Type 5 LSAs. Areas that redistribute information between
the OSPF central site (area 0) and an external routing protocol domain can be configured
as NSSAs.

You may ask, "Why use an NSSA?" As shown in Figure 9-20, if you are an Internet service
provider (ISP) or a network administrator who has to connect a central site using OSPF to
a remote site that is using a different protocol, such as RIP or EIGRP, you can use NSSA
to simplify the administration of this kind of topology.

Figure 9-20 *NSSAs—Why Use Them?*

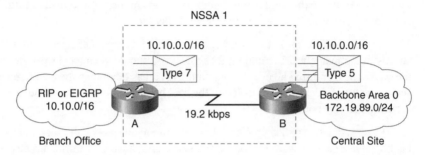

Prior to NSSA, the connection between the corporate-site ABR and the remote router used RIP or EIGRP. This meant maintaining two routing protocols. Now, with NSSA, you can extend OSPF to cover the remote connection by defining the area between the corporate router and the remote router as an NSSA, as shown in the graphic. You cannot expand the normal OSPF area to the remote site because the Type 5 external will overwhelm both the slow link and the remote router.

DESIGN RULE   From experience, NSSAs are powerful, but can get sloppy and confusing to work with if you are not careful. Don't arbitrarily use NSSAs unless you know exactly what you are trying to accomplish.

OSPF Backbone Design

A LAN backbone is ideal for OSPF because the diameter is always one hop. Latency introduced by the backbone is minimized for traffic and for routing information. The LAN backbone design is simple and converges quickly. Figure 9-21 shows this type of OSPF topology design. Be sure to avoid a complex mesh design in your LAN backbone.

Figure 9-21 *Use Simple OSPF Backbone Design*

In Figure 9-21, if your OSPF backbone is in one building, many engineers choose a topology like Fast Ethernet for maximum transport. In the not-too-distant future, we will see more OSPF area 0 designs with Gigabit Ethernet.

You can put workgroups in the backbone if it is the only area. Otherwise, use the backbone strictly as a transit area. As Figure 9-22 shows, you should keep local workgroup traffic off the backbone by putting all client workstations in areas other than the backbone. Doing this serves the two-fold purpose of isolating the backbone from intra-area traffic, and physically securing the backbone.

Good design practice will keep the backbone components physically secure if possible. The backbone is a critical shared resource and should not have user traffic directly attached, except in very rare situations. In most cases, it is beneficial to segment user segments as separate, summarized OSPF areas.

Figure 9-22 *Isolate Backbone from Traffic and Trouble*

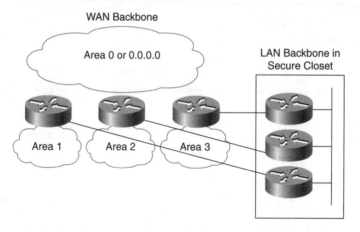

Scalable OSPF Internetworks: Design Golden Rules

To build a scalable OSPF internetwork, there are some general rules to follow:

- Each area should contain fewer than 100 routers.
- Keep the backbone topology simple.
- Keep the backbone diameter small.
- Use TSAs.
- Maximize summarization at ABRs.
- Maximize summarization at ASBRs.

For more details, see the *Internetwork Design Guide*, available on the Cisco Documentation CD-ROM.

OSPF Convergence, Load Balancing, and Resource Utilization

The three components of OSPF convergence are as follows:

- The time it takes to detect a link failure
- The time it takes the routers to exchange routing information and build a new routing table
- A built-in delay of 5 seconds, which, depending on the stability of your network, may be changed with the **timer spf** command

As stated earlier in the chapter in the section, "OSPF Link-State Advertisements," the SPF delay timer is important because it prevents rapid changes from causing unstable routing. The following outlines the time that it takes to detect a link failure, which is the first component in network convergence:

- Instantaneous for FDDI, Token Ring, or CD failures
- Two to three times the keepalive timers for Ethernet or other types of serial failures
- The OSPF dead timer amount if the OSPF hello timer is less than the interface keepalive timer
- Time for OSPF to propagate LSAs and compute the Dijkstra algorithm: Approximately 1 second
- The SPF delay timer: 5 seconds by default

Therefore, OSPF convergence can be anything from 6 to 46 seconds, depending on the type of failure, the timer settings, and the size of the network. The worst-case scenario is when a routing node fails and the destination is still reachable, because the 40-second default dead timer will expire before SPF is recalculated.

OSPF routing on the Cisco router supports up to six equal-cost routes to a destination. It is important to maximize multiple-path routing. If several entries exist in the routing table, switching to remaining paths begins immediately when a link failure is recognized.

The OSPF cost metric is derived from the interface bandwidth. Before IOS Release 10.3, the default cost was calculated by dividing 100,000,000 by the default bandwidth of the interface. With Release 10.3 and later, the cost is calculated by dividing 100,000,000 by the configured bandwidth of the interface. Manually configure the bandwidth or cost to ensure valid routing metrics. To control how OSPF calculates default metrics for the interface, use the **ospf auto-cost reference-bandwidth** router configuration command.

The question of how much bandwidth and CPU that an OSPF network requires is a commonly asked question. OSPF routers exchange Hellos with the DR and BDR as determined by the Hello interval. OSPF routers send LSAs whenever a link changes state. OSPF routers exchange the complete link-state table update every 30 minutes. This equates to CPU and bandwidth utilization. The exact amount will vary, depending on the size of the link-state database and the Hello interval settings.

Furthermore, note that route summarization directly affects the amount of bandwidth, CPU, and memory resources consumed by the OSPF process. Therefore, it is recommended to use maximum route summarization whenever possible.

Additional OSPF References

The following are some good OSPF resources should you need more detailed information about deploying OSPF in your internetwork:

- OSPF internetwork design guidelines, which you can find at www.cisco.com/univercd/cc/td/doc/cisintwk/idg4/nd2003.htm#xtocid1338322

- OSPF Design Guide, which you can find at www.cisco.com/warp/customer/104/1.html#I00

- *OSPF Network Design Solutions*, by Tom Thomas, published by Cisco Press

Summary

Because it is an open standard, OSPF is a very popular in many internetwork designs, especially those that support a multivendor router environment. Regardless of vendor or platform, OSPF has a set of design guidelines that should be followed for maximum uptime and network availability. Some of those areas discussed in this chapter were as follows:

- Maximize summarization.
- Allocate addresses in contiguous blocks.
- Use totally stubby areas.
- Use a simple backbone topology.
- Limit areas to fewer than 100 routers.
- Limit number of areas to fewer than 28.
- Keep local traffic off the backbone.

OSPF can scale to thousands of routers, provided you follow proper summarization and hierarchy guidelines. In summary, as long you play by the rules, OSPF can be just what you need to keep your network running at peak routing efficiency.

Chapter Review Questions

1 What are the four different classifications of routers in OSPF?

2 What is the recommended maximum number of routers in an OSPF area, specifically the backbone area?

3 When using OSPF, is area 0.0.0.0 the same as area 0? Should the backbone always be area 0?

4 Describe the different types of link-state advertisements used by OSPF.

5 What is an external LSA?

6 What is a discontiguous subnet? Does OSPF support discontiguous subnets?

7 What is the name of the algorithm that OSPF uses to calculate a routing table?

8 What is the significance of the spf holdtime?

9 What does OSPF "full state" mean?

10 Should end users be connected directly into area 0?

We did not create this market. We enabled it. Routing was a natural next step. The amazing thing is that more people didn't realize that at the time.

—John P. Morgridge, Chairman of Cisco Systems

Upon completion of this chapter, you will be able to do the following:

- Determine IGRP convergence time for various internetwork configurations

- Describe how to use IGRP for path determination in IP internetworks

- Describe how to use EIGRP for path determination in internetworks that support IP, IPX, and AppleTalk

CHAPTER 10

IGRP/EIGRP Design

Interior Gateway Routing Protocol (IGRP) and Enhanced IGRP (EIGRP) are proprietary protocols that have been developed by Cisco Systems for routing internetwork traffic. Today, many large customer locations still use IGRP extensively. However, more and more, organizations are shifting toward EIGRP, if they have not done so already. You may wonder why this is the case. Because IGRP network convergence time is much greater than with EIGRP and EIGRP supports multiple protocols whereas IGRP only supports IP, EIGRP has some clear advantages over its classful predecessor. This chapter describes how to use IGRP for path determination in IP internetworks, and Enhanced IGRP for path determination in internetworks that support IP, IPX, and AppleTalk.

Cisco Connection Online (CCO) has a number of good white papers on IGRP and EIGRP that give design tips. As appropriate, these URLs are listed at the end of the chapter. Both IGRP and EIGRP are simple to deploy, but a few simple misconfigurations could potentially cause major network problems. As a design engineer, you need to be concerned with several topics. They include convergence time, summarization issues, and support (or lack thereof) for discontiguous networks, all of which is discussed in this chapter.

IGRP Characteristics

IGRP is a Cisco-proprietary Interior Gateway Protocol (IGP). Although there are a large number of networks running IGRP today, this base is dwindling as internetworks have become much larger and much more complex. As a design engineer, you should think of IGRP as, more or less, a stepping stone away from RIP v1, which was popular in the late 1980s and early 1990s. In that regard, IGRP, too, is still somewhat dated with respect to some of the more commonly deployed protocols such as OSPF and EIGRP. Further, IGRP can be characterized as follows:

- Distance vector routing protocol
- Uses a 24-bit metric to find the best route to destination networks
- Easy to implement and easy to troubleshoot
- Can advertise and select from a number of candidate default networks
- Scales up to handle the path determination for medium-to-large internetworks

- Lack of support for VLSM
- Lack of support for discontiguous subnets

A distance vector protocol, IGRP summarizes at network boundaries. This means that IGRP is a *classful* protocol. Subnets are not advertised across different major networks, but are always advertised within the same major network. This means that IGRP, like RIP, does not support discontiguous subnets. Although IGRP is tolerant of arbitrary mesh topologies, as with most IGPs, highly complex mesh topologies make convergence slower because periodic routing updates propagate inconsistent information for a short time. An inherent limitation to IGRP is its inability to support discontiguous subnets or VLSM. These limitations are some design pitfalls when using IGRP.

As depicted in Figure 10-1, IGRP resource requirements depend on the update interval and the number of routes in the routing table.

Figure 10-1   *IGRP Update Traffic: Bigger Routing Table = More Bandwidth*

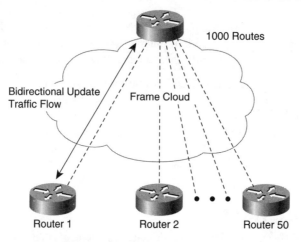

A 1500-byte IGRP routing update packet holds up to 104 routes. The key point to remember is that the entire routing table is sent on each update. The update timer is set by default at 90 seconds. The figure further illustrates that the updates are bidirectional (that is, each IGRP neighbor updates its adjacent neighbor with a full routing table every 90 seconds).

This consideration is useful when considering how best to size the circuits between routers based on routing overhead.

Suppose, for example, that in Figure 10-1, you have a Frame Relay network with 50 remote sites and a network routing table consisting of 1000 routes. IGRP updates flow every 90 seconds by default. Each IGRP packet can contain 104 route entries for a total of 1492 bytes; 38 of this is header information, and each route entry is 14 bytes. If you advertised

1000 routes over a Frame Relay link configured with 50 DLCIs, you would end up with approximately 720 KB of routing update data every 90 seconds, or 64 kbps of bandwidth consumed. On a T1 link, this would represent 4.2% of the bandwidth, with each update duration being 3.7 seconds. At this level, this is an acceptable amount of overhead but, as you start increasing routes, you start increasing the amount of overhead and bandwidth required.

The mathematics of this calculation are as follows:

1000/104 = 9 packets × 38 = 342 header bytes
1000 × 14 = 14,000 B of route entries
Total 14,342 B × 50 DLCIs = 717 KB of IGRP updates every 90 seconds
717,000 B / 90 × 8 bits = 63.7 kbps

IGRP Routing

Split horizon is a routing technique in which information about routes is prevented from exiting the router interface through which that information was received. Split-horizon updates are useful in preventing routing loops. Split horizon is on by default for IGRP, except for Frame Relay and Switched Multimegabit Data Service (SMDS). With Frame Relay and SMDS, each virtual circuit needs routing updates in nonbroadcast multiaccess (NBMA) WAN environments. So, to achieve proper routing table exchanges in those environments, split horizon is off by default.

As Figure 10-2 shows, split horizon dictates that updates from Ann for Network 1 will not ever be sent out Ann's Ethernet0 interface that connects to Joe's Ehternet0 interface.

Figure 10-2 *IGRP Prevents Loops with Split Horizon*

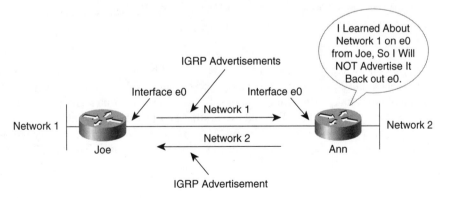

NOTE	Although split horizon should prevent routing loops between adjacent routers, poison-reverse updates are necessary to defeat larger routing loops. For example, increases in routing metrics generally indicate routing loops. Poison-reverse updates then are sent to remove the route and place it in holddown. In Cisco's implementation of IGRP, poison-reverse updates are sent if a route metric has increased by a factor of 1.1 or greater.

IGRP Load Balancing

IGRP supports load balancing over unequal paths. The proportion of the network traffic load that is balanced is defined by *variance*. Setting a variance value lets the router determine the feasibility of a potential route. A route is feasible if the next router in the path is closer to the destination than the current router and if the metric for the entire path is within the variance. Only paths that are feasible can be used for load balancing and included in the routing table. Variance is set at one by default, which means there is load balancing over equal-cost paths. If variance is set at two, the IGRP metric can vary by a factor of two, and load balancing still takes place.

IGRP does load balancing over variant paths in proportion to the bandwidth of the link. Figure 10-3 shows a typical configuration setup that warrants the use of variance.

Figure 10-3   *IGRP Variance*

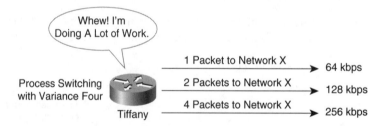

In process-switched mode (that is, per-packet load balancing), router Tiffany sends four packets to the 256-kbps link and two packets to the 128-kbps link for every packet sent to a 64-kbps link. In fast- or autonomous-switched mode, router Tiffany caches four destinations to a 256-kbps link and two destinations to a 128-kbps link for every destination cached to a 64-kbps link. In this scenario, you have three unequal circuit speeds to a destination, and variance is manipulated to load balance traffic over these links.

TIP	If you are using fast or autonomous switching, do not set variance greater than one, because a high-traffic destination might get cached with the slower path, causing what is known as "pinhole congestion." In this scenario, your end user will likely experience many retransmissions and unacceptable network performance. If you must use process switching, a variance of two is generally considered acceptable.

Variance is set by the **variance** *multiplier* command, used under the **router igrp** *autonomous-system* in your configuration. The *multiplier* is the metric value used for load balancing. It can be a value from 1 to 128. The default is 1, which means equal-cost load balancing.

As in Figure 10-3, the following example sets a variance value of 4:

```
!
router igrp 99
variance 4
!
```

DESIGN RULE	Today, because most routers are configured for fast switching or better, the use of variance is not generally recommended anymore. In the event that you are process switching a large percentage of traffic, however, the use of variance may still make sense.

IGRP Routing Metrics

By default, IGRP uses a combination of bandwidth and delay to create its routing metric. In total, IGRP actually tracks six different types of data elements, which can be used in any combination to customize the routing metric. The metrics that IGRP uses are as follows:

- **Bandwidth (static)**—Smallest bandwidth link from here to destination.
- **Delay (static)**—Interface delay is additive along the whole path. Interface delay on each link is inversely proportional to the bandwidth. Delay is the sum of the delays of all *outgoing* interfaces between source and destination.
- **Reliability (dynamic)**—Worst reliability from here to destination based on keepalives.
- **Loading (dynamic)**—Heaviest load from here to destination based on bits per second.
- **MTU (static)**—Smallest MTU from here to destination. MTU is used to avoid sending a frame that is too large when the IP "don't-fragment bit" is set, but cannot be used in the metric computation.

- **Hops (static)**—Total hop count from here to destination. Hop count is used to prevent count to infinity, but cannot be used in the metric computation.

Figure 10-4 illustrates the how the IGRP metrics work. In this example, the sum of all delays is the total delay (D1 + D2 + D3) used in the IGRP delay component of metric calculation from Point A to Point B. The smallest bandwidth between Point C and Point D is used as the bandwidth variable (64 kbps).

You can see that bandwidth dominates in the metric calculation of short paths, whereas delay tends to dominate in the calculation of longer paths. Knowing this, you can set the metrics to your design requirement when you are designing policy decisions.

Figure 10-4   *How the IGRP Metrics Work*

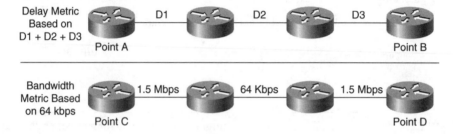

IGRP Metric Calculation

As stated earlier, in the simplest (and default) IGRP metric calculation, the two metrics used for path determination are bandwidth and delay. There actually is a complex formula that IGRP uses for metric calculation that is listed in the note that follows this section. By default, several coefficients are set to zero, and IGRP will use the smallest bandwidth and the sum of all delays from all the outgoing interfaces between a source and destination to calculate the metric. In the example, 64 kbps is the bandwidth used in the metric calculation; the sum total of D1, D2, and D3 constitute the delay metric component.

IGRP calculates the metric by adding together weighted values of different characteristics of the link to the network in question. These values (bandwidth, bandwidth divided by load, and delay) are weighted with the constants K1, K2, and K3. The formula is as follows:

Metric = K1 × BandW + (K2 × BandW)/(256 − load) + K3 × Delay

The default constant values are K1 = K3 = 1 and K2 = K4 = K5 = 0, so:

Metric = BandW + Delay

If K5 does not equal 0, an additional operation is done:

Metric = Metric × (K5/[reliability + K4])

To find BandW, find the smallest of all the bandwidths from outgoing interfaces and divide 10,000,000 by that number. (The bandwidth is scaled by 10,000,000 in kps.)

To find Delay, add all the delays from the outgoing interfaces and divide this number by 10. (The delay is in 10s of spout→microseconds.)

Remember, the path with the smallest metric is the best path.

IGRP Convergence

IGRP convergence depends on the following sequence of events.

Step 1 **A link failure is detected**—This is usually instant for FDDI, Token Ring, or carrier loss. For other topologies, two to three times the interface keepalive timer will trigger a link failure.

Step 2 **The router sends a triggered update, indicating the unreachable network(s)**— The triggered update is sent immediately to adjacent routers. All adjacent routers generate triggered updates in turn. Routers continue to send routing tables at the normal update interval.

Step 3 **Periodic updates transmit the entire routing table**—As shown in Figure 10-5, triggered (flash) updates reduce traffic by transmitting only changes. Triggered updates reduce the time that a router would otherwise have to wait to send the changes to their neighbor. If triggered updates did not exist, for example, the IGRP router four hops away might need to wait 360 seconds for the route-change information. With triggered updates, this time is reduced to only a few seconds. Remember that triggered updates are link-state changes only and full convergence still depends on the network diameter.

Figure 10-5 *IGRP Triggered Updates Speed Convergence*

TIP IGRP routing updates are easy to interpret with a protocol analyzer, especially if you are seeing triggered updates. Capturing these small updates could help you to isolate a flapping network.

IGRP Timers

IGRP maintains a number of timers and variables containing time intervals. These include an update timer, an invalid timer, a hold-time period, and a flush timer. You can tune these IGRP timers if faster convergence is required. Fast LANs may require only a 10-second update, for example, whereas slower LANs may need a 90-second update. To adjust IGRP network timers, use the **timers basic** router configuration command. The syntax of the **timers basic** command is as follows:

```
timers basic update invalid holddown flush
```

IGRP timers are described as follows, with the default value indicated in parentheses:

- **Update interval**—Time between routing updates (90 seconds)
- **Invalid timer**—Three times update interval (270 seconds)
- **Holddown timer**—Three times update interval plus 10 (280 seconds)
- **Flush timer**—Seven times the update interval (630 seconds)

Update Interval

The IGRP update timer specifies how frequently routing update messages should be sent. The IGRP default for this variable is 90 seconds.

Example 10-1 sets updates to be broadcast every 5 seconds.

Example 10-1   *Setting the Update Interval*

```
!
router igrp 109
  timers basic 5  15  15  30
!
```

Note that by setting a short update period, you run the risk of congesting slow-speed serial lines; however, this is not a big concern on faster-speed Ethernets and T1-rate serial lines. Also, if you have many routes in your updates, you can cause the routers to spend an excessive amount of time processing updates.

Invalid Timer

The invalid timer specifies how long a router should wait, in the absence of routing-update messages about a specific route before declaring that route invalid. The IGRP default for this variable is three times the update period. In Example 10-1, if a router is not heard from in 15 seconds (the invalid timer), the route is declared unusable.

Holddown Timer

The hold-time variable specifies the holddown period. The IGRP default for this variable is three times the update timer period plus 10 seconds. By default, the holddown timer is 280 seconds. This holddown timer value equals three times the default update interval (90 seconds) plus 10 seconds. The holddown timer allows routing information to propagate several hops by triggered updates. The holddown timer is set conservatively to allow for gateways that might send out a regularly scheduled routing update at the same time that a triggered update is propagating (that is, this timer is set conservatively for "worst-case scenarios").

A route that is in holddown is flagged and advertised with an unreachable metric is also called a *poisoned route*. A route is poisoned when the local interface goes down, or when an unreachable network is advertised by a peer. A poisoned route can only be replaced in the routing table after holddown expires or when a route with a lower administrative distance arrives.

Sometimes it is advisable to turn off holddowns with the **no metric holddown** command. IGRP will then converge much more quickly.

By turning off holddowns, you trade bandwidth for fast convergence. The extra traffic caused by temporary routing loops is of less concern with high-bandwidth links. Routing loops can, however, cause significant temporary congestion over slow 64-kbps links, for example. If you are doing dynamic IGRP routing over slow WAN links, it is generally recommended to reduce holddowns rather than eliminate them altogether.

When holddowns are disabled, IGRP routers use a strict rule about route poisoning to prevent count-to-infinity loops. If the hop count to a destination network increases, the route is poisoned. Eliminating or even reducing holddown timers should be used with extreme care. If a change is necessary, the holddown timer needs to be changed network-wide to prevent any major convergence issues.

Note, that when a route is in holddown, the route is marked inaccessible and advertised as unreachable. However, the route is still used for forwarding packets.

Flush Timer

The flush timer indicates how much time should pass before a route should be flushed from the routing table. The IGRP default is seven times the routing update period. Once the flush time is reached, the route is purged from the routing table.

Remember that if you change these timer settings, you need to document the changes carefully and maintain strict control of configuration changes. Otherwise, you will likely run into convergence problems in your network. Generally speaking, you should not have to adjust update timers unless absolutely necessary.

EIGRP Routing

We now switch gears to EIGRP. EIGRP is quite different from IGRP. EIGRP has several very favorable characteristics for building scalable internetworks, including the following:

- Sophisticated 32-bit metric based on the IGRP metric
- Easy to install
- Supports VLSM
- Supports discontiguous subnets
- Scales without tuning to support large internetworks
- Uses a reliable transport protocol
- Converges within 1 second of detecting a link failure
- Supports multiple protocols
- Combines the best of link-state and distance vector protocols

EIGRP has protocol-dependent modules (PDMs) that support routing for IP, IPX, and AppleTalk. The IPX module also supports the Novell Service Advertisement Protocol (SAP). Each client protocol has its own separate hellos, timers, and metrics. Figure 10-6 shows this separation of EIGRP by protocol function in block format.

Figure 10-6   *EIGRP Maintains Separate Tables*

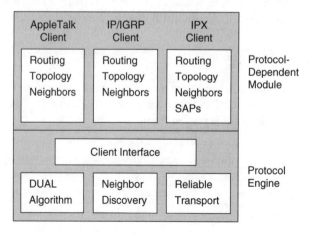

As Figure 10-6 shows, DUAL, RTP, and neighbor discovery are at the heart of EIGRP; the PDMs are snap-in modules for each protocol. This modular design of EIGRP makes it a very attractive architecture for future protocols to "plug in" to the EIGRP model, if necessary.

The following list documents the roles that DUAL, RTP, and neighbor discovery play in EIGRP:

- The DUAL finite state machine embodies the decision process for all route computations. It tracks all routes advertised by all neighbors.

- RTP is responsible for guaranteed, ordered delivery of EIGRP packets to all neighbors. It supports intermixed transmission of multicast or unicast packets.

- Neighbor discovery is the process that routers use to dynamically learn of other routers on their directly attached networks.

The common protocol engine includes the diffusion update algorithm (DUAL), neighbor discovery, and the reliable transport protocol for routing updates. EIGRP is considered to be a "Ships-In-The-Night" (SIN) routing protocol because Datagram Discovery Protocol (DDP), IPX, and IP each maintain separate routing tables and use separate hellos to discover neighbors. EIGRP automatically redistributes routing and SAP tables to the appropriate client protocol.

Fortunately, Cisco was thinking interoperability with IGRP and common desktop protocols when they invented EIGRP. By default, EIGRP advertises full RIP, SAP, and RTMP updates on LAN interfaces and reliable updates only on WAN interfaces. Figure 10-7 illustrates the different options for IPX and AppleTalk routing, including where and when updates are sent out based on LAN or WAN location. Full updates are sent by default on LANs, whereas incremental and reliable updates are sent by default on WANs.

Figure 10-7   *EIGRP for IPX, RIP/SAP, and RTMP*

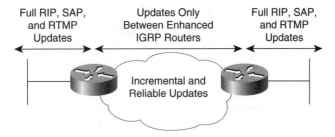

EIGRP Route Summarization

By default, EIGRP summarizes automatically on network boundaries. Alternatively, you can manually configure summarization of address blocks with prefix routing (also referred to as classless routing). VLSM is supported because subnet mask information is transmitted with routing information.

One good place to configure manual summarization of contiguous blocks is at the distribution or core layers. For an example of this feature, consider Figure 10-8.

Figure 10-8 *Configure Prefix Route Summarization at Distribution or Core Tier*

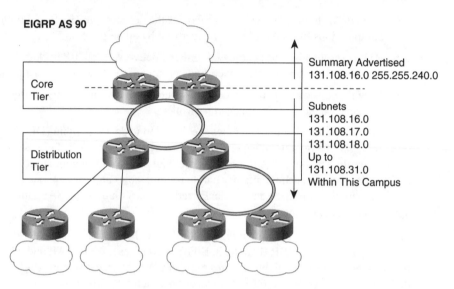

Figure 10-8 illustrates a case where address blocks are allocated at the campus level (connecting the core and FDDI rings). Here, an EIGRP manual summary is configured, which is summarizing networks 131.108.16.0 to 131.108.31.0 with a 20-bit mask. This is done by configuring **ip summary-address eigrp 90 131.18.16.0 255.255.240.0** on the core interfaces. It is important to note that EIGRP always summarizes at a "class boundary" by default, but can also summarize at any bit boundary.

NOTE	You need to remember to apply the **no auto-summary** command to configure a manual EIGRP summary address. Also, manual summaries are done on an interface level rather than a global (router) basis.

EIGRP Support for Mobile Hosts

EIGRP supports the mobile host feature. With this feature, an exception route is propagated for a host that moves away from its subnet. The host route is more specific than the subnet route, so traffic still gets to the host. Local mobility works as long as the host moves within the same major network number. Exception routing is more scalable than bridging and less scalable than conventional classful routing.

Local mobility is included with Cisco IOS Release 10.2 and later, and is shown in Figure 10-9.

Figure 10-9   *EIGRP Supports Mobile Hosts*

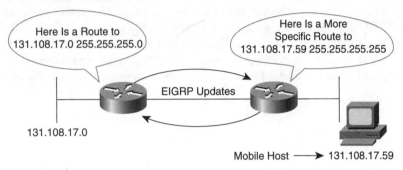

EIGRP Support for Discontiguous Subnets

Another key by-product of EIGRP manual summarization is that it allows subnet information to be advertised across a different major network and therefore makes discontiguous subnets possible. This is an extremely powerful and flexible advantage over traditional distance vector protocols such as RIP or IGRP. Figure 10-10 shows an example of manual summarization. Here, the subnets 131.108.32.0 and 131.08.75.0 can be successfully propagated over the 144.254.100.0 network. In a RIP or IGRP environment, this type of configuration is not supported, and if attempted, it can be a recipe for disaster.

Figure 10-10   *EIGRP Supports Discontiguous Subnets*

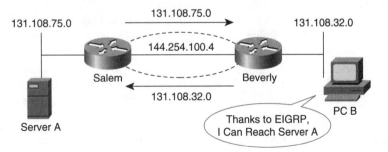

EIGRP Supports VLSM

By default, EIGRP routers summarize automatically on network boundaries. A key reason why EIGRP can be configured to do arbitrary, manual, bit-level summarization is its capability to support VLSM. Figure 10-11 shows a typical example of VLSM with manual summarization. Router Grant summarizes 131.108.75.0, 131.108.75.4, 131.108.75.8, and 131.108.75.12 (all with a 255.255.255.252 mask) as 131.108.75.0 255.255.255.0. Router Sue just receives the summary address rather than all the specific routes (that is, all the 255.255.255.252 routes) in that range. In short, VLSM allows the 131.108.0.0 major network to be bit-wise subnetted into several smaller for very efficient use of IP address space. In light of the IP address depletion and the sheer size of large corporate internetworks, VLSM is a required feature in most networks today so that address space is most efficiently used.

Figure 10-11   *EIGRP Supports VLSM*

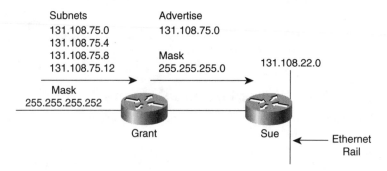

Enhanced IGRP Convergence

The DUAL algorithm makes EIGRP converge quickly. As shown in Figure 10-12, the whole process takes less than 1 second for most failures. The worse-case scenario for a disconnected node is 16 seconds, assuming a 5-second hello interval plus 1 second to run DUAL (that is, $3 \times$ hello interval + time for DUAL to run = $5 \times 3 + 1 = 16$ seconds).

Here is what happens:

Step 1   A local interface is flagged as down (instantaneous for Carrier Detect failure or beaconing Token Rings; three times the 5-second hello timer for other links).

Step 2   The router looks at local and neighbor routing tables for an alternate route.

Step 3   The router switches to alternate route immediately if found locally.

Step 4   The router sends query to neighbors except the one that it learned from if no alternate route is found locally.

Step 5   The query propagates until a new route is found.

Step 6   Affected routers update their routing tables.

Step 7   Enhanced IGRP convergence is fast and quiet because changed routing
information propagates immediately to affected nodes.

Figure 10-12   *Enhanced IGRP Converges Quickly*

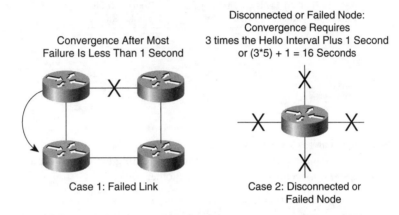

Convergence After Most
Failure Is Less Than 1 Second

Disconnected or Failed Node:
Convergence Requires
3 times the Hello Interval Plus 1 Second
or (3*5) + 1 = 16 Seconds

Case 1: Failed Link

Case 2: Disconnected or
Failed Node

If all queries for a given active route are not replied to within about 3 minutes
(configurable), the router will declare that route Stuck In Active (SIA). When an SIA
occurs, all adjacencies to unresponsive neighbor(s) are reset, forcing new adjacencies to be
formed and increasing network convergence time. Occasional SIAs are not really a bad
thing; if you get them on a regular basis, however, that is certainly cause for concern.

Some possible causes of SIAs are old (pre 11.1) IOS code, low memory, low-end platforms
such as 2500s carrying large neighbor counts and routing table sizes, circuits with 0K CIRs,
and unstable network links.

DUAL

The heart of Enhanced IGRP is DUAL, whose characteristics are the following:

- Convergence within 1 second of detecting link failure.
- Route filtering at any node.
- Hello protocol prevents black holes.
- Sequenced and acknowledged updates guarantee convergence.
- Routing information propagates to affected nodes only.

In addition to the local routing table, EIGRP keeps the active routing table of each adjacent
router, which gives the EIGRP router a fast way to predict how routing will change when a

network link changes state. Figure 10-13 depicts normal EIGRP table behavior. Here, router X has not only his own routing table, but also contains a mirror copy of router Y and Z's routing table. This allows a process, known as *local computation*, to quickly occur without impacting any network bandwidth.

Figure 10-13   *Database Used for Local Computations*

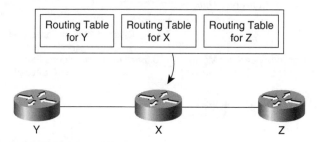

When a link changes state, the router can immediately change the active routing table based on information in the local copy of a neighbor's routing table. This capability is called a *local computation* because it does not affect other routers.

When the neighbor routing tables do not have a feasible successor route, a *diffused computation* takes place. A route is flagged active, and the router sends a query. The query propagates until a new route is found.

In Figure 10-14, active routes to network N are marked with arrows. The active routes shown assume that the route from router C to router D to router A has a lower metric than the route from router C to router B to router A.

Figure 10-14   *Enhanced IGRP: Convergence Example*

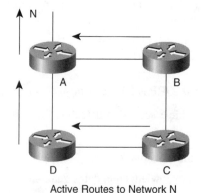

Active Routes to Network N

In Figure 10-15, you can see how EIGRP deals with a link failure, and how it quickly uses first a local computation to find a feasible successor. If that is not successful, the same router does a diffusing calculation to find a feasible successor for a given network, network N. Assuming that the link failure is detected within 1 second by the CD lead dropping, the following occurs:

Step 1 Link L fails.

Step 2 Router D fails to find an alternate route to network N in its copy of router C's routing table.

Step 3 Router D sends a query to router C.

Step 4 Router C looks in its local copy of router B's routing table.

Step 5 Router C finds a route to network N and immediately changes its local routing table.

Step 6 Router C sends a reply to router D, indicating the new route to network N.

Step 7 Router D immediately updates its local routing table.

Step 8 Routers D and C send updates to their neighbors to indicate the change.

Step 9 Total convergence time in this typical case is about 1 second.

Figure 10-15 *Enhanced IGRP: Convergence Example, Continued*

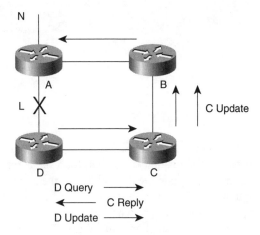

EIGRP Load Balancing

EIGRP supports load balancing on up to six variant paths. Follow the same design rules for variance as discussed in the IGRP section.

Hierarchical Networks and EIGRP

As with most IGPs, the use of complex or highly redundant mesh designs should be moderated with concerns for convergence time. As shown in Figure 10-16, use hierarchical topologies in place of mesh designs. (As was previously mentioned, this also applies for IGRP.)

Figure 10-16 *Hierarchical Networks Perform Best*

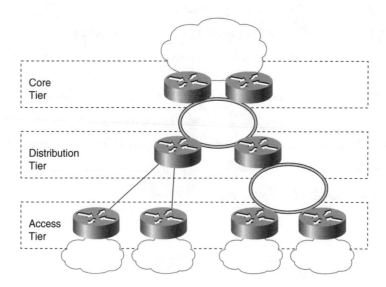

EIGRP Design

You should always design redundancy where failures occur or you expect them or for critical sites. EIGRP summarization is essential for a stable internetwork design. This can be achieved through careful planning and abiding to the core/distribution/access hierarchical design model. This is because EIGRP queries need to go to all neighbors, except for those through the interface where the original route was learned. You can therefore deduce that the more neighbors and alternative routes you have, the longer it will take for all queries to be returned to the source router when link instability occurs.

Techniques, including route filtering and active timer adjustments, to minimize query ranges are important considerations to take into account when designing EIGRP networks. Those topics, however, although very important, are beyond the scope of this book and the CID course. You can find more information about these in Jeff Doyle's excellent book titled *Routing TCP/IP* (Cisco Press). Also, *Advanced IP Network Design*, by Don Slice, Alvaro Retana, and Russ White is another outstanding reference.

Additional References for IGRP/EIGRP Information

Some good IGRP/EIGRP links include the following:

- **Introduction to Enhanced IGRP (EIGRP)**—www.cisco.com/warp/customer/103/1.html

- **Configuration Notes for the Enhanced Implementation of EIGRP**—www.cisco.com/warp/customer/103/12.html

- **Basic Terminology for EIGRP**—www.cisco.com/warp/customer/103/11.html

- **EIGRP Deployment Guides**—www.cisco.com/warp/customer/103/9.html

- **EIGRP Design Guide on CCO**—www.cisco.com/univercd/cc/td/doc/cisintwk/idg4/nd2003.htm#xtocid1338311

- **An Introduction to IGRP on CCO**—www.cisco.com/warp/public/103/5.html

- **IGRP Metric**—www.cisco.com/warp/customer/103/3.html

- **Interior Gateway Routing Protocol**—www.cisco.com/univercd/cc/td/doc/cisintwk/ito_doc/igrp.htm

Summary

IGRP and EIGRP are proprietary protocols that have been developed by Cisco Systems for routing internetwork traffic. Beyond their similar sounding names, EIGRP and IGRP have little in common. For example, IGRP networks cannot support discontiguous networks or multiple protocols; EIGRP networks can. IGRP is being phased out of most networks, especially large, dynamic internetworks that are a result of mergers or acquisitions and require the use of VLSM.

Although EIGRP is easy to deploy, a few simple misconfigurations can potentially cause major network meltdowns. Design networks with the protocols with care and forethought, and you will see extremely good convergence.

Chapter Review Questions

1   Is IGRP a classless or classful routing protocol?

2   What is the default update timer for IGRP?

3   Discuss IGRP variance as it relates to load sharing.

4   Name and describe the different IGRP metrics.

5   By default, how long is the IGRP invalid timer?

6   Why is EIGRP considered to be a "Ships-In-The-Night" protocol?

7 What are the methods that EIGRP uses for broadcasting RTMP and IPX RIP/SAP updates across the LAN and WAN?

8 What makes EIGRP converge so quickly? How long does convergence generally take for most failures?

9 What is meant by an EIGRP local computation?

10 What is meant by an EIGRP diffused computation?

PART IV

Desktop Protocol Design

Q: How many Macintosh Division employees do you need to change a light bulb?

A: One. He holds the light bulb up and lets the universe revolve around him.

—From *The Macintosh Way* by Guy Kawasaki, trumpeting the Apple-centric approach to desktop computing in the 1980s.

Upon completion of this chapter, you will be able to do the following:

- Explain the requirements of the client/server model as implemented by different desktop protocols

- Explain how clients send out broadcasts to locate servers for Novell IPX, AppleTalk, and Microsoft Windows networks

- Describe the elements involved in desktop protocol design

CHAPTER 11

Desktop Design Overview

Desktop protocols are based on a client/server model. These protocols are primarily designed to enable clients and servers to communicate across a LAN. Generally, it is assumed that the LAN consists of a single shared or switched medium, such as Ethernet or Fast Ethernet, and it provides connections for multiple hosts. A shared medium, whether or not it is switched, should be designed as a single broadcast domain. The reason is that the desktop protocols discussed in this section rely heavily on broadcasts to advertise and locate services on the network.

The desktop protocols are defined at OSI Layers 3, 4, and higher. Like TCP/IP, they should be considered not as single protocols but as protocol suites comprised of multiple individual protocols at various OSI layers that work together to provide seamless connectivity between clients and servers. The individual protocols that make up the protocol suites are described in more detail in the following chapters: IPX in Chapter 12, AppleTalk in Chapter 13, and Windows Networking in Chapter 14.

Desktop Protocols Use Broadcasts

The desktop protocols are designed to provide host access to a shared medium in a LAN environment. In the hierarchical design model, they are primarily at the access tier. However, as you will see, they can also traverse the WAN. Because servers and clients find each other via a packet broadcast method, it is understood that these protocols optimally should be deployed on a shared medium in a single broadcast domain.

AppleTalk and IPX are routable protocols and, hence, could be routed across a campus backbone or a point-to-point WAN link. In practice, however, many internetwork designers avoid this because of the large WAN bandwidth overhead of broadcasts that these protocols require. NetBIOS and NetBEUI (Microsoft Windows protocols) are by definition nonroutable protocols because they have no network component and, therefore, are reserved for use on the local network. They could be bridged across backbone or WAN links, but this practice is definitely not recommended because all broadcasts will be sent across the link, unless carefully designed filters are deployed on the WAN interfaces. Also, the overhead for Spanning Tree BPDUs contribute to wasted bandwidth.

Broadcast packets (as distinct from unicast or multicast) are Layer 2 frames that use a hardware destination address with a special meaning: typically, all 1s in binary

(FFFFFF:FFFFFF in hex). The broadcast destination address ensures that the broadcast packet is seen and processed by every host on the local network.

In a client/server architecture, clients must have a way of locating servers, as well as specific resources located on those servers (disk volumes, printers, application gateways, and so on). Broadcast service advertisements are one way of accomplishing this. IPX-based Novell servers, for instance, send a broadcast packet onto the local network every 60 seconds by default (configurable) to alert clients of their location and services available. Clients passively listen and are updated as to services and routes available on the local network on this regular schedule.

Figure 11-1 shows that the use of broadcasts for such routing tasks results in high traffic volume traveling at regular intervals across the network. In a relatively high-speed LAN environment, the impact may be negligible. However, the impact of periodic broadcasts is likely to degrade performance considerably across lower-speed WAN links (for example, 28.8-kbps or 56-kbps dialup or leased lines, or across ISDN links). Moreover, dial-on-demand links that would otherwise drop during periods of inactivity may be kept up by continuous and, hence, expensive broadcasts. Broadcasts are design considerations that you must take into consideration, especially as the desktop protocols extend across the WAN.

Figure 11-1 *Broadcasts, Broadcasts Everywhere!*

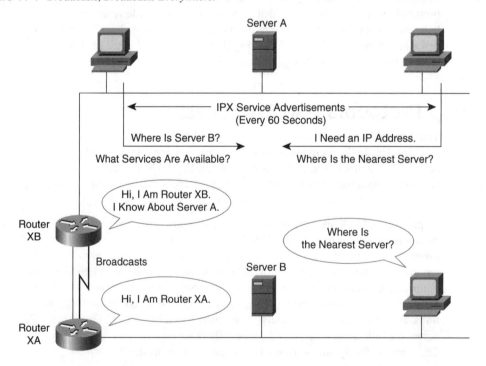

WAN Concerns with the Broadcast Model

Modern routers, gateways, and switches often provide ways to filter unwanted broadcasts away from particular links where they are not desired. When mixing broadcast protocols in an internetwork that is dependent on slow or expensive WAN links, one critical internetwork design principle is to make certain that the equipment has this filtering capability. The bottom line is that you want to try to keep broadcasts off a WAN segment whenever possible.

Novell IPX Considerations

The Routing Information Protocol (RIP) and the Service Advertisement Protocol (SAP) generate most of the broadcast traffic in the Novell IPX environment. There may also be some broadcast traffic associated with NetBIOS emulation (if configured) as well as NetWare server serialization packets.

Design strategies for containment include protocol filters, which are most effective in a hierarchical design, and more advanced routing protocols, such as EIGRP and NLSP.

NOTE   Desktop protocols rely heavily on broadcasts in their normal operation. Broadcasts can impose large-scale network problems, especially across a WAN.

AppleTalk Considerations

In AppleTalk networks, the following three protocols generate most of the broadcast traffic:

- **Routing Table Maintenance Protocol (RTMP)**—The AppleTalk routing protocol based on the distance vector method. RTMP periodically broadcasts the entire routing table (following split-horizon rules) every 10 seconds by default.

- **Zone Information Protocol (ZIP)**—Involved in client/server communication—specifically, zone information. ZIP is a session layer protocol in the AppleTalk protocol suite that maintains network number-to-zone name mappings in AppleTalk routers. ZIP is used primarily by AppleTalk routers.

- **Name Binding Protocol (NBP)**—Involved in client/server communication—specifically, name-to-number translation. NBP is a transport layer protocol in the AppleTalk protocol suite that maps the addresses used at lower layers to AppleTalk names.

As a network designer for AppleTalk, you need to plan out zones based on a number of factors that will be discussed in Chapter 13, "AppleTalk Design." In addition, Cisco routers implement filters that can be used to contain the broadcast traffic. The deployment of these features is much more effective in a hierarchical design. Alternative routing protocols, such

Apple/EIGRP and AppleTalk Update Routing Protocol (AURP), are also available for deployment in the WAN.

Windows Networking Considerations

NetBIOS and NetBEUI can be among the most troublesome of protocols to contend with in a network design. Not only do these protocols make extensive use of broadcasts, they also must be bridged because they cannot be routed. Pertinent Windows Networking design options found in Cisco routers include filters, name caches, and proxy response methods. Also, today, there is an option to encapsulate NetBIOS in IP. Although this appears to be a good solution, the same broadcast issues remain. In the case of IP encapsulation, NetBIOS broadcasts are encapsulated in the User Datagram Protocol (UDP) and can impact your entire WAN, if you are not careful. I have seen several "directed broadcast" storms that have turned out to be NetBIOS hidden in IP packets. The bottom line is that you should take special care whenever you are looking at WAN deployment of any desktop (LAN-based) protocol, especially NetBIOS.

Summary

Traditional LAN-based protocols use a large number of broadcasts to locate their services. In the days before the WAN was prevalent, broadcasts really were not a big concern. Today, however, broadcasts are of primary concern in the WAN environment, and legacy LAN protocols need to be optimized to work in the world of enterprise internetworking. Without special care, these protocols can severely degrade WAN performance. AppleTalk, Novell IPX, and Windows with NetBIOS are all covered in greater detail in the following chapters.

Chapter Review Questions

1   Describe the general model used for the design of most desktop-based network operating systems.

2   What common problem do most desktop systems present to network designers?

3   What is the impact of protocols that use periodic broadcasts in the WAN environment?

4   What protocols generate the majority of the broadcast traffic in the Novell IPX environment?

5   What is ZIP?

6   Does NetBIOS encapsulation into IP solve the broadcast issues with native NetBIOS?

Because this is engineering and not mathematics, infinity turns out to be 15.

—Radia Perlman, in reference to the infamous 15-hop radius of an IPX internetwork

Upon completion of this chapter, you will be able to do the following:

- Examine a client's requirements and construct an appropriate IPX design solution
- Choose the appropriate routing protocol for an IPX internetwork
- Describe how to design scalable and manageable IPX internetworks by controlling RIP and SAP traffic

CHAPTER 12

IPX Design

Designing an IPX network is often incorrectly viewed as a trivial task. However, many IPX networks today are extremely bandwidth-intensive, especially on slow-speed WAN links. With SAP tables of sizes well into the thousands quite common in today's large internetworks, the construction of an appropriate IPX network design solution is extremely important. Several routing protocols for an IPX internetwork are available today. This chapter discusses available IPX routing options and also how to design scalable and manageable IPX internetworks by controlling RIP and SAP traffic.

Novell Network Protocols

Novell servers support several protocol stacks. They can appear as AppleShare servers, Network File System (NFS) servers, and IBM Systems Network Architecture (SNA) gateways.

However, the majority of Novell traffic occurs in the "native IPX stack" between client PCs and servers. As in TCP/IP, each layer in the IPX stack performs a different and complementary function. The application layer is the NetWare Core Protocol (NCP), which provides session and sequence control.

Novell's Routing Information Protocol (RIP) and Service Advertising Protocol (SAP) are native protocols active on all IPX interfaces of routers and servers.

Figure 12-1 shows the different possible stacks that can be supported in a Novell NetWare file server. A wide range of supported interfaces, topologies, and protocols make the NetWare server flexible and adaptable in most LAN environments.

Figure 12-1 *Novell Servers Support Several Client Stacks*

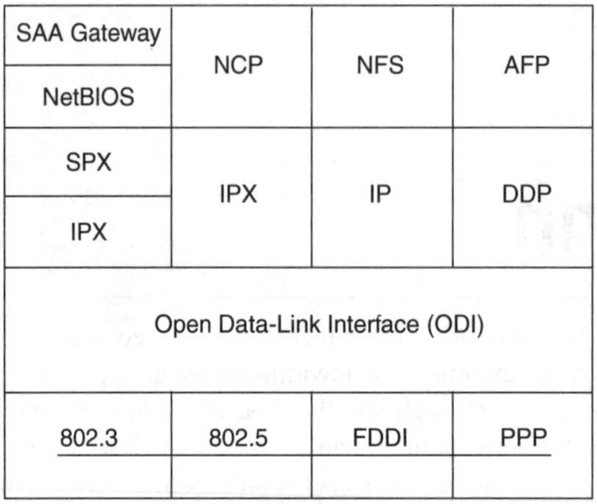

SAA Gateway	NCP	NFS	AFP
NetBIOS			
SPX	IPX	IP	DDP
IPX			
Open Data-Link Interface (ODI)			
802.3	802.5	FDDI	PPP

Novell Encapsulations

The original default IPX encapsulation for Ethernet is called Raw Ethernet. Raw Ethernet is also known as ETHERNET_802.3 in IPX configuration and **novell-ether** in Cisco configuration. Raw Ethernet is a nonstandard encapsulation that resembles IEEE 802.3, with FFFF in place of a normal 802.3 destination service access point (DSAP) and source service access point (SSAP), and with no Logical Link Control (LLC) layer.

As of NetWare 4.x, the new default is known as ETHERNET_802.2 in IPX configuration and *iso1* or *sap* in Cisco configuration. This default is standard IEEE 802.2 with the value E0E0 for DSAP/SSAP.

When bridging IPX, all possible encapsulations must be supported. When routing IPX, each network uses one type of encapsulation.

Novell Encapsulations for Ethernet

Table 12-1 shows all the Novell encapsulations for Ethernet that are supported by Cisco.

Table 12-1 *Novell Encapsulations for Ethernet*

Novell Term	Cisco Term	Encapsulation
ETHERNET_802.3	novell-ether	802.3 with FFFF
ETHERNET_SNAP	snap	802.2 SNAP with 8137
ETHERNET_802.2	sap or iso1	802.2 with E0E0 sap
ETHERNET_II	arpa	arpa with 8137 type

They key is to remember that the IPX encapsulation on the router needs to match the IPX encapsulation being used on the network. Otherwise, you will not achieve IPX connectivity. You will see many of "format errors" under the **show ipx traffic** IOS command output when this condition is present.

NOTE	Although synchronizing the IPX encapsulation on the router with the IPX encapsulation on the network is helpful, this is not 100% foolproof. Keep in mind that format errors will also occur when the length of the received packet is smaller than 30 bytes or larger than the interface MTU.

Novell Encapsulations for Token Ring and FDDI

Table 12-2 shows standard encapsulations for routing IPX over Token Ring and FDDI.

Table 12-2   *FDDI and Token Ring Encapsulations*

Novell Term	Cisco Term	Encapsulation
FDDI_SNAP	snap	802.2 SNAP with 8137
FDDI_802.2	sap or iso1	802.2 with E0E0 saps
TOKEN-RING	novell-tr	802.2 with E0E0 saps
TOKEN-RING_SNAP	snap	802.2 SNAP with 8137

Raw Token Ring and Raw FDDI are supported when bridging IPX, and a default encapsulation is assumed for any Media Access Control (MAC) address not in the switching cache.

As with Ethernet encapsulations, you need to remember to set the Token Ring or FDDI encapsulations to match the encapsulation of the IPX network to which it is attached. Otherwise, you will not achieve IPX connectivity.

Support for Multiple IPX Encapsulations on the Same Interface

At some point, you may be faced with the issue of how to support multiple IPX encapsulations on the same interface. Subinterfaces can be configured on the router to support several IPX networks on the same LAN. Hosts on different networks do not communicate directly and can use different encapsulations.

In Figure 12-2, IPX network 100 uses SNAP, and Network 200 uses Raw Ethernet. Network 100 is configured on subinterface E0.1, and Network 200 is configured on subinterface E0.2. All traffic between networks 100 and 200 is relayed by the router because the router automatically converts the encapsulation. You should also make sure to enable fast switching of IPX on the relay interface with the **ipx route-cache same-interface** command.

Figure 12-2 *IPX Subinterfaces Connect Networks*

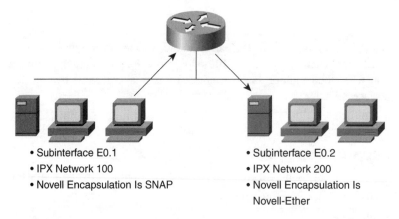

- Subinterface E0.1
- IPX Network 100
- Novell Encapsulation Is SNAP

- Subinterface E0.2
- IPX Network 200
- Novell Encapsulation Is
  Novell-Ether

TIP   As a rule of thumb, you should configure all the Novell devices on the LAN as part of the same network using the same encapsulation for efficiency. Using the router as a relay introduces extra delay and traffic. You should only use subinterfaces as a workaround or an interim solution.

Novell Routing

IPX/RIP is similar in functionality to IP/RIP. Whereas IP/RIP uses hop count as its metric, the IPX routing metric is delay as measured in ticks. A tick is defined as 1/18 second. IPX/RIP has a 60-second update interval and flushes routes in 180 seconds.

Just like IP/RIP, IPX/RIP uses split horizon to prevent counting to infinity. Split horizon cannot be disabled, so connectivity is limited to directly connected peers in nonbroadcast multiaccess (NBMA) packet-switched WAN configurations. This is discussed in Chapter 17, "Frame Relay Design."

NOTE   In 12.0 code, IPX Enhanced IGRP (EIGRP) split horizon is off for WAN interfaces and on for LAN interfaces. The global default stays off. The interface setting takes precedence when the interface setting is modified or when both the global and interface settings are unmodified. The global setting is used only when the global setting is modified and the interface setting is unmodified.

Also, in 12.0 code, IPX EIGRP incremental SAP now has split horizon, which instructs the routers not to advertise the SAP to the same interface from where that SAP is received. It also enables you to display the EIGRP neighbor server table using regular expressions.

As Figure 12-3 shows, a router receives an update that network ABC has failed. The receiving router then sends a RIP broadcast with the network flagged unreachable. The router waits for 10 ticks and checks the routing table for an alternative route. This period of 10 ticks is called *holddown*. Routers use what is called the *lost route algorithm* to find an alternative route if required. The lost route algorithm prevents routing loops.

Figure 12-3   *Novell Routing Updates and Split Horizon*

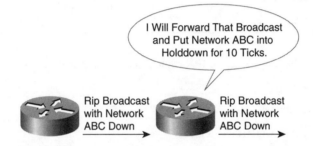

IPX/RIP tracks delay as measured in ticks and hop count. LAN hops are counted as 1 tick, and WAN links are counted as 6 ticks by default. The hop count is used to break ties when ticks are equal. As shown in Figure 12-4, the Ethernet, FDDI, and Token Ring segments are LAN media, so the metric is one tick per LAN. For any wide-area link of any speed, the metric is treated as 6 ticks.

Figure 12-4   *Default Routing Metrics for LAN and WAN*

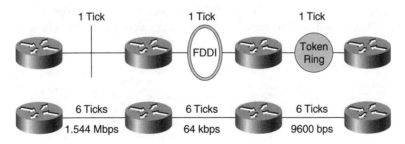

The assigned IPX interface delay is used to break ties when the number of ticks and hops are equal and the number of routes in the routing table has reached the value determined by the **ipx maximum-paths** command.

Example 12-1 shows how the IOS is configured to use up to three parallel paths. Notice, however, we have two Ethernets and one FDDI. If, for example, we received three equal-cost paths from each interface, in fact we would only use the FDDI link, because it has the lowest intrinsic delay (100 microseconds, whereas Ethernet is 1000 microseconds).

Example 12-1   **ipx maximum-paths** *Configuration to Use Three Parallel Paths*

```
!
interface e0
ipx network 123
!
interface e1
ipx network 345
!
interface fddi1
ipx network 346
!
ipx maximum-paths 3
```

Therefore, the precedence of IPX route selection is as follows:

1 Lowest ticks

2 Lowest hops

3 Lowest IPX interface delay

IPXWAN

IPXWAN is a handshake protocol that establishes an accurate routing metric when a dialup link is established. As of Cisco IOS Release 10.0, both IP and IPX are supported over PPP between Cisco routers and Novell servers. IPXWAN over HDLC is supported between two Cisco routers.

Figure 12-5 shows a typical use of IPXWAN with PPP. Here, a Novell server is connected to a Cisco router, and the metric is dynamically calculated for full connectivity.

Figure 12-5   *Use IPXWAN Protocol over PPP*

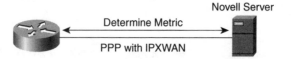

Novell High-Level Data Link Control (HDLC) encapsulation is not compatible with Cisco HDLC. To connect a Novell server to a Cisco router, use the Point-to-Point Protocol (PPP).

The IPX tick represents a transmission delay of 1/18 second. To allow for better routing decisions, let IPXWAN determine an accurate value for delay. Alternatively, adjust ticks with the **ipx delay** command based on the bandwidth of the interface.

The following suggested delay values are based on the formula that Novell and Cisco use to calculate ticks with IPXWAN 2.0:

- 2.04 Mbps: 6 ticks
- 1.544 Mbps: 6 ticks
- 256 kbps: 6 ticks
- 128 kbps: 12 ticks
- 56 kbps: 18 ticks
- 38.4 kbps: 24 ticks
- 19.2 kbps: 60 ticks
- 9600 bps: 108 ticks

These fine-tuned metrics make IPXWAN weigh links more accurately than IPX RIP.

IPX Switching Modes/Load Balancing

Switching modes for IPX do not correspond exactly to switching modes for IP on the router because unique data structures are involved.

The characteristics of the switching modes are as follows:

- **Process switching**—Load balancing is done packet by packet (like IP).
- **Fast switching**—Load balancing is still done packet by packet (different from IP).
- **Autonomous/silicon switching**—Load balancing is done by destination (like IP).

The key point to remember is that the switching mode determines IPX load balancing. Also note that with fast switching you still get packet-by-packet load balancing. This is opposite of IP-based load balancing with fast switching.

The default for IPX routing is no load balancing. You can adjust **maximum paths** on the Cisco router to permit load balancing on two to four equal-cost paths concurrently. You would use the configuration **ipx-maximum paths 4** to load balance over four equal-cost paths.

One-Path IPX Routing

Although simple to configure, the disadvantage to one-path IPX routing is that there is no load balancing. Also, because there is only one path, this means slower network convergence times for your end users.

Multipath IPX Routing

The advantage to multipath IPX routing is that there can be load balancing. In this case, many paths lead to much faster network convergence times.

IPX Routing with NLSP

Version 1.0 of NetWare Link Services Protocol (NLSP) runs with NetWare 3.11 or higher and is similar to OSI's Intermediate System-to-Intermediate System (IS-IS) hierarchical link-state protocol, except that only one area can be defined. This release of NLSP has been supported since Cisco IOS Release 10.3. In Cisco IOS Release 11.2, however, support for NLSP V1.1's multiple areas allows a routing hierarchy for NLSP.

As of 11.1 code, Cisco's implementation of Novell NLSP route aggregation extends the choices for connecting areas from the standard IPX/RIP to NLSP and Cisco's EIGRP. Benefits of Cisco NLSP route aggregation include more efficient network operation because of reduced routing traffic and reduced use of system resources. You can find out more about NLSP route aggregation at www.cisco.com/warp/public/732/Novell/nlsp_wp.htm.

NLSP has faster convergence than IPX/RIP. It only advertises routing and services incrementally. The shortest path first (SPF) algorithm used by NLSP is CPU-intensive compared to IPX/RIP.

In general, you should limit the size of one NLSP process (area) to about 400 routing nodes. The computational overhead of running the SPF algorithm varies according to the formula $n \times \log(n)$, where n is the number of adjacency relationships between routing nodes. Figure 12-6 shows a typical NLSP area topology. The key thing to remember about NLSP is that it offers fast convergence with redundant mesh topologies.

Figure 12-6   *NetWare Link Services Protocol*

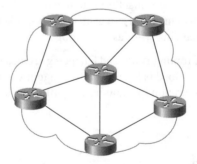

The geographic dispersion of networks is more important than the number of routing nodes. Each campus in a large IPX internetwork should probably be in a separate area.

The routing metric for NLSP is cost. The cost for an interface is an integer from 1 to 63. The total number of hops allowed by NLSP is 1023. Using the **ipx nlsp** *metric* command causes NLSP to prefer some links over others. A link with a lower metric is more preferable than one with a higher metric. Typically, it is not necessary to configure the metric; however, it may be desirable in some cases when there are considerable differences in link bandwidths.

Although NLSP supports paths up to 1023 hops, most clients and some servers continue to rely on RIP and SAP updates. The limit of 15 routing hops still applies to RIP-based path determination. Figure 12-7 shows a typical example where NLSP is used in the network core; IPX RIP/SAP is used at the edges. It is important to note that if you have any IPX/RIP running in your NLSP network, the maximum number of hops is still only 15. NLSP essentially defaults to the lowest common denominator for hop count. You really need a "pure" NLSP environment to gain all of NLSP's benefits, which is not commonly deployed.

Figure 12-7   *Connectivity Is Limited with NLSP and RIP*

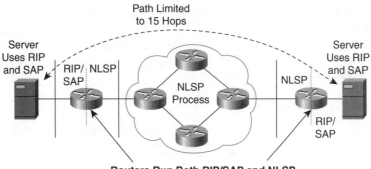

The redistribution between NLSP and RIP is handled automatically. While allowing redundant paths, loops are prevented by an algorithm that may sometimes result in suboptimal routes. No configuration of route filtering with access lists is required. Figure 12-8 shows a RIP-NLSP network with automatic redistribution occurring. The benefit of this configuration choice is its simplicity, and it guards against potential routing loops caused by feedback.

Figure 12-8 *No Filtering Is Required for NLSP to RIP*

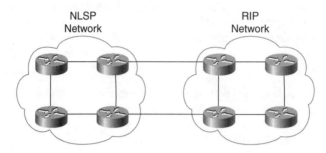

IPX Routing with EIGRP

IPX EIGRP dramatically reduces bandwidth consumption by transmitting incremental changes to routing information and services. EIGRP peers exchange only reliable updates over WAN interfaces by default. The default for LAN interfaces is to transmit the full RIP and SAP tables. Redistribution between EIGRP and RIP and SAP is automatic. Figure 12-9 shows this level of redistribution where the core routers are running IPX/EIGRP on their WAN interfaces and running IPX/RIP on their LAN interfaces. This design makes for a very easy configuration for legacy Novell networks.

Figure 12-9 *Use Enhanced IGRP for Scalable IPX*

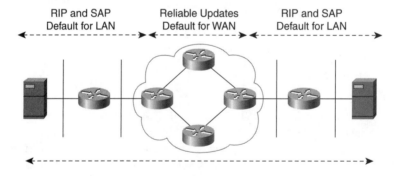

NOTE   Route redistribution is disabled between instances of NLSP Version 1.1 and EIGRP to minimize the possibility of routing loops in certain topologies. To add an EIGRP area, you must explicitly instruct the router to redistribute the route entry from an NLSP 1.1 area to an EIGRP area, and vice versa.

You should use IPX EIGRP in the WAN to get the benefits of fast convergence and low bandwidth consumption. It may be necessary to use the **delay** command when configuring the routers at the edge of the WAN cloud because the cloud topology is transparent to the LAN environment. Delay is used because it is a key metric that EIGRP uses for metric calculation. IPX/EIGRP is very commonly deployed in many network designs.

EIGRP tracks the IPX routing metrics as external metrics. The hop count is incremented by two as the route passes from IPX/RIP to EIGRP and back to IPX/RIP. The tick metric is not incremented, so the EIGRP cloud appears to be zero ticks.

When a route is originally an EIGRP route, the metric in ticks is derived from the interface delay. The tick value is redistributed correctly to IPX RIP routers. The tick is defined as 1/18 second. For LAN interfaces, Cisco follows the Novell convention of one tick per hop. Figure 12-10 shows an example of a RIP-to-EIGRP-to-RIP design. Here, as RIP network 100 passes into EIGRP and back into RIP network 300, we see that the tick count stays the same, although the hop count increases by two.

Figure 12-10   *EIGRP and IPX Metrics*

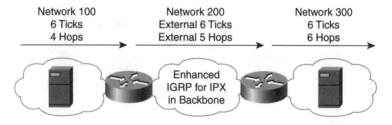

RIP and SAP Issues

SAP advertisements work like RIP advertisements. Both send the whole table to adjacent routers every 60 seconds. SAP generates more traffic than RIP because more services are on the internetwork than network numbers. As shown in Figure 12-11, SAPs occur by default every 60 seconds, and each SAP packet contains seven SAPs by default. RIP also updates every 60 seconds and each RIP packet contains entries for 50 networks. These timers are all tunable in IOS.

Figure 12-11   *RIP and SAP Overhead*

In Figure 12-11, the 480 B (SAP update traffic) and 432 B (RIP update traffic) indicate the number of bytes per update. By default, the maximum size of RIP updates sent out an interface is 432 bytes. This size allows for 50 routes at 8 bytes each, plus a 32-byte IPX/RIP header. By default, the maximum size of SAP updates sent out an interface is 480 bytes. This size allows for seven servers (64 bytes each), plus a 32-byte IPX/SAP header.

IPX traffic can be controlled with IPX access lists. As shown in Figure 12-12, policy decisions can be implemented using IPX access lists on distribution layer routers. This is appropriate because there are relatively few distribution layer routers.

Figure 12-12 *Implement Policy with IPX Access Lists*

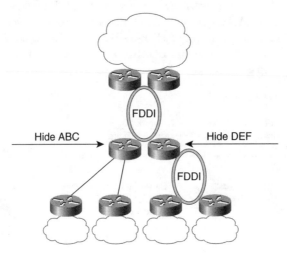

There are different types of IPX access lists. First, the *simple access list* (in the router configuration, simple IPX access lists range from 800 to 899) filters are based on the traffic source and destination addresses. Next, the *extended access list* (in the router configuration, extended IPX access lists range from 900 to 999) is based on source address, destination address, port, and socket number.

NOTE There are actually two other types of IPX access lists. One is for IPX NLSP route aggregation filtering and the other is for SAP filtering. For more information on access lists available for IPX, check out www.cisco.com/univercd/cc/td/doc/product/software/ios112/112cg_cr/6rbook/6ripx.htm.

You can be very creative with these access lists to suit your design needs. For example, a common access list is one that blocks all type 107 SAPS (Novell RCONSOLE) from leaving a building. That will only allow locally connected supervisors to gain access to a local Novell server console.

With some designs, you may want to use the access list at the access layer IPX router. This will allow only certain SAPs or RIPs to leave a particular access LAN, saving bandwidth on the WAN. One drawback to implementing access lists at this level is that this can impose a high level of network administration, to maintain and update the IPX access lists. This approach may vary from design to design, however, based on requirements.

There is no impact on the switching performance because SAP packets are handled by the route processor anyway.

SAP access lists can be applied in two ways:

- **On input**—input-sap-filter
- **On output**—output-sap-filter

As shown in Figure 12-13, you should try to control SAP packets as close to the source as possible. Also, note that you should use SAP access lists based on network numbers rather than specific host addresses. The reason for this use is because host addresses for IPX are derived from the MAC address and will change if the network interface card is replaced. That would increase administrative duties.

DESIGN RULE   In many cases, we recommend a permissive filtering strategy—in other words, we permit only specific SAPs out of a region. This prevents new IPX applications from being proliferated network-wide without the designers knowledge or input.

Figure 12-13   *Control SAP Packets at the Source*

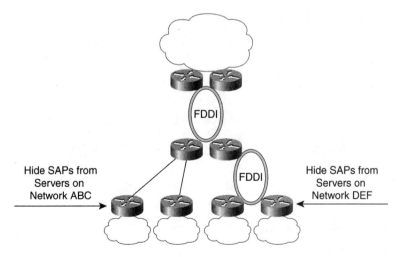

Get Nearest Server Queries

A Cisco router can respond to Get Nearest Server (GNS) queries on serverless networks. By default, the GNS response delay is zero on serverless networks. If the response is too fast for slow clients, the response delay time can be configured. Note that the router will not respond to GNS queries if there is a server on the network.

As of Cisco IOS Software Release 9.21, the router can be configured to respond to GNS queries in a round-robin fashion if several equidistant servers are in the SAP table. The command to configure this behavior is **ipx gns-round-robin**. Per Cisco documentation, in the normal server selection process, requests for service are responded to with the most recently learned, closest server. If you enable the round-robin method, Cisco IOS software maintains a list of the nearest servers eligible to provide specific services. The router uses this list when responding to GNS requests. Responses to requests are distributed in a round-robin fashion across all active IPX interfaces on the router.

Eligible servers are those that satisfy the "nearest" requirement for a given request and that are not filtered either by a SAP filter or by a GNS filter. If this is not configured, the router responds with the first service in its SAP table. Figure 12-14 shows two separate scenarios.

Figure 12-14 *Use Router to Respond to GNS Queries*

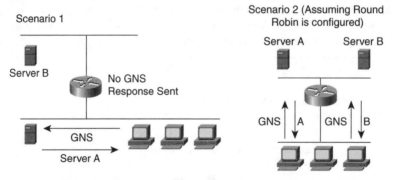

As shown in Scenario 1, a router is on the same segment as a server. By seeing the server's SAPs, the router knows that the server is local. Therefore, it will *not* reply to GNS requests. In Scenario 2, there are clients on a serverless network. The router will reply to the GNS requests by providing the name of the nearest server. There is zero delay on serverless networks. Remember that **ipx output-gns-filter** enables you to filter which servers a router uses in its GNS reply.

To create filters for controlling which servers are included in the GNS responses sent by Cisco IOS software, perform the following tasks:

Step 1 Create a SAP access list.

Step 2 Apply a GNS filter to an interface.

Example 12-2 demonstrates how to carry out these tasks.

Example 12-2   *Creating Filters for Controlling Which Servers Are Included in the GNS Responses Sent by IOS*

```
!Step 1: Create the access-list
access-list 1001 permit FEEDFACE
access-list 1001 deny -1
!Step 2: Apply the access-list to an interface
int e0
ipx output-gns-filter 1001
!
```

Example 12-2 says that on interface e0, only respond to GNS requests with servers whose address is on network FEEDFACE.

IPX with NetBIOS

NetBIOS applications running over IPX are subject to the same scaling issues as NetBIOS over LLC2. NetBIOS uses network-wide broadcasts to find other servers.

NetBIOS clients use IPX port 20 broadcasts to find a server. Type 20 broadcasts must be flooded for NetBIOS connectivity. Use the **ipx type-20-propagation** command to forward NetBIOS broadcasts and block all other IPX broadcasts. This command is configured on an interface basis. Chapter 14, "Windows Networking Design," contains examples of type 20 propagation when using IPX as a transport in a Windows environment. You can also forward type 20 packets with helper addresses, using the **ipx type-20-helpered** and **ipx helper-address** *network.node* commands. You can find more information about IPX helper addresses at www.cisco.com/univercd/cc/td/doc/product/software/ios112/112cg_cr/6rbook/6ripx.htm#xtocid2046437.

The local router closest to the sending IPX host floods the type 20 broadcast to all IPX networks. Figure 12-15 shows a typical routed network that allows for IPX type 20 propagation to occur. This is necessary for an IPX/NetBIOS client to receive a reply to its FindName query broadcasts.

Fortunately, Cisco IOS software supports filtering NetBIOS by name for NetBIOS over IPX. This is similar to filtering NetBIOS by name over LLC2. Filtering by name is the most scalable way to control NetBIOS. Of course, you should implement a good naming convention for optimal access list design. Figure 12-16 shows an example of a NetBIOS name filter.

Figure 12-15   *NetBIOS over IPX Broadcast Behavior*

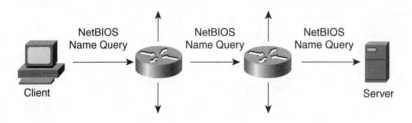

Figure 12-16   *Filter NetBIOS over IPX by Name*

In Figure 12-16, incoming IPX NetBIOS FindName messages are applied using the **ipx netbios input-access-filter** and **ipx netbios output-access-filter** interface configuration commands. Note that wildcards are available for use, which simplifies IPX NetBIOS filter creation. For instance, Example 12-3 uses a NetBIOS host name to filter IPX NetBIOS frames. The example denies all outgoing IPX NetBIOS frames with a NetBIOS host name of Boston on Ethernet interface 0.

Example 12-3   *Filtering IPX NetBIOS Frames with a NetBIOS Host Name*

```
netbios access-list host token deny Boston
netbios access-list host token permit *
!
ipx routing 0000.0c17.d45d
!
interface ethernet 0
 ipx network 155 encapsulation ARPA
 ipx type-20-propagation
 ipx netbios output-access-filter host token
 no mop enabled
!
interface ethernet 1
 no ip address
 ipx network 105
!
```

Configuration Considerations

NetWare servers send a keepalive message to all connected clients every 5 minutes. If clients are connected by dial-on-demand routing (DDR) circuits, the keepalive acts as an interesting packet and keeps the DDR link open indefinitely.

Use a technique called *watchdog spoofing* on the router at the server end. The command to use is **ipx watchdog-spoof**, which will have the router answer session keepalives locally, and the DDR link will be allowed to drop. This will save dialup line costs.

Applications that use SPX, such as SAA and Novell RCONSOLE, can use SPX keepalives. An *SPX keepalive* is an unsolicited ACK. After a timeout, the SPX software sends the same ACK and sequence number that it sent in the previous ACK when it acknowledged receipt of data. The sender expects an ACK to the keepalive. SPX spoofing, enabled with the command **ipx spx-spoof**, causes the router to send the ACK so that no packet goes on the WAN link.

Watchdog spoofing has been available since Cisco IOS Release 9.1.9. SPX spoofing is a feature introduced in Cisco IOS Release 11.0. Figure 12-17 depicts a network that employs both SPX spoofing and IPX watchdog spoofing. These features are most critical in dialup and DDR type networks.

Figure 12-17   *Use Spoofing to Drop DDR Links*

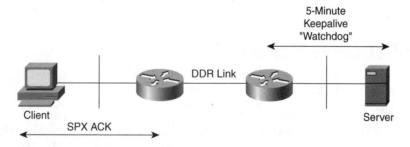

IPX/IP Gateways

When enabling users to access the Internet or local TCP/IP applications, you have the following two choices:

- Implement a TCP/IP stack on each PC.
- Implement a TCP/IP gateway at a central location.

Users of other protocol suites do not have native access to the Internet.

The IPeXchange IPX-to-IP Gateway product (shown in Figure 12-18) requires only one IP address for all PC clients in the network. Running TCP/IP on each client generates additional administrative overhead caused by dual protocol stacks and IP addressing requirements.

Figure 12-18 *IPX Access to IP Networks*

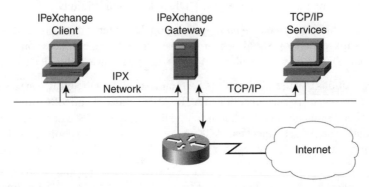

The Cisco IPeXchange Internet Gateway is both a client and a server product. The client image executes on a Windows-based PC utilizing IPX. The server image executes on a workstation or server running Windows NT; the server image can execute on a PC running the NetWare Server software. With these configurations, the IPeXchange Gateway software runs over both IPX and TCP/IP. This design solution produces Internet connectivity for IPX clients.

New Enhancements to IPX

As of IOS Release 12.0, the IPX trace route probes all the intermediate IPX routers and servers traversed along the path to the final destination; it measures round-trip delays and displays them. This is extremely useful in troubleshooting IPX networks end to end.

Also, as mentioned earlier in the chapter, in IOS 12.0, IPX EIGRP incremental SAP now has split horizon, which instructs the routers not to advertise the SAP to the same interface from where that SAP is received. It also enables you to display the EIGRP neighbor server table using regular expressions.

Summary

IPX network design, like any other protocol, requires careful planning and consideration. IPX, if not implemented correctly, can cause network performance bottlenecks. With proper SAP filtering at the access and distribution layers with SAP access lists and routing protocols that use incremental updates, however, your IPX network can let you sleep at night. Whenever possible, use EIGRP to reduce routing overhead and convergence time. Although not often used, IPXWAN is also a choice when accurate routing metrics for WAN interfaces are essential. Finally, load balancing is a hot topic these days. You can load balance IPX by increasing maximum paths with the **ipx maximum-paths** command. This allows IPX to load balance and ultimately yield fastest network convergence.

Chapter Review Questions

1 Describe the different IPX encapsulations that are available on Cisco routers.

2 Is it possible to support multiple IPX encapsulations on the same physical interface? If so, how?

3 How often does IPX RIP send out routing updates?

4 What is IPXWAN?

5 How is IPX fast switching different from IP fast switching?

6 Describe the advantages and disadvantages of using NLSP over IPX/RIP for your routing protocol.

7 When an IPX packet is routed from IPX to EIGRP back to IPX, how is the metric handled?

8 How often do NetWare servers send a keepalive message to all connected clients?

9 What is SPX spoofing?

Once we have thousands of ideas to harvest, we may have the chance once again to create a second Renaissance, perhaps every bit as important as the first.

—John Sculley, former CEO of Apple Computer

Upon completion of this chapter, you will be able to do the following:

- Examine a sample client's requirements and construct an appropriate AppleTalk design solution

- Determine which addressing and naming conventions are used to build manageable and scalable AppleTalk internetworks

- Describe how to use Cisco IOS software features to design scalable AppleTalk internetworks

CHAPTER 13

AppleTalk Design

Although AppleTalk is becoming less and less prevalent in enterprise networks, the requirement is still fairly common in smaller LAN networks where AppleTalk users reside. As a design engineer, it is important to understand the issues that you will face when beginning an AppleTalk network design.

Just as you would approach any other design, you should carefully define the customer's major objectives for the design before designing an AppleTalk network. In the end, the network should be easy to use, configure, and maintain. This chapter discusses the building blocks of effective AppleTalk network design, including the fundamentals of the AppleTalk protocol suite, protocol choices, and best practices.

AppleTalk Protocol Suite

Apple designed the AppleTalk protocols with ease of use as the main goal, so developing an AppleTalk design that benefits from the inherent simplicity of AppleTalk should be easy. Figure 13-1 shows the AppleTalk protocol suite.

Figure 13-1   *AppleTalk Protocol Suite*

IP Network Applications	AppleTalk Network Applications		Routing	Chooser
	AppleTalk Higher Layers			
Mac TCP Supports IP Stack	ATP	ADSP	RTMP	NBP
			ZIP	
DDP				AARP
Physical and Data Link Layers				

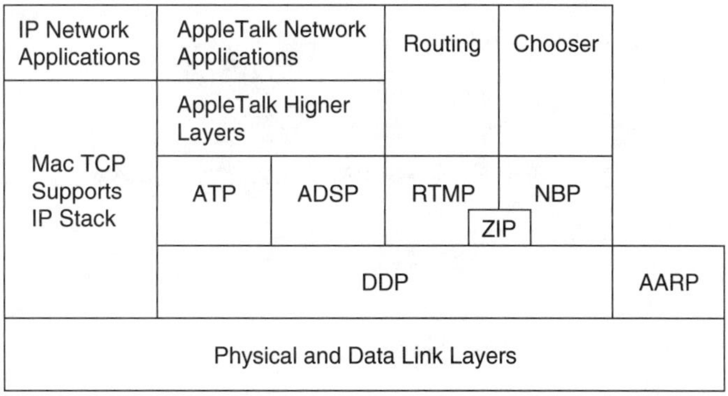

The AppleTalk protocol suite consists of several layers, including the following:

- AARP (AppleTalk Address Resolution Protocol)
- DDP (Datagram Delivery Protocol)
- NBP (Name Binding Protocol)
- RTMP (Routing Table Maintenance Protocol)
- ZIP (Zone Information Protocol)
- ADSP (AppleTalk Data Stream Protocol)
- ATP (AppleTalk Transaction Protocol)

Like other protocols such as TCP/IP, each element within the AppleTalk model serves a unique purpose in delivering packets from source to destination. Many of these elements are discussed later in the chapter.

The original version of AppleTalk is now called Phase 1. Phase 1 and transition networks between Phase 1 and Phase 2 are fully supported by Cisco. Transition networks are complex to design, configure, and troubleshoot, so it is recommended that you use Phase 2 exclusively. Phase 2 supports cable ranges that permit more than 253 devices on a LAN segment. This and other improvements make Phase 2 internetworks more scalable than Phase 1 internetworks. AppleTalk Phase 1 supported only one zone per LAN segment consisting of up to 127 servers and 127 hosts, and used Ethernet II frames. Above all, AppleTalk Phase 1 just wasn't very scalable.

AppleTalk Phase 2 supports multiple zones per LAN segment consisting of up to 253 nodes (servers or hosts), and typically uses Ethernet SNAP frames. The network number can range from 1 to 65,535.

Figure 13-2 shows a typical AppleTalk Phase 2 environment. Among the other advantages mentioned, AppleTalk Phase 2 also supports multiple physical topologies, including FDDI, Token Ring, and Ethernet.

Figure 13-2   *AppleTalk Phase 2 Network Topology*

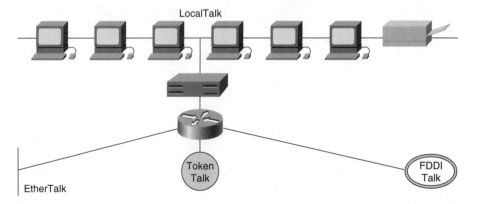

NOTE	One of my favorite reference Web sites on AppleTalk is at www.neon.com/atalk_routing.html. This site discusses the technical details of RTMP, ZIP, and the basics of AppleTalk routing. This is also a good site if you need a quick refresher.

AppleTalk Routing

AppleTalk's routing protocol, RTMP, is similar to Routing Information Protocol (RIP). Like RIP, the maximum hop count is 15. However, AppleTalk is very chatty. Whereas IP/ RIP broadcasts routing updates every 30 seconds, AppleTalk routing updates occur every 10 seconds. As shown in Figure 13-3, a routing packet contains routing tuples. A routing tuple is basically a table of cable range and hop counts used to create routing table entries.

Figure 13-3   *AppleTalk Routing Protocol Is RTMP*

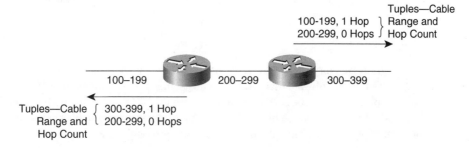

As illustrated in Figure 13-3, the router on the left advertises Network 200-299 as 0 hops, which means that the network is directly attached, and the tuple for Network 300-399 is advertised as being 1 hop (1 router) away. The router on the right advertises Network 200-299 as 0 hops, which means that the network is directly attached, and the tuple for Network 100-199 is advertised as being 1 hop (1 router) away.

RTMP always uses split horizon, which limits connectivity in certain partial mesh, packet-switched WAN configurations. The effect of split horizon on nonbroadcast multiaccess (NBMA) WAN design is discussed in Chapter 17, "Frame Relay Design." The fact that AppleTalk employs split horizon can be very critical if you are deploying a multipoint Frame Relay interface. If you have multiple Frame Relay destinations defined on the same interface, for example, you will run into a split-horizon issue. As discussed later in this chapter, this problem is addressed in the AppleTalk version of EIGRP.

A Cisco router does not advertise an AppleTalk network until the corresponding zone information is known. This slows the propagation of routing information, but prevents ZIP storms that result if routing information races ahead of zone information. ZIP queries for a network are only sent after the routing tuples are received for that same network. If a router does not have a route for a given AppleTalk network, there will not be any zones within that network that will be available from that router. We'll later see that controlling the routing updates sent and received can be effective in controlling the zone traffic.

AARP

AppleTalk Address Resolution Protocol (AARP) is a network layer protocol in the AppleTalk protocol suite that associates AppleTalk network addresses with hardware addresses. AARP services are used by other AppleTalk protocols. When an AppleTalk protocol has data to transmit, for example, it specifies the network address of the destination. It is the job of AARP to find the hardware address associated with the device using that network address.

AARP uses a request-response process to learn the hardware address of other network nodes. Because AARP is a media-dependent protocol, the method used to request a hardware address from a node varies depending on the data link layer implementation. Typically, a broadcast message is sent to all AppleTalk nodes on the network.

DDP

The Datagram Delivery Protocol (DDP) is the primary network layer routing protocol in the AppleTalk protocol suite that provides a best-effort connectionless datagram service between AppleTalk sockets. As with protocols such as TCP, no virtual circuit or connection is established between two devices. The function of guaranteeing delivery instead is handled by upper-layer protocols of the AppleTalk protocol suite.

DDP performs two key functions: packet transmission and receipt.

- **Transmission of packets**—DDP receives data from socket clients, creates a DDP header by using the appropriate destination address, and passes the packet to the data link layer protocol.
- **Reception of packets**—DDP receives frames from the data link layer, examines the DDP header to find the destination address, and routes the packet to the destination socket.

DDP maintains the cable range of the local network and the network address of a router attached to the local network in every AppleTalk node. In addition to this information, AppleTalk routers must maintain a routing table by using the Routing Table Maintenance Protocol (RTMP).

DDP Transmission Process

DDP operates much like any routing protocol. Packets are addressed at the source, passed to the data link layer, and transmitted to the destination. When DDP receives data from an upper-layer protocol, it determines whether the source and destination nodes are on the same network by examining the network number of the destination address. If the destination network number is within the cable range of the local network, the packet is encapsulated in a DDP header and is passed to the data link layer for transmission to the destination node. If the destination network number is not within the cable range of the local network, the packet is encapsulated in a DDP header and is passed to the data link layer for transmission to a router. Intermediate routers use their routing tables to forward the packet toward the destination network. When the packet reaches a router attached to the destination network, the packet is transmitted to the destination node.

NBP

The Name Binding Protocol (NBP) is a transport layer protocol in the AppleTalk protocol suite that maps the addresses used at lower layers to AppleTalk names. Socket clients within AppleTalk nodes are known as network-visible entities (NVEs). An NVE is a network-addressable resource, such as a print service, that is accessible over the internetwork. NVEs are referred to by character strings known as entity names. NVEs also have a zone and various attributes, known as entity types, associated with them.

Two key reasons exist for using entity names rather than addresses at the upper layers:

- Network addresses are assigned to nodes dynamically and, therefore, change regularly. Entity names provide a consistent way for users to refer to network resources and services, such as a file server.

- Using names rather than addresses to refer to resources and services preserves the transparency of lower-layer operations to end users.

In the past, the Chooser application in Mac OS caused significant traffic because it generated an NBP (Name Binding Protocol) broadcast every 3 seconds as long as the window was open and a zone and device driver were selected. When Apple released version System 7.0 of the Mac OS, it included an exponential timing delay so that NBP broadcasts go out far less frequently. Figure 13-4 shows a typical setup of NBP.

Here, an end-user station has its Chooser dialog box open. The key to remember that is that the Chooser will generate NBP broadcasts that have three components: object name, type, and zone.

Additionally, the NBP query contains two fields. The responses fill in the missing field. In the case of the Chooser, the missing field is the object name. The responder daemon in each host matches replies to the NBP query.

| NOTE | Remember that older versions of Mac OS (before 7.0) should be upgraded to decrease the potential large amount of NBP traffic from passing on your network. |

Figure 13-4   *AppleTalk Chooser Uses NBP*

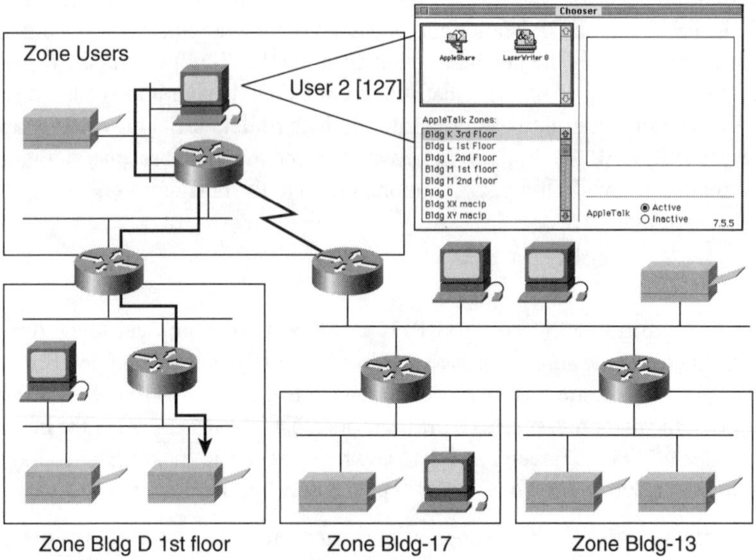

ZIP and ADSP

The Zone Information Protocol (ZIP) is a session layer protocol in the AppleTalk protocol suite that maintains network number–to–zone name mappings in AppleTalk routers. ZIP is used primarily by AppleTalk routers. Other network nodes, however, use ZIP services at startup to choose their zone. ZIP maintains a zone information table (ZIT) in each router. ZITs are lists maintained by ZIP that map specific network numbers to one or more zone names. Each ZIT contains a network number–to–zone name mapping for every network in the internetwork. As discussed later in this chapter, ZIP information can be filtered in many different ways.

The AppleTalk Data Stream Protocol (ADSP) is a session layer protocol in the AppleTalk protocol suite that establishes and maintains full-duplex communication between two AppleTalk sockets. ADSP guarantees that data is correctly sequenced and that packets are not duplicated. ADSP also implements a flow-control mechanism that allows a destination to slow source transmissions by reducing the size of the advertised receive window. ADSP runs directly on top of the DDP.

Routing Overhead Calculation

Routing overhead for WAN links can be determined by using the following numbers:

- An RTMP packet contains 100 to 200 routing tuples, depending on whether the update carries Phase I or Phase II routes. Phase I can carry 200 routing tuples, but Phase II can carry only 100 routing tuples. You may see a mixture of both kinds of routes—that is, a packet may contain 100 to 200 routing tuples.

- RTMP transmits the routing table to each interface every 10 seconds.

- RTMP generates one routing tuple (a cable range and a hop count) for every AppleTalk cable range (using split horizon).

- A DDP packet can be up to 600 bytes long.

If we had 600 AppleTalk routing tuples, for example, this would require three AppleTalk update packets. Because DDP uses up to 600 bytes per packet (with no fragmentation), this means that there is a bandwidth requirement of 1800 bytes of AppleTalk RTMP overhead traffic every 10 seconds. In LAN environments, this is not a big issue. As we look into the WAN environment, however, the overhead presents some bandwidth, which ultimately leads to potential business (financial) burdens.

To solve the WAN bandwidth dilemma prevalent in RTMP networks, Cisco invented EIGRP with added support for AppleTalk routing. By enabling EIGRP for AppleTalk in your backbone, these routers will still redistribute native RTMP to local routers at the access layer. The configuration in Example 13-1 shows how to enable EIGRP for AppleTalk routing. In this example, Ethernet interface 0 is configured for both EIGRP and RTMP routing, and serial interface 0 is configured for only AppleTalk EIGRP routing.

Example 13-1   *Enabling EIGRP for AppleTalk Routing*

```
!
appletalk routing eigrp 90
appletalk route-redistribution
!
Interface e0
Description LAN Interface EIGRP & RTMP
Appletalk network 100-100 100.5
appletalk protocol eigrp
!
Interface s0
Description WAN Interface Apple/EIGRP Only (no RTMP)!
Appletalk network 200-200 200.2
appletalk protocol eigrp
no appletalk protocol rtmp
!
```

There are a number of advantages to using EIGRP for AppleTalk routing in the WAN, including the following:

- EIGRP saves bandwidth because it only sends routing updates when changes occur.

- EIGRP converges within 1 second after a link failure.

- EIGRP supports disabling split horizon.
- EIGRP sends Hello packets to maintain neighbor relationships.
- EIGRP provides automatic redistribution into RTMP and vice versa.

The formulas for EIGRP and RTMP metric conversions for making routing calculations, as illustrated in Figure 13-5, are as follows:

- From RTMP to EIGRP:
  - Metric = hops $\times$ 25,652,400 (the value 25,652,400 is a predefined constant)
  - Each hop looks like a 9600-bps link
- From EIGRP to RTMP:
  - End-to-end hop count maintained across the EIGRP core

Figure 13-5   *EIGRP Reduces Routing Traffic on WAN*

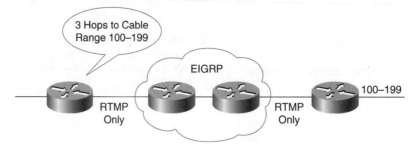

DESIGN RULE   Use EIGRP for AppleTalk routing in the WAN.

AURP

The AppleTalk Update Routing Protocol (AURP) was designed by Apple with the Internet Engineering Task Force (IETF) and is intended to be an open standard. AURP provides enhancements that are compatible with AppleTalk Phase 2. Figure 13-6 shows a typical setup where AURP can be deployed.

Figure 13-6   *AURP Reduces Routing Traffic on WAN*

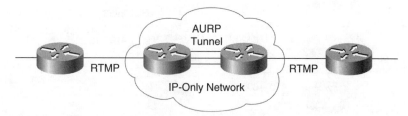

Figure 13-6 shows two RTMP routers that interface to an IP-only network. The IP network carries AURP traffic tunnel to tunnel where RTMP is de-encapsulated on the other side. Like AppleTalk/EIGRP, the benefit is that there is reduced routing traffic on WAN links because only updates are sent. Additionally, tunneling through IP internetworks and other network systems yields basic security, including device and network hiding, as well as hop-count reduction to allow the creation of larger internetworks.

AURP is designed to handle routing update traffic over WAN links more efficiently than RTMP.

NOTE   AURP does not replace RTMP in the LAN environment. It is intended strictly for WAN environments only.

AppleTalk Administrative Choices

To effectively design an AppleTalk network, you must first consider several administrative choices. For example, network numbering schemes, floating static routes, NVEs, naming conventions, and zones are all areas that you should look into. Each of the following sections address these key classes of administrative decisions.

AppleTalk Network Number Allocation

An AppleTalk network number is a 16-bit integer, which is analogous to that of a "natural" Class B IP network; more than 64,000 network numbers are available. In my experiences, I have never seen address-space depletion as an issue in an enterprise AppleTalk environment.

As shown in Figure 13-7, a good practice is to administer AppleTalk numbers in a way that facilitates troubleshooting.

Figure 13-7   *Allocate Network Numbers by Location*

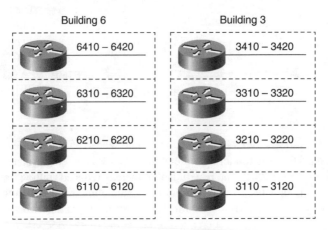

Networks are commonly allocated by building, floor, row, or office. Generally, each LAN can have several network numbers with AppleTalk Phase 2. The network numbers are called a cable range. In Figure 13-7, cable ranges are allocated by building number and by floor. The Building 6 networks all start with a 6, for example, and then are followed by the floor number, and end with 10–20. Remember that cable ranges must be unique and not overlap. As a good practice, you should always document the ranges in use. In the event of an AppleTalk problem sometime in the future, you will then be able to troubleshoot and correct it quickly and effectively.

Floating Static Routes

A floating static route has a higher administrative distance than dynamically learned routes and is only used as a last resort. Floating static routes for AppleTalk and IPX are available in Release 11.0 and later of the Cisco IOS software. Figure 13-8 shows a typical scenario where floating AppleTalk static routes could be used.

Figure 13-8   *Use Floating Static Routes for Backup*

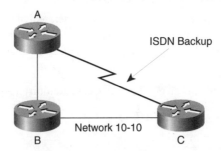

As illustrated in Figure 13-8, the primary path for Network 10-10 with respect to router A is through router B (through RTMP over an Ethernet segment). The floating static is put in place between router A and router C across a slower-speed serial link. In the event that the Ethernet segment between router A and router B fails, the route to Network 10-10 through router B would disappear from router A's AppleTalk routing table. At that point, the floating static to network 10-10 through router C would appear in router A's routing table and connectivity would be preserved. Note that service to network 10-10 will undoubtedly be slower, but at least the network is not "down hard."

Network-Visible Entities

Much like TCP/IP and IPX, AppleTalk communication takes place between devices with defined network number, host number, and port number. In AppleTalk, these are referred to as network-visible entities (NVEs). An NVE is identified by the following three parameters:

- **Network number**—16 bits
- **Node number**—8 bits
- **Socket number**—8 bits

The socket number identifies an application. For example, socket 4 is used by the AppleTalk Echo Protocol (ping).

NVEs can be named. An entity name is a 32-character string consisting of three fields: object, type, and zone, separated with punctuation. For example, DocPrinter:LaserWriter@Tech Pubs identifies a printer in the Tech Pubs zone. Notice that special characters can be included in this 32-character string.

AppleTalk Naming Conventions

End users locate resources on the network using the Chooser application. As shown in Figure 13-9, to make this search as efficient as possible, it is important that every computer and service have a readily identifiable and unique name.

Figure 13-9   *Use Unambiguous Names for Nodes*

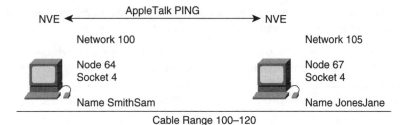

AppleTalk PING

NVE ◄──────────────► NVE

Network 100	Network 105
Node 64	Node 67
Socket 4	Socket 4
Name SmithSam	Name JonesJane

Cable Range 100–120

Use a simple convention for names so that end users can quickly scan the list to find a resource. In this example, the Macintosh on the left is named SmithSam and the Macintosh on the right is named JonesJane. The list appears in alphabetical order, so end users should identify their Macintosh with their last name followed by their first name.

NOTE	AppleTalk naming conventions should not be overlooked. You may end up saving yourself hours of time if you implement a logical naming and numbering convention. Sometimes, you may find it easy to use a portion of the IP network address (that is, the subnet number) as the AppleTalk network number. This practice is commonly done in IPX networks as well.

AppleTalk Zones

An AppleTalk zone name is used to describe a functional unit within the organization.

If a zone is localized, use a naming convention that describes the group's function as well as location. As shown in Figure 13-10, it is good practice to use short names so that users can immediately grasp the function and location when scanning through zones in the Chooser. Here, zone names such as Marketing HQ make resource identification quick and easy for end users to locate.

Figure 13-10   *Use Descriptive Names for Zones*

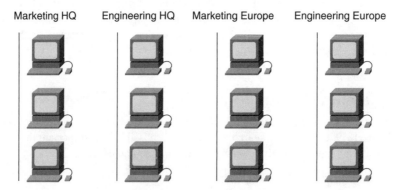

Marketing HQ   Engineering HQ   Marketing Europe   Engineering Europe

A zone can be dispersed across many physical locations. In this case, the zone name does not represent the functional unit's physical location.

It may be useful to put serial links into a zone whose name starts with several repetitions of the letter Z so that the serial link zones come up last as users scroll through the list of zones in the Chooser window. A serial link probably does not have any services on it and is irrelevant to the Chooser user. Likewise, if there is one particular zone that the majority of users access repeatedly, they will appreciate your design efforts (and consideration) if you name it with the letter A so that it is at the top of the Chooser listing.

NOTE   Multiple cable ranges can use the same zone name. In addition, a cable range can have multiple names.

In a large internetwork, it is not a good idea to put all the WAN links in one zone because of the propagation of NBP lookups that this would cause if the user searched for services in the zone. Therefore, it is recommended that you divide up the WAN links geographically. A later section in this chapter discusses configuring a zone filter (GetZoneList filter) so that zones for WAN links do not appear in the Chooser.

Although not generally recommended, a zone that spans many networks can be used to provide corporate information services that everyone needs. This condition makes widely distributed resources easily accessible. Outside of this requirement, it is highly advisable to keep zones localized. Widely distributed zones generate NBP traffic whenever someone uses the Chooser to search for services in the zone.

As a rule, you should try to limit the number of zones that cross WANs. When using dial-on-demand routing (DDR), make sure zones are localized so that unnecessary NBP traffic does not bring up the DDR line. Referring back to Figure 13-10, dividing zones by department and geographically with corporate resources distributed within each zone keeps the zones localized. Keeping the zones localized prevents unnecessary NBP traffic on the WAN links, and, arguably can save you time and resources later on down the road while troubleshooting AppleTalk issues.

When the Chooser is opened (as illustrated in Figure 13-4), a GetZoneList query goes to a router to populate the zone list at the lower left. The box at the upper left is populated with all the network drivers loaded on the Macintosh. The user selects a zone and a driver, and an NBP query goes out. The responses to the NBP query populate the window on the right with the names of the NVEs that offer the selected service in the selected zone.

As a design rule, it is highly advisable to keep the sizes of the zones relatively small to reduce the amount of NBP queries that need to traverse your network. Figure 13-11 illustrates an inefficient zone setup because the zone spans multiple cable ranges.

Figure 13-11 *Use Small Zones to Reduce NBP Traffic*

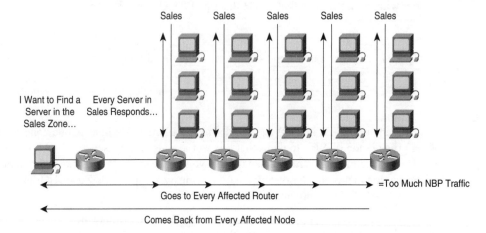

AppleTalk Filtering Options

To effectively deal with the issue of NBP traffic and zone queries, several methods of filtering have been added to Cisco IOS. You can filter network and zone information in AppleTalk in the following four ways:

- GZL filters
- ZIP reply filters
- NBP filters
- Distribute lists

Each type of filter is used in a slightly different manner to give you control of the AppleTalk protocol traffic.

GetZoneList Filters

The GetZoneList (GZL) filters ZIP information locally between a router and Macintosh hosts. The result is that specific zones can be hidden from users on specific networks. This works fine for small AppleTalk networks, but it does not scale because each router must be configured making administration burdensome. In Figure 13-12, a GZL filter is applied to the router's Ethernet (LAN) interface to block predefined zones from being sent after receiving a GZL request. This feature works well for small networks, but does not scale very well.

Figure 13-12 *AppleTalk GZL Filtering*

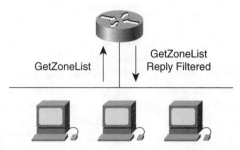

When defining GZL filters, you should ensure that all routers on the same internetwork filter GZL replies identically. Otherwise, the Chooser will list different zones depending on which router responded to the request. Also, inconsistent filters can result in zones appearing and disappearing every few seconds when the user remains in the Chooser.

TIP	Because of these inconsistencies, you should normally use the **appletalk getzonelist-filter** command only when all routers in the internetwork are Cisco routers, unless the routers from other vendors have a similar feature.

Example 13-2 demonstrates configuration of a GZL filter. (The zone NSA in GZL replies sent out Token Ring interface 0 are not included in Example 13-2.)

Example 13-2 *Configuring a GZL Filter*

```
!
access-list 600 deny zone NSA
interface token 0
appletalk getzonelist-filter 600
!
```

NBP Filters

NBP filters are a Cisco IOS Software Release 11.0 feature used to filter NBP packets to hide services. This filter will allow only predefined AppleTalk devices to propagate through a router after a NBP request has been sent from an end device. Example 13-3 adds entries to access list number 607 to allow forwarding of NBP packets from specific sources and deny forwarding of NBP packets from all other sources.

Example 13-3 *Configuring an NBP Filter*

```
!
access-list 607 permit nbp 1 type LaserWriter
access-list 607 permit nbp 2 type AFPServer
```

continues

Example 13-3   *Configuring an NBP Filter (Continued)*

```
access-list 607 permit nbp 3 object HotShotPaint
access-list 607 deny other-nbps
!
```

The first command in Example 13-3 adds an entry that allows NBP packets from all printers of type LaserWriter. The second command adds an entry that allows NBP packets from all AppleTalk file servers of type AFPServer. The third command adds an entry that allows NBP packets from all applications called HotShotPaint. An application might have a zone name of Accounting, for example, and an application might have a zone name of Engineering, both having the object name of HotShotPaint. NBP packets forwarded from both applications will be allowed.

The final **deny other-nbps** command denies forwarding of NBP packets from all other sources.

To use the 607 access list to filter NBP packets on Ethernet interface 0, apply it to the interface using the commands in Example 13-4.

Example 13-4   *Applying an Access List to Another Interface*

```
!
appletalk routing
interface ethernet 0
 appletalk cable-range 55-55
 appletalk zone No Parking
 appletalk access-group 607
!
```

TIP   You can filter on object, type, or zone names. This enables you to isolate a specific device or group of devices in many ways.

ZIP Reply Filters

ZIP reply filters are a Cisco IOS Software Release 10.2 feature used to hide zone information between areas. This basically stops a router from replying to a ZIP request, which essentially hides zones between router devices.

As shown in Figure 13-13, the ZIP reply filter can be used to hide zones when connecting two AppleTalk administrative domains. Here, we have two AppleTalk autonomous systems. Full RTMP routing knowledge is passed between the two ASs, but only a filtered zone list is shared between each other.

Figure 13-13   *ZIP Reply Filtering Hides Services*

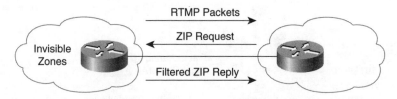

The ZIP reply filter allows RTMP tuples to propagate between RTMP peers, but blocks specific zones when the routers reach back for zone information. The filtered zones are invisible to all downstream routers and nodes. Zones can then be "leaked" as needed between the ASs by adding them to the "permitted list" in the GZL reply filter. Example 13-5 shows a simple example of a ZIP reply filter where the ethernet 0 interface will hide the Engineering and Accounting zones from other AppleTalk routers.

Example 13-5   *Applying a ZIP Reply Filter*

```
!
access-list 650 deny zone Engineering
access-list 650 deny zone Accounting
access-list 650 permit additional-zones
access-list 650 permit other-access
!
interface ethernet 0
appletalk zip-reply-filter 650
!
```

DESIGN RULE   Use the ZIP reply filter to hide zones where two administrative domains touch.

Distribute Lists

The distribute list feature is used to block cable range (network) RTMP broadcasts between routers. In general, you should not use distribute lists to hide zones because complex iterations can result. If your intent is to block zones, you should use a ZIP reply filter. As shown in Figure 13-14, a **distribute-list out** is configured on Router A to block cable range 10 from being advertised to router B.

Figure 13-14   *Distribute List Filtering*

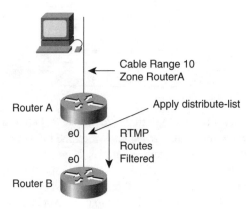

Example 13-6 shows a sample distribute list.

Example 13-6   *Applying a Distribute List*

```
!
access-list 612 deny network 10
access-list 612 permit other-access
interface ethernet 0
 appletalk distribute-list 612 out
!
```

NOTE   Note that the **appletalk distribute-list** is an interface configuration command.

AppleTalk and IP

Native DDP is faster than tunneling DDP in IP datagrams. However, sometimes using a tunnel is preferable to running AppleTalk in a backbone network.

If you decide to allow DDP on the backbone, you should still use EIGRP for routing table updates in the core WAN. EIGRP provides faster convergence and generates less overhead than native RTMP. Figure 13-15 shows a typical use for AppleTalk tunneling. Using a star topology, your tunnels will connect isolated AppleTalk LANs over a WAN.

Figure 13-15   *AppleTalk EIGRP over GRE IP Tunneling*

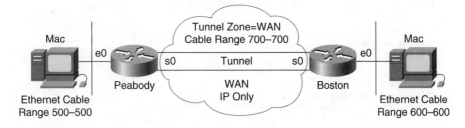

Example 13-7 shows the configuration for AppleTalk EIGRP over GRE IP tunneling configuration as illustrated in Figure 13-15.

Example 13-7   *Configuring AppleTalk EIGRP over GRE IP Tunneling*

```
For Peabody:
!
appletalk routing
appletalk routing eigrp 1
appletalk route-redistribution
!
interface Serial 0
ip address 150.100.1.2 255.255.255.252
!
interface Ethernet 0
ip address 130.108.1.1 255.255.255.0
appletalk cable-range 500-500
appletalk zone Engineering
!
interface Tunnel 0
no ip address
tunnel source 150.100.1.2
tunnel destination 150.100.1.1
tunnel mode gre ip
appletalk protocol eigrp
no appletalk protocol rtmp
appletalk cable-range 700-700
appletalk zone WAN

For Boston:
!
appletalk routing
appletalk routing eigrp 2
appletalk route-redistribution
!
interface Serial 0
ip address 150.100.1.1 255.255.255.252
!
interface Ethernet 0
ip address 207.100.2.1 255.255.255.0
appletalk cable-range 600-600
```

continues

Example 13-7   *Configuring AppleTalk EIGRP over GRE IP Tunneling (Continued)*

```
appletalk zone Marketing
!
interface Tunnel 0
no ip address
tunnel source 150.100.1.1
tunnel destination 150.100.1.2
tunnel mode gre ip
appletalk protocol eigrp
no appletalk protocol rtmp
appletalk cable-range 700-700
appletalk zone WAN
!
```

Although you might encounter some tunneling performance overhead, many newer routers (for example, 7206 VXR chassis) can handle the tunneling quite well. Many customers are moving to IP-only cores so that they can deliver QoS to their end users. As a result, "legacy" protocols, such as AppleTalk and IPX are often being tunneled across IP-based core infrastructures through GRE tunnels. Larger routers such as the Gigabit Switch Router (GSR) support only IP; therefore, if you have an AppleTalk requirement, tunneling in IP is a logical choice.

Summary

A base of networks still has a requirement to support AppleTalk. If you are faced with such a project, you should follow some basic rules:

- Use descriptive naming conventions for nodes and zones. This will make your network easier to support later on down the road.

- Although almost second nature, you should ensure cable range numbers are unique and meaningful on your internetwork.

- Minimize the number of different zones in the internetwork.

- Design your network with special attention to the direction in which traffic will flow. You should use filtering for security and policy-based routing and to reduce traffic. The type of filter will vary depending on the policies you are trying to implement.

- Probably most importantly, whenever possible, you should use Enhanced IGRP on WAN links.

Success is measured in the end, if the network is user friendly and "supportable" by your network-operations team.

Chapter Review Questions

1 List the protocols that make up the AppleTalk protocol suite.

2 How often does AppleTalk RTMP send its updates?

3 Why don't Cisco routers advertise an AppleTalk network until the corresponding zone information is known?

4 What are the formulas for Enhanced IGRP and RTMP metric conversions for making routing calculations?

5 Name two methods of reducing consumption of bandwidth in WANs by AppleTalk protocols.

6 What is a GZL filter?

7 What is a ZIP reply filter and what is its purpose?

The Internet can be compared to the arrival of the printing press, the telephone, and the radio.

—Bill Gates, Chairman and CEO of Microsoft Corporation

Upon completion of this chapter, you will be able to do the following:

- Identify the design requirements of deploying Windows-based internetworks

- Describe the network architecture used by Microsoft clients and servers

- Describe the operation of the NetBIOS and NetBEUI protocol stacks

- Identify the operational impact that NetBIOS and NetBEUI have on network design

- Describe design practices that allow efficient deployment of NetBIOS and NetBEUI

CHAPTER 14

Windows Networking Design

Microsoft Networking can be implemented fairly easily in your network. Unfortunately, however, design issues such as bandwidth requirements and decisions such as whether to use routing or bridging are often forgotten or overlooked. This can potentially lead to big problems down the road. In the past, I have dealt with large NetBIOS over TCP/IP (NBT) implementations that needed a complete redesign to effectively scale. Much like AppleTalk, Microsoft Networking was designed to be user-friendly, but, depending on the configuration, it is not always "network-friendly."

This chapter discusses the design requirements of deploying Windows-based internetworks, including a discussion of the network architecture used by Microsoft clients and servers and the protocol stacks of NetBIOS and NetBEUI. This chapter also discusses the best practices to allow efficient deployment of Microsoft Networking. Furthermore, Appendix D, "Design and Implementation Guide: Designing Networks with Windows Networking," contains useful information and should be used a supplement to the material covered in this chapter.

Windows Networking Concepts

Windows Networking (also referred to as Microsoft Networking) refers to the networking capabilities shared by Microsoft operating systems and servers. Figure 14-1 shows a typical LAN configuration where Windows OSs are prevalent.

Figure 14-1   *Windows Networking Components in a Workgroup*

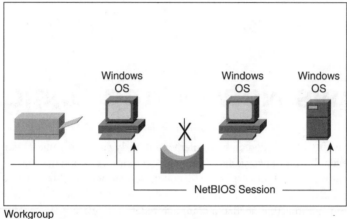

Workgroup

As Figure 14-1 illustrates, clients and servers using Windows operating systems communicate and share resources (such as files and printers) as facilitated by Microsoft Networking.

Before proceeding any further, you need to understand two key concepts at the outset of this discussion:

- The architectural grouping of network devices into domains and workgroups.
- The role of NetBIOS is critical to designing Microsoft networks.

The following sections expand on each of these concepts.

Domains and Workgroups

Microsoft Networking with Windows allows clients and servers of different platforms to be loosely organized into workgroups. All the Microsoft operating systems can interoperate across the local network. The network-enabling NetBIOS software is supplied as part of the bundled operating system, whether it is Windows for Workgroups, Windows 95, Windows 98, Windows NT, or Windows 2000.

Windows Networking employs two concepts of a group of related computers—namely, workgroups and domains. Workgroups can be any logical collection of computers. Any computer can join an existing workgroup or can be used to create a new one. Domains are a more formal entity. Figure 14-2 shows a sample domain.

Figure 14-2   *Domains Versus Workgroups*

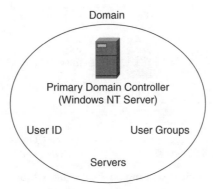

Domains are created and managed by a process called a Primary Domain Controller (PDC), which runs on a Windows NT Server. As shown in the figure, the domain has an NT Server that has administrative and security properties that workgroups do not have. (A domain is required to have at least one PDC.) The term *domain* as used here should not be confused with the Internet domain structure used by the Domain Name System (DNS).

NetBIOS Protocol

NetBIOS was originally created by IBM as an application programming interface (API) to create LAN applications in environments such as IBM LAN Server, Microsoft LAN Manager, and OS/2. It is therefore very difficult to compartmentalize NetBIOS directly into the OSI model. In fact, parts of NetBIOS can reside on Layer 4 through Layer 7, depending on the implementation. However, the exact placement of NetBIOS in the OSI model is not as important to network design as the simple fact that NetBIOS allows end stations to address servers by name. For the sake of simplicity, this book discusses NetBIOS functions as a session layer protocol with respect to the OSI reference model. NetBIOS frequently shows up in source-route bridge networks with SNA gateway devices implemented in PCs.

Windows Networking uses NetBIOS for all of its operation, including client access to devices such as file and print servers. The NetBIOS protocol requires additional software at the transport layer.

NetBIOS was originally designed to provide an extension to the basic I/O system of a PC. Its goal was to provide applications with a standard interface to lower-level network functions. For the routed environment, the biggest problem is that NetBIOS was designed on the premise that PCs need to talk only to other PCs on the same LAN. Consequently, there is no network layer functionality to provide logical addressing and routing. Instead, as shown in Figure 14-3, the NetBIOS design makes heavy use of data link layer broadcasts for a number of things.

Figure 14-3   *NetBIOS*

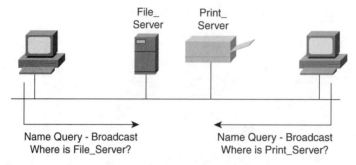

Name Query - Broadcast
Where is File_Server?

Name Query - Broadcast
Where is Print_Server?

Figure 14-3 shows devices sending out NameQuery broadcasts to locate a particular file or print server. Other examples of NetBIOS application traffic include messaging, name resolution, and authentication. No matter how large or small your network is, excessive broadcasts can become a drain on network bandwidth.

As Figure 14-4 shows, NetBIOS operates at the session layer of the OSI reference model as an API that sets up communication between networked computers.

Figure 14-4   *NetBIOS Protocol Stack*

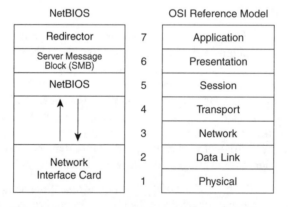

Because no network layer is provided, NetBIOS was designed to talk directly to network interface cards (NICs) through the extensive use of data link broadcasts. The protocol stack does include some higher-level components.

A software component called the Redirector directs network requests to network servers and local commands to the local operating system. The Redirector effectively sits at the application layer of the OSI model.

The Server Message Block (SMB) provides the peer-to-peer language and formats required for communication between applications. SMB effectively is located at the presentation layer of the OSI model. Note that there is no "Layer 3 and Layer 4" in the NetBIOS protocol stack. Although this certainly keeps the protocol simple, at the same time, it also inhibits "native" NetBIOS for use in larger, routed internetworks.

Transport Protocols

NetBIOS must be transported across the network, and, in general, there are two ways to accomplish this: bridging or routing. NetBEUI is bridged; IPX and TCP/IP are supported for routing. Figure 14-5 shows the transport mechanisms that can carry NetBIOS through your network. If you had an IPX-only network, for example, you would choose to encapsulate NetBIOS in IPX, using the NWLINK feature. NetBIOS over TCP/IP (NBT) is a very common Windows Networking implementation in large IP-based networks.

Figure 14-5   *Network Transport Mechanisms*

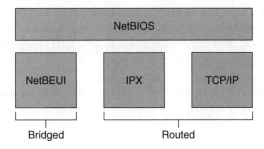

NetBEUI

NetBEUI is a transport and network layer protocol, but it still does not include a logical addressing scheme. As shown in Figure 14-6, NetBEUI interfaces directly to the data link layer, using MAC addresses and relying heavily on data-link broadcasts.

Figure 14-6   *NetBEUI Protocol Stack*

NetBEUI		OSI Reference Model
Redirector	7	Application
Server Message Block (SMB)	6	Presentation
NetBIOS	5	Session
NetBEUI	4	Transport
	3	Network
	2	Data Link
Network Interface Card	1	Physical

The key point to remember is that the "void" at Layer 3 and Layer 4 seemingly has been filled by NetBEUI in this model. However, this is not really true. NetBEUI still does not have a network component, so it is not routable. Therefore, all native NetBEUI application traffic must be bridged.

For these reasons, NetBEUI is the least scalable of the three transport methods and is only intended for use on small LANs and to support older services (for example, older versions of LAN Manager). One advantage of NetBEUI is that no end-station network address configuration is required.

NWLINK

NetBIOS over IPX is referred to as NWLINK. This protocol is recommended for small- to medium-sized networks, especially if IPX is already in use. Like NetBEUI, NWLINK requires no end-station address configuration. NWLINK uses IPX type 20 packets to exchange registration and browsing information. To forward these packets through a Cisco router, use the **ipx type-20-propagation** command on each interface. Also, Cisco added two global commands, **ipx type-20-input-checks** and **ipx type-20-output-checks**, to ensure that packets are accepted only on the primary interface (per the routing table) and also to prevent packets from being sent out an interface that is the path back to the source network so that routing loops cannot occur. Figure 14-7 shows the OSI protocol stack for NWLINK.

Figure 14-7   *NetBIOS over IPX-NWLINK*

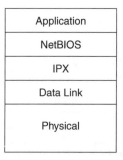

In Figure 14-7, NetBIOS is just encapsulated in IPX. Therefore, IPX functionality and its inherent routing capabilities are inherited by NetBIOS. Example 14-1 shows a sample configuration using **ipx type-20-propagation**.

Example 14-1   *Forwarding Type 20 Packets Through a Cisco Router*

```
ipx routing
ipx type-20-input-checks
ipx type-20-output-checks
!
int e 0
```

Example 14-1   *Forwarding Type 20 Packets Through a Cisco Router (Continued)*

```
ipx network 10
ipx type-20-propagation
!
int ethernet 1
ipx network 40
ipx type-20-propagation
!
```

NBT

Microsoft recommends NBT for medium-sized and large networks, or anytime the network has a WAN connection. This is especially true if you are already using TCP/IP as your primary network transport protocol. Because NBT uses TCP/IP, each computer must, as always, be properly configured with a valid IP address.

As Figure 14-8 shows, there are two general methods for configuring machines with IP addresses in the Windows environment:

- A static configuration at each computer, as shown on the computer on the left
- A dynamic configuration via Dynamic Host Configuration Protocol (DHCP), as done for the computer on the right

Figure 14-8   *IP Addressing for NBT*

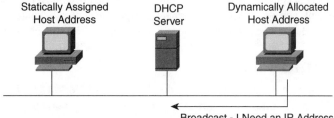

DHCP is designed to provide clients with a valid IP address, along with other options previously discussed in Chapter 7, "TCP/IP Addressing Design." DHCP requires a device that is configured as a DHCP server (examples are Windows NT Server and Novell NetWare).

LAN Services Browser

In any client/server environment, there must be some method to allow clients to find servers and for servers to make their presence known to clients. The Microsoft LAN Services Browser was designed for this purpose. The browser enables a user to get a list of all computers available on the network. Each Windows Networking client registers its NetBIOS name periodically by sending broadcasts. Every computer also has to send broadcasts to elect a browse master for the network. As shown in Figure 14-9, the browse master (and several backup browse masters) maintains a list of computers and their addresses. When a user browses a network, the client sends a broadcast request, and one of the browse masters responds. The presence of a browse master eliminates the need for all devices to respond to broadcast requests.

Figure 14-9   *LAN Services Browser*

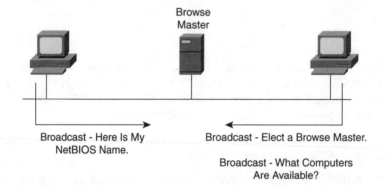

Windows Networking was originally designed to run on a single LAN segment or flat (bridged) network, and only NetBEUI was supported. Support was added later for IPX and TCP/IP, but Windows Networking still assumes that all nodes are on the same logical IPX or IP network; devices still send broadcasts to register and find computers on that network. Without a concept known as WINS configured, this can become a problem over routed environments because encapsulated broadcasts are sent across the routed domain, which could span the world. The next section addresses more about WINS and name resolution techniques.

Name Resolution

Name resolution is very important in the Windows Networking environment because it allows PCs to communicate with another device solely by knowing the name of the device with which it wishes to communicate. Without some form of name resolution, every PC would have to have full knowledge of every other device in the network—not a good idea. Fortunately, Windows Networking clients have four methods for name resolution. Some, of course, are better than others. They are as follows:

- Broadcasts
- LMHOSTS
- WINS
- Internet DNS

Broadcasts

Figure 14-10 shows the broadcast method for name resolution.

Figure 14-10   *Name Resolution—Broadcasts*

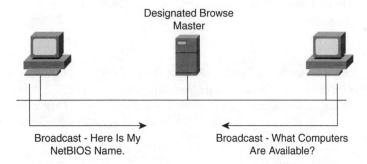

By sending broadcasts on a subnet, Windows clients cause a browser election. The designated browse master maintains a list of all the resources available on that subnet. Because registrations, browser elections, and name queries all generate broadcasts, this method does not scale well and is not recommended.

TIP   Broadcast is the default on all Microsoft products. It is strongly recommended that you turn this feature off by setting the BrowseMaster setting to Disabled (the default is Automatic), because good designs should always strive to reduce unnecessary broadcasts.

LMHOSTS

In the LMHOSTS method, as illustrated in Figure 14-11, clients consult a static table maintained on the PDC. For this method to scale at all, the PDC must maintain not only a static list of all computers and IP addresses in that domain, but also the names and addresses of the PDCs for all other domains in the network. All clients must be configured with an LMHOSTS file containing the IP address of their local PDC and the path to the master LMHOSTS file on it.

Figure 14-11   *Name Resolution—LMHOSTS*

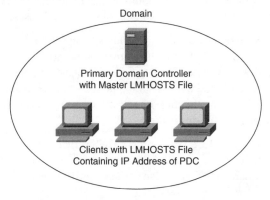

Because of the extensive manual configuration required, the LMHOSTS file approach does not scale well and is recommended only for small networks.

WINS

Windows Internet Name Service (WINS), shown in Figure 14-12, was created to allow clients on different IP subnets to dynamically register and browse the network without sending broadcasts. Clients send unicast packets to the WINS server at a well-known address. The WINS server in turn does a NetBIOS name–to–IP address translation for the clients.

Figure 14-12   *Name Resolution—WINS*

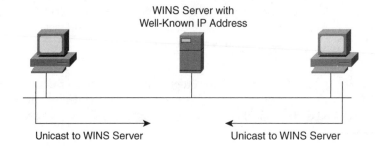

You should remember that, for compatibility with older Windows Networking clients, broadcast name resolution is still turned on by default, even when WINS is configured. WINS is the best method to properly scale a Microsoft network because it cuts back on the inherent broadcasting native to NetBIOS.

DNS

DNS is a common TCP/IP application that provides Internet name–to–IP address translation. Most DNS servers are configured statically, with tables of manually assigned device names associated with manually assigned IP addresses.

WINS provides NetBIOS name–to–IP address translation. It is very similar in function to DNS but uses NetBIOS (rather than Internet) names to form its name/address translation tables. Thus, it can associate a NetBIOS name request with a valid IP address. To reiterate, NetBIOS name–to–IP address translation is important because it allows clients to communicate with each other or with servers without requiring them to have specific IP address knowledge of the destination.

As shown in Figure 14-13, a Windows NT DNS server can be set up to query a WINS server (in this case, itself) for addresses or names that were not entered statically. This is useful in environments where WINS is used to register NetBIOS names and DHCP is used to assign

IP addresses. WINS and DNS work in conjunction with one another to provide fast and effective DNS-to-NetBIOS-to-IP name lookup as needed by the end-user devices. The typical operational steps are as follows:

Step 1   Client gets IP address from DHCP server.

Step 2   Client registers NetBIOS name with WINS server.

Step 3   DNS server queries WINS server for names.

Figure 14-13   *Name Resolution—Internet DNS*

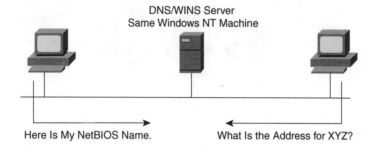

DNS/WINS Server
Same Windows NT Machine

Here Is My NetBIOS Name.   What Is the Address for XYZ?

Domain Models

To effectively scale your network, you should design your Windows network around one of several distinct domain models.

There are four domain models. They are shown in Figures 14-14 through 14-17 and described in the following list. These models follow a hierarchy and can scale to fit into many different-sized networks:

- **Single domain model**—A simple design adequate for small or medium-sized networks.

- **Master domain model**—A master domain (containing users) is trusted by all other domains (containing resources). The master domain trusts no one and retains centralized control over user administration and authentication. The departments or divisions (resource domains) retain control over their own resources.

- **Multiple master domain model**—This method is used for large networks where centralized user or resource management is not feasible. The master domains (users) fully trust each other; the departmental domains (resources) trust each master domain, but not vice versa.

- **Complete trust domain model**—Under this method, there can be distribution of users and resources into many domains that maintain a complete set of two-way trust relationships. This is not a secure method of setting up Windows NT domains, but it allows for administration from many places.

If you create multiple domains, for example, each domain exchanges data with other domains on the network. Trust relationships are a way to gain or grant access to a domain without having to manage each user individually.

Figure 14-14   *Single Domain Model*

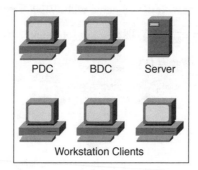

Figure 14-15   *Master Domain Model*

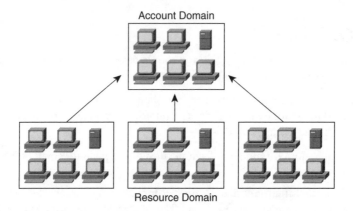

Figure 14-16 *Multiple Master Domain Model*

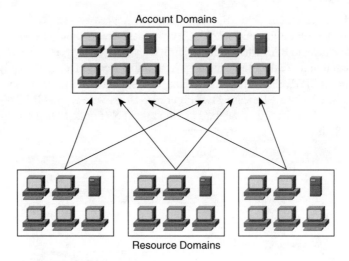

Figure 14-17 *Complete Trust Domain Model*

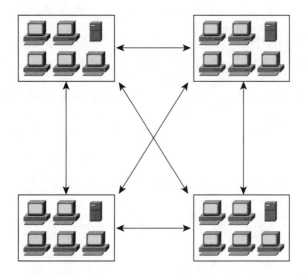

Remote Access Server

Windows NT comes with Microsoft's Remote Access Server (RAS), which is based on the Point-to-Point Protocol (PPP). Cisco access servers should generally be used as an alternative to RAS when higher dial-in density or better performance is required. This is discussed in more detail in Chapter 19, "Remote Access Design." The NT platform supports TCP/IP, IPX, and NetBEUI, as do Cisco products (such as AS5300) starting with Cisco IOS Software Release 11.1. Figure 14-18 shows a typical RAS configuration where a remote set of users use standard dialin via PSTN (Public Switched Telephone Network) to reach the Windows NT RAS server.

Figure 14-18   *Remote Access*

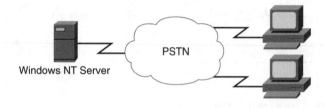

Design Examples

Figure 14-19 shows a small single-domain network using NWLINK (NetBIOS over IPX). The central router is configured with an IPX network number on each interface. Each interface is also configured for IPX type 20 propagation. An access server provides connections for remote clients, and Internet access is provided by a Cisco IPeXchange gateway router. Local hosts are connected through Catalyst switches.

Figure 14-19   *Design Example 1*

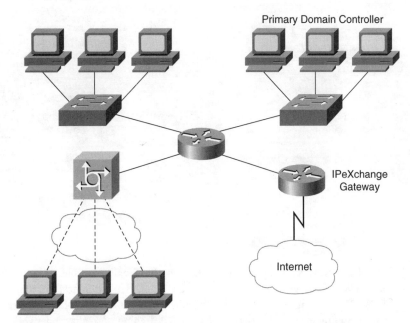

Figure 14-20 shows a medium-sized network using NBT and static name resolution (LMHOSTS). Engineering, Marketing, IS, Sales, and Finance each has its own PDC. Each client in the domain is statically configured with the IP address of its associated PDC. The PDCs, in turn, are configured with the addresses of all the other PDCs, along with the addresses of the clients in their domains. A single WINS server is provided for use by all PDCs to resolve NetBIOS name-to-address mappings. Note that all components are at a single campus; no WAN link is involved.

Figure 14-20   *Design Example 2*

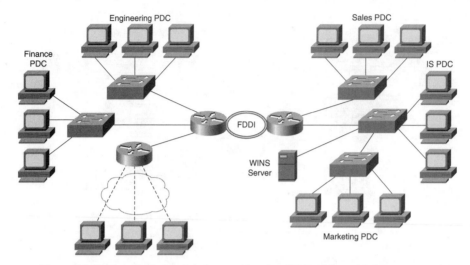

Figure 14-21 shows a large global network using NBT with multiple master domains and replicated WINS servers. Major sites are located in the United States, Europe, and Asia, with a core WAN providing connectivity among all sites. A PDC and WINS server are provided for each area, adding the scalability required when designing such a large network.

Figure 14-21   *Design Example 3*

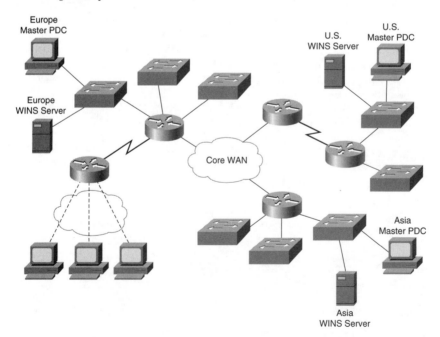

Summary

Microsoft Networking was designed to be user-friendly. Be careful, however: It is not always network-friendly. Key concepts to remember include the fact that NetBIOS is the commonly used session layer protocol and it is not routable. Three transport methods are available for NetBIOS, with TCP/IP (NBT) being the most favorable and scalable. Details such as address assignment and name resolution via WINS servers are very critical in helping eliminate the broadcast mechanisms.

Further, this chapter explored the best design practices that allow efficient deployment of Microsoft Networking based on the available options. In most cases today, NBT is deployed with a hierarchical domain model for maximum scalability.

Chapter Review Questions

1 At what layer does NetBIOS function with respect to the OSI networking model?

2 How are domains created and managed?

3 What various NetBIOS transport methods are available?

4 What IPX packet type does NWLINK require to exchange registration and browsing information?

5 What are the name resolution methods for Windows clients?

6 What is the default name-resolution method, and should it always be left as the default?

7 What is meant by a *master domain*? When is this option useful?

8 What is the function of WINS?

9 What is Microsoft RAS? Is RAS always a preferred design solution?

WAN Design

We're going from the circuit-switched world to a packet world. We all know that it's happening—but why? First, because it costs less for the infrastructure. And second, because you get better network utilization. So for those very fundamental business economics of cost/performance, we will see packet switching prevail. And the beauty of that packet-switched world is that it looks like we have a common protocol called IP that can take us across those smokestacks that created those various businesses called telephony, entertainment, and information.

—C. Michael Armstrong, Chairman and CEO, AT&T

Upon completion of this chapter, you will be able to do the following:

- List common concerns that customers have about WAN designs

- Examine sample customer statements and distinguish issues that affect the choice of WAN designs

- Describe how to design core WAN connectivity to maximize availability and optimize utilization of resources

CHAPTER 15

WAN Design Overview

When designing most wide-area network (WAN) implementations, *reliability* is the most important goal because the WAN is often a part of the backbone of the internetwork. WAN resources are expensive, however. Designing a fully redundant network to maximize availability is a tradeoff to designing a cost-effective network. You need to factor in the cost of downtime whenever making business and technical decisions. Other WAN design issues that you need to consider include the following:

- Latency issues
- Cost of WAN resources
- Amount of traffic that will traverse the WAN
- Which protocols will be allowed on the WAN
- Compatibility with standards of legacy systems
- Simplicity and ease of configuration of your proposed solution
- Support for remote offices and telecommuters

The bottom line is that, if the WAN is nonfunctional, how many people are unable to work and how much revenue is lost during this time? The remaining content of this chapter addresses the issue of WAN reliability.

DESIGN RULE   Reliability in a WAN design is the most important goal.

Optimizing Core WAN Availability

As shown in Figure 15-1, in general, two types of options are available for wide-area networking—dedicated lines or switched connections. Switched connections may be circuit-switched or packet-/cell-switched.

Figure 15-1   *WAN Technology Options*

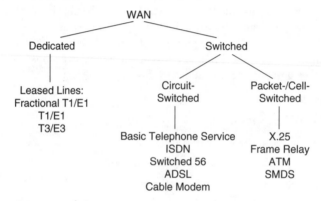

Table 15-1 documents the primary characteristics of the WAN connection options. Chapters 16–20 cover all these options in greater detail.

Table 15-1   *Wan Connection Options*

| | Dedicated Lines | | | Switched Connections | | | | |
	T1	T3	Fractional T1	Frame Relay (Packet-Switched)	X.25 (Packet-Switched)	ATM (Cell-Switched)	SMDS (Cell-Switched)	Dialup
Transmission Speed	1.544 Mbps	45 Mbps	Increments of 64 kbps up to T1 speed	Operates up to T1 speed most commonly but can go higher	Operates up to T1 speed	T1 T3 OC-3 and higher	T1 T3 speeds	28 kbps (without compression) 56 kbps (limited availability) 64–128 kbps (ISDN)
Primary Connectivity Characteristics	Core connectivity between large sites or campuses LAN-to-LAN connectivity	Core connectivity between large sites or campuses LAN-to-LAN connectivity	Core connectivity between medium-sized to large sites or campuses LAN-to-LAN connectivity	Core connectivity between large sites or campuses LAN-to-LAN connectivity	Core connectivity between large sites or campuses LAN-to-LAN connectivity	Core connectivity between large sites or campuses LAN-to-LAN connectivity Client support with LANE (LAN Emulation)	Core connectivity between large sites or campuses LAN-to-LAN connectivity	Connect remote users and mobile users to corporate LANs
Type of Data Transmitted	Data, voice, and occasionally video	Data, voice, and occasionally video	Data, voice, and occasionally video	Data, voice, and occasionally video	Data	Data, voice, and video	Data, occasionally voice and video	Data, occasionally voice and video

continues

Table 15-1 *Wan Connection Options (Continued)*

	Dedicated Lines			Switched Connections				
	T1	T3	Fractional T1	Frame Relay (Packet-Switched)	X.25 (Packet-Switched)	ATM (Cell-Switched)	SMDS (Cell-Switched)	Dialup
Advantages	Pre-established bandwidth Widely deployed Simple configuration	Widely deployed Simple configuration	Widely deployed Simple configuration	Point-to-point Multipoint Widely deployed Can easily increase bandwidth (CIR) as needed Very streamlined (little overhead due to error checking)	Point-to-point End-to-end reliability built in Widely available since the 1970s	Point-to-point Multipoint Class of Service Quality of service	Point-to-point Multipoint configurations	Relatively low bandwidth Connections on demand
Disadvantages	Point-to-point only Expensive if not fully utilized	Point-to-point only Expensive if not fully utilized	Point-to-point only Expensive if not fully utilized	Slow speeds relative to ATM	Slow speeds Older technology developed when WAN lines were lower speed and less reliable Extensive error checking causes slowdowns	Can be complex to troubleshoot	Not widely available or deployed for WAN access Can be complex to troubleshoot	Slow speeds relative to dedicated circuits

Optimizing Core WAN Performance

Goals for designing the WAN core at the micro level should focus on the following three components:

- **Maximization** of throughput over WAN circuits
- **Minimization** of delay over WAN circuits
- **Minimization** of overhead traffic over WAN circuits

Many choices contribute to using the WAN efficiently. These choices involve host applications and protocols, some of which we've already discussed, such as IPX SAP filtering and Cisco IOS software features on the routers. You may or may not be able to change or tune host applications and protocols to make them more internetwork-friendly. A list of items that should be checked to optimize your WAN follows:

- Implement quieter (less network-intensive) applications such as client/server applications.
- Tune protocol window sizes for optimal transport.
- Implement quieter routing protocols that update only when changes occur.
- Use bandwidth on demand so that links are most efficiently utilized.
- Use protocol-prioritization methods so that mission-critical applications get guaranteed bandwidth.
- Use filtering to keep unnecessary traffic off the WAN.
- Use compression to maximize line efficiency.

Agents that yield optimized bandwidth utilization include compression, filtering, bandwidth on demand, window-size tuning, and traffic prioritization. Here are some host protocol-related factors to consider in your design:

- Reliable transport protocols may adjust window size in response to congestion.
- Larger packet size may be more efficient.
- Sending repeated broadcasts can generate excess traffic.
- The unit of recovery may be a large block of data or a single packet.
- Many value-added Cisco IOS features are available to optimize the use of WAN resources in the core. Use smart protocols such as Enhanced IGRP to reduce routing traffic. Use features such as prioritization and compression as appropriate.

Backbone-Routing Protocol Choices

In some internetworks, there may be a requirement that only native IP can be used in the WAN backbone. This *IP-only* requirement may occur because a separate department is responsible for maintaining the backbone, or WAN resources may be leased from an IP service provider, or perhaps you are considering deployment of IP-based QoS. In either case, all other protocols must be encapsulated in IP datagrams and tunneled between sites.

The WAN is easier to manage when IP is the only protocol used in the core. Addressing and configuration issues related to other protocols are avoided. One cost for this simplicity is increased router CPU overhead at the ends of the tunnels. Another cost is the WAN bandwidth needed to accommodate the additional bandwidth overhead of encapsulated datagrams.

As shown in Figure 15-2, you can use Cisco's generic routing encapsulation (GRE) to tunnel protocols through IP. In many designs, it is becoming more and more common to tunnel AppleTalk or IPX across an IP core network.

Figure 15-2 *GRE Tunneling*

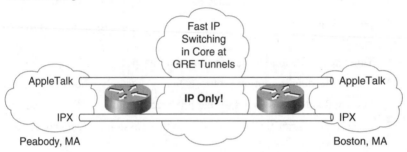

A good rule of thumb for GRE tunneling is to use it for non-IP protocols across the core if IP is the predominant protocol in your network. Certainly, although some tunneling overhead at the edges will occur, the final result is that you need only to have a single-protocol administration in the core. Furthermore, the technique of GRE tunneling across an *IP-only* backbone is extremely useful for QoS purposes. Many of the queuing mechanisms are defeated by non-IP protocols that are FIFO-based. So, the trade-off for minor performance degradation on the edge tunnel routers is the capability to implement QoS.

NOTE Cisco IOS 11.1 and higher support fast switching over GRE tunnels.

DESIGN RULE Use a single-protocol IP backbone if IP traffic predominates.

Summary

When designing WAN implementations, reliability is often the most important goal. However, issues such as latency and availability are also very important. Design options such as whether to choose leased lines, packet- or cell-switched, or circuit-switched network architectures are important decisions you will need to make based on the user's technical and business requirements. Designing a fully redundant network to maximize availability is a trade-off with designing a cost-effective network. Chapters 16–20 cover all the WAN options discussed in this chapter in greater detail.

Chapter Review Questions

1   Name the design issues associated with WANs.

2   What Cisco IOS software features would be options for deployment in WAN environments to improve performance?

3   What is an advantage of using ATM in your network design?

4   What is a disadvantage of using X.25 in your network design?

5   What are the three goals for designing the WAN core?

If you see a company that is investing in circuit switches, then you know immediately that it is a company that is investing in the past.

—William T. Esrey, CEO of Sprint

Upon completion of this chapter, you will be able to do the following:

- Identify the components required for leased line connections
- Compare different leased line topology methods
- Describe different encapsulation methods and the benefits of each

CHAPTER 16

Design Using Dedicated Lines

Leased lines are a tried-and-true method for interconnecting networks across a wide area. They are deployed heavily today, with speeds now reaching OC-48 (2.4 Gbps) and higher in many carrier networks. Whether you use high- or low-speed links, there are leased line topology methods and encapsulation methods that have different benefits for the problems you are trying to solve.

This chapter discusses the design basics of leased lines, including connections, usage, architecture, and encapsulation methods. All these areas are important as you ensure that your "Layer 3 and higher" design will be optimized in your Layer 1 and Layer 2 infrastructure.

Leased Line Overview

When leased line connections are made, a router port is required for each connection, along with either a separate or integrated CSU/DSU (channel service unit/digital service unit) as well as the circuit from the service provider, as illustrated in Figure 16-1.

Figure 16-1 *Leased Line Connections*

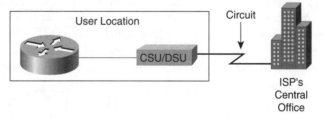

Here, the circuit from the Central Office (CO) is terminated on the CSU/DSU and then carried via V.35 into the router's WAN port. The cost of dedicated-line solutions can become significant when deployed to connect many sites, which is especially true if full meshing is desired. If full meshing is required among *n* nodes, for example, you will require $(n \times [n - 1])/2$ circuits, which can be expensive. The number of circuits required for a full mesh for 10 nodes, for example, is as follows:

$$(10 \times [10 - 1])/2 = (10 \times 9)/2 = 45 \text{ links}$$

NOTE	Several variations of leased lines now exist. Channelized interfaces do not require external CSU/DSU equipment, for example, because they have this functionality built in. It is also possible to have a single T3 or T1 Channelized card at a central site fanning out to dozens of field units. Packet of Sonet (POSIP) is another leased service that does not require external CSU/DSU equipment.

Dedicated leased lines are generally considered as reasonable design options for the core WAN. As mentioned, this design requires a router port and circuit for each remote site. The important thing to consider is the reliability of your carrier's network, especially when designing core network links. In many cases, you will want to negotiate an SLA (service level agreement) based on your business requirements. The bottom line is that SLAs on leased lines are all about uptime—how often a circuit goes down relative to the length of time that it is up.

NOTE	Leased lines have low latency, as well as fast error and fault detection.

Architecture

It is often too expensive to design a full-mesh WAN core. Instead, a partial mesh that provides for multiple equal-cost paths between sites can be used. The definition of equal-cost paths depends on the routing protocol. Ideally, two sites should be directly connected to minimize delay. Multiple-hop paths can be put between sites that generate less traffic, if your budget cannot provide for a full mesh.

Figure 16-2 demonstrates a network that implements multiple paths in the core WAN. The sites that have high traffic between them (Campus A to B, Campus A to C, Campus D to B, and Campus D to C) have equal-cost paths with direct links; the sites that have low traffic between them (Campus A to Campus D and Campus B to Campus C) do not, and therefore, require a router hop via an intermediate router. The result is a savings in network-circuit link costs.

Figure 16-2 *Plan Multiple Paths in the Core WAN*

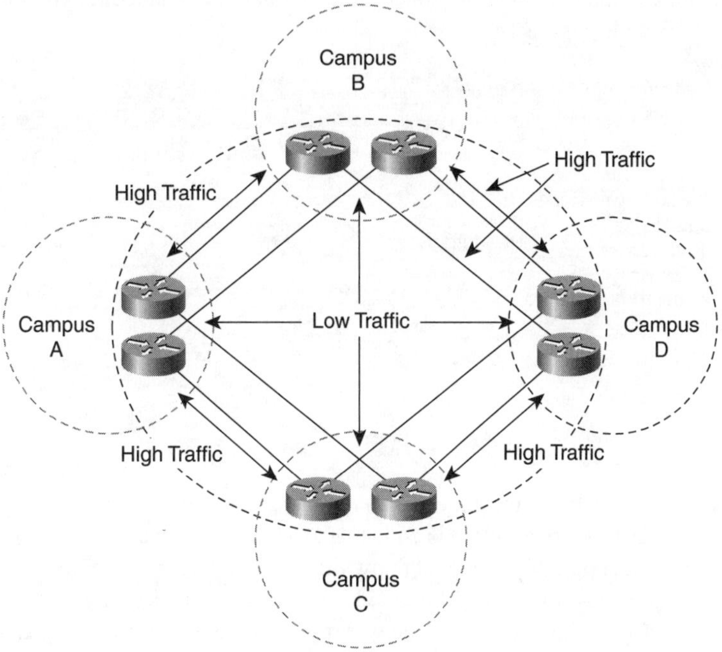

NOTE   As discussed in Chapter 2, "Hierarchical Design," whenever possible, it is recommended to keep all the bandwidths consistent across the core WAN. This helps to optimize routing decisions, and, in the event of a circuit failure, service degradation will not be noticed by the end users. More and more, the requirement for "99.999% uptime" is becoming more prevalent in large internetworks and, simply put, users will not accept anything except full service levels, especially at the core layer.

DESIGN RULE Although parallel paths support load balancing, they also imply instant convergence. This is true because both routes are cached as equal-cost paths, so no routing protocol convergence is required. Many designs use this and maintain less than 50% load on trunks to permit this feature.

In an example of a typical redundant hierarchical WAN design, two routers are placed at headquarters, one router is placed at each regional office, and one router is at a branch site, as illustrated in Figure 16-3.

Figure 16-3 *Typical Redundant Hierarchical WAN*

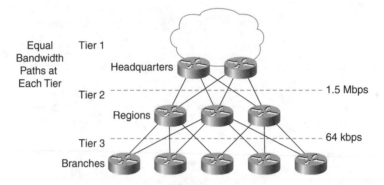

Here, each branch site is connected to two regional offices. (This technique is called *dual homing.*) Each regional office is connected to both headquarters' routers. Both links from a remote site should be of equal bandwidth. Both links from a regional office should also be of equal bandwidth. Equal-bandwidth links allow equal-cost load balancing. Further, equal-bandwidth links means no degradation of network performance in the event of a single path failure. The net result is that every remote site has four equal-cost paths to reach headquarters.

Encapsulation Methods

Four different serial-line encapsulations are widely deployed and each one offers certain benefits:

- **SDLC**—SDLC supports a variety of link types and topologies. It can be used with point-to-point and multipoint links, bounded and unbounded media, half-duplex and full-duplex transmission facilities, and circuit-switched and packet-switched networks. Often used in SNA environments.

- **HDLC**—HDLC is a connectionless datagram delivery mechanism with minimal overhead and supports the AutoInstall feature of IOS. Used in Cisco-specific networks over reliable media.

- **PPP**—An open standard, PPP supports many protocols, including IP, Novell's Internetwork Packet Exchange (IPX), AppleTalk, and DECnet. Often used for dialup and ISDN connections and for mixed vendor WANs.

- **LAPB**—LAPB is a connection-oriented protocol which ensures that frames are correctly ordered and error free. Often used for unreliable media and X.25 support.

All four encapsulations were originally derived from Synchronous Data Link Connection (SDLC) and share a common frame format. SDLC encapsulation is used in SNA environments and it is discussed more in upcoming chapters.

As shown in Figure 16-4, the SDLC frame has six different fields, each of which is designed for a special purpose.

- **Flag**—Indicates the beginning of the frame and is set to a hexadecimal pattern of 7F.

- **Address**—A 1- or 2-byte field to address the end station in multidrop environments.

- **Control**—Indicates whether the frame is an information, supervisory, or unnumbered frame type. It also contains specific function codes.

- **Data**—The encapsulated data.

- **FCS**—The frame-check sequence.

- **Flag**—The trailing 7E flag identifier.

Figure 16-4 *SDLC Encapsulation*

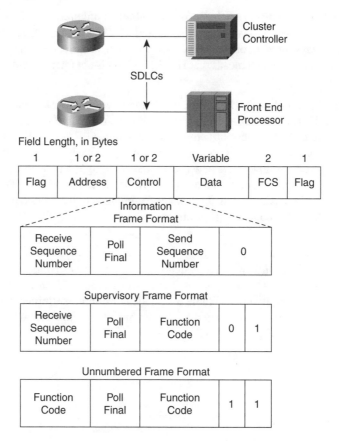

HDLC

High-Level Data Link Control (HDLC) is Cisco's default encapsulation for serial lines. This implementation is very streamlined. There is no windowing or flow control and only point-to-point connections are allowed (no multipoint). Figure 16-5 shows a very common use for HDLC, namely Cisco-to-Cisco point-to-point connectivity.

Figure 16-5 *Cisco's HDLC Encapsulation*

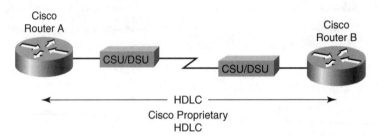

Here, two routers that are point-to-point are both configured by default to HDLC encapsulation. This is a very simple setup and widely used. With Cisco HDLC, the Address field is always set to all ones. Furthermore, a 2-byte proprietary Type code is inserted after the Control field, which means that HDLC framing is not interoperable with other vendors' equipment.

Another benefit of using HDLC encapsulation in your network is the support of an IOS feature called AutoInstall. AutoInstall enables you to configure a new router automatically and dynamically with very little to no human interaction. The AutoInstall procedure involves connecting a new Cisco router to a network where an existing router is preconfigured, turning on the new router, and enabling it with a configuration file that is automatically downloaded from a Trivial File Transfer Protocol (TFTP) server. You can learn more about AutoInstall at www.cisco.com/univercd/cc/td/doc/product/software/ios112/112cg_cr/1cbook/1cclkstr.htm.

NOTE   Many vendors, including Cisco Systems, use some form of HDLC framing, but often do not support the full HDLC protocol. The exact specifics of each vendor's implementation of HDLC is generally not available for public consumption. Suffice it to say that Cisco-HDLC, for example, is optimized for use within a Cisco-to-Cisco environment and is subject to change if ever required.

PPP

The Point-to-Point Protocol (PPP) is a standard serial-line encapsulation method and is defined in RFC 1332 and RFC 1661. As depicted in Figure 16-6, PPP includes a Protocol type field along with a Link Control Protocol. This protocol can, among other things, check for link quality during connection establishment. In addition, there is support for authentication through the Password Authentication Protocol (PAP) and the Challenge Handshake Authentication Protocol (CHAP). PPP is therefore used for dialup and ISDN connections.

NOTE   PPP is often the only choice in mixed-vendor WAN point-to-point network connectivity (for example, T1 links). To have a Bay BCN router connect to a Cisco 2500 access router, for example, you would most likely configure the link for PPP.

Figure 16-6 *PPP Encapsulation*

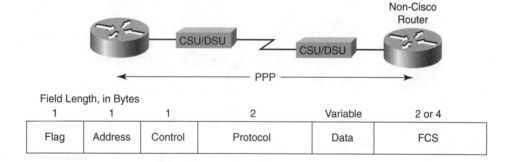

NOTE   PPP is a standards-based (RFC-based) serial-line encapsulation.

LAPB

LAPB encapsulation is recommended for unreliable media because it provides a more efficient way to recover from frequent errors at the link level. For reliable media such as fiber-optic transmission systems (FOTS), it is more efficient to use a stripped down data-link protocol, such as PPP, and let a reliable transport protocol such as Transmission Control Protocol (TCP) recover errors. Because X.25 is inherently reliable, it is a good data link over unreliable links. Figure 16-7 shows a typical use of X.25 over satellite links.

Figure 16-7 *LAPB over Satellite Links*

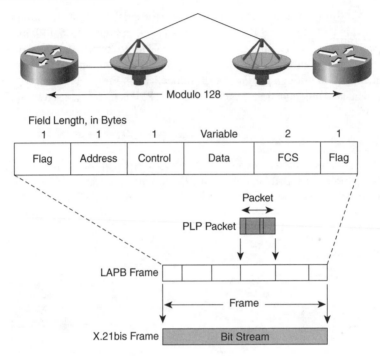

LAPB is reliable, supports analog lines and link compression, and provides a data link for X.25 access. LAPB should be used over unreliable links.

LAPB Modulo Types

Cisco IOS software supports Modulo 128 LAPB and Modulo 8. As shown in Figure 16-7, you should use Modulo 128 for higher throughput over high-bandwidth or high-delay media. Some public data networks support Modulo 128 LAPB for X.25 access.

Modulo 8 (basic mode) is widely available, because it is required for all standard LAPB implementations and is sufficient for most links. Modulo 128 (extended mode) can achieve greater throughput on high-speed links that have a low error rate (some satellite links, for example) by increasing the number of frames that can be transmitted before waiting for acknowledgment (as configured by the LAPB window parameter, k). By its design, LAPB's k parameter can be at most one less than the operating modulo. Modulo 8 links can typically send seven frames before an acknowledgment must be received; modulo 128 links can set k to a value as large as 127. By default, LAPB links use the basic mode with a window of 7.

Summary

Leased lines of various speeds are widely deployed in enterprise networks everywhere. As a designer, you need to understand the connection types, bandwidth selection criteria, architecture, and encapsulation methods. In many network design projects, you will often need to interface with the "Layer 2" organization, which will determine what technologies to deploy. You will need to make sure to pay attention to overhead issues (that is, when to choose PPP versus HDLC, and so on) and make sure the Layer 2 choices fit the rest of your network design. With these building blocks, you have the transport for your "Layer 3" design to rest on.

Chapter Review Questions

1 What is required to install a leased line connection?

2 From a traffic-design perspective, why should both links from a regional office should be of equal bandwidth?

3 Which four different serial-line encapsulations are widely deployed?

4 What is the default encapsulation for Cisco point-to-point circuits?

5 When is PPP most often used?

6 What is an advantage to using modulo 128?

The 21st century is the century of visual communications, like the 20th century was the century of voice communications.

—Joseph P. Nacchio, Chairman and CEO, Qwest Communications International, Inc.

Upon completion of this chapter, you will be able to do the following:

- Understand Frame Relay terminology

- Describe the components and terminology used in Frame Relay networks

- Compare different topology options available in Frame Relay designs, recognizing the costs and the benefits of each

CHAPTER 17

Frame Relay Design

Frame Relay is widely used in many large enterprise internetworks. The motivation for using a packet-switched WAN architecture such as Frame Relay is to save money and reduce latency, two characteristics that make Frame Relay one of the most popular WAN connection options. As a design engineer, you will certainly be involved in a Frame Relay network design project sooner or later. This chapter discusses the components and terminology used in Frame Relay networks, and the different topology options available in Frame Relay designs. This chapter discusses Frame Relay services, including data-link connection identifier (DLCI), Local Management Interface (LMI), and Inverse Address Resolution Protocol (Inverse ARP). Furthermore, Appendix C, "Design and Implementation Guide: Frame Relay," contains useful information and should be used as a supplement to the material covered in this chapter.

Frame Relay Overview

Figure 17-1 shows a typical partial-mesh WAN comprised of point-to-point circuits. To provide redundancy, each router has several physical serial interfaces, and each site is connected to several other sites. To move data from Chicago to Los Angeles, three router hops are required. Because each hop introduces delay (both a router forwarding delay and the inherent High-Level Data Link Control [HDLC] circuit delay), you can reduce the latency by connecting all the sites in a full mesh, but this will increase the cost.

Figure 17-1   *Cost and Latency of a Leased-Line Point-to-Point WAN*

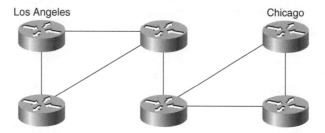

Frame Relay was envisioned as a cost-effective alternative to leased-line point-to-point WAN designs. As shown in Figure 17-2, each site can be connected to every other site by a virtual circuit (VC), creating a full logical mesh of Frame Relay VCs. Further, each router needs only one physical interface to the carrier. Latency in the cloud is seen by the router as just the time it takes to travel from one site to another. You still could design this network with Frame Relay in a partial mesh, and you would very likely see substantial cost savings over a point-to-point leased-line, partial-mesh design. In Frame Relay partial-mesh solutions, however, you will likely see higher round-trip delays because Frame Relay is inherently slower than point-to-point leased lines.

Figure 17-2   *Frame Relay: Cost-Effective Connectivity*

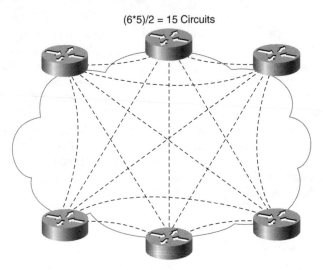

(6*5)/2 = 15 Circuits

NOTE   The actual latency in the Frame Relay cloud depends on the underlying technology. Some Frame Relay services operate over cell switching or ATM, which makes the latency very low. Note, however, that Frame Relay still has higher latency than leased-line services. Latency in the leased-line example is a function of cumulative circuit distance (remember latency ≈8 ms per 1000 fiber miles) and the number of router hops.

The number of PVCs required for a full mesh is $[n \times (n-1)]/2$ where n is the number of connections to the Frame Relay network. It is interesting to note that $n-1$ equals the number of permanent virtual circuits (PVCs) that are active on any router interface. This is an important consideration when you consider broadcast traffic, such as routing updates generated by the router.

Frame Relay is implemented often as a carrier-provided service, (that is, MCI Worldcom and AT&T), but can also be used for private networks. Examples of commonly deployed Frame Relay switches, both in public and private networks, are the Cisco BPX and Nortel BNX platforms.

Frame Relay is a packet-switched data network designed to be simpler and faster than X.25. Frame Relay has none of the reliability features or the complexity of X.25, and the inherent simplicity of Frame Relay is due to the vastly improved error rates with fiber-optic transmission systems (FOTS).

Frame Relay defines the connection between customer data terminal equipment (DTE) and carrier data circuit-terminating equipment (DCE). Typically, the DTE is a router, and the DCE is a Frame Relay switch. Other examples of DTE devices are terminals, personal computers, routers, and bridges. The purpose of DCE equipment is to provide clocking and switching services in a network, which are the devices that actually transmit data through the WAN.

Frame Relay access is most commonly provided at 56 kbps, 64 kbps, or 1.544 Mbps, although some providers offer $N \times T - 1$ or up to T3 speed (45 Mbps). Examples of Frame Relay DTEs are routers, Frame Relay Access Devices (FRADs), or IBM front-end processors (FEPs). A FRAD is a device that provides only the function of connecting to the Frame Relay network, it does not provide a feature-rich IOS as in a router. FRADs generally connect one particular kind of system to the Frame Relay network (for example, a PC or a LAN segment). Chapter 21, "SNA Design Overview," discusses FEPs in more detail. Figure 17-3 illustrates each type of Frame Relay DTE.

If basic connectivity to a Frame Relay network is all that is required, a FRAD would make sense; if you need to connect different types of LANs and need features such as routing protocols and filters, a router would make more sense.

Figure 17-3   *Frame Relay Access Devices*

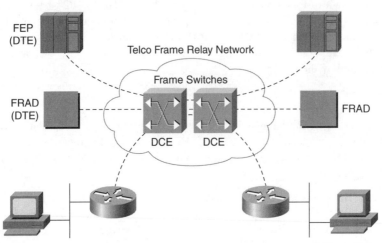

Frame Relay Services: DLCIs

The typical unit of Frame Relay service is the PVC. A PVC is an unreliable data link and is identified by a data-link connection identifier (DLCI). DLCI values typically are assigned by the Frame Relay service provider (for example, the telephone company). Frame Relay DLCIs have local significance, which means that the values themselves are not unique in the Frame Relay WAN. Two DTE devices connected by a virtual circuit, for example, may use a different DLCI value to refer to the same connection.

The DLCI contract between the customer and the carrier specifies the committed information rate (CIR) provided by the carrier. The CIR (in bits per second) is defined as the rate at which the ingress and egress (incoming and outgoing) Frame Relay ports transfer information to the end system under normal conditions. Any data stream above the CIR will be marked discard eligible (DE) by the Frame Relay switch. In the case of Frame Relay cloud congestion, DE packets will always be dropped before non-DE traffic. If you notice much DE traffic (and drops) on a Frame Relay DLCI of your network, for example, it may be time to consider increasing your CIR on that circuit to decrease the likelihood of the carrier dropping your traffic.

TIP

You can observe the number of DE packets on your PVC by issuing the **show frame pvc** command on the router. This is a useful technique to use in isolating performance problems in the Frame Relay cloud.

In Figure 17-4, a CIR of 56 kbps is defined on the PVC between Router A and Router B. In this example, the circuit's access speed could range anywhere from 56 kbps up to DS3, provided the carrier's Frame Relay service supports that line rate. Router A's DLCI is 99; Router B has a DLCI of 96. The PVC defined between the two routers becomes a logical circuit through which data will pass.

Figure 17-4   *Frame Relay Service and Circuits*

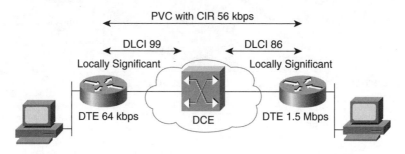

NOTE   A DLCI is locally significant between the router and the switch it directly attaches to. Also, the access circuit speed rate for Frame Relay ranges all the way from 56 kbps to 45 Mbps. Sprint offers up to T3 (45 Mbps) frame port, whereas MCI Worldcom often offers up to 12 Mbps maximum port speed access.

The Frame Relay switching table consists of four entries, two of which represent the incoming port and DLCI, and the other two represent the outgoing port and DLCI. The DLCI could therefore be remapped as it passes through each switch. Furthermore, the fact that the port reference can be changed is why the DLCI is "locally significant." Figure 17-5 shows a typical Frame Relay switching table. Here, the switching table consists of entries for all locally attached DLCIs and ports. Essentially, the Frame Relay switch device has static frame mappings that route DLCIs from one interface to another interface.

Figure 17-5 *Frame Relay Operation—Switching*

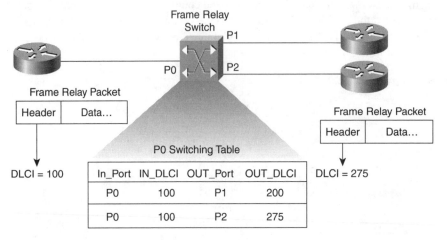

NOTE	An excellent resource for Frame Relay tips can be found at www.mot.com/networking/ frame-relay/resources.html.

Frame Relay Services: LMI

Frame Relay signaling reports the status of PVCs. The original Frame Relay signaling specification is called the Link Management Interface (LMI). LMI was proposed by the Frame Relay Forum. Subsequently, the American National Standards Institute (ANSI) and the International Telecommunication Union Telecommunication Standardization Sector (ITU-T) have standardized slightly different versions of LMI. (ITU-T was formerly called the CCITT.) As shown in Figure 17-6, LMI is passed between the switch and the router. LMI carries PVC status information, and also serves as a keepalive mechanism between the router and switch.

Figure 17-6 *Frame Relay Operation—LMI*

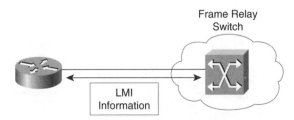

Cisco supports all three versions of LMI (ANSI T1.617 Annex D, ITU-T Q.933 Annex A, and Frame Relay Forum LMI). The Frame Relay Forum version is the default. For compatibility, you must use whichever one is specified by the Frame Relay service provider. As of IOS Release 11.2, the routers autosense the LMI type being used by the Frame Relay switch. This feature proves quite valuable when you are unsure about the configured LMI type on a switch.

NOTE   You can find out more about Frame Relay standards at www.frforum.com.

Router Interaction

RFC 1490 describes an encapsulation method for carrying network interconnect traffic over a Frame Relay backbone. It covers aspects for both bridging and routing, as well as a simple fragmentation procedure for carrying large frames over a Frame Relay network with a smaller maximum transmission unit (MTU).

NOTE   You can find RFC 1490 at ftp://ftp.isi.edu/in-notes/rfc1490.txt.

RFC 1490 defines a header that includes the Network Level Protocol ID (NLPID) field for identifying the upper-layer protocol encapsulated in the Frame Relay header. The NLPID field is administered by ISO and contains values for different protocols including IP, Connectionless Network Protocol (CLNP), and IEEE Subnetwork Access Protocol (SNAP).

Because the NLPID numbering space is limited, not all protocols have specific NLPID values assigned to them. When packets of such protocols are routed over Frame Relay networks, they are sent using the NLPID that indicates a SNAP header follows. The SNAP header specifies the upper-layer protocol contained in the packet. This is analogous in function to an Ethernet frame that has a SNAP header.

RFC 1490 also specifies how to dynamically resolve a protocol address. Address resolution can be accomplished using the standard Address Resolution Protocol (ARP) encapsulated within a SNAP-encoded Frame Relay packet. Inverse ARP is also supported for finding the protocol address when a DLCI is known. (Inverse ARP is discussed in further detail in the section titled "Inverse ARP.")

The router next-hop address determined from the routing table must be resolved to a Frame Relay DLCI. The resolution is done through a data structure called a *Frame Relay map*. This data structure may be statically configured in the router, or the Inverse ARP feature can be used for automatic setup of the map. Figure 17-7 shows a typical example of a Frame Relay map configuration.

Figure 17-7   *Frame Relay Mapping*

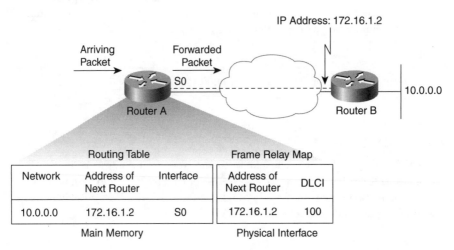

By way of analogy, Frame Relay mapping of logical (for example, IP) addresses to DLCIs is similar to the ARP operation in Ethernet. So, somehow this mapping must be set up. This setup can be done statically with the Cisco IOS software configuration commands. Example 17-1 shows the configuration for Router A in Figure 17-7.

Example 17-1   *Setting Up a Frame Relay Map*

```
Router A
interface serial 0
encapsulation frame-relay
frame-relay map ip 172.16.1.2 100 broadcast
```

You may ask, "How do I know what to use for a DLCI value?" The answer is: The Frame Relay service provider will tell you. When this information is provided, however, it may be terms of a geographic location; the person doing the router configuration must relate that to an IP address. As the next section shows, we can also get this mapping done by the Inverse ARP protocol.

A Frame Relay map specifies a DLCI that will carry a specific protocol and network host. In this example, an IP address (172.16.1.2) is mapped to a DLCI (100). Other Frame Relay maps can be defined to carry AppleTalk, VINES, IPX, and so on.

Inverse ARP

The Inverse ARP mechanism allows the router to automatically build the Frame Relay map, as illustrated in Figure 17-8. The router learns the DLCIs that are in use from the switch during the initial LMI exchange. The router then sends an Inverse ARP request to each DLCI for each protocol configured on the interface if the protocol is supported. The return information from the Inverse ARP is then used to build its Frame Relay map.

Figure 17-8   *Inverse ARP*

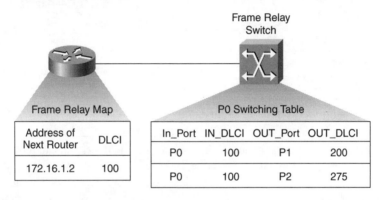

TIP	Often, Inverse ARP is used when many remote devices are all coming to a centralized hub location. This makes the hub design and configuration very simple. However, the "cost" of using Inverse ARP rather than static mapping is ease of troubleshooting. Because the remote DLCIs are dynamically (rather than statically) defined, they are subject to change and subject to error, which could potentially put your network at risk. A good documentation strategy must be adopted when implementing an Inverse ARP design.

Interaction with Routing Protocols

When doing a Frame Relay design, you must consider the interaction with the routing protocol. Distance vector routing protocols, such as RIP and IGRP, enforce the split-horizon rule. This rule prevents information learned at an interface from being advertised back out that interface, even though the information was learned over a different virtual circuit. Figure 17-9 shows the case where split horizon prevents network 10.0.0.0 and network 12.0.0.0 from being advertised out the same interface where they were learned.

Figure 17-9   *Split Horizon's Interaction with Routing Protocols*

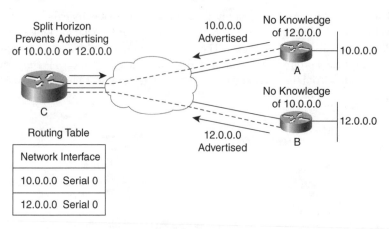

TIP	Because split horizon may not be desirable in all situations, you can turn off split horizon for IP on Frame Relay interfaces. Note, however, that you cannot turn off split horizon for IPX RIP or AppleTalk RTMP. In these cases, you need to run EIGRP because it can turn off split horizon for these two protocols. The other choice is to use point-to-point subinterfaces. This will solve the split-horizon issue because the interfaces are no longer multipoint. Subinterfaces are discussed in more detail later in this chapter.

Network Types

Routers connected by a mesh of Frame Relay circuits can be modeled as a network or subnet. However, the Frame Relay network, like most WANs, is based on star topologies, and does not support one-to-any broadcasting. To simulate a broadcast LAN, the Frame Relay network is configured as a full mesh of VCs between router peers. Every broadcast is copied to every peer. This configuration is known as the nonbroadcast multiaccess (NBMA) model. A multiaccess model implies that all routers are configured as one logical subnet, so the Frame Relay topology is very much like that of a LAN. Copying broadcasts has three major impacts:

* The route processor must copy each broadcast.
* Broadcasts must traverse each virtual circuit.
* All VCs must traverse the same access link, causing an overall performance issue (number of the DLCIs multiplied by the number of broadcasts) on the access link.

All these factors add up to a potential for router and network performance degradation. If a router has to send out 2000 IPX SAPs across the Frame Relay network to 10 peers, for example, the router must broadcast the equivalent of 10×2000, or 20,000 SAPs. This process is very CPU and network bandwidth intensive. To remedy this problem, a special queue known as the *Frame Relay broadcast queue* was created.

The Frame Relay broadcast queue is managed independently of the normal interface queue. It has its own buffers and a configurable service rate. A broadcast queue is given a maximum transmission rate (throughput) limit measured in bytes per second and packets per second. The queue is serviced to ensure that only this maximum is provided. The broadcast queue has priority when transmitting at a rate below the configured maximum, and hence has a guaranteed minimum bandwidth allocation. The two transmission rate limits are intended to avoid flooding the interface with broadcasts. The actual limit in any second is the first rate limit that is reached.

DESIGN RULE Create a broadcast queue for a specified interface to hold broadcast traffic that has been replicated for transmission on multiple DLCIs using the **frame-relay broadcast-queue** interface configuration command.

Figure 17-10 shows a typical NBMA network setup for Frame Relay.

Figure 17-10 *NBMA Network Type*

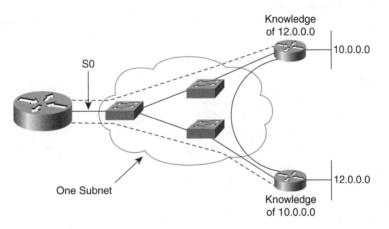

Knowledge
of 12.0.0.0
10.0.0.0

S0

One Subnet

12.0.0.0
Knowledge
of 10.0.0.0

Subinterfaces

Subinterfaces are a feature of Cisco IOS software that makes Frame Relay configuration and scaling much easier. The capability to forward traffic to multiple logical interfaces representing the same physical interface is also called *virtual circuit routing*.

With subinterface configuration, each PVC maps to a different network or subnet. The result is that Frame Relay works like several point-to-point links, and is therefore no longer mapped to a LAN.

As shown in Figure 17-11, Router A has multiple logical interfaces (subinterfaces) defined on its physical interface s0. Because each of these subinterfaces maps to a separate subnet, there are no split-horizon problems.

Figure 17-11 *Subinterfaces*

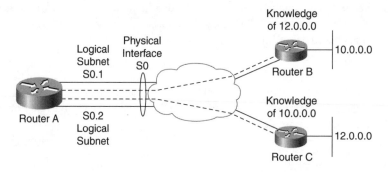

Example 17-2 shows the configuration for all three routers shown in Figure 17-11.

Example 17-2 *Configuring Subinterfaces*

```
Router A
!
int s0
encapsulation frame-relay
no ip address
frame-relay lmi-type ansi
!
int s0.1
ip address 150.100.1.1 255.255.255.252
frame-relay interface-dlci 100 broadcast
!
int s0.2
ip address 150.100.1.5 255.255.255.252
frame-relay interface-dlci 200 broadcast
!
Router B
!
int s0
encapsulation frame-relay
no ip address
frame-relay lmi-type ansi
!
int s0.1
ip address 150.100.1.2 255.255.255.252
```

Example 17-2   *Configuring Subinterfaces (Continued)*

```
frame-relay interface-dlci 150 broadcast
!

Router C
!
int s0
encapsulation frame-relay
no ip address
frame-relay lmi-type ansi
!
int s0.1
ip address 150.100.1.6 255.255.255.252
frame-relay interface-dlci 250 broadcast
!
```

Topology Options

Several Frame Relay design topology options exist that allow deployment of the NBMA or the subinterface model as required to meet the business objectives of the design.

As shown in Figure 17-12, in the full-mesh NBMA design, the number of PVCs is based on the $n \times (n-1) / 2$ rule, where there are 6 PVCs, 1 subnet, and the number of hops from Router A to Router B is 1.

Figure 17-12   *NBMA Using Full Mesh*

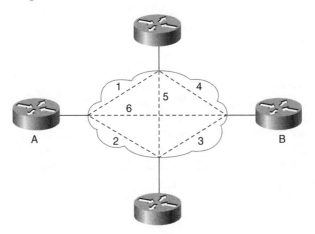

As Figure 17-12 illustrates, because we have 4 routers that require a full mesh, we need $4 \times (4-1) / 2 = 6$ PVCs. This rule means the full-mesh design will not scale well because of the large number of PVCs that may be required. As discussed earlier, there is also an issue with this design because of the burden of broadcast replication. In addition, routing protocols such as EIGRP may be unstable with older router hardware in this design due to the processor power required to process so many redundant paths. With some of the faster 75xx RSP4 and 7200 NPE 200 platforms, however, this issue is not as crucial anymore.

Subinterfaces Using Full Mesh

In the design in Figure 17-13, using full mesh, each PVC is mapped to a separate subnet. Using subinterfaces means that the design will require a subnet for each PVC, and the allocation of IP address (scaling) issues apply. Here, we need 6 PVCs built; therefore, we need 6 IP networks. The number of hops from Router A to Router B is 1. This topology would be more stable for routing protocols.

Figure 17-13 *Subinterfaces Using Full Mesh*

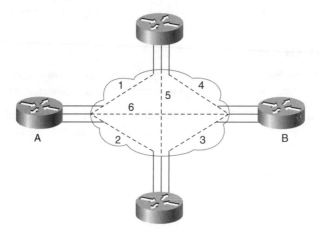

DESIGN RULE For the WAN links, you should always use a 255.255.255.252 mask because you need only two hosts for the link. From a design perspective, this conserves IP address space and reserves a block of addresses solely for WAN links. For a given Class C address, for example, you can create up to 64 networks for serial links—that is, 161.21.4.0, 161.21.4.4, 161.21.4.8, 161.21.4.12, and so on, all sharing a 255.255.255.252 subnet mask.

Subinterfaces Using Hub-and-Spoke

As shown in Figure 17-14, in the hub-and-spoke topology, a group of smaller remote sites is connected to a central hub site. This design uses 3 PVCs, and 3 subnets, and the number of hops between Router A and Router B is 2.

Figure 17-14   *Subinterfaces Using Hub-and-Spoke*

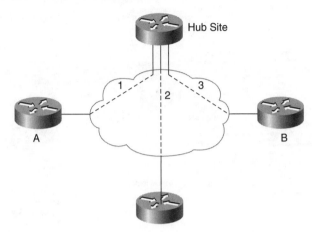

Servers needed throughout the organization are generally deployed at the hub site. Little, if any, direct communication is required between the remote sites (characteristic of this design approach). Any communication that does occur requires a hop through the hub site. Generally speaking, this design maps well to the business model employed by most organizations and is therefore commonly deployed in many enterprise networks. This is because in most organizations, the majority of network traffic comes from the remote access sites (branches) to the main sites (regional office or headquarters) rather than between remote offices.

DDR for PVC Backup

Dial backup (using the **interface backup dialer0** command) is not generally recommended for backing up a single PVC, because this technique is used to provide backup for the full frame port. Rather, dial-on-demand routing (DDR) is generally recommended for this task, specifically for backing up the spokes of a hub-and-spoke network design.

To use DDR to back up a PVC, you create a floating static route to the destination. To create the floating static, you need to make sure that the static route has a greater administrative distance than the dynamic routing protocol. The floating static route is used only if the dynamic route goes away. In Figure 17-15, we are running with IGRP with an administrative distance of 100.

Figure 17-15   *DDR as Backup for Frame Relay*

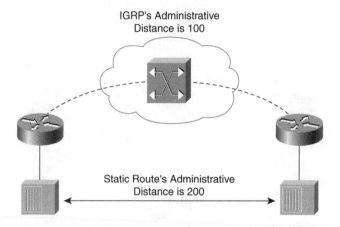

If the IGRP route disappears because of a Frame Relay failure, the floating static administrative distance of 150 "drops" into the routing table and the circuit is used to maintain network connectivity. For example, this configuration would resemble Example 17-3:

Example 17-3   *Configuration for Figure 17-15*

```
ROUTER1# (router on the left)
!
hostname ROUTER1
!
username ROUTER2 password same
isdn switch-type basic-dms100
!
interface Ethernet 0
ip address 172.16.15.1 255.255.255.0
!
interface serial 0
ip address 172.16.24.129 255.255.255.128
encapsulation FRAME-RELAY
frame-relay local-dlci 106
frame-relay map IP 172.16.24.130 102 broadcast
!
interface BRI0
description Backup ISDN for frame-relay
ip address 172.16.12.1 255.255.255.0
encapsulation PPP
dialer idle-timeout 240
dialer wait-for-carrier-time 60
dialer map IP 172.16.12.2 name ROUTER2 broadcast 14152728032
ppp authentication chap
dialer-group 1
isdn spid1 12125267013 5267013
isdn spid2 12125267014 5267014
```

Example 17-3   *Configuration for Figure 17-15 (Continued)*

```
!
router igrp 1
network 172.16.0.0
!
ip route 172.16.16.0 255.255.255.0 172.16.12.2 150 <--Floating static route
!
access-list 101 deny   igrp 0.0.0.0 255.255.255.255 0.0.0.0 255.255.255.255
access-list 101 permit ip 0.0.0.0 255.255.255.255 0.0.0.0 255.255.255.255
dialer-list 1 LIST 101
!

ROUTER2#(router on the right)
!
hostname ROUTER2
!
username ROUTER1 password same
isdn switch-type basic-dms100
!
interface Ethernet 0
ip address 172.16.16.1 255.255.255.0
!
interface Serial 0
ip address 172.16.24.130 255.255.255.128
encapsulation FRAME-RELAY
frame-relay local-dlci 102
frame-relay map IP 172.16.24.129 106 broadcast
!
interface BRI0
description ISDN backup interface for frame-relay
ip address 172.16.12.2 255.255.255.0
encapsulation PPP
dialer idle-timeout 240
dialer map IP 172.16.12.1 name ROUTER1 broadcast 12125267013
ppp authentication chap
pulse-time 1
dialer-group 1
isdn spid1 1415272803200 2728032
isdn spid2 1415272802500 2728025
!
router igrp 1
network 172.16.0.0
!
ip route 172.16.15.0 255.255.255.0 172.16.12.1 150  <--Floating static route
!
access-list 101 deny   igrp 0.0.0.0 255.255.255.255 0.0.0.0 255.255.255.255
access-list 101 permit ip 0.0.0.0 255.255.255.255 162.27.9.0 0.0.0.255
dialer-list 1 LIST 101
!
```

Summary

Frame Relay provides a flexible, cost-effective method of connecting LANs over WAN links. Several topology options exist for Frame Relay designs, including partial mesh, hub-and-spoke, and full mesh. Each topology has its benefits and drawbacks. Frame Relay interaction with routing protocols must be considered, particularly when designing backup strategies for Frame Relay networks. When designed effectively, Frame Relay networks can be very cost effective and can be relatively easy to maintain over the long term.

Chapter Review Questions

1 What is the unit of Frame Relay service?

2 What is the biggest design advantage presented by Frame Relay when compared to leased lines?

3 What are the components of a Frame Relay switching table?

4 What is the purpose of RFC 1490?

5 Describe the Inverse ARP mechanism.

6 What is the purpose of the Link Management Interface?

7 What are the benefits of using subinterfaces in Frame Relay designs?

8 What Frame Relay design topology options exist?

9 How do you configure DDR to back up a Frame PVC?

Be liberal in what you receive and conservative in what you send.

—Jon Postel, Father of the IANA, referring to the design and implementation of computer protocols

Upon completion of this chapter, you will be able to do the following:

- Design scalable internetwork WANs with nonbroadcast multiaccess X.25

- Design scalable internetwork WANs with X.25 subinterface configuration

- Describe how to use X.25 switching to provide X.25 service over an integrated IP backbone

CHAPTER 18

X.25 Design

Designing scalable WANs solely with nonbroadcast multiaccess (NBMA) X.25 is still used for legacy applications that require X.25 services or in areas of the world that have only X.25 available. In the banking industry, in particular, many ATMs are still connected via X.25. Also, X.25 is used in the packet-switched networks (PSNs) of common carriers, such as the telephone companies, as well as retail environments for bank credit-card verification. X.25 is often selected when there is no need for a high-speed, dedicated circuit. Cisco routers provide subinterfaces to easily terminate multiple X.25 virtual circuits on a single physical port. Still, in most cases, X.25 is used only when it is the only choice. This chapter discusses the X.25 service fundamentals, X.25 NBMA, X.25 subinterfaces, and X.25 switching.

X.25 Service Fundamentals

X.25 network devices fall into three general categories: data terminal equipment (DTE), data circuit-terminating equipment (DCE), and packet switch exchange (PSE). DTE devices are end systems that communicate across the X.25 network. They are usually terminals, personal computers, or network hosts, and are located on the premises of individual subscribers. DCE devices are communications devices, such as modems and packet switches, that provide the interface between DTE devices and a PSE and are generally located in the carrier's facilities. PSEs are switches that compose the bulk of the carrier's network. They transfer data from one DTE device to another through the X.25 PSN.

The X.25 Protocol Suite

The X.25 protocol suite maps to the lowest three layers of the OSI reference model. The following protocols are typically used in X.25 implementations:

- Packet level protocol (PLP)
- Link Access Procedure, Balanced (LAPB)
- Protocols found among other physical layer serial interfaces (such as EIA/TIA-232, EIA/TIA-449, EIA-530, and G.703)

Figure 18-1 maps the key X.25 protocols to the layers of the OSI reference model.

Figure 18-1 *Key X.25 Protocols Map to the Three Lowest Layers of the OSI Reference Model*

OSI Reference Model

Application	Other Services
Presentation	
Session	
Transport	PLP
Network	LAPB
Data Link	X.21bis, EIA/TIA-232,
Physical	EIA/TIA-449, EIA-530,
	G.703

X.25 is a packet-switched data network that can be either public or private. Public X.25 networks are known as public data networks (PDNs). Because early X.25 networks were built over unreliable analog circuits, reliability was built in to X.25 at the data link layer and at the network layer.

As shown in Figure 18-2, X.25 uses the reliable data link protocol LAPB. The X.25 PLP also provides reliable virtual circuits at the network layer. Because complex sliding-window protocols are used at two layers, X.25 networks have low throughput and high latency compared to Frame Relay.

Figure 18-2 *X.25 Is Based on Reliable Protocols*

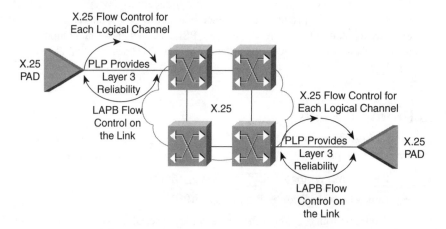

Every individual virtual circuit has its own sliding-window flow control at the X.25 layer. The window is local between the packet assembler/disassembler (PAD) (or router) and the X.25 switch.

Because X.25 service is available in many countries, it is the least common denominator (and most cost-effective method) for building international internetworks. International X.25 connectivity is provided by X.75 gateways.

As shown in Figure 18-3, a router is the logical DTE. The logical DCE is a concentrator or switch located at the carrier.

Figure 18-3   *Use X.25 Circuits as WAN Data Links Using Routers*

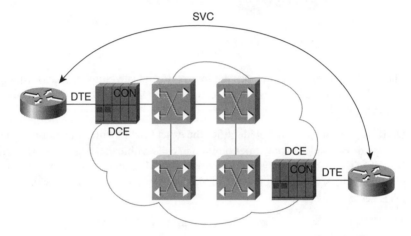

In internetworking, the X.25 virtual circuit (VC) is used like a data link. For protocols such as TCP/IP, X.25 is over-engineered because transport protocols, such as TCP, also provide reliability. The trade-off is performance.

Routers usually dial up switched virtual circuit (SVC) connections to other routers. The X.121 address of peer routers is mapped to the network protocol address. An X.121 address is assigned by the X.25 network service provider and can have a variable length.

X.121 Address Format

X.121 addresses are used by the X.25 PLP in call-setup mode to establish SVCs. Figure 18-4 illustrates the format of an X.121 address.

Figure 18-4   *The X.121 Address Includes an IDN Field*

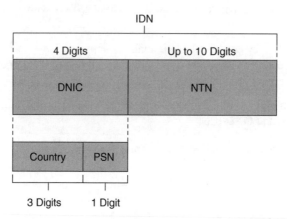

The X.121 Address field includes the International Data Number (IDN), which consists of two fields: the Data Network Identification Code (DNIC) and the National Terminal Number (NTN).

DNIC is an optional field that identifies the exact PSN in which the destination DTE device is located. This field is sometimes omitted in calls within the same PSN. The DNIC has two subfields: Country and PSN. The Country subfield specifies the country in which the destination PSN is located. The PSN field specifies the exact PSN in which the destination DTE device is located.

The NTN identifies the exact DTE device in the PSN for which a packet is destined. This field varies in length.

X.25 networks do not have the inherent reliability that allows them to reroute in the event of network failures. Because of this and the slow speeds that accompany X.25 networks, it is often appropriate to use static routing and static Novell Service Advertising Protocol (SAP) definitions between routers, especially because X.25 networks charge per packet, and routing broadcasts and multicast hellos generate many packets. In Figure 18-5, a static route is configured to 131.108.8.0 and to 131.108.9.0, because dynamic routing would not be an effective use of available bandwidth.

Figure 18-5 *Use Static Routing and Static IPX SAPs*

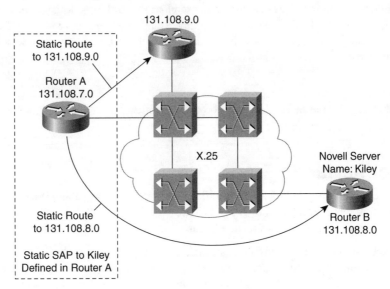

X.25 Nonbroadcast Multiaccess

Prior to Cisco IOS Release 10.0, X.25 was always treated as an NBMA network. The design considerations with X.25 NBMA are similar to those discussed with Frame Relay in Chapter 17. The biggest difference is that X.25 uses a reliable data link, whereas Frame Relay does not. Figure 18-6 shows a typical X.25 network data hierarchy.

Figure 18-6 *X.25 NBMA for Cost-Effective Access*

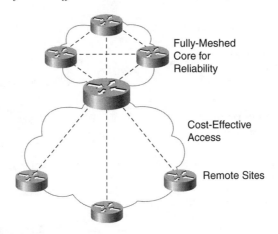

While X.25 as a type of network transport is generally being phased out, the model it follows for hierarchical structure is the same as that of Frame Relay. This hierarchical model is cost-effective because, like Frame Relay, any given end router needs only a single X.25 connection to the central hub to achieve reachability to any other device in the network.

DESIGN RULE   Use fully meshed X.25 in the core for reliability.

X.25 Subinterfaces

Cisco IOS Software Release 10.0 and later releases support subinterface configuration for X.25, sometimes referred to as *per-virtual-circuit routing*. Subinterface configuration eliminates NBMA matters related to partial-mesh connectivity and split horizon.

Each subinterface is configured as a different subnetwork or network. Therefore, the X.25 virtual circuit acts like a point-to-point link. The main advantage of point-to-point subinterfaces is robust routing. However, the benefit for the network engineer is the fact that multiple logical VCs can be easily configured on the same physical interface.

Sample X.25 Back-to-Back Configuration

It is possible to use X.25 encapsulation with subinterfaces on two back-to-back routers. This may be especially helpful for CCIE lab preparation. Example 18-1 shows how to do this.

Example 18-1   *X.25 Encapsulation with Subinterfaces on Back-to-Back Routers*

```
Router1 (DCE) :
int e 0
  ip address 10.1.1.1 255.255.255.0
int s 0
  clock rate 64000
  enca x25 dce
  x25 address 1111
  x25 htc 10
  no shut
int s 0.1 point-to-point
    ip unnumbered e 0
x25 map ip 10.1.2.1 2222 broadcast
```

Example 18-1 *X.25 Encapsulation with Subinterfaces on Back-to-Back Routers (Continued)*

```
ip route 10.1.2.0 255.255.255.0 s 0.1

Router2 (DTE) :
int e 0
  ip address 10.1.2.1 255.255.255.0
int s 0
  enca x25
  x25 address 2222
  x25 htc 10
  no shut
int s 0.1 point-to-point
    ip unnumbered e 0
x25 map ip 10.1.1.1 1111 broadcast
ip route 10.1.1.0 255.255.255.0 s 0.1
!
```

X.25 Switching

The Cisco router supports local X.25 switching between serial interfaces. The interfaces are dedicated to LAPB and X.25 and cannot carry other encapsulations. Both PVCs and SVCs are supported. Figure 18-7 shows an example of an X.25 switch setup where two Cisco routers are configured as X.25 DCE devices that can route PVCs and SVCs. In this example, each router has a static mapping (that is, static X.25 route) to the given X.121 addresses.

XOT (Remote) X.25 Router

New enhancements in IOS Release 11.3 have seen improvements to X.25 in the area of XOT (remote X.25 routing). A remote X.25 route is one that crosses a TCP connection. Such routes are called X.25 over TCP (XOT) routes (formerly remote routes or tunneled routes). The beauty of XOT is that it enables you to tunnel X.25 over a TCP/IP backbone. This is becoming increasingly popular in many large internetworks that are deploying *IP-only* core topologies. You can find out more about XOT at www.cisco.com/univercd/cc/td/doc/product/software/ios11/cbook/cx25.htm#xtocid2349651. Figure 18-7 demonstrates how XOT works.

Figure 18-7   *Configure Router as an X.25 Packet Switch*

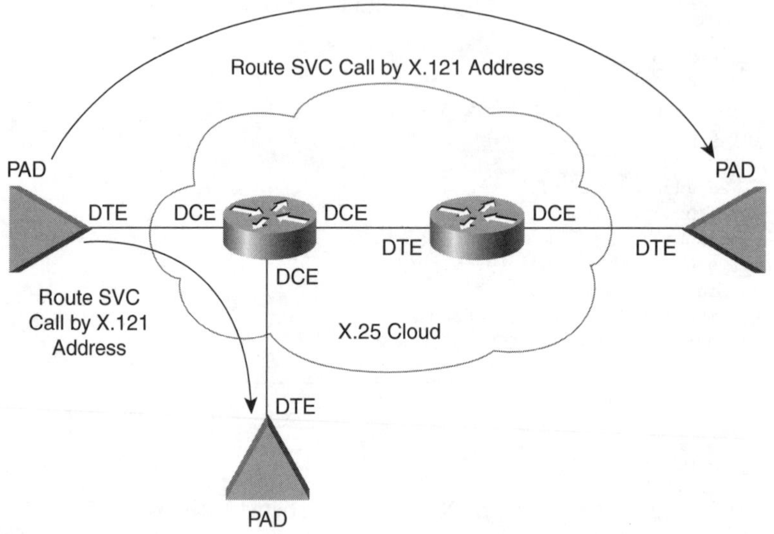

Summary

As a network designer, you might have the opportunity to work with X.25. X.25 is often selected when there is no need for a high-speed, dedicated circuit or if it is the "least common denominator" of WAN connectivity options available to you. Like Frame Relay and other protocols, you should use the hierarchical design to scale an X.25 NBMA WAN. Techniques such as using static routing and static SAPs over reliable X.25 WAN circuits should be implemented to save bandwidth used for protocol overhead. For robust routing over an X.25 WAN core, you should use a point-to-point subinterface configuration. With all these tools at your disposal, you should be able to implement a cost-effective and scalable X.25 design.

Chapter Review Questions

1 Into which general categories can X.25 network devices be classified?

2 What is a PDN?

3 How is X.25 different from Frame Relay?

4 What problems do X.25 subinterface configurations solve?

5 Can a Cisco router be configured as an X.25 switch? If so, can it support PVCs and SVCs?

Media and distribution have historically proven to be a winning model since the earliest days of television. At this point in the evolution of the Internet, with dialup access within the reach of most U.S. consumers, the emphasis of growth will shift to the fast-expanding footprint of broadband.

—George Bell, president of Excite@Home

Upon completion of this chapter, you will be able to do the following:

- Identify the major business and technology issues that relate to designing remote access networks
- Describe the dialup connection methods and the benefits of each
- Identify four methods to connect remote users
- Select equipment to be deployed at the remote user site
- Select equipment to be deployed at the central site
- Describe remote access security techniques
- Describe security and Internet design options

CHAPTER 19

Remote Access Design

Remote access refers to any technology that enables you to connect users in geographically dispersed locations. This access has typically been achieved over some kind of dialup connection using either basic telephone service or via ISDN connections. However, more recently, in addition to traditional analog and ISDN connectivity options, several newer dialup connectivity options are available, including digital subscriber line (DSL) and cable modem technology that will be introduced in this chapter. We'll see that 56 kbps is probably the practical limit for analog modems, and ISDN can increase this to 128 kbps. These technologies are still slow compared to the emerging asymmetric DSL (ADSL) technologies that are currently offering speeds between 1.5 Mbps and 8.0 Mbps, and cable modem speeds up to 30 Mbps. All hardware, software, and protocol choices aside, how you measure your remote access design's success is in the capability to securely and reliably connect any user or customer from any location into your corporate network.

Remote Access Issues

Remote access involves connecting users located at remote locations through dialup connections. The remote location may be a telecommuter's home, a mobile user's hotel room, or a small remote office. The dialup connection may be made via an analog connection using basic telephone service, Integrated Services Digital Networks (ISDNs), xDSL, or a cable modem. Connectivity is affected by speed, cost, distance, and availability, as illustrated by Table 19-1. The term xDSL actually covers a number of similar yet competing forms of DSL, including ADSL, SDSL, HDSL, RADSL, and VDSL. xDSL is drawing significant attention from implementers and service providers because it promises to deliver high-bandwidth data rates to dispersed locations with relatively small changes to the existing telco infrastructure. Currently, the primary focus in xDSL is the development and deployment of ADSL and VDSL technologies and architectures, so they will be covered in this chapter.

Remote access links generally represent the lowest-speed link in the enterprise. Any improvements in speed are desirable. The cost of remote access tends to be relatively low, especially for basic telephone service. ISDN, ADSL, and cable modem service fees can vary widely depending on the geographic area, the service availability, and the billing method. There may be distance limitations with regard to dialup services, especially with ISDN.

Table 19-1   *Remote Access Technology Characteristics*

	Speed	Cost	Distance	Availability	Advantages	Disadvantages
Analog Connection	14–56 kbps	Inexpensive	20,000 feet	Widespread	Modems are inexpensive. Availability anywhere. Standards based. When configured, usually, no maintenance is required.	Slow speeds, slow connect times. Prone to noise and line-quality problems. Long-distance charges may apply.
ISDN	56–128 kbps	Relatively inexpensive	18,000 feet	Moderate	ISDN modems are inexpensive. ISDN is simple to set up. Proven technology. Standards based. Most ISPs support ISDN. Channels can be used for voice or data.	Setup of ISDN calls is much slower than cable or DSL. Only moderate availability. Per-minute connect time applies.
*x*DSL	1.5–8 Mbps	Moderately expensive	18,000 feet	Limited	High speed. Secure connection. Uses the existing phone wire. Distance is a limiting factor of bandwidth. No dialup needed—"always on."	Currently, there is no guarantee of interoperability among different vendors' DSL equipment. Lack of availability. Cost. Speed depends on distance.

Table 19-1   *Remote Access Technology Characteristics*

	Speed	Cost	Distance	Availability	Advantages	Disadvantages
Cable Modem	30 Mbps	Moderately expensive	Cable modem rates do not depend on coaxial cable distance, as amplifiers in the cable network boost signal power sufficiently to give every user enough. Variation in cable modem capacity will depend rather on ingress noise in the line itself and the number of simultaneous users seeking access to a shared line.	Limited	No dialup needed— "always on." Distance is not a limiting factor of bandwidth. High speed.	Lack of availability. Small portion of cable companies offer two-way service. As more users are added, bandwidth is lowered. Shared access means potential for security issues.

NOTE   Source: *Time* Magazine, September 23, 1996 (page 55)

- A cable modem could transmit all 857 pages of Melville's *Moby Dick* in about 2 seconds.
- In the same time, a high-speed ISDN phone line could move 10 pages.
- And a 28.8 modem, the most common way of accessing the Internet today, wouldn't get past page 3.

Connection Technology

From the perspective of connection technology, two areas need to be examined:

- The remote access component, which is the end user or users out in the field requiring network resources

- The centralized-site access component, which serves as a concentration point for all remote access users

The sections that follow discuss the components of all four connection technology options in detail.

Analog Services

Dialup connections using analog, or basic telephone service, represent one of the least expensive and widely available methods of providing connectivity for remote access. Figure 19-1 illustrates a typical analog connection.

Figure 19-1   *Analog Overview*

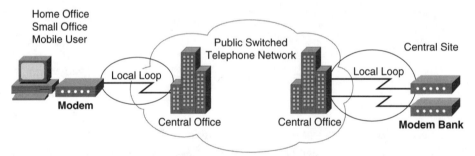

Home offices and small offices connect through the public switched telephone network. Although generally reliable for lower-speed connections (28.8 kbps and below), most connection problems for both high- and low-speed analog dialup occur in what is known as the *local loop*. As Figure 19-1 shows, the local loop is the circuit between your modem and the nearest telephone company switch.

The downside of this method has traditionally been the relatively low speed. Even with the latest state-of-the-art analog modem technology, the average connect rate is still 28.8 kbps or 33.6 kbps and, in a few but growing number of instances, up to 56 kbps. The road to 56 kbps in modem technology has been a rocky one. Prior to 1998, there were several "competing standards" as modem speeds closed in on the "Holy Grail" of analog modem speeds: 56 kbps. Prior to 1998, some of the competing (and proprietary) technologies were K56plus (Rockwell), K56Flex (Lucent and Rockwell), and X2 (3Com). Through hard work and compromise, the ITU-T standard, coined "V.90" was born in February 1998, in none other than the land of neutrality, Geneva, Switzerland.

At the central site, the modem may be a standalone device; much more often, however, it is integrated with other equipment, such as routers, into an access server, such as an AS5300. As with other design issues, the decision of which remote access technology to use is generally driven by the number of connections and port densities required.

ISDN Services

ISDN was developed by the telephone companies with the intention of creating a totally digital network. Because it is end-to-end digital, ISDN is a technology well suited for data, fax, voice, and video streams. ISDN is often used for videoconferencing (an example is the Intel ProShare videoconferencing product line). Figure 19-2 shows a typical ISDN setup.

Figure 19-2   *ISDN Overview*

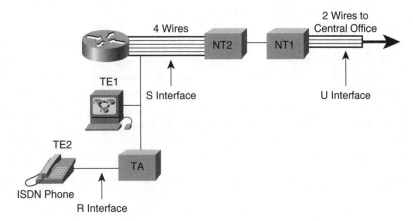

As shown in Figure 19-2, ISDN devices include the following:

- **Terminal Equipment 1 (TE1)**—Designates a device compatible with the ISDN network. A TE1 connects to a Network Termination of either Type 1 or Type 2.

- **Terminal Equipment 2 (TE2)**—Designates a device not compatible with ISDN and requires a Terminal Adapter (that is, non-ISDN terminals such as DTE that predate the ISDN standards are referred to as Terminal Equipment Type 2 [TE2]).

- **Terminal Adapter (TA)**—Converts standard electrical signals from non-ISDN devices into the proper signal form used by ISDN.

- **Network Termination Type 1 (NT1)**—Connects four-wire ISDN subscriber wiring to the conventional two-wire local loop facility.

- **Network Termination Type 2 (NT2)**—Directs traffic to and from different subscriber devices and the NT1. The NT2 is an intelligent device that performs switching and concentrating.

- **ISDN interface reference points**—Include the following:
    - The S/T interface defines the interface between a TE1 and an NT. The S/T is also used to define the TA-to-NT interface.
    - The R interface defines the interface between a TE2 and the TA.
    - The U interface defines the two-wire interface between the NT and the ISDN "cloud."

As a design engineer, you may be faced with choosing an ISDN service for your design. With an understanding of the basic terminology of ISDN, we can now proceed with an examination of ISDN services. Decisions, such as when to use PRI or BRI for router backup or remote access, require an understanding of these services for cost-effective ISDN designs.

ISDN Basic Rate Interface

There are two ISDN services: Basic Rate Interface (BRI) and Primary Rate Interface (PRI). ISDN BRI operates over most of the copper twisted-pair telephone wiring in place today. ISDN BRI consists of three separate channels. As shown in Figure 19-3, two of the channels, called B (bearer) channels, operate at 64 kbps and are used to carry voice or data traffic. The third channel, the D (data) channel, is a 16-kbps signaling channel used to carry instructions that tell the telephone network how to handle each of the B channels. The D channel signaling protocol comprises Layers 1 through 3 of the OSI reference model, bringing its total bit rate to 144 kbps. ISDN BRI is often referred to as "2B+D."

ISDN provides great flexibility to the network designer because of its capability to use each of the B channels for separate voice or data applications; for example, a long document can be downloaded from the corporate network over one ISDN 64-kbps B channel while the other B channel is being used to connect to browse the Web. Care should be taken in the design phase to ensure that the equipment selected has the feature set that takes advantage of ISDNs flexibility.

Figure 19-3   *ISDN Services—Basic Rate Interface*

ISDN Primary Rate Interface

ISDN PRI (Primary Rate Interface) is often referred to as "23B+D" (United States and Japan) running at 1.544 Mbps or "30B+D" (Europe, Australia, and other parts of the world) running at 2.048 Mbps. Figure 19-4 shows a typical PRI configuration, depending on geographic location. PRI is designed to carry large numbers of incoming ISDN calls at corporate offices or other central-site locations. PRI will use either T1 or E1 circuits as its underlying bit-transport layer. T1 uses in-band signaling and E1 uses out-of-band signaling. This signaling difference accounts for the different line capacities.

Figure 19-4   *ISDN Service—Primary Rate ISDN*

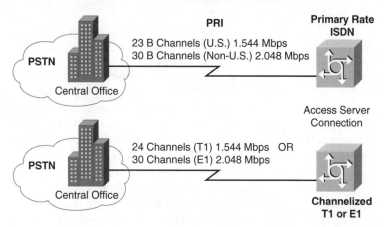

¥ U.S.: 23 Bearer + 1 Shared Signaling (D) Channel
¥ Non-U.S.: 30 Bearer + 1 Shared Signaling (D) Channel

ISDN offers several advantages over analog basic telephone service. Based on speed alone, ISDN outperforms analog, even using the latest V.90 technology, by more than two times. Furthermore, ISDN lines provide practically error-free digital transmission, whereas analog calls are subject to interference from static and other line problems. Also, call setup with ISDN is much faster than with analog service.

ISDN also has disadvantages to be considered in a design. ISDN service is not as widely available as analog service. ISDN has limitations with distance from the central office, and can sometimes be expensive, depending on your physical location. ISDN also tends to be more complex to order and set up, although after it is configured, it requires little to no administrative overhead.

Digital Subscriber Line

Digital Subscriber Line (DSL) technology is a modem technology that uses existing twisted-pair telephone lines to transport high-bandwidth data, such as multimedia and video, to service subscribers. The term *x*DSL covers a number of similar yet competing forms of DSL, including asymmetric digital subscriber lines (ADSL), single-pair high-bit-rate digital subscriber lines (SDSL), high-bit-rate digital subscriber lines (HDSL), rate adaptive digital subscriber lines (RADSL), and very high-bit-rate digital subscriber lines

(VDSL). *x*DSL is drawing significant attention from implementers and service providers because it promises to deliver high-bandwidth data rates to dispersed locations with relatively small changes to the existing telco infrastructure. *x*DSL services are dedicated, point-to-point, public network access over twisted-pair copper wire on the local loop ("last mile") between a network service provider's (NSP) central office and the customer site, or on local loops created either intra-building or intra-campus. Because the primary focus in *x*DSL is currently the development and deployment of ADSL and VDSL technologies and architectures, they are discussed next.

ADSL

ADSL technology is asymmetric. It allows more bandwidth downstream—from an NSPs central office to the customer site—than upstream from the subscriber to the central office. This asymmetry, combined with always-on access (which eliminates call setup), makes ADSL ideal for Internet/intranet surfing, video-on-demand, and remote LAN access. Users of these applications typically download much more information than they send. ADSL transmits between the customer-provided equipment (CPE) and the telco equipment (known as a DSL Access Multiplexer (DSLAM)) more than 6 Mbps to a subscriber, and as much as 640 kbps or more in both directions, as shown in Figure 19-5. Such rates expand existing access capacity by a factor of 50 or more without new cabling. ADSL can literally transform the existing public information network from one limited to voice, text, and low-resolution graphics to a powerful, ubiquitous system capable of bringing multimedia, including full-motion video, to every home in the near future.

Figure 19-5   *The Components of an ADSL Network Include a Telco and a CPE*

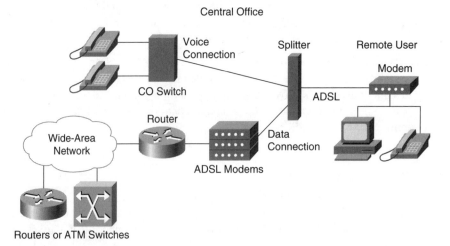

ADSL Standards and Associations

The American National Standards Institute (ANSI) Working Group T1E1.4 recently approved an ADSL standard at rates up to 6.1 Mbps (ANSI Standard T1.413). The European Technical Standards Institute (ETSI) contributed an annex to T1.413 to reflect European requirements. T1.413 currently embodies a single terminal interface at the premises end. Issue II, now under study by T1E1.4, will expand the standard to include a multiplexed interface at the premises end, protocols for configuration and network management, and other improvements.

The ATM Forum and the Digital Audio-Visual Council (DAVIC) have both recognized ADSL as a physical layer transmission protocol for unshielded twisted-pair (UTP) media. The ADSL Forum was formed in December 1994 to promote the ADSL concept and facilitate development of ADSL system architectures, protocols, and interfaces for major ADSL applications. The forum has more than 200 members, representing service providers, equipment manufacturers, and semiconductor companies throughout the world.

You can find out more about the ADSL Forum at www.adsl.com/adsl_forum.html.

VDSL

In simple terms, VDSL transmits high-speed data over short reaches of twisted-pair copper telephone lines, with a range of speeds depending on actual line length. The maximum downstream rate under consideration is between 51 and 55 Mbps over lines up to 1000 feet (300 meters) in length. Downstream speeds as low as 13 Mbps over lengths beyond 4000 feet (1500 meters) are also common. Upstream rates in early models will be asymmetric, just like ADSL, at speeds from 1.6 to 2.3 Mbps. Both data channels will be separated in frequency from bands used for basic telephone service and Integrated Services Digital Network (ISDN), enabling service providers to overlay VDSL on existing services. At present the two high-speed channels are also separated in frequency. As needs arise for higher-speed upstream channels or symmetric rates, VDSL systems may need to use echo cancellation.

The battle between VDSL and ADSL is on. However, costs cannot be ignored—VDSL has a much lower cost target than ADSL because VDSL may connect directly from a wiring center or cable modems, which also have much lower common equipment costs per user. Watch for these emerging technologies.

Cable Modem Technology

Although products are shipping today, cable modem technology is still in its infancy. Today, several trials are being conducted by leading cable companies such as Cox, Excite@Home, and Time Warner. Why the hype? Cable modem technology, with a standard called DOCSIS (Data Over Cable Service Interface Specification) promises to deliver 30 Mbps of throughput downstream to the end user, essentially providing all the bandwidth that an end station can handle. With all this downstream speed, there is a bottleneck problem with most of today's PCs. Namely, the vast majority of cable modem users will have 10BaseT or 10-Mbps connections attached to their PCs, yielding approximately 1.5 Mbps.

The speed of the cable modem is only one part of the equation. "There are a combination of factors," according to David Gingold from MIT's Research Program on Communications Policy, "starting with how fast your PC can handle Internet Protocol (IP) traffic, then how fast your PC to cable modem interface is, then how fast the cable modem system runs and how much congestion there is on the cable network, then how big a pipe there is at the head end to the rest of the Internet."

You can learn more about DOCSIS at www.CableLabs.com/.

What's Ahead for Cable Modem Technology

First and foremost, cable companies must first design their infrastructures so that two-way transactions are enabled. Furthermore, cable operators need to select a vendor that can deliver on time with a product that works. Many vendors are currently designing and shipping cable modems. They include Cisco, General Instrument, Motorola, and Terayon. The Cisco UBR904 and UBR924 cable modems are supported in Cisco IOS Release 12.0 and higher.

NOTE   Data-over-cable systems can provide access speeds up to 36 Mbps. That bandwidth, however, is shared by multiple subscribers because very few computers today can connect to a network at such high speeds. Typical connection speeds to be expected are 5 Mbps downstream and 1 Mbps upstream per subscriber.

To compare data-over-cable speeds with other Internet access technologies available today, a file that would take 8 minutes to download over standard telephone lines with a 28.8 kbps modem would take 2 minutes to download over ISDN. The same file would take approximately 8 seconds to download over a data-over-cable system.

In the near term, the battle for remote access will likely shift to ADSL versus cable modem technology. Reality shows that only 10 million homes today can support two-way cable modem transmissions, a prerequisite for cable modem technology. This number will certainly continue to expand, but it will not catch up with telephone lines for many years.

You can find out more about the cable modem technology at the following sites:

> www.cablemodemhelp.com/
> www.cablemodeminfo.com/CableModemFAQ.html

Remote Access Methods

Keeping the technology options already discussed in mind, the methods by which remote users are connected into the corporate LAN usually fall into one of three major categories:

- Remote gateway
- Remote control
- Remote node

Each of these methods can be implemented over analog, ISDN, ADSL, or cable modem service connections. As discussed in the following sections, each access class has advantages and disadvantages.

Remote Gateway

Remote gateway is usually meant to serve one particular need. Assume, for example, that a company has many remote representatives that frequently work out of their cars or in hotel rooms. As shown in Figure 19-6, if these users need to access e-mail only, a remote e-mail gateway solution would be adequate, which is nothing more than a mail program on the users' laptops that can access a modem. The modem then dials up a remote mail server, and the remote user gets the mail. Novell GroupWise is a popular e-mail and scheduling program that offers a remote gateway for the end users.

This solution has the advantages of being very easy to implement and being inexpensive. This solution only solves one particular problem, however, namely remote e-mail access. There is no capability to access corporate databases or "surf" the Web, for example.

Figure 19-6   *Remote Gateway*

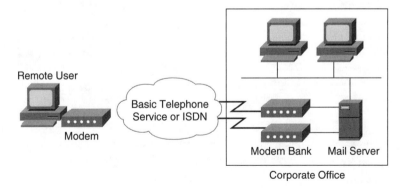

Remote Control

In the *remote-control* method, the remote gains control of the PC attached to the LAN at the central site. The remote user then has all the capabilities normally available when using the office PC. This solution offers some significant advantages. It is widely available and is quite inexpensive. In addition to running the remote-control software on both ends of the connection, all that is required for additional hardware is a modem at each end.

However, there are several disadvantages to the remote-control method. Remote control is quite wasteful of bandwidth, and performance can be very bad on low-bandwidth links. This solution is very difficult to secure because anyone could dial in to the modem. There is no easy way to globally enforce password checking or to set up audit trails. A popular and effective remote-control package is called PC AnyWhere by Symmantec, and a newer package that can be integrated in your Web browser for IP-based remote control is called pcAnywhere EXPRESS. This solution also requires that two PCs be allocated to the user, and the PC at the office must always be powered up. A downside to remote control sometimes occurs when there is a problem with the remote-control server or if someone else is connected to it. You may face performance problems or no access at all. Check out Symantec's Web site at www.symantec.com/pcanywhere/ for more details.

Remote Node

With the *remote-node* method, the users connect to the local LAN at the central site for the duration of the call. Shown in Figure 19-7, aside from having a lower-speed connection via remote node, the remote user sees the same environment the local user sees.

Figure 19-7   *Remote Node*

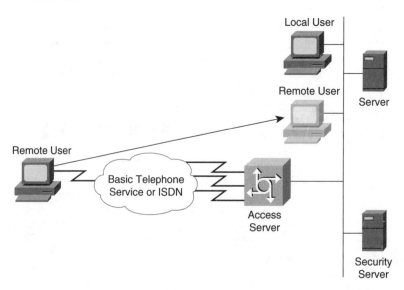

The connection to the corporate network is typically through an access server. This device usually combines the functions of the incoming modem and a router. The remote user can be screened through a security server (generally a TACACS+ server, as discussed in the security section of this chapter) before login is complete, and an audit trail can be easily established. When logged in, the remote user can access servers at the corporate LAN as if they were local.

The remote node method offers many advantages. It is the most secure and flexible of the three methods, and it is the most scalable. Only one PC is required for the remote user, and many client software solutions are available. The only additional hardware required at the remote location is a modem. The main disadvantage of this method is the additional administrative overhead required to support the remote user. Because of its many advantages, this solution tends to be the standard and will be used in the remainder of the design examples.

Equipment Deployment Based on User Category

When considering equipment to deploy at the remote-user location, it is extremely important to first consider the user requirements. Users can be grouped based on how often they use the remote connection and whether the remote site is a single computer or a LAN. Based on these considerations, as shown in Figure 19-8, three categories of users emerge: occasional telecommuter/mobile user, dedicated telecommuter/teleworker, and small office/home office (SOHO) with LAN presence.

The category of users will affect the type of equipment you choose to deploy.

Figure 19-8   *Remote User Access Equipment*

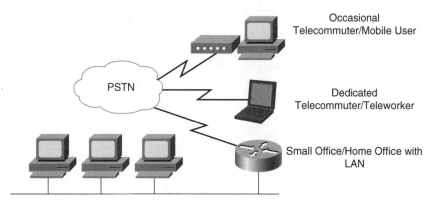

Occasional Telecommuters/Mobile Users

Occasional telecommuters or mobile users are those who need infrequent dial-in access to the enterprise network. An example might be the mobile user on the road who dials in to the enterprise network in the mornings and evenings to check e-mail or to access corporate database information throughout the day. Another example is the person who occasionally takes work home in the evenings or on weekends. As shown in Figure 19-9, such a requirement will likely point to analog modem as the connection method. In many implementations, the occasional telecommuter is given a laptop with a PCMCIA modem card that is capable of V.90 support. This type of connectivity is usually sufficient for most occasional users.

Figure 19-9   *Occasional Telecommuter/Mobile User Using Analog Dial*

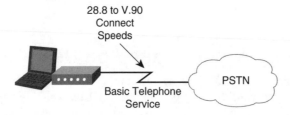

Full-Time Telecommuter/Teleworker

The full-time telecommuter/teleworker normally works out of the home. This user is more of a power user who needs access to the enterprise networks for a longer period of time. This connection should be reliable and available at all times. Notice that the ISDN router in Figure 19-10 has connections for the user workstation or PC and for an analog telephone or fax line. The user can set up an ISDN connection and use both lines to provide 128-kbps access to the central site. If a phone call comes in during the data transmission, the router or access server (at the central site) will drop one of the ISDN B channels to receive the call. The B channel will be reactivated when the call is finished. This feature is helpful if you are on a conference call and also dialed in to your network, troubleshooting a problem, or getting sales data.

Figure 19-10   *Dedicated Telecommuter/Teleworker*

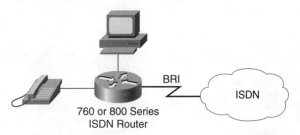

760 or 800 Series
ISDN Router

Note, however, that although very widely deployed, ISDN still is not readily available for some users who live in rural areas. Other choices may include ADSL and cable modem technology, but chances are fairly good right now that if your telco cannot provide you with ISDN service, they won't have ADSL or cable modems yet.

Both technologies are still fairly new, however, and don't have much exposure yet. You should check with your telephone company and cable company to see what their plans are for these technologies. For example, BellSouth has a great Web page that describes the local availability for ADSL in the BellSouth area (www.buzz.bellsouth.net/external/adsl/city_availability.html).

On the cable modem front, Cox@Home, at www.cox.com/CoxatHome/ has a listing of some cities that currently have cable modem technologies deployed. Check with your local cable company for availability.

SOHO

A small office or home office consisting of a few power users requires a connection that provides branch office-type access. The Cisco 1600 series router is shown as a solution in Figure 19-11, using an ISDN BRI connection. If sufficient demand exists, the Cisco 1600 could be connected to other services such as Frame Relay, leased lines, SMDS, or X.25. The Cisco 1600 has an integrated 56-kbps CSU/DSU to reduce the amount of equipment required at the remote site.

Figure 19-11 *SOHO with LAN*

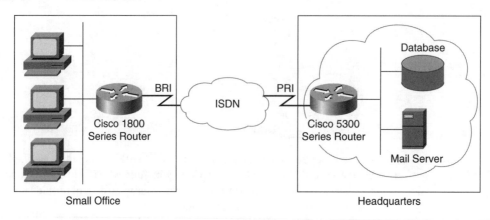

Central-Site Equipment

The equipment at the central site may consist of routers, modems, or access servers. The selection of specific components is driven by the number and type of connections required, along with the number and type of LANs connected at the central site. Figure 19-12 shows several different concentrator-class access points for different remote access technologies. A new concentrator for cable modem technology is the UBR7246 router, for example, and is shown in Figure 19-12. You can find out more about the UBR7246 at www.cisco.com/warp/public/cc/cisco/mkt/access/index.shtml.

Figure 19-12 *Central-Site Access Equipment*

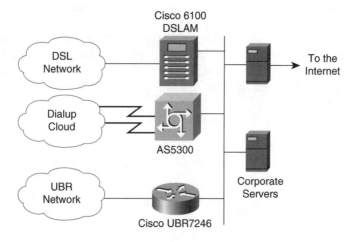

For ADSL, Cisco offers the 6100 (shown in Figure 19-12), 6130, and 6200, and 6260 architectures, which are built for rapid deployment of large-scale DSL concentration points (known as DSLAMS), and are targeted toward the consumer and commercial markets.

For analog dial, Cisco offers the AS5200, AS5300, and AS5800, as shown in the Figure 19-13.

Figure 19-13   *Basic Telephone Service Design with AS5200 or AS5300 at the Central Location*

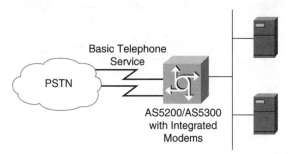

When the incoming connections are analog (basic telephone service) connections and are relatively low in density (8 to 16 connections), in the past, Cisco 2500 series routers would be deployed. Today, more and more Cisco AS5300s are being deployed because they are RISC based and can offer higher port densities than the 2500 series for future expandability. Because the routers have additional LAN and synchronous WAN connections, they could be deployed as a remote office. The LAN connections could provide access to servers locally; the WAN connections could provide access to a central site. In "old world" designs, external modems were often deployed, but because this solution is not easily scalable, "new world" remote access design use access servers such as the AS5300 with integrated modems.

A design that incorporates a higher-density analog (basic telephone service) connection would likely call for an access server, such as the AS5300 or 3640, with modem modules installed. These access servers contain integrated modem banks, thus reducing the number of components required at the central site.

Sizing Your Hardware at the Central Site

If ISDN dialup is being deployed, as shown in Figure 19-14, some general hardware sizing rules of thumb are given. If the number of connections is relatively small (typically fewer than 20), multiple BRI connections could be used with a Cisco 3600 or 4000 series router. When a higher density of connections is required, an ISDN PRI interface would be a better solution. In this case, a 7200 or 7500 series router could be used, especially if a large number of additional LAN and WAN interfaces are required. Otherwise, the AS5300 provides a highly scalable solution. In addition, the AS5300 can accommodate a mixture of analog (basic telephone service) and ISDN connections. The exact hardware configuration will vary by design, based on speed requirements of other interfaces that the remote router will need to handle. Often Fast Ethernet or FDDI connectivity may be required on the access server, thus requiring a faster processor.

Figure 19-14   *ISDN Design Rules of Thumb*

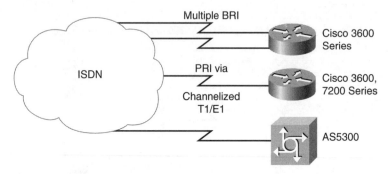

Data Encapsulation Issues

When deploying remote access solutions, several encapsulation choices are available. The most common is the Point-to-Point Protocol (PPP), as illustrated by Figure 19-15. Although there are others such as Serial Line Internet Protocol (SLIP) and High-Level Data Link Control (HDLC), PPP is much more robust and offers significant advantages; therefore, PPP is the only encapsulation discussed in this book.

Figure 19-15   *Data-Link Encapsulation*

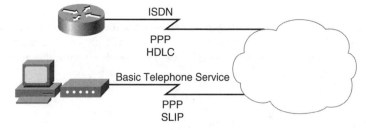

PPP is an open standard specified by RFC 1661. PPP was designed with several features that make it particularly useful in remote access applications:

- PPP uses Link Control Protocol to initially establish the link and agree on configuration (such as packet-framing methods to use).

- PPP's built-in security features such as the Password Authentication Protocol (PAP) and the Challenge Handshake Authentication Protocol (CHAP) make robust security design easier.

- PPP's Multilink PPP enhancement provides a standard way of combining two channels, such as the B channels, in an ISDN BRI connection.

- Multilink Multichassis PPP (MMP) is an enhancement to the MP standard which gives the permitting MLP links from a single client to terminate at different access servers. Although individual MLP links of the same bundle may actually terminate at different access servers, it appears to the Multilink PPP client as if they are terminating at a single access server.

PPP Link Control Protocol

The PPP LCP provides a method of establishing, configuring, maintaining, and terminating the point-to-point connection. LCP goes through four distinct phases:

Step 1 Link establishment and configuration negotiation occurs. Before any network layer datagrams (for example, IP) can be exchanged, LCP first must open the connection and negotiate configuration parameters. This phase is complete when a configuration-acknowledgment frame has been both sent and received.

Step 2 Link-quality determination allows an optional link-quality determination phase following the link-establishment and configuration-negotiation phase. In this phase, the link is tested to determine whether the link quality is sufficient to bring up network layer protocols. This phase is optional. LCP can delay transmission of network layer protocol information until this phase is complete.

Step 3 Network layer protocol configuration negotiation occurs. After LCP has finished, the link-quality determination phase, network layer protocols can be configured separately by the appropriate NCP and can be brought up and taken down at any time. If LCP closes the link, it informs the network layer protocols so that they can take appropriate action.

Step 4 Link termination occurs. LCP can terminate the link at any time. This usually will be done at the request of a user but can happen because of a physical event, such as the loss of carrier or the expiration of an idle-period timer.

PPP Security Features

PPP can be configured to use either PAP or CHAP. PAP, defined in RFC 1334, is a weak authentication method, because the password is sent in clear-text. It is also limited to only being used once, at link establishment. CHAP, on the other hand, defined in RFC 1994, is a strong authentication method, because the password is not ever sent in clear-text. CHAP, unlike PAP, has the built-in capability to periodically confirm the identity of the connected client; however, this is not supported in all client software.

Multilink PPP

Multilink PPP (MP), as specified in RFC 1717 (www.isi.edu/in-notes/rfc1717.txt), is designed to fragment packets and transmit the fragments over parallel connections, such as ISDN BRI and PRI access lines. As shown in Figure 19-16, the MP-compliant implementation segments and sequences the packets before transmission, and reassembles the packets on the other end. The sequencing is done through a 4-byte field added to the frame header. These additional bytes also identify the first and last packet fragment in a group.

Figure 19-16   *Multilink Point-to-Point Protocol*

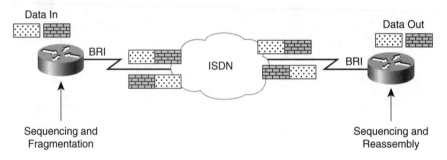

Multilink Multichassis PPP

An enhancement to the MP standard provided in Cisco IOS Software Release 11.2 is called Multilink Multichassis PPP (MMP). As shown in Figure 19-17, this feature provides a mechanism to aggregate B channels transparently across multiple routers or access servers, which means that fragments from one client could terminate at different access servers. MMP is important because now scaling up of the central site is more flexible, and more access servers can be added as needed.

Figure 19-17   *Multilink Multichassis PPP*

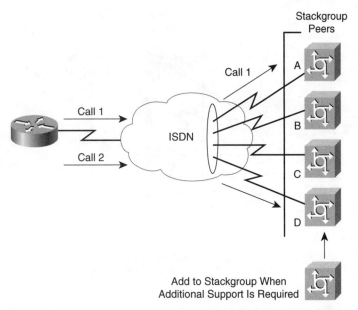

A benefit of MMP is that call-aggregation processing can be distributed evenly among peers, or weighted to favor a certain device in the stackgroup. The Stackgroup Bidding Protocol (SGBP) "bidding" process defines the MMP process server in a manner that the process server wins the bidding for call processing. For example, a high-performance access device such as the RISC-based Cisco 4700 or 3640 can be used as the MMP process server to process call packet reassembly. In this scenario, the AS5300 can concentrate on answering the high number of dialup calls, while the "back-end" call processor handles reassembly. Figure 19-18 shows a typical MMP process server setup. In this case, you have four AS5300 stackgroup peers that terminate all their calls into the Cisco 3640 process server. The process server performs all packet reassembly.

An excellent document on CCO goes into MMP technology in much more detail. You can find this document at www.cisco.com/warp/public/131/3.html.

Figure 19-18   *MMP Process Server*

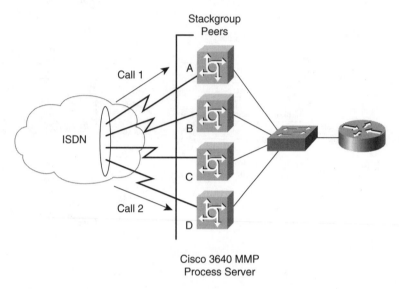

Security and Internet Considerations for Remote Access Design

A number of security challenges arise when dial access connectivity is added to an enterprise network. Incoming connections must be policed to ensure that only authorized users are gaining access to the network through the dialup connections. Several options are available to the network designer to meet this objective.

As mentioned earlier, the PPP data-link protocol has two security features built in: PAP and CHAP. Cisco IOS software features at the access server, such as per-user access lists, can also aid in implementing security. In addition, a security server may be implemented using Enhanced Terminal Access Controller Access Control System (TACACS+) or Remote Access Dial-In User Service (RADIUS). Cisco also offers the CiscoSecure package for UNIX environments and a TACACS+ for NT package to provide additional security. As shown in Figure 19-19, a typical user connects to the access server, and then is authenticated using either PPP CHAP or PAP. Then, after the physical link is established, the user is asked for a login name and password. The CiscoSecure database server will maintain an audit trail of all user attempts to the network and has the option of logging all user activities for future auditing purposes.

Figure 19-19   *Security*

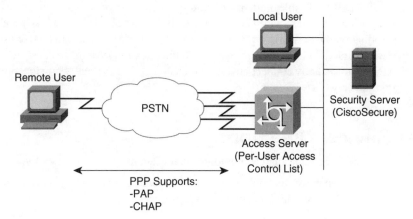

The Internet and Virtual Private Networks

Another popular option to consider in design and implementation of a remote access solution is to use the Internet. This option has several benefits, including low cost and ease of implementation. The cost is low because the remote user dials in to a local point of presence for the Internet service provider (ISP). This option is especially useful if the remote user is mobile and the ISP has locations in most geographic areas. The tunnel operation is accomplished by a transport protocol, such as Layer 2 Forwarding (L2F), operating at the data link layer. L2F and Point-to-Point Tunneling Protocol (PPTP) protocols merged, resulting in the proposed IETF protocol, Layer 2 Tunneling Protocol (L2TP). The Cisco implementation of L2TP support is based on the latest draft of the L2TP standard, available on the Web at www.townsley.net/mark/l2tp/l2tp-latest.txt.

The L2TP option effectively implements a virtual private network (VPN) through the Internet. Remote users gain secure, easy access to corporate networks through existing public infrastructures, while retaining control of security and management. VPNs are a key example of a "new world" service because they enable companies to connect their offices, mobile workers, and business partners with dramatically reduced costs by leveraging the shared communications infrastructure of the Internet or a service provider shared backbone. You can find out more about remote VPNs by checking out the following document on the Cisco 1720 VPN router: www.cisco.com/warp/public/cc/cisco/mkt/access/1700/index.shtml.

Summary

Remote access refers to any technology that enables you to connect users in geographically dispersed locations. Today, with the Internet craze, in addition to traditional analog and

ISDN connectivity options, there are several emerging dialup connectivity options including DSL and cable modem technology. Regardless of which technology prevails, the issues of remote access hardware, software, and protocol selection are key and will vary depending on the network requirements. Most remote access designs today use PPP and CHAP, coupled with some form of a user-authentication system, such as TACACS+ or RADIUS, to securely connect any user or customer from virtually any location into your corporate network.

Chapter Review Questions

1   Name three traditional technologies that often used dialup networking.

2   Name two newer technologies that are becoming increasingly more popular, due to their very high bandwidth capabilities.

3   What is MP and why is important?

4   What is MMP and why is important?

5   Identify three implementation methods that designers have for connecting remote users.

6   Describe three categories of dialup users.

7   What is remote-control network access?

8   What are some advantages to remote-node network access?

9   What is a VPN?

We believe successful service providers will deliver networks centered around a broadband optical core. There will be a variety of access mechanisms available for business and residences, including wireline and wireless, carrying voice, data, and video.

We believe service providers must have advanced software platforms that will enable customers to create rich new services through the interworking of existing networks with open applications interfaces.

And finally, we believe that service providers will deploy merged IP and ATM network protocols.

—Richard A. McGinn, Chief Executive Officer & Chairman, Lucent Technologies

Upon completion of this chapter, you will be able to do the following:

- Describe issues related to using cell-based services for WAN connections
- Describe how to implement router- and ATM-based designs for ATM WAN connectivity
- Describe how to deploy SMDS technology in a WAN design
- Describe key issues in ATM WAN design
- Describe the different StrataCom (Cisco) ATM WAN nodes and their major features

CHAPTER 20

ATM Internetwork Design

Asynchronous Transfer Mode (ATM) is an evolving technology designed for the high-speed transfer of voice, video, and data through public and private networks in a cost-effective manner. ATM is based on the efforts of Study Group XVIII of the International Telecommunication Union Telecommunication Standardization Sector (ITU-T, formerly the Consultative Committee for International Telegraph and Telephone [CCITT]) and the American National Standards Institute (ANSI) to apply Very Large-Scale Integration (VLSI) technology to the transfer of data within public networks. Officially, the ATM layer of the Broadband Integrated Services Digital Network (BISDN) model is defined by CCITT I.361. Current efforts to bring ATM technology to private networks and to guarantee interoperability between private and public networks is being done by the ATM Forum, which was jointly founded by Cisco Systems, NET/ADAPTIVE, Northern Telecom, and Sprint in 1991.

Role of ATM in Internetworks

Today, 90 percent of computing power resides on desktops, and that power is growing exponentially. Distributed applications are increasingly bandwidth hungry, and the emergence of the Internet is driving most LAN architectures to the limit. Voice communications have increased significantly with increasing reliance on centralized voice-mail systems for verbal communications. The internetwork is the critical tool for information flow. Internetworks are being pressured to cost less yet support the emerging applications and a higher number of users with increased performance.

To date, local-area and wide-area communications have remained logically separate. In the LAN, bandwidth is "free" and connectivity is limited only by hardware and implementation cost. Traditionally, the LAN carried data only. In the WAN, bandwidth has been the overriding cost, and delay-sensitive traffic such as voice has remained separate from data. New applications and the economics of supporting them, however, are forcing these conventions to change.

The Internet is the first source of multimedia to the desktop and immediately breaks the rules. Such Internet applications as voice and real-time video require better, more predictable LAN and WAN performance. In addition, the Internet also necessitates that the WAN recognize the traffic in the LAN stream, thereby driving LAN/WAN integration.

Multiservice Networks

ATM has emerged as one of the technologies for integrating LANs and WANs. ATM networks are often called a multiservice networks because can support any traffic type in separate or mixed streams, delay-sensitive traffic, and non-delay-sensitive traffic. Figure 20-1 illustrates a private ATM network and a public ATM network carrying voice, video, and data traffic.

Figure 20-1   *ATM Support of Various Traffic Types*

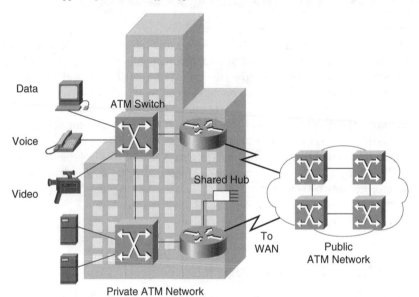

ATM can also scale from low to high speeds. It has been adopted by all the industry's equipment vendors, from LAN to private branch exchange (PBX). With ATM, network designers can integrate LANs and WANs, support emerging applications with economy in the enterprise, and support legacy protocols with added efficiency.

ATM Concepts

Several key characteristics of ATM are important to keep in mind as you design an ATM network:

- ATM is a hardware and software architecture that switches small units of data called cells. Each cell consists of 53 octets: 5 octets of header information and 48 octets of data. In contrast, Ethernet uses frames (rather than cells), which range in size from 64 bytes to 1500 bytes.

- ATM is a multiplexing and switching technology designed for flexibility and performance. ATM supports Quality of Service (QoS) options for flexibility and high-bandwidth options for performance.

- ATM supports environments where applications with different performance requirements need to be executed on the same computer, multiplexer, router, switch, and network. The flexibility of ATM means that voice, video, data, and future payloads that require isochronous access can be transported. Isochronous access is guaranteed access time to the network under all conditions.

- ATM has worldwide support. The ATM Forum, an industry forum made up of many companies including Cisco, works with formal standards bodies to specify ATM.

- The latency of an ATM cell in a switch is very small because of the short cell size. Short cells result in a tiny store-and-forward delay. Cells are switched very quickly in hardware.

ATM offers both permanent virtual circuits (PVCs), as when an engineer sets up static connections, and switched virtual circuits (SVCs) that are automatically set up and torn down when data needs to be transferred. As discussed in the next section, ATM (like Frame Relay) uses SVCs and PVCs for end-to-end ATM connectivity.

NOTE   The latency in an ATM network is very low due to the high speed and short cells.

PVCs

A PVC allows direct connectivity between sites. In this way, a PVC is similar to a leased line. Among its advantages, a PVC guarantees availability of a connection and does not require call setup procedures between switches. Disadvantages of PVCs include static connectivity and manual setup.

The protocol stack shown in Figure 20-2 applies to the ATM PVC, which Cisco uses for data transmission. Everything is statically configured, and no signaling is involved. The PVC is mapped to a network in a subinterface point-to-point configuration.

Figure 20-2 *PVCs*

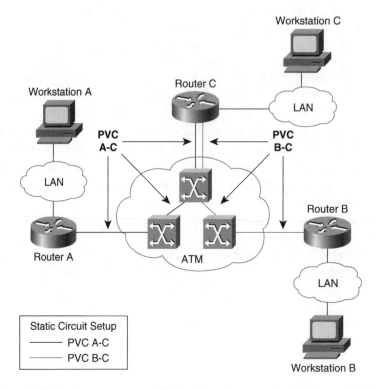

Example 20-1 demonstrates an ATM subinterface configuration, connecting two routers with the ATM Deluxe port adapter back to back.

Example 20-1 *ATM Subinterface Configuration*

```
First router:
interface ATM3/0
no keepalive
atm clock internal
!
interface ATM3/0.1
ip address 10.0.0.1 255.0.0.0
atm pvc 1 1 5 aal5snap
!
Second router:
interface ATM3/0
no keepalive
!
interface ATM3/0.1
ip address 10.0.0.2 255.0.0.0
atm pvc 1 1 5 aal5snap
```

The logical data link layer uses Subnetwork Access Protocol (SNAP) encapsulation, as defined in RFC 1483 (www.isi.edu/in-notes/rfc1483.txt), which allows multiple protocols to be multiplexed over one PVC. Each Layer 3 network protocol understands the ATM PVC as a network or subnetwork. Data across a PVC is statically switched in a series of steps that includes the examination of a Virtual Channel Identifier (VCI) and Virtual Path Identifier (VPI) fields. The VPI and VCI fields of the cell header identify the next network segment that a cell needs to transmit on its way to its final destination.

When configuring routers, only the local VPI/VCI at each end is relevant. To a native ATM computer or router, the VPI/VCI number can be thought of as a single logical channel number. The VPI field is 8 bits at the User-to-Network Interface (UNI) or 12 bits at the Network-to-Network Interface (NNI). The VCI field is 16 bits. Groups of VCI are bundled and switched together as VPI trunk groups. The VPI equals zero for most local applications.

SVCs

A SVC is created and released dynamically and remains in use only as long as data is being transferred. In this sense, it is similar to a telephone call. Therefore, establishing an ATM SVC involves an agreement between the end nodes and all the switches in between. Each end node has a special signaling channel to the connected switch called the User-Network Interface (UNI). Switches have a signaling channel between them called the Network-to-Network Interface (NNI). Cells that arrive on the signaling channel are reassembled into frames. After an SVC is established, it functions like a PVC. As discussed later in this chapter, SVCs can be used in point-to-point subinterface configuration or point-to-multipoint nonbroadcast multiaccess (NBMA) configuration. To effectively do an ATM design, more theory about how ATM works is in order. Figure 20-3 illustrates SVCs in an ATM network.

Figure 20-3 *SVCs*

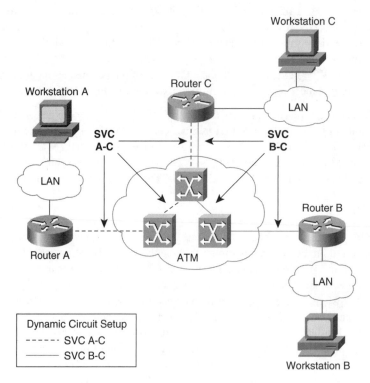

PVC/SVC Summary

To summarize this section, a PVC allows direct connectivity between sites. In this way, a PVC is similar to a leased line. Among its advantages, a PVC guarantees availability of a connection and does not require call setup procedures between switches. Disadvantages of PVCs include static connectivity and manual setup.

An SVC is created and released dynamically and remains in use only as long as data is being transferred. In this sense, it is similar to a telephone call. Dynamic call control requires a signaling protocol between the ATM endpoint and the ATM switch. The advantages of SVCs include connection flexibility and call setup that can be handled automatically by a networking device. Disadvantages include the extra time and overhead required to set up the connection.

We'll now move up the ATM model to the ATM adaptation layer (AAL), which is roughly analogous to the data link layer of the OSI model. The AAL is responsible for isolating higher-layer protocols from the details of the ATM processes.

ATM Adaptation Layers

The ATM reference model, as illustrated in Figure 20-4, is composed of the following ATM layers:

- **Physical layer**—Analogous to the physical layer of the OSI reference model, the ATM physical layer manages the medium-dependent transmission.

- **ATM layer**—Combined with the ATM adaptation layer, the ATM layer is roughly analogous to the data link layer of the OSI reference model. The ATM layer is responsible for establishing connections and passing cells through the ATM network. To do this, it uses information in the header of each ATM cell.

- **ATM adaptation layer (AAL)**—Combined with the ATM layer, the AAL is roughly analogous to the data link layer of the OSI model. The AAL is responsible for isolating higher-layer protocols from the details of the ATM processes. The most commonly deployed AALs are AAL1, AAL3/4, and AAL5. AAL1, a connection-oriented service, is suitable for handling circuit-emulation applications, such as voice and videoconferencing. Circuit-emulation service also accommodates the attachment of equipment currently using leased lines to an ATM backbone network. AAL1 requires timing synchronization between the source and destination. AAL3/4 supports both connection-oriented and connectionless data. It was designed for network service providers and is closely aligned with Switched Multimegabit Data Service (SMDS). AAL3/4 is used to transmit SMDS packets over an ATM network. AAL5 is the primary AAL for data and supports both connection-oriented and connectionless data. It is used to transfer most non-SMDS data, such as classical IP over ATM and LAN Emulation (LANE).

- Finally, the higher layers residing above the AAL accept user data, arrange it into packets, and hand it to the AAL.

Figure 20-4   *The ATM Reference Model Relates to the Lowest Two Layers of the OSI Reference Model*

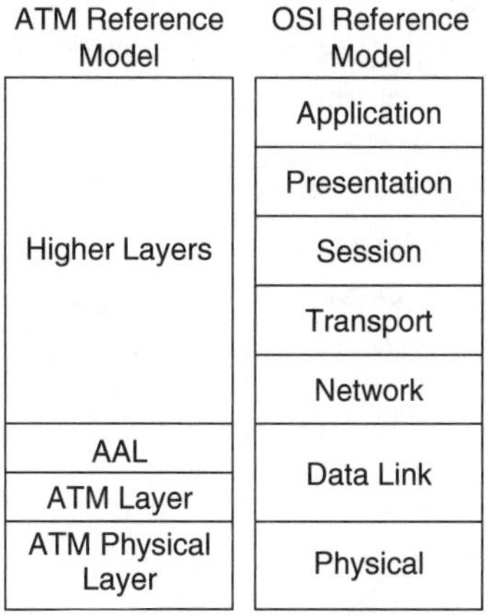

The ATM Physical Layer

The ATM physical layer has four functions:

- Conversion of bits into cells
- Control of transmission and receipt of bits on the physical medium
- Tracking of ATM cell boundaries
- Packaging of cells into the appropriate types of frames for the physical medium

The ATM physical layer is divided into two parts: the physical medium dependent (PMD) sublayer and the transmission convergence (TC) sublayer.

The PMD sublayer synchronizes transmission and reception by sending and receiving a continuous flow of bits with associated timing information. In addition, the PMD sublayer specifies the physical media for the physical medium used, including connector types and cable. Examples of physical medium standards for ATM include the following:

- Synchronous Optical Network/Synchronous Digital Hierarchy (SONET/SDH)
- DS-3/E3
- 155 Mbps over multimode fiber (MMF) using the 8B/10B encoding scheme
- 155 Mbps 8B/10B over shielded twisted-pair (STP) cabling

The TC sublayer has four functions:

- **Cell delineation**—Maintains ATM cell boundaries, allowing devices to locate cells within a stream of bits
- **Header error-control (HEC) sequence generation and verification**—Creates and checks the header error-control code to ensure valid data
- **Cell-rate decoupling**—Maintains synchronization and inserts or suppresses idle(unassigned) ATM cells to adapt the rate of valid ATM cells to the payload capacity of the transmission system
- **Transmission-frame adaptation**—Packages ATM cells into frames acceptable to the particular physical layer implementation

Voice Applications: Use AAL1

AAL1, a connection-oriented service, is suitable for handling circuit-emulation applications, such as voice and video conferencing. Circuit-emulation service also accommodates the attachment of equipment currently using leased lines to an ATM backbone network. AAL1 requires timing synchronization between the source and destination.

ATM Adaptation Layers: AAL3/4

AAL3/4 supports both connection-oriented and connectionless data. It was designed for network service providers and is closely aligned with Switched Multimegabit Data Service (SMDS). AAL3/4 is used to transmit SMDS packets over an ATM network.

SMDS Applications: Use AAL3/4

ATM adaptation layer (AAL) 3/4 supports connectionless SMDS service. To support SMDS, a message identifier (MID) and a sequence number are added to the AAL3/4 cell. Therefore, the payload portion is reduced to 44 bytes from 48 bytes.

Because of the additional header overhead the following rules come into play when you are looking to design an SMDS network:

- Cells from several sources can arrive on a connectionless channel simultaneously. The receiver can reassemble frames based on the MID and sequence number.
- More delay overhead is required for segmentation and re-assembly (SAR).
- Message identifier is added.
- Sequence number is added.
- Cyclic redundancy check 10 (CRC-10) is added.

SMDS Implementation

In a metropolitan-area network (MAN) environment, SMDS offers a very flexible service with connection options that can support changing business needs. It is a connectionless, cell-based transport service that can provide any-to-any connections between a variety of sites with no call setup or tear-down procedures. The SMDS network looks like a LAN service to the connecting routers.

As shown in Figure 20-5, the SMDS DSU receives a Layer 3 protocol data unit (L3_ PDU) such as an IP packet. This packet is then segmented into 53-octet cells at the SDSU and forwarded to the SMDS network. An SDSU on the receiving end performs packet reassembly.

Figure 20-5   *SMDS Connections*

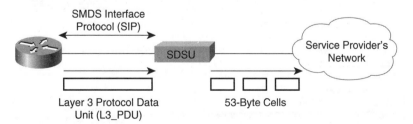

All major protocols are supported for SMDS by Cisco routers. Address mapping is one configuration matter to be considered during the design. The specifics of address mapping are protocol dependent. As illustrated in Figure 20-6, some protocols require static entries to be defined in the router; other protocols, such as TCP/IP, however, take advantage of SMDS's multicast addressing using ARP capability.

Figure 20-6   *SMDS Configuration*

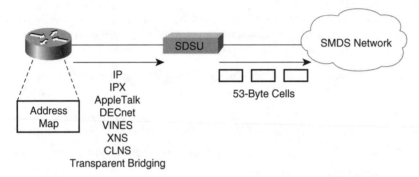

Example 20-2 demonstrates an SMDS multiprotocol configuration. This example is a typical interface configured for IP, DECnet, ISO CLNS, Novell IPX, XNS, and AppleTalk. DECnet needs to be configured globally and at the interface level.

Example 20-2   *SMDS Multiprotocol Configuration*

```
interface serial 4
ip address 1.1.1.2 255.0.0.0
decnet cost 4
appletalk address 92.1
appletalk zone smds
clns router igrp FOO
ipx net 1a
xns net 17
encapsulation SMDS
! SMDS configuration follows
smds address c120.1580.4721
smds static-map APPLETALK 92.2 c120.1580.4592.FFFF
smds static-map APPLETALK 92.3 c120.1580.4593.FFFF
smds static-map APPLETALK 92.4 c120.1580.4594.FFFF
smds static-map NOVELL 1a.0c00.0102.23ca c120.1580.4792.FFFF
smds static-map XNS  17.0c00.0102.23ca c120.1580.4792.FFFF
smds static-map NOVELL 1a.0c00.0102.23dd c120.1580.4728.FFFF
smds static-map XNS 17.0c00.0102.23aa c120.1580.4727.FFFF
smds multicast NOVELL e180.0999.9999.FFFF
smds multicast XNS e180.0999.9999.FFFF
smds multicast ARP e180.0999.9999.FFFF
smds multicast IP e180.0999.9999.FFFF
smds multicast APPLETALK e180.0999.9999.FFFF
smds multicast AARP e180.0999.9999.FFFF
smds multicast CLNS_IS e180.0999.9990.FFFF
```

Example 20-2   *SMDS Multiprotocol Configuration (Continued)*

```
smds multicast CLNS_ES e180.0999.9990.FFFF
smds multicast DECNET_ROUTER e180.0999.9992.FFFF
smds multicast DECNET_NODE e180.0999.9992.FFFF
smds multicast DECNET e180.0999.9992.FFFF
smds enable-arp
```

Example 20-3 illustrates a remote peer on the same SMDS network. DECnet needs to be configured globally and at the interface level.

Example 20-3   *Remote Peer Configuration on SMDS Network*

```
interface serial 0
ip address 1.1.1.1 255.0.0.0
decnet cost 4
appletalk address 92.2
appletalk zone smds
clns router igrp FOO
ipx net 1a
xns net 17
encapsulation SMDS
! SMDS configuration follows
smds address c120.1580.4792
smds static-map APPLETALK 92.1 c120.1580.4721.FFFF
smds static-map APPLETALK 92.3 c120.1580.4593.FFFF
smds static-map APPLETALK 92.4 c120.1580.4594.FFFF
smds static-map NOVELL 1a.0c00.0102.23cb c120.1580.4721.FFFF
smds static-map XNS 17.0c00.0102.23cb c120.1580.4721.FFFF
smds static-map NOVELL 1a.0c00.0102.23dd c120.1580.4728.FFFF
smds static-map XNS 17.0c00.0102.23aa c120.1580.4727.FFFF
smds multicast NOVELL e180.0999.9999.FFFF
smds multicast XNS e180.0999.9999.FFFF
smds multicast IP e180.0999.9999.FFFF
smds multicast APPLETALK e180.0999.9999.FFFF
smds multicast AARP e180.0999.9999.FFFF
smds multicast CLNS_IS e180.0999.9990.FFFF
smds multicast CLNS_ES e180.0999.9990.FFFF
smds multicast DECNET_ROUTER e180.0999.9992.FFFF
smds multicast DECNET_NODE e180.0999.9992.FFFF
smds multicast DECNET e180.0999.9992.FFFF
smds enable-arp
```

Logical Independent Subnets

The easiest way to organize the topology of an SMDS network is to treat the SMDS network cloud as a single subnet. For more flexible network designs, the SMDS network can be divided into multiple logical IP subnets (LISs), as illustrated in Figure 20-7. Configuring the subinterface feature on the router enables the association of one serial interface with multiple logical networks.

Figure 20-7   *Logical IP Subnets*

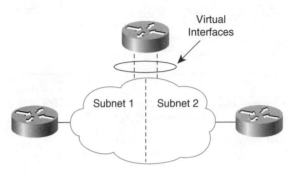

Data Applications: Use AAL5

AAL5 is the primary AAL for data and supports both connection-oriented and
connectionless data. The segmentation and reassembly (SAR) is simple because there is no
MID or sequence number. It is used to transfer most non-SMDS data, such as classical IP
over ATM and LANE. AAL5 also is known as the simple and efficient AAL (SEAL)
because the SAR sublayer just accepts the convergence sublayer-protocol data unit (CS-
PDU) and segments it into 48-octet SAR-PDUs without adding any additional fields. Cells
from two sources must not be mixed together on the same virtual circuit with AAL5. Figure
20-8 shows a typical AAL5 cell where the payload frame is broken down into a 48-byte
chunk through the SAR process and packaged into a 53-byte ATM cell.

Figure 20-8   *Use AAL5 for Data Applications*

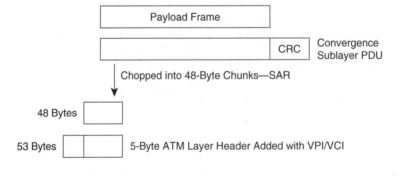

DESIGN RULE   AAL5 is used extensively for data virtual circuits.

ATM Routing in Private Networks

Private ATM networks use a 20-octet or 40-hex character address at the UNI. The address is significant from the left. Private Network-Network Interface (PNNI), described in the next section, will use prefix or best-fit routing.

A network of three routers could be identified as

1xxxxxxxxxxxxxxxxxxxxxxxxxxxxxxxxxxxxxxxx
2xxxxxxxxxxxxxxxxxxxxxxxxxxxxxxxxxxxxxxxx
3xxxxxxxxxxxxxxxxxxxxxxxxxxxxxxxxxxxxxxxx

The *x* represents a "don't-care" bit. The first hex character is sufficient to distinguish the three routers. Figure 20-9 shows a typical example of ATM prefix routing using network service access point (NSAP) addresses, which are the ATM address format defined by the ATM Forum. In LAN terminology, you can roughly think of the NSAP as an IP address because NSAPs are used for ATM node identification. NSAPs and the protocol for routing ATM cells (PNNI) is discussed in the next section.

Figure 20-9   *ATM Prefix Routing in Private Networks*

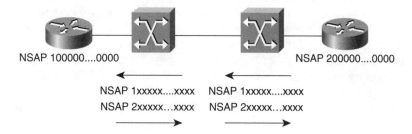

NOTE   ATM uses prefix routing. ATM routing does a best-fit match starting with the most significant character at the left.

PNNI

Private Network Node Interface (PNNI) provides dynamic ATM routing with QoS support. The PNNI protocol is used as the dynamic routing protocol for the global ATM internetwork and, therefore, has been specified as a hierarchical routing protocol. The number of hierarchical levels can vary from network to network. PNNI is dynamic because it learns the network topology and reachability information with minimal configuration. It automatically adapts to network changes by advertising topology state information.

PNNI uses prefix routing and supports an arbitrary address hierarchy. Routing aggregation takes place at any point in the address field. PNNI hierarchy has some advantages and disadvantages that should be considered before you decide to implement it in your network.

An advantage of PNNI hierarchy is its capability to scale to very large networks. This scalability is because of the exponential reduction in size of the visible topology and amount of received topology state information at each switch in the network. These reductions improve the effectiveness of your network by reducing the control traffic, memory, and processing required by each switch in the network.

A disadvantage of PNNI hierarchy is the loss of information caused by topology aggregation. PNNI performs route computations based on its view of the network topology. Because a hierarchical view of the network is restricted, compared to a nonhierarchical (flat topology) view, routing decisions are not as effective as in a flat topology. In both cases, a path to the destination is selected; however, in most cases the path selected in a flat topology is more efficient. This tradeoff between routing efficiency and scalability is not specific to PNNI; it is a known limitation of any hierarchical routing protocol.

The decision to implement a PNNI hierarchy depends on many factors, including the size of the network, type of network traffic, call setup activity, and the amount of processing and memory required to handle the PNNI control traffic. Because you must consider several factors, and their interdependency is not easily quantifiable, it is not possible to specify the exact number of nodes above which a flat network must be migrated to a hierarchical network. A high CPU load caused by PNNI control traffic can be a strong indication that a hierarchical organization of the topology is needed. Figure 20-10 depicts an example of PNNI routing where the ATM switches are sending aggregate link-state advertisements (similar to OSPF summary addresses) to one another for dynamic routing between ATM network 75*xxx....xxx* and 99*xxx....xxxx*.

Figure 20-10 *ATM Routing—PNNI*

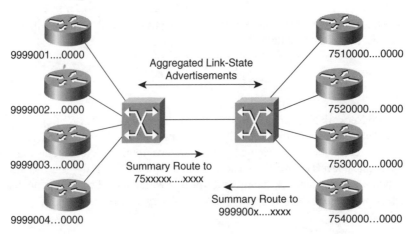

PNNI is complex because it supports routing for public and private networks:

- Switch to switch
- Private networks—NSAP addresses 20 bytes in length
- Public networks—E.164 addresses 20 bytes in length
- Network to network
- Logical NNI
- Private network-to-private network across a public network
- NSAP and E.164 addressing

NOTE   The primary goal of the PNNI hierarchy is scalability. A side effect of this scalability, however, is complexity.

The first adopted standard for ATM routing is Interim Inter-Switch Signaling Protocol (IISP), formerly called PNNI-0. IISP routing is configured statically on ATM switches. As shown in Figure 20-11, an NSAP route has a primary path and a backup path. If the primary path is down, an incoming SVC request routes to the backup path.

Figure 20-11   *Establish Static ATM Routing with IISP*

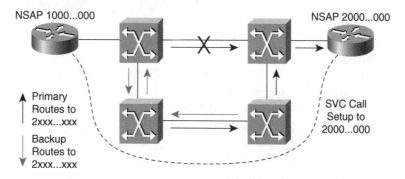

NOTE   The IISP protocol was recently approved by the ATM Forum and is supported in the Cisco LightStream 1010 switch. It uses UNI signaling for switch-to-switch communication, with nodes arbitrarily taking the role of the network and user side across IISP links.

LANE: ATM as a Virtual LAN

LANE is a standard defined by the ATM Forum that gives to stations attached via ATM the same capabilities they normally obtain from legacy LANs, such as Ethernet and Token Ring. As the name suggests, the function of the LANE protocol is to emulate a LAN on top of an ATM network. Specifically, the LANE protocol defines mechanisms for emulating either an IEEE 802.3 Ethernet or an 802.5 Token Ring LAN. The current LANE protocol does not define a separate encapsulation for FDDI. (FDDI packets must be mapped into either Ethernet or Token Ring emulated LANs [ELANs] by using existing translational bridging techniques.) Fast Ethernet (100BaseT) and IEEE 802.12 (100VG-AnyLAN) both can be mapped unchanged because they use the same packet formats.

Figure 20-12 illustrates a single ELAN, which consists of several entities.

Figure 20-12 *LANE Components*

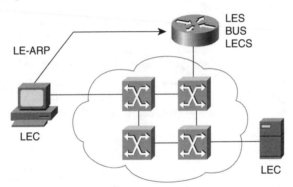

Note that the router is serving as the LAN Emulation Server (LES), Broadcast and Unknown Server (BUS), and LAN Emulation Configuration Server (LECS). The LECS and LES/BUS could exist on other LANE devices in the cloud, if desirable. Also, assume that this interface is connected to a switch.

- **LE Client (LEC)**—An entity in an endpoint such as a workstation or router that performs data forwarding, address resolution, and other control functions for a single endpoint in a single ELAN. The LEC provides a standard LAN service to any higher layers that interface to it. A router can have multiple resident LECs, each connecting with different emulated LANs. The LEC registers its MAC address with the LAN Emulation server.

- **LE Server (LES)**—Provides a registration facility for clients to register unicast and multicast MAC addresses. The LES controls "joins" to the ELAN. The LES handles LAN Emulation ARP (LE-ARP) requests and maintains a list of LAN destination MAC addresses.

- **Broadcast and Unknown Server (BUS)**—A multicast server that floods unknown destination traffic and forwards multicast and broadcast traffic to clients within an ELAN.

- **LE Configuration Server (LECS)**—Assigns individual LECs to particular emulated LANs by directing them to the LES that corresponds to the emulated LAN. The LECS maintains a database of LEC ATM or MAC addresses and associated ELANs. Only one LECS exists per ATM switch cloud and it can serve multiple ELANs.

When a workstation wants to connect to another station, the following transactions take place:

Step 1   The LEC software in the workstation sends an LE-ARP to the LES.

Step 2   The LES responds with the OSI NSAP address of the destination, if known.

Step 3   The LEC establishes an SVC to communicate with the destination MAC address.

Step 4   If the LES does not know the destination address, it can send the ARP to all other LECs.

Step 5   The destination can respond to the LES or directly to the sending workstation.

NOTE   LANE uses specialized client and server software to emulate the broadcast functions of a LAN.

ATM Design Models

When doing network designs with routers connecting to ATM service provider networks, the topology issues are similar to those in Frame Relay. Two primary topologies emerge: nonbroadcast multiaccess (NBMA) and hub-and-spoke, using subinterfaces. The NBMA model requires a full mesh of PVCs for complete connectivity; the hub-and-spoke model facilitates full connectivity with a partial mesh.

The connection scenario shown in Figure 20-13 more accurately reflects the long-term goals of ATM: end-to-end connectivity using ATM. The private network switch equipment attaches to the service provider switch over the public UNI just as the router did. Using this connection, a network designer could conceivably extend LAN Emulation over a WAN. The edge switch would have to set up an SVC tunnel through the service provider network for this operation.

Figure 20-13   *ATM Design Models*

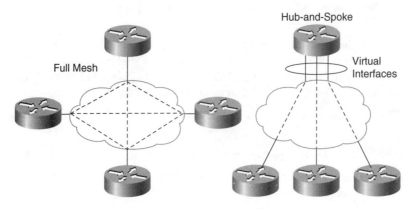

NOTE   Some ATM experts call ATM a data link protocol. Others call it a network layer protocol. Anthony Alles, Cisco Systems' ATM Product Line Manager, makes a good case for ATM being a network layer protocol in his white paper, "ATM Internetworking," available at http://cio.cisco.com. ATM specifies end-to-end addressing, but data link layer addresses are only significant between nodes. ATM addresses are hierarchical, similar to other network layer addresses such as IP and IPX addresses. From a layering standpoint, ATM is similar to X.25. IP and other network layer protocols will be carried by ATM, using what the ATM Forum calls the *overlay model.*

WAN Design Considerations

In WAN design, you must deal with a wide variety of media and traffic types. Each of these traffic types typically has its own requirements, such as constant or variable bit rate, circuit bandwidth, and class of service (CoS). The traditional requirements have been for data and voice. There is an emerging need to support video over these same networks. The data methods can include Frame Relay, T1, E1, ISDN, and X.25.

ATM is the preferred transport mechanism, with its capability to integrate this wide variety of traffic types and to support their unique requirements

StrataCom Nodes

StrataCom's networking system supports multiband ATM applications in private WANs and public carrier service offerings such as Frame Relay and native ATM. StrataCom's product family includes the BPX/AXIS, IGX, and IPX. These switches are used to implement digital high-speed, wide-area private and public networks (WANs) for interconnecting customers' LANs. These cell relay networks are created by interconnecting StrataCom network switches with high-speed digital trunks provided by most public common carriers or private network service providers. You can find out more information about the StrataCom (Cisco acquired StrataCom in 1996), including the StrataCom Strategic Wide Area ATM networking, "carrier class" products including an overview of the Cisco IPX, MGX 8220 and 8800, IGX 8400, BPX 8600, AXIS, Access products, INS, and StrataSphere NMS at www.cisco.com/univercd/cc/td/doc/product/wanbu/82/switch/sysm/sysmch01.htm.

Many of Cisco's newer WAN switches now support a new tag-switching standard called Multiprotocol Label Switching (MPLS). Service providers benefit from IP+ATM switching by being able to deploy emerging services such as voice over IP and VPNs without requiring multiple overlay networks. You can learn more about MPLS in the document, "Multiprotocol Label Switching (MPLS) Traffic Engineering," located at www.cisco.com/univercd/cc/td/doc/product/software/ios120/120newft/120limit/120s/120s5/mpls_te.htm.

Summary

ATM is an efficient technology to integrate LANs and WANs, as well as to combine multiple networks into one multiservice network. This chapter described the current ATM technologies that network designers can use in their networks. ATM has many options available to design engineers. Experience has shown that knowing and understanding ATM theory, as well as the customer requirements, is key to making your design a success.

Chapter Review Questions

1 What is an ATM PVC?

2 What is an ATM SVC?

3 Identify the OSI reference model layers of ATM and the function of each layer.

4 What is AAL1? Give an example of an application requiring AAL1.

5 What are three considerations for a design that may include SMDS?

6 What is AAL5? Give an example of an application requiring AAL5.

7 What is LANE?

8 What WAN-based design models are commonly deployed in ATM internetwork designs?

9 What are some of StrataCom's product family of switches and what are they used for?

SNA Design

Information technology—and specifically network technology—represents the most powerful tool we've ever had for change. It is a new engine for real economic growth, a new medium that will redefine the nature of relationships among governments, among institutions and businesses of all kinds—and the people they serve now, and might serve tomorrow. This powerful tool is here for all of us today.

—Lou Gerstner, CEO, IBM Corporation, CBIT, 1998

Upon completion of this chapter, you will be able to do the following:

- Identify the components that make up the SNA environment and the function of each
- Compare different methods of doing SNA internetworking and list the benefits of each
- Describe different topologies used in SNA designs

CHAPTER 21

SNA Design Overview

IBM introduced SNA in 1974. Even today, it is still alive and well in many networks. SNA is popular in many financial institutions, such as banks and brokerage houses, and in the retail environment, where it is commonly used to connect users to mainframes for order and inventory tracking.

Because of this, it is very important for every network engineer to have a solid understanding of the technology and the design guidelines for proper SNA network implementation. Certainly, older technologies, such as RSRB, have been replaced with DLSw and DLSw+ (Cisco's enhancement to the DLSw standard) in many implementations, but most of the same concepts still apply. This chapter deals with SNA as a technology and offers some design guidelines for each approach discussed.

SNA Components

SNA is a host-centric, hierarchical network architecture. Early implementations of SNA required the host to handle a large amount of overhead processing, such as polling and character-handling functions. These overhead functions later moved to a 37x5 communications device called a front-end processor (FEP). Figure 21-1 shows a typical SNA environment with three components: the host, the FEP, and the cluster controller, where the end terminals would attach to the network. To achieve connectivity and also handle the overhead required to manage the end nodes, the 37x5 devices were programmable and ran system software called the Network Control Program (NCP). Host software later evolved into the virtual telecommunications access method (VTAM).

Figure 21-1   *SNA Introduction*

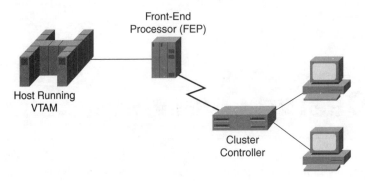

Network Addressable Units

All communication within SNA occurs between devices called network addressable units (NAUs). Furthermore, as shown in the following list, three kinds of NAUs are defined in SNA networks. Each type with its functional characteristics is as follows:

- System services control point (SSCP) software is part of VTAM on the host computer and controls the following:

  — Physical configuration of resources in its domain

  — Addition and removal of resources activation and deactivation of resources

  — Establishment of communication paths

  — Testing of resources

  — Recovery from problems with resources

- Logical unit (LU) software controls the following:

  — Interaction with end users

  — Interaction with host-based applications

- Physical unit (PU) controls the following:

  — Activation, deactivation, and operation of resources within a node

  — Operation of data links within a node

  — Loading of software within a node

  — Providing diagnostic information for a node

  — Communication with SSCP

SNA Hierarchy: Subarea Nodes and Peripheral Nodes

SNA hierarchy defines four types of nodes—types 1, 2, 4, and 5. The node types are distinguished by their functions and their associated NAU types. Types 4 and 5 are called *subarea nodes*, and types 1 and 2 are called *peripheral nodes*. Subarea nodes have routing capabilities, whereas peripheral nodes have little or no message-routing capabilities. The sections that follow discuss both node types.

Subarea Nodes

There are different types of subarea nodes, namely host and communication-controller subarea nodes. An example of host subarea node is a mainframe running ACF/VTAM. An example of a communication-controller subarea node is a communication controller (that is, 3705, 3725, 3745/46) running ACF/NCP. A subarea node owns its peripheral nodes and it provides network services for the peripheral nodes. This means that all traffic must pass through the subarea node and the peripheral node can be attached to only one subarea node.

Each subarea node has a unique subarea number. All communication in the SNA network is controlled by software on the mainframe (host) computer. All the resources associated with a particular host are said to be within the same domain. The NAU that controls the domain is the SSCP.

Peripheral Nodes

Peripheral nodes can transmit or receive messages to or from their subarea node only. Each peripheral node must be attached to a subarea node via components in the path control network. As shown in Figure 21-2, the cluster controller, known as a 3174, is considered as a *peripheral* node (PU type 2) in SNA. 3270 terminals that attach directly to the cluster controller are called a secondary logical unit (SLU).

Figure 21-2   *Peripheral Nodes*

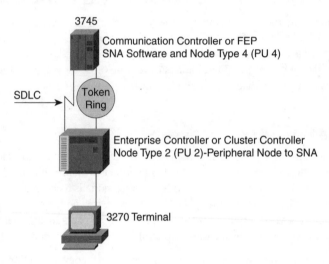

3745

Communication Controller or FEP
SNA Software and Node Type 4 (PU 4)

SDLC

Token
Ring

Enterprise Controller or Cluster Controller
Node Type 2 (PU 2)-Peripheral Node to SNA

3270 Terminal

SNA Subareas

An SNA subarea is a subarea node (host or communications controller) plus the peripheral nodes directly attached to it. It is defined in NCP and is usually associated with a FEP and the cluster controllers and other devices attached to it; a subarea could also be just a single FEP, however. A single FEP is also known as an Internetwork Node (INN), which effectively is an SNA router with a static routing table.

Subareas are the basis of SNA logical addressing. In subarea SNA, all routes are statically defined. Between any two subareas up to eight explicit routes can be defined. Each subarea has its own subarea number; devices are numbered within that area. Figure 21-3 shows five defined subareas, and each one is attached to a FEP link for SNA routing between subareas. In this setup, user sessions could be established in an "any-subarea-to-any-subarea" fashion. End user communication is discussed in the section that follows.

Figure 21-3 *The SNA Subarea*

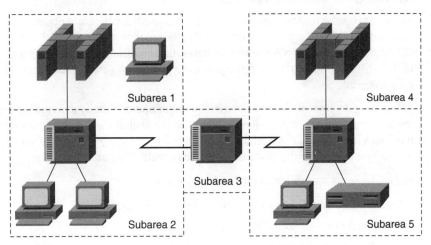

SNA End-User Session Setup and Communication

End-user communication is achieved through LU-LU sessions. When a user accesses an application on the mainframe, for example, an LU-LU session must be established. You can think of an LU-LU session as being roughly analogous to an end-to-end TCP connection when a Telnet user establishes communication with a Telnet host.

However, establishing an LU-LU connection is not as simple as it sounds. Before an LU-LU session can take place, other types of sessions must first be established:

Step 1 An SSCP must establish an SSCP-PU session with the PU that is resident in the type 5 node that contains the SSCP.

Step 2 After the SSCP-PU type 5 session is established, the SSCP must establish SSCP-PU sessions with the PUs of the nodes that contain the LUs that want to communicate.

Step 3 After Step 2, the SSCP can issue SSCP-LU session-activation requests for the LUs that want to communicate.

Step 4 At this point, the primary LU can activate an LU-LU session with the secondary LU.

If an LU-LU session is required between two LUs that belong to different domains, an SSCP-SSCP session is also required between the two SSCPs that control the domains.

It is very important to understand that all these sessions must successfully be created to allow for SNA session establishment, especially as you are designing and later troubleshooting SNA network problems.

Token Ring SNA Gateways

The most popular desktop terminal is a PC. PCs in SNA environments are typically attached to a Token Ring. As was described in the preceding section, a Token Ring–attached PC cannot just access SNA resources (that is, the mainframe) without its session being initialized. To do so, it must go through some type of SNA gateway for the required session establishment.

Token Ring devices are defined as switched major nodes in the system generation (sysgen) macros (that is, the host configuration files) on the host. A switched major node identifies the Token Ring station physical units, and their associated logical units, that can connect to the host mainframe or the host mainframe may "call" the station.

In fact, there are two different types of SNA gateways:

- **PU gateway**—Token Ring device appears as PU node type 2.
- **LU gateway**—Token Ring device appears as LU.

Figure 21-4 shows the two different types of gateways.

Figure 21-4   *Access to SNA by Token Ring Gateways*

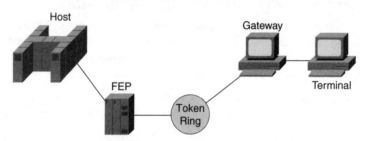

Token Ring Devices Can Appear as PU Type 2 or as Just an LU

The sections that follow discuss the SNA gateway types in further detail.

Pass Through Gateways

Several IBM products can be Token Ring gateways. The benefit of a pass through (PU) gateway is that it is invisible to the Token Ring–attached PC and the SNA host, because every Token Ring–attached PC must be manually defined in a switched major node in VTAM. Unfortunately, because of all these switched major node definitions, the downside is that PU gateways result in more overhead and administration on the host. The 3745 FEP, the 3172 gateway, and the 3174 controller all function as PU gateways.

Every PC is defined as a node type 2 and is in session directly with the SSCP. As Figure 21-5 shows, every PU in every PC gateway has a direct session with SSCP at the host.

Figure 21-5   *PU Gateway: Pass-Through Gateway*

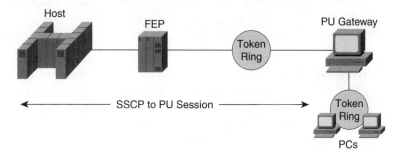

PU in Every PC in Session with SSCP

LU Gateways

Logical unit (LU) gateways solve the host overhead problem associated with PU gateways because the SSCP is only in session with the PU in the gateway. Furthermore, the amount of definition required for the node configurations in VTAM is reduced. As discussed later in this section, LU gateways can be collocated with either the host or the clients.

The other option is to locate the LU with the clients. As shown in Figure 21-6, gateway servers are collocated with the client PCs. This configuration reduces traffic across the WAN because the only session that needs to constantly poll is the host to the LU. The downside is that maintenance costs might be higher because the servers are all distributed.

Figure 21-6   *LU Gateway: Collocated with Client*

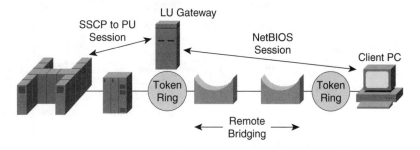

There are always pros and cons to any network decision. Placement of your LU gateway will vary and will depend on other things, such as bandwidth and staffing, which ultimately point to overall network cost.

LU gateways are available from several vendors. The desktop PC has client software, and a gateway PC has server software. The protocol between the gateway and the client PC is often NetBIOS or a derivative. For example,

- Novell SAA gateways can use NetBIOS over IPX or native SPX/IPX.
- Attachmate gateways can use NetBIOS over LLC2.
- Mitec gateways can use NetBIOS over TCP/IP.

A Third Option: DSPU

Another option to using a PU or LU gateway is to use a downstream PU (DSPU) concentrator. Cisco IOS software supports a Cisco router acting as a DSPU concentrator. Using this feature reduces the number of PU definitions required in the mainframe, thereby conserving mainframe resources, simplifying administrative tasks, and reducing polling overhead.

The DSPU concentration feature provides a network access and concentration point for SNA devices to communicate with an upstream mainframe. The Cisco router provides the appearance of a single device (PU 2.0) to the mainframe and simulates the mainframe (PU 5) to the downstream devices.

Features and benefits of the DSPU concentration option include the following:

- Reduces costs and complexity associated with using LU gateways for DSPU concentration
- Multiplexes multiple downstream PUs and LUs over a single upstream PU on the mainframe
- Supports Token Ring and remote source-route bridging (RSRB) connections to downstream SNA PU 2.0 and PU 2.1 devices
- Supports Token Ring and RSRB connections upstream to SNA hosts
- Passes alerts from downstream devices upstream to IBM's NetView
- Allows dynamic registration of downstream SNA devices
- Minimizes SNA host resource definitions
- Adds flexibility to transparently reconfigure the downstream SNA network to the host
- Conserves WAN resources by reducing traffic overhead
- Speeds up recovery of SNA sessions after a 3745 Token Ring interface coupler (TIC) failure

SNA Internetworking

Just like any other protocol discussed in this book, to make SNA internetworking work in your environment, you need to examine business and technical requirements. Design decisions, such as when to use serial tunneling for SDLC, SDLLC (SDLC-to-LAN Conversion), data-link switching (DLSw), Advanced Peer-to-Peer Networking (APPN), or Cisco Channel Interface Processor (CIP), can be daunting tasks for those faint of heart. This section tries to sort out these SNA internetworking choices so you are prepared to use them in their appropriate places in your design.

Business and Technical Requirements

In the past, the mainframe data center was characterized by centralized computing, separate PC/mini/mainframe strategies, interactive terminal-oriented applications, and centralized management. Today, the mainframe is often considered a corporate data repository that can support large-scale client/server applications. Further, resource management is becoming more distributed and often more cost effective because multipurpose routers can take the place of expensive, dedicated communication equipment.

There is no evidence that companies are replacing their mainframes with other types of equipment, despite some exaggerated claims to the contrary in magazine articles in the early 1990s. However, companies are repositioning the use of the mainframe as a huge data repository with enormous processing power and user-access support and integrating it with their enterprise networks. Goals for merging the mainframe environment and the internetwork environment include the following:

- Unified software strategy
- User access through the media of choice
- User access through the protocol of choice
- Client/server communication support
- New business applications support
- Support for new types of data, including video and voice
- Support for network backups
- Lower cost of ownership
- Compatibility with IBM
- Comprehensive service
- Effective mainframe MIPS usage
- High-throughput network connections
- Scalable designs
- Resources that are manageable from the mainframe or from the network

SNA Design Migration

"Old World" SNA network structures consisted of many distributed FEPs across an enterprise network. As shown in Figure 21-7, in these designs, in addition to the FEPs, there also were many SDLC links, some BSC (bisync) links, and Token Ring support. This type of design, aside from being difficult to manage, was also costly.

Figure 21-7   *Migration Strategy—Old World*

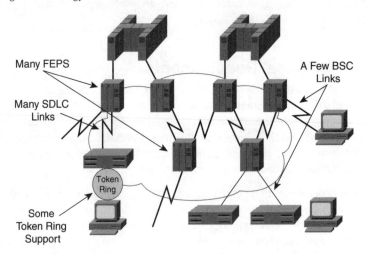

In the early 1990s, SNA networks began to deploy Frame Relay (RFC 1490), which offers support for SNA, so that many of the remote FEPs could be replaced (retired) with substantially lower-cost Cisco routers.

Cisco routers have two distinct applications that can result in substantial cost savings over multiple leased SDLC lines. In one application, RFC 1490 is an optional encapsulation scheme for RSRB over Frame Relay. The second application provides direct connection to RFC 1490–compliant IBM FEPs. The same SNA network pictured in Figure 21-7 now has routers and Frame Relay links where there used to be SDLC and FEPs, as illustrated in Figure 21-8. The end result is better performance and substantial cost savings, but in the evolution of SNA, this was the first step.

Figure 21-8   *Migration Strategy Part 1—Cost Savings*

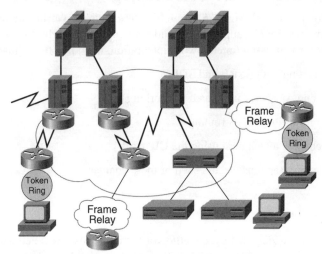

The next step toward a "New World" network architecture after introducing routers with Frame Relay was to move to a multiprotocol network. In this environment, the rest of the remote FEPs were replaced with Cisco routers, DLSw+ (data-link switching, discussed later in this chapter) was deployed, and BSC was tunneled. In this environment, as shown in Figure 21-9, protocols such as TCP/IP and IPX simultaneously share the same network that the SNA is running on. The multiprotocol infrastructure was important because no longer did corporations have a requirement for a "monolithic" SNA network, but rather they could run SNA across their multiprotocol networks.

Figure 21-9   *Migration Strategy Part 2—Multiprotocol Network = "New World" Network*

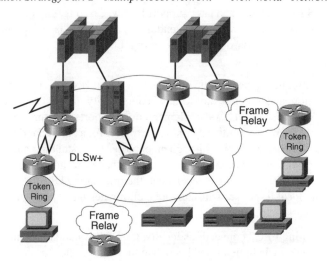

SNA Token Ring Internetworking

Migration from "Old World" SNA architecture to "New World," multiprotocol internetworks that still support SNA did not happen overnight. In reality, there were many enablers for mainframe/internetwork integration, including the following:

SNA tunneling with RSRB and SDLC

DLSw+ and APPN for integrated networking

APPN for multihost SNA routing

Router channel attachment using the CIP card

The following sections discuss each of these enablers.

Data-Link Switching

Today's most widely deployed method of tunneling SNA is called data-link switching (DLSw). DLSw provides a standard for integrating SNA and NetBIOS over TCP/IP. It reduces SNA overhead and minimizes SNA session timeouts. Although other enablers have been important over the past several years, today they are really historical in nature, because DLSw is the current enabler for many enterprise SNAs to scale. Because many networks still run RSRB and STUN, they are covered in the following sections.

In October 1994, the DLSw Working Group of the APPN Implementers' Workshop (AIW) completed a standard definition of DLSw that replaced the first-generation specification described in RFC 1434. The new standard brought increased functionality and interpretability. In May 1995, the new standard became RFC 1795 (which you can find at www.isi.edu/in-notes/rfc1795.txt).

Cisco IOS Release 10.3 and later support DLSw. Cisco is fully compliant with DLSw and is therefore compatible with other vendors. In addition, Cisco supports some valuable extensions to the standard DLSw. The term DLSw+ is used to represent all the standard features plus extensions.

DLSw+ introduces a peer-group concept that optimizes explorer processing, simplifies configuration, and enables "any-to-any" connectivity in networks that comprise many routers. Also, Cisco's DLSw+ implementation supports a feature called explorer firewalls. An explorer firewall permits only a single explorer for a particular destination MAC address to be sent across the WAN. Although an explorer is outstanding and awaiting a response from the destination, subsequent explorers for that MAC address are merely remembered. When the explorer response is received at the originating DLSw+, all explorers receive an immediate local response. This technique eliminates the start-of-day explorer storm that many networks experience.

By terminating LLC2 connections locally, the DLSw standard eliminates the requirement for LLC2 acknowledgments and keepalive messages to flow across the WAN. In addition, because routers acknowledge frames locally, LLC2 timeouts should not occur. The DLSw routers take responsibility for multiplexing the traffic of multiple LLC connections into TCP pipes and transporting the data reliably across an IP backbone.

RSRB supports Routing Information Field (RIF) pass-through, where the entire router cloud appears as one ring in the RIF. The complete RIF is visible to a protocol analyzer. This method allows only seven SRB hops along the entire path.

As shown in Figure 21-10, in DLSw+, the RIF terminates in the virtual ring. This technique scales up to longer paths than RSRB, allowing six additional SRB hops on either end. It does not allow the entire path to be visible to a protocol analyzer.

Figure 21-10 *RIF Termination Allows Longer Paths*

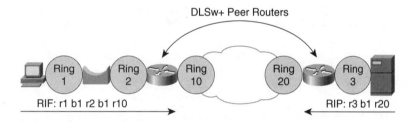

DLSW Circuit Establishment

DLSw circuits are established based on the fact that SNA devices on a LAN find other SNA devices by sending an explorer test frame with the MAC address of the target SNA device. When a DLSw router receives an explorer frame, the router sends a query frame to each of its DLSw partners to determine whether the partner can reach the target device. If one of its DLSw partners can reach the specified MAC address, the partner replies. This information can be cached to reduce the number of future broadcasts.

At this point, the DLSw partners establish a circuit that consists of the data-link control connection between each router and the locally attached SNA end system, and the TCP connection between the DLSw partners. After the circuit is established, SNA information frames can flow over it.

NetBIOS circuit establishment is fairly similar, except in this case, DLSw routers send a name query to their partners. Again, the standard does not describe how to cache NetBIOS names; if NetBIOS names are cached, however, subsequent searches for a given NetBIOS name will not require that the NetBIOS name query be sent to all DLSw partners.

An excellent resource for DLSW, "Designing DLSw+ Internetworks" can be found at www.cisco.com/univercd/cc/td/doc/cisintwk/idg4/nd2007.htm.

DESIGN RULE   Whenever possible, use DLSw+ for SNA transport across an IP-based WAN.

SNA Tunneling with RSRB

SNA tunneling with RSRB is one of the oldest and now less frequently used techniques for tunneling SNA. However, it is still found in a large number of networks today.

Because LLC2 peers communicate from end to end, the routers and the tunnel need to be transparent to the end-to-end timing. As shown in Figure 21-11, in steady state, all LLC2 Information (I) frames and ACKs must flow uninterrupted from end to end across the tunnel between the host and the end user.

Figure 21-11   *RSRB Tunnel in Steady State*

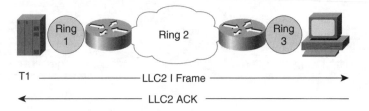

Normally, this end-to-end tunnel operation works well. If slow WAN links get congested, however, delays might trigger the LLC2 T1 timer. The T1 timer is used to control how long the router waits for an acknowledgment after an I frame is transmitted. The default is 1000 ms. When the T1 timer expires, the LLC2 station retransmits the original frame. Retransmission in turn causes more congestion. If the T1 (retries) timer expires, the end-to-end SNA session fails. These timeout problems, nonetheless, are important design considerations when choosing the transport for SNA. Several encapsulation options are available for SNA. The following is a list of technology options available in SRB networks:

- Direct encapsulation
    - Encapsulates LLC2 frames in a data-link frame (for example, HDLC for point-to-point link)
- Frame Relay encapsulation
    - Encapsulates LLC2 frame in Frame Relay per RFC 1490 specification
- IP encapsulation with Fast-Sequenced Transport (FST)
    - Encapsulates LLC2 frame in IP datagrams
    - Use if packets never arrive out of sequence and will not be fragmented
- TCP transport
    - Encapsulates LLC2 frame in TCP segment

— Use if packets can arrive out of sequence and might be fragmented and if local acknowledgment (ACK) is required

The "chatty" keepalive mechanisms inherent to LLC2 are a big problem with SNA in the WAN with direct, Frame Relay, or IP FST encapsulations mentioned in the preceding list. With these methods, LLC2 acknowledgements can be easily lost during periods of congestion in large WAN environments. A technique that uses TCP transport known as *local ACK* solves this problem. It is discussed in the following section.

Local ACK

Local ACK means that the Cisco router at either end locally terminates the LLC2 session with the SNA device. All LLC2 timing is now local between the Cisco router and the TIC-attached FEP. All LLC2 timing is also local between the Cisco router and the Token Ring–attached cluster controller or PC.

The benefit of local ACK is that it prevents any T1 timeouts from end to end. Local ACK does not affect response time to the 3270 end user because the SNA RUs still traverse from end to end to get to the terminal screen.

TCP encapsulation is always used for local ACK because TCP, unlike UDP, guarantees delivery of the data. TCP matches the reliable, connection-oriented characteristics of LLC2. As shown in Figure 21-12, local ACK basically "segments" the LL2 connection from Figure 21-11 into three distinct virtual sessions. There is an LLC session between the host and its adjacent router, and another LLC session between the client and its adjacent router. A TCP session between routers is used for reliable delivery of packets across the WAN.

Figure 21-12 *Local Acknowledgment Is LLC2 Termination*

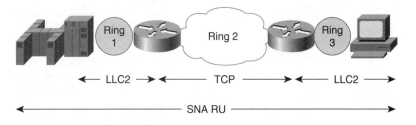

DESIGN RULE Use Local ACK when LLC2 endpoints are separated by unreliable WAN circuits.

Serial Tunneling Options

Serial tunneling (STUN) is another, older option for SNA encapsulation over the WAN. It actually has fewer encapsulation options than RSRB, which will be presented here mainly for a historical perspective. The characteristics of STUN are as follows:

- Serial direct between serial ports on the router
- Use to attach local controllers
- Best performance over a serial line
- TCP encapsulation between routers across an arbitrary IP internetwork
- Robust
- Routable
- Supports local ACK
- More overhead than HDLC or serial direct

DESIGN RULE You should use local ACK for TCP STUN connections in cases where congestion and delay in the WAN cause SNA sessions to drop. Local ACK for STUN is less critical than local ACK for RSRB because remote SDLC timers are larger due to the slower media involved.

Local ACK can provide better performance with TCP encapsulation because the router always accepts the whole SDLC window of data from the primary link station (PLS) or secondary link station (SLS). As shown in Figure 21-13, SDLC with local ACK allows both end SNA devices to "feel" like the network is very responsive, thus improving performance and preventing session loss across a congested WAN.

Figure 21-13 *Reasons to Use Local ACK with STUN*

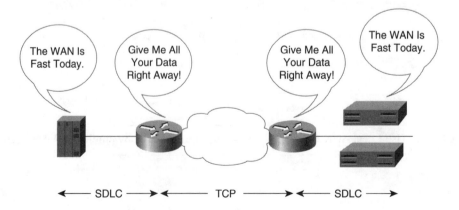

SDLLC Conversion

There has been a strong incentive for users to upgrade the FEP to include a Token Ring interface coupler (TIC). One key reason is that many SDLC interfaces can be consolidated because the throughput of a single 16-Mbps Token Ring is so high. A technique known as SDLC-to-LAN conversion (SDLLC) enables you to conserve precious FEP ports and connect remote SDLC devices, thus saving money and improving performance. SDLLC offers protocol conversion so that legacy SDLC controllers can connect to TIC-attached FEPs.

The SDLLC conversion is a local process on the Cisco router at the SDLC end of the connection. The Cisco router at the Token Ring end is not aware of the protocol conversion because the tunnel between the routers is RSRB.

As shown in Figure 21-14, the SDLLC router terminates LLC2 on one side and SDLC on the other side.

Figure 21-14 *Use SDLLC to Access TIC-Attached FEP*

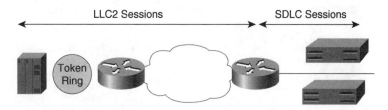

Local ACK can be used with SDLLC. The SDLC session always terminates at the SDLLC router. The SDLC end is always locally terminated. The LLC2 RSRB session from the TIC-attached FEP to the protocol conversion router can use local ACK.

As with STUN, local ACK breaks the end-to-end SNA session into three separate, reliable connections. Figure 21-15 shows how LLC2 is locally terminated between the FEP and the router at the Token Ring end. In this figure, a TCP tunnel running RSRB connects the peer routers. The protocol conversion router terminates SDLC at the other end.

Figure 21-15 *SDLLC with RSRB Local ACK*

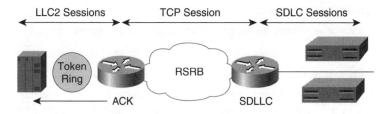

Load Balancing

Peer routers maintain a cache with the location of local and remote Token Ring devices. With load balancing enabled, the router caches equal-cost paths to a destination and allocates new sessions to each path on a round-robin basis.

If load balancing is not enabled, each router uses the preferred path for all explorers to one destination.

In Figure 21-16, new sessions coming from MAC A and MAC B and going to MAC 1 are allocated to the two paths to Routers Y and Z in a round-robin fashion. If a session connection goes to Router Z, it is mapped to either the Ring 3 path or the Ring 4 path to get to MAC 1.

Figure 21-16 *Load Balancing by Connection*

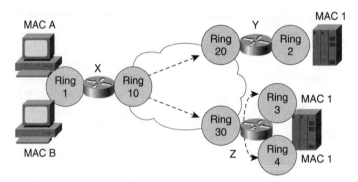

Advanced Peer-to-Peer Networking

APPN was developed by IBM to meet the following requirements:

- Provide an effective routing protocol to allow SNA traffic to flow natively and concurrently with other protocols
- Allow sessions to be established between end users without the involvement of the mainframe
- Reduce requirements for predefined resources and paths
- Maintain and enhance class of service (CoS) to provide prioritizing within SNA traffic
- Provide an environment that supports both legacy and APPN traffic

APPN provides peer-to-peer networking and dynamic locating of resources and routes. Sessions can be established between any two logical units in the network without involving a mainframe.

Directory services are distributed, so that a network node need remember only those resources that use its services. (Directory services can be centralized on VTAM, however.)

Each APPN router maintains a complete map of the network topology of all network nodes (routers) and links. Maintaining this map allows each router to select the best path through the network at any time, based on CoS. The topology is updated as changes in the network occur.

CoS is carried forward from legacy SNA and, in fact, is improved. In APPN, CoS extends to the end nodes in the network, instead of being used just between FEPs. Additionally, CoS can now be defined to a more granular level by explicitly defining line speeds, cost, and other characteristics

Different types of elements or APPN "node types" can be part of a given APPN topology. The next section discusses these node types.

APPN Node Types

In APPN, the Control Point (CP) is responsible for activating and deactivating resources within a node or between a node and adjacent nodes. The CP is also responsible for exchanging information, such as topology, with adjacent nodes. As shown in Figure 21-17, APPN defines four types of nodes:

- **Network node (NN)**—A router in an APPN network. Other resources go to the NN when activation of sessions and location of resources are required.

- **End node (EN)**—Can be thought of as an application host, accessing the network through its network node server. An EN contains a subset of APPN functionality, eliminating functions such as network topology maintenance and rerouting.

- **Low entry node (LEN)**—The original peer node that IBM defined for AS/400s and S/36s. It allowed communication between two nodes without the intervention of VTAM. Unfortunately, it did not provide for intermediate routing, so relay applications or direct connections were required for LEN nodes. APPN nodes are the extensions added to LEN nodes to provide this added functionality. LEN nodes can access an APPN network through an NN server, but resources must be predefined.

- **Composite network node (CNN)**—Invented to describe the APPN functionality implemented in VTAM and NCP. Working together, NCP and CNN can represent a single NN.

Figure 21-17   *APPN Terminology*

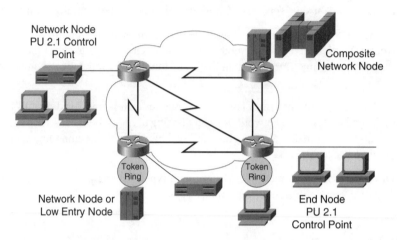

APPN routing is dynamic and is based on a least-weight path calculated from input received from all APPN network nodes. Each APPN network node is responsible for reporting changes in its local topology (that is, the node itself and the attached links). Topology information is passed until all APPN nodes receive it.

When a node receives data it already has, it stops forwarding the data to other nodes. Duplicate information is recognized via a check of update sequence numbers. Several underlying functions and capabilities enable APPN routing. These include Node Type 2.1 routing, Dependent Logical-Unit Requester/Server (DLUR/S) routing, connection networks, and border nodes. Discussion of all these topics are beyond the scope of this book. However, an excellent guide on CCO for designing APPN networks can be found at www.cisco.com/univercd/cc/td/doc/cisintwk/idg4/nd2006.htm.

Channel Interface Processor

With the Channel Interface Processor (CIP), a Cisco 7200 or 7500 series router combines the functionality of the IBM 3172 or 3745 gateway with multiprocessor routing. CIP combines the power and redundancy of the Cisco 7000 with a direct mainframe channel attachment delivering high-speed network access to the mainframe. By using the CIP's support of IBM's 17-Mbps ESCON channel with Cisco's 155-Mbps ATM interface processor, the Cisco 7000 provides very high bandwidth mainframe networking capability for both SNA and TCP/IP networks. Figure 21-18 shows a typical CIP configuration where the CIP transparently offloads work that the host or FEP would otherwise need to do.

Figure 21-18   *Typical CIP Configuration*

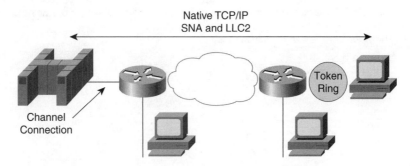

Cisco IOS Release 10.2 and later provide IP datagram support, and Cisco IOS Release 11.0 provides TCP/IP offload and SNA communication support.

TCP/IP offload moves the TCP layer and below from the mainframe into the router. This offload removes a significant amount of cycle overhead from the mainframe host processor.

Additionally, the implementation of TN3270 server on a channel-attached router, using the CIP or 7200-based CIP port adapter (CPA), provides an efficient method of removing the processing of TN3270 sessions from the costly mainframe cycles to a faster, more efficient router.

Each CIP takes a single slot in a Cisco 7000 series or Cisco 7500 series router and can support up to two IBM mainframe channel connections. Channel connections can be a mix of Bus and Tag or Enterprise System Connect (ESCON). As alluded to in this section, there is now a Cisco 7200 port adapter version of the CIP available.

For a good URL for CIP frequently asked questions, check out www.cisco.com/warp/public/458/19.html.

SNA Internetworking Topologies

You may ask yourself at this point, "How do I use these technologies in my network? How do I build reliable SNA networks? What connectivity models should I use? Should I implement a hierarchical model for SNA? What queuing mechanisms are available for SNA and what are their benefits and drawbacks?" These questions are addressed in the following sections:

- Reliable SNA Internetworks
- Connectivity Models
- Hierarchical Design Model for SNA
- Prioritization of SNA

Reliable SNA Internetworks

Figure 21-19 shows a typical redundant FEP, redundant Token Ring design.

Figure 21-19   *Use Dual FEP Design for Redundancy*

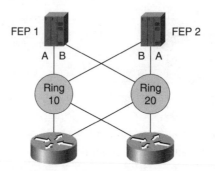

The same locally administered MAC address appears on both FEPs and allows for redundant Token Ring paths from clients to the host. When a client PC or downstream physical unit (DSPU) sends an explorer, it connects to the first FEP that responds.

The administrator configures half the gateways or DSPUs with MAC address A and the other half with MAC address B. About half connect to FEP 1, and the rest connect to FEP 2. In addition,

> 25% attach to MAC A on FEP 1 through Ring 20.
> 25% attach to MAC A on FEP 2 through Ring 10.
> 25% attach to MAC B on FEP 1 through Ring 10.
> 25% attach to MAC B on FEP 2 through Ring 20.

NOTE   This design provides load balancing and redundancy. The connection establishment still works if one of the FEPs is down.

Both FEPs are assigned MAC address A. Both FEPs are assigned MAC address B. This works because the two A addresses are not on same ring and the two B addresses are not on the same ring. Problems would occur if for some reason the two rings were merged.

Connectivity Models

Figure 21-20 shows a typical dual backbone Token Ring design. Clients reside on floor rings, and servers are attached to backbone rings in the risers of the building. Dual redundant FEPs are shown attached to the backbone rings.

Figure 21-20 *Dual Backbone Token Ring Design*

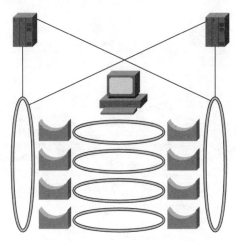

Explorers are controlled at the bridges between the client rings and the server rings. The bridges examine the number of hops in the RIF and decide to filter or forward the frame. The normal seven-hop limit can be configured to a lower number.

With maximum hops set to one, the clients can communicate with servers or FEPs one hop away. Clients cannot communicate with clients that are two hops away. Explorer multiplication and the extra traffic they impose are therefore curtailed.

NOTE   The dual backbone rings design is a traditional design that IBM has recommended for years. Its main feature is redundancy. A client on a floor ring can reach servers and FEPs in multiple ways, so connectivity is possible even when rings or bridges have problems.

Dual Collapsed Backbone Design

Dual collapsed backbone (illustrated in Figure 21-21) is an alternative to the conventional dual backbone Token Ring design. The backbone Token Rings are collapsed into the backplanes of two routers. Each router has an internal virtual ring bridged to the client rings.

Figure 21-21 *Use Dual Collapsed Backbone for Control*

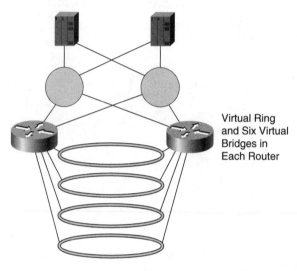

Virtual Ring
and Six Virtual
Bridges in
Each Router

Hierarchical Design Model for SNA

More than one virtual ring must be built to connect many sites. Configure a two-layer hierarchy if all the remote sites connect to one or two data centers, as shown in Figure 21-22.

Figure 21-22 *Use Two-Layer Hierarchy for Larger Scale*

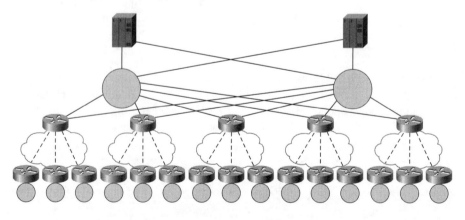

Because each virtual ring has a unique number, connectivity and explorer traffic can be controlled by setting the maximum hops value for explorers. Explorers pick up two hops on their way in from client rings to the central ring. Explorers should be blocked from being copied back out to all the other client rings: otherwise, a single explorer would result in 12 duplicate copies in Figure 21-22.

Prioritization of SNA

Cisco IOS software offers *priority queuing* and *custom queuing* as methods to prioritize time-critical SNA traffic across slow WAN links in the core. Both priority queuing and custom queuing are CPU intensive and therefore suitable for slow serial links.

Priority queuing works by setting up four interface output queues. The processor puts frames in either the high, medium, normal, or low queue. The high-priority queue is always emptied before any traffic in the medium-priority queue can be transmitted. Priority queuing is based on CPU queues and works with process switching only. In Figure 21-23, priority queuing is used. Here, you run the risk of starving lower-priority traffic if high-priority traffic is on the network.

Figure 21-23   *Priority Queuing for Mission-Critical SNA*

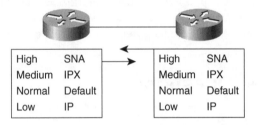

Priority queuing is a drastic prioritization scheme. Use priority queuing if SNA is your mission-critical traffic and you are not worried about other protocols potentially getting blocked. Queuing is not a substitute for adding more bandwidth to your network. The reality of "fancy queuing" is that if high-priority traffic always fills the pipe, more bandwidth is likely required.

DESIGN RULE   Use priority queuing if SNA is your mission-critical traffic and you are not worried about other protocols potentially getting blocked. Use priority queuing only on slow WANs. Do not use it on LANs.

Custom queuing works by establishing up to 16 interface output queues. The transmission window size of each queue is specified in bytes. When the appropriate number of frames is transmitted from a queue, the next queue is checked. Custom queuing is more fair than priority queuing because each queue gets a chance to send at least one frame each time.

Custom queuing is appropriate for prioritizing SNA traffic without excluding other traffic. The difference between custom queuing and priority queuing occurs when the link is heavily congested.

NOTE   Fancy queuing only "kicks in" when congestion is present. By far, that is one of the most often overlooked aspects in queuing theory. You can find an excellent discussion on custom queuing tuning by Paul Harris at www.cisco.com/warp/public/784/packet/jan99/17.html.

Summary

SNA is a host-centric, hierarchical, network architecture that has been in corporate networks since the mid-1970s. SNA can be integrated into router-based multiprotocol LANs through the use of SDLC tunneling, RSRB, DLSW, and SDLLC2. Many key topology options center around redundancy, as well as Cisco IOS software features, such as maximum hops and priority/custom queuing, that should be used to improve designs and help overall performance. With an understanding of the business and technical requirements of a design, you have the tools to make your SNA network a success.

Chapter Review Questions

1 What node type is an FEP and what kind of software runs on it?

2 What are the three network addressable units in the SNA architecture?

3 What is the function of SSCP?

4 What is a type 5 node? What software runs on a type 5 node?

5 When would you use DLSw+ rather than RSRB to internetwork SNA?

6 In APPN, what is an end node?

7 What is CIP and why is it useful?

8 What is a redundant Token Ring/redundant FEP design and how does it work?

9 How does custom queuing work?

CID Course Summary and Case Studies

100% of the shots you don't take don't go in.

—Wayne Gretzky

CHAPTER 22

Internetworking Design Summary

The goal of an internetwork design is a fully functional network that meets a client's business and technical objectives. The design should be adaptable as the client's requirements change and should use state-of-the-art technologies that will scale as the internetwork grows. The design should also use the client's resources effectively. To achieve this level of success, you should follow several key steps.

Steps for Designing Internetworks

This book has identified six key steps that you should follow to design a scalable internetwork. Figure 22-1 charts this design methodology.

Figure 22-1   *Internetwork Design Methodology*

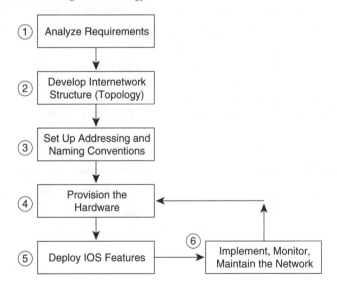

The Rubber Meets the Road: Measuring Your Internetwork's Performance with Network Management

Network management is probably one of the most overlooked areas, but yet arguably the most important after a network design has been implemented. I have seen many network-management systems that are so inefficient and reactive that the NMS operators essentially "wait" for a remote site to call them to tell them that their site is down. Being proactive benefits end users in many ways; however, don't expect a thank-you from them, because most of the time, they were not aware that you were even working on their behalf. Spotting and correcting potential problems before they happen is the key to being truly proactive.

To proactively measure the effectiveness of your network design, you should use network-management applications based on Simple Network Management Protocol (SNMP) and Remote Monitoring (RMON) to improve availability. The CiscoWorks 2000 set of applications has many specialized features for managing internetworks of Cisco products. CiscoWorks 2000 applications communicate with routers using SNMP and RMON to extract management information, upload and download configurations, and display real-time data.

CiscoWorks 2000 on a UNIX platform optionally records many levels of informational and debug messages remotely from the router consoles. Other SNMP platforms are available, including the popular HP OpenView and NetView 6000 environments.

Cisco products support the Cisco Management Information Base (MIB) and most industry-standard MIBs, such as MIB II and RMON groups 1–9.

In addition to CiscoWorks 2000, you should use protocol analyzers such as the Network Associates Sniffer or NETscout RMON probes, as well as other tools, such as the Fluke LanMeter, to monitor and troubleshoot your internetwork design. Table 22-1 lists those tools specific to CiscoWorks 2000, as well as some other excellent tools for monitoring and managing your network, including the Cisco **debug** and **show** commands, Syslogd, TACACS+, and homegrown scripts written in Perl or Expect.

Table 22-1 *Network-Management Tools*

CiscoWorks 2000 Tools	Other Monitoring and Management Applications
Relational database	Cisco **debug** and **show** commands
Router configuration management	Syslogd
Router health monitoring	Protocol analyzers
Real-time network analysis	DNS

Table 22-1   *Network-Management Tools*

CiscoWorks 2000 Tools	Other Monitoring and Management Applications
Performance data collection	TFTP and FTP
	DHCP and BOOTP
	Telnet
	RMON probes
	TACACS+
	Scripts (Expect, Perl, UNIX Shell)

Performance demands are greatest in the workgroup and the backbone. Router switching performance is critical at the point where a router connects client LANs to a high-speed backbone such as Gigabit Ethernet, FDDI, or ATM. Switching performance onto the high-speed medium is important because the router aggregates traffic from many slower media. As shown in Figure 22-2, workgroups and backbones are key concentration areas for large user-traffic volumes. As a rule, you should monitor switching performance wherever you aggregate traffic, which generally occurs in the workgroups and on the backbone.

Figure 22-2   *Monitor the Strategic Points of the Internetwork*

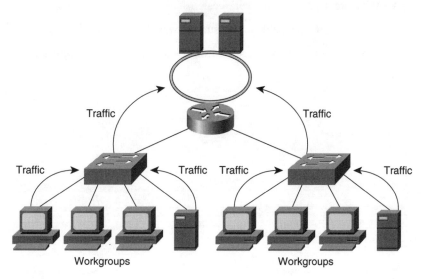

Summary

Internetwork design is not a perfect science. Many guidelines have been described in this book, but every network is different. The goal of an internetwork design is a fully functional network that is both cost-effective and scalable while simultaneously meeting a client's business and technical objectives. The design should be adaptable as the client's requirements change and should use state-of-the-art technologies that will scale as the internetwork grows. The design should also use the client's resources effectively. To achieve this level of success, several key internetwork design steps should be followed. Furthermore, your network-management strategy should consist of tools to ensure that your internetwork design functions as intended.

To further enhance your design abilities, the appendixes contain several design and implementation guides. You are encouraged to study these design guides and refer to them as needed. Although there will undoubtedly be "exceptions to the rules," for the majority of network designs, the points discussed in this book should enable you to build a cost-effective and scalable internetwork—one that you can be proud of.

Chapter Review Questions

1   What is the primary goal of a good internetwork design?

2   What are the six internetwork design steps?

3   What tools are available to measure network performance?

4   Where in your network are performance demands generally greatest?

Although Harvard Business School employs a variety of teaching methods, our hallmark—the case study method—fuses analysis and action. Our goal is to create an environment where students learn how to tackle difficult, complex problems—by probing, discussing, and integrating, working together toward an understanding much deeper than ever could be achieved on their own.

—Kim B. Clark, Dean of Harvard Business School

Upon completion of this chapter, you will be able to do the following:

- Use the technical tips and tools learned in this book to effectively put network design into practice

CHAPTER 23

Case Studies

We have spent 22 chapters on network design principles for you to use in your networks. As the adage says, "This is where the rubber meets the road." Becoming proficient in network design takes practice and creative thinking. Much like Harvard Business School's case study method used for reinforcing business concepts, I can't stress enough that book knowledge alone is not sufficient to become proficient in the area of network design. Just like any career path, for the network designer, the challenge of finding solutions to complex internetwork problems should be something that you fully enjoy.

This chapter goes through six different case studies, each of which has multiple answers, found in Appendix B, "Solutions to Case Studies" (in network design, there really never is one right answer). I encourage you to spend time thinking about your own creative solutions before looking at the answers. They will profoundly affect your ability when testing under the pressure cooker of the CCIE lab and, more importantly, in real-world design scenarios.

Case Study 1: Virtual University

Virtual University (VU) is an urban university with five buildings. As shown in Figure 23-1, the buildings are designated Physics, Math, Chemistry, Philosophy, and Admin. These buildings are all within a few hundred meters of each other, and the university has control of the rights of way between the buildings. VU needs a substantial upgrade to its network. This network upgrade should lay the foundation for three to five years of growth. It should be expected that demanding high-bandwidth applications will be deployed.

Figure 23-1 *Current Design: Virtual University*

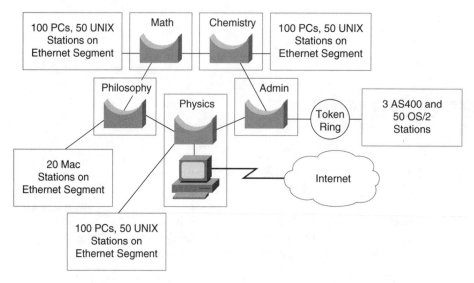

Current Network

The current network is a flat, all-bridged network. There is no isolation through filters. The primary networking protocol is TCP/IP, although VU also has AppleTalk and SNA. The physical and data link layers are primarily Ethernet. Token Ring is used in the SNA network, which is isolated from the remainder of the network. The following sections detail the network layout.

Physics

- Ten floors strung together with 10Base2 Ethernet.
- A cluster of multiprocessor UNIX servers.
- One hundred PCs running TCP/IP distributed throughout the building.
- Fifty UNIX workstations distributed throughout the building.
- Traffic patterns are fairly stable; 80% of the traffic is to the local servers.
- Connection to the Internet is available in the Physics building through three dedicated PCs with V.34 modems; a user must physically go to Physics to use the Internet connection.
- Bridged to Philosophy and Admin.

Philosophy

- Twenty Apple Macintosh computers running AppleTalk.
- Five laser printers.
- Bridged to Physics and Math.

Math

- Ten floors with a 10BaseT hub on every second floor.
- A cluster of multiprocessor UNIX servers.
- One hundred PCs running TCP/IP distributed throughout the building.
- Fifty UNIX workstations distributed throughout the building.
- Traffic patterns are fairly stable; 80% of the traffic is to the local servers.
- Bridged to Philosophy and Chemistry.

Chemistry

- Five large floors bridged through a Cisco AGS+ router with routing disabled.
- One hundred PCs running TCP/IP distributed throughout the building.
- Fifty UNIX workstations distributed throughout the building.
- Some end stations are connected through 10BaseT hubs; others are attached to thick Ethernet that runs throughout the building.
- Traffic patterns are fairly stable; 80% of the traffic is to the local servers.
- Bridged to Math and Admin.

Admin

- There is a Token Ring network with the following components attached:
  - Three AS400 minicomputers
  - Fifty IBM PCs running OS/2
- Fifty IBM 5250 terminals access the AS400 over daisy-chained twin-axial cable.
- The Token Ring network does not attach to the campus Ethernet-bridged LAN. The Ethernet is just passing through this building, going to Chemistry and Physics. Any access to the Admin systems requires that you be in the Admin area.

New Network Requirements

Virtual University is seeking a complete redesign of its network. Caveats for the new design are as follows:

- In general, any network user, in any building or department, must be able to communicate with any other user via e-mail. In addition, all users, including Admin and Philosophy, must have access to the Internet.

- The usage of the buildings by departments will remain the same. There may be a need for more end stations in each building, but not at this time.

- The positioning of servers may change. It is desirable to have the servers as centralized as possible for ease of management.

- The redesign can include upgrades to the cable plant.

- All users of the network must be able to access the Internet. Any user must be able to send e-mail to and receive e-mail from any other user.

- Professors must be able to access the IBM applications in Admin via TCP/IP. Gateways will be provided for this purpose; this design need only provide the path to the gateway device. Students must not be able to access Admin.

- There must be a future upgrade path that can support new technology, more bandwidth demands, and possible remote users or other campuses via WAN connections.

Case Study Task

Design a network solution that fully addresses these new network requirements for Virtual University.

Case Study 2: Simple Minds

Simple Minds is a benefits administration company that has 10 sites throughout the United States in major metropolitan areas. Each site has the same layout, shown in Figure 23-2. There is a building with 10 floors and a basement. Workers in the buildings use PCs primarily to do word processing, database access, and e-mail. The database is primarily ASCII text in nature. TCP/IP is used as the network protocol; the addresses are manually administered. The company is using an arbitrarily selected Class B address and is not connected to the Internet.

Figure 23-2 *Current Design: Simple Minds*

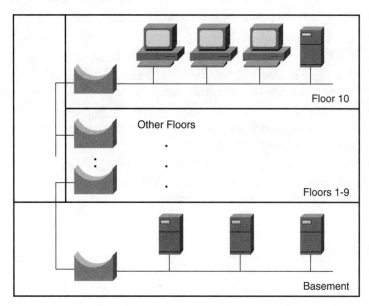

Current Network

Each floor has about 40 to 50 PCs and four to five servers that are Ethernet-attached. The servers on the floor are accessed only by users on that floor. There are also 10 servers in the basement, which are accessed by all users in the building. All floors are connected by bridges to the basement. The individual sites are not currently connected to each other. Any communication that must occur between sites is done via telephone (voice), conventional mail, or overnight express service.

Each PC generates about 100 kbps of traffic. Most of the traffic (about 90%) is for the local servers; 10% is for a shared server in the basement.

New Network Requirements

Simple Minds is experiencing extensive growth. It anticipates that there will be up to 100 user PCs and 10 servers per floor. In addition, the company is performing application upgrades. These new packages will do much more graphical presentation of data. Simple Minds is finding that the addition of more users and newer applications is resulting in severe access-performance problems in its network. It also sees a need to interconnect the major sites, anticipating that 1% of the traffic from each building will go to some other building. Future company growth is expected to result in more sites being added, up to a maximum of 30, with the same end-user requirements.

The new design must provide the following:

- A highly scalable interconnection method within the building.

- Logical isolation between workgroups (floors) for the purpose of administrative control.

- A detailed recommendation for IP addressing of the network with the possibility of future connection to the Internet. Present alternatives for the Internet connection.

- A recommendation regarding routing protocols required, including at least one sample configuration script for the recommended protocol. The company is willing to consider readdressing its network.

- Details regarding the method of interconnecting sites (that is, WAN connections) are not required. Any protocols recommended must be open (nonproprietary) standards readily available from multiple vendors.

Case Study Task

Design a network solution that fully addresses these new network requirements for Simple Minds.

Case Study 3: ABC Advertising

ABC Advertising is located in three buildings. As shown in Figure 23-3, two of the buildings, Building A and Building B, are close together; Building C is about a quarter mile away. ABC uses a combination of network systems that includes Novell IPX, AppleTalk, and UNIX workstations using TCP/IP. IPX is used primarily for PC-based accounting and billing applications; AppleTalk is used for graphics layout; high-end users employ UNIX workstations.

Figure 23-3 *Current Campus Design: ABC Advertising*

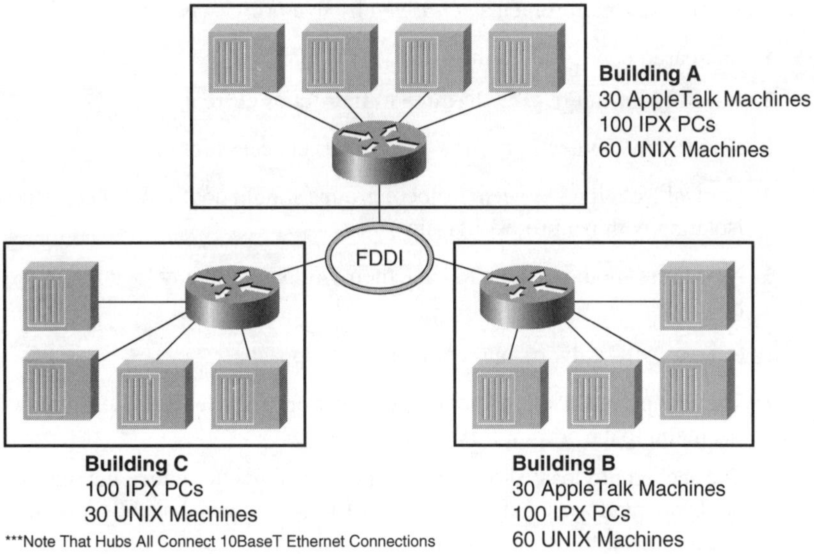

Building A
30 AppleTalk Machines
100 IPX PCs
60 UNIX Machines

FDDI

Building C
100 IPX PCs
30 UNIX Machines
***Note That Hubs All Connect 10BaseT Ethernet Connections

Building B
30 AppleTalk Machines
100 IPX PCs
60 UNIX Machines

Current Network

The current campus backbone is a FDDI ring that goes between the three buildings. There is a router in each building that connects to the FDDI ring. Each router also has four Ethernet interfaces. 10BaseT hubs attach to the router Ethernet interfaces. Table 23-1 shows the current population of users.

Table 23-1   *ABC Advertising User Population*

	Building A	Building B	Building C	Total
AppleTalk	30	30	0	60
Novell	100	100	100	300
UNIX	60	60	30	150
Total	190	190	130	510

The AppleTalk users have high-end Power Macintosh computers; IPX users have PCs with Windows 3.1. The company is migrating to Windows 98. The UNIX users have high-end SPARCstations. Each protocol group has its own set of applications, including e-mail, and there is little communication between groups.

New Network Requirements

The new network requirements are driven by five primary needs:

1   Increased bandwidth to the end-user stations.

2   Capacity for future growth (three to four times current).

3   Any-to-any connectivity for e-mail; Internet access for all.

4   Logical isolation between protocol groups should continue. There is no need for isolation within a protocol group.

5   New users should be able to have their workspace in any location in the three buildings.

Furthermore, ABC Advertising requires two proposals:

1   The first proposal should address the network requirements described while maintaining the current mix of protocols.

2   The second proposal should be a longer-term plan to reduce the number of different hardware platforms and, especially, software systems that are supported. ABC would like to standardize on applications, operating systems, and network protocols as much as possible. It requires details regarding how this standardization might be done.

Case Study Task

Design a network solution that fully addresses these new network and proposal requirements for ABC Advertising.

Case Study 4: Widespread, Inc.

Widespread, Inc., is a diversified company with locations throughout the United States. The sites are distributed as follows:

* Two large data centers located 10 miles apart.

* Four large regional centers located 500 miles from the large data centers.

* Sixteen local offices located 200 miles from the closest regional center.

The traffic patterns between the sites, as shown in Figure 23-4, are well known and are as follows:

* The *Data Centers* generate a constant 2 Mbps of traffic between them doing real-time database backup. Each is always online.

* The *Regional Offices* generate an average of 96 kbps of traffic for the active data center during business hours.

- The *Local Offices* generate an average of 48 kbps for the active data center during business hours. An additional 12 kbps of traffic leaves each local office for another local office.

Figure 23-4 *Current Bandwidth Requirements: Widespread, Inc.*

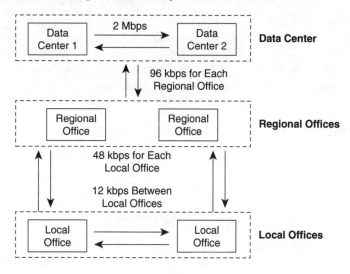

Current Network

The network is undergoing complete redesign.

New Network Requirements

Assume that the following cost structure is in place from the service provider, and only these offerings are available:

- Leased lines are priced as follows:
    - 64 kbps circuits cost $4 per mile per month for the first 100 miles and $1 per mile after that.
    - 128 kbps circuits cost $8 per mile per month for the first 100 miles and $2 per mile after that.
    - 1544 kbps circuits cost $16 per mile per month for the first 100 miles and $4 per mile after that.

- Frame Relay is priced as follows:
    - Access at 64 kbps costs $400 per month.
    - Access at 1544 kbps costs $1200 per month.
    - PVCs cost $40 per month (one charge end-to-end, not CIR-dependent).

Widespread, Inc. requires a network using any combination of leased lines and Frame Relay. The data centers must have circuits for their real-time database backup. The regional and local offices must have redundant access to each data center to support the traffic loads described. All applications are TCP/IP-based. Make recommendations regarding addressing and routing protocols as part of the design.

Case Study Task

Design a network solution that fully addresses these new network requirements for Widespread, Inc.

Case Study 5: TurtleNet Consulting

TurtleNet Consulting has two major lines of business. It provides technical and management training to Fortune 1000 companies and does custom application development for PC and UNIX environments.

The company headquarters is in San Francisco, and it has a large training center located in San Jose, California. The company has field offices in Los Angeles, Chicago, Dallas, New York City, and Washington, D.C. Figure 23-5 shows each of these locations.

Figure 23-5 *Current Design: TurtleNet Consulting*

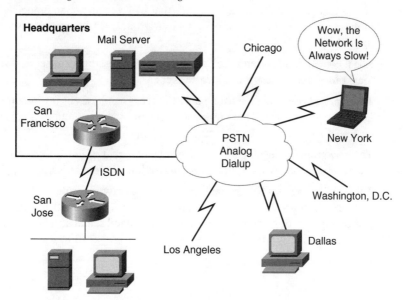

Current Network

The critical data for the company is kept at the office in San Francisco. There are 35 PC users who use IPX to communicate with 5 servers. These are all connected on a single LAN segment. There is another LAN in San Jose with 12 users and 2 servers. There is an ISDN link between San Francisco and San Jose. There is a mail server in San Francisco. Users at other locations do not have network connections except for dialup access to the mail server. The mail system is often used to transport large data files as attachments. The mail server is often down or unavailable due to the volume of traffic it is supporting.

New Network Requirements

TurtleNet Consulting is in a rapid-growth phase and requires a reliable, high-performance network to support this growth. The company is expected to grow from the current user population of approximately 65 users to at least 500 to 1000 users. The new users will be primarily trainer/consultant and program-development personnel. The company is open to any ideas because they are essentially building a new network.

General caveats for the new network are as follows:

- Every user must be able communicate with every other user via e-mail. This connection must be a reliable connection and have high availability.

- Administrative, technical, and management personnel at each site must be able to access databases at the corporate office that will remain in San Francisco. The access to these servers must be controlled by user groups. A backup strategy is needed for these databases.

- Local connection is required in each office for accessing local servers. All users at a local office may access these local servers.

- Trainers and consultants must be able to access databases of information from anywhere at any time. These users are frequently working out of hotel rooms or at customer sites.

- The new program developers may live anywhere in the United States and work out of their homes. They will require more time online, but not continuously.

- The company would like to standardize on one network protocol and is open to recommendations. Any recommendation must be very detailed and include protocols, addressing, server placement, management strategies, and access methods. All recommendations must be justified.

- Every user must be able to get to the Internet.

Case Study Task

Design a network solution that fully addresses these new network requirements for TurtleNet Consulting. (After your successful redesign, the CEO promised to meet with you to consider changing the company name to Jaguar Consulting and granting you some stock options.)

Case Study 6: National Mathematical Bank

National Mathematical Bank (NMB) is a small bank whose network has been evolving over the past few years. Originally, its network consisted of all SNA 3270 applications that ran on an IBM mainframe computer. During the past two years, it has been migrating to distributed Windows-based applications accessed through Novell IPX. The bank is experiencing sluggish response and generally poor performance in its network as it grows. Figure 23-6 shows the current network setup.

Figure 23-6 *Current Network Design Hierarchy: NMB*

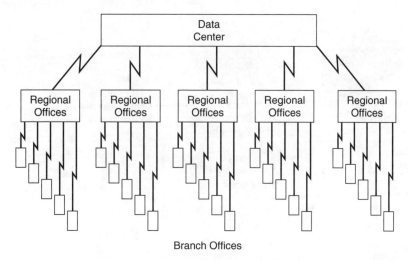

Branch Offices

Current Network

The current network hierarchy, as shown in Figure 23-6, consists of a main data center, 5 regional offices, and 25 local offices. The local offices are clustered in groups of 5 around the regional offices.

The details of the network, shown in Figure 23-7, are as follows:

- Headquarters office/data center is in one building that spans four floors.
- Client PCs Token Ring are attached on each floor.
- Dual-backbone Token Rings (identified as Ring A and Ring B) in the data center are bridged to floor rings.
- ES9000 is in the data center, running batch and online 3270 applications.
- One 3745 FEP in the data center dual-attached to the backbone rings.
- The FEP is also attached to FEPs at the regional offices via an SDLC line at 19.2 kbps.
- Four 3174 cluster controllers are attached to backbone ring A and serve a total of 100 3270 terminals.
- One hundred PCs are attached to the floor rings.
- Four Novell servers are attached to backbone ring B.
- Four SNA gateways are attached to backbone ring B; the PCs use NetBIOS to reach the gateways.

Figure 23-7   *Current Design: NMB HQ*

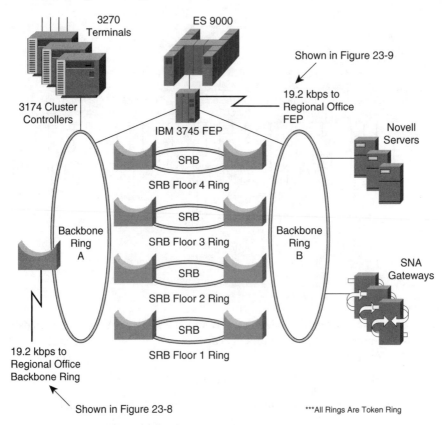

Each regional office, the topology of which is shown in Figure 23-8, is in a four-story building with the same configuration:

- Token Ring LANs are on each floor.
- One backbone ring is bridged to the floor rings.
- Backbone ring is bridged to Backbone Ring A at the data center using a 19.2 kbps line.
- Forty PCs are attached to the floor rings.
- Four Novell and four SNA Gateway servers are attached to the backbone.
- A 3745 FEP is SDLC-attached to local 3174 controllers and the SNA Gateways.
- The FEP is attached to the FEP at the data center as described in the Headquarters with a 19.2 kbps line.
- Three IBM 3174 controllers serve a total of 30 type 3270 terminals.

Figure 23-8 *Current Design: NMB Region*

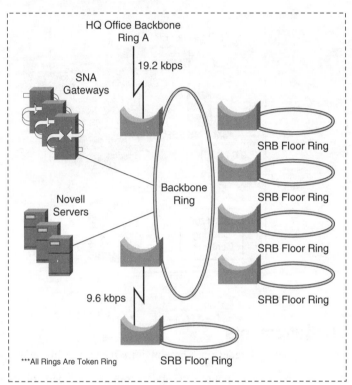

Each of the 25 branches, the topology of which is shown in Figure 23-9, has the same configuration, as described in the following list:

- A banking controller with ATMs is SDLC-attached to the FEP at the regional office over a 9.6 kbps line.

- Four IBM PCs and 1 server are attached to a local Token Ring.

- The local Token Ring is bridged to the backbone ring at the regional center over a 9.6 kbps line.

Figure 23-9 *Current Design: NMB Branch*

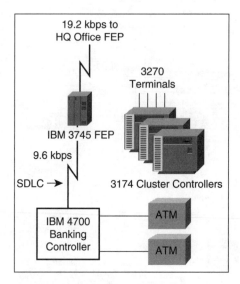

New Network Requirements

NMB requires a network redesign. Three major issues drive this redesign:

1 It needs to improve response time and overall network performance.

2 NMB is merging with another bank that is larger and will have more influence in technology directions. This other bank has gone much further in migration to client/server. It has standardized on TCP/IP as its network protocol for new applications; existing applications are tunneled until they can be rewritten.

3 The new bank's router-based TCP/IP network must be integrated with NMB's network.

Case Study Task

Design a network solution that fully addresses these new network requirements for National Mathematical Bank.

PART VIII

Appendixes

Answers to Chapter Review Questions

Chapter 1

1   List and describe five goals of a sound network design.

The five goals of sound network design are as follows:

- Functionality
- Scalability
- Adaptability
- Manageability
- Cost Effectiveness

2   What is the key tradeoff that must be made in most network designs?

The key tradeoff is cost versus availability. Face it, there always is room for improvement in any network design. An understanding of what a network costs to operate and, more importantly, the total cost of network ownership is vital to justifying technology costs.

3   Describe the steps that need to take place in a good network design methodology.

The steps for a good network design methodology are as follows:

Step 1   Analyze requirements.

Step 2   Develop the internetwork structure.

Step 3   Set up addressing and naming conventions.

Step 4   Provision the hardware.

Step 5   Deploy Cisco IOS software features to implement, manage, and monitor the network.

Step 6   Implement, monitor, and maintain the network.

4   At which tier of the hierarchical model is QoS usually deployed?

QoS can be found at any tier of the hierarchical model, but it is usually found at the core tier; however, this function is getting pushed to the distribution tier and eventually will move to the access tiers, especially as voice-based applications such as IP telephony propagate.

5   Why is scalability so important in good network design?

Scalability of your network design determines how much and how fast your network can grow. A highly scalable network can adapt implicitly to a large increase in end locations, which is generally a characteristic of corporate acquisitions or expansion initiatives.

6   Why is adaptability so important in good network design?

Adaptability of a network design governs how well new technologies can be absorbed. Designing a network that is adaptable will allow your network to react to Voice over IP and other multicast applications that are ready to dominate "New World" network infrastructures.

7   At which tier of the hierarchical model are firewalls most often deployed?

Firewalls are often found at the distribution tier of the hierarchical model because it is much easier to control and enforce policy at this tier. Firewalls can also be found at the access tier.

Chapter 2

1   What three components comprise the hierarchical model?

The three components that comprise the hierarchical model are the core, distribution, and access tiers.

2   What is the primary function of the core tier in a hierarchical network design?

The core tier provides optimal wide-area transport between geographically remote sites, while tying a number of campus networks together in a corporate or enterprise WAN.

3   Describe the functions performed at the distribution tier of a hierarchical network design.

The distribution tier is often where network policy is implemented (for example, security with IOS firewall feature set, access lists, Network Address Translation, network naming and numbering conventions, encryption).

4   Describe the elements that comprise the access tier of a hierarchical network design.

The access tier is usually a LAN or a group of LANs, typically Ethernet or Token Ring, that provides users with local access to network services. The access tier is where almost all hosts are attached to the network, including servers of all kinds and user workstations.

5   Identify six benefits of using a hierarchical design model.

The six benefits of using a hierarchical design model are scalability, ease of implementation, ease of troubleshooting, predictability, protocol support, and manageability.

6   List some common variations on the three-tier hierarchy using only one or two tiers of the model.

The variations of three-tier hierarchy using only one or two tiers of the model are one-tier design distributed, one-tier design hub-and-spoke, and two-tier designs.

7   What are the general hierarchical design guidelines?

The general hierarchical design guidelines are as follows: Choose a hierarchical model that best fits your requirements; do not completely mesh the network; do not place end stations on backbones; and keep as much as 80 percent of traffic local to a workgroup.

8 What are some IOS features commonly found in the core tier design?

Some IOS features commonly found in core network designs are Cisco Express Forwarding (CEF), Weighted Random Early Detection (WRED), and route aggregation via Border Gateway Protocol (BGP).

Chapter 3

1 Name two general methods of implementing campus backbones.

The two general methods of implementing campus backbones are to use either a distributed or a collapsed backbone architecture.

2 Name a benefit in deploying a collapsed campus backbone.

A benefit in deploying a collapsed campus backbone is that a collapsed backbone makes problem isolation relatively simple. Note, however, that actually finding a problem's root cause can sometimes be difficult or may require network-wide downtime because any troubleshooting changes can potentially impact other segments attached to the same device.

3 Name a drawback in deploying a distributed campus backbone.

Distributed backbones require extra input and output ports for each component of the distributed backbone. These extra ports can have an adverse impact on cost, especially with some of the newer technologies such as Gigabit Ethernet. You may find that some devices need to have forklift upgrades to support the core technology that is being distributed.

4 What is an end-user issue as you design a campus LAN topology?

End-station issues include hardware and software issues such as choice of the operating system (OS) version and NICs, the level of use of broadcasts by the client for device discovery and normal operation, and implementation of Quality of Service (QoS) mechanisms.

5 What is a server issue as you design a campus LAN topology?

Server-station issues include hardware and software issues such as choice of the network operating system (NOS) version, NICs, broadcast issues associated with protocol choices, server placement, and whether to deploy Quality of Service (QoS).

6 What are the general design recommendations for implementation of cabling in campus network designs?

The physical cable is one the most important issues to consider when designing a network. Design issues include the type of cabling to be used (typically copper or fiber) and the overall structure of the cable topology. In addition to distance limitations, carefully evaluate the strengths and weaknesses of various wiring topologies. Make certain that your cable infrastructure meets or exceeds cable specifications.

7 Compare bridging/switching and routing as interconnect methods.

Bridging/switching is useful for small Layer 2 designs that have very minor requirements for scalability, whereas routing is extremely useful for Layer 3 (logical network) designs that have large requirements for network scalability and growth. In reality, a combination of both routing and switching is present in nearly all network designs.

8 What is a typical media problem and how can it be corrected?

A typical media problem is bandwidth contention on a local segment. This type of problem can be resolved through the use of a switch.

9 What is a typical protocol problem and how can it be corrected?

A typical protocol problem is excessive broadcasts on a local segment. A router will not forward broadcasts, so provides separation of broadcast domains through the analysis of the logical network number.

10 What is a typical transport issue and how can be it corrected?

A typical transport problem is that of Quality of Service (QoS). If there is a requirement to transport voice across a data network, a certain guarantee must be given to the voice traffic above the data traffic. Technologies, such as ATM, will allow classes of service to be defined so that mission-critical data will get preference over noncritical data flows.

Chapter 4

1 Describe the operation of Token Ring.

Token Ring passes tokens over a ring topology running at 4 or 16 Mbps.

2 What is a cut-through switch?

Ethernet switches employ one of two kinds of switching methods: *cut-through* or *store-and-forward*. In cut-through switching, the frame is forwarded as soon as the first 48 bits (that is, the destination address [DA]) are read, which means that no packet integrity or cyclic redundancy check (CRC) functions are performed.

3 What is a store-and-forward switch?

In store-and-forward switching, the entire frame is first copied into a buffer, where frame checks are performed before the frame is forwarded to its destination.

4   What is a key characteristic of a VLAN?

A key characteristic of a VLAN is that every VLAN represents a separate broadcast domain.

5   What is an ELAN?

LANE defines the operation of a single emulated LAN (in a similar style to a VLAN), also known as an ELAN. An ELAN emulates either an Ethernet or a Token Ring and consists of a LAN Emulation Client (LEC), a LAN Emulation Server (LES), a Broadcast and Unknown Server (BUS), and a LAN Emulation Configuration Server (LECS).

6   Why is the 802.1Q standard important?

802.1Q facilitates multivendor VLAN interoperability. Prior to 802.1Q, all VLAN information was propagated via proprietary vendor protocols, such as ISL (Cisco) and Lattisnet (Nortel Networks).

7   What are some ATM design guidelines?

Use a full-mesh virtual circuit (VC) configuration between routers. Each router can transmit directly to every other router over ATM. Use of a full mesh is almost always a requirement because a full-mesh topology avoids an extra router hop that introduces latency because of repeated segmentation and re-assembly (SAR).

8   What is a major topological difference between 10Base2 and 10BaseT?

Ethernet remains a logical bus topology, even though the physical configuration since the advent of 10BaseT describes not a bus, but a physical star.

Chapter 5

1   An organization requires a network that will permit any user within a building to be in any logical workgroup. It also requires that all servers in the building be centrally located. What design would you recommend to meet these needs?

A collapsed backbone approach is a viable solution for these design requirements. User workstations can be physically placed anywhere in the building and still remain in the same VLAN. The server farm in the building can be placed in one physical location, but still remain logically in separate LANs.

2   How would you extend the design in Question 1 so that a user could be located anywhere within a campus?

If you add in fiber connectivity between buildings in the campus, you could set up trunking between building switches so that all VLAN information is shared and propagated to campus routers. Moves/adds/changes from any campus VLAN would then be propagated to all campus switches.

3   What is DHCP?

Dynamic Host Configuration Protocol (DHCP) is a reliable method for automatically assigning IP addresses to hosts on your network.

4 Why do cabling recommendations in general call for multimode fiber in the risers between floors and in the tunnels that typically connect buildings in a campus environment?

Fiber allows the bandwidth to be scaled up as far as necessary (FDDI, 100BaseFX, fiber-based ATM, Gigabit Ethernet) while providing reliable links that are resistant to sources of electromagnetic interference (EMI).

5 What is LANE?

LANE is a standard defined by the ATM Forum that gives to stations attached via ATM the same capabilities they normally obtain from legacy LANs, such as Ethernet and Token Ring.

6 What is Hot Standby Router Protocol (HSRP) and how can it be used in a VLAN design?

Hot Standby Router Protocol (HSRP) is often used in distributed backbones and solves the age-old problem of the router being a single point of failure. HRSP automatically detects a network or router failure, and subsequently switches to the alternate router without the end-user systems noticing that a problem has ever occurred.)

7 What is a widely deployed high-speed upgrade path for existing legacy FDDI distributed backbones?

In the case where a distributed campus backbone is used, an ATM switch, such as a Cisco LightStream, replaces the FDDI ring. The ATM network generally is fully meshed and represents one logical subnet, just as the FDDI ring did.

Chapter 6

1 What are some major issues in strategic design of TCP/IP networks?

Clearly defining the physical and logical components of the network design with an eye toward future scalability.

2 Name two general choices for selection of IP addresses.

Whether to use public (that is, IANA assigned) or private (RFC 1918) address space in your design.

3 Name three considerations for routing protocols.

Addressing, routing, and security choices.

4 What is subnetting?

Subnetting enables you to make the most efficient use of your granted IP address space.

5 What is a routing protocol?

Routing protocols are the language by which routers exchange this routing information.

6   Name a commonly deployed Exterior Gateway Protocol.

Border Gateway Protocol (BGP).

7   What is the key to implementing IP security?

The key to implementing security is the establishment of a corporate policy.

8   What is the difference between a distance vector and a link-state routing protocol?

Link-state protocols advertise to the internetwork only those networks physically attached to it. Distance vector protocols advertise remote nets learned about through other routers' advertisements, sometimes also referred to as "routing by rumor."

9   Why is IP address uniqueness important?

Without address uniqueness on the Internet, there would be no way to reliably route packets to a given destination. A situation of a duplicate IP address would be analogous to having two mailing addresses. To which would the post office deliver your mail?

Chapter 7

1   What is meant by classful routing?

Classful routing does not transmit any information about the IP address prefix length. Quite simply, prefix length was calculated from the first few bits of the classful IP address.

2   Give examples of classless routing protocols.

OSPF, EIGRP, and RIP-2 are examples of classless routing protocols because they allow for variable-length subnet masks.

3   What is Network Registrar?

A Cisco product called Cisco Network Registrar (acquired in 1998 from American Internet Corporation) is a scalable DNS and DHCP system for very large IP networks, including large enterprises, cable Internet service providers, and Internet service providers (ISPs). CDDM will be replaced by Cisco Network Registrar (CNR).

4   What is the first and most important design step to determine the security policy of your company or organization?

The first and most important design step is to determine the policy of your company or organization.

5   What is IGMP and what is its importance?

Multicast routers use the Internet Group Management Protocol (IGMP) to learn whether any hosts on a given segment want to join or leave a given multicast group.

6   What is meant by route summarization?

Route summarization is also called aggregation or supernetting. Route summarization refers to allocating multiple IP addresses in a way that allows aggregation of multiple networks into a smaller number of routing-table entries.

7   What are two key benefits of route summarization?

Summarization reduces memory usage on routers and reduces routing-protocol traffic.

8   What routing protocol is commonly used in implementing IP-based multicasting?

Cisco implemented Protocol-Independent Multicast (PIM) as a pivotal routing component of its IP multicast support. PIM provides a scalable, multi-enterprise solution for multicast capability that enables networks running any unicast routing protocol to support IP multicast. PIM can be integrated into existing networks running IGRP, EIGRP, IS-IS, OSPF, or RIP routing protocols.

9   Describe general functionality requirements that are important to look for in a firewall system.

Some key features to look for in a firewall system are NAT, support for application proxy, support for ad-hoc packet filtering, support for audit trails, and login protection.

10   What are some commonly blocked ports on a firewall?

Table A-1 lists the well-known ports that are commonly blocked on a firewall.

Table A-1   *Commonly Blocked Ports on a Firewall*

Application	Protocol	Transport	Port Number(s)
E-mail	SMTP	TCP	25
Domain Name System	DNS	UDP or TCP	53
Terminal access	telnet	TCP	23
File transfer	FTP	TCP	20, 21
File transfer	TFTP	UDP	69
Web browser	HTTP	TCP	80

You can also find an excellent list of well-known UDP/TCP ports at www.netanalysis.org/docs/ portnumbers.txt.

Chapter 8

1   What are the tasks that a router must accomplish?

A router has two separate tasks: relaying or switching packets, and path determination.

2   What is the difference between process switching and fast switching?

In *process switching*, the first packet is copied to the system buffer. The router looks up the Layer 3 network address in the routing table and initializes the fast-switch cache. The frame is rewritten with the destination address and sent to the exit interface that services that destination. Subsequent packets for that destination are sent by the same switching path. The route processor computes the cyclic redundancy check (CRC). When packets are *fast switched*, the first packet is copied to packet memory and the destination network or host is found in the fast-switching cache. The frame is rewritten and sent to the exit interface that services the destination. Subsequent packets for the same destination use the same switching path. The interface processor computes the CRC.

3 What does the term "routing by rumors" mean and what is an example of a protocol that uses this mechanism?

Distance vector routing protocols are also known as "routing by rumors," meaning that routers pass routing information gathered from neighbors.

4 What is meant by administrative distance?

The administrative distance is a measure of the "trustworthiness" of a routing information source and can be altered by using the **distance** command, but this is not recommended.

5 Describe the operation and purpose of the split horizon mechanism.

Put simply, split horizon enforces the rule that a router should never re-advertise a route out the same interface it learned it on. Split horizon prevents short routing loops.

6 What is meant by convergence time?

Convergence is the time it takes when a route currently in the forwarding table is invalidated until an alternate is installed. During the interim, packets will be discarded or may loop.

7 What is an EGP? Give an example of a common EGP.

An Exterior Gateway Protocol (EGP) connects autonomous systems (ASs) together. A common example of an EGP is the Border Gateway Protocol, also known as BGP v4.

8 What is the significance of RFC 1923?

RFC 1923, "RIP1: Applicability Statement for Historic Status," was published in 1996. It declares RIP Version 1 a historic document and essentially restates that RIP is an "Old World" protocol with no support of classless updates.

Chapter 9

1 What are the four different classifications of routers in OSPF?

The four classes of routers are Internal Routers, Area Border Routers, Backbone Routers, and Autonomous System Border Routers.

2   What is the recommended maximum number of routers in an OSPF area, specifically the backbone area?

It depends on how stable your network is. If it is extremely stable, with no flapping links, you can get by with more routers in an area. Forty is a conservative number.

3   When using OSPF, is area 0.0.0.0 the same as area 0? Should the backbone always be area 0?

Yes. Area 0 is also displayed as area 0.0.0.0.

Yes. Area 0 is the backbone area, and it is mandatory.

4   Describe the different types of link-state advertisements used by OSPF.

The different types of link-state advertisements used by OSPF are router, network, summary, and external link states. There are also other kinds, such as NSSA link states, opaque link states, and multicast link states, but they are less commonly deployed.

5   What is an external LSA?

An external link advertisement describes a route to a destination in another autonomous system or separate routing process

6   What is a discontiguous subnet? Does OSPF support discontiguous subnets?

Subnets become discontiguous when they are separated by one or more segments represented by a different major network number. Discontiguous subnets are supported by OSPF because subnet masks are part of the link-state database (LSDB).

7   What is the name of the algorithm that OSPF uses to calculate a routing table?

The shortest path first (SPF) algorithm, also called the Dijkstra algorithm (named after the computer scientist who invented it).

8   What is the significance of the spf holdtime?

The **spf holdtime** command limits how often the SPF algorithm is computed. By default, the SPF hold time is 10 seconds. LSAs are collected for a period of 10 seconds before a new routing table is calculated.

9   What does OSPF "full state" mean?

When two OSPF routers are in "full state," they have successfully established an adjacency.

10   Should end users be connected directly into area 0?

Good design practice will keep the backbone components physically secure if possible. The backbone is a critical shared resource and should not have user traffic directly attached, except in very rare situations. In most cases, it is beneficial to segment user segments as separate, summarized OSPF areas.

Chapter 10

1 Is IGRP a classless or classful routing protocol?

IGRP is a classful protocol. As a distance vector protocol, IGRP summarizes at network boundaries.

2 What is the default update timer for IGRP?

The default update timer for IGRP is set by default at 90 seconds.

3 Discuss IGRP variance as it relates to load sharing?

IGRP does load sharing over variant paths in proportion to the bandwidth of the link. If you are using process switching, the router sends two packets to a 128-kbps link for every packet sent to a 64-kbps link. If you are using fast or autonomous switching, the router caches two destinations to a 128-kbps link for every destination cached to a 64-kbps link.

4 Name and describe the different IGRP metrics.

A summary of each IGRP metric type follows:

- **Bandwidth (static)**—Smallest bandwidth link from here to destination.
- **Delay (static)**—Interface delay is additive along the whole path. Interface delay on each link is inversely proportional to the bandwidth. Delay is the sum of the delays of all *outgoing* interfaces between source and destination.
- **Reliability (dynamic)**—Worst reliability from here to destination based on keepalives.
- **Loading (dynamic)**—Heaviest load from here to destination based on bits per second.
- **MTU (static)**—Smallest MTU from here to destination. MTU is used to avoid sending a frame that is too large when the IP "don't-fragment bit" is set, but cannot be used in the metric computation.
- **Hops (static)**—Total hop count from here to destination. Hop count is used to prevent count to infinity, but cannot be used in the metric computation.

5 By default, how long is the IGRP invalid timer?

By default, the IGRP invalid timer is three times the update interval. Therefore, because the update interval is 90 seconds, the invalid timer is 270 seconds by default.

6 Why is EIGRP considered to be a "Ships-In-The-Night" protocol?

Enhanced IGRP is considered to be a "Ships-In-The-Night" (SIN) routing protocol because DDP, IPX, and IP each maintain separate routing tables and use separate hellos to discover neighbors.

7 What are the methods that EIGRP uses for broadcasting RTMP and IPX RIP/SAP updates across the LAN and WAN?

By default, Enhanced IGRP advertises full RIP, SAP, and RTMP updates on LAN interfaces and reliable updates only on WAN interfaces.

8 What makes EIGRP converge so quickly? How long does convergence generally take for most failures?

The DUAL algorithm makes Enhanced IGRP converge quickly. The whole process takes less than 1 second for most failures.

9 What is meant by an EIGRP local computation?

When a link changes state, the router can immediately change the active routing table based on information in the local copy of a neighbor's routing table. This capability is called a *local computation* because it does not affect other routers.

10 What is meant by an EIGRP diffused computation?

When the neighbor routing tables do not have a feasible successor route, a *diffused computation* takes place. A route is flagged active, and the router sends a query. The query propagates until a new route is found.

Chapter 11

1 Describe the general model used for design of most desktop-based network operating systems.

Desktop protocols are based on a client/server model. These protocols are primarily designed to enable clients and servers to communicate across a LAN. Generally, it is assumed that the LAN consists of a single shared or switched medium such as Ethernet or Fast Ethernet, and it provides connections for multiple hosts.

2 What common problem do most desktop systems present to network designers?

Broadcasts are design considerations that you must take into consideration, especially as the desktop protocols extend across the WAN.

3 What is the impact of protocols that use periodic broadcasts in the WAN environment?

The impact of periodic broadcasts in the WAN environment is likely to degrade performance considerably, especially across lower-speed links.

4 What protocols generate the majority of the broadcast traffic in the Novell IPX environment?

The Routing Information Protocol (RIP) and the Service Advertisement Protocol (SAP) generate most of the broadcast traffic in the Novell IPX environment.

5 What is ZIP?

ZIP is a session layer protocol in the AppleTalk protocol suite that maintains network number-to-zone name mappings in AppleTalk routers.

6   Does NetBIOS encapsulation into IP solve the broadcast issues with native NetBIOS?

Although this appears to be a good solution, the same NetBIOS broadcast issues remain. In the case of IP encapsulation, NetBIOS broadcasts are encapsulated in the User Datagram Protocol (UDP) and broadcasts (now UDP-based broadcasts) can impact your entire WAN, if you are not careful.

Chapter 12

1   Describe the different IPX encapsulations that are available on Cisco routers.

The original default IPX encapsulation for Ethernet was called Raw Ethernet. Raw Ethernet is also known as ETHERNET_802.3 in IPX configuration and novell-ether in Cisco configuration. Raw Ethernet is a nonstandard encapsulation that resembles IEEE 802.3, with FFFF in place of a normal 802.3 destination service access point (DSAP) and source service access point (SSAP), and with no Logical Link Control (LLC) layer.

2   Is it possible to support multiple IPX encapsulations on the same physical interface? If so, how?

You may be faced with an issue of how to support multiple IPX encapsulations on the same interface. Subinterfaces can be configured on the router to support several IPX networks on the same LAN. Hosts on different networks do not communicate directly and can use different encapsulations.

3   How often does IPX RIP send out routing updates?

IPX/RIP has a 60-second update interval.

4   What is IPXWAN?

IPXWAN is a handshake protocol that establishes an accurate routing metric when a dialup link is established.

5   How is IPX fast switching different from IP fast switching?

In IPX-based fast switching, the load balancing is still done packet by packet, which is different from IP.

6   Describe the advantages and disadvantages of using NLSP over IPX/RIP for your routing protocol.

NLSP has faster convergence than IPX/RIP. It only advertises routing and services incrementally. The shortest path first (SPF) algorithm is CPU intensive, compared to IPX/RIP.

7   When an IPX packet is routed from IPX to EIGRP back to IPX, how is the metric handled?

Enhanced IGRP tracks the IPX routing metrics as external metrics. The hop count is incremented by two as the route passes from IPX/RIP to Enhanced IGRP and back to IPX/RIP. The tick metric is not incremented, so the Enhanced IGRP cloud appears to be zero ticks.

8 How often do NetWare servers send a keepalive message to all connected clients?

NetWare servers send a keepalive message to all connected clients every 5 minutes.

9 What is SPX spoofing?

SPX spoofing, enabled with the command **ipx spx-spoof**, causes the router to send the ACK, so that no packet goes on the WAN link.

Chapter 13

1 List the protocols that make up the AppleTalk protocol suite.

The AppleTalk protocols consist of several layers, including AARP (AppleTalk Address Resolution Protocol), DDP (Datagram Delivery Protocol), NBP (Name Binding Protocol), ZIP (Zone Information Protocol), RTMP (Routing Table Maintenance Protocol), ADSP (AppleTalk Data Stream Protocol) and ATP (AppleTalk Transaction Protocol).

2 How often does AppleTalk RTMP send its updates?

Whereas IP RIP broadcasts routing updates every 30 seconds, AppleTalk routing updates occur every 10 seconds.

3 Why don't Cisco routers advertise an AppleTalk network until the corresponding zone information is known?

To prevent ZIP storms that could result if routing information races ahead of zone information, Cisco routers do not advertise an AppleTalk network until the corresponding zone information is known.

4 What are the formulas for Enhanced IGRP and RTMP metric conversions for making routing calculations?

The formulas for EIGRP and RTMP metric conversions for making routing calculations from RTMP to EIGRP are as follows:

- From RTMP to EIGRP—Metric = hops × 25,652,400, where each hop looks like a 9600-bps link
- From EIGRP to RTMP—End-to-end hop count maintained across the Enhanced IGRP core

5 Name two methods of reducing consumption of bandwidth in WANs by AppleTalk protocols.

AURP is designed to handle routing update traffic over WAN links more efficiently than RTMP. Another option would be to deploy Apple/EIGRP in the WAN.

6 What is a GZL filter?

The GetZoneList (GZL) filters ZIP information locally between a router and Macintosh hosts. The result is that specific zones can be hidden from users on specific networks.

7 What is a ZIP reply filter and what is its purpose?

The ZIP reply filter allows RTMP tuples to propagate between RTMP peers, but blocks specific zones when the routers reach back for zone information. The filtered zones are invisible to all downstream routers and nodes. Zones can then be "leaked" as needed between the ASs by adding them to the "permitted list" in the GZL reply filter.

Chapter 14

1 At what layer does NetBIOS function with respect to the OSI networking model?

NetBIOS functions primarily as a session layer protocol with respect to the OSI reference model.

2 How are domains created and managed?

Domains are created and managed by a process called a Primary Domain Controller (PDC), which runs on a Windows NT Server.

3 What various NetBIOS transport methods are available?

NetBIOS must be transported across the network, and in general there are two ways to accomplish this: bridging and routing. NetBEUI is a bridged method; IPX and TCP/IP are supported for routing.

4 What IPX packet type does NWLINK require to exchange registration and browsing information?

NWLINK requires IPX type 20 packets to exchange registration and browsing information.

5 What are the name resolution methods for Windows clients?

Windows Networking clients have a choice of four methods for name resolution:

- Broadcasts
- LMHOSTS
- WINS
- Internet DNS

6 What is the default name-resolution method and should it be left as the default always?

Broadcast is the default on all Microsoft products. It is strongly recommended that you turn this feature off by setting the BrowseMaster setting to Disabled (the default is Automatic).

7 What is meant by a *master domain*? When is this option useful?

A master domain is trusted by all other domains, but the master domain trusts no one. This option is useful when departments or divisions want to control their own resources but still want to authenticate centrally.

8 What is the function of WINS?

WINS provides NetBIOS name–to–IP address translation. It is similar in function to DNS, but uses NetBIOS (rather than Internet) names to form its name/address translation tables. Thus, it can associate a NetBIOS name request with a valid IP address.

9 What is Microsoft RAS? Is RAS always a preferred design solution?

Windows NT comes with Microsoft's Remote Access Server (RAS), which is based on the Point-to-Point Protocol (PPP). Cisco access servers should generally be used as an alternative when higher dial-in density or better performance is required.

Chapter 15

1 Name the design issues associated with WANs.

WAN design issues that you need to consider include the following: reliability, latency issues, costs of WAN resources, amount of traffic that will traverse the WAN, which protocols will be allowed on the WAN, compatibility with standards of legacy systems, simplicity and ease of configuration, and support for remote offices and telecommuters.

2 What Cisco IOS software features would be options for deployment in WAN environments to improve performance?

Many value-added Cisco IOS features are available to optimize the use of WAN resources in the core. Use smart protocols, such as Enhanced IGRP, to reduce routing traffic. Use features such as prioritization and compression as appropriate. Further, use GRE tunnels in network core designs where IP predominates.

3 What is an advantage to using ATM in your network design?

Some advantages to using ATM in your network design include its capability to support either point-to-point or multipoint links, Class of Service (CoS), Quality of Service (QoS), and the capability to transport data, voice, and video.

4 What is a disadvantage of using X.25 in your network design?

Some disadvantages of using X.25 in your network design include support for slow speeds, the fact that it uses extensive error checking (causing slowdowns), and it is an older technology developed when WAN lines were lower speed and less reliable. (X.25 is not a modern-day WAN transport!)

5 What the three goals for designing the WAN core?

Goals for designing the WAN core at the micro level focus on the following three components:

- Maximization of throughput over WAN circuits
- Minimization of delay over WAN circuits
- Minimization of overhead traffic over WAN circuits

Chapter 16

1 What is required to install a leased line connection?

When leased line connections are made, a router port is required for each connection, along with a CSU/DSU (channel service unit/digital service unit) and the actual circuit from the service provider.

2 From a traffic-design perspective, why should both links from a regional office should be of equal bandwidth?

Both links from a regional office should be of equal bandwidth to allow for equal-cost load balancing.

3 Which four different serial-line encapsulations are widely deployed?

The four different serial line encapsulations that are widely deployed are SDLC, HDLC, PPP, and LAPB.

4 What is the default encapsulation for Cisco point-to-point circuits?

HDLC is Cisco's default encapsulation for serial lines.

5 When is PPP most often used?

PPP is often the only choice in mixed-vendor WAN point- to-point network connectivity. To have a Bay BCN router connect to a Cisco 2500 access router on a T1 circuit, for example, you would configure the link for PPP.

6 What is an advantage to using modulo 128?

Use modulo 128 for higher throughput over high-bandwidth or high-delay media.

Chapter 17

1 What is the unit of Frame Relay service?

The unit of Frame Relay service is the permanent virtual circuit (PVC). A PVC is an unreliable data link and is identified by a data-link connection identifier (DLCI).

2 What is the biggest design advantage presented by Frame Relay when compared to leased lines?

The biggest advantage is that Frame Relay was envisioned as a cost-effective alternative to point-to-point WAN designs.

3 What are the components of a Frame Relay switching table?

The Frame Relay switching table consists of four entries, two of which represent the incoming port and DLCI, and the other two represent outgoing the port and DLCI.

4 What is the purpose of RFC 1490?

RFC 1490 describes an encapsulation method for carrying network interconnect traffic over a Frame Relay backbone. It covers aspects for both bridging and routing as well as a simple fragmentation procedure for carrying large frames over a Frame Relay network with a smaller MTU.

5 Describe the Inverse ARP mechanism.

The Inverse ARP mechanism allows the router to automatically build the Frame Relay map. The router learns the DLCIs that are in use from the switch during the initial LMI exchange.

6 What is the purpose of the Link Management Interface?

LMI carries PVC status information, and also serves as a keepalive mechanism between the router and switch.

7 What are the benefits of using subinterfaces in Frame Relay designs?

With subinterface configuration, each PVC maps to a different network or subnet. The result is that Frame Relay works like several point-to-point links, and is therefore no longer mapped to a LAN.

8 What Frame Relay design topology options exist?

The topologies that exist are full mesh, partial mesh, and hub-and-spoke.

9 How do you configure DDR to back up a Frame PVC?

To use DDR to back up a PVC, you create a floating static route to the destination. To create the floating static, you need to make sure that the static route has a greater administrative distance than the dynamic routing protocol. The floating static route is used only if the dynamic route goes away.

Chapter 18

1 Into which general categories can X.25 network devices be classified?

X.25 network devices fall into three general categories: data terminal equipment (DTE), data circuit-terminating equipment (DCE), and packet switch exchange (PSE).

2 What is a PDN?

Public X.25 networks are known as public data networks (PDNs).

3 How is X.25 different from Frame Relay?

The biggest difference is that X.25 uses a reliable data link, whereas Frame Relay does not.

4 What problems do X.25 subinterface configurations solve?

Subinterface configuration eliminates NBMA matters related to partial-mesh connectivity and split horizon.

5 Can a Cisco router be configured as an X.25 switch? If so, can it support PVCs and SVCs?

The Cisco router supports local X.25 switching between serial interfaces. The interfaces are dedicated to LAPB and X.25, and cannot carry other encapsulations. Both permanent virtual circuits (PVCs) and switched virtual circuits (SVCs) are supported.

Chapter 19

1 Name three traditional technologies that often used dialup networking.

Analog, ISDN BRI (Basic Rate Interface), and ISDN PRI (Primary Rate Interface)

2 Name two newer technologies that are becoming increasingly more popular, due to their very high bandwidth capabilities.

ADSL (asynchronous digital subscriber line) and cable modem technology.

3 What is MP and why is important?

Multilink PPP (MP), as specified in RFC 1717, is designed to fragment packets and transmit the fragments over parallel connections, such as ISDN BRI and PRI access lines.

4 What is MMP and why is important?

Multilink Multichassis PPP (MMP) is an enhancement to the MP standard provided in Cisco IOS Software Release 11.2. MMP provides a mechanism to aggregate B channels transparently across multiple routers or access servers, which means that fragments from one client could terminate at different access servers. MMP is very important because now scaling up of the central site is more flexible and more access servers can be added as needed.

5 Identify three implementation methods that designers have for connecting remote users.

The methods by which remote users are connected into the corporate LAN usually fall into the categories of either remote gateway, remote control, or remote node.

6 Describe three categories of dialup users.

Three general categories of users require some type of remote access: occasional telecommuter/mobile user, dedicated telecommuter/teleworker, and small office/home office with LAN presence.

7 What is remote-control network access?

In the remote-control method, the remote gains control of the PC attached to the LAN at the central site. The remote user then has all the capabilities normally available when using the office PC.

8 What are some advantages to remote-node network access?

Remote node offers many advantages. It is the most secure and flexible of the three methods, and it is the most scalable. Only one PC is required for the remote user, and many client software solutions are available. The only additional hardware required at the remote location is a modem.

9 What is a VPN?

Virtual private networks (VPNs) are a key example of a "New World" service because they enable companies to connect their offices, mobile workers, and business partners with dramatically reduced costs by leveraging the shared communications infrastructure of the Internet or a service provider shared backbone.

Chapter 20

1 What is an ATM PVC?

PVC allows direct connectivity between sites. In this way, a PVC is similar to a leased line. Among its advantages, a PVC guarantees availability of a connection and does not require call setup procedures between switches.

2 What is an ATM SVC?

An SVC is created and released dynamically and remains in use only as long as data is being transferred. In this sense, it is similar to a telephone call.

3 Identify the OSI reference model layers of ATM and the function of each layer.

The OSI reference model layers of ATM are the physical layer, ATM layer, and the ATM adaptation layer. The physical layer is analogous to the physical layer of the OSI reference model; the ATM physical layer manages the medium-dependent transmission. The ATM layer is roughly analogous to the data link layer of the OSI reference model. The ATM layer is responsible for establishing connections and passing cells through the ATM network. To do this, it uses information in the header of each ATM cell. Finally, the ATM adaptation layer (AAL) is roughly analogous to the data link layer of the OSI model. The AAL is responsible for isolating higher-layer protocols from the details of the ATM processes.

4 What is AAL1? Give an example of an application requiring AAL1.

AAL1, a connection-oriented service, is suitable for handling circuit-emulation applications, such as voice and video conferencing. Circuit-emulation service also accommodates the attachment of equipment currently using leased lines to an ATM backbone network. AAL1 requires timing synchronization between the source and destination.

5 What are three considerations for a design that may include SMDS?

Three considerations for a design that may include SMDS include: First, cells from several sources can arrive on a connectionless channel at the same time. The receiver can reassemble frames based on the MID and sequence number. Second, more delay overhead is required for segmentation and reassembly (SAR), and third, a message identifier, CRC, and sequence number are all added.

6 What is AAL5? Give an example of an application requiring AAL5.

AAL5 is the primary AAL for data and supports both connection-oriented and connectionless data. The segmentation and reassembly (SAR) is simple because there is no MID or sequence number. It is used to transfer most non-SMDS data, such as classical IP over ATM and LAN Emulation (LANE).

7 What is LANE?

LANE is a standard defined by the ATM Forum that gives to stations attached via ATM the same capabilities they normally obtain from legacy LANs, such as Ethernet and Token Ring.

8 What WAN-based design models are commonly deployed in ATM internetwork designs?

ATM design and topology issues are similar to those in Frame Relay. Two primary topologies emerge: nonbroadcast multiaccess (NBMA), and hub-and-spoke, using subinterfaces.

9 What are some of StrataCom's product family of switches and what are they used for?

StrataCom's networking system supports multiband ATM applications in private WANs and public carrier service offerings, such as Frame Relay and native ATM. StrataCom's product family includes the BPX/AXIS, IGX, and IPX. These switches are used to implement digital high-speed, wide-area private and public networks (WANs) for interconnecting customers' LANs.

Chapter 21

1 What node type is an FEP and what kind of software runs on it?

A front-end processor (FEP) is a type 4 SNA device and runs system software called the Network Control Program (NCP).

2 What are the three network addressable units in the SNA architecture?

The three types of NAUs are logical units (LUs), physical units (PUs), and system services control point (SSCP).

3 What is the function of SSCP?

The system services control point (SSCP) is a part of VTAM on the host computer that controls and manages SNA network resources in the SNA domain.

4 What is a type 5 node? What software runs on a type 5 node?

In SNA, the host computer is known as a node type 5 and is the top layer of the hierarchy. The software that runs on the node type 5 is called VTAM.

5 When would you use DLSw+ rather than RSRB to internetwork SNA?

In DLSw+, the RIF terminates in the virtual ring. This technique scales up to longer paths than RSRB, allowing six additional SRB hops on either end. It does not allow the entire path to be visible to a protocol analyzer. Therefore, if you had more than six hops, that would be a reason to go with DLSW+ over RSRB.

6 In APPN, what is an end node?

An APPN end node (EN) can be thought of as an application host, accessing the network via its network node server. An EN contains a subset of APPN functionality, eliminating functions such as network topology maintenance and rerouting.

7 What is the CIP and why is it useful?

With the Channel Interface Processor (CIP), a Cisco 7000 series or Cisco 7500 series router combines the functionality of the IBM 3172 or 3745 gateway with multiprocessor routing. CIP transparently offloads work that the host or FEP would otherwise need to do, thereby saving the end user a large amount of money that would otherwise be spent on FEPs.

8 What is a redundant Token Ring/redundant FEP design and how does it work?

The same locally administered MAC address appears on both FEPs and allows for redundant Token Ring paths from clients to the host. When a client PC or downstream physical unit (DSPU) sends an explorer, it connects to the first FEP that responds.

9 How does custom queuing work?

Custom queuing works by establishing up to 16 interface output queues. The transmission window size of each queue is specified in bytes. When the appropriate number of frames is transmitted from a queue, the next queue is checked. Custom queuing is more fair than priority queuing because each queue gets a chance to send at least one frame each time.

Chapter 22

1 What is the primary goal of a good internetwork design?

The key goal of an internetwork design is a fully functional network that meets a client's business and technical objectives.

2 What are the six internetwork design steps?

   Step 1 Analyze requirements.

   Step 2 Develop internetwork structure (topology).

   Step 3 Set up addressing and naming conventions.

   Step 4 Provision the hardware.

   Step 5 Deploy IOS features

   Step 6 Implement, monitor, and maintain the internetwork (this step cycles back to Step 4).

3 What tools are available to measure network performance?

In addition to CiscoWorks 2000, you should use protocol analyzers such as the Network Associates Sniffer or Netscout probes, as well as other tools such as the Fluke LanMeter to monitor and troubleshoot your internetwork design. Other excellent tools for monitoring and managing your network include Cisco **debug** and **show** commands, Syslogd, TACACS+, and homegrown scripts written in Expect or UNIX Shells that query SNMP information.

4 Where in your network are performance demands generally greatest?

Performance demands are greatest in the workgroup and the backbone because this is typically where traffic aggregation occurs.

Solutions to Case Studies

Chapter 23, "Case Studies," provides all the details of the six case studies, the solutions for which appear in this appendix. You may want to refer back to Chapter 23 to review the initial network setup and statistics, as well as the new network requirements before reviewing the solutions in this appendix.

Solutions to Case Study 1: Virtual University

In the original design as shown in Figure B-1, the entire campus is set up as a single flat, bridged network with five buildings. Coaxial cable runs between buildings, and the Physics building has access to the Internet through standalone PCs.

Figure B-1   *Virtual University—Original Design*

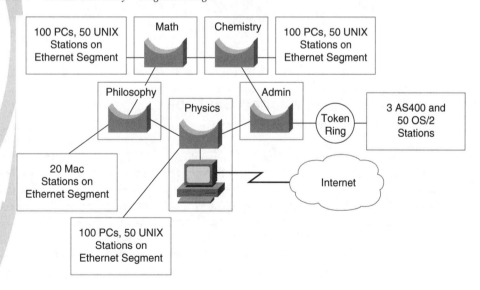

New Design 1: Switched Fast Ethernet Backbone

A more cost-effective design may be achieved by using Fast or Gigabit Ethernet, as illustrated in the first design proposal in Figure B-2. In fact, as we discussed in the book, FDDI would have been chosen in the past, but now it is quickly becoming surpassed by Fast and now even by Gigabit Ethernet technologies in new designs. This is due in part to cost (Fast Ethernet is cheaper to deploy than FDDI) and also due in part to complexity. Additionally, Fast Ethernet is easier to troubleshoot than FDDI. Gigabit Ethernet may be a little more expensive than FDDI today, but it offers speeds 10 times that of FDDI. A benefit to this design is that VLAN information will pass between either Gigabit or Fast Ethernet switches.

Figure B-2   *Virtual University—New Design 1*

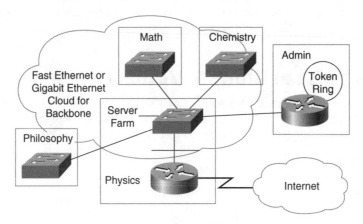

New Design 2: ATM Cell-Switched Backbone

The collapsed switch backbone design can then be migrated to ATM, as illustrated in the fourth design proposal in Figure B-3. In this case, an ATM switch is used for the campus backbone connection. This switch would run LAN Emulation (or MPOA) to extend the virtual LANs (VLANs) across buildings on the campus. The LAN switches would now require ATM up-links and the router, acting as a route server, would attach to the ATM switch. This design would allow Virtual University to eventually create a truly virtual classroom environment because multimedia class sessions could be broadcast across the new ATM core, providing end-to-end Quality of Service. The cost of ATM will be higher than that of the other solutions, but it will give the most flexibility as newer technologies such as VoIP are added.

Figure B-3   *Virtual University—New Design 2*

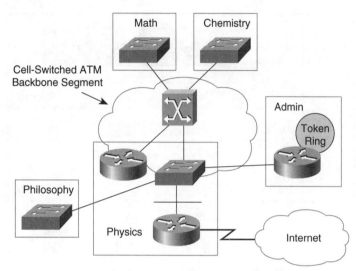

DESIGN RULE   Don't forget about the Layer 2 design! If not in place already, Virtual University needs to lay in a fiber plant to permit these designs. Don't forget to factor in the cost of fiber and labor to install it. Most likely, a star-based fiber topology will be most effective, given the building locations and connectivity requirements.

Solutions to Case Study 2: Simple Minds

In the original design for Simple Minds, as shown in Figure B-4, each floor has thin wire Ethernet (10BaseT) running along the floor. Each floor is then daisy-chain bridged to each adjacent floor and eventually to the basement. This means that each building is a single flat network; broadcasts from any end station are propagated throughout the building.

Figure B-4 *Simple Minds—Original Design*

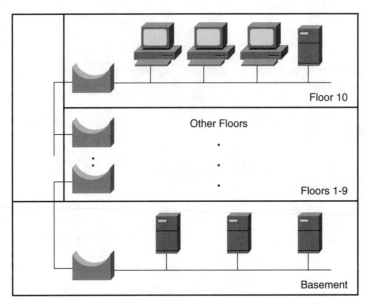

New Design 1: Collapsed Router Backbone

The design illustrated in Figure B-5 uses a collapsed router backbone. An Ethernet switch is deployed on each floor. This provides connectivity for the end stations on the floor. Providing dedicated bandwidth will ensure capacity for growth. One 10BaseT port on each floor switch is then connected to a dedicated 10 Mbps port on the router, and the router backplane now provides the backbone for the building. With each workgroup attached to a separate router port, there is isolation between the groups on each floor. Broadcasts are isolated to the workgroup and administrative controls may be implemented through Cisco IOS software features such as access lists. The router also provides the WAN connection. The downside to this design is that users on other floors cannot be dynamically moved to another VLAN, because VLAN information is not passed between switches.

Figure B-5 *Simple Minds—Collapsed Router Backbone Solution*

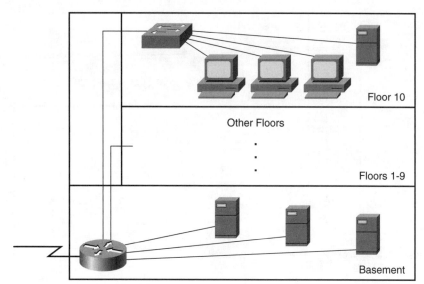

New Design 2: Collapsed Switch Backbone

The design illustrated in Figure B-6 is similar to the collapsed router backbone solution except that an Ethernet switch in the basement now provides the building backbone. This would permit the implementation of VLANs throughout the building and centralized servers in the basement. Because VLANs can be propagated everywhere, this design allows user VLAN moves/adds/changes to occur dynamically. The router would now have a single 100BaseT interface to connect to the basement Ethernet switch and this serves as the routing capability between VLANs. This routing is done via Inter-Switch Link (ISL) or 802.1Q framing, as discussed in earlier chapters. The router also provides the WAN connection as before.

Figure B-6 *Simple Minds—Collapsed Switch Backbone Solution*

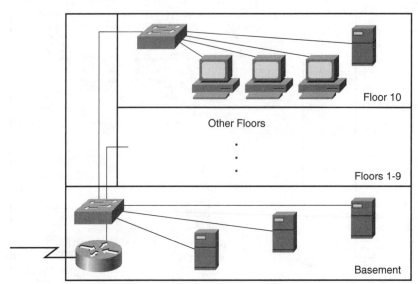

Routing/Addressing Solutions for Simple Minds

The routing/addressing portion of the solution applies regardless of whether the router or switch solution is applied. OSPF and RIP would be possible candidates for routing protocols because the customer specified that an open protocol would be required. Of the two, OSPF would be a better choice because it provides better convergence characteristics, lower link utilization, and a better metric.

OSPF also provides more addressing flexibility. In this case, that advantage would not be critical because they could go to private addressing. By using Class A address 10.0.0.0, they would have ample space for allocation of addresses. Each building could be set up as an OSPF area. By using a 16-bit subnet mask, and then dividing that in half to indicate area and subnet in the area, we get the following capabilities:

- 254 hosts in a subnet

- 256 areas (buildings and backbone)

- 256 subnets per area (really only 255 subnets, assuming we do not use subnet 0)

Configuration for ABR in Simple Minds Network

Figure B-7 shows the configuration script at the Area Border Router between Area 0 and Area 1. The ABR is the router that is in the basement.

Figure B-7   *Simple Minds—ABR Configuration*

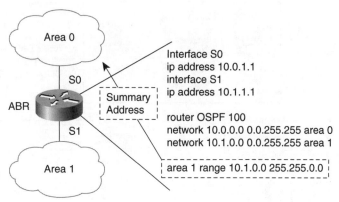

Interface S0
ip address 10.0.1.1
interface S1
ip address 10.1.1.1

router OSPF 100
network 10.0.0.0 0.0.255.255 area 0
network 10.1.0.0 0.0.255.255 area 1

area 1 range 10.1.0.0 255.255.0.0

Interface S0 is placed in Area 0 and interface Fast Ethernet 0 is placed in Area 1. OSPF is started, and we identify which interfaces are associated with which area. Finally, we provide the summarization command to cause a single summary link-state advertisement (LSA) to be sent into Area 0 from Area 1.

Some key things to remember with this OSPF design follow:

- The Area 0 links must be reliable (in general, do not implement this design over international links that are known to be unstable at times).

- Summarization should be used heavily.

- The number of routers in Area 0 is kept to a minimum. There will be 10 in this case, which is within design specifications.

Solutions to Case Study 3: ABC Advertising

In the original design for ABC Advertising, as shown in Figure B-8, there is a fiber (FDDI) backbone going between the buildings. A router in each building connects the LAN segments to the backbone. The LANs in the building are used for AppleTalk, IPX, and TCP/IP traffic. The LANs are connected to Ethernet ports on the routers. Each Ethernet port carries a combination of the three protocols.

Figure B-8 *ABC Advertising—Original Design*

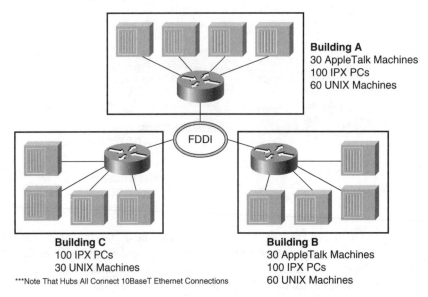

Building A
30 AppleTalk Machines
100 IPX PCs
60 UNIX Machines

FDDI

Building C
100 IPX PCs
30 UNIX Machines
***Note That Hubs All Connect 10BaseT Ethernet Connections

Building B
30 AppleTalk Machines
100 IPX PCs
60 UNIX Machines

New Design—Proposal 1

The first part of this design addresses the network requirements for ABC Advertising. Figure B-9 shows this topology with a FDDI Dual Ring with proposed solutions to address the requirements laid out to us. Note that there is no requirement for the end stations to upgrade to a single protocol stack, so this network must be "multilingual." This is truly a multiprotocol network design that provides optimal performance and any-to-any connectivity based on the requirements (and restrictions) ABC currently defined.

NOTE   More often than not, you need to retrofit existing network infrastructure to meet the new demands of the customer. Remember that you won't always have a "blank sheet" to start your design from. This is, therefore, a major reason to design for scalability and future upgrades!

Figure B-9   *ABC Advertising—New Design, Proposal 1*

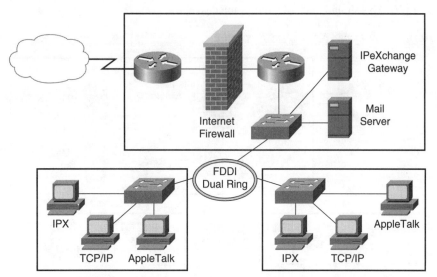

The new proposal for ABC Advertising has requirements that could be addressed as follows:

- **Increased bandwidth to end stations with capacity for growth**—This indicates a need to go to Ethernet switching. Although the current FDDI backbone may be adequate, for reasons mentioned earlier, FDDI installations are being replaced quite rapidly with either Gigabit Ethernet or ATM.

- **Any-to-any connectivity for e-mail and Internet access**—We could standardize on a mail system and use the current transports to reach multiprotocol-aware servers. A better plan, because we need Internet access anyway, is to go to an SNMP-based server that is reached via TCP/IP. Provide gateways, such as IPeXchange, for IPX traffic to get to IP. Either use gateways for AppleTalk, or put a native IP stack on the MAC. The second option represents a better strategic solution.

- **Logical isolation between the groups; no isolation within a group; user mobility throughout the campus**—Use VLANs. Place each protocol group in a separate VLAN and let each VLAN be a flat network. Centralize all servers in one building, and install network management systems to manage VLANs.

New Design—Proposal 2

The second part of this design, as illustrated in Figure B-10, requires a long-term plan to migrate to the single-protocol environment. The protocol should be TCP/IP. End-station clients that are not IP should migrate. The server strategy could consider going to Windows NT as the platform, using NetBIOS over TCP/IP.

The network infrastructure from Part 1 is still appropriate in this migration. In fact, use of VLANs should make the migration easier.

Figure B-10 *ABC Advertising—New Design, Proposal 2*

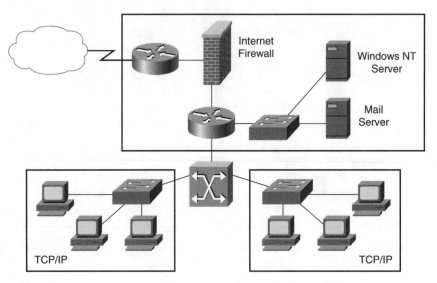

Solutions to Case Study 4: Widespread, Inc.

Because Widespread is starting the design from scratch, we will assume it has no network. Figure B-11 shows the traffic distribution.

Figure B-11 *Widespread, Inc.—Traffic Distribution*

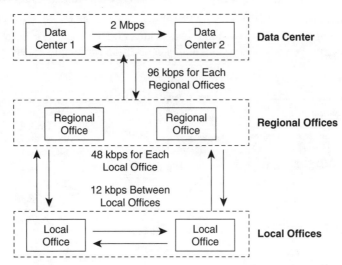

Proposed Design for Widespread, Inc.

The most cost-effective design that would meet the requirements would be deployment of T1 leased-line circuits between the two main data centers, and use Frame Relay everywhere else, as illustrated in Figure B-12. The access speed should be T1 for the main data centers and regional offices. The local offices could get 64 kbps. A total of 40 PVCs are required to meet the redundancy requirements.

Figure B-12 *Widespread, Inc. Design Proposal*

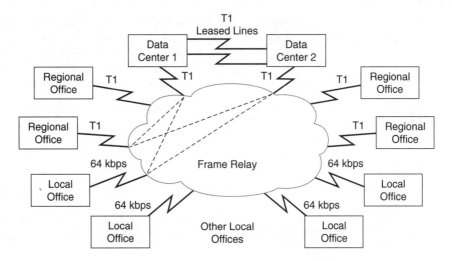

Solutions to Case Study 5: TurtleNet Consulting

The original design for TurtleNet Consulting, as illustrated in Figure B-13, consisted of LANs at San Francisco and San Jose, with an ISDN connection between them. An e-mail server is available through dialup connection for remote access.

Figure B-13 *TurtleNet Consulting—Original Design*

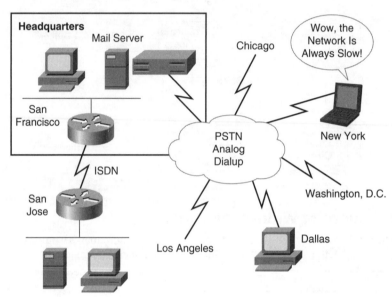

New Core Design

The new core design for TurtleNet Consulting would be best accomplished through Frame Relay. The ISDN backup line could be left in place so that the two most critical sites would have a connection should there be an outage of the Frame Relay network. Figure B-14 shows the proposed core design for TurtleNet Consulting.

Figure B-14 *TurtleNet Consulting—New Core Design*

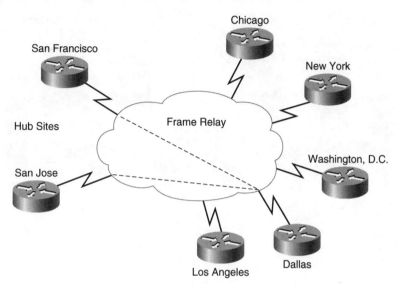

New HQ Design

The two main sites in the company are San Francisco and San Jose. It would, therefore, make sense to make these locations the primary and backup sites for the company's main database servers. Access for local users would be 10BaseT connections to an Ethernet switch. Servers and the router would connect through 100BaseTX (or FX). Remote users would come in through an access server either using ISDN or basic telephone service. A TACACS+ or RADIUS server is provided to secure these connections. Figure B-15 illustrates the proposed HQ design for TurtleNet Consulting.

Figure B-15 *TurtleNet Consulting—New HQ Design*

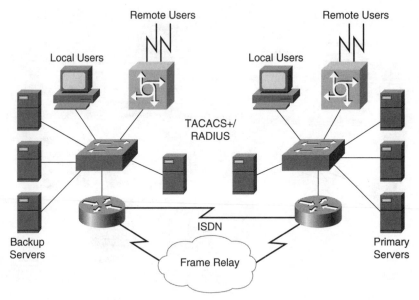

New Local Office Design

The local sites require a WAN connection to Frame Relay and a switched LAN connection for each local user. A combination switch/router device could serve this purpose. The local LAN could be a flat network. Remote users that are local to this office could come in through an access server. Figure B-16 illustrates the proposed HQ design for TurtleNet Consulting.

Figure B-16 *TurtleNet Consulting—New Local Office Design*

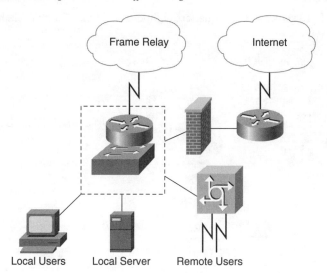

Solutions to Case Study 6: National Mathematical Bank

Figure B-17 shows a "big picture" that clearly reveals the hierarchical structure of the National Mathematical Bank network.

Figure B-17 *National Mathematical Bank—Original Overall Design*

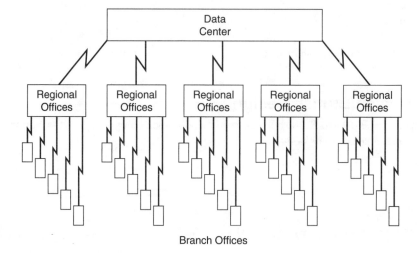

Original HQ Design

Figure B-18 shows the headquarters components of the National Mathematical Bank network.

Figure B-18 *National Mathematical Bank—Original HQ Design*

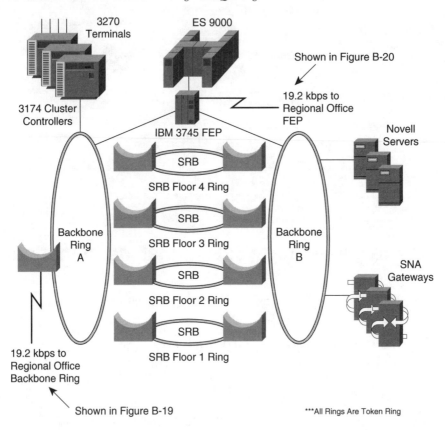

Original Region/Branch Design

Figures B-19 and B-20 show the region and branch components of the National Mathematical Bank network.

Figure B-19 *National Mathematical Bank—Original Region Design*

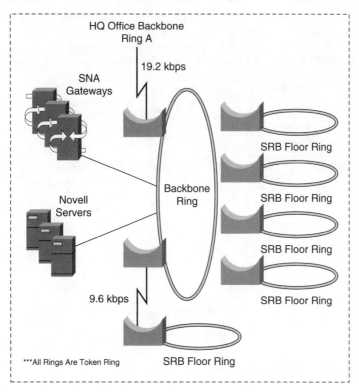

Figure B-20 *National Mathematical Bank—Original Branch Design*

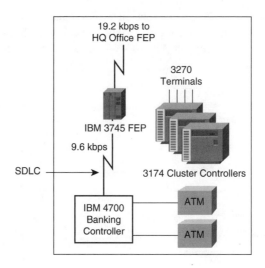

New Overall Design—Phase 1

The first phase of the new overall design, as illustrated in Figure B-21, replaces part of the WAN network with Frame Relay.

Figure B-21 *National Mathematical Bank—New Overall Design, Phase 1*

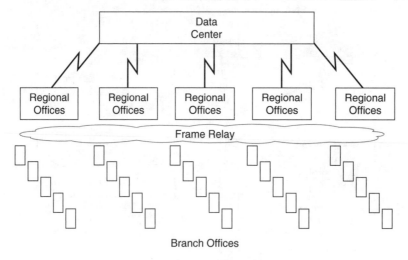

New HQ Design—Phase 1

The Phase 1 new HQ design, as illustrated in Figure B-22, uses the dual router, dual FEP, dual-ring topology recommended for maximum redundancy in the network. The source-route bridges (SRBs) have been eliminated and replaced by a collapsed router backbone. The IBM 3174 cluster controllers, SNA gateways, and Novell servers are equally distributed among the two backbone rings. Leased lines from the HQ routers connect to the regional centers. All the SNA gateways are reached by routed IPX. No NetBIOS is used.

Figure B-22 *National Mathematical Bank—New HQ Design, Phase 1*

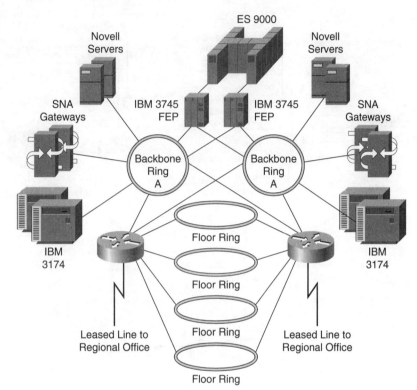

New Region/Branch Design—Phase 1

The regional office SRBs are replaced by routers; the floor rings, along with the backbone ring, collapse into the router. Dual routers provide redundancy back to the data center at HQ. The IBM 3174 cluster controllers are distributed between the two routers; SDLLC is used to convert protocols. Everything that goes up to the data center is now LLC2.

At the branch, a router with two serial interfaces and one Token Ring interface provides connectivity. The local Token Ring attaches to the router. The local IBM 4700 banking controller is SDLC attached to the router, and SDLLC converts this to LLC2. The other serial line is used to connect to the Frame Relay network. Two Frame Relay PVCs are used, one going to each router at the regional center. Figure B-23 shows the Phase 1 portion of the proposed region/branch design.

Figure B-23 *National Mathematical Bank—New Region/Branch Design, Phase 1*

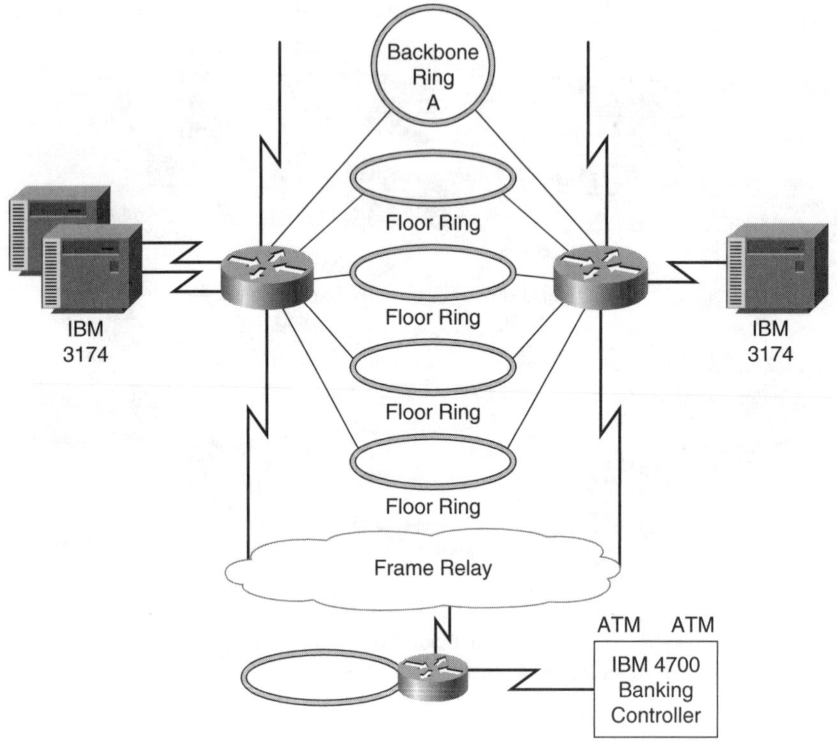

New Overall Design—Phase 2

In Phase 2, all WAN connectivity is through a Frame Relay network in a hub-and-spoke configuration, with the data center as the hub site. Each remote site (region and local offices) has two PVCs to the data center. Figure B-24 shows the Phase 2 portion of the proposed overall design.

Figure B-24 *National Mathematical Bank—New Overall Design, Phase 2*

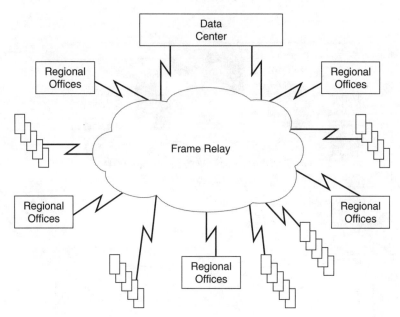

New HQ Design—Phase 2

As illustrated in Figure B-25, the data center FEPs are replaced by channel-attached routers. The routers used own-stream PU concentration features to bring the local and remote gateways into the main frame. The IBM 3174 cluster controllers and 3270 terminals could be replaced by PCs and SNA gateways. Token Ring switching could be used to increase bandwidth in the Token Ring network, or we could migrate to Ethernet switches.

Figure B-25 *National Mathematical Bank—New HQ Design, Phase 2*

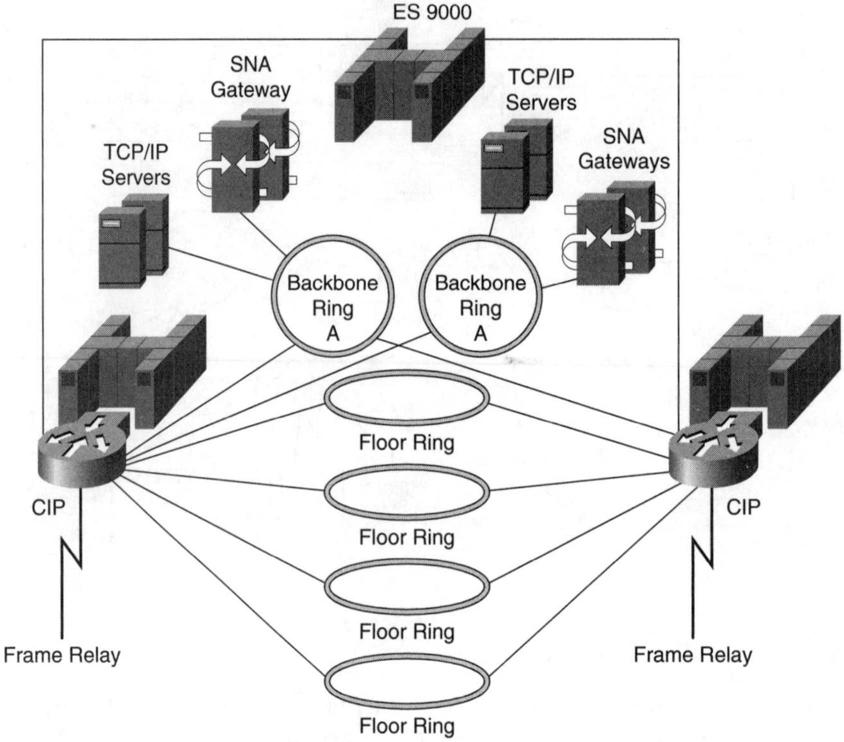

New Region/Branch Design—Phase 2

As illustrated in Figure B-26, the IBM 3174 cluster controllers have been eliminated, and the 3270 terminals have been replaced with PCs that access SNA gateways using TCP/IP. The original PCs also use TCP/IP now, and all PCs are attached to dedicated Ethernet switch ports. If redundancy is still deemed necessary, two routers running HSRP can be deployed. Multiple switches can also be deployed for redundancy using STP.

The branch could migrate from an SDLC-attached ATM controller to a LAN-connected controller (Token Ring or Ethernet). If Ethernet were selected, the PCs on the Token Rings would also be migrated.

Figure B-26 *National Mathematical Bank—New Region/Branch Design, Phase 2*

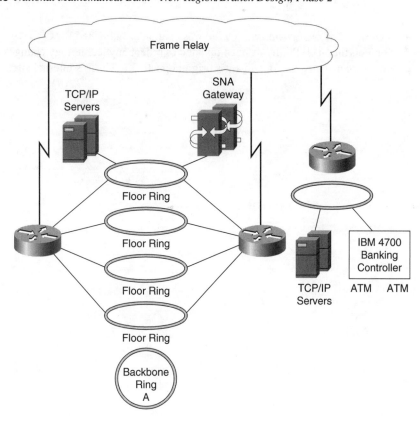

This *Design and Implementation Guide* was originally published for Cisco Systems by Adrien Fournier in 1996. It has been updated to reflect any technology changes during the past three years since this document's original posting to Cisco's internal site.

Design and Implementation Guide: Frame Relay

Frame Relay Networks are growing at an unprecedented rate and are quickly becoming the wide-area networking solution of choice in the Fortune 1000 marketplace and beyond. This document contains a discussion of Frame Relay technology, an analysis of protocol overhead associated with Frame Relay networks, memory usage requirements by platform, and a discussion of features associated with a Frame Relay network. A companion Excel spreadsheet can be used to determine total overhead for your network based on routing, routed, and bridged protocols.

The use of Frame Relay technology in today's networks varies significantly as to how it is deployed. Many players in this arena offer a multitude of solutions. This appendix focuses on primarily on router-based Frame Relay networks.

Overview

Frame Relay provides a packet-switching data communications capability used across the interface between user devices (for example, routers, bridges, and host machines) and network equipment (for example, switching nodes), and operates at Layer 2 of the seven-layer OSI model. The network providing the Frame Relay interface can be either a carrier-provided public network or a network of privately owned equipment serving a single enterprise.

As an interface to a network, Frame Relay is a similar type of protocol as X.25. However, Frame Relay differs significantly from X.25 in its functionality and format. In particular, Frame Relay is a more streamlined protocol, facilitating higher performance and greater efficiency. With the introduction of digital transmission technology, far less error detection and correction was required compared to that of analog technology commonly seen in X.25 networks. The elimination of this redundant error control at this layer and allowing the layers above to handle error detection and retransmission allowed greater performance and efficiency to be realized with Frame Relay.

In comparison to a dedicated leased-line network, the main attraction to migrate to Frame Relay is cost. This is true in terms of recurring costs and connectivity requirements such as number of physical ports and CSU/DSUs. In a competitive market, the delta in cost savings is typically higher.

As an interface between user and network equipment, Frame Relay provides a means for statistically multiplexing many logical data conversations (referred to as virtual circuits [VCs]) over a single physical transmission link. This contrasts with systems that use only time-division multiplexing (TDM) techniques for supporting multiple data streams. Frame Relay's statistical multiplexing provides more flexible and efficient use of available bandwidth.

Frame Relay Basics

Frame Relay Terms

Many terms apply to Frame Relay networking. The basic, generic ones that apply to this discussion are defined here. There are many vendors out there, each with its own implementations and naming conventions. The description of these terms will shed some light.

Link access rate—This is the clock speed of the connection (local loop) to the Frame Relay network. The clock can be provided by the CSU/DSU or by the Frame Relay switch itself. This is the rate at which data travels into or out of the network, regardless of other settings.

DLCI (data-link connection identifier)—Contained in every Frame Relay header to identify the logical circuit between the CPE and the Frame Relay switch. The switch then maps (through configuration) the DLCIs at both ends to create a permanent virtual circuit (PVC). Each PVC has configuration parameters (described later); these parameters usually include CIR, committed burst, and excess burst.

CIR (committed information rate)—This is the rate in bits per second (bps) that the Frame Relay switch agrees to transfer data. This rate is usually averaged over a minimum increment of the Committed Rate Measurement Interval (T^c). The CIR is configurable on the Frame Relay switch on an individual PVC basis, and can be any value between 0 and the actual link speed. Service providers' options differ.

B^c (committed burst)—the maximum number of bits that the switch agrees to transfer during any Committed Rate Measurement Interval (T^c). Typical values of T^c are .5 to 2 seconds. Here is the formula for calculating (B^c). In this example, assume a CIR of 32 kbps, and a T^c of 2 seconds:

$T^c = B^c$ / CIR (B^c is typically a multiple of CIR.)

or

$B^c = T^c \times$ CIR
64 kbps = 2 secs $\times$ 32 kbps

The significance of this is that the higher the B^c-to-CIR ratio is, the longer the switch can handle a sustained burst. This means larger input buffer resources are needed. Although latency may grow as more frames are buffered, in most cases this, is not a problem. The very nature of Frame Relay technology allows for buffering elasticity for handling differing link access rates, and makes it possible to handle bursts of data. Vendors' implementations differ, however, as do service providers' options.

B^e (excess burst)—The maximum number of uncommitted bits that the switch will attempt to transfer beyond the CIR. Excess burst is limited by the link access rate. The formula for this is as follows:

$([B^c + B^e \ ]/\ B^c\ ) \times CIR$ = link access rate
$([64 + 64)/64\ ] \times 32) = 64$ kbps (This configuration would not work for a link access rate of 56 kbps.)

The percentage of successfully transmitted frames in the excess burst region depends entirely on the provisioning and configuration of the Frame Relay network. Obviously, if the switches are heavily configured and/or switch-to-switch network bandwidth is limited, congestion is more likely (along with the resultant higher probability of dropped frames).

DE (discard eligible)—This bit in the Frame Relay header, when set, indicates that the frame is eligible for discard in the event of network congestion. The bit is set when a frame entering the switch is determined to be in excess of the committed information rate (CIR), but less than the excess burst limit. If the B^e (excess burst) limit is exceeded, the frame should be dropped in normal operation. The option to not enforce this is available in some Frame Relay switches and may be useful where ingress and egress access speeds are equal where full bandwidth could be used when available. This scenario would mostly apply to private Frame Relay networks. The DE bit can also be set before entering the Frame Relay switch by CPE equipment, such as a router. Cisco IOS allows the setting of DE bit for packets classified through standard access lists.

FECN (forward explicit congestion notification)—This bit in the Frame Relay header is set by the network Frame Relay switch to notify the end station receiving the frame that the frame has been delivered through a congested path of the network. How the destination end station or intervening router/FRAD reacts to the notification is of no consequence to the switch. It's sole function is to notify. It's up to the destination end station or intervening router/FRAD to take action if any is required.

BECN (backward explicit congestion notification)—This bit in the Frame Relay header is set by the network Frame Relay switch to notify the source (sending) station that congestion exists in the path it is transmitting into. The source end station or intervening router/FRAD should take immediate action to reduce data being sent into the network while the congestion condition continues. (A discussion of traffic shaping follows in the section titled "Key Cisco Features and When to Use.") To put some of these terms into perspective, consider the following. When transmitting data across the physical link into the Frame Relay switch, it is transferred at the link access rate. The switch counts the incoming bits on a per-VC basis as committed burst (B^c) bits within time interval T^c. Any bits arriving in excess of the B^c limit are counted as excess burst (B^e) bits and the frame containing these bits will have the DE bit set. These frames are forwarded if there is no congestion detected in the network. When you go beyond the excess burst limit, the switch discards new incoming frames. Of course, as the frames on the input queue within the committed burst region get forwarded, the B^c bit counter decrements, allowing room for more committed data. This scheme is sometimes referred to as a "leaky bucket" algorithm, which is well suited for handling bursty traffic.

Frame Format

Figure C-1 shows the components of and format for a Frame Relay frame.

Figure C-1   *Frame Relay Frame Format (ANSI T1.618)*

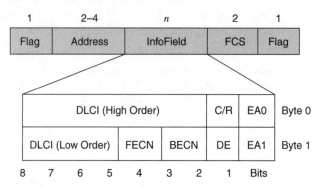

DLCI: Data Link Connection Identifier
C/R: Command Response Field
FECN: Forward Explicit Congestion Notify
BECN: Backward Explicit Congestion Notify
DE: Discard Eligible
EA: Address Field Extension

Congestion

As illustrated in Figure C-2, congestion is monitored by the Frame Relay switch(es) in the network. One of the ways this is done is by examining the queue depths of the transmit queues on an individual VC basis. When the average queue size exceeds its optimal threshold, over some predefined period of time, frames entering this queue will have the FECN bit set. This will continue to happen until the queue depth falls below the suboptimal threshold. Remember, this is only a notification. Ideally, the destination end station's protocol stack receiving this notification could initiate a throttling mechanism, such as a window-size reduction signal, back to the source end station. Regardless of the existence of this capability, when congestion persists, the Frame Relay switch will notify the source end station or intervening router/FRAD by setting the BECN bit on frames going back to that source.

Figure C-2   *Congestion on Transmit Queue Causes FECN to Be Set on Frames to Destination, and Eventually BECN Set on Frames Back to Source*

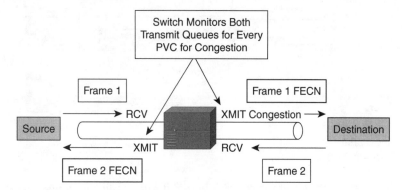

Managing congestion in a Frame Relay network is a cooperative effort between switch vendors, router/FRAD vendors, and end-station protocols. Pushing the capacity limits of Frame Relay networks will certainly require this cooperative effort to produce effective congestion management, which in turn will reduce the cost of running the network.

Planning

Frame Relay Subscription

The majority of deployed Frame Relay networks are star (or hub-and-spoke) topologies. This fits the model of host-based application access, or central-server access. When provisioning Frame Relay services for a topology of this kind, care must be taken to provide adequate bandwidth and resources to handle all the traffic needs of your organization and any protocol overhead. Oversubscription in these environments is quite common and, if not carefully planned, can lead to adverse network performance including poor interactive response times. The underlying problem associated with this poor performance can mostly be attributed to underestimating the actual volume of traffic and traffic patterns that exists on the network. Successful oversubscribed services contain enough bandwidth and buffering capacity to handle the traffic. Using the star (or hub-and-spoke) topology, let's examine the subscription issues associated with deploying a simple network.

Figure C-3 *Star Topology Using a 2-Mbps Link Access Rate at the Central Site with Remote Sites Using 64 kbps*

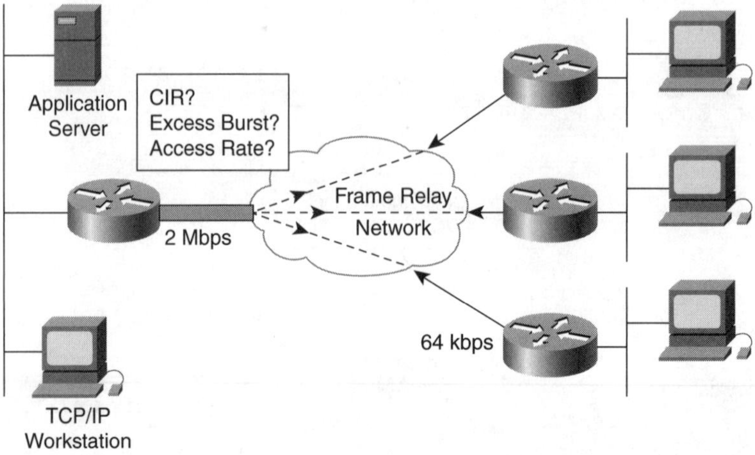

The central (hub) site physical link connection will typically have link speeds of fractional T1/E1, or T1/E1 (64 kbps to 2.0 Mbps); common access (spoke) link speeds are 56/64 kbps. This is where the question of over/undersubscription comes into play. Consider the following scenarios.

Scenario 1: Subscribing to Physical-Link Access Rates

This is where you aggregate the available bandwidth of all the access (spoke) sites into the central (hub) site.

- Central-site link rate of 2 Mbps.
- 30 X Access sites each with link rate of 64 kbps.
- If all access sites burst to 100 percent, the central hub site can theoretically handle all traffic.

With knowledge of overall bandwidth requirements and with sufficient router resources (memory), yet with little knowledge of what the protocol mix is and of the link overhead used, this level of subscription is safe. Many will argue overkill. A major factor to consider when subscribing at this level is network congestion. If all available bandwidth is to be used, CIR should be high, if not equal to access link speed, and committed burst B^c set to allow for sustained bursts. Of course, the cost of doing this can be quite high. Depending on the service provider, the costs may be close to leased-line connectivity.

Scenario 2: Subscribing to a Moderate CIR

This is where you aggregate the CIRs of all VCs into the central hub site's BW capacity. Assume a CIR of 32 kbps on each VC.

- Central-site link rate of 2 Mbps.

- 60 X Access sites each with link rate of 64 kbps, and CIR of 32 kbps.

- If all access sites burst over their respective CIRs, congestion will occur at the egress point of the Frame Relay network; in this case, the switch interface to the central hub site. Frames will get dropped.

- If the central hub site bursts beyond all the individual CIRs, congestion occurs at the access spoke interfaces of the Frame Relay network and potentially overwhelms the ingress point of the Frame Relay network. Remember that the central hub connection is a single physical interface multiplexing multiple virtual circuits; in this case, 60 PVCs.

Of course, this scenario required that the CIR be chosen correctly based on knowledge of bandwidth requirements for the traffic patterns and protocols used. Choosing a CIR of 32 kbps should mean that the requirement is to have a guaranteed bandwidth available to pass at least 32 kbps worth of data, with the flexibility of bursting above this rate, but not for a sustained period of time. This is what makes Frame Relay technology suitable for bursty traffic applications. It is unlikely in this scenario that all access sites would burst at the same time, although certain traffic patterns may indeed be occurring, such as broadcasts (see "Consider User Traffic Mix and Patterns" later in this appendix). If your bandwidth requirements are low (that is, small amounts of single protocol traffic and no broadcasts), you can increase the number of access spoke sites that you aggregate into the central hub site. This is *oversubscription*. The issues now move into the router and how many VCs it can effectively handle. This will be discussed in more detail later.

Scenario 3: Subscribing with 0 CIR

Some service providers offer a zero committed information rate (0 CIR) provisioning that typically includes a separate service-level agreement (that is, if you are dropping packets consistently, they will do something about it). To offer this kind of provisioning, the service providers design the Frame Relay network with sufficient resources to handle the traffic loads (bandwidth, and buffers). The pricing for 0 CIR is typically very attractive. The use of the Frame Relay traffic shaping features in IOS 11.2 to control the amount of data flowing into the network are of great value when provisioning for 0 CIR.

NOTE   The same parameter requirements exist here as did for Scenario 2. The major difference here is that all frames entering the network are beyond committed burst; however, the switches are typically configured to not drop frames until there is significant congestion.

Consider User Traffic Mix and Patterns

Assume a network in a banking environment, where each branch supports a router that is Frame Relay connected to a central hub router. Each branch supports a LAN port that connects to branch PCs and a serial link connecting the Automated Teller Machines (ATMs). The applications on the PCs are primarily interactive (query/response), but are also used for file transfer, the latter for uploading the day's business to the central site. Because this is done after hours, interactive response times during the daytime meets or exceeds requirements. The file transfers can be quite lengthy, especially on major payroll days. There is also a peak usage on the ATMs on these days, and the line-ups can be long. If the file transfers are running during this peak period, ATM response times will be adversely affected. ATMs have quite low bandwidth demands, because the frames generated are quite small and infrequent (relatively speaking). The other consideration is what's happening at the central hub site? Many sites in the same time zones are all file transferring data in, and are likely exceeding the excess burst rates on all PVC's. Frames are getting dropped and retransmissions are rampant. When subscribing Frame Relay circuits, look for worst-case scenarios and their risks and plan accordingly. In this example, custom queuing on a per-VC basis (IOS 11.2) could be configured to prioritize interactive traffic over file transfers. Alternatively, provision separate VCs for interactive traffic, subscribe additional CIR and excess burst on a single VC, or modify scheduled times of file transfers. Know your traffic!

Router DLCI Capacity

How many DLCIs can one configure per physical interface? How many DLCIs can one configure in a specific router? These are two very frequently asked questions. Disappointingly, the answer is, "It depends." (And this is one of the most frequently used answers.) I will first review the technical limits, which are beyond the practical maximum. Then, we'll look at the factors associated with practical limitations.

Technical Limits

DLCI Address Space—Approximately 1000 DLCIs can be configured on a single physical link given a 10-bit address. Due to certain DLCIs being reserved (vendor-implementation dependent), the maximum is about 1000.

LMI Status Update— The LMI protocol (ANSI Annex D, and ITU-T standards also) requires that all PVC status reports fit into a single packet and generally limits the number of DLCI's to less than 800. This is dependent on the MTU size:

- (MTU – 20)/5 = Max DLCIs (approximately)
- (4000 – 20) /5 = 796 DLCIs, where 20 = Frame Relay and LMI header
- The default MTU on serial interfaces is 1500 bytes. This yields a maximum of 296 DLCIs per interface.

NOTE   These numbers vary slightly depending on LMI type.

Practical Limitations

User Data—How much and what kind of user data is expected to travel across each VC? The answer to this question is necessary to determine initial provisioning of the Frame Relay service. File transfers will quickly consume CIR and excess burst limits. If the requirement is to configure many DLCIs into a physical link, we must eliminate broadcasts and avoid multiple protocols.

Broadcast Traffic—Two implications here: 1) bandwidth consumption for broadcast traffic, and 2) broadcast replication in central hub router. To avoid broadcast traffic

- Use default or static routes.
- Filter SAPs.

See the next section for details on broadcast traffic analysis.

Memory Constraints—What else are you running on the router? Routing protocols? How big is your routing table? Do you have enough memory for all the DLCI's (see Memory calculation section).

Processor Constraints—Avoid the use of processor-intensive features such as compression, prioritization, or process-switched protocols when maximizing the number of virtual circuits in a router. From IOS Release 11.0 and higher, many of these features have moved to the fast-switching path.

Guidelines—Efficiency of Frame Relay software can be compromised when stretching the limits. The general guidelines for maximum numbers of DLCIs per interface as per the *Internet Design Guide* are between 10 and 50, depending on the traffic and constraints previously listed. If you choose to go beyond this, consider the following guidelines and measure as you go. Making guesses as to what you think your traffic is and what it actually is can cost an extra router or two.

Step 1   Determine the user traffic requirements. From this, determine by how much you can safely oversubscribe the central hub link. Consider the previous 2-Mbps link subscription scenarios and do not exceed a 3:1 oversubscription. That's 120 DLCIs, in which each VC's normal traffic level seldom exceeds 16 kbps. This precludes the use of file transfer on these VCs. Typical low-traffic applications could be ATMs, paging systems, or network-management SNMP updates. If you don't know what your traffic patterns and link overhead will be, don't oversubscribe.

Step 2 Eliminate all broadcasts on the Frame Relay link. If you must run a routing protocol, carefully plan to use route summarization, and minimize routing table size by advertising (for example, a single default route).

Step 3 Implement the maximum DLCIs per router platform guideline, based on extrapolation from empirical data established on a Cisco 7000 router platform:

2500: 1 × T1/E1 link @ 60 DLCIs per interface = 60 total
4000: 1 × T1/E1 link @ 120 DLCIs per interface = 120 total
4500: 3 × T1/E1 links @ 120 DLCIs per interface = 360 total
4700: 4 × T1/E1 links @ 120 DLCIs per interface = 480 total
7000: 4 × T1/E1/T3/E3 links @ 120 DLCIs per interface = 480 total
7200: 5 × T1/E1/T3/E3 links @ 120 DLCIs per interface = 600 total
7500: 6 × T1/E1/T3/E3 links @ 120 DLCIs per interface = 720 total

NOTE   These are guidelines only; assume that all traffic is fast switched.

Broadcast Traffic Analysis

Bandwidth consumption by broadcast traffic is a major concern in router-based Frame Relay networks because packet replication occurs on a single physical interface. This replication is most common at the central site, where the concentration of VCs onto physical links is much higher than at the access or distribution sites. Using a simple hub-and-spoke topology (refer to Figure C-3), analysis of WAN traffic is performed on the hub (core) router link that connects to the Frame Relay switch. Multiple protocols are configured on the routers and the resulting overhead data is observed. To fully analyze the traffic, we must consider broadcasts from the following:

- Routing protocols
- Routed protocols
- Transparent bridging
- Remote SRB

Routing Protocols

Routing updates in a Frame Relay network can significantly impact performance, because routing updates go out on a per-PVC (DLCI) basis. Therefore, when you configure multiple DLCIs on a single WAN Frame Relay interface, routing updates will be replicated for each DLCI. Although distance vector routing protocols, such as RIP and IGRP, are easily predictable in that updates go out at regular intervals, the same is not true of link-state protocols, such as OSPF and IS-IS. EIGRP, an advanced distance vector routing protocol, also falls in the same behavior category as OSPF. Although EIGRP is not a link-state protocol, routing updates are propagated in a similar way to a link-state protocol—that is, flooding occurs when adjacencies are lost (see the sections "Routing with OSPF" and "Routing with EIGR"). The following subsections discuss, on a per-protocol basis, the overhead consumed when these protocols are configured.

RIP

RIP updates flow every 30 seconds. Each RIP packet can contain up to 25 route entries for a total of 536 bytes—36 bytes of this is header information, and each route entry is 20 bytes. Therefore, if you were to advertise 1000 routes over a Frame Relay link configured for 50 DLCIs, you would end up with 1 MB of routing update data every 30 seconds, or 285 kbps of bandwidth consumed. On a T1 link, this represents 18.7% of the bandwidth, with each update duration being 5.6 seconds. This is a considerable amount of overhead (borderline acceptable), but CIR would have to be in the region of the access speed. Obviously, anything less than a T1 would incur too much overhead.

$1000/25 = 40$ packets $\times 36 = 1440$ header bytes
1000×20 bytes $= 20,000$ bytes of route entries
Total $21,440$ bytes $\times 50$ DLCIs $= 1072$ MB of RIP updates every 30 seconds
$1,072,000$ bytes / 30 secs $\times 8$ bits $= 285$ kbps

IGRP

IGRP updates flow every 90 seconds (configurable). Each IGRP packet can contain 104 route entries for a total of 1492 bytes—38 of this is header information, and each route entry is 14 bytes. If you were to advertise 1000 routes over a Frame Relay link configured with 50 DLCIs, you would end up with approximately 720 KB of routing update data every 90 seconds, or 64 kbps of bandwidth consumed. On a T1 link, this represents 4.2% of the bandwidth, with each update duration being 3.7 seconds. This is an acceptable amount of overhead.

$1000/104 = 9$ packets $\times 38 = 342$ header bytes
$1000 \times 14 = 14,000$ bytes of route entries
Total $14,342$ bytes $\times 50$ DLCIs $= 717$ KB of IGRP updates every 90 seconds
$717,000$ bytes / 90×8 bits $= 63.7$ kbps

Routed Protocols

AppleTalk (Extended)

RTMP routing updates occur every 10 seconds (configurable). Each RTMP packet can contain up to 94 extended route entries for a total of 564 bytes—23 bytes of header information, and each route entry is 6 bytes. If you were to advertise 1000 AppleTalk networks over a Frame Relay link configured for 50 DLCIs, you would end up with approximately 313 KB of RTMP updates every 10 seconds, or 250 kbps of bandwidth consumed. To remain within an acceptable level of overhead (15% or less), a T1 rate is required.

1000/94 = 11 packets × 23 bytes = 253 header bytes
1000 × 6 = 6000 bytes of route entries
Total = 6253 × 50 DLCIs = 313 KB of RTMP updates every 10 seconds
313,000 / 10 secs × 8 bits = 250 kbps

DECnet

DECnet routing updates occur every 40 seconds (configurable). Each DECnet routing packet can contain up to 368 route entries for a total of 1490 bytes—25 bytes of header information, and each route entry is 4 bytes. If you were to advertise 1000 DECnet routes over a Frame Relay link configured for 50 DLCIs, you would end up with 203 KB of DECnet updates every 40 seconds, or 40.8 kbps of bandwidth consumed. To remain within an acceptable level of overhead (15% or less), a rate of 256 kbps is required.

1000/368 = 3 packets × 25 bytes = 75 bytes of header
1000 × 4 = 4000 bytes of route entries
Total = 4075 × 50 DLCIs = 203,750 bytes of DECnet updates every 40 seconds
203,750 / 40 secs × 8 bits = 40.8 kbps

IPX RIP

IPX RIP packet updates occur every 60 seconds (configurable). Each IPX RIP packet can contain up to 50 route entries for a total of 536 bytes—38 bytes of header information, and each route entry is 8 bytes. If you were to advertise 1000 IPX routes over a Frame Relay link configured for 50 DLCIs, you would end up with 536 KB of IPX updates every 60 seconds, or 58.4 kbps of bandwidth consumed. To remain within an acceptable level of overhead (15% or less), a rate of 512 kbps is required.

1000/50 = 20 packets × 38 bytes = 760 bytes of header
1000 × 8 = 8000 bytes of route entries
Total = 8760 × 50 DLCIs = 438,000 bytes of IPX updates every 60 seconds
438,000 / 60 secs × 8 bits = 58.4 kbps

IPX SAP

IPX SAP packet updates occur every 60 seconds (configurable). Each IPX SAP packet can contain up to 7 advertisement entries for a total of 536 bytes—38 bytes of header information, and each advertisement entry is 64 bytes. If you were to broadcast 1000 IPX advertisements over a Frame Relay link configured for 50 DLCIs, you would end up with 536 KB of IPX updates every 60 seconds, or 58.4 kbps of bandwidth consumed. To remain within an acceptable level of overhead (15% or less), a rate of greater than 2 Mbps is required. Obviously, SAP filtering would be required in this scenario. In comparison to all other protocols mentioned here, IPX SAP updates require the most bandwidth.

1000/7 = 143 packets $\times$ 38 bytes = 5434 bytes of header
1000 $\times$ 64 = 64,000 bytes of route entries
Total = 69,434 $\times$ 50 DLCIs = 3,471,700 bytes of IPX service advertisements every 60 seconds
3,471,700 / 60 secs $\times$ 8 bits = 462 kbps

VINES

VINES RTP packet updates occur every 90 seconds (configurable). Each RTP packet can contain up to 104 route entries for a total of 1492 bytes—28 bytes of header information, and each route entry is 8 bytes. If you were to advertise 1000 VINES routes over a Frame Relay link configured for 50 DLCIs, you would end up with 415 KB of VINES updates every 90 seconds. Using the same math as in the other examples, this gives you 37 kbps of bandwidth consumed. To remain within an acceptable level of overhead (15% or less), a rate of 256 kbps is required.

1000/104 = 10 packets $\times$ 28 bytes = 280 bytes of header
1000 $\times$ 8 = 8000 bytes of route entries
Total = 8280 $\times$ 50 DLCIs = 414,000 bytes of IPX updates every 60 seconds
414,000 / 90 secs $\times$ 8 bits = 37 kbps

XNS

XNS RIP packet updates occur every 30 seconds (configurable). Each XNS RIP packet can contain up to 25 route entries, for a total of 536 bytes—46 bytes of header information, and each route entry is 20 bytes. If you were to advertise 1000 XNS routes over a Frame Relay link configured for 50 DLCIs, you would end up with 1.08 MB of XNS updates every 30 seconds. Using the same math, this gives you 291 kbps of bandwidth consumed. To remain within an acceptable level of overhead (15% or less), a rate of 2 Mbps is required.

1000/25 = 40 packets $\times$ 46 = 1840 header bytes
1000 $\times$ 20 = 20,000 bytes of route entries
Total = 21,840 $\times$ 50 DLCIs = 1,092,000 bytes of IPX updates every 30 seconds
1,092,000 / 30 secs $\times$ 8 bits = 291 kbps

Inverse ARP Traffic at Startup

Address resolution is done on a DLCI basis for each protocol at startup time. It takes three packets to resolve addresses for each protocol on each DLCI. If you were to configured 50 DLCIs, each carrying three protocols (say IP,IPX, and AppleTalk), 450 packets would flow (ranging between 30 and 46 bytes each depending on protocol address length). Inverse ARP protocol is turned on by default when Frame Relay is configured on a link. The target hardware address used is the Frame Relay address field, which includes the DLCI. This traffic is bursty for a short period of time and could cause minor congestion during startup (when powering everything up on a Monday morning, for example, or following a power outage). After addresses are resolved, no more broadcasts are expected. In the event of an unstable environment where there are line transitions, a repetition of the Inverse ARP process will occur.

Transparent Bridging: Spanning-Tree Protocol

Configuration messages, called bridge protocol data units (BPDUs), used in the Spanning-Tree Protocols supported in Cisco bridge/routers flow at regular intervals between bridges. These constitute a fair amount of traffic because of their frequent occurrence. The Spanning-Tree Protocol used in transparent bridging comes in two flavors. Digital Equipment Corp. (DEC) first introduced it and the algorithm was subsequently revised by the IEEE 802 committee and published in the IEEE 802.1d specification. The DEC Spanning-Tree Protocol issues BPDUs at 1-second intervals; the IEEE issues BPDU's at 2-second intervals. Each packet is 41 bytes: a 35-byte configuration BPDU message, a 2-byte Frame Relay header, a 2-byte Ethernet type, and 2-byte frame-check sequence.

Remote Source-Route Bridging

Remote source-route bridging (RSRB) configured with TCP/IP encapsulation occurs on a router-to-router peer basis. Therefore, in a typical hub-and-spoke Frame Relay network configuration, the hub router will be peered to each of the spoke site routers. TCP/IP keepalive request/response packets will flow between these peers every 60 seconds.

Routing with OSPF

Overhead associated with OSPF is not as obvious and predictable as that with traditional distance vector routing protocols. The unpredictability comes from whether the OSPF network links are stable. If all adjacencies to a Frame Relay router are stable, only neighbor Hello packets (keepalives) will flow, which is comparatively much less overhead than that incurred with a distance vector protocol (RIP, IGRP). If routes (adjacencies) are unstable, however, link-state flooding will occur and bandwidth can quickly be consumed. OSPF is also processor-intensive when running the Dijkstra algorithm (used for computing routes).

When configuring OSPF in a Frame Relay environment, consider the following subsections, summarized from the *OSPF Design Guide*, authored by Sam Halibi, of Cisco. You can find the entire guide at www.cisco.com/warp/public/104/1.html.

Adjacencies on Nonbroadcast Multiaccess

In earlier releases of IOS, special care had to be taken when configuring OSPF over nonbroadcast multiaccess (NBMA) media, such as Frame Relay, X.25, and ATM. The OSPF protocol considers these media, like any other broadcast media, such as Ethernet. NBMA clouds are typically built in a hub-and spoke topology. PVCs or SVCs are laid out in a partial mesh and the physical topology does not provide the multiaccess that OSPF believes is out there. In the case of point-to-point serial interfaces, OSPF will always form an adjacency between the neighbors. OSPF adjacencies exchange database information. To minimize the amount of information exchange on a particular segment, OSPF elects one router to be a designated router (DR) and one router to be a backup designated router (BDR) on each multiaccess segment. The BDR is elected as a backup mechanism in case the DR goes down. The idea behind this is that routers have a central point of contact for information exchange. The selection of the DR became an issue because the DR and BDR needed to have full physical connectivity with all routers that exist on the cloud. Also, because of the lack of broadcast capabilities, the DR and BDR needed to have a static list of all other routers attached to the cloud. This was achieved using the **neighbor** command:

```
neighbor ip-address [priority number] [poll-interval seconds]
```

In more recent releases, different methods can be used to avoid the complications of configuring static neighbors and having specific routers becoming DRs or BDRs on the nonbroadcast cloud. Which method to use is influenced by whether we are starting the network from scratch or rectifying an already existing design.

Method 1: Point-to-Point Subinterfaces

A subinterface is a logical way of defining an interface. The same physical interface can be split into multiple logical interfaces, with each subinterface being defined as point to point. This was originally created to better handle issues caused by split horizon over NBMA and vector-based routing protocols. A point-to-point subinterface has the properties of any physical point-to-point interface. As far as OSPF is concerned, an adjacency is always formed over a point-to-point subinterface with no DR or BDR election. OSPF will consider the cloud as a set of point-to-point links rather than one multiaccess network. The only drawback for the point-to-point link is that each segment will belong to a different subnet. This might not be acceptable (for example, if some administrators have already assigned one IP subnet for the whole cloud).

Method 2: IP Unnumbered

Another workaround is to use IP unnumbered interfaces on the cloud. This also might be a problem for some administrators who manage the WAN based on IP addresses of the serial lines.

Method 3: Selecting Interface Network Types

The following command is used to set the network type of an OSPF interface:

```
ip ospf network {broadcast | non-broadcast | point-to-multipoint}
```

Point-to-Multipoint Interfaces

An OSPF point-to-multipoint interface is defined as a numbered point-to-point interface having one or more neighbors. This concept takes the previously discussed point-to-point concept one step further. Administrators do not have to worry about having multiple subnets for each point-to-point link. The cloud is configured as one subnet. This should work well for people who are migrating into the point-to-point concept with no change in IP addressing on the cloud. Also, they would not have to worry about DRs and neighbor statements. OSPF point-to-multipoint works by exchanging additional link-state updates that contain a number of information elements that describe connectivity to the neighboring routers.

Broadcast Interfaces

This approach is a workaround for using the **neighbor** command, which statically lists all existing neighbors. The interface will be logically set to broadcast and will behave as if the router were connected to a LAN. DR and BDR election will still be performed, so special care should be taken to ensure either a full-mesh topology or a static selection of the DR based on the interface priority.

Dealing with Large OSPF Networks

Careful planning is required for larger networks in the area of addressing and bandwidth constraints. Use of variable-length subnet masks (VLSMs) and OSPF route summarization can respectively deal with these issues.

VLSM

The idea behind variable-length subnet masks is to offer more flexibility when dividing a major network into multiple subnets while maintaining an adequate number of hosts in each subnet. Without VLSM, only one subnet mask can be applied to a major network. Given the number of subnets required, this limitation restricts the number of hosts. If you were to pick the mask such that you have enough subnets, you would not be able to allocate enough hosts in each subnet. The same is true for the hosts; a mask that allows enough hosts might not provide enough subnet space. Using VLSM saves on available address space. Refer to the *OSPF Design Guide* for more information

Route Summarization

Summarizing is the consolidation of multiple routes into one single advertisement. This is normally done at the boundaries of area border routers (ABRs). Although summarization can be configured between any two areas, it is better to summarize in the direction of the backbone. This way the backbone receives all the aggregate addresses and in turn will inject them, already summarized, into other areas. Clearly, reducing the amount of information contained in route advertisements will make more efficient use of the available bandwidth. Refer to the *OSPF Design Guide* for more information.

Full Mesh Versus Partial Mesh

NBMA clouds, such as Frame Relay or X.25, are always a challenge. The combination of low bandwidth and too many link states is a recipe for problems. A partial-mesh topology has proven to behave much better than a full-mesh topology. A carefully laid out point-to-point or point-to-multipoint network works much better than multipoint networks that have to deal with DR issues.

Routing with EIGRP

EIGRP was significantly enhanced in Releases 10.3(11), 11.0(8), 11.1(3), and all later releases. The implementation was changed to improve the performance on low-speed networks (including Frame Relay) and in configurations with many neighbors. For the most part, the changes are transparent. Most existing configurations should continue to operate as before. To take advantage of the improvements for low-speed links and Frame Relay networks, however, it is important to properly configure the bandwidth on each interface on which EIGRP is running. Although the enhanced implementation will interoperate with the earlier version, the full benefits of the enhancements may not be realized until the entire network is upgraded.

Bandwidth Control

The enhanced implementation uses the configured interface bandwidth to determine how much EIGRP data to transmit in a given amount of time. By default, EIGRP will limit itself to using no more than 50% of the available bandwidth. The primary benefit of controlling EIGRP's bandwidth usage is to avoid losing EIGRP packets, which can occur when EIGRP generates data faster than the line can absorb it. This is of particular benefit on Frame Relay networks, where the access-line bandwidth and the PVC capacity may be very different. A secondary benefit is to allow the network administrator to ensure that some bandwidth remains for passing user data, even when EIGRP is very busy.

Configuration Commands

The amount of bandwidth is controlled by two interface subcommands:

```
bandwidth kilobits
```

and one of the following:

```
ip bandwidth-percent eigrp as-number percent
```

```
appletalk eigrp-bandwidth-percent percent
```

```
ipx bandwidth-percent eigrp as-number percent >
```

for IP, AppleTalk, and IPX EIGRP, respectively.

The **bandwidth-percent** command tells EIGRP what percentage of the configured bandwidth it may use. The default is 50%. Because the bandwidth command is also used to set the routing protocol metric, it may be set to a particular value for policy reasons. The **bandwidth-percent** command can have values greater than 100 if the bandwidth is configured artificially low due to such policy reasons.

Configuration Problems

If the bandwidth is configured to be a small value relative to the actual link speed, the enhanced implementation may converge at a slower rate than the earlier implementation. If the value is small enough and there are enough routes in the system, convergence may be so slow that it triggers Stuck In Active (SIA) detection, which may prevent the network from ever converging. This state is evidenced by repeated messages of the following form:

```
%DUAL-3-SIA: Route XXX stuck-in-active state in IP-EIGRP YY. Cleaning up
```

The workaround for this problem is to raise the value of the active timer for EIGRP by configuring the following:

```
router eigrp
timers active-time
```

The default value in the enhanced code is 3 minutes; in earlier releases, the default is 1 minute. You must raise this value throughout the network. If the bandwidth is configured to be too high (greater than the actual available bandwidth), the loss of EIGRP packets may occur. The packets will be retransmitted, but this may degrade convergence. The convergence in this case will be no slower than the earlier implementation, however.

Configuration Guidelines

The following guidelines give recommendations for configuration on NBMA interfaces (Frame Relay, X.25, and ATM). The recommendations are described in terms of configuring the interface *bandwidth* parameter (with EIGRP being able to use 50% of that bandwidth by default). If the interface bandwidth configuration cannot be changed because of routing policy considerations, or for any other reason, the **bandwidth-percent** command should be used to control the EIGRP bandwidth. On low-speed interfaces, raising the available bandwidth for EIGRP above the default of 50% is advisable to improve convergence.

It is particularly critical to configure NBMA interfaces correctly; otherwise, many EIGRP packets may be lost in the switched network. There are three basic rules:

1 The traffic that EIGRP is allowed to send on a single VC cannot exceed the capacity of that VC.

2 The total EIGRP traffic for all VCs cannot exceed the access-line speed of the interface.

3 The bandwidth allowed for EIGRP on each virtual circuit must be the same in each direction.

There are three different scenarios for NBMA interfaces:

- Pure multipoint configuration (no subinterfaces)
- Pure point-to-point configuration (each VC on a separate subinterface)
- Hybrid configuration (point-to-point and multipoint subinterfaces)

The following sections examine each configuration separately.

Pure Multipoint Configuration (No Subinterfaces)

In this configuration, EIGRP divides the configured bandwidth evenly across each VC. You must ensure that this will not overload each VC. If you have a T1 access line with four 56-KB VCs, for example, you should configure the bandwidth to be 224 kbps (4×56 KB) to avoid dropping packets. If the total bandwidth of the VCs equals or exceeds the access-line speed, configure the bandwidth to equal the access-line speed. Note that if the VCs are of different capacities, the bandwidth must be set to take into account the lowest capacity VC. If a T1 access line has three 256-KB VCs and one 56-KB VC, the bandwidth should be set to 224 kbps (4×56 KB). In such configurations, putting at least the slow VC onto a point-to-point subinterface is strongly recommended (so that the bandwidth can be raised on the others).

Pure Point-to-Point Configuration (Each VC on a Separate Subinterface)

This configuration allows maximum control because the bandwidth can be configured separately on each subinterface, and is the best configuration if the VCs have different capacities. Each subinterface bandwidth should be configured to be no greater than the available bandwidth on the associated VC, and the total bandwidth for all subinterfaces cannot exceed the available access-line bandwidth. If the interface is oversubscribed, the access line bandwidth must be divided across each of the subinterfaces. If a T1 access line (1544 kbps) has 10 VCs with a capacity of 256 kbps, for example, the bandwidth on each subinterface should be configured to be 154 kbps (1544/10).

Hybrid Configuration (Point-to-Point and Multipoint Subinterfaces)

Hybrid configurations should use combinations of the two individual strategies, while ensuring that the three basic rules are followed.

Oversubscribed Hub-and-Spoke Frame Relay Configuration (Subinterfaces)

A fairly common configuration in networks with light amounts of transaction traffic is a hub-and-spoke configuration on which the access line to the hub is oversubscribed (because there is usually not enough data traffic to cause this to be a problem). In this scenario, assume a 256-kbps access line to the hub, with 56-kbps access lines to each of 10 spoke sites. IP EIGRP process 123 is configured. Because a maximum of 256 kbps is available, we cannot allow any individual PVC to handle more than 25 kbps (256/10). Because this data rate is fairly low and we don't expect very much user data traffic, we can allow EIGRP to use up to 90% of the bandwidth. Example C-1 shows what the hub configuration would look like.

Example C-1 *Hub Configuration for an Oversubscribed Hub-and-Spoke Frame Relay Network*

```
interface Serial 0
encapsulation frame-relay
interface Serial 0.1 point-to-point
bandwidth 25
ip bandwidth-percent eigrp 123 90
interface Serial 0.2 point-to-point
bandwidth 25
ip bandwidth-percent eigrp 123 90
...
```

Each spoke router must be configured to limit EIGRP traffic to the same rate as that of the hub, to satisfy the third rule listed earlier. Example C-2 shows what the spoke configuration would look like.

Example C-2   *Spoke Configuration for an Oversubscribed Hub-and-Spoke Frame Relay Network*

```
interface Serial 0
encapsulation frame-relay
interface Serial 0.1 point-to-point
bandwidth 25
ip bandwidth-percent eigrp 123 90
```

Note that EIGRP will not use more than 22.5 kbps (90% of 25 KB) on this interface, even though its capacity is 56 kbps. This configuration will not affect user data capacity, which will still be able to use the entire 56 kbps. Alternatively, if you want to set the interface bandwidth to reflect the PVC capacity, you can adjust the bandwidth percentage for EIGRP. In this example, the desired bandwidth for EIGRP is (256 KB/10) × .9 = 23.04 KB; the bandwidth percentage would be 23.04 KB/56 KB = .41 (41%). Therefore, the same effect results from using the configuration in Example C-3.

Example C-3   *Alternative Spoke Configuration for an Oversubscribed Hub-and-Spoke Frame Relay Network Based on Total PVC Capacity*

```
interface Serial 0.1 point-to-point
bandwidth 56
ip bandwidth-percent eigrp 123 41
```

Memory Utilization for Frame Relay Configured Resources

Memory consumption for Frame Relay resources occurs in three areas:

- Each DLCI—216 bytes
- Each **map** statement—96 bytes (or dynamically built map)
- Each IDB (H/W interface + encapsulated Frame Relay)—5040 + 8346 = 13,386 bytes
- Each IDB (S/W subinterface)—2260 bytes

Assuming, for example, a 2501 using two Frame Relay interfaces, each with 4 subinterfaces, total of 8 DLCIs, and associated maps, would result in the following:

2 interface IDB × 13,386 = 26,772 (physical I/F)
8 subinterface IDB × 2260 = 18,080 (subinterfaces)
8 DLCIs × 216 = 1728 (DLCIs)
8 maps × 96 = 768 (map statements or dynamic)
Total = 47,348 bytes of RAM used

NOTE   The values used here are based on IOS Release 11.1. Other releases will vary slightly.

Key Cisco Features and When to Use

The following is a discussion of key features that can be used to solve problems associated with designing scalable Frame Relay networks. For a full description of these features, refer to the published documentation available through CCO or in training documentation.

Traffic Shaping over Frame Relay

Congestion management in Frame Relay networks has been a challenge for some time now. Frame Relay technology does have congestion notification mechanisms built in to the specifications, and most switch vendors implement them. The notifications were mainly intended for end systems, however, which are most often the source of the congestion condition to begin with. The intervening routers connecting the end stations to the Frame Relay network have largely played a passive role in Frame Relay switch congestion—except, of course, promoting the congestion notifications to protocols having a congestion indicator, namely DECnet IV, OSI CLNS, and BECN support for SNA. In large part, however, other protocols cannot be notified because their protocol headers contain no congestion indication. This driving need for more control in this area has led to the development of a congestion-management feature that also includes the prioritization of data going into a Frame Relay network.

Description

The traffic shaping over Frame Relay feature is available in IOS Release 11.2 and higher. This feature allows the router to regulate and prioritize the transmission of frames on a per-VC basis to the network as well as react to congestion notification from the Frame Relay network. Traffic shaping for Frame Relay can be broken down into three main components:

- **Rate enforcement on a per-VC basis**—Define and enforce a rate on the VC at which the router will send traffic into the network.

- **Generalized BECN support on a per-VC basis**—Enable router to dynamically fluctuate the rate at which it sends packets depending on the BECNs it receives. If the router begins receiving numerous BECNs, for example, it will reduce the frame transmit rate. As BECNs become more intermittent, the router will increase the frame transmission rate.

- **VC queuing (custom, priority, and FIFO)**—For circuits carrying more than one protocol, queuing can be applied on a per-VC basis. This can be accomplished by configuring queuing as in earlier releases, and then applying either the **queue-list** for custom queuing or **priority-group** for priority queuing to the **map-class** command used in traffic shaping (as discussed later). For proper operation, queuing must be defined the same on sending and receiving routers.

Additional overall feedback is provided to the traffic-shaping algorithm by monitoring the queue depth of the physical interface.

NOTE   Frame Relay traffic shaping can be applied to both PVCs and SVCs.

The rate-enforcement algorithm used incorporates a two-stage queuing process. The first level is where the queuing on a VC basis is implemented (using either custom, priority, or the default first-come, first-served mechanism). The output of these first-stage queues feed into a single interface-level queue. Traffic is metered at the output of the per-VC queues based on the configuration parameters specified for each of these queues.

Weighted fair queuing (WFQ) and traffic shaping over Frame Relay are mutually exclusive.

Configurable Parameters

For each Frame Relay VC, the user may configure the following parameters:

- CIR—Committed information rate
- B^c—Committed burst size
- B^e—Excess burst size
- Q—Queuing algorithm to be used within the VC

Facilities are provided so that a user may configure a default profile for all VCs at the interface, or subinterface level, which can be overridden at the individual VC level if required.

End-User Interface

The interface-level command that turns on traffic shaping and per-VC queuing on a Frame Relay interface is **frame-relay traffic-shaping**. Use the **no** form of the command to disable traffic shaping and per-VC queuing.

To configure all the traffic-shaping characteristics of a VC in a single command, use the **frame-relay traffic-rate** *average* [*peak*] command where *average* is the average rate equivalent to CIR in bps and [*peak*] is the peak rate equivalent to $CIR + B^e/t = CIR(1 + B^e/B^c)$. If [*peak*] is omitted, the default value used is derived from the BW (interface bandwidth) parameter.

NOTE   If EIGRP (new) is configured, it is advisable to configure the [*peak*] parameter, as opposed to letting it default. EIGRP can also be dependent on BW parameter.

Other related commands for the end-user interface are as follows:

- **frame-relay custom-queue-list** *list-number*—Used to specify a custom queue to be used for the VC queuing associated with a specified map class.

- **frame-relay priority-group** *list-number*—Used to assign a priority queue to VCs associated with a map class.

- **frame-relay adaptive-shaping**—Used to select the type of backward notification you want to use. This command replaced the **frame-relay becn-response-enable** command.

- **frame-relay class** *name*—Used to associate a map class with an interface or subinterface.

- **show frame-relay pvc**—Extended to include specified parameters and queuing used. Used to display statistics about PVC's for Frame Relay interfaces.

- **map-class frame-relay** *map-class-name*—Used to specify a map class to define Quality of Service (QoS) values for an SVC.

Problems Solved

Traffic shaping over Frame Relay solves four problems, as documented in the paragraphs that follow.

Prioritization of packets on a per-VC basis solves a major problem when multiple protocols are configured on the same DLCI. The capability to prioritize—for example, SNA data over IP and other protocols—to preserve session response time for legacy applications allows new IP-based applications to share the same resources safely.

Frame Relay traffic entering a Frame Relay network does so at the link access rate, regardless of any parameters set on the switch (such as CIR, excess burst, or committed burst). Of course, the rate and volume of traffic entering the switch will be monitored at the input, and decisions will be made on what to do with the traffic based on these parameters. Incoming packets can be propagated into the network, which is the case for all traffic entering within CIR. Alternatively, packets can be marked as discard eligible (for those packets entering between CIR and the excess burst limit), and thus subject to being dropped if network congestion exists. And finally, packets can just be dropped at the input if excess burst is exceeded. The Frame Relay traffic-shaping rate-enforcement feature provides control over how much data is sent into the network. It can allow packets to enter the Frame Relay network within CIR, for example, and thus guarantee their propagation through the network. It can further ensure that traffic enters the network within the excess burst limit so that immediate drops do not occur.

For 0 CIR service offered by some service providers, the traffic-shaping rate-enforcement feature could provide a level of control at the router. If you are experiencing drops in the 0 CIR environment, some parameter experimentation and monitoring may be in order to identify at what level the Frame Relay switch begins to drop data. Finding the correct rate enforcement parameters for this particular environment can result in maximizing the available resources while minimizing the amount of dropped frames.

In the event of congestion within the Frame Relay network where BECN is provided to the source (in this case, the router), a further throttling of network-bound data will occur. The problem solved here is that the congestion in the Frame Relay network now has a much better chance of decongesting quickly, without dropping as many DE packets as it might have.

Configuration Example: Router FR45 Is Hub Router; FR3 Is Spoke Router

Example C-4 provides a sample configuration for the FR45 hub router.

Example C-4 *FR45 Router Configuration*

```
Current configuration:
!
version 11.2
!
hostname FR45
!
!
interface Ethernet0
ip address 192.150.42.61 255.255.255.248
media-type 10BaseT
!
!
interface Serial0
no ip address
encapsulation frame-relay
no fair-queue
frame-relay traffic-shaping **Enable Traffic Shaping on interface**
!
interface Serial0.1 point-to-point
ip address 171.68.157.113 255.255.255.240
ipx network AB449D80
frame-relay class 32cir **Here, the map-class defined below is assigned to subinterface**
frame-relay interface-dlci 101 broadcast
!
interface Serial0.2 point-to-point
ip address 171.68.157.129 255.255.255.240
frame-relay class 16cir **Here, the map-class defined below is assigned to subinterface**
frame-relay interface-dlci 102 broadcast
!
```

Example C-4 *FR45 Router Configuration (Continued)*

```
interface Serial0.3 point-to-point
ip address 171.68.157.145 255.255.255.240
frame-relay class bc64 **Here, the map-class defined below is assigned to subinterface**
frame-relay interface-dlci 103 broadcast
!
!
router eigrp 44
network 171.68.0.0
!
ip route 171.69.1.129 255.255.255.255 192.150.42.62
!
map-class frame-relay 32cir
frame-relay traffic-rate 32000 64000 **Here, the average & peak rates are set to the
VC's CIR, and Excess Burst**
frame-relay custom-queue-list 1 **Here, a custom queue list is also assigned to this
map class**
!
map-class frame-relay 16cir
frame-relay traffic-rate 16000 64000 **Here, the average & peak rates are set to the
VC's CIR, and Excess Burst**
!
map-class frame-relay bc64
frame-relay cir in 32000 **Here, specific control of parameters is possible on a bi-directional
basis**
frame-relay cir out 32000
frame-relay bc in 32000
frame-relay bc out 64000
frame-relay be in 64000
frame-relay be out 64000
!
queue-list 1 protocol ip 1
queue-list 1 protocol ipx 2
queue-list 1 queue 1 byte-count 4200
queue-list 1 queue 2 byte-count 1400
!
!
end
```

Example C-5 provides a sample configuration for the FR3 spoke router.

Example C-5 *FR3 Configuration*

```
Current configuration:
!
version 11.2
!
hostname FR3
!
enable password cisco
!
ipx routing 0000.0c18.d70c
!
interface Ethernet0
ip address 198.19.1.1 255.255.255.0
```

Example C-5 *FR3 Configuration (Continued)*

```
ip helper-address 171.68.159.82
ipx network C6130301
!
!
interface Serial0
ip address 171.68.157.146 255.255.255.240
encapsulation frame-relay
ipx network AB449D90
frame-relay traffic-shaping
frame-relay class 32cir **Here, the map-class defined below is assigned to interface**
!
router eigrp 44
network 171.68.0.0
!
!
no ip classless
ip route 171.69.1.129 255.255.255.255 192.150.42.161
!
map-class frame-relay 32cir
frame-relay traffic-rate 32000 64000 **Here, the average & peak rates match those in the
Hub router**
frame-relay custom-queue-list 1 **Here, the custom queue list matches that in the
Hub router**
!
queue-list 1 protocol ip 1
queue-list 1 protocol ipx 2
queue-list 1 queue 1 byte-count 4200
queue-list 1 queue 2 byte-count 1400
!
!
end
```

Dial Backup per DLCI

To back up an individual DLCI, a separate interface must be used as backup. This feature works by detecting that the VC is no longer available; this is learned through either the LMI (Local Management Interface) status updates from the switch, or from not receiving keepalives on the physical link (the latter case would apply if the physical link goes down). In a typical hub-and-spoke scenario, as shown in Figure C-4, the spoke or access site should initiate the backup. This eases resources required at the central site. The backup can be done through a separate serial interface, or an Async port, or over an ISDN link. For ISDN, some service providers offer media support backup into a Frame Relay switch port. This will become more popular with the availability of SVCs. Otherwise, backup is typically achieved by bypassing the entire Frame Relay network and connecting directly to the central hub site.

If the serial interface option is used, the interface could be brought up, which would in turn initiate a switched synchronous connection to be made on the access device's serial interface. You would require a dedicated serial port at the hub site or a switched connection into a multichannel interface (MIP card). This strategy could be expensive in resources. If the ISDN option is used, a good strategy is to use PRI - ISDN at the central site. Concentration of multiple ISDN circuits in a single router is achievable and more cost effective.

Figure C-4 *Dial Backup Initiated from Spoke Site Router upon Detection of VC Failure Either Locally or Remotely*

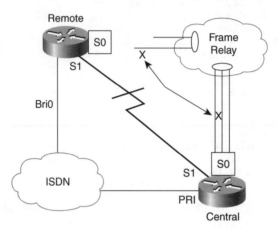

If the Aysnc interface is used, dialing in to a terminal access server located at the hub or central site will work well. Example C-6 shows a configuration example using the async line.

Example C-6 *Spoke Router Dial Backup Using Async Interface When DLCI 207 Goes Down*

```
Current configuration:
!
version 11.1
!
hostname fr7
!
enable password cisco
!
!
interface Ethernet0
ip address 8.51.12.33 255.255.255.224
!
interface Serial0
no ip address
encapsulation frame-relay
no fair-queue
!
interface Serial0.2 point-to-point **Note that a sub-interface is used when backup is
defined.**
backup delay 0 0 **A failed DLCI causes the subinterface to go down, thus **
backup interface Async1 **triggering the backup of interface async 1. **
ip address 171.68.157.226 255.255.255.240
```

Example C-6 *Spoke Router Dial Backup Using Async Interface When DLCI 207 Goes Down (Continued)*

```
frame-relay interface-dlci 207 broadcast
!
interface Async1
ip address 172.58.157.112 255.255.255.0
dialer in-band
dialer string 18005551212
!
router eigrp 44
network 171.68.0.0
!
!
line con 0
exec-timeout 0 0
password cisco
line aux 0
line vty 0 4
password cisco
login
!
end
```

Broadcast Queue

This is a major feature for use in medium to large IP and/or IPX networks where routing and SAP broadcasts must flow across the Frame Relay network. As shown in Figure C-5, the broadcast queue is managed independently of the normal interface queue, has its own buffers, and has a configurable size and service rate. This broadcast queue is not used for bridging Spanning Tree updates (BPDUs) due to timing sensitivities. These packets will flow through the normal queues. The **frame-relay broadcast-queue** *size byte-rate packet-rate* interface command enables the broadcast queue.

Figure C-5 *Broadcast Queue Separate from Normal Traffic*

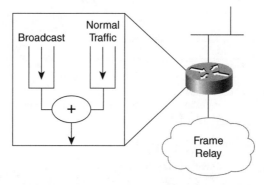

A broadcast queue is given a maximum transmission-rate (throughput) limit measured in bytes per second and packets per second. The queue is serviced to ensure that only this maximum is provided. The broadcast queue has priority when transmitting at a rate below the configured maximum, and hence has a guaranteed minimum bandwidth allocation. The two transmission rate limits are intended to avoid flooding the interface with broadcasts. The actual limit in any second is the first rate limit that is reached. Given the transmission-rate restriction, additional buffering is required to store broadcast packets. The broadcast queue is configurable to store large numbers of broadcast packets. The queue size should be set to avoid loss of broadcast routing update packets. The exact size will depend on the protocol being used and the number of packets required for each update. To be safe, set the queue size so that one complete routing update from each protocol and for each DLCI can be stored. As a general rule, start with 20 packets per DLCI. Also, as a general rule, the byte rate should be less than both of the following:

- $N/4$ times the minimum remote access rate (measured in bytes per second), where N is the number of DLCIs to which the broadcast must be replicated

- 1/4 the local access rate (measured in bytes per second)

The packet rate is not critical if you set the byte rate conservatively. As a general rule, set the packet rate assuming 250-byte packets. The defaults are 64 queue size, 256,000 bytes per second (2,048,000 bps), and 36 packets per second.

Example C-7 shows a configuration example with the broadcast queue set for interface Serial0.

Example C-7 *Broadcast Queue Set for Interface Serial0*

```
Current configuration:
!
version 11.2
!
hostname FR45
!
!
interface Ethernet0
ip address 192.150.42.61 255.255.255.248
media-type 10BaseT
!
interface Serial0
description T1 HUB LINK TO TELCO
no ip address
encapsulation frame-relay
no fair-queue
frame-relay traffic-shaping
frame-relay broadcast-queue 80 48000 160 **Queue size=80, byte rate=48KBps
(384kbps), packet rate=160 pps**
!
interface Serial0.1 point-to-point
ip address 171.68.157.113 255.255.255.240
frame-relay interface-dlci 101 broadcast
!
interface Serial0.2 point-to-point
ip address 171.68.157.129 255.255.255.240
```

Example C-7 *Broadcast Queue Set for Interface Serial0 (Continued)*

```
frame-relay interface-dlci 102 broadcast
!
router eigrp 44
network 171.68.0.0
!
end
```

Subinterfaces

Frame Relay networks provide multiple point-to-point links, or PVCs, through the same physical serial interface. Subinterfaces allow blocks of one or more VCs to be treated as separate subnetworks. A subinterface with a single VC is modeled as a point-to-point link. A subinterface with multiple VCs is modeled as a LAN. Protocols such as IP, IPX, and bridging view each subinterface as a separate interface with its own address and protocol assignments. In Example C-8, subinterface 1 models a point-to-point subnet and subinterface 2 models a broadcast subnet.

Example C-8 *Subinterfaces Are Flexible Because They Can Be Used as Either Point-to-Point Links or Multipoint Networks*

```
interface serial 0
encapsulation frame-relay
!
interface serial 0.1 point-to-point
ip address 10.0.1.1 255.255.255.0
frame-relay interface-dlci 42
!
interface serial 0.2 multipoint
ip address 10.0.2.1 255.255.255.0
frame-relay map 10.0.2.1 255.255.255.0 17 broadcast
frame-relay map 10.0.2.2 255.255.255.0 18
```

Subinterfaces provide a mechanism for supporting partially meshed Frame Relay networks. In the past, a single network number (such as an IP subnet or an IPX network number) was assigned to an entire Frame Relay or X.25 network. Most protocols assume transitivity on a logical network; that is, if station A can talk to station B, and station A can talk to station C, then station B should be able to talk to station C directly. This is true on LANs, but was not true on public switched networks unless they were fully meshed. Additionally, certain protocols such as IPX and AppleTalk could not be supported on partially meshed networks because they require split horizon, in which a routing protocol packet received on an interface cannot be transmitted out the same interface even if the packet is received and transmitted on different VCs. As shown in Figure C-6, subinterfaces fully address these limitations by providing a way to subdivide a partially meshed Frame Relay network into a number of smaller, fully meshed (or point-to-point) subnetworks. Transitivity is, therefore, a direct benefit of the subinterface approach (without the requirement of a full Frame Relay PVC mesh).

Figure C-6   *Routers B, C, and D Can Have Connectivity with Each Other Through Router A Using Subinterfaces*

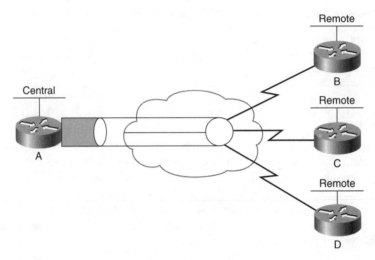

Example C-9 shows a configuration with the point-to-point subinterfaces configured at the hub site.

Example C-9   *Point-to-Point Subinterfaces Configured at Hub Site*

```
Current configuration:
!
version 11.2
!
hostname Router-A
!
!
interface Ethernet0
ip address 192.150.42.61 255.255.255.248
media-type 10BaseT
!
interface Serial0
no ip address
encapsulation frame-relay
no fair-queue
frame-relay traffic-shaping
frame-relay broadcast-queue 64 48000 36
!
interface Serial0.1 point-to-point **To Router B**
ip address 171.68.157.113 255.255.255.240
frame-relay interface-dlci 101 broadcast
!
interface Serial0.2 point-to-point **To Router C**
ip address 171.68.157.129 255.255.255.240
frame-relay interface-dlci 102 broadcast
!
interface Serial0.3 point-to-point **To Router D**
```

Example C-9 *Point-to-Point Subinterfaces Configured at Hub Site (Continued)*

```
ip address 171.68.157.145 255.255.255.240
frame-relay interface-dlci 103 broadcast
!
!
router eigrp 44 **When using a routing protocol, full mesh connectivity**
network 171.68.0.0 **is attained amongst routers A,B,C,& D with very **
! **little configuration.
!
!
line con 0
exec-timeout 0 0
line aux 0
line vty 0 4
login
!
end
FR45#
```

Inverse ARP

Inverse ARP allows a router running Frame Relay to dynamically discover the protocol address of a device associated with the VC. The use of Inverse ARP greatly reduces the configuration task of specifying map statements and includes the following protocols: IP, IPX, XNS, AppleTalk, DECnet and VINES. Inverse ARP is on by default.

This implementation of Inverse ARP is based on RFC 1293. As shown in Figure C-7, it allows a router or access server running Frame Relay to discover the protocol address of a device associated with the VC. In Frame Relay, PVC's are identified by a DLCI, which is the equivalent of a hardware address. By exchanging signaling messages, a network announces a new VC, and with Inverse ARP, the protocol address at the other side of the circuit can be discovered.

Figure C-7 *Frame Relay Inverse ARP Exchange*

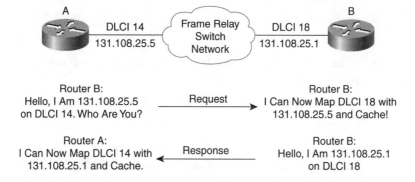

Example C-10 sets Inverse ARP on an interface running AppleTalk.

Example C-10 *Setting ARP on an Interface Running Appletalk*

```
interface serial 0
frame-relay inverse-arp appletalk 100
```

AutoInstall

The feature allows for simple router installation at a remote site from a centralized management location. The central location connects to the remote router via the Frame Relay link and downloads a configuration file. This results in considerable time and cost savings because users at remote sites do not need any specialized training to install a router. The central management location has complete control of the process, and the remote user needs only to power up the remote router, configure encapsulation as Frame Relay, and connect the serial line.

AutoInstall Steps

Step 1 New unconfigured (write erase) router's lowest-numbered serial interface is configured for encapsulation Frame Relay and is connected to Frame Relay network. LMI will resolve what the DLCI is.

Step 2 The new router will now find an IP address through BOOTP. This requires a gateway router at the other end and a TFTP server. The gateway router must be configured to map DLCI to IP addresses.

Step 3 The gateway router acts as BOOTP server, with an IP helper address pointing to TFTP server.

Step 4 The new router, upon receipt of IP address for the serial interface, and TFTP server address provided by BOOTP server will now automatically send TFTP request for configuration file. The gateway router forwards the request to TFTP server.

Step 5 TFTP server sends *network-confg* to requester, which in turn tries to resolve the host name.

Step 6 If the host name is resolved, *hostname-confg* is sent and we're done. If not...

Step 7 TFTP server sends *router-confg*, a basic default configuration.

Design Topologies and Strategies

Several common techniques are commonly used in Frame Relay network design. By far, the "star/hub-and-spoke" topology is most commonly deployed; but full-mesh, partial-mesh, and hierarchical-mesh topologies also are utilized. As the tradeoffs between cost and availability are analyzed, the business and technical requirements will drive each network design team's own selection. The following sections discuss each of the design topologies and strategies.

Star Topology (Hub-and-Spoke)

Hub-and-spoke is the topology referred to most in this design guide, and is the most common Frame Relay network design found today. It accounts for more than 65% of all Frame Relay networks, and spans from as few as two remote sites to several hundred. This topology can be scaled somewhat by using multiple central-site router interfaces, and/or multiple central-site routers to split the network into multiple segments. A pure hub-and-spoke topology requires no spoke-to-spoke connectivity. Occasional spoke-to-spoke connectivity can be achieved by the use of SVCs available in IOS Release 11.2 and higher. To scale to larger networks, a hierarchical design, as illustrated in Figure C-8, is recommended

Figure C-8   *Multiple Branch (Spoke) Sites Communicate to Single Central (Hub) Site*

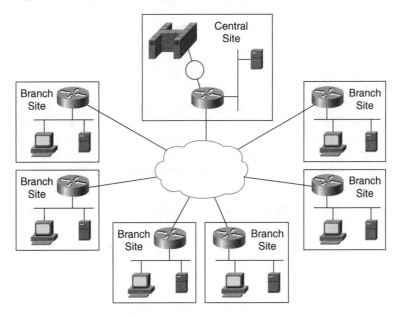

Full-Mesh Topology

For full connectivity requirements, a full-mesh topology is required. In a Frame Relay environment, VCs must be provisioned to all destination routers from each router. In a large full-mesh network, this can be costly in PVC's; however, not as costly as leased-line circuits, which would require sufficient router interface ports as well as CSU/DSUs for each interface. Full-mesh connectivity is typically required when designing the core portion of a wide-area network, where a distributed server design exists. To calculate how many VCs are required for full connectivity, refer to Figure C-9.

Figure C-9 *Full-Mesh Topology for Any-to-Any Connectivity*

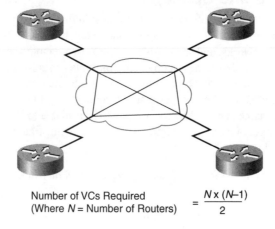

Number of VCs Required
(Where *N* = Number of Routers) $= \dfrac{N \times (N-1)}{2}$

Partial-Mesh Topology with Redundant Central

Partial-mesh topologies incorporate a basic hub-and-spoke design, where a central site exists, but where connectivity between spoke sites is also required. This design is common in the retail environments where both centralized warehousing and store-to-store inventories can be accessed from any location. The use of point-to-point subinterfaces facilitates this kind of design by providing any-to-any connectivity through the central hub router.

Figure C-10 shows a partial-mesh design that also has a redundant centralized router for backup.

Figure C-10 *Each Access Site Has Two Paths to Redundant Central Router*

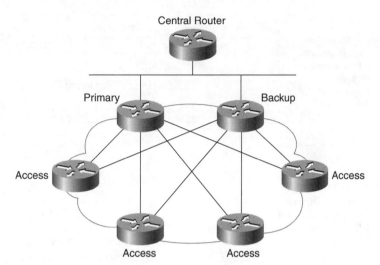

Different strategies could be used in this example:

1 Have spoke-site routers connected to both primary and backup hub routers through separate PVCs and configure HSRP at hub.

2 Trigger ISDN dial backup to occur at access site when either Frame Relay network or primary router goes down. Taking this a step further, with dual hub routers, split the VC connections to all the spoke sites between the two hub routers, and back up each hub router's VCs to the alternate hub router using ISDN PRI.

3 Trigger Frame Relay SVC connection to backup router.

Hierarchical Mesh

A hierarchical design is required for building large Frame Relay networks or integrating separate networks into a larger single network, as is the case in business mergers. The idea is to split the network into different layers, where each layer has distinct connectivity functions. The three layers are the core, the distribution layer, and the access layer, each of which is described in the sections that follow. Figure C-11 shows a typical hierarchical-mesh topology.

Figure C-11 *Hierarchical Design Separates Network Segments*

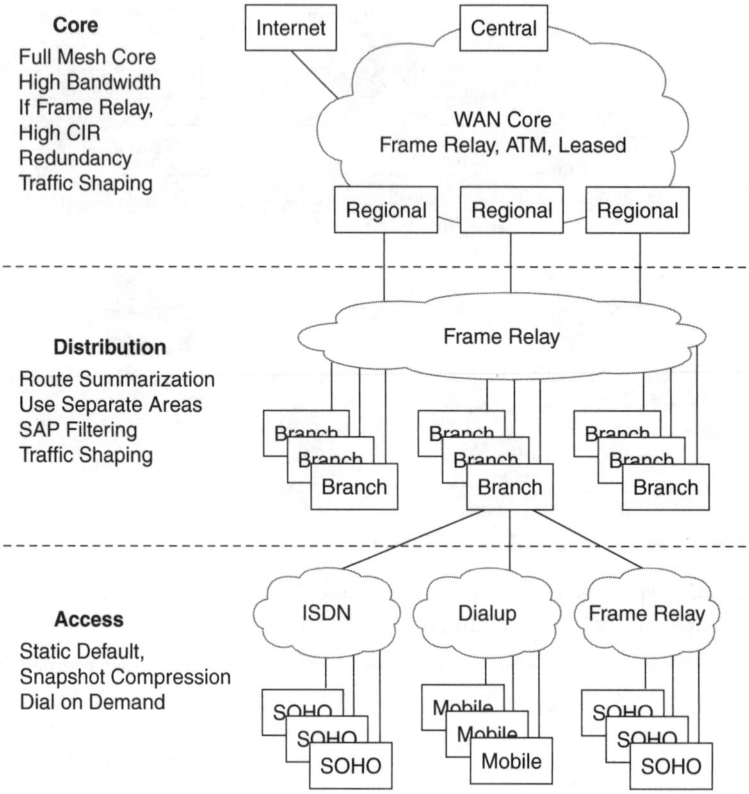

Core Tier

The core makes up the corporate backbone whereby dispersed central or large regional offices are interconnected through high-speed links in a full-mesh topology. From a router perspective, this means that certain interfaces will be dedicated to connecting to other core routers and local servers, as well as connections to the distribution tier, which may or may not be collocated.

Distribution Tier

The distribution tier will be the connection point to the core and access sites. The distribution tier can provide isolation of unnecessary broadcast traffic entering the core tier and can enable bandwidth, security, and other processor-intensive features to the access tier.

Access Tier

The access tier is primarily where end stations will connect; however, extensions beyond this tier (access subtiers) are quite common. The connection to the distribution tier is often relatively slow speed, so efficient use of bandwidth is important. Features that can be employed effectively at this level include data/payload compression, local acknowledgment, the use of static or default routes.

Conclusion

Designing successful Frame Relay networks requires planning and efficient use of features. With the implementation variations that exist among Frame Relay equipment vendors and the many different options offered by each service provider, predicting performance is difficult at best. Knowledge of what your traffic is and how much of it needs to be moved is a good start in the planning process. Narrowing down your choice of network and technologies will be easier with this knowledge.

As Frame Relay and related technologies such as ATM mature, the focus is changing to interworking, bandwidth efficiency, and QoS. Integrating data, voice, and video is the key driver for this focus, and it is in these areas where the greatest improvements will be seen.

Frame Relay–Related Standards Supported in Cisco's IOS

RFCs and other Frame Relay–related standards include the following:

- RFC 1144—*TCP/IP Header Compression*
- RFC 1293—*Frame Relay Inverse ARP*
- RFC 1315—*Frame Relay MIB*
- RFC 1490—*Multiprotocol Encapsulation*

FRF Implementation Agreements:

- FRF 1.1—*User-to-Network Interface (UNI)*
- FRF 2.1—*Frame Relay Network-to-Network Interface (NNI)*
- FRF 3.1—*Multiprotocol Encapsulation*
- FRF 4—*Switched Virtual Circuits*
- FRF 6—*Frame Relay Service Customer Network Management (MIB)*

"Gang Of Four" LMI:

- Q.922 Annex A
- ANSI T1.617 Annex D
- ANSI T1.618, T1.606
- ITU-T Q.933, Q.922

This Design and Implementation Guide: Designing Networks with Windows Networking was originally written by Cisco. It has been edited here for formatting reasons.

Although this guide contains some information on older products and software and refers to some "future" products, which are, in fact, now available, this guide does provide useful information regarding the design and implementation of Windows networks. Refer to the Cisco IOS and other product documentation for information on the latest products and features available.

Design and Implementation Guide: Designing Networks with Windows Networking

The term "networking" covers a broad range of technologies that, when combined, allow computers to share information. Networking components can be segmented into end system applications, network operating systems, and networking equipment.

A network operating system is software run on all interconnected systems. Examples include Novell NetWare, Sun's Network File System (NFS), AppleShare, and Microsoft's implementation of a network operating system commonly called *Windows Networking*. Windows Networking is now extensively deployed, with over 100 million nodes.

This design guide explains the basic concepts of Windows Networking and provides insight on how to design networks (LANs and WANs) to best utilize Windows Networking. The guide also explains Windows protocols, naming, and scaling issues associated with Windows Networking.

What Is Windows Networking?

Windows Networking refers to the networking system shared by the software that comes with all the following Microsoft operating systems or servers:

- Microsoft LAN Manager
- MS-DOS with LAN Manager client
- Windows for Workgroups
- Windows 95
- Windows NT
- Windows 98
- Windows 2000

Microsoft LAN Manager, the LAN Manager client for MS-DOS, and Windows NT 3.1 will not be discussed in this document except in an historical context.

Domains Versus Workgroups

Windows Networking has two concepts of a group of related computers—workgroups and domains. Workgroups can be any logical collection of computers; any computer on the network can join an existing workgroup or create a new one. More formal entities, domains, are created and managed by a Primary Domain Controller (PDC) process that runs on a Windows NT server. A domain has security and administrative properties that a workgroup does not. Each domain must have at least one NT server. Windows Networking domains are not the same as Internet domain names, as used by Domain Naming System (DNS).

What Protocol Does It Use?

Windows Networking uses the NetBIOS protocol for file sharing, printer sharing, messaging, authentication, and name resolution. NetBIOS is a session layer protocol that can run on any of these transport protocols:

- NetBEUI
- NWLink (NetBIOS over IPX)
- NetBIOS over TCP (NBT)

Although Microsoft recommends that clients use only one transport protocol at a time for maximum performance, this is not the default. You should pick a protocol to use for your entire network and then turn off the other protocols.

NetBEUI is the least scalable of the three protocols because it must be bridged. NetBEUI is only included to support very old services (for example, old versions of LAN manager). NetBEUI does not require any client address configuration.

NWLink is recommended for small- to medium-sized networks, especially if they are already running IPX. Like NetBEUI, NWLink requires no client address configuration. NWLink uses IPX type-20 packets to exchange registration and browsing information. To forward type-20 IPX packets across Cisco routers, you must configure **ipx type-20-propagation** on each interface on every router on your network.

Microsoft recommends NetBIOS over TCP (NBT) for medium-sized and large networks, or anytime the network includes a wide-area network (WAN). Because NBT uses TCP/IP, each computer must be configured to use a static IP address or to fetch an IP address dynamically with the Dynamic Host Configuration Protocol (DHCP).

Dynamic IP Addressing

Manually addressing TCP/IP clients is both time consuming and error-prone. To solve this problem, the Internet Engineering Task Force (IETF) developed DHCP, the Dynamic Host Configuration Protocol. DHCP is designed to automatically provide clients with a valid IP address and related configuration information (see the section "DHCP Options"). Each range of addresses that a DHCP server manages is called a *scope*.

DHCP Scopes

You must configure a range of addresses for every IP subnet where clients will request a DHCP address. Each range of addresses is called a DHCP scope. You can configure a DHCP server to serve several scopes because the DHCP server or servers do not need to be physically connected to the same network as the client. If the DHCP server is on a different IP subnet from the client, then you need to use DHCP Relay to forward DHCP requests to your DHCP server.

DHCP Relay

DHCP Relay typically runs on a router. You can turn on DHCP Relay on a Cisco Internetwork Operating System (Cisco IOS) router by configuring **ip helper-address** with the address of the DHCP server on each interface that will have DHCP clients. To prevent forwarding other broadcasts to the DHCP server, add the **ip forward-protocol udp bootpc** global command to the router configuration. DHCP Relay on the Cisco 700 series is planned for the last quarter of 1996.

DHCP Options

In addition to its IP address, a DHCP client can get other TCP/IP configuration information from a DHCP server, including the subnet mask, default gateway, and DNS information. These pieces of information, called DHCP Options, can be configured in the DHCP Manager on your Windows NT DHCP server (see Figure D-1).

Figure D-1   *Microsoft's DHCP Manager*

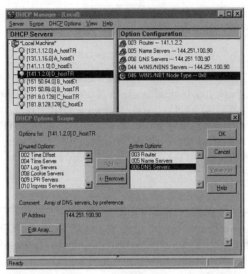

If your clients are using Windows Internet Name Service (WINS) for name resolution, discussed later, you should configure the address of the WINS server and the WINS node type. A brief list of node types is included in the Name Resolution section. p-node (0x2) is strongly recommended.

Network Registrar

Cisco Network Registrar (CNR) is a full-featured, scalable DNS and DHCP system for large IP networks. It provides the key benefits of stabilizing the IP infrastructure, automating networking services including client configuration and provisioning cable modems, and providing the foundation of user-based policies.

With unique features that enable integration with other network infrastructure software and business applications, CNR enables enterprise and service provider users to better manage their networks.

The Cisco Technical Assistance Center (TAC) will continue to support Cisco DNS/DHCP Manager until July 31, 2001. No new features will be added to the Cisco DNS/DHCP Manager.

Microsoft LAN Services Browser

Windows Networking was originally designed to run on a single LAN segment or a bridged (flat) network. At that time, only the NetBEUI protocol was supported.

Microsoft developed the LAN Services Browser to enable the user to browse a list of all computers available on the network. Each Windows Networking client registered its NetBIOS Name periodically by sending broadcasts.

Every computer also had to send broadcasts to elect a browse master for the network. The browse master (and several backup browse masters) maintained the list of computers and their addresses. When a user browsed the network, the client would send a broadcast request, and one of the browse masters would respond.

Eventually, Microsoft added support for NetBIOS over IPX and NetBIOS over TCP/IP, but Windows Networking still assumed that all clients and servers were on the same logical IPX network or IP subnet—they still sent broadcasts to register and find computers on the network.

This architecture, although simple to implement, generated an enormous burden on the network and on the CPU of each client on the network. Because of these scalability problems, Microsoft began to offer other methods of browsing and name resolution—ways for clients to map a name to the IP address of other computers on the network. Eventually, Microsoft also provided a way to browse and resolve names without broadcasts.

Name Resolution

As of the release of Microsoft Windows NT 3.51, Windows Networking clients have a choice of four methods of name resolution:

- Broadcasts
- LMHOSTS
- WINS
- Internet DNS

Broadcasts

By sending broadcasts on a subnet, Windows Networking clients cause a browser election. The designated browse master maintains a list of all the resources available on that subnet. Because registrations, browser elections, and name queries all generate broadcasts, use of this method is not recommended.

Because this method is used by default on all Microsoft products, it is strongly recommended that you turn this feature off by setting the BrowseMaster setting to Disabled (the default is Automatic). For specific details, see Appendix A, "Turning Off Broadcast Name Resolution," in this document.

LMHOSTS

Windows Networking can consult a static table in a file called LMHOSTS. To use this method, the Primary Domain Controller (PDC) should maintain at least a static list of all computers and their IP addresses in that domain, and the names and addresses of the PDCs for all other domains in the network. All clients must then have an LMHOSTS file with the IP address of their PDC and the path to the master LMHOSTS file on the PDC.

Using this method alone, however, does not allow clients to browse the network. Because of the obvious administrative burden, this method of resolving NetBIOS names is recommended only if you are using a router running EveryWare (Cisco 700 series) and you need to control line charges. (See the section "Dial-on-Demand Routing" for more details.)

Windows Internet Name Service

WINS was created to allow clients on different IP subnets to dynamically register and browse the network without sending broadcasts. Clients send unicast packets to the WINS server at a well-known address. For compatibility with older MS Networking clients, however, broadcast name resolution is still turned on by default, even when WINS is also configured.

NOTE   *Important*: As shown in Figure D-2, browsing will not work on a subnet if any Windows 3.1 or Windows 95 computer on the subnet has broadcast name resolution turned on (that is, Browse Master setting to Automatic). Individual servers, however, are still reachable by name.

Figure D-2   *With WINS, Broadcast Name Resolution Must Be Turned Off*

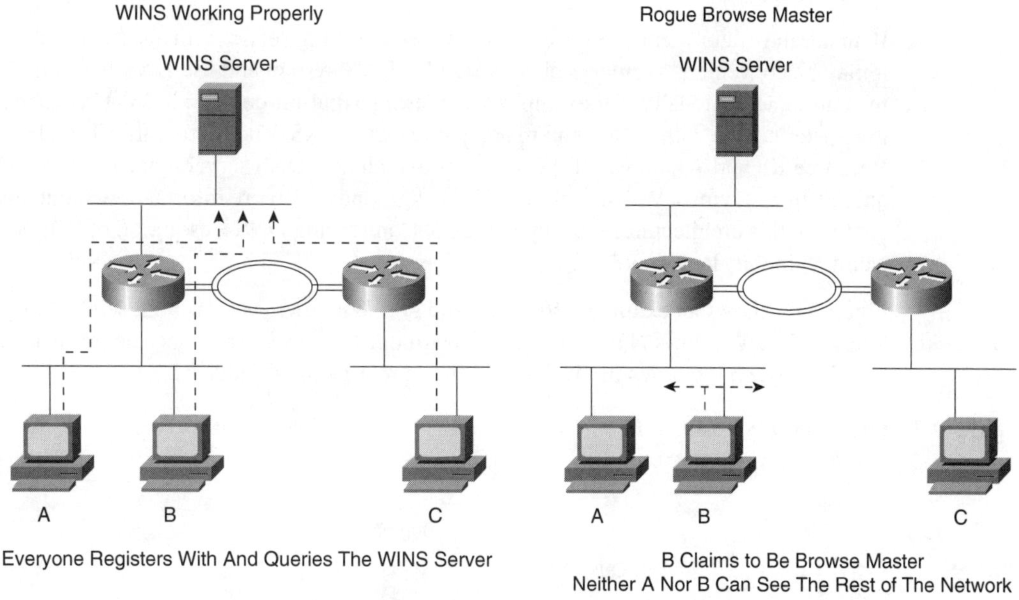

In Windows for Workgroups 3.11, broadcasts are turned off by adding a command to the system.ini file. (See Appendix A in this document for details.) In Windows 95, the Browse Master setting in Advanced File and Print Sharing Properties must be set to Disabled. Administrators can control broadcasts sent by DHCP clients by selecting the appropriate WINS node-type (p-node: 0x2). Table D-1 provides a complete list of WINS node types.

Table D-1   *WINS Node Types*

WINS Node Type	Name Search Order
b-node (0x1)	Broadcast only
p-node (0x2)	WINS only
m-node (0x4)	Broadcast, then WINS
h-node (0x8)	WINS, then broadcast

Internet DNS

Any DNS server can be configured statically to answer queries for computers with fixed IP addresses. This is useful if computers in your network have fixed IP addresses. When Windows systems use DHCP to get an IP address and WINS to register a NetBIOS name, you can set up a Windows NT DNS server to query a WINS server for names or addresses that were not entered statically. In both cases, Windows and non-Windows systems can resolve IP addresses correctly.

If an administrator configures each Windows Networking server with a static IP address, it may be convenient to enter each server in the DNS system and use DNS for name resolution. Occasionally (for example, when using a dial-on-demand link), it is convenient to register clients with WINS and make queries with DNS. The Microsoft NT 3.51 Resource Kit and Windows NT 4.0 server both include a DNS server that can answer DNS queries by querying a WINS server in the background. For more information about how to configure this architecture, see Appendix B, "Configuring DNS Resolution of WINS Names," in this document.

Figure D-3 shows an example. Windows and non-Windows systems both send DNS lookups for a Windows NT server named Warthog. The DNS server does not have an entry for Warthog, so it queries the WINS server and returns the IP address.

Figure D-3   *WINS and DNS Servers Can Work Together to Answer Queries from Windows and Non-Windows Systems*

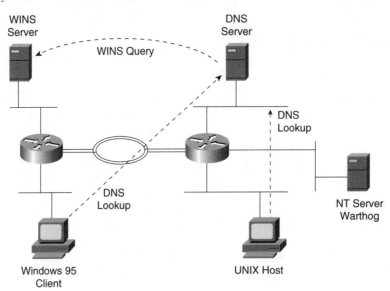

Scaling to Larger Networks—Trusted Domains

When planning a Windows network, consideration of what domain model to use is important. The following list discusses the benefits and drawbacks of several domain models. If you have several domains, you probably want to exchange data with other domains in your network. Trust relationships are a way to gain or grant access to a domain without having to manage each user individually. Each relationship permits trust in only one direction. For more information, see the *Windows NT Resource Kit, Volume II,* Chapter 4.

- **Single domain model**—A simple design that is adequate for small or medium-sized networks.

- **Master domain model**—A master domain (containing users) is trusted by all other domains (containing resources). The master domain trusts no one and retains centralized control over user administration and authentication. The departments or divisions (resource domains) retain control over their own resources.

- **Multiple master domain model**—This method is used for large networks where centralized user or resource management is not feasible. The master domain (users) fully trust each other, while the departmental domains (resources) trust each master domain, but not vice versa.

- **Complete trust domain model**—Under this method, there can be distribution of users and resources into many domains that maintain a complete set of two-way trust relationships. This is not a secure method of setting up Windows NT domains, but it allows for administration from many places.

Replicating WINS

For redundancy or to optimize WAN traffic, sometimes having several WINS servers is desirable. Windows NT servers can replicate or resynchronize WINS databases in either or both directions. In Figure D-4, a large multinational company has several distributed WINS servers so that WINS queries do not have to travel across continents.

Figure D-4 *Example of an Enterprise-Wide Configuration for WINS Replication*

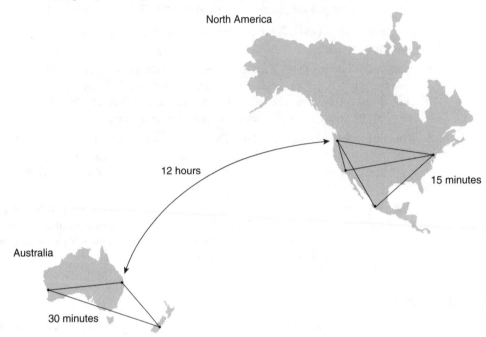

Modem Access

Windows NT comes with Microsoft's remote-access server (RAS), which uses the Point-to-Point Protocol (PPP). Customers often want to use Cisco access servers instead of NT RASs for their dial-in pools because of the better dial-in density and performance available on Cisco access servers.

NT supports TCP/IP, IPX, and NetBEUI (IPCP, IPXCP, and NBFCP control protocols for PPP). NetBEUI dial-in support was added to the Cisco IOS™ in Release 11.1. For NetBEUI dial-in, use the **netbios nbf** command (as shown in Example D-1) on each async interface or on a group-async interface on the access server.

Example D-1 *Enabling NetBEUI Dial-In*

```
interface group-async 0
  group-range 1 16
  netbios nbf
```

To configure IPX dial-in, use the **ipx ppp-client** command (as shown in Example D-2) on each async interface or on a group-async interface on the access server. This command requires you to configure an IPX network address on a loopback interface. Dial-in clients do not need to hear Service Advertisement Protocol (SAP) messages, so these messages should be turned off with the **ipx sap-interval 0** command.

Example D-2 *Enabling IPX Dial-In*

```
interface loopback 0
  ipx network <network number>
interface group-async 0
  group-range 1 16
  ipx ppp-client loopback 0
  ipx sap-interval 0
```

In order to assign IP addresses to dial-in clients, Cisco access servers can use a pool of local addresses or act as a proxy for a DHCP server. The access server requests an address from the DHCP server and uses that address during PPP negotiation. The client can also negotiate the address of its WINS server. Example D-3 illustrates this process.

Example D-3 *Assigning IP Addresses to Dial-In Clients*

```
ip dhcp-server n.n.n.n
async-bootp nbns-server m.m.m.m
async-bootp dns-server p.p.p.p
ip address-pool dhcp-proxy-client
!
interface group-async 0
  group-range 1 16
  peer default ip address dhcp
```

Dial-on-Demand Routing

Dial-on-demand routing (DDR) provides network connections across Public Switched Telephone Networks (PSTNs). Traditionally, WAN connections have been dedicated leased lines. DDR provides low-volume, periodic network connections, allowing on-demand services and decreasing network costs. ISDN is a circuit-switched technology. Like the analog telephone network, ISDN connections are made only when there is a need to communicate.

Cisco routers use DDR to determine when a connection needs to be made to another site. Packets are classified as either interesting or uninteresting based on protocol-specific access lists and dialer lists. Uninteresting packets can travel across an active DDR link, but they do not bring up the link or keep it up.

As shown in Figure D-5, Windows for Workgroups and Windows 95 clients using WINS try to register themselves on the network every 10 minutes by sending a unicast packet to the WINS server (on User Datagram Protocol [UDP] port 137—the NetBIOS Name Service port).

Figure D-5   *Dial-on-Demand Link Up All the Time*

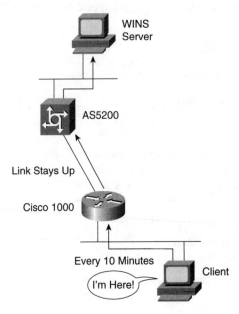

Sending a packet to the WINS server normally brings up the dial-on-demand link. If, however, this port is classified as uninteresting to the Cisco IOS software, as shown in the configuration in Example D-4 and in Figure D-6, then the router will neither bring up nor keep up the link. This feature is not currently available on the Cisco 700 series.

Example D-4   *Making Packets to the WINS Server Uninteresting*

```
interface bri 0
  dialer-group 1
!
dialer-list 1 protocol ip list 101
access-list 101 deny udp any any eq netbios-ns
access-list 101 permit ip any any
```

Figure D-6   *UDP Port 137 Is Uninteresting; Link Is Down*

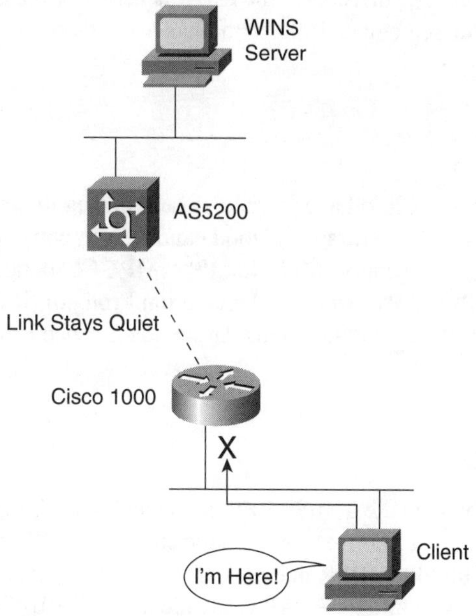

Unfortunately, making NetBIOS name service packets uninteresting can cause initial logins to time out or fail completely. The only reliable way to ensure that Windows for Workgroups and Windows 95 logins succeed while controlling line usage is to use the DNS method of NetBIOS name resolution.

Windows NT workstations and servers regularly send security messages to the domain controllers in their domain. This traffic is not spoofable. To prevent this traffic from keeping up your dial-on-demand connection, Cisco recommends that you create a separate trusted domain at the remote site. You might also want to use separate WINS servers on each side of the ISDN line and periodically replicate them.

ISDN Access

This section covers ISDN cards and terminal adapters (TAs). For information about using Windows networking with ISDN routers, see the previous section on DDR.

Cisco 200

Cisco 201 and 202 are ISDN cards for Industry-Standard Architecture (ISA) bus computers. Open Data-Link Interface (ODI) drivers are available for Windows 3.1 and

Windows 95, which support IP and IPX DDR. Network driver interface specification (NDIS) 3.1 drivers and drivers for the ISDN accelerator pack (both for Windows 95) were made available in September 1996. Windows NT drivers were released in the third quarter of 1996.

Adtran

Because Adtran and Cisco have worked closely during interoperability testing (PPP bakeoffs, for example), Adtran is a good candidate to consider for external terminal adapters. Adtran TAs support Multilink PPP (MP), Challenge Handshake Authentication Protocol (CHAP) and Password Authentication Protocol (PAP), synchronous or asychronous serial interfaces, and the Automatic Service Profile Identifier (AutoSPID) configuration.

Motorola BitSURFR

The simplest way to make a BitSURFR connected to a PC interoperate with a Cisco router is to turn on async/sync conversion with the command **AT%A2=95** (for more information, see page 7-1 of the BitSURFR manual). If you are using a BitSURFR Pro and want to use both B channels, you must use PAP authentication. The BitSURFR Pro cannot correctly answer the CHAP challenge sent when bringing up the second B channel. To place a call using two B channels, you must enter the phone number twice. For example, if the phone number is 555-1212, you would enter **ATD555-1212&555-1212**. Table D-2 lists the commands to enter for several types of connections.

Table D-2 *Commands to Establish Connections on a Motorola BitSURFR*

Type of Connection	Command
Connect using PPP	%A2=95
Use both B channels (MP)	@B0=2
Use PAP authentication	@M2=P
Data Termination Equipment (DTE) Speed (PC COM port)	&M
Place 64 kbps calls	%A4=0
Place 56 kbps calls	%A4=1
Place voice calls	%A98

Client Software

This section covers some Windows client software products available from Cisco.

CiscoRemote and CiscoRemote Lite

CiscoRemote Lite is a free TCP/IP stack and dialer application for Windows 3.1 and Windows for Workgroups.

CiscoRemote is a complete set of applications for "dial-up" remote computing in one package for the PC Windows and Apple Macintosh environments. All applications are optimized, tested, and supported by Cisco. This single product will link PCs with other computing resources within an enterprise network or across the worldwide Internet. CiscoRemote also includes the industry's first remote node accelerator to dramatically improve dial-up performance.

Cisco TCP/IP Suite 100

This TCP/IP stack for Windows 3.1 and Windows 95 directly replaces the Microsoft stack and adds features like router discovery and extensive configuration and management facilities. The full suite of TCP/IP applications include a Serial Line Internet Protocol (SLIP) and PPP dialer; a graphical File Transfer Protocol (FTP) client (with passive-mode support); a Telnet client with full VT420, tn3270, and tn5250 emulation and Kerberos support; a World Wide Web browser; Post-Office Protocol (POP) mail client; a Network File System (NFS) client; line printer daemon (LPD), Stream and PCNFSd printing; and best-in-class technical support.

IPeXchange Gateways

Customers using NWLink (NetBIOS over IPX) who want Internet access but do not want the complexity of configuring TCP/IP on each computer can use a Cisco IPeXchange gateway to run TCP/IP applications on a computer configured only with IPX. Only the IPeXchange Gateway requires a TCP/IP address.

Examples

This section shows four examples of Windows networks that include Cisco routers and access servers. Configurations are also provided for some of the devices.

Example 1

Example 1 (see Figure D-7) shows a small, single-domain network using NWLink (NetBIOS over IPX).

Figure D-7 *Small, Single-Domain Network Using NWLink*

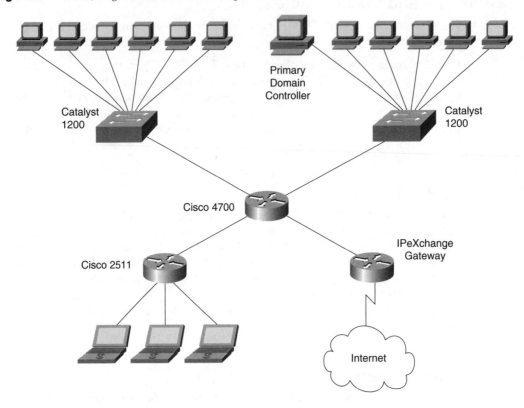

Configuration of Cisco 4700 Router

Example D-5 shows a sample configuration of the Cisco 4700 router in the network depicted in Figure D-7.

Example D-5 *Configuration of the Cisco 4700 Router in Figure D-7*

```
hostname 4700
ipx routing
!
interface ethernet 0
  ipx network 50
  ipx type-20-propagation
```

Example D-5 *Configuration of the Cisco 4700 Router in Figure D-7 (Continued)*

```
interface ethernet 1
  ipx network 60
  ipx type-20-propagation
interface ethernet 2
  ipx network 7B
  ipx type-20-propagation
interface ethernet 3
  ipx network 95
  ipx type-20-propagation
```

Configuration of Cisco 2511 Access Server

Example D-6 shows a sample configuration of the Cisco 2511 Access Server in the network depicted in Figure D-7.

Example D-6 *Configuration of the Cisco 2511 Access Server in Figure D-7*

```
hostname 2511
ipx routing
!
interface ethernet 0
 ipx network 98
interface loopback 0
 ipx network 163
interface group-async 0
 group-member 1 16
 ipx ppp-client loopback 0
 ipx sap-interval 0
 encapsulation ppp
 async mode dedicated
!
line 1 16
  modem inout
  speed 115200
  flowcontrol hardware
```

Example 2

Example 2 (see Figure D-8) shows a medium-sized network using NBT (NetBIOS over TCP) and static name resolution (LMHOSTS).

Figure D-8 *Medium-Sized Network Using NBT and LMHOSTS*

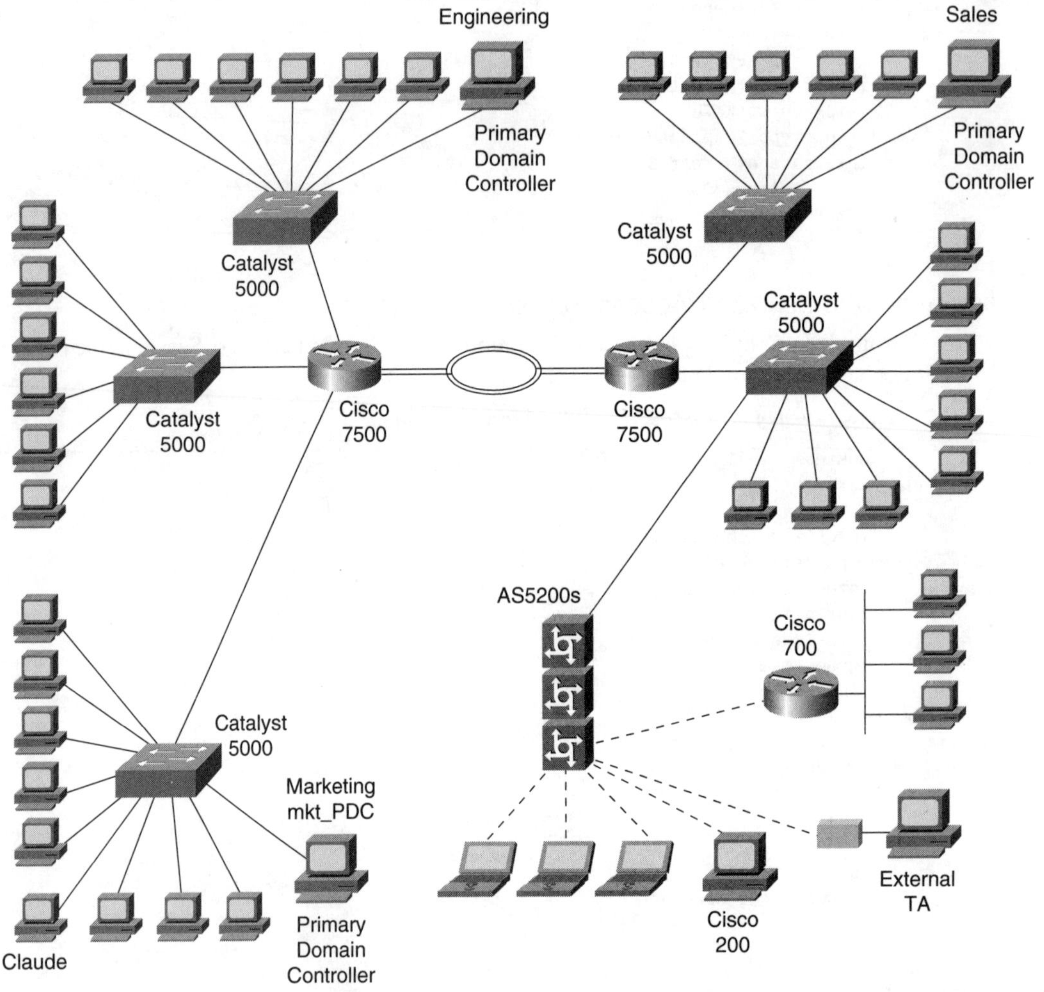

LMHOSTS Configuration on Claude (a Client in the Marketing Domain)

Example D-7 shows a sample LMHOSTS configuration for the client "Claude" in the network depicted in Figure D-8.

Example D-7 *LMHOSTS Configuration for Client "Claude" in Figure D-8*

```
1.2.1.8    mkt_PDC    #PRE
1.2.7.3    mkt_BDC    #PRE
#BEGIN ALTERNATE
  #INCLUDE \\mkt_pdc\public\lmhosts
  #INCLUDE \\mkt_bdc\public\lmhosts
#END ALTERNATE
```

LMHOSTS Configuration on mkt_PDC (Primary Domain Controller for the Marketing Domain)

Example D-8 shows a sample LMHOSTS configuration for the mkt_PDC in the network depicted in Figure D-8.

Example D-8 *LMHOSTS Configuration for the Marketing Domain PDC in Figure D-8*

```
1.1.1.3    eng_PDC     #PRE #DOM:eng
1.1.4.5    sales_PDC   #PRE #DOM:sales
1.2.1.4    sleepy
1.2.1.5    sneezy
1.2.6.2    martin
1.2.6.78   theresa
1.2.6.89   claude
```

Configuration of Cisco 7500 Router

Example D-9 shows a sample configuration for a 7500 router in the network depicted in Figure D-8.

Example D-9 *Configuration for a Cisco 7500 Router in Figure D-8*

```
hostname 7500
ip forward-protocol udp bootpc
!
interface ethernet 0
 ip address 1.5.6.1 255.255.255.0
 ip helper-address n.n.n.n
...
interface ethernet 23
 ip address 1.5.56.1 255.255.255.0
 ip helper-address n.n.n.n
```

Configuration of an AS5200 in a Stack Group

Example D-10 shows a sample configuration for an AS5200 in the stack group in the network depicted in Figure D-8.

Example D-10 *Configuration for an AS5200 in the Stack Group in Figure D-8*

```
hostname as5200-1
!
controller t1 0
 framing esf
 linecode b8zs
 pri-group
controller t1 1
 framing esf
 linecode b8zs
  pri-group
!
sgbp group as5200s
sgbp member as5200-2
sgbp member as5200-3
username as5200s password stackpassword
!
ip dhcp-server n.n.n.n
ip wins-server m.m.m.m
ip address-pool dhcp-proxy-client
!
interface ethernet 0
 ip address 192.168.2.1 255.255.255.0
!
interface group-async 0
 group-member 1 48
 peer default ip address dhcp
!
interface serial 0:23
 dialer rotary-group 1
 isdn incoming-voice modem
interface serial 1:23
 dialer rotary-group 1
 isdn incoming-voice modem
interface dialer 1
 ip unnumbered ethernet 0
 encapsulation ppp
 ppp multilink
 ppp authentication chap
 ppp use-tacacs
 dialer-group 1
!
dialer-list 1 protocol ip permit
!
line 1 48
 modem inout
 modem autoconfigure type microcom-hdms
 speed 115200
 flowcontrol hardware
```

Configuration of Cisco 700 Router

Example D-11 shows a sample configuration for the Cisco 700 router in the network depicted in Figure D-8.

Example D-11 *Configuration for the Cisco 700 Router in Figure D-8*

```
set system 700
cd LAN
 set ip address 1.4.3.1
 set ip netmask 255.255.255.248
 set ip routing on
 set ip rip update periodic
cd
set user as5200s
 set encapsulation ppp
 set ip framing none
 set ip routing on
set number 5551212
set ip route destination 0.0.0.0/0 gateway 0.0.0.0
cd
set active as5200s
set bridging off
```

Example 3

Example 3 shows a medium-sized network using NBT (NetBIOS over TCP) and a single WINS server (see Figure D-9).

Figure D-9 *Medium-Sized Network Using NBT and a Single WINS Server*

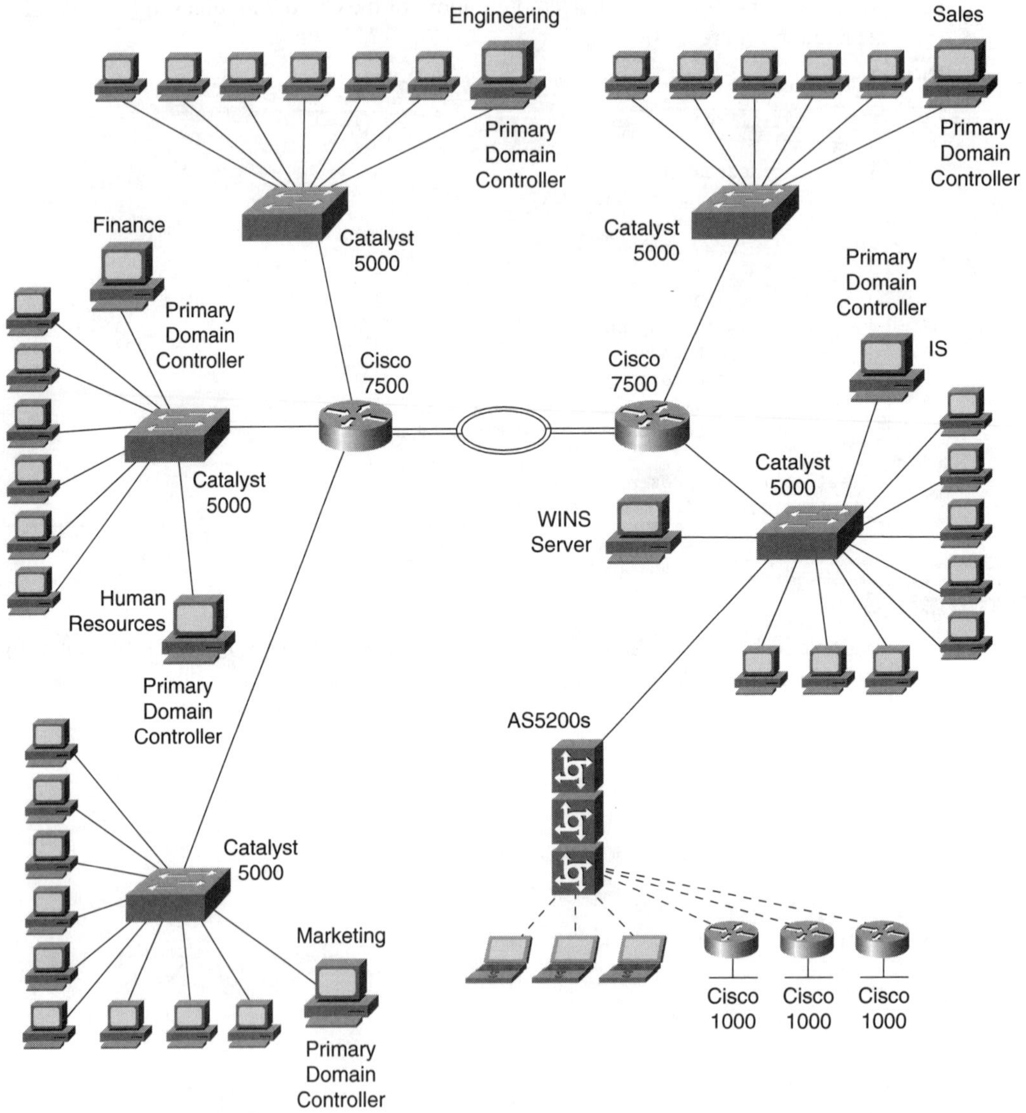

Configuration of a Cisco 1000 Router

Example D-12 shows a sample configuration for a Cisco 1000 router in the network depicted in Figure D-9.

Example D-12 *Configuration for a Cisco 1000 Router in Figure D-9*

```
hostname 1000
username as5200s password secret
!
interface ethernet 0
 ip address 1.4.3.1 255.255.255.248
interface bri 0
 ip unnumbered ethernet 0
 encapsulation ppp
 ppp multilink
 dialer string 5551212
 dialer-group 1
!
dialer-list 1 protocol ip list 101
access-list 101 deny udp any any eq netbios-ns
access-list 101 permit ip any any
```

Example 4

Figure D-10 shows a large network using NBT (NetBIOS over TCP) with multiple master domains and replicated WINS servers.

Figure D-10 *Large Network Using NBT with Multiple Master Domains and Replicated WINS Servers*

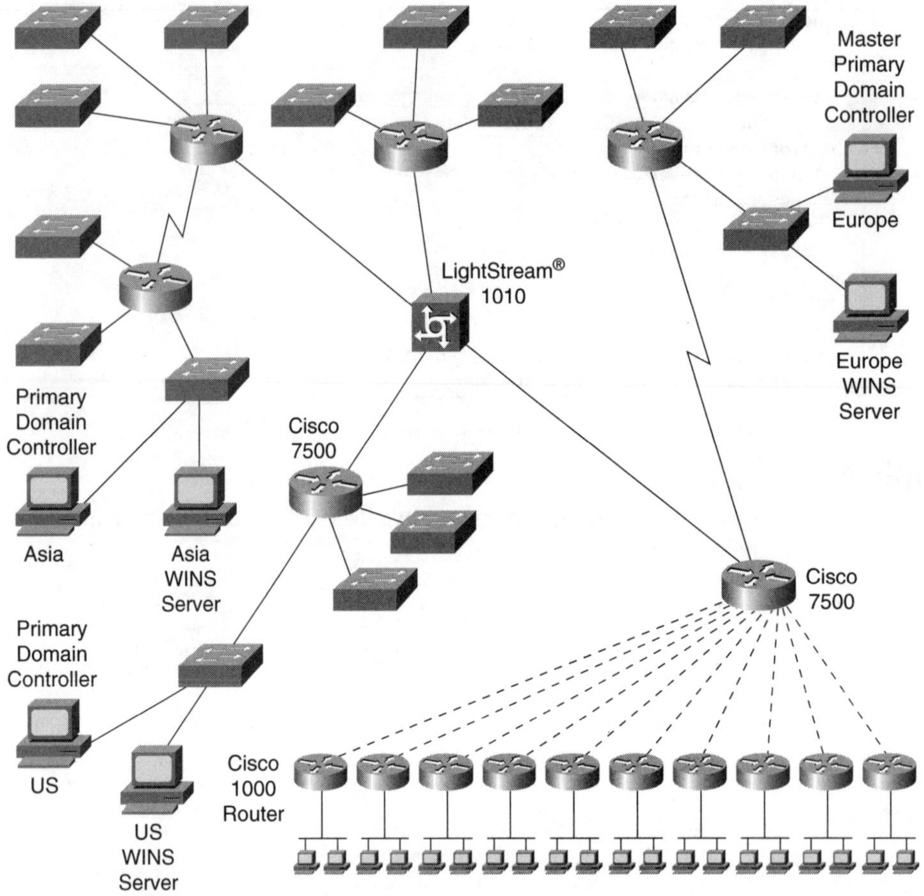

Appendix A: Turning Off Broadcast Name Resolution

This appendix covers how to turn off broadcast name resolution for the following systems:

- Windows for Workgroups 3.11
- Windows 95
- Windows NT 3.51

In addition, this appendix covers the proper Windows NT Registry settings to use to disable broadcast name resolution, as well as how to locate Windows 3.1 and Windows 95 workstations that are attempting to function as browse masters.

When Using Windows for Workgroups 3.11

When using Windows for Workgroups 3.11, a new browser file, VREDIR.386, which is included with Windows NT 3.5, must be used to allow browsing to work correctly. Windows 95 already includes this modified browser. The VREDIR.386 file is typically located in the C:\WINDOWS\SYSTEM directory.

Windows for Workgroups clients should make the change to the SYSTEM.INI file that is illustrated in Example D-13:

Example D-13 *SYSTEM.INI File Changes for Windows for Workgroups Clients*

```
; SYSTEM.INI
;
[Network]
MaintainServerList=No
```

Windows 95

Figure D-11 illustrates how to disable the Browse Master on Windows 95 client machines.

Figure D-11 *Turning Off Browse Master in Windows 95*

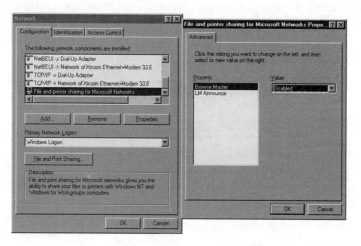

Windows NT 3.51

Windows NT 3.51 Workstations and Servers which are configured for WINS name resolution do not send broadcasts unless other computers on the network request a browser election. No action is required.

Windows NT Registry Entries

These entries in the hkey_local_machine\system\currentcontrolset\services\
browser\parameters area of the Registry should be set as follows. MaintainServerList
should be set to Yes, and IsDomainMaster should be set to False. These are the default
settings.

The MasterPeriodicity setting (in seconds) specifies how often subnet browse servers query
the domain master to obtain a browse list. When subnet browse servers and the domain
master are separated by a low-speed or charge-per-packet link, you can set this to an hour
or more.

Finding Rogue Browse Masters

Windows 3.1 and Windows 95 workstations cannot function as browse masters in a
Windows NT network because they do not handle NT server and domain information.
Unfortunately, by default, Windows 95 will attempt to become a browse master. A single
workstation incorrectly claiming to be the browse master will hinder browsing for every
computer on that entire subnet.

The Windows NT Server Resource Kit contains a utility called BROWSTAT. The easiest
way to find a rogue broadcaster on a subnet is to run BROWSTAT on a Windows NT
computer on the affected subnet.

Appendix B: Configuring DNS Resolution of WINS Names

The Microsoft NT 3.51 Resource Kit and Windows NT 4.0 server both include a DNS
server that can answer DNS queries by querying a WINS server in the background. The
WINS server and the DNS server must be on the same Windows NT machine. All DNS
queries to a subdomain (in this example, wins.cisco.com) should be delegated to the DNS/
WINS server.

For more information about DNS, see *DNS and Bind* by Paul Albitz and Cricket Liu
(O'Reilly and Associates, 1992).

Example D-14 shows an example of a DNS boot file.

Example D-14 *The DNS Boot File*

```
;BOOT
cache    .       CACHE
primary  domain.com      domain.dom
primary  8.17.1.in-addr.arpa     1-17-8.rev
```

Example D-15 shows the DNS File for cisco.com.

Example D-15 *The DNS File for cisco.com*

```
;domain.dom
@   IN   SOA   ns.domain.com.   rohan.domain.com. (
        1  ; Serial Number
        10800   ; Refresh [3h]
        3600   ; Retry [1h]
        604800   ; Expire [7d]
        86400)   ; Minimum [1d]
@   IN   WINS   1.1.4.6 1.2.7.4
wins-server   IN   A 1.1.4.6
wins-server2   IN   A 1.2.7.4
```

This OSPF Design Guide was originally written by Sam Halabi of Cisco Systems, Network Consulting Engineer—NSA group, and edited by Laura McCarty on April 9, 1996. This guide can also be found on Cisco's Web site at http://www.cisco.com/warp/public/104/1.html. It has been edited here for formatting reasons.

Design and Implementation Guide: OSPF

OSPF (Open Shortest Path First) protocol was developed due to a need in the internet community to introduce a high functionality nonproprietary Internal Gateway Protocol (IGP) for the TCP/IP protocol family. The discussion of creating a common interoperable IGP for the Internet started in 1988 and did not get formalized until 1991. At that time, the OSPF Working Group requested that OSPF be considered for advancement to Draft Internet Standard.

The OSPF protocol is based on link-state technology, which is a departure from the Bellman-Ford vector-based algorithms used in traditional Internet routing protocols, such as RIP. OSPF has introduced new concepts, such as authentication of routing updates, Variable Length Subnet Masks (VLSM), route summarization, and so forth.

This paper addresses the OSPF terminology, algorithm, and the pros and cons of the protocol in designing the large and complicated networks of today.

OSPF and RIP

The rapid growth and expansion of today's networks has pushed RIP to its limits. RIP has certain limitations that could cause problems in large networks:

- **RIP has a limit of 15 hops**—A RIP network that spans more than 15 hops (15 routers) is considered unreachable.

- **RIP cannot handle Variable Length Subnet Masks (VLSM)**—Given the shortage of IP addresses and the flexibility VLSM gives in the efficient assignment of IP addresses, this is considered a major flaw.

- **Periodic broadcasts of the full routing table will consume a large amount of bandwidth**—This is a major problem with large networks, especially on slow links and WAN clouds.

- **RIP converges more slowly than OSPF**—In large networks, convergence gets to be in the order of minutes. RIP routers will go through a period of a hold-down and garbage collection and will slowly time-out information that has not been received recently. This is inappropriate in large environments and could cause routing inconsistencies.

- **RIP has no concept of network delays and link costs**—Routing decisions are based on hop counts. The path with the lowest hop count to the destination is always preferred, even if the longer path has a better aggregate link bandwidth and slower delays.

- **RIP networks are flat networks**—There is no concept of areas or boundaries. With the introduction of classless routing and the intelligent use of aggregation and summarization, RIP networks seem to have fallen behind.

Some enhancements were introduced in a new version of RIP called RIP Version 2. RIP Version 2 addresses the issues of VLSM, authentication, and multicast routing updates. RIP Version 2 is not a big improvement over RIP (now called RIP Version 1) because it still has the limitations of hop counts and slow convergence, which are essential in today's large networks.

OSPF, on the other hand, addresses most of the issues presented in the preceding list on the limitations of RIP, including:

- With OSPF, there is no limitation on the hop count.

- The intelligent use of VLSM is useful in IP address allocation.

- OSPF uses IP multicast to send link-state updates. This ensures less processing on routers that are not listening to OSPF packets. With IP multicasting, OSPF sends updates only when routing changes occur, instead sending updates periodically. This ensures a better use of bandwidth.

- OSPF has better convergence than RIP because routing changes are propagated instantaneously and not periodically.

- OSPF allows for better load balancing based on the actual cost of the link. Link delays are a major factor in deciding where to send routing updates.

- OSPF allows for a logical definition of networks where routers can be divided into areas. This will limit the explosion of link state updates over the whole network. This also provides a mechanism for aggregating routes and cutting down on the unnecessary propagation of subnet information.

- OSPF allows for routing authentication by using different methods of password authentication.

- OSPF allows for the transfer and tagging of external routes injected into an autonomous system (AS). This keeps track of external routes injected by exterior protocols, such as BGP.

This, of course, would lead to more complexity in configuring and troubleshooting OSPF networks. Administrators that are used to the simplicity of RIP will be challenged with the amount of new information they have to learn in order to keep up with OSPF networks. Also, this will introduce more overhead in memory allocation and CPU utilization. Some of the routers running RIP might have to be upgraded in order to handle the overhead caused by OSPF.

What Do We Mean by Link States?

OSPF is a link-state protocol. We could think of a link as being an interface on the router. The state of the link is a description of that interface and of its relationship to its neighboring routers. A description of the interface would include, for example, the IP address of the interface, the mask, the type of network it is connected to, the routers connected to that network and so on. The collection of all these link-states would form a link-state database.

OSPF uses a link-state algorithm in order to build and calculate the shortest path to all known destinations. The algorithm by itself is quite complicated. The following is a high-level, simplified way of looking at the various steps of the algorithm:

Step 1   Upon initialization or due to any change in routing information, a router will generate a link-state advertisement (LSA). This advertisement will represent the collection of all link-states on that router.

Step 2   All routers will exchange link-states by means of flooding. Each router that receives a link-state update should store a copy in its link-state database and then propagate the update to other routers.

Step 3   After the database of each router is completed, the router will calculate a Shortest Path Tree to all destinations. The router uses the Dijkstra algorithm to calculate the Shortest Path Tree. The destinations, the associated cost, and the next hop to reach those destinations will form the IP routing table.

Step 4   In case no changes in the OSPF network occur, such as cost of a link or a network being added or deleted, OSPF should be quiet. Any changes that occur are communicated through link-state packets, and the Dijkstra algorithm is recalculated to find the shortest path.

Shortest Path Algorithm

The shortest path is calculated using the Diskjtra algorithm. The algorithm places each router at the root of a tree and calculates the shortest path to each destination based on the cumulative cost required to reach that destination. Each router will have its own view of the topology, even though all the routers will build a shortest path tree using the same link-state database. The following sections indicate what is involved in building a shortest path tree.

OSPF Cost

The cost (also called metric) of an interface in OSPF is an indication of the overhead required to send packets across a certain interface. The cost of an interface is inversely proportional to the bandwidth of that interface. A higher bandwidth indicates a lower cost.

There is more overhead (higher cost) and time delays involved in crossing a 56 kbps serial line than crossing a 10 MB ethernet line. The formula used to calculate the cost is:

Cost=100,000,000/bandwith in bps

For example, it will cost $10^8/10^7 = 10$ to cross a 10 Mbps Ethernet line and will cost $10^8/1544000 = 64$ to cross a T1 line.

By default, the cost of an interface is calculated based on the bandwidth; you can force the cost of an interface by using the **ip ospf cost** *cost* interface subcommand.

Shortest Path Tree

Assume we have the network diagram in Figure E-1 with the indicated interface costs. In order to build the shortest path tree for Router A, we would have to make Router A the root of the tree and calculate the smallest cost for each destination.

Figure E-1 *Building the Shortest Path Tree for Router A*

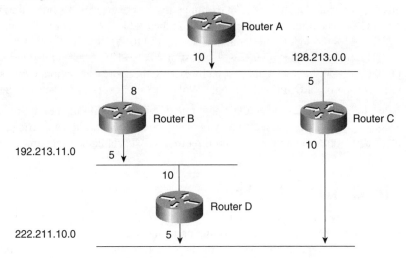

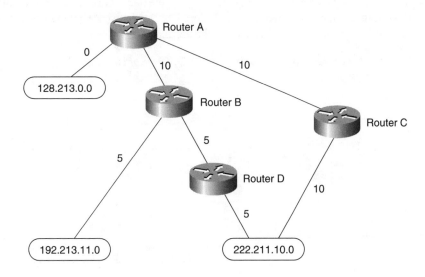

Figure E-1 is the view of the network as seen from Router A. Note the direction of the arrows in calculating the cost. For example, the cost of Router B's interface to network 128.213.0.0 is not relevant when calculating the cost to 192.213.11.0. Router A can reach 192.213.11.0 through Router B with a cost of 15 (10+5). Router A can also reach 222.211.10.0 through Router C with a cost of 20 (10+10) or through Router B with a cost of 20 (10+5+5). In case equal cost paths exist to the same destination, Cisco's implementation of OSPF will keep track of up to six next hops to the same destination.

After the router builds the shortest path tree, it will start building the routing table accordingly. Directly connected networks will be reached through a metric (cost) of 0, and other networks will be reached according to the cost calculated in the tree.

Areas and Border Routers

As previously mentioned, OSPF uses flooding to exchange link-state updates between routers. Any change in routing information is flooded to all routers in the network. Areas are introduced to put a boundary on the explosion of link-state updates. Flooding and calculation of the Dijkstra algorithm on a router is limited to changes within an area. All routers within an area have the exact link-state database. Routers that belong to multiple areas, called area border routers (ABR), have the duty of disseminating routing information or routing changes between areas. Figure E-2 shows two ASs that have been divided into OSPF areas and the ABRs between the areas.

Figure E-2 *OSPF Uses Areas Within an AS To Limit the Explosion of Link-State Updates*

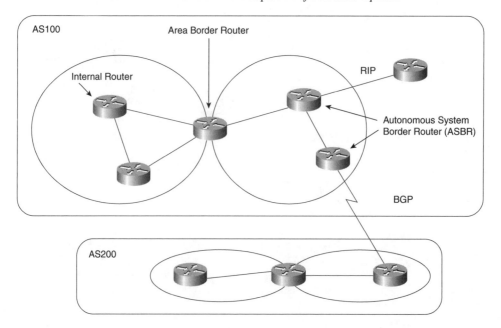

An area is interface specific. A router that has all of its interfaces within the same area is called an internal router (IR). A router that has interfaces in multiple areas is called an area border router (ABR). Routers that act as gateways (redistribution) between OSPF and other routing protocols (IGRP, EIGRP, IS-IS, RIP, BGP, static) or other instances of the OSPF routing process are called autonomous system border routers (ASBR). Any router can be an ABR or an ASBR.

Link-State Packets

There are different types of link-state packets; those are what you normally see in an OSPF database (see Appendix A, "Link-State Database Synchronization," in this document). Figure E-3 illustrates the different types of link-state packets.

Figure E-3 *Link-State Packet Types*

Router Links

Describe The State And Cost
of The Router's Links (Interfaces)
to The Area (Intra-Area).

Summary Links

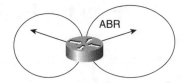

Originated by ABRs Only.
Describe Networks in The AS
But Outside of An Area (Interarea).
Also Describe The Location of The ASBR.

Network Links

Originated for Multiaccess Segments
with More Than One Attached Router.
Describe All Routers Attached to The
Specific Segment. Originated by A
Designed Router (Discussed Later On).

External Links

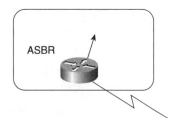

Originated by An ASBR.
Describe Destinations External
to The AS or A Default Route
to The Outside Autonomous System.

Router links are an indication of the state of the interfaces on a router belonging to a certain area. Each router will generate a router link for all of its interfaces.

Summary links are generated by ABRs; this is how network reachability information is disseminated between areas. Normally, all information is injected into the backbone (area 0), and, in turn, the backbone will pass it on to other areas. ABRs also have the task of propagating the reachability of the ASBR. This is how routers know how to get to external routes in other ASs.

Network links are generated by a designated router (DR) on a segment (DRs will be discussed later). This information is an indication of all routers connected to a particular multi-access segment, such as Ethernet, Token Ring, and FDDI (NBMA also).

External links are an indication of networks outside of the AS. These networks are injected into OSPF through redistribution. The ASBR has the task of injecting these routes into an AS.

Enabling OSPF on the Router

Enabling OSPF on the router involves the following two steps in configuration mode:

Step 1   Enable an OSPF process via the **router ospf** *process-id* command.

Step 2   Assign areas to the interfaces via the **network** {*network or IP address*} *mask* **area** *area-id* command.

The OSPF *process-id* is a numeric value local to the router. It does not have to match *process-id*s on other routers. It is possible to run multiple OSPF processes on the same router, but it is not recommended because it creates multiple database instances that add extra overhead to the router.

The **network** command is a way of assigning an interface to a certain area. The *mask* is used as a shortcut, and it helps when putting a list of interfaces in the same area with a one-line configuration. The *mask* contains wildcard bits, where 0 is a match and 1 is a "do not care" bit. For example, 0.0.255.255 indicates a match in the first two bytes of the network number.

The *area-id* is the area number we want the interface to be in. The *area-id* can be an integer between 0 and 4,294,967,295 or can take a form similar to an IP address A.B.C.D.

Figure E-4 shows an example of an ABR, Router A, between area 23 and area 0.0.0.0.

Figure E-4   *Example OSPF Area Configuration*

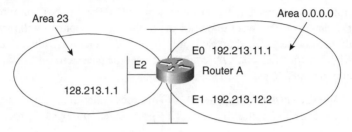

Example E-1 shows the configuration of OSPF on Router A in Figure E-4.

Example E-1   *Configuring OSPF on Router A in Figure E-4*

```
Router A#
interface Ethernet0
 ip address 192.213.11.1 255.255.255.0

interface Ethernet1
 ip address 192.213.12.2 255.255.255.0

interface Ethernet2
 ip address 128.213.1.1 255.255.255.0

router ospf 100
 network 192.213.0.0 0.0.255.255 area 0.0.0.0
 network 128.213.1.1 0.0.0.0 area 23
```

The first network statement will put both Ethernet0 and Ethernet1 in the same area (0.0.0.0), and the second network statement will put Ethernet2 in area 23. Note the mask of 0.0.0.0, which indicates a full match on the IP address. This is an easy way to put an interface in a certain area if you are having problems figuring out a mask.

OSPF Authentication

It is possible to authenticate the OSPF packets so that routers can participate in routing domains based on predefined passwords. By default, a router uses a Null authentication, which means that routing exchanges over a network are not authenticated. Two other authentication methods exist: simple password authentication and Message Digest authentication (MD5).

Simple Password Authentication

Simple password authentication allows a password (key) to be configured per area. Routers in the same area that want to participate in the routing domain will have to be configured with the same key. The drawback of this method is that it is vulnerable to passive attacks. Anybody with a link analyzer could easily get the password off the wire. The following commands enable password authentication:

> **ip ospf authentication-key** *key* (This goes under the specific interface.)
> **area** *area-id* **authentication** (This goes under **router ospf** *process-id.*)

Example E-2 shows the configuration of simple OSPF password authentication on a router.

Example E-2   *Configuring Simple OSPF Authentication*

```
interface Ethernet0
 ip address 10.10.10.10 255.255.255.0
 ip ospf authentication-key mypassword

router ospf 10
 network 10.10.0.0 0.0.255.255 area 0 area 0 authentication
```

Message Digest Authentication

Message Digest Authentication is a cryptographic authentication. A key (password) and key-ID are configured on each router. The router uses an algorithm based on the OSPF packet, the key, and the key-ID to generate a "message digest," which gets appended to the packet. Unlike the simple authentication, the key is not exchanged over the wire. A nondecreasing sequence number is also included in each OSPF packet to protect against replay attacks.

This method also allows for uninterrupted transitions between keys. This is helpful for administrators who want to change the OSPF password without disrupting communication. If an interface is configured with a new key, the router will send multiple copies of the same packet, each authenticated by different keys. The router will stop sending duplicate packets after it detects that all its neighbors have adopted the new key. The commands used for message digest authentication follow:

> **ip ospf message-digest-key** *keyid* **md5** *key* (used under the interface)
> **area** *area-id* **authentication message-digest** (used under **router ospf** *process-id)*

Example E-3 shows the configuration of Message Digest OSPF password authentication on a router.

Example E-3 *Configuring OSPF Message Digest Authentication*

```
interface Ethernet0
 ip address 10.10.10.10 255.255.255.0
 ip ospf message-digest-key 10 md5 mypassword

router ospf 10
 network 10.10.0.0 0.0.255.255 area 0
 area 0 authentication message-digest
```

The Backbone and Area 0

OSPF has special restrictions when multiple areas are involved. If more than one area is configured, one of these areas has to be area 0. This is called the backbone. When designing networks, it is good practice to start with area 0 and then expand into other areas later.

The backbone has to be at the center of all other areas. That is, all areas have to be physically connected to the backbone. The reasoning behind this is that OSPF expects all areas to inject routing information into the backbone, and the backbone will, in turn, disseminate that information into other areas. Figure E-5 illustrates the flow of information in an OSPF network.

Figure E-5 *Information Flow in an OSPF Network*

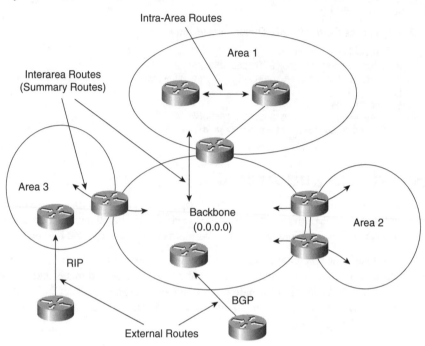

In Figure E-5, all areas are directly connected to the backbone. In the rare situations where a new area is introduced that cannot have a direct physical access to the backbone, a virtual link will have to be configured. Virtual links are discussed in the next section. Note the different types of routing information. Routes that are generated from within an area (the destination belongs to the area) are called *intra-area routes*. These routes are normally represented by the letter **O** in the IP routing table. Routes that originate from other areas are called *interarea* or *summary routes*. The notation for these routes is **O IA** in the IP routing table. Routes that originate from other routing protocols (or different OSPF processes) and that are injected into OSPF via redistribution are called *external routes*. These routes are represented by **O E2** or **O E1** in the IP routing table. Multiple routes to the same destination are preferred in the following order: intra-area, interarea, external E1, and external E2. External types E1 and E2 will be explained later.

Virtual Links

Virtual links are used for two purposes:

- Linking an area that does not have a physical connection to the backbone
- Patching the backbone in case discontinuity of area 0 occurs

Areas Not Physically Connected to Area 0

As mentioned earlier, area 0 has to be at the center of all other areas. In some rare case where it is impossible to have an area physically connected to the backbone, a virtual link is used. The virtual link will provide the disconnected area a logical path to the backbone. The virtual link has to be established between two ABRs that have a common area, with one ABR connected to the backbone. Figure E-6 illustrates an example of establishing a virtual link between two ABRs.

Figure E-6   *Establishing a Virtual Link between Two ABRs*

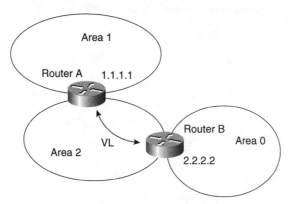

In this example, area 1 does not have a direct physical connection into area 0. A virtual link has to be configured between Router A and Router B. Area 2 is to be used as a transit area, and Router B is the entry point into area 0. In this way, Router A and area 1 will have a logical connection to the backbone. In order to configure a virtual link, use the **area** *area-id* **virtual-link** *router-id* subcommand on both Router A and Router B.

The *area-id* parameter represents the transit area. In Figure E-6, this is area 2. The OSPF *router-id* is usually the highest IP address on the box or the highest loopback address if one exists. The *router-id* is only calculated at boot time or anytime the OSPF process is restarted. In order to find the *router-id*, you can do a **show ip ospf interface**. Assuming that 1.1.1.1 and 2.2.2.2 are the respective *router-id*s of Router A and Router B, the OSPF configuration for both routers would look like Example E-4:

Example E-4   *Configuring Virtual Areas on the Routers in Figure E-6*

```
Router A#
router ospf 10
 area 2 virtual-link 2.2.2.2

Router B#
router ospf 10
 area 2 virtual-link 1.1.1.1
```

Partitioning the Backbone

OSPF allows for linking discontinuous parts of the backbone by using a virtual link. In some cases, different area 0s need to be linked together. This can occur if, for example, a company is trying to merge two separate OSPF networks into one network with a common area 0. In other instances, virtual links are added for redundancy in case some router failure causes the backbone to be split into two. Whatever the reason might be, a virtual link can be configured between separate ABRs that touch area 0 from each side and having a common area (see Figure E-7).

Figure E-7 *Configuring a Virtual Link to Link the Backbone*

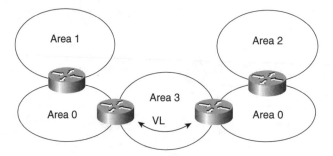

As depicted in Figure E-7, two area 0s are linked together through a virtual link. In case a common area does not exist, an additional area, such as area 3, could be created to become the transit area.

In case any area that is different than the backbone becomes partitioned, the backbone will take care of the partitioning without using any virtual links. One part of the partioned area will be known to the other part through interarea routes rather than intra-area routes.

Neighbors

Routers that share a common segment become neighbors on that segment. Neighbors are elected through the Hello protocol. Hello packets are sent periodically out of each interface using IP multicast (see Appendix B, "OSPF and IP Multicast Addressing," in this document). Routers become neighbors as soon as they see themselves listed in the neighbor's Hello packet. This way, a two-way communication is guaranteed. Neighbor negotiation applies to the *primary address* only. Secondary addresses can be configured on an interface with a restriction that they have to belong to the same area as the primary address.

Two routers will not become neighbors unless they agree on the following criteria:

- **Area-id**—Two routers having a common segment; their interfaces have to belong to the same area on that segment. Of course, the interfaces should belong to the same subnet and have a similar mask.

- **Authentication**—OSPF allows for the configuration of a password for a specific area. Routers that want to become neighbors have to exchange the same password on a particular segment.

- **Hello and Dead Intervals**—OSPF exchanges hello packets on each segment. This is a form of keepalive used by routers to acknowledge their existence on a segment and to elect a designated router (DR) on multiaccess segments. The hello interval specifies the length of time, in seconds, between the hello packets that a router sends on an OSPF interface. The dead interval is the number of seconds that a router's hello packets have not been seen before its neighbors declare the OSPF router down.

  OSPF requires these intervals to be exactly the same between two neighbors. If any of these intervals are different, these routers will not become neighbors on a particular segment. The router interface commands used to set these timers are **ip ospf hello-interval** *seconds* and **ip ospf dead-interval** *seconds.*

- **Stub area flag**—Two routers also have to agree on the stub area flag in the hello packets in order to become neighbors. Stub areas are discussed later. Keep in mind for now that defining stub areas will affect the neighbor election process.

Adjacencies

An adjacency is the next step after the neighboring process. Adjacent routers are routers that go beyond the simple Hello exchange and proceed into the database exchange process. In order to minimize the amount of information exchange on a particular segment, OSPF elects one router to be a DR, and one router to be a backup designated router (BDR) on each multi-access segment. The BDR is elected as a backup mechanism in case the DR goes down. The idea behind this is that routers have a central point of contact for information exchange. Instead of each router exchanging updates with every other router on the segment, every router will exchange the information with the DR and BDR. The DR and BDR will relay the information to everybody else. In mathematical terms, this would cut the information exchange from O(n*n) to O(n), where n is the number of routers on a multi-access segment. The router model in Figure E-8 illustrates the DR and BDR.

Figure E-8 *A Router Model Shows the DR and BDR on a Multi-Access Segment, Used to Minimize the Required Information Exchange*

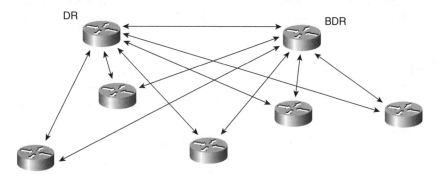

In Figure E-8, all routers share a common multi-access segment. Due to the exchange of hello packets, one router is elected DR, and another is elected BDR. Each router on the segment (which already became a neighbor) will try to establish an adjacency with the DR and BDR.

DR Election

DR and BDR election is done through the Hello protocol. Hello packets are exchanged through IP multicast packets on each segment. The router with the highest OSPF priority on a segment will become the DR for that segment. The same process is repeated for the BDR. In case of a tie, the router with the highest RID will win. The default for the interface OSPF priority is 1. Remember that the DR and BDR concepts are per multi-access segment. Setting the OSPF priority on an interface is done with the **ip ospf priority** *value* interface command.

A priority value of 0 indicates an interface that is not to be elected as DR or BDR. The state of the interface with priority 0 will be *DROTHER*. Figure E-9 illustrates the DR election.

Figure E-9 *Designated Router Election Process*

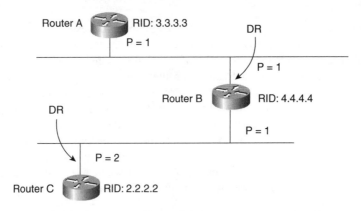

In Figure E-9, Router A and Router B have the same interface priority, but Router B has a higher RID. Router B would be DR on that segment. Router C has a higher priority than Router B. Router C is DR on that segment.

Building the Adjacency

The adjacency building process takes effect after multiple stages have been fulfilled. Routers that become adjacent will have the exact link-state database. The following is a brief summary of the states an interface passes through before becoming adjacent to another router:

Step 1 **Down**—No information has been received from anybody on the segment.

Step 2 **Attempt**—On nonbroadcast, multi-access clouds, such as Frame Relay and X.25, this state indicates that no recent information has been received from the neighbor. An effort should be made to contact the neighbor by sending hello packets at the reduced rate *PollInterval*.

Step 3 **Init**—The interface has detected a hello packet coming from a neighbor, but bidirectional communication has not yet been established.

Step 4 **Two-way**—There is bidirectional communication with a neighbor. The router has seen itself in the hello packets coming from a neighbor. The DR and BDR election would have been done at the end of this stage. At the end of the two-way stage, routers will decide whether to proceed in building an adjacency or not. The decision is based on whether one of the routers is a DR or BDR or the link is a point-to-point or a virtual link.

Step 5 **Exstart**—Routers are trying to establish the initial sequence number that is going to be used in the information exchange packets. The sequence number insures that routers always get the most recent information. One router will become the primary, and the other will become secondary. The primary router will poll the secondary for information.

Step 6 **Exchange**—Routers will describe their entire link-state database by sending database description packets. At this state, packets could be flooded to other interfaces on the router.

Step 7 **Loading**—At this state, routers are finalizing the information exchange. Routers have built a link-state request list and a link-state retransmission list. Any information that looks incomplete or outdated will be put on the request list. Any update that is sent will be put on the retransmission list until it gets acknowledged.

Step 8 **Full**—At this state, the adjacency is complete. The neighboring routers are fully adjacent. Adjacent routers will have a similar link-state database.

Figure E-10 shows an example of a multi-access network running OSPF.

Figure E-10 *OSPF on a Multi-Access Segment*

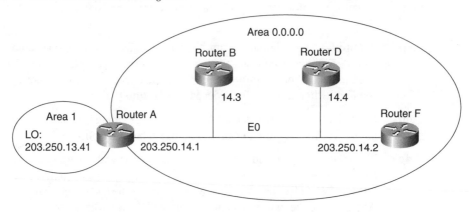

Router A, Router B, Router D, and Router F share a common segment (E0) in area 0.0.0.0. Example E-5 shows the configurations of Router A and Router F. Router B and Router D should have a similar configuration to Router F and will not be included.

Example E-5 *Configuring OSPF on Router A and Router F in Figure E-10*

```
Router A#
hostname Router A

interface Loopback0
 ip address 203.250.13.41 255.255.255.0

interface Ethernet0
 ip address 203.250.14.1 255.255.255.0

router ospf 10
 network 203.250.13.1 0.0.0.0 area 1
 network 203.250.0.0 0.0.255.255 area 0.0.0.0

Router F#
hostname Router F
interface Ethernet0
 ip address 203.250.14.2 255.255.255.0

router ospf 10
 network 203.250.0.0 0.0.255.255 area 0.0.0.0
```

The example shown in Figure E-10 and Example E-5 can be used to demonstrate a couple of commands that are useful when debugging OSPF networks: **show ip ospf interface** *interface* and **show ip ospf neighbor.**

The **show ip ospf interface** *interface* command is a quick check to see if all of the
interfaces belong to the areas they are supposed to be in. The sequence in which the OSPF
network commands are listed is very important. In Router A's configuration, if the "network
203.250.0.0 0.0.255.255 area 0.0.0.0" statement was put before the "network
203.250.13.41 0.0.0.0 area 1" statement, all the interfaces would be in area 0, which is
incorrect because the loopback is in area 1. Example E-6 shows the output for the **show ip
ospf interface** command on Router A, Router F, Router B, and Router D.

Example E-6 *Output of the **show ip ospf interface** Command for the Routers in Figure E-10*

```
Router A#show ip ospf interface e 0
Ethernet0 is up, line protocol is up
  Internet Address 203.250.14.1 255.255.255.0, Area 0.0.0.0
  Process ID 10, Router ID 203.250.13.41, Network Type BROADCAST, Cost:
10
  Transmit Delay is 1 sec, State BDR, Priority 1
  Designated Router (ID) 203.250.15.1, Interface address 203.250.14.2
  Backup Designated router (ID) 203.250.13.41, Interface address
203.250.14.1
  Timer intervals configured, Hello 10, Dead 40, Wait 40, Retransmit 5
    Hello due in 0:00:02
  Neighbor Count is 3, Adjacent neighbor count is 3
    Adjacent with neighbor 203.250.15.1  (Designated Router)
Loopback0 is up, line protocol is up
  Internet Address 203.250.13.41 255.255.255.255, Area 1
  Process ID 10, Router ID 203.250.13.41, Network Type LOOPBACK, Cost: 1
  Loopback interface is treated as a stub Host

Router F#show ip ospf interface e 0
Ethernet0 is up, line protocol is up
  Internet Address 203.250.14.2 255.255.255.0, Area 0.0.0.0
  Process ID 10, Router ID 203.250.15.1, Network Type BROADCAST, Cost: 10
  Transmit Delay is 1 sec, State DR, Priority 1
  Designated Router (ID) 203.250.15.1, Interface address 203.250.14.2
  Backup Designated router (ID) 203.250.13.41, Interface address
203.250.14.1
  Timer intervals configured, Hello 10, Dead 40, Wait 40, Retransmit 5
    Hello due in 0:00:08
  Neighbor Count is 3, Adjacent neighbor count is 3
    Adjacent with neighbor 203.250.13.41  (Backup Designated Router)

Router D#show ip ospf interface e 0
Ethernet0 is up, line protocol is up
  Internet Address 203.250.14.4 255.255.255.0, Area 0.0.0.0
  Process ID 10, Router ID 192.208.10.174, Network Type BROADCAST, Cost:
10
  Transmit Delay is 1 sec, State DROTHER, Priority 1
  Designated Router (ID) 203.250.15.1, Interface address 203.250.14.2
  Backup Designated router (ID) 203.250.13.41, Interface address
203.250.14.1
  Timer intervals configured, Hello 10, Dead 40, Wait 40, Retransmit 5
    Hello due in 0:00:03
  Neighbor Count is 3, Adjacent neighbor count is 2
```

continues

Example E-6 *Output of the **show ip ospf interface** Command for the Routers in Figure E-10 (Continued)*

```
      Adjacent with neighbor 203.250.15.1  (Designated Router)
      Adjacent with neighbor 203.250.13.41  (Backup Designated Router)

Router B#show ip ospf interface e 0
Ethernet0 is up, line protocol is up
  Internet Address 203.250.14.3 255.255.255.0, Area 0.0.0.0
  Process ID 10, Router ID 203.250.12.1, Network Type BROADCAST, Cost: 10
  Transmit Delay is 1 sec, State DROTHER, Priority 1
  Designated Router (ID) 203.250.15.1, Interface address 203.250.14.2
  Backup Designated router (ID) 203.250.13.41, Interface address
203.250.14.1
    Timer intervals configured, Hello 10, Dead 40, Wait 40, Retransmit 5
      Hello due in 0:00:03
    Neighbor Count is 3, Adjacent neighbor count is 2
      Adjacent with neighbor 203.250.15.1  (Designated Router)
      Adjacent with neighbor 203.250.13.41  (Backup Designated Router)
```

The output in Example E-6 shows important information. Take a look at Router A's output. Ethernet0 is in area 0.0.0.0. The process ID is 10 (router ospf 10), and the router ID is 203.250.13.41. Remember that the RID is the highest IP address on the box or the loopback interface, calculated at boot time or whenever the OSPF process is restarted. The state of the interface is BDR. Because all routers have the same OSPF priority on Ethernet 0 (default is 1), Router F's interface was elected as DR because of the higher RID. In the same way, Router A was elected as BDR. Router D and Router B are neither a DR nor a BDR, and their state is DROTHER.

Also note the neighbor count and the adjacent count. Router D has three neighbors and is adjacent to two of them, the DR and the BDR. Router F has three neighbors and is adjacent to all of them because it is the DR.

The information about the network type is important and will determine the state of the interface. On broadcast networks such as Ethernet, the election of the DR and BDR should be irrelevant to the end user. It should not matter who the DR or BDR are. In other cases, such as NBMA media such as Frame Relay and X.25, this becomes important for OSPF to function correctly. Fortunately, with the introduction of point-to-point and point-to-multipoint subinterfaces, DR election is no longer an issue. OSPF over NBMA is discussed in the next section.

show ip ospf neighbor is another command we need to look at. Example E-7 looks at Router D's output after executing the **show ip ospf neighbor command**.

Example E-7 *Output of the **show ip ospf neighbor** Command for Router D in Figure E-10*

```
Router D#show ip ospf neighbor

Neighbor ID    Pri State        Dead Time  Address       Interface

203.250.12.1    1  2WAY/DROTHER  0:00:37    203.250.14.3  Ethernet0
203.250.15.1    1  FULL/DR       0:00:36    203.250.14.2  Ethernet0
203.250.13.41   1  FULL/BDR      0:00:34    203.250.14.1  Ethernet0
```

The **show ip ospf neighbor** command shows the state of all the neighbors on a particular segment. Do not be alarmed if the *Neighbor ID* does not belong to the segment you are looking at. In our case, 203.250.12.1 and 103.250.15.1 are not on Ethernet0. This is okay because the *Neighbor ID* is actually the Router ID, which could be any IP address on the box. Router D and Router B are just neighbors, which is why the state is *2WAY/DROTHER*. Router D is adjacent to Router A and Router F, and the state is *FULL/DR* and *FULL/BDR*.

Adjacencies on Point-to-Point Interfaces

OSPF will always form an adjacency with the neighbor on the other side of a point-to-point interface, such as point-to-point serial lines. There is no concept of DR or BDR. The state of the serial interfaces is point-to-point.

Adjacencies on NBMA

Special care should be taken when configuring OSPF over multi-access, nonbroadcast medias, such as Frame Relay, X.25, and ATM. The protocol considers these media like any other broadcast media, such as Ethernet. NBMA clouds are usually built in a hub-and-spoke topology. PVCs or SVCs are laid out in a partial mesh, and the physical topology does not provide the multi-access that OSPF believes is out there. The selection of the DR becomes an issue because the DR and BDR need to have full physical connectivity with all routers that exist on the cloud. Also, because of the lack of broadcast capabilities, the DR and BDR need to have a static list of all other routers attached to the cloud. This is achieved using the **neighbor** *ip-address* [**priority** *number*] [**poll-interval** *seconds*] command, where the *ip-address* and **priority** are the IP address and the OSPF priority given to the neighbor. A neighbor with priority 0 is considered ineligible for DR election. The "poll-interval" is the amount of time an NBMA interface waits before polling (sending a hello) to a presumably dead neighbor. The neighbor command applies to routers with a potential of being DRs or BDRs (interface priority not equal to 0). Figure E-11 shows a network diagram where DR selection is very important.

Figure E-11 *OSPF DR Selection on an NBMA Network*

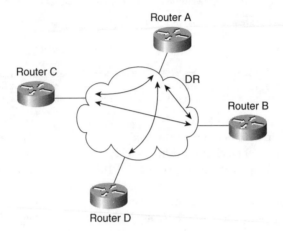

In Figure E-11, it is essential for Router A's interface to the cloud to be elected DR because Router A is the only router that has full connectivity to other routers. The election of the DR could be influenced by setting the OSPF priority on the interfaces. Routers that do not need to become DRs or BDRs will have a priority of 0; other routers could have a lower priority.

Do not dwell too much on the use of the **neighbor** command because it is becoming obsolete with the introduction of new means of setting the interface Network Type to whatever we want, irrespective of what the underlying physical media are. This is explained in the following section.

Avoiding DRs and the neighbor Command on NBMA

Different methods can be used to avoid the complications of configuring static neighbors and having specific routers becoming DRs or BDRs on the nonbroadcast cloud. Specifying which method to use is influenced by whether we are starting the network from scratch or rectifying an already existing design.

Point-to-Point Subinterfaces

A subinterface is a logical way of defining an interface. The same physical interface can be split into multiple logical interfaces, with each subinterface being defined as point-to-point. This was originally created in order to better handle issues caused by split horizon over NBMA and vector-based routing protocols.

A point-to-point subinterface has the properties of any physical point-to-point interface. As far as OSPF is concerned, an adjacency is always formed over a point-to-point subinterface with no DR or BDR election. Figure E-12 provides an illustration of point-to-point subinterfaces.

Figure E-12 *Point-to-Point Subinterfaces*

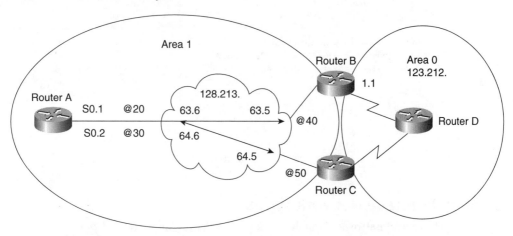

In Figure E-12, on Router A, we can split Serial 0 into two point-to-point subinterfaces, S0.1 and S0.2. This way, OSPF will consider the cloud as a set of point-to-point links rather than one multi-access network. The only drawback for the point-to-point is that each segment will belong to a different subnet. This might not be acceptable because some administrators have already assigned one IP subnet for the whole cloud.

Another workaround is to use IP unnumbered interfaces on the cloud. This also might be a problem for some administrators who manage the WAN based on IP addresses of the serial lines. Example E-8 shows a typical configuration for Router A and Router B.

Example E-8 *Configuring Subinterfaces on Router A and Router B in Figure E-12*

```
Router A#

interface Serial 0
 no ip address
 encapsulation frame-relay

interface Serial0.1 point-to-point
 ip address 128.213.63.6 255.255.252.0
 frame-relay interface-dlci 20

interface Serial0.2 point-to-point
 ip address 128.213.64.6 255.255.252.0
 frame-relay interface-dlci 30

router ospf 10
```

continues

Example E-8 *Configuring Subinterfaces on Router A and Router B in Figure E-12 (Continued)*

```
 network 128.213.0.0 0.0.255.255 area 1

Router B#

interface Serial 0
 no ip address
 encapsulation frame-relay

interface Serial0.1 point-to-point
 ip address 128.213.63.5 255.255.252.0
 frame-relay interface-dlci 40

interface Serial1
 ip address 123.212.1.1 255.255.255.0

router ospf 10
 network 128.213.0.0 0.0.255.255 area 1
 network 123.212.0.0 0.0.255.255 area 0
```

Selecting Interface Network Types

The **ip ospf network** {**broadcast** | **non-broadcast** | **point-to-multipoint**} command is used to set the network type of an OSPF interface.

Point-to-Multipoint Interfaces

An OSPF point-to-multipoint interface is defined as a numbered point-to-point interface having one or more neighbors. This concept takes the previously discussed point-to-point concept one step further. Administrators do not have to worry about having multiple subnets for each point-to-point link. The cloud is configured as one subnet. This should work well for people who are migrating into the point-to-point concept with no change in IP addressing on the cloud. Also, they would not have to worry about DRs and neighbor statements. OSPF point-to-multipoint works by exchanging additional link-state updates that contain a number of information elements that describe connectivity to the neighboring routers. Figure E-13 shows a point-to-multipoint interface.

Figure E-13 *Point-to-Multipoint Interfaces*

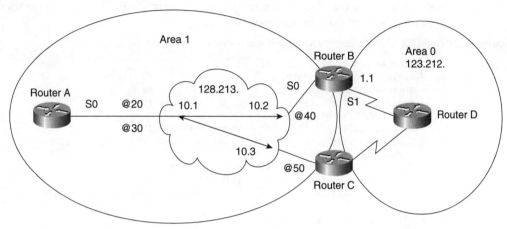

Example E-9 shows the configuration of Router A and Router B in Figure E-13.

Example E-9 *Configuring Point-to-Multipoint Interfaces on Router A and Router B in Figure E-13*

```
Router A#

interface Loopback0
 ip address 200.200.10.1 255.255.255.0

interface Serial0
 ip address 128.213.10.1 255.255.252.0
 encapsulation frame-relay
 ip ospf network point-to-multipoint

router ospf 10
 network 128.213.0.0 0.0.255.255 area 1

Router B#
interface Serial0
 ip address 128.213.10.2 255.255.255.0
 encapsulation frame-relay
 ip ospf network point-to-multipoint

interface Serial1
 ip address 123.212.1.1 255.255.255.0

router ospf 10
 network 128.213.0.0 0.0.255.255 area 1
 network 123.212.0.0 0.0.255.255 area 0
```

Note that no static **frame-relay map** statements were configured; this is because Inverse ARP takes care of the DLCI to IP address mapping. Example E-10 presents some **show ip ospf interface** and **show ip ospf route** outputs.

Example E-10 *Output of show Commands for Router A and Router B in Figure E-13*

```
Router A#show ip ospf interface s0
Serial0 is up, line protocol is up
  Internet Address 128.213.10.1 255.255.255.0, Area 0
  Process ID 10, Router ID 200.200.10.1, Network Type
POINT_TO_MULTIPOINT, Cost: 64
  Transmit Delay is 1 sec, State POINT_TO_MULTIPOINT,
  Timer intervals configured, Hello 30, Dead 120, Wait 120, Retransmit 5
    Hello due in 0:00:04
  Neighbor Count is 2, Adjacent neighbor count is 2
    Adjacent with neighbor 195.211.10.174
    Adjacent with neighbor 128.213.63.130Router A#show ip ospf neighbor


Router B#show ip ospf neighbor

Neighbor ID     Pri   State           Dead Time    Address        Interface
128.213.10.3     1    FULL/   -       0:01:35      128.213.10.3   Serial0
128.213.10.2     1    FULL/   -       0:01:44      128.213.10.2   Serial0

Router B#show ip ospf interface s0

Serial0 is up, line protocol is up
  Internet Address 128.213.10.2 255.255.255.0, Area 0
  Process ID 10, Router ID 128.213.10.2, Network Type
POINT_TO_MULTIPOINT, Cost: 64
  Transmit Delay is 1 sec, State POINT_TO_MULTIPOINT,
  Timer intervals configured, Hello 30, Dead 120, Wait 120, Retransmit 5
    Hello due in 0:00:14
  Neighbor Count is 1, Adjacent neighbor count is 1
    Adjacent with neighbor 200.200.10.1

Router B#show ip ospf neighbor

Neighbor ID     Pri   State           Dead Time    Address        Interface
200.200.10.1     1    FULL/   -       0:01:52      128.213.10.1   Serial0
```

The only drawback for point-to-multipoint is that it generates multiple Hosts routes (routes with mask 255.255.255.255) for all the neighbors. Note the Host routes in the IP routing table for Router B and Router C shown in Example E-11.

Example E-11 *Routing Tables for Router B and Router C in Figure E-13*

```
Router B#show ip route
  Codes: C - connected, S - static, I - IGRP, R - RIP, M - mobile, B - BGP
         D - EIGRP, EX - EIGRP external, O - OSPF, IA - OSPF inter area
         E1 - OSPF external type 1, E2 - OSPF external type 2, E - EGP
         i - IS-IS, L1 - IS-IS level-1, L2 - IS-IS level-2, * - candidate default

Gateway of last resort is not set

      200.200.10.0 255.255.255.255 is subnetted, 1 subnets
O        200.200.10.1 [110/65] via 128.213.10.1,  Serial0
         128.213.0.0 is variably subnetted, 3 subnets, 2 masks
O        128.213.10.3 255.255.255.255
            [110/128] via 128.213.10.1, 00:00:00, Serial0
O        128.213.10.1 255.255.255.255
            [110/64] via 128.213.10.1, 00:00:00, Serial0
C        128.213.10.0 255.255.255.0 is directly connected, Serial0
      123.0.0.0 255.255.255.0 is subnetted, 1 subnets
C        123.212.1.0 is directly connected, Serial1
Router C#show ip route
      200.200.10.0 255.255.255.255 is subnetted, 1 subnets
O        200.200.10.1 [110/65] via 128.213.10.1, Serial1
      128.213.0.0 is variably subnetted, 4 subnets, 2 masks
O        128.213.10.2 255.255.255.255 [110/128] via 128.213.10.1,Serial1
O        128.213.10.1 255.255.255.255 [110/64] via 128.213.10.1, Serial1
C        128.213.10.0 255.255.255.0 is directly connected, Serial1
      123.0.0.0 255.255.255.0 is subnetted, 1 subnets
O        123.212.1.0 [110/192] via 128.213.10.1, 00:14:29, Serial1
```

Note that in Router C's IP routing table, network 123.212.1.0 is reachable through next hop 128.213.10.1 and not through 128.213.10.2, as you normally see over Frame Relay clouds sharing the same subnet. This is one advantage of the point-to-multipoint configuration because you do not need to resort to static mapping on Router C to be able to reach next hop 128.213.10.2.

Broadcast Interfaces

This approach is a workaround for using the **neighbor** command, which statically lists all existing neighbors. The interface will be logically set to broadcast and will behave as if the router were connected to a LAN. DR and BDR election will still be performed, so special care should be taken to assure either a full mesh topology or a static selection of the DR based on the interface priority. The **ip ospf network broadcast** command sets the interface to broadcast.

OSPF and Route Summarization

Summarizing is the consolidation of multiple routes into one single advertisement. This is normally done at the boundaries of area border routers (ABRs). Although summarization could be configured between any two areas, it is better to summarize in the direction of the backbone. This way, the backbone receives all the aggregate addresses and, in turn, will inject them, already summarized, into other areas. There are two types of summarization:

- Interarea route summarization
- External route summarization

Interarea Route Summarization

Interarea route summarization is done on ABRs, and it applies to routes from within the AS. It does not apply to external routes injected into OSPF through redistribution. In order to take advantage of summarization, network numbers in areas should be assigned in a contiguous way to be able to lump these addresses into one range. To specify an address range, execute the **area** *area-id* **range** *address mask* command in router configuration mode.

The *area-id* parameter is the area containing networks to be summarized. The *address* and *mask* parameters specify the range of addresses to be summarized in one range. Figure E-14 shows an example of summarization.

Figure E-14 *Interarea Route Summarization*

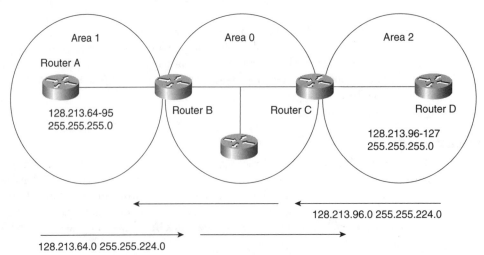

In Figure E-14, Router B is summarizing the range of subnets from 128.213.64.0 to 128.213.95.0 into one range: 128.213.64.0 255.255.224.0. This is achieved by masking the first three left bits of 64 using a mask of 255.255.224.0. In the same way, Router C is generating the summary address 128.213.96.0 255.255.224.0 into the backbone. Note that this summarization was successful because we have two distinct ranges of subnets, 64–95 and 96–127.

It would be hard to summarize if the subnets between area 1 and area 2 were overlapping. The backbone area would receive summary ranges that overlap, and routers in the middle would not know where to send the traffic based on the summary address.

Example E-12 presents the relative configuration of Router B.

Example E-12 *Configuring Router B in Figure E-14 for Interarea Route Summarization*

```
Router B#
router ospf 100
 area 1 range 128.213.64.0 255.255.224.0
```

External Route Summarization

External route summarization is specific to external routes that are injected into OSPF through redistribution. Also, make sure that external ranges that are being summarized are contiguous. Summarization overlapping ranges from two different routers could cause packets to be sent to the wrong destination. Summarization is done through the **summary-address** *ip-address mask* command.

This command is effective only on ASBRs doing redistribution into OSPF. Figure E-15 shows a network with two ASBRs, Router A and Router D.

Figure E-15 *External Route Summarization*

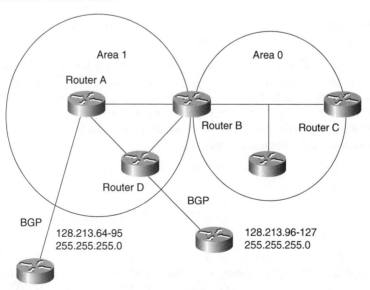

In Figure E-15, Router A and Router D are injecting external routes into OSPF by redistribution. Router A is injecting subnets in the range 128.213.64-95, and Router D is injecting subnets in the range 128.213.96-127. Example E-13 demonstrates what we can do to summarize the subnets into one range on each router.

Example E-13 *Summarizing Subnets into One Range on Router A and Router D in Figure E-15*

```
Router A#
router ospf 100
 summary-address 128.213.64.0 255.255.224.0
 redistribute bgp 50 metric 1000 subnets

Router D#
router ospf 100
 summary-address 128.213.96.0 255.255.224.0
 redistribute bgp 20 metric 1000 subnets
```

This will cause Router A to generate one external route 128.213.64.0 255.255.224.0 and will cause Router D to generate 128.213.96.0 255.255.224.0.

Note that the **summary-address** command has no effect if it is used on Router B; Router B is not doing the redistribution into OSPF.

Stub Areas

OSPF allows certain areas to be configured as stub areas. External networks, such as those redistributed from other protocols into OSPF, are not allowed to be flooded into a stub area. Routing from these areas to the outside world is based on a default route. Configuring a stub area reduces the topological database size inside an area and reduces the memory requirements of routers inside that area.

An area could be qualified a stub when there is a single exit point from that area or if routing to the outside of the area does not have to take an optimal path. The latter description is just an indication that a stub area that has multiple exit points will have one or more ABRs injecting a default into that area. Routing to the outside world could take a suboptimal path in reaching the destination by going out of the area through an exit point that is farther to the destination than other exit points.

Other stub area restrictions are that a stub area cannot be used as a transit area for virtual links. Also, an ASBR cannot be internal to a stub area. These restrictions are made because a stub area is mainly configured not to carry external routes, and any of the previous situations cause external links to be injected in that area. The backbone, of course, cannot be configured as stub.

All OSPF routers inside a stub area have to be configured as stub routers because whenever an area is configured as stub, all interfaces that belong to that area will start exchanging hello packets with a flag that indicates that the interface is stub. Actually, this is just a bit in the hello packet (E bit) that gets set to 0. All routers that have a common segment have to agree on that flag. If they do not, they will not become neighbors, and routing will not take effect.

An extension to stub areas is what is called *totally stubby areas*. Cisco indicates this by adding a **no-summary** keyword to the stub area configuration. A totally stubby area is one that blocks external routes and summary routes (interarea routes) from going into the area. This way, intra-area routes and the default of 0.0.0.0 are the only routes injected into that area.

The **area** *area-id* **stub [no-summary]** command configures an area as stub. The **area** *area-id* **default-cost** *cost* command configures a default-cost into an area. If the cost is not set using the **area** *area-id* **default-cost** *cost* command, a cost of 1 will be advertised by the ABR.

Figure E-16 shows an example of an OSPF network with a stub area.

Figure E-16 *A Network with a Stub Area*

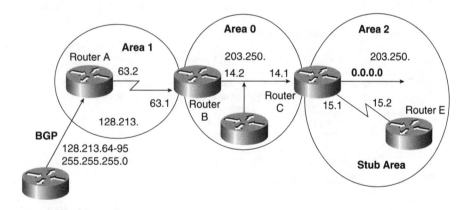

Assume that area 2 is to be configured as a stub area. Example E-14 shows the configuration of Router C and the routing table of Router E before configuring area 2 as a stub.

Example E-14 *Before Configuring a Stub Area in Figure E-16*

```
Router C#

interface Ethernet 0
 ip address 203.250.14.1 255.255.255.0

interface Serial1
 ip address 203.250.15.1 255.255.255.252

router ospf 10
 network 203.250.15.0 0.0.0.255 area 2
 network 203.250.14.0 0.0.0.255 area 0

Router E#show ip route
 Codes: C - connected, S - static, I - IGRP, R - RIP, M - mobile, B - BGP
        D - EIGRP, EX - EIGRP external, O - OSPF, IA - OSPF inter area
        E1 - OSPF external type 1, E2 - OSPF external type 2, E - EGP
        i - IS-IS, L1 - IS-IS level-1, L2 - IS-IS level-2, * - candidate default

Gateway of last resort is not set

     203.250.15.0 255.255.255.252 is subnetted, 1 subnets
C       203.250.15.0 is directly connected, Serial0
O IA 203.250.14.0 [110/74] via 203.250.15.1, 00:06:31, Serial0
     128.213.0.0 is variably subnetted, 2 subnets, 2 masks
O E2    128.213.64.0 255.255.192.0
           [110/10] via 203.250.15.1, 00:00:29, Serial0
O IA    128.213.63.0 255.255.255.252
           [110/84] via 203.250.15.1, 00:03:57, Serial0
     131.108.0.0 255.255.255.240 is subnetted, 1 subnets
O       131.108.79.208 [110/74] via 203.250.15.1, 00:00:10, Serial0
```

Router E has learned the interarea routes (O IA) 203.250.14.0 and 128.213.63.0 and it has learned the intra-area route (O) 131.108.79.208 and the external route (O E2) 128.213.64.0.

Example E-15 shows the necessary configuration to make area 2 a stub.

Example E-15 *Configuring a Stub Area on the Routers in Figure E-16*

```
Router C#

interface Ethernet 0
 ip address 203.250.14.1 255.255.255.0

interface Serial1
 ip address 203.250.15.1 255.255.255.252

router ospf 10
 network 203.250.15.0 0.0.0.255 area 2
 network 203.250.14.0 0.0.0.255 area 0
 area 2 stub

Router E#

interface Ethernet0
 ip address 203.250.14.2 255.255.255.0

interface Ethernet1
 ip address 131.108.79.209 255.255.255.240

interface Serial1
 ip address 203.250.15.1 255.255.255.252

router ospf 10
 network 203.250.15.0 0.0.0.255 area 2
 network 203.250.14.0 0.0.0.255 area 0
 network 131.108.0.0 0.0.255.255 area 2
 area 2 stub
```

Note that the **stub** command is also configured on Router E; otherwise, Router E would never become a neighbor to Router C. The default cost was not set, so Router C will advertise 0.0.0.0 to Router E with a metric of 1. Example E-16 shows the routing table for Router E now that area 2 is a stub area.

Example E-16 *Router E's Routing Table after Configuring a Stub Area*

```
Router E#show ip route
Codes: C - connected, S - static, I - IGRP, R - RIP, M - mobile, B - BGP
       D - EIGRP, EX - EIGRP external, O - OSPF, IA - OSPF inter area
       E1 - OSPF external type 1, E2 - OSPF external type 2, E - EGP
       i - IS-IS, L1 - IS-IS level-1, L2 - IS-IS level-2, * - candidate default

Gateway of last resort is 203.250.15.1 to network 0.0.0.0

     203.250.15.0 255.255.255.252 is subnetted, 1 subnets
C       203.250.15.0 is directly connected, Serial0
O IA 203.250.14.0 [110/74] via 203.250.15.1, 00:26:58, Serial0
     128.213.0.0 255.255.255.252 is subnetted, 1 subnets
O IA    128.213.63.0 [110/84] via 203.250.15.1, 00:26:59, Serial0
     131.108.0.0 255.255.255.240 is subnetted, 1 subnets
O       131.108.79.208 [110/74] via 203.250.15.1, 00:26:59, Serial0
O*IA 0.0.0.0 0.0.0.0 [110/65] via 203.250.15.1, 00:26:59, Serial0
```

Note that all the routes show up except the external routes, which were replaced by a default route of 0.0.0.0. The cost of the route happened to be 65 (64 for a T1 line plus 1 advertised by Router C).

Example E-17 shows how to configure area 2 to be totally stubby and change the default cost of 0.0.0.0 to 10.

Example E-17 *Configuring a Totally Stubby Area on the Routers in Figure E-16*

```
Router C#

interface Ethernet 0
 ip address 203.250.14.1 255.255.255.0

interface Serial1
 ip address 203.250.15.1 255.255.255.252

router ospf 10
 network 203.250.15.0 0.0.0.255 area 2
 network 203.250.14.0 0.0.0.255 area 0
 area 2 stub no-summary

Router E#show ip route


 Codes: C - connected, S - static, I - IGRP, R - RIP, M - mobile, B - BGP
        D - EIGRP, EX - EIGRP external, O - OSPF, IA - OSPF inter area
        E1 - OSPF external type 1, E2 - OSPF external type 2, E - EGP
        i - IS-IS, L1 - IS-IS level-1, L2 - IS-IS level-2, * - candidate default

 Gateway of last resort is not set

     203.250.15.0 255.255.255.252 is subnetted, 1 subnets
```

Example E-17 *Configuring a Totally Stubby Area on the Routers in Figure E-16 (Continued)*

```
C       203.250.15.0 is directly connected, Serial0
        131.108.0.0 255.255.255.240 is subnetted, 1 subnets
O       131.108.79.208 [110/74] via 203.250.15.1, 00:31:27, Serial0
O*IA 0.0.0.0 0.0.0.0 [110/74] via 203.250.15.1, 00:00:00, Serial0
```

Note that the only routes that show up are the intra-area routes (O) and the default-route 0.0.0.0. The external and interarea routes have been blocked. The cost of the default route is now 74 (64 for a T1 line + 10 advertised by Router C). No configuration is needed on Router E in this case. The area is already stubbed, and the **no-summary** command does not affect the hello packet at all, which the **stub** command does.

Redistributing Routes into OSPF

Redistributing routes into OSPF from other routing protocols or from static will cause these routes to become OSPF external routes. To redistribute routes into OSPF, use the **redistribute** *protocol* [*process-id*] [**metric** *value*] [**metric-type** *value*] [**route-map** *map-tag*] [**subnets**] command in router configuration mode.

The *protocol* and *process-id* parameters indicate the protocol that is injected into OSPF and its process-id if it exits. The **metric** is the cost we assign to the external route. If no metric is specified, OSPF puts a default value of 20 when redistributing routes from all protocols except BGP routes, which get a metric of 1. The **metric-type** is discussed in the next section.

The **route-map** is a method used to control the redistribution of routes between routing domains. The format of a route map follows:

```
route-map map-tag [[permit | deny] | [sequence-number]]
```

When redistributing routes into OSPF, only routes that are not subnetted are redistributed if the **subnets** keyword is not specified.

E1 Versus E2 External Routes

External routes fall under two categories, external type 1 and external type 2. The difference between the two is in the way the cost (metric) of the route is calculated. The cost of a type 2 route is always the external cost, irrespective of the interior cost to reach that route. A type 1 cost is the addition of the external cost and the internal cost used to reach that route. A type 1 route is always preferred over a type 2 route for the same destination (see Figure E-17).

Figure E-17 *Type E1 and E2 External OSPF Routes*

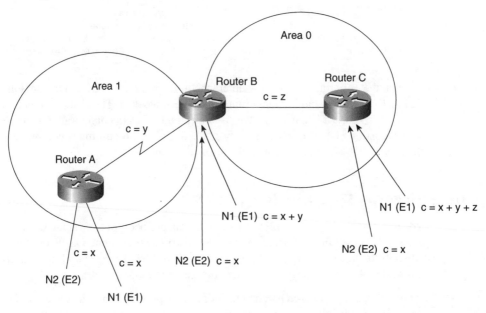

As Figure E-17 shows, Router A is redistributing two external routes into OSPF. N1 and N2 both have an external cost of **x**. The only difference is that N1 is redistributed into OSPF with a **metric-type** 1, and N2 is redistributed with a **metric-type** 2. If we follow the routes as they flow from Area 1 to Area 0, the cost to reach N2 as seen from Router B or Router C will always be **x**. The internal cost along the way is not considered. On the other hand, the cost to reach N1 is incremented by the internal cost. The cost is **x+y** as seen from Router B and **x+y+z** as seen from Router C. Type 2 routes are preferred over type 1 routes in case two same-cost routes exist to the destination. The default is type 2.

Figure E-18 shows another example of redistribution, with static routes.

Figure E-18 *Static Routes Configured on an OSPF Router*

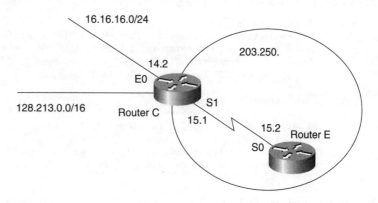

Suppose we added two static routes pointing to E0 on Router C: 16.16.16.0 255.255.255.0 (the /24 notation indicates a 24-bit mask starting from the far left) and 128.213.0.0 255.255.0.0. To show the different behaviors when different parameters are used in the **redistribute** command on Router C, start with the configurations in Example E-18.

Example E-18 *Configuring Router C and Router E in Figure E-18*

```
Router C#
interface Ethernet0
 ip address 203.250.14.2 255.255.255.0

interface Serial1
 ip address 203.250.15.1 255.255.255.252

router ospf 10
 redistribute static
 network 203.250.15.0 0.0.0.255 area 2
 network 203.250.14.0 0.0.0.255 area 0

ip route 16.16.16.0 255.255.255.0 Ethernet0
ip route 128.213.0.0 255.255.0.0 Ethernet0

Router E#

interface Serial0
 ip address 203.250.15.2 255.255.255.252

router ospf 10
 network 203.250.15.0 0.0.0.255 area 2
```

Example E-19 shows the output of the **show ip route** command on Router E.

Example E-19 *The Routing Table on Router E in Figure E-18*

```
Router E#show ip route
 Codes: C - connected, S - static, I - IGRP, R - RIP, M - mobile, B - BGP
        D - EIGRP, EX - EIGRP external, O - OSPF, IA - OSPF inter area
        E1 - OSPF external type 1, E2 - OSPF external type 2, E - EGP
        i - IS-IS, L1 - IS-IS level-1, L2 - IS-IS level-2, * - candidate default

Gateway of last resort is not set

     203.250.15.0 255.255.255.252 is subnetted, 1 subnets
C       203.250.15.0 is directly connected, Serial0
O IA 203.250.14.0 [110/74] via 203.250.15.1, 00:02:31, Serial0
O E2 128.213.0.0 [110/20] via 203.250.15.1, 00:02:32, Serial0
```

Note that the only external route that has appeared is 128.213.0.0 because we did not use the **subnet** keyword. Remember that if the **subnet** keyword is not used, only routes that are not subnetted will be redistributed. In our case, 16.16.16.0 is a class A route that is subnetted, and it did not get redistributed. Because the **metric** keyword was not used (or a **default-metric** statement under router OSPF), the cost allocated to the external route is 20 (the default is 1 for BGP). If we use the **redistribute static metric 50 subnets** command on Router C, Example E-20 shows the resulting change to the routing table on Router E.

Example E-20 *The Routing Table on Router E in Figure E-18 with Router C Redistributing Subnets*

```
Router E#show ip route
 Codes: C - connected, S - static, I - IGRP, R - RIP, M
 - mobile, B - BGP
        D - EIGRP, EX - EIGRP external, O - OSPF, IA - OSPF inter area
        E1 - OSPF external type 1, E2 - OSPF external type 2, E - EGP
        i - IS-IS, L1 - IS-IS level-1, L2 - IS-IS level-2, * - candidate default

Gateway of last resort is not set

     16.0.0.0 255.255.255.0 is subnetted, 1 subnets
O E2    16.16.16.0 [110/50] via 203.250.15.1, 00:00:02, Serial0
     203.250.15.0 255.255.255.252 is subnetted, 1 subnets
C       203.250.15.0 is directly connected, Serial0
O IA 203.250.14.0 [110/74] via 203.250.15.1, 00:00:02, Serial0
O E2 128.213.0.0 [110/50] via 203.250.15.1, 00:00:02, Serial0
```

Note that 16.16.16.0 has shown up now, and the cost to external routes is 50. Because the external routes are of type 2 (E2), the internal cost has not been added. Suppose we now change the type to E1 in the redistribute command on Router C, as follows: **redistribute static metric 50 metric-type 1 subnets.** Example E-21 shows the resulting change to the routing table on Router E.

Example E-21 *The Routing Table on Router E in Figure E-18 with Router C Redistributing Type 1 Routes*

```
Router E#show ip route
 Codes: C - connected, S - static, I - IGRP, R - RIP, M - mobile, B - BGP
        D - EIGRP, EX - EIGRP external, O - OSPF, IA - OSPF inter area
        E1 - OSPF external type 1, E2 - OSPF external type 2, E - EGP
        i - IS-IS, L1 - IS-IS level-1, L2 - IS-IS level-2, * - candidate default

Gateway of last resort is not set

     16.0.0.0 255.255.255.0 is subnetted, 1 subnets
O E1    16.16.16.0 [110/114] via 203.250.15.1, 00:04:20, Serial0
     203.250.15.0 255.255.255.252 is subnetted, 1 subnets
C       203.250.15.0 is directly connected, Serial0
O IA 203.250.14.0 [110/74] via 203.250.15.1, 00:09:41, Serial0
O E1 128.213.0.0 [110/114] via 203.250.15.1, 00:04:21, Serial0
```

Note that the type has changed to E1 and the cost has been incremented by the internal cost of Serial0 which is 64; the total cost is 64 + 50 = 114.

Assuming we added a route map to Router C's configuration, we would get the configuration shown in Example E-22.

Example E-22 *Configuring a Route Map on Router C in Figure E-18*

```
Router C#
interface Ethernet0
 ip address 203.250.14.2 255.255.255.0

interface Serial1
 ip address 203.250.15.1 255.255.255.252

router ospf 10

 redistribute static metric 50 metric-type 1 subnets route-map STOPUPDATE
 network 203.250.15.0 0.0.0.255 area 2
 network 203.250.14.0 0.0.0.255 area 0

ip route 16.16.16.0 255.255.255.0 Ethernet0
ip route 128.213.0.0 255.255.0.0 Ethernet0

access-list 1 permit 128.213.0.0 0.0.255.255

route-map STOPUPDATE permit 10
 match ip address 1
```

The route map in Example E-22 will only permit 128.213.0.0 to be redistributed into OSPF and will deny the rest. This is why 16.16.16.0 does not show up in Router E's routing table anymore, as shown in Example E-23.

Example E-23 *The Routing Table on Router E in Figure E-18 with Router C Configured with a Route Map*

```
Router E#show ip route
Codes: C - connected, S - static, I - IGRP, R - RIP, M - mobile, B - BGP
       D - EIGRP, EX - EIGRP external, O - OSPF, IA - OSPF inter area
       E1 - OSPF external type 1, E2 - OSPF external type 2, E - EGP
       i - IS-IS, L1 - IS-IS level-1, L2 - IS-IS level-2, * - candidate default

Gateway of last resort is not set

     203.250.15.0 255.255.255.252 is subnetted, 1 subnets
C       203.250.15.0 is directly connected, Serial0
O IA 203.250.14.0 [110/74] via 203.250.15.1, 00:00:04, Serial0
O E1 128.213.0.0 [110/114] via 203.250.15.1, 00:00:05, Serial0
```

Redistributing OSPF into Other Protocols

When redistributing OSPF into other protocols, consider the following:

- The use of a valid metric
- The effect of using VLSM
- The effect of mutual redistribution

Use of a Valid Metric

Whenever you redistribute OSPF into other protocols, you have to respect the rules of those protocols. In particular, the metric applied should match the metric used by that protocol. For example, the RIP metric is a hop count ranging between 1 and 16, where 1 indicates that a network is one hop away and 16 indicates that the network is unreachable. On the other hand, IGRP and EIGRP require a metric in this form:

default-metric *bandwidth delay reliability loading mtu*

VLSM

Another issue to consider is VLSM (see the Variable Length Subnet Guide, covered in Appendix C, "Variable Length Subnet Masks [VLSM],"). OSPF can carry multiple subnet information for the same major net, but other protocols, such as RIP and IGRP (EIGRP is okay with VLSM), cannot. If the same major net crosses the boundaries of an OSPF and RIP domain, VLSM information redistributed into RIP or IGRP will be lost, and static routes will have to be configured in the RIP or IGRP domains. Figure E-19 illustrates this problem.

Figure E-19 *Example Using RIP and OSPF with VLSMs*

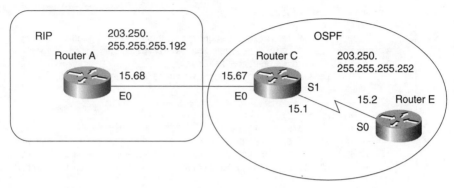

In Figure E-19, Router E is running OSPF, and Router A is running RIP. Router C is doing the redistribution between the two protocols. The problem is that the class C network 203.250.15.0 is variably subnetted; it has two different masks, 255.255.255.252 and 255.255.255.192. Example E-24 shows the configuration for Routers A, C, and E, and the routing tables of Router E and Router A.

Example E-24 *Configuration and Routing Tables for the Routers in Figure E-19*

```
Router A#
interface Ethernet0
 ip address 203.250.15.68 255.255.255.192

router rip
 network 203.250.15.0

Router C#
interface Ethernet0
 ip address 203.250.15.67 255.255.255.192

interface Serial1
 ip address 203.250.15.1 255.255.255.252

router ospf 10
 redistribute rip metric 10 subnets
 network 203.250.15.0 0.0.0.255 area 0

router rip
 redistribute ospf 10 metric 2
 network 203.250.15.0

Router E#show ip route
Codes: C - connected, S - static, I - IGRP, R - RIP, M - mobile, B - BGP
       D - EIGRP, EX - EIGRP external, O - OSPF, IA - OSPF inter area
       E1 - OSPF external type 1, E2 - OSPF external type 2, E - EGP
       i - IS-IS, L1 - IS-IS level-1, L2 - IS-IS level-2, * - candidate default
```

continues

Example E-24 *Configuration and Routing Tables for the Routers in Figure E-19 (Continued)*

```
       Gateway of last resort is not set

            203.250.15.0 is variably subnetted, 2 subnets, 2 masks
       C        203.250.15.0 255.255.255.252 is directly connected, Serial0
       O        203.250.15.64 255.255.255.192
                   [110/74] via 203.250.15.1, 00:15:55, Serial0


       Router A#show ip route
       Codes: C - connected, S - static, I - IGRP, R - RIP, M - mobile, B - BGP
              D - EIGRP, EX - EIGRP external, O - OSPF, IA - OSPF inter area
              E1 - OSPF external type 1, E2 - OSPF external type 2, E - EGP
              i - IS-IS, L1 - IS-IS level-1, L2 - IS-IS level-2, * - candidate default

       Gateway of last resort is not set

            203.250.15.0 255.255.255.192 is subnetted, 1 subnets
       C        203.250.15.64 is directly connected, Ethernet0
```

Note that Router E has recognized that 203.250.15.0 has two subnets, whereas Router A thinks that it has only one subnet (the one configured on the interface). Information about subnet 203.250.15.0 255.255.255.252 is lost in the RIP domain. In order to reach that subnet, a static route needs to be configured on Router A, as in Example E-25.

Example E-25 *Configuring a Static Route on Router A in Figure E-19*

```
       Router A#
       interface Ethernet0
        ip address 203.250.15.68 255.255.255.192

       router rip
        network 203.250.15.0

       ip route 203.250.15.0 255.255.255.0 203.250.15.67
```

It is in this way that Router A will be able to reach the other subnets.

Mutual Redistribution

Mutual redistribution between protocols should be done carefully and in a controlled manner. Incorrect configuration could lead to potential looping of routing information. A rule of thumb for mutual redistribution is not to allow information learned from a protocol to be injected back into the same protocol. Passive interfaces and distribute lists should be applied on the redistributing routers. Filtering information with link-state protocols, such as OSPF, is a tricky business. The **distribute-list out** command works on the ASBR to filter redistributed routes into other protocols; **distribute-list in** works on any router to prevent routes from being put in the routing table, but it does not prevent link-state packets from being propagated—downstream routers would still have the routes. It is better to avoid OSPF filtering as much as possible if filters can be applied on the other protocols to prevent loops. Figure E-20 shows an example of a network with RIP and OSPF configured.

Figure E-20 *Example of Mutual Redistribution between OSPF and RIP*

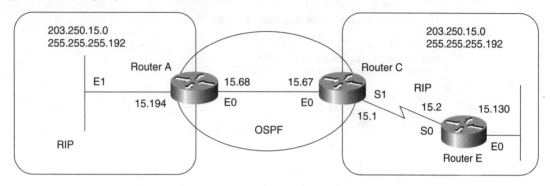

To illustrate, suppose Router A, Router C, and Router E are running RIP. Router A and Router C are also running OSPF. Both Router A and Router C are doing redistribution between RIP and OSPF. Let us assume that you do not want the RIP coming from Router E to be injected into the OSPF domain, so you put a passive interface for RIP on E0 of Router C. However, you have allowed the RIP coming from Router A to be injected into OSPF. Example E-26 shows the outcome. (Do not use this configuration.)

Example E-26 *Configurations and Routing Table for Routers in Figure E-20*

```
Router E#
interface Ethernet0
 ip address 203.250.15.130 255.255.255.192

interface Serial0
 ip address 203.250.15.2 255.255.255.192

router rip
 network 203.250.15.0

Router C#
interface Ethernet0
 ip address 203.250.15.67 255.255.255.192

interface Serial1
 ip address 203.250.15.1 255.255.255.192

router ospf 10
 redistribute rip metric 10 subnets
 network 203.250.15.0 0.0.0.255 area 0

router rip
 redistribute ospf 10 metric 2
```

continues

Example E-26 *Configurations and Routing Table for Routers in Figure E-20 (Continued)*

```
 passive-interface Ethernet0
 network 203.250.15.0

Router A#
interface Ethernet0
 ip address 203.250.15.68 255.255.255.192

router ospf 10
 redistribute rip metric 10 subnets
 network 203.250.15.0 0.0.0.255 area 0

router rip
 redistribute ospf 10 metric 1
 network 203.250.15.0

Router C#show ip route
 Codes: C - connected, S - static, I - IGRP, R - RIP, M - mobile, B - BGP
        D - EIGRP, EX - EIGRP external, O - OSPF, IA - OSPF inter area
        E1 - OSPF external type 1, E2 - OSPF external type 2, E - EGP
        i - IS-IS, L1 - IS-IS level-1, L2 - IS-IS level-2, * - candidate default

Gateway of last resort is not set

     203.250.15.0 255.255.255.192 is subnetted, 4 subnets
C       203.250.15.0 is directly connected, Serial1
C       203.250.15.64 is directly connected, Ethernet0
R       203.250.15.128 [120/1] via 203.250.15.68, 00:01:08, Ethernet0
                       [120/1] via 203.250.15.2, 00:00:11, Serial1
O       203.250.15.192 [110/20] via 203.250.15.68, 00:21:41, Ethernet0
```

Note that Router C has two paths to reach the 203.250.15.128 subnet: Serial1 and Ethernet0 (Ethernet0 is obviously the wrong path). This happened because Router C gave that entry to Router A through OSPF, and Router A gave it back through RIP because Router A did not learn it through RIP. This example is a very small scale of loops that can occur because of an incorrect configuration. In large networks, this situation gets even more aggravated.

In order to fix the situation in the example, you could stop RIP from being sent on Router A's Ethernet0 through a passive interface. This might not be suitable in case some routers on the Ethernet are RIP-only routers. In this case, you could allow Router C to send RIP on the Ethernet; this way, Router A will not send it back on the wire because of split-horizon (this might not work on NBMA media if split horizon is off). Split-horizon does not allow updates to be sent back on the same interface they were learned from (through the same protocol). Another good method is to apply distribute-lists on Router A to deny subnets learned via OSPF from being put back into RIP on the Ethernet. The latter, illustrated in Example E-27, is the one we will be using.

Example E-27 *Configuring Distribute-List on Router A in Figure E-20*

```
Router A#
interface Ethernet0
 ip address 203.250.15.68 255.255.255.192

router ospf 10
 redistribute rip metric 10 subnets
 network 203.250.15.0 0.0.0.255 area 0

router rip
 redistribute ospf 10 metric 1
 network 203.250.15.0
 distribute-list 1 out ospf 10
```

Example E-28 shows the output of Router C's routing table.

Example E-28 *Router C's Routing Table with a Distribute-List on Router A*

```
Router C#show ip route
Codes: C - connected, S - static, I - IGRP, R - RIP, M - mobile, B - BGP
       D - EIGRP, EX - EIGRP external, O - OSPF, IA - OSPF inter area
       E1 - OSPF external type 1, E2 - OSPF external type 2, E - EGP
       i - IS-IS, L1 - IS-IS level-1, L2 - IS-IS level-2, * - candidate default

Gateway of last resort is not set

     203.250.15.0 255.255.255.192 is subnetted, 4 subnets
C       203.250.15.0 is directly connected, Serial1
C       203.250.15.64 is directly connected, Ethernet0
R       203.250.15.128 [120/1] via 203.250.15.2, 00:00:19, Serial1
O       203.250.15.192 [110/20] via 203.250.15.68, 00:21:41, Ethernet0
```

Injecting Defaults into OSPF

An autonomous system boundary router (ASBR) can be forced to generate a default route into the OSPF domain. As discussed earlier, a router becomes an ASBR whenever routes are redistributed into an OSPF domain. However, by default, an ASBR does not generate a default route into the OSPF routing domain.

To have OSPF generate a default route use the following command:

default-information originate [always] [metric *metric-value*] **[metric-type**
type-value] **[route-map** *map-name*]

There are two ways to generate a default. The first is to advertise 0.0.0.0 inside the domain, but only if the ASBR itself already has a default route. The second is to advertise 0.0.0.0, regardless of whether the ASBR has a default route. The latter can be set by adding the keyword **always**—but be careful when using the **always** keyword. If your router advertises a default (0.0.0.0) inside the domain and does not have a default itself or a path to reach the destinations, routing will be broken.

The **metric** and **metric-type** are the cost and type (E1 or E2) assigned to the default route. The **route-map** specifies the set of conditions that need to be satisfied in order for the default to be generated.

Figure E-21 shows an example network using OSPF and RIP.

Figure E-21 *Example of Injecting a Default Route into OSPF*

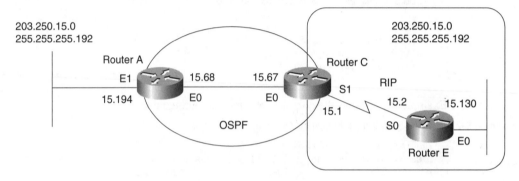

Assume that Router E is injecting a default-route 0.0.0.0 into RIP. Router C will have a gateway of last resort of 203.250.15.2. Router C will not propagate the default to Router A until we configure Router C with a **default-information originate** command as in Example E-29.

Example E-29 *Routing Tables and Configuration for Routers in Figure E-21 when Injecting a Default Route*

```
Router C#show ip route
 Codes: C - connected, S - static, I - IGRP, R - RIP, M - mobile, B - BGP
        D - EIGRP, EX - EIGRP external, O - OSPF, IA - OSPF inter area
        E1 - OSPF external type 1, E2 - OSPF external type 2, E - EGP
        i - IS-IS, L1 - IS-IS level-1, L2 - IS-IS level-2, * - candidate default

 Gateway of last resort is 203.250.15.2 to network 0.0.0.0

      203.250.15.0 255.255.255.192 is subnetted, 4 subnets
 C       203.250.15.0 is directly connected, Serial1
 C       203.250.15.64 is directly connected, Ethernet0
 R       203.250.15.128 [120/1] via 203.250.15.2, 00:00:17, Serial1
 O       203.250.15.192 [110/20] via 203.250.15.68, 2d23, Ethernet0
 R*   0.0.0.0 0.0.0.0 [120/1] via 203.250.15.2, 00:00:17, Serial1
             [120/1] via 203.250.15.68, 00:00:32, Ethernet0

Router C#interface Ethernet0
 ip address 203.250.15.67 255.255.255.192
```

Example E-29 *Routing Tables and Configuration for Routers in Figure E-21 when Injecting a Default Route (Continued)*

```
 interface Serial1
  ip address 203.250.15.1 255.255.255.192

 router ospf 10
  redistribute rip metric 10 subnets
  network 203.250.15.0 0.0.0.255 area 0
  default-information originate metric 10

 router rip
  redistribute ospf 10 metric 2
  passive-interface Ethernet0
  network 203.250.15.0

Router A#show ip route

Codes: C - connected, S - static, I - IGRP, R - RIP, M - mobile, B - BGP
       D - EIGRP, EX - EIGRP external, O - OSPF, IA - OSPF inter area
       E1 - OSPF external type 1, E2 - OSPF external type 2, E - EGP
       i - IS-IS, L1 - IS-IS level-1, L2 - IS-IS level-2, * - candidate default

Gateway of last resort is 203.250.15.67 to network 0.0.0.0

     203.250.15.0 255.255.255.192 is subnetted, 4 subnets
O       203.250.15.0 [110/74] via 203.250.15.67, 2d23, Ethernet0
C       203.250.15.64 is directly connected, Ethernet0
O E2    203.250.15.128 [110/10] via 203.250.15.67, 2d23, Ethernet0
C       203.250.15.192 is directly connected, Ethernet1
O*E2 0.0.0.0 0.0.0.0 [110/10] via 203.250.15.67, 00:00:17, Ethernet0
```

Note that Router A has learned 0.0.0.0 as an external route with metric 10. The gateway of last resort is set to 203.250.15.67, as expected.

OSPF Design Tips

The OSPF RFC (1583) did not specify any guidelines for the number of routers in an area, the number of neighbors per segment, or what is the best way to architect a network. People have different approaches to designing OSPF networks. The important thing to remember is that any protocol can fail under pressure. The idea is not to challenge the protocol, but to work with it in order to get the best behavior. The following sections discuss things to consider.

Number of Routers per Area

Experience has shown that 40 to 50 routers per area is the upper bound for OSPF. That does not mean that networks with 60 or 70 routers in an area won't function, but why experiment with stability if you don't need to? One of the main problems is that administrators let their backbone area grow too large. Try to outline the logical view of the network from the start, and remember that it doesn't hurt to start creating that other area.

Number of Neighbors

The number of routers connected to the same LAN is also important. Each LAN has a DR and BDR that build adjacencies with all other routers. The fewer neighbors that exist on the LAN, the smaller the number of adjacencies a DR or BDR have to build. That depends on how much power your router has. You could always change the OSPF priority to select your DR. Also, if possible, try to avoid having the same router be the DR on more than one segment. If DR selection is based on the highest RID, then one router could accidentally become a DR over all segments it is connected to. This router would be doing extra effort while other routers are idle. Figure E-22 shows two segments with four routers; a different router is chosen as the DR on each segment.

Figure E-22 *Try To Avoid Having the Same Router Be the DR on More than One Segment*

More Neighbors = More Work for DR/BDR

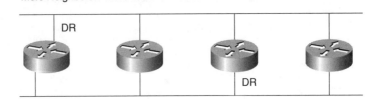

Number of Areas per ABR

ABRs will keep a copy of the database for all areas they service. If, for example, a router is connected to five areas, it will have to keep a list of five different databases. It is better not to overload an ABR. You could always spread the areas over other routers. The ideal design is to have each ABR connected to two areas only: the backbone and another area, with three areas being the upper limit. Figure E-23 shows the difference between one ABR holding five different databases (including area 0) and two ABRs holding three databases each. Again, these are just guidelines. The more areas you configure per ABR, the lower the performance you get. In some cases, the lower performance can be tolerated.

Figure E-23 *Try To Avoid Having One Router Be the ABR for More than Two Areas*

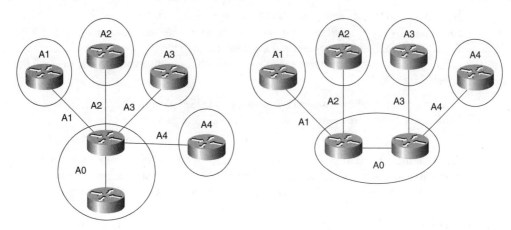

Full Mesh Versus Partial Mesh

Non broadcast Multiaccess (NBMA) clouds such as Frame Relay or X.25, are always a challenge. The combination of low bandwidth and too many link-states is a recipe for problems. A partial mesh topology has proven to behave much better than a full mesh. A carefully laid out point-to-point or point-to-multipoint network works much better than multipoint networks that have to deal with DR issues, as shown in Figure E-24.

Figure E-24 *Partial Mesh Has Proven To Behave Much Better than Full Mesh for OSPF*

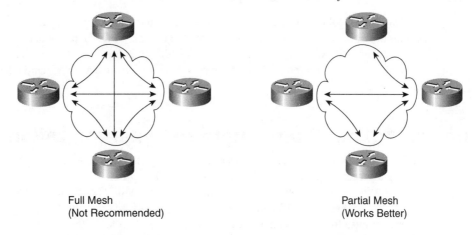

Memory Issues

It is not easy to figure out the memory needed for a particular OSPF configuration. Memory issues usually come up when too many external routes are injected in the OSPF domain. A backbone area with 40 routers and a default route to the outside world would have less memory issues compared with a backbone area with four routers and 33,000 external routes injected into OSPF.

Memory could also be conserved by using a good OSPF design. Summarization at the area border routers and use of stub areas could further minimize the number of routes exchanged.

The total memory used by OSPF is the sum of the memory used in the routing table (**show ip route summary**) and the memory used in the link-state database. The following numbers are a rule-of-thumb estimate. Each entry in the routing table will consume between approximately 200 and 280 bytes, plus 44 bytes per extra path. Each LSA will consume a 100-byte overhead, plus the size of the actual link state advertisement, possibly another 60 to 100 bytes. (For router links, this depends on the number of interfaces on the router.) This should be added to memory used by other processes and by the IOS itself. If you really want to know the exact number, you can do a **show memory** with and without OSPF being turned on. The difference in the processor memory used would be the answer (keep a backup copy of the configurations).

Normally, a routing table with less than 500,000 bytes could be accommodated with 2 to 4 MB of RAM; large networks greater than 500,000 mighy need 8 to 16 MB (maybe 32 to 64 MB if full routes are injected from the Internet).

Summary

The OSPF protocol defined in RFC 1583 provides a high functionality open protocol that enables multiple-vendor networks to communicate using the TCP/IP protocol family. Some of the benefits of OSPF are fast convergence, VLSM, authentication, hierarchical segmentation, route summarization, and aggregation, which are needed to handle large and complicated networks.

Appendix A: Link-State Database Synchronization

As Figure E-25 shows, routers on the same segment go through a series of states before forming a successful adjacency. The neighbor and DR election are done through the Hello protocol. Whenever a router sees itself in his neighbor's hello packet, the state transitions to "2-Way." At that point, DR and BDR election is performed on multi-access segments. A router continues forming an adjacency with a neighbor if either of the two routers is a DR or BDR or they are connected through a point-to-point or virtual link.

Figure E-25 *Router OSPF State Transitions*

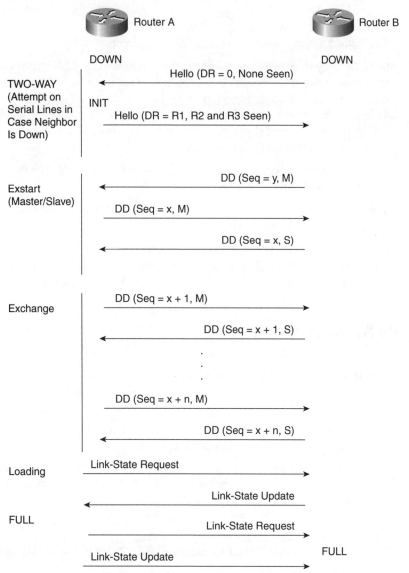

In the *Exstart* state, the two neighbors form a Master/Slave relationship, where they agree on a initial *sequence number*. The sequence number is used to detect old or duplicate link-state advertisements (LSA).

In the *Exchange* state, Database Description Packets (DD) will get exchanged. These are abbreviated link-state advertisements in the form of link-state headers. The header supplies enough information to identify a link. The master node sends DD packets, which are acknowledged with DD packets from the slave node. All adjacencies in exchange state or greater are used by the flooding procedure. These adjacencies are fully capable of transmitting and receiving all types of OSPF routing protocol packets.

In the *Loading* state, link-state request packets are sent to neighbors, asking for more recent advertisements that have been discovered but not yet received. Each router builds a list of required LSAs to bring its adjacency up to date. A *Retransmission* List is maintained to make sure that every LSA is acknowledged. To specify the number of seconds between link-state advertisement retransmissions for the adjacency, you can use the **ip ospf retransmit-interval seconds** command.

Link-state update packets are sent in response to request packets. The link-state update packets will be flooded over all adjacencies.

In the *Full* state, the neighbor routers are fully adjacent. The databases for a common area are an exact match between adjacent routers.

Each LSA has an *age* field that gets periodically incremented while it is contained in the database or as it gets flooded throughout the area. When an LSA reaches a *Maxage*, it gets flushed from the database if that LSA is not on any neighbors retransmission list.

Link-State Advertisements

Link-state advertisements (LSAs) are broken into five types:

- **Router Links** (RL) are generated by all routers. These links describe the state of the router interfaces inside a particular area. These links are only flooded inside the router's area.

- **Network Links** (NL) are generated by a DR of a particular segment; these are an indication of the routers connected to that segment.

- **Summary Links** (SL) are the interarea links (type 3); these links will list the networks inside other areas but still belonging to the autonomous system. Summary links are injected by the ABR from the backbone into other areas and from other areas into the backbone. These links are used for aggregation between areas.

- **ASBR-summary** are the other types of summary links. These are type 4 links that point to the ASBR. This is to make sure that all routers know the way to exit the autonomous system.

- **External Links** (EL) are the last type of links (type 5). ELs are injected by the ASBR into the domain.

Figure E-26 illustrates these five different types of LSAs.

Figure E-26 *The Five Types of Link-State Advertisements*

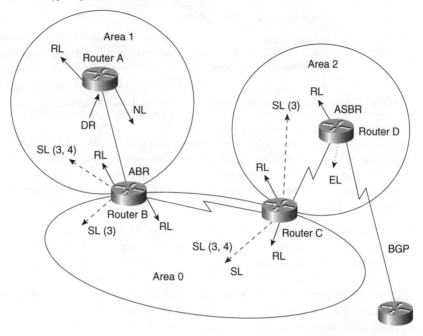

Router A generates a RL into area 1, and it also generates a NL because it happens to be the DR on that particular segment. Router B is an ABR, and it generates a RL into area 1 and area 0. Router B also generates summary links into area 1 and area 0. These links are the list of networks that are interchanged between the two areas. An ASBR summary link is also injected by Router B into area 1. This is an indication of the existence of Router D, the ASBR. Similarly, Router C, which is another ABR, generates a RL for area 0 and area 2, and an SL (3) into area 2 (because it is not announcing any ASBR), and an SL (3,4) into area 0 announcing Router D. Router D generates an RL for area 2 and generates an EL for external routes learned through BGP. The external routers will be flooded all over the domain.

Table E-1 provides a summary of the LSAs.

Table E-1   *Link-State Advertisements*

LS Type	Advertisement Description
1	RL advertisements. Generated by each router for each area it belongs to. They describe the states of the router's link to the area. These are only flooded within a particular area.
2	NL advertisements. Generated by DRs. They describe the set of routers attached to a particular network. Flooded in the area that contains the network.

continues

Table E-1   *Link-State Advertisements (Continued)*

LS Type	Advertisement Description
3 or 4	SL advertisements. Generated by ABRs. They describe inter-area (between areas) routes. Type 3 describes routes to networks, also used for aggregating routes. Type 4 describes routes to ASBR.
5	AS external link advertisements. Originated by ASBR. They describe routes to destinations external to the AS. Flooded all over except stub areas.

If you look at the OSPF database in detail, using **show ip ospf d d**, you will see different keywords, such as *Link-Data*, *Link-ID*, and *Link-state ID*. These terms become confusing because the value of each depends on the link-state type and the link-type. We will go over this terminology and will provide a detailed example on the OSPF database as seen from the router.

The Link-State ID basically defines the identity of the link-state, depending on the LS type. RLs are identified by the router ID (RID) of the router that originated the advertisement. NLs are identified by the relative IP address of the DR. This makes sense because NLs are originated by the Designated Router. SLs (type 3) are identified by the IP network numbers of the destinations they are pointing at. ASBR SLs (SLs type 4) are identified by the RID of the ASBR. Finally, ELs are identified by the IP network numbers of the external destinations they are pointing at. Table E-2 summarizes this information.

Table E-2   *Interpreting Link State ID in **show ip ospf** Commands, Based on Link-State Type*

LS Type	Link-State ID
1	The originating router's router ID (RID)
2	The IP interface address of the network's designated router
3	The destination network number
4	The router ID of the described AS boundary router
5	The external network number

In the high-level view of the database when referencing a router, the Link-State ID is referred to as the Link ID.

The following list describes the different links available:

- **Stub network links**—This term has nothing to do with stub areas. A stub segment is a segment that has one router only attached to it. An Ethernet or Token Ring segment that has one attached router is considered a link to a stub network. A loopback interface is also considered a link to stub network with a 255.255.255.255 mask (Host route).

- **Point-to-point links**—These could be physical or logical (subinterfaces) point-to-point serial link connections. These links could be numbered (an IP address is configured on the link) or unnumbered.

- **Transit links**—These are interfaces connected to networks that have more than one router attached, hence the name transit.

- **Virtual links**—These are logical links that connect areas that do not have physical connections to the backbone. Virtual links are treated as numbered point-to-point links.

The link-ID is an identification of the link itself. This is different for each link type. A transit link is identified by the IP address of the DR on that link. A numbered point-to-point link is identified by the RID of the neighbor router on the point-to-point link. Virtual links are identical to point-to-point links. Finally, links to stub networks are identified by the IP address of the interface to the stub network. Table E-3 summarizes this information.

Table E-3 *Interpreting Link ID in **show ip ospf** Commands, Based on Link Type*

Link Type	Link ID
Point-to-Point	Neighbor Router ID
Link to transit network	Interface address of DR
Link to stub network (In case of loopback, mask is 255.255.255.255)	Network/subnet number
Virtual Link	Neighbor router ID

The Link ID applies to individual links in this case.

The *Link Data* is the *IP address of the link, except for stub network* where the link data is the *network mask*. Table E-4 summarizes this information.

Table E-4 *Interpreting Link Data in **show ip ospf** Commands, Based on Link Type*

Link Type	Link Data
Stub network	Network Mask
Other networks (applies to router links only)	Router's associated IP interface address

Finally, an *Advertising Router* is the RID of the router that has sent the LSA.

OSPF Database Example

Given the topology in Figure E-27 and the configurations and IP route tables in Example E-30, let us look at different ways of understanding the OSPF database.

Figure E-27 *Example OSPF Network*

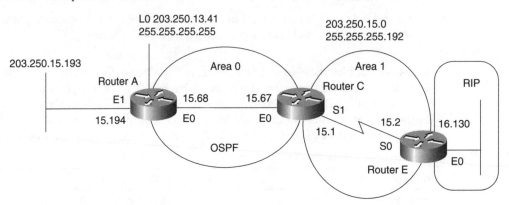

Example E-30 *Configurations and Routing Tables for Routers in Figure E-27*

```
Router A#
interface Loopback0
 ip address 203.250.13.41 255.255.255.255

interface Ethernet0
 ip address 203.250.15.68 255.255.255.192

interface Ethernet1
 ip address 203.250.15.193 255.255.255.192

router ospf 10
 network 203.250.0.0 0.0.255.255 area 0

Router A#show ip route
 Codes: C - connected, S - static, I - IGRP, R - RIP, M - mobile, B - BGP
        D - EIGRP, EX - EIGRP external, O - OSPF, IA - OSPF inter area
        E1 - OSPF external type 1, E2 - OSPF external type 2, E - EGP
        i - IS-IS, L1 - IS-IS level-1, L2 - IS-IS level-2, * - candidate default

Gateway of last resort is 203.250.15.67 to network 0.0.0.0

      203.250.16.0 255.255.255.192 is subnetted, 1 subnets
O E2    203.250.16.128 [110/10] via 203.250.15.67, 00:00:50, Ethernet0
      203.250.13.0 255.255.255.255 is subnetted, 1 subnets
C       203.250.13.41 is directly connected, Loopback0
      203.250.15.0 255.255.255.192 is subnetted, 3 subnets
O IA    203.250.15.0 [110/74] via 203.250.15.67, 00:00:50, Ethernet0
C       203.250.15.64 is directly connected, Ethernet0
```

Example E-30 *Configurations and Routing Tables for Routers in Figure E-27 (Continued)*

```
C       203.250.15.192 is directly connected, Ethernet1
O*E2 0.0.0.0 0.0.0.0 [110/10] via 203.250.15.67, 00:00:50, Ethernet0

Router E#
ip subnet-zero

interface Ethernet0
 ip address 203.250.16.130 255.255.255.192
interface Serial0
 ip address 203.250.15.2 255.255.255.192

router ospf 10
 redistribute rip metric 10 subnets
 network 203.250.15.0 0.0.0.63 area 1
 default-information originate metric 10

router rip
 network 203.250.16.0

ip route 0.0.0.0 0.0.0.0 Ethernet0

Router E#show ip route
 Codes: C - connected, S - static, I - IGRP, R - RIP, M - mobile, B - BGP
        D - EIGRP, EX - EIGRP external, O - OSPF, IA - OSPF inter area
        E1 - OSPF external type 1, E2 - OSPF external type 2, E - EGP
        i - IS-IS, L1 - IS-IS level-1, L2 - IS-IS level-2, * - candidate default

 Gateway of last resort is 0.0.0.0 to network 0.0.0.0

      203.250.16.0 255.255.255.192 is subnetted, 1 subnets
 C       203.250.16.128 is directly connected, Ethernet0
      203.250.13.0 is variably subnetted, 2 subnets, 2 masks
 O IA    203.250.13.41 255.255.255.255
             [110/75] via 203.250.15.1, 00:16:31, Serial0
      203.250.15.0 255.255.255.192 is subnetted, 3 subnets
 C       203.250.15.0 is directly connected, Serial0
 O IA    203.250.15.64 [110/74] via 203.250.15.1, 00:16:31, Serial0
 O IA    203.250.15.192 [110/84] via 203.250.15.1, 00:16:31, Serial0
 S*    0.0.0.0 0.0.0.0 is directly connected, Ethernet0

Router C#
ip subnet-zero

interface Ethernet0
 ip address 203.250.15.67 255.255.255.192

interface Serial1
 ip address 203.250.15.1 255.255.255.192

router ospf 10
 network 203.250.15.64 0.0.0.63 area 0
 network 203.250.15.0 0.0.0.63 area 1
```

continues

Example E-30 *Configurations and Routing Tables for Routers in Figure E-27 (Continued)*

```
Router C#show ip route
  Codes: C - connected, S - static, I - IGRP, R - RIP, M - mobile, B - BGP
         D - EIGRP, EX - EIGRP external, O - OSPF, IA - OSPF inter area
         E1 - OSPF external type 1, E2 - OSPF external type 2, E - EGP
         i - IS-IS, L1 - IS-IS level-1, L2 - IS-IS level-2, * - candidate default

Gateway of last resort is 203.250.15.2 to network 0.0.0.0

     203.250.16.0 255.255.255.192 is subnetted, 1 subnets
O E2    203.250.16.128 [110/10] via 203.250.15.2, 04:49:05, Serial1
     203.250.13.0 255.255.255.255 is subnetted, 1 subnets
O       203.250.13.41 [110/11] via 203.250.15.68, 04:49:06, Ethernet0
     203.250.15.0 255.255.255.192 is subnetted, 3 subnets
C       203.250.15.0 is directly connected, Serial1
C       203.250.15.64 is directly connected, Ethernet0
O       203.250.15.192 [110/20] via 203.250.15.68, 04:49:06, Ethernet0
O*E2 0.0.0.0 0.0.0.0 [110/10] via 203.250.15.2, 04:49:06, Serial1
```

General View of the Database

Example E-31 is a general look at the whole OSPF database. The database is listed according to the areas. In this case, we are looking at router C's database, which is an ABR. Both area 1 and area 0's databases are listed. Area 1 is composed of RLs and SLs. No network links exist because no DR exists on any of the segments in area 1. No Summary ASBR links exist in area 1 because the only ASBR happens to be in area 0. ELs do not belong to any particular area because they are flooded all over. Note that all the links are the cumulative links collected from all routers in an area.

Example E-31 *OSPF Database on Router C in Figure E-27*

```
Router C#show ip ospf database

        OSPF Router with ID (203.250.15.67) (Process ID 10)

             Router Link States (Area 1)

Link ID          ADV Router       Age    Seq#        Checksum Link count
203.250.15.67    203.250.15.67    48     0x80000008 0xB112    2
203.250.16.130   203.250.16.130   212    0x80000006 0x3F44    2

             Summary Net Link States (Area 1)

Link ID          ADV Router       Age    Seq#        Checksum
203.250.13.41    203.250.15.67    602    0x80000002 0x90AA
203.250.15.64    203.250.15.67    620    0x800000E9 0x3E3C
203.250.15.192   203.250.15.67    638    0x800000E5 0xA54E

             Router Link States (Area 0)
```

Example E-31 *OSPF Database on Router C in Figure E-27 (Continued)*

```
Link ID           ADV Router        Age    Seq#        Checksum Link count
203.250.13.41     203.250.13.41     179    0x80000029  0x9ADA   3
203.250.15.67     203.250.15.67     675    0x800001E2  0xDD23   1


                  Net Link States (Area 0)


Link ID           ADV Router        Age    Seq#        Checksum
203.250.15.68     203.250.13.41     334    0x80000001  0xB6B5

                  Summary Net Link States (Area 0)


Link ID           ADV Router        Age    Seq#        Checksum
203.250.15.0      203.250.15.67     792    0x80000002  0xAEBD


                  Summary ASB Link States (Area 0)


Link ID           ADV Router        Age    Seq#        Checksum
203.250.16.130    203.250.15.67     579    0x80000001  0xF9AF


                  AS External Link States


Link ID           ADV Router        Age    Seq#        Checksum Tag
0.0.0.0           203.250.16.130    1787   0x80000001  0x98CE   10
203.250.16.128    203.250.16.130    5      0x80000002  0x93C4   0
```

We will mainly concentrate on the database in area 0. The Link-ID indicated here is actually the Link-State ID. This is a representation of the whole router, not a particular link. This is a bit confusing, but just remember that this high-level Link-ID (should be Link-State ID) represents the whole router and not just a link.

Router Links

In Example E-32, we start with the router links.

Example E-32 *Router Link States for Area 0 on Router C in Figure E-27*

```
                  Router Link States (Area 0)

Link ID           ADV Router        Age    Seq#        Checksum Link count
203.250.13.41     203.250.13.41     179    0x80000029  0x9ADA   3
203.250.15.67     203.250.15.67     675    0x800001E2  0xDD23   1
```

There are two entries listed for 203.250.13.41 and 203.250.15.67 ; these are the RIDs of the two routers in area 0. The number of links in area 0 for each router is also indicated. Router A has three links to area 0, and Router C has one link. Example E-33 provides a detailed view of router C's router links (in area 1).

Example E-33 *Detailed Router Link States for Router C Area 1 in Figure E-27*

```
Router C#show ip ospf database router 203.250.15.67

        OSPF Router with ID (203.250.15.67) (Process ID 10)

                   Router Link States (Area 1)
    LS age: 1169
    Options: (No TOS-capability)
    LS Type: Router Links
    Link State ID: 203.250.15.67
    Advertising Router: 203.250.15.67
    LS Seq Number: 80000008
    Checksum: 0xB112
    Length: 48
    Area Border Router
     Number of Links: 2

       Link connected to: another Router (point-to-point)
        (Link ID) Neighboring Router ID: 203.250.16.130
        (Link Data) Router Interface address: 203.250.15.1
         Number of TOS metrics: 0
          TOS 0 Metrics: 64

       Link connected to: a Stub Network
        (Link ID) Network/subnet number: 203.250.15.0
        (Link Data) Network Mask: 255.255.255.192
         Number of TOS metrics: 0
          TOS 0 Metrics: 64
```

One thing to note here is that OSPF generates an extra stub link for each point-to-point interface. Do not get confused if you see the link count larger than the number of physical interfaces. Example E-34 is a continuation of the output in Example E-33 and provides a detailed view of router C's router links (in area 0).

Example E-34 *Detailed Router Link States for Router C Area 0 in Figure E-27*

```
                   Router Link States (Area 0)

    LS age: 1227
    Options: (No TOS-capability)
    LS Type: Router Links
    Link State ID: 203.250.15.67
    Advertising Router: 203.250.15.67
    LS Seq Number: 80000003
    Checksum: 0xA041
    Length: 36
    Area Border Router
     Number of Links: 1

       Link connected to: a Transit Network
        (Link ID) Designated Router address: 203.250.15.68
```

Example E-34 *Detailed Router Link States for Router C Area 0 in Figure E-27 (Continued)*

```
(Link Data) Router Interface address: 203.250.15.67
  Number of TOS metrics: 0
   TOS 0 Metrics: 10
```

Note that the Link ID is equal to the IP address (not the RID) of the attached DR; in this case, it is 203.250.15.68. The Link Data is router C's own IP address.

Network Links

In Example E-35, we again see the network links part of the OSPF database for area 0 for router C.

Example E-35 *Network Link States for Area 0 on Router C in Figure E-27*

```
               Net Link States (Area 0)

  Link ID          ADV Router      Age    Seq#        Checksum
  203.250.15.68    203.250.13.41   334    0x80000001  0xB6B5
```

One network link is listed, indicated by the interface IP address (not the RID) of the DR—in this case, 203.250.15.68. Example E-36 presents a detailed view of this entry.

Example E-36 *Detailed Network Link States for Area 0 for Router C in Figure E-27*

```
Router C#show ip ospf database network

        OSPF Router with ID (203.250.15.67) (Process ID 10)

               Net Link States (Area 0)

  Routing Bit Set on this LSA
  LS age: 1549
  Options: (No TOS-capability)
  LS Type: Network Links
  Link State ID: 203.250.15.68 (address of Designated Router)
  Advertising Router: 203.250.13.41
  LS Seq Number: 80000002
  Checksum: 0xB4B6
  Length: 32
  Network Mask: 255.255.255.192

        Attached Router: 203.250.13.41
        Attached Router: 203.250.15.67
```

Note that the network link lists the RIDs of the routers attached to the transit network; in this case, the RIDs of router A and router C are listed.

Summary Links

In Example E-37, we again see the summary network links part of the ospf database for area 0 for router C.

Example E-37 *Summary Network Link States for Area 0 on Router C in Figure E-27*

```
                   Summary Net Link States (Area 0)

   Link ID       ADV Router      Age    Seq#       Checksum
   203.250.15.0  203.250.15.67   792    0x80000002 0xAEBD
```

Area 0 has one summary link represented by the IP network address of the link 203.250.15.0. This link was injected by the ABR router C from area 1 into area 0. Example E-38 shows a detailed view of this summary link (summary links for area 1 are not listed here).

Example E-38 *Detailed Summary Network Link States for Area 0 for Router C in Figure E-27*

```
   Router C#show ip ospf database summary (area 1 is not listed)

                  Summary Net Link States (Area 0)

     LS age: 615
     Options: (No TOS-capability)
     LS Type: Summary Links(Network)
     Link State ID: 203.250.15.0 (summary Network Number)
     Advertising Router: 203.250.15.67
     LS Seq Number: 80000003
     Checksum: 0xACBE
     Length: 28
     Network Mask: 255.255.255.192 TOS: 0  Metric: 64
```

Summary ASBR Links

In Example E-39, we again see the summary ASB links part of the OSPF database for area 0 for Router C.

Example E-39 *Summary ASB Link States for Area 0 on Router C in Figure E-27*

```
                   Summary ASB Link States (Area 0)

   Link ID        ADV Router      Age    Seq#       Checksum
   203.250.16.130 203.250.15.67   579    0x80000001 0xF9AF
```

Example E-39 provides an indication of who the ASBR is. In this case, the ASBR is router E represented by its RID 203.250.16.130. The advertising router for this entry into area 0 is router C with RID 203.250.15.67. Example E-40 shows a detailed view of the summary ASBR entry.

Example E-40 *Detailed Summary ASB Link States for Area 0 for Router C in Figure E-27*

```
Router C#show ip ospf database asbr-summary

        OSPF Router with ID (203.250.15.67) (Process ID 10)

              Summary ASB Link States (Area 0)

    LS age: 802
    Options: (No TOS-capability)
    LS Type: Summary Links(AS Boundary Router)
    Link State ID: 203.250.16.130 (AS Boundary Router address)
    Advertising Router: 203.250.15.67
    LS Seq Number: 80000003
    Checksum: 0xF5B1
    Length: 28
    Network Mask: 0.0.0.0 TOS: 0  Metric: 64
```

External Links

In Example E-41, we again see the external link states part of the ospf database on router C.

Example E-41 *External Link States on Router C in Figure E-27*

```
              AS External Link States

    Link ID       ADV Router      Age    Seq#       Checksum Tag
    0.0.0.0       203.250.16.130  1787   0x80000001 0x98CE   10
    203.250.16.128 203.250.16.130 5      0x80000002 0x93C4   0
```

We have two external Links: the first is the 0.0.0.0 injected into OSPF via the **default-information originate** command, and the other entry is network 203.250.16.128, which is injected into OSPF by redistribution. The router advertising these networks is 203.250.16.130, the RID of router E. Example E-42 shows a detailed view of the external routes.

Example E-42 *Detailed External Link States on Router C in Figure E-27*

```
Router C#show ip ospf database external

        OSPF Router with ID (203.250.15.67) (Process ID 10)

              AS External Link States

    Routing Bit Set on this LSA
    LS age: 208
    Options: (No TOS-capability)
    LS Type: AS External Link
    Link State ID: 0.0.0.0 (External Network Number )
```

continues

Example E-42 *Detailed External Link States on Router C in Figure E-27 (Continued)*

```
        Advertising Router: 203.250.16.130
        LS Seq Number: 80000002
        Checksum: 0x96CF
        Length: 36
        Network Mask: 0.0.0.0
              Metric Type: 2 (Larger than any link state path)
              TOS: 0
              Metric: 10
           Forward Address: 0.0.0.0
           External Route Tag: 10
      Routing Bit Set on this LSA
       LS age: 226
       Options: (No TOS-capability)
       LS Type: AS External Link
       Link State ID: 203.250.16.128 (External Network Number)
       Advertising Router: 203.250.16.130
       LS Seq Number: 80000002
       Checksum: 0x93C4
       Length: 36
       Network Mask: 255.255.255.192
              Metric Type: 2 (Larger than any link state path)
              TOS: 0
              Metric: 10
           Forward Address: 0.0.0.0
           External Route Tag: 0
```

Please note the forward address. Whenever this address is 0.0.0.0, it indicates that the external routes are reachable via the advertising router—in this case, 203.250.16.130. This is why the identity of the ASBR is injected by ABRs into other areas using ASBR summary links.

This forward address is not always 0.0.0.0. In some cases, it could be the IP address of another router on the same segment. Figure E-28 illustrates this situation.

Figure E-28 *Example of when OSPF Forwarding Address Is Not 0.0.0.0*

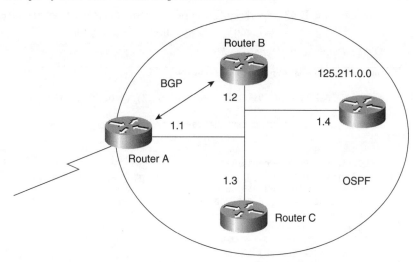

In the network in Figure E-28, Router B is running BGP with Router A and OSPF with the rest of the domain. Router A is not running OSPF. Router B is redistributing BGP routes into OSPF. According to OSPF, Router B is an ASBR advertising external routes. The forwarding address, in this case, is set to 125.211.1.1 and not to the advertising router (0.0.0.0) router B. This makes sense because there is no need to make the extra hop.

NOTE   An important thing to remember is that routers inside the OSPF domain should be able to reach the forwarding address through OSPF in order for the external routes to be put in the IP routing table. If the forwarding address is reached through some other protocol or not accessible, the external entries would be in the database but not in the IP routing table.

Another situation would arise if both router B and router C are ASBRs (router C is also running BGP with router A). In this situation, in order to eliminate the duplication of the effort, one of the two routers will not advertise (will flush) the external routes. The router with the higher RID will win.

The Full Database

Finally, Example E-43 provides a listing of the whole database as an exercise. You should now be able to go over each entry and explain what is going on.

Example E-43 *Full OSPF Database on Router C in Figure E-27*

```
Router C#show ip ospf database router

          OSPF Router with ID (203.250.15.67) (Process ID 10)

                Router Link States (Area 1)

    LS age: 926
    Options: (No TOS-capability)
    LS Type: Router Links
    Link State ID: 203.250.15.67
    Advertising Router: 203.250.15.67
    LS Seq Number: 80000035
    Checksum: 0x573F
    Length: 48
    Area Border Router
     Number of Links: 2

      Link connected to: another Router (point-to-point)
        (Link ID) Neighboring Router ID: 203.250.16.130
        (Link Data) Router Interface address: 203.250.15.1
         Number of TOS metrics: 0
          TOS 0 Metrics: 64

      Link connected to: a Stub Network
        (Link ID) Network/subnet number: 203.250.15.0
        (Link Data) Network Mask: 255.255.255.192
         Number of TOS metrics: 0
          TOS 0 Metrics: 64

    Routing Bit Set on this LSA
    LS age: 958
    Options: (No TOS-capability)
    LS Type: Router Links
    Link State ID: 203.250.16.130
    Advertising Router: 203.250.16.130
    LS Seq Number: 80000038
    Checksum: 0xDA76
    Length: 48
    AS Boundary Router
     Number of Links: 2

      Link connected to: another Router (point-to-point)
        (Link ID) Neighboring Router ID: 203.250.15.67
        (Link Data) Router Interface address: 203.250.15.2
         Number of TOS metrics: 0
          TOS 0 Metrics: 64
```

Example E-43 *Full OSPF Database on Router C in Figure E-27 (Continued)*

```
          Link connected to: a Stub Network
           (Link ID) Network/subnet number: 203.250.15.0
           (Link Data) Network Mask: 255.255.255.192
            Number of TOS metrics: 0
             TOS 0 Metrics: 64

                    Router Link States (Area 0)

      Routing Bit Set on this LSA
      LS age: 1107
      Options: (No TOS-capability)
      LS Type: Router Links
      Link State ID: 203.250.13.41
      Advertising Router: 203.250.13.41
      LS Seq Number: 8000002A
      Checksum: 0xC0B0
      Length: 60
      AS Boundary Router
       Number of Links: 3

         Link connected to: a Stub Network
          (Link ID) Network/subnet number: 203.250.13.41
          (Link Data) Network Mask: 255.255.255.255
           Number of TOS metrics: 0
            TOS 0 Metrics: 1

         Link connected to: a Stub Network
          (Link ID) Network/subnet number: 203.250.15.192
          (Link Data) Network Mask: 255.255.255.192
           Number of TOS metrics: 0
            TOS 0 Metrics: 10

         Link connected to: a Transit Network
          (Link ID) Designated Router address: 203.250.15.68
          (Link Data) Router Interface address: 203.250.15.68
           Number of TOS metrics: 0
            TOS 0 Metrics: 10

      LS age: 1575
      Options: (No TOS-capability)
      LS Type: Router Links
      Link State ID: 203.250.15.67
      Advertising Router: 203.250.15.67
      LS Seq Number: 80000028
      Checksum: 0x5666
      Length: 36
      Area Border Router
       Number of Links: 1

         Link connected to: a Transit Network
          (Link ID) Designated Router address: 203.250.15.68
          (Link Data) Router Interface address: 203.250.15.67
```

continues

Example E-43 *Full OSPF Database on Router C in Figure E-27 (Continued)*

```
              Number of TOS metrics: 0
              TOS 0 Metrics: 10


Router C#show ip ospf database network

          OSPF Router with ID (203.250.15.67) (Process ID 10)

                  Net Link States (Area 0)

    Routing Bit Set on this LSA
    LS age: 1725
    Options: (No TOS-capability)
    LS Type: Network Links
    Link State ID: 203.250.15.68 (address of Designated Router)
    Advertising Router: 203.250.13.41
    LS Seq Number: 80000026
    Checksum: 0x6CDA
    Length: 32
    Network Mask: 255.255.255.192
          Attached Router: 203.250.13.41
          Attached Router: 203.250.15.67


Router C#show ip ospf database summary

          OSPF Router with ID (203.250.15.67) (Process ID 10)

                  Summary Net Link States (Area 1)
    LS age: 8
    Options: (No TOS-capability)
    LS Type: Summary Links(Network)
    Link State ID: 203.250.13.41 (summary Network Number)
    Advertising Router: 203.250.15.67
    LS Seq Number: 80000029
    Checksum: 0x42D1
    Length: 28
    Network Mask: 255.255.255.255 TOS: 0  Metric: 11


    LS age: 26
    Options: (No TOS-capability)
    LS Type: Summary Links(Network)
    Link State ID: 203.250.15.64 (summary Network Number)
    Advertising Router: 203.250.15.67
    LS Seq Number: 80000030
    Checksum: 0xB182
    Length: 28
    Network Mask: 255.255.255.192 TOS: 0  Metric: 10


    LS age: 47
    Options: (No TOS-capability)
    LS Type: Summary Links(Network)
    Link State ID: 203.250.15.192 (summary Network Number)
    Advertising Router: 203.250.15.67
```

Example E-43 *Full OSPF Database on Router C in Figure E-27 (Continued)*

```
              LS Seq Number: 80000029
              Checksum: 0x1F91
              Length: 28
              Network Mask: 255.255.255.192 TOS: 0  Metric: 20

                          Summary Net Link States (Area 0)

              LS age: 66
              Options: (No TOS-capability)
              LS Type: Summary Links(Network)
              Link State ID: 203.250.15.0 (summary Network Number)
              Advertising Router: 203.250.15.67
              LS Seq Number: 80000025
              Checksum: 0x68E0
              Length: 28
              Network Mask: 255.255.255.192 TOS: 0  Metric: 64

Router C#show ip ospf asbr-summary

            OSPF Router with ID (203.250.15.67) (Process ID 10)

                          Summary ASB Link States (Area 0)

              LS age: 576
              Options: (No TOS-capability)
              LS Type: Summary Links(AS Boundary Router)
              Link State ID: 203.250.16.130 (AS Boundary Router address)
              Advertising Router: 203.250.15.67
              LS Seq Number: 80000024
              Checksum: 0xB3D2
              Length: 28
              Network Mask: 0.0.0.0 TOS: 0  Metric: 64

Router C#show ip ospf database external

            OSPF Router with ID (203.250.15.67) (Process ID 10)

                          AS External Link States

              Routing Bit Set on this LSA
              LS age: 305
              Options: (No TOS-capability)
              LS Type: AS External Link
              Link State ID: 0.0.0.0 (External Network Number)
              Advertising Router: 203.250.16.130
              LS Seq Number: 80000001
              Checksum: 0x98CE
              Length: 36
              Network Mask: 0.0.0.0
                    Metric Type: 2 (Larger than any link state path)
                    TOS: 0
                    Metric: 10
```

continues

Example E-43 *Full OSPF Database on Router C in Figure E-27 (Continued)*

```
                          Forward Address: 0.0.0.0
                          External Route Tag: 10


               Routing Bit Set on this LSA
               LS age: 653
               Options: (No TOS-capability)
               LS Type: AS External Link
               Link State ID: 203.250.16.128 (External Network Number)
               Advertising Router: 203.250.16.130
               LS Seq Number: 80000024
               Checksum: 0x4FE6
               Length: 36
               Network Mask: 255.255.255.192
                          Metric Type: 2 (Larger than any link state path)
                          TOS: 0
                          Metric: 10
                          Forward Address: 0.0.0.0
                          External Route Tag: 0
```

Appendix B: OSPF and IP Multicast Addressing

OSPF used IP multicast to exchange hello packets and link state updates. An IP multicast address is implemented using class D addresses. As shown in Figure E-29, the most significant four bits in a class D address are set to binary 1110; thus, a class D address ranges from 224.0.0.0 to 239.255.255.255.

Figure E-29 *The Most Significant Four Bits for a Class D IP Address*

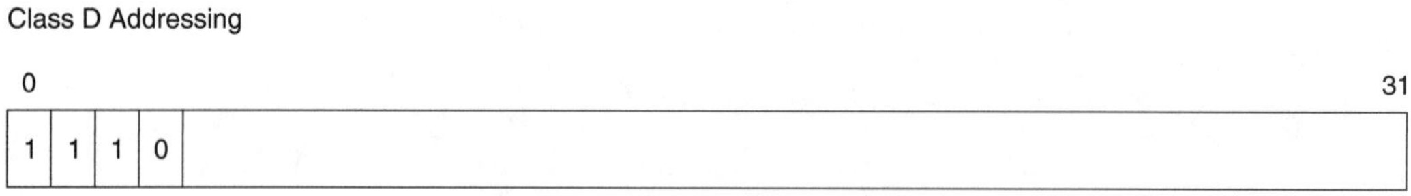

Class D Addressing

Some special IP multicast addresses are reserved for OSPF:

- **224.0.0.5**—All OSPF routers should be able to transmit and listen to this address.
- **224.0.0.6**—All DR and BDR routers should be able to transmit and listen to this address.

The mapping between IP multicast addresses and MAC addresses has the following rule:

For multi-access networks that support multicast, the low order 23 bits of the IP address are used as the low order bits of the MAC multicast address 01-00-5E-00-00-00.

For example:

224.0.0.5 would be mapped to 01-00-5E-00-00-05 and
224.0.0.6 would be mapped to 01-00-5E-00-00-06

OSPF uses broadcast on Token Ring networks.

Appendix C: Variable Length Subnet Masks

Table E-5 provides a binary to decimal conversion chart, useful in IP addressing and Variable Length Subnet Masks (VLSM) calculations.

Table E-5   *Binary/Decimal Conversion Chart*

	0000		0001		0010		0011		0100		0101		0110		0111
0	0000	16	0000	32	0000	48	0000	64	0000	80	000 0	96	0000	112	0000
1	0001	17	0001	33	0001	49	0001	65	0001	81	000 1	97	0001	113	0001
2	0010	18	0010	34	0010	50	0010	66	0010	82	001 0	98	0010	114	0010
	0000		0001		0010		0011		0100		0101		0110		0111
3	0011	19	0011	35	0011	51	0011	67	0011	83	001 1	99	0011	115	0011
4	0100	20	0100	36	0100	52	0100	68	0100	84	010 0	100	0100	116	0100
5	0101	21	0101	37	0101	53	0101	69	0101	85	010 1	101	0101	117	0101
6	0110	22	0110	38	0110	54	0110	70	0110	86	011 0	102	0110	118	0110
7	0111	23	0111	39	0111	55	0111	71	0111	87	011 1	103	0111	119	0111
8	1000	24	1000	40	1000	56	1000	72	1000	88	100 0	104	1000	120	1000
9	1001	25	1001	41	1001	57	1001	73	1001	89	100 1	105	1001	121	1001
10	1010	26	1010	42	1010	58	1010	74	1010	90	10 10	106	1010	122	1010
11	1011	27	1011	43	1011	59	1011	75	1011	91	10 11	107	1011	123	1011
12	1100	28	1100	44	1100	60	1100	76	1100	92	11 00	108	1100	124	1100
13	1101	29	1101	45	1101	61	1101	77	1101	93	11 01	109	1101	125	1101
14	1110	30	1110	46	1110	62	1110	78	1110	94	11 10	110	1110	126	1110
15	1111	31	1111	47	1111	63	1111	79	1111	95	11 11	111	1111	127	1111
	1000		1001		1010		1011		1100		1101		1110		1111
128	0000	144	0000	160	0000	176	0000	192	0000	208	0000	224	0000	240	0000
129	0001	145	0001	161	0001	177	0001	193	0001	209	0001	225	0001	241	0001
130	0010	146	0010	162	0010	178	0010	194	0010	210	0010	226	0010	242	0010
131	0011	147	0011	163	0011	179	0011	195	0011	211	0011	227	0011	243	0011

continues

Table E-5 *Binary/Decimal Conversion Chart (Continued)*

132	0100	148	0100	164	0100	180	0100	196	0100	212	0100	228	0100	244	0100
133	0101	149	0101	165	0101	181	0101	197	0101	213	0101	229	0101	245	0101
134	0110	150	0110	166	0110	182	0110	198	0110	214	0110	230	0110	246	0110
135	0111	151	0111	167	0111	183	0111	199	0111	215	0111	231	0111	247	0111
136	1000	152	1000	168	1000	184	1000	200	1000	216	1000	232	1000	248	1000
137	1001	153	1001	169	1001	185	1001	201	1001	217	1001	233	1001	249	1001
138	1010	154	1010	170	1010	186	1010	202	1010	218	1010	234	1010	250	1010
139	1011	155	1011	171	1011	187	1011	203	1011	219	1011	235	1011	251	1011
140	1100	156	1100	172	1100	188	1100	204	1100	220	1100	236	1100	252	1100
141	1101	157	1101	173	1101	189	1101	205	1101	221	1101	237	1101	253	1101
142	1110	158	1110	174	1110	190	1110	206	1110	222	1110	238	1110	254	1110
143	1111	159	1111	175	1111	191	1111	207	1111	223	1111	239	1111	255	1111

The idea behind VLSM is to offer more flexibility in dealing with dividing a major net into multiple subnets and still being able to maintain an adequate number of hosts in each subnet. Without VLSM, only one subnet mask can be applied to a major network. This would restrict the number of hosts given the number of subnets required. If we pick the mask so that we have enough subnets, we wouldn't be able to allocate enough hosts in each subnet. The same is true for the hosts; a mask that allows enough hosts might not provide enough subnet space.

For example, suppose you were assigned a class C network 192.213.11.0 and you needed to divide that network into three subnets with 100 hosts in one subnet and 50 hosts for each of the remaining subnets. Ignoring the two end limits of 0 and 255, you theoretically have 256 addresses (192.213.11.0–192.213.11.255) available to you. This cannot be done without VLSM. Figure E-30 shows an example network, with the maximum number of host addresses on each network noted.

Figure E-30 *Example Network Requiring VLSM*

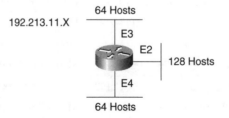

There are a handful of subnet masks that can be used; remember that a mask should have a contiguous number of 1s starting from the left and the rest of the bits being all 0s. The last octet of the available subnet mask could be as follows:

-252 (1111 1100) The address space is divided into 64.
-248 (1111 1000) The address space is divided into 32.
-240 (1111 0000) The address space is divided into 16.
-224 (1110 0000) The address space is divided into 8.
-192 (1100 0000) The address space is divided into 4.
-128 (1000 0000) The address space is divided into 2.

Without VLSM, we have the choice of using mask 255.255.255.128 and dividing the addresses into two subnets with 128 hosts each or using 255.255.255.192 and dividing the space into four subnets with 64 hosts each. This would not meet the requirement. By using multiple masks, we can use mask 128 and further subnet the second chunk of addresses with mask 192. Figure E-31 shows how we have divided the address space accordingly.

Figure E-31 *Division of the Address Space for the Network in Figure E-30, Using VLSM*

VLSM

128 Addresses (E2) (Mask 255.255.255.128)	
64 Addresses (E3) (Mask 255.255.255.192)	64 Addresses (E4) (Mask 255.255.255.192)

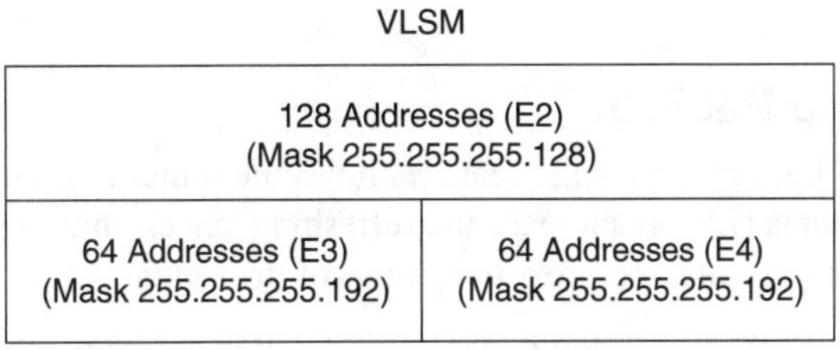

Now, be careful in allocating the IP addresses to each mask. After you assign an IP address to the router or to a host, you have used up the whole subnet for that segment. For example, if you assign 192.213.11.10 255.255.255.128 to E2, the whole range of addresses between 192.213.11.0 and 192.214.11.127 is consumed by E2. Likewise, if you assign 192.213.11.160 255.255.255.128 to E2, the whole range of addresses between 192.213.11.128 and 192.213.11.255 is consumed by the E2 segment.

Example E-44 is an illustration of how the router will interpret these addresses. Please remember that any time you are using a mask different than the natural mask—for instance, when you are subnetting—the router will complain if the combination IP address and mask will result in a subnet zero. To resolve this issue, use the command **ip subnet-zero** on the router.

Example E-44 *Configuration of the Router in Figure E-30, Using VLSM*

```
Router A#
ip subnet-zero
interface Ethernet2
  ip address 192.213.11.10 255.255.255.128
interface Ethernet3
```

continues

Example E-44 *Configuration of the Router in Figure E-30, Using VLSM*

```
 ip address 192.213.11.160 255.255.255.192
interface Ethernet4
 ip address 192.213.11.226 255.255.255.192

Router A#show ip route connected
     192.213.11.0 is variably subnetted, 3 subnets, 2 masks
C       192.213.11.0 255.255.255.128 is directly connected, Ethernet2
C       192.213.11.128 255.255.255.192 is directly connected, Ethernet3
C       192.213.11.192 255.255.255.192 is directly connected, Ethernet4
```

Appendix D: OSPF New 12.0 Enhancements

Since the initial publication of this OSPF Design Guide, there have been some IOS 12.0 enhancements to OSPF, including:

- OSPF LSA group pacing
- OSPF point-to-multipoint features

OSPF LSA Group Pacing

The OSPF LSA group pacing feature allows the router to group together OSPF link-state advertisements (LSAs) and pace the refreshing, checksumming, and aging functions. The group pacing results in more efficient use of the router.

Prior to the LSA group pacing feature, Cisco IOS software would perform refreshing on a single timer, and checksumming and aging on another timer. In the case of refreshing, for example, the software would scan the whole database every 30 minutes, refreshing every LSA the router generated, no mater how old it was.

This problem is now solved by each LSA having its own timer. Again using the example of refreshing, each LSA gets refreshed when it is 30 minutes old, independent of other LSAs. So, CPU is used only when necessary. However, LSAs being refreshed at frequent, random intervals would require many packets for the few refreshed LSAs the router must send out. That would be inefficient use of bandwitdth. Therefore, the router delays the LSA refresh function for an interval of time instead of performing it when the individual timers are reached. The accumulated LSAs constitute a group, which is then refreshed and sent out in one packet or more. Thus, the refresh packets are paced, as are the checksumming and aging. The pacing interval is configurable; it defaults to 4 minutes, which is randomized to further avoid synchronization.

The router groups together OSPF LSAs and paces the refreshing, checksumming, and aging functions so that sudden hits on CPU usage and network resources are avoided. This feature is most beneficial to large OSPF networks.

OSPF Point-to-Multipoint

OSPF has two new features related to point-to-multipoint networks. One feature applies to broadcast networks; the other feature applies to nonbroadcast networks.

- On point-to-multipoint broadcase networks, there is no need to specifiy neighbors. However, you can specify neighbors with the **neighbor** command, in which case, you should specify a cost to that neighbor.

- On point-to-multipoint nonbroadcast networks, you now use the **neighbor** command to identify neighbors. Assigning a cost to a neighbor is optional.

Before this feature, some OSPF point-to-multipoing protocol traffic was treated as multicast traffic. Therefore, the **neighbor** command was not needed for point-to-multipoing interfaces because multicast took care of the traffic. Hellos, updates, and acknowledgments were sent using multicast. In particular, multicast hellos discovered all neighbors dynamically. However, some customers were using point-to-multipoint on nonbroadcast media (such as classic IP over ATM), so their routers could not dynamically discover their neighbors. This feature allows the **neighbor** command to be used on point-to-multipoint interfaces.

On any point-to-multipoint interface (broadcast or not), Cisco IOS software assumed the cost to each neighbor was equal. The cost was configured with the **ip ospf cost** command. In reality, the bandwidth to each neighbor is different, so the cost should be different. With this feature, you can configure a separate cost to each neighbor. This feature applies to point-to-multipoint interfaces only.

This feature allows you to configure neighbors on point-to-multipoint interfaces and assign a cost to each neighbor. These capabilities allow the router to dynamically discover neighbors over nonbroadcast media and to prefer some routes over others by assigning different costs to neighbors.

INDEX

Numerics

1-tier hierarchical model, 25–26
2B+D, 328
2-tier hierarchical model, 27
3-tier hierarchical model, 17
    access tier, 19
    core tier, 18
    distribution tier, 19
    implementing, 23–24
    manageability, 25
    predictability, 24
    protocol support, 24
    scalability, 23
    troubleshooting, 24
80/20 rule, 49
802.1Q, 431

A

AAL (ATM Adaptation Layer), 355
    applications, 356–359
    SAR (segmentation and re-assembly), 360
    SEAL (simple and efficient AAL), 360
AARP (AppleTalk Address Resolution Protocol), 236
ABC Advertising (case study), solutions, 457, 459
ABRs (area border routers), 159, 548–549
    areas, density, 590
    class B addresses, summarizing, 167
    promiscuous mode, 173
    summarization, 170–171
    summary links, 550
    virtual links, 554–555
access lists, IPX, 223–225
access management, 117
access servers, 335
    placement, 339
    scalability, 339–340
access speeds (Internet), comparing, 332
access tier (hierarchical design model), 428
    desktop protocols, 19, 207–208
    Frame Relay hierarchical topology, 512
    hierarchical model, 11

    functionality, 21–22
    segmentation, 22
accounting, audit trails, 118
acknowledgement, LSAs, 144
ACKs (acknowledgements), SPX keepalives, 229
adaptability as design goal, 6, 427
Address field (X.121), 316
address space
    DLCIs, 482
    OSPF, allocating, 166–167
addressing schemes
    aggregation, 109–110
    AppleTalk
        cable ranges, 242
        naming conventions, 243
    CIDR (Classless Interdomain Routing), 108
    developing, 11–12
    DHCP (Dynamic Host Configuration Protocol), 86
    hierarchical addressing, 101
    IP (Internet Protocol), 92–93
        binary to decimal conversion chart, 613
        CIDR (Classless Interdomain Routing), 109
        IANA (Internet Assigned Numbers Authority), 93
        NAT (Network Address Translation), 93
        private addresses, 93, 122
        selecting design, 101
        subnetting, 93–94
    IPX (Internetwork Packet Exchange)
        enhancements, 230
        helper addresses, 227
        IPeXchange Internet Gateway, 229–230
    multicast routing, 113, 115
    name resolution
        broadcasts, 263
        DNS, 264
        LMHOSTS, 263
        Windows, 262
        WINS, 264
    network layer, affect on network design, 45
    NVEs (network-visible entities), 237
    OSPF, 166, 490
    prefix routing, 102–103
    secondary addressing, 101, 110

B

K-L

M

O

P

T

W

X

Z

CCIE Professional Development

Cisco LAN Switching

Kennedy Clark, CCIE; Kevin Hamilton, CCIE

1-57870-094-9 • AVAILABLE NOW

This volume provides an in-depth analysis of Cisco LAN switching technologies, architectures, and deployments, including unique coverage of Catalyst network design essentials. Network designs and configuration examples are incorporated throughout to demonstrate the principles and enable easy translation of the material into practice in production networks.

Advanced IP Network Design

Alvaro Retana, CCIE; Don Slice, CCIE; and Russ White, CCIE

1-57870-097-3 • AVAILABLE NOW

Network engineers and managers can use these case studies, which highlight various network design goals, to explore issues including protocol choice, network stability, and growth. This book also includes theoretical discussion on advanced design topics.

Large-Scale IP Network Solutions

Khalid Raza, CCIE; and Mark Turner

1-57870-084-1 • AVAILABLE NOW

Network engineers can find solutions as their IP networks grow in size and complexity. Examine all the major IP protocols in-depth and learn about scalability, migration planning, network management, and security for large-scale networks.

Routing TCP/IP, Volume I

Jeff Doyle, CCIE

1-57870-041-8 • AVAILABLE NOW

This book takes the reader from a basic understanding of routers and routing protocols through a detailed examination of each of the IP interior routing protocols. Learn techniques for designing networks that maximize the efficiency of the protocol being used. Exercises and review questions provide core study for the CCIE Routing and Switching exam.

CISCO SYSTEMS

CISCO PRESS

www.ciscopress.com

Cisco Career Certifications

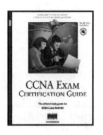

CCNA Exam Certification Guide
Wendell Odom, CCIE

0-7357-0073-7 • AVAILABLE NOW

This book is a comprehensive study tool for CCNA Exam #640-407 and part of a recommended study program from Cisco Systems. *CCNA Exam Certification Guide* helps you understand and master the exam objectives. Instructor-developed elements and techniques maximize your retention and recall of exam topics, and scenario-based exercises help validate your mastery of the exam objectives.

Advanced Cisco Router Configuration
Cisco Systems, Inc., edited by Laura Chappell

1-57870-074-4 • AVAILABLE NOW

Based on the actual Cisco ACRC course, this book provides a thorough treatment of advanced network deployment issues. Learn to apply effective configuration techniques for solid network implementation and management as you prepare for CCNP and CCDP certifications. This book also includes chapter-ending tests for self-assessment.

Introduction to Cisco Router Configuration
Cisco Systems, Inc., edited by Laura Chappell

1-57870-076-0 • AVAILABLE NOW

Based on the actual Cisco ICRC course, this book presents the foundation knowledge necessary to define Cisco router configurations in multiprotocol environments. Examples and chapter-ending tests build a solid framework for understanding internetworking concepts. Prepare for the ICRC course and CCNA certification while mastering the protocols and technologies for router configuration.

Cisco CCNA Preparation Library
Cisco Systems, Inc., Laura Chappell, and Kevin Downes, CCIE

1-57870-125-2 • AVAILABLE NOW • CD-ROM

This boxed set contains two Cisco Press books—*Introduction to Cisco Router Configuration* and *Internetworking Technologies Handbook,* Second Edition— and the *High-Performance Solutions for Desktop Connectivity* CD.

CISCO SYSTEMS

CISCO PRESS

www.ciscopress.com

Cisco Press Solutions

Enhanced IP Services for Cisco Networks
Donald C. Lee, CCIE

1-57870-106-6 • AVAILABLE NOW

This is a guide to improving your network's capabilities by understanding the new enabling and advanced Cisco IOS services that build more scalable, intelligent, and secure networks. Learn the technical details necessary to deploy Quality of Service, VPN technologies, IPsec, the IOS firewall and IOS Intrusion Detection. These services will allow you to extend the network to new frontiers securely, protect your network from attacks, and increase the sophistication of network services.

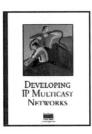

Developing IP Multicast Networks, Volume I
Beau Williamson, CCIE

1-57870-077-9 • AVAILABLE NOW

This book provides a solid foundation of IP multicast concepts and explains how to design and deploy the networks that will support appplications such as audio and video conferencing, distance-learning, and data replication. Includes an in-depth discussion of the PIM protocol used in Cisco routers and detailed coverage of the rules that control the creation and maintenance of Cisco mroute state entries.

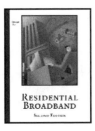

Residential Broadband, Second Edition
George Abe

1-57870-177-5 • AVAILABLE DECEMBER 1999

This book will answer basic questions of residential broadband networks such as: Why do we need high speed networks at home? How will high speed residential services be delivered to the home? How do regulatory or commercial factors affect this technology? Explore such networking topics as xDSL, cable, and wireless.

Designing Network Security
Merike Kaeo

1-57870-043-4 • AVAILABLE NOW

Designing Network Security is a practical guide designed to help you understand the fundamentals of securing your corporate infrastructure. This book takes a comprehensive look at underlying security technologies, the process of creating a security policy, and the practical requirements necessary to implement a corporate security policy.

www.ciscopress.com

Cisco Press Solutions

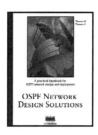

OSPF Network Design Solutions
Thomas M. Thomas II
1-57870-046-9 • **AVAILABLE NOW**

This comprehensive guide presents a detailed, applied look into the workings
of the popular Open Shortest Path First protocol, demonstrating how to
dramatically increase network performance and security, and how to most
easily maintain large-scale networks. OSPF is thoroughly explained through
exhaustive coverage of network design, deployment, management, and
troubleshooting.

Top-Down Network Design
Priscilla Oppenheimer
1-57870-069-8 • **AVAILABLE NOW**

Building reliable, secure, and manageable networks is every network
professional's goal. This practical guide teaches you a systematic method for
network design that can be applied to campus LANs, remote-access networks,
WAN links, and large-scale internetworks. Learn how to analyze business and
technical requirements, examine traffic flow and Quality of Service requirements, and select protocols and technologies based on performance goals.

Internetworking SNA with Cisco Solutions
George Sackett and Nancy Sackett
1-57870-083-3 • **AVAILABLE NOW**

This comprehensive guide presents a practical approach to integrating
SNA and TCP/IP networks. It provides readers with an understanding of
internetworking terms, networking architectures, protocols, and
implementations for internetworking SNA with Cisco routers.

For the latest on Cisco Press resources and Certification and

Training guides, or for information on publishing opportunities, visit

www.ciscopress.com.

CISCO SYSTEMS

CISCO PRESS

**Cisco Press books are available at your local bookstore,
computer store, and online booksellers.**